BRYN THOMAS was born in Zimbabwe where he grew up on a farm. Since graduating from Durham University with a degree in anthropology, travel on five continents has included a Saharan journey in a home-built kit-car, a solo 2500km cycle ride through the Andes, seven Himalayan treks and 40,000km of rail travel.

The first edition of this book, shortlisted for the Thomas Cook Travel and Guide Book Awards, was the result of several trips on the Trans-Siberian and six months in the Reading Room of the British Library. Subsequent publications have included *Trekking in the Annapurna Region*, also published by Trailblazer, and guides to India, Goa and Britain which he co-authored for Lonely Planet.

In 1992 he set up Trailblazer, to produce the series of route guides for adventurous travellers that has now grown to almost 30 titles.

NICK HILL updated this fifth edition of the *Trans-Siberian Handbook*. After completing a design degree at university, Nick headed off into Asia for a short trip; several fascinating years later he had crossed the continent overland four times.

Russia has long intrigued Nick and it proved to be amongst the most interesting and thought-provoking places he has visited – and the people the most friendly. He currently lives in Bangkok.

Trans-Siberian Handbook
First edition 1988; this fifth edition 2001

Publisher
Trailblazer Publications
The Old Manse, Tower Rd, Hindhead, Surrey, GU26 6SU, UK
Fax (+44) 01428-607571
info@trailblazer-guides.com
www.trailblazer-guides.com

British Library Cataloguing in Publication Data
A catalogue record for this book is available from the British Library

ISBN 1-873756-42-9

Editor: Patricia Major
Typesetting: Anna Jacomb-Hood
Cartography: Nick Hill and Jane Thomas
Illustrations: Nick Hill
Index: Jane Thomas

Printed on chlorine-free paper from farmed forests by
Kelso Graphics (☎ 01573-223214) The Knowes, Kelso, Scottish Borders TD5 7BH

TRANS-SIBERIAN HANDBOOK

BRYN THOMAS

FIFTH EDITION RESEARCHED AND UPDATED BY
NICK HILL

TRAILBLAZER PUBLICATIONS

For my long-suffering Editor

Acknowledgements

From Nick: Thanks to Bill and Jenny Hill for their support and interest. Thanks also (in no particular order) to Ogi Ulzhima, Ray Rudowksi, Kunkun, Rob Phair, Sascha and Lena, Anastasia, Max Kovalov, Oksana, Marina and Nara, Evgueni and Gleb, Nikolai, Sergei, Nika, Olga, Brian McLaren, Sindbad Travel, most of the provodniks and provodnitsas and the countless other people who helped me to understand more about this fascinating region but whose names I never knew. Thanks also to Bryn for giving me this opportunity.

From Bryn: I am greatly indebted to the numerous people who have helped me with the research and execution of this project in its five editions since the first publication in 1988. First, I should like to thank Jane Thomas for her extensive work in drawing the strip maps and original town plans (without which this guide would be incomplete) and for the index. I'd also like to thank Patricia Thomas for her scrupulous editing of the text. Thanks to Nick Hill for updating this fifth edition, and for all his work in producing the digitized town plans and excellent line drawings, to Athol Yates and Tatyana Pozar-Burgar for photographs and for expanding and updating the fourth edition of the book, to Athol Yates for the carriage plan on p117 and to Athol Yates and Nicholas Zvegintsov for the railway dictionary on p418-9, to Dominic Streatfeild-James who updated the third edition (and whose wry comments survive) and to Doug Streatfeild-James for the Chinese words and phrases section. I'm also grateful to Neil McGowan (The Russia Experience) for the Moscow restaurant review, the section on Internet resources and for other advice, to André de Smet (Monkey Business) for visa advice and information on Beijing bars and restaurants, Neil Taylor (Regent Holidays) for general tips and advice, to Anna Udagawa for updating the travel agents' section and other help with the book, to Colin Taylor for world's longest rail journey route, to Ramsey Zarifeh for information on Japan. Thanks, again, to Ron Ziel for the cover photograph.

Among the readers who wrote: thanks to Asger Christiansen (Denmark) for his detailed post-watching notes, Joe Davies (Russia) for last-minute price checks in Moscow, David and Janet Carr (UK), Andrew Wingham (UK), Gordon Gill (USA), Laurens den Dulk (Netherlands), for general information and the piece on dachas: Nancy Scarth (Canada), Werner Verschueren and Nieves Blasco (Belgium), Dr Malcolm Hannan (UK), Laura Hamelen (UK), Angela Hollingsworth (UK), Matz Lonnedal Risberg (Norway), Howard Dymock (UK) and Dmitri Gorokhov (Russia), Stephen McLaughlin (UK), Reijo Härkönen (Finland), Mike Matthews (UK). For feedback from readers and help on previous editions thanks to: Jacinta Nelligan, Darko Burgar, Elena Vvedenskaia, Ilya and Inna Karachevtsev, Jan Wigsten (Eco Tour Productions), Susie Drost (The Mongolian Society), Becky Last (Monkey Business), Youry and Dennis Nemirovsky (Baikal Complex), Darcey Dahl, Frank Becker, Iko and Ann-Marie Burgar, Earlam Matthew, Herbert Groot Jebbink, Konstantine Tchervinski, J Ward Hills, Helen Fuge, Brent McCunn and Craig Patterson, Brian and Val Colyer (Australia), Kenneth Lymer, Anthony Kay, Edward Wilson (UK), Werner Verschueren and Nieves Blasco (Belgium), Rodney Pinder (Hong Kong), Stuart Wilde, Dick Thompson, Jim Millar and Bob Huntley (UK), Lawrence R Cotter (USA), David Cowans (Australia), Guy de Bruyn (Netherlands), Abigail Browne, David and Janet Carr, Julian Wathen, Keith Walker, SCL Phillips (UK), Becky Last (Hong Kong), Christopher Knight (UK), Elizabeth Hehir (Netherlands), Annabel Boyes, Mary Fox, Susan Sexton (UK), Dolf van der Haven (Netherlands), David and Siriporn Brian (Hong Kong), Jacqui Williams (UK), Graham and Sue Small (New Zealand), Steven Caron, Boris Samarianov, Helen Nehonova, Ludmilla, Lingard and Maxim, Svetlana Rabdanova (Russia), Huang Rui Li (Beijing), Alex Malone and Rupert Dunbar-Rees (UK), Angels Castro and Genis Aymerich (Spain), Anne Lavelle and Pauline Wilson, Nick and Hilma (UK), Sandy Macmillan and John Podgora, Hal Sharpe (USA), Felix Patton (Australia), Andre Lvov (Russia), Ian Button (UK), Philip Robinson (UK, for the aside on Siberian post past), James Cherkoff (UK), Matthew Parsons (UK), Jovita da Silva (South Africa), Michael Crick (UK), Maarten Langemeijer (Netherlands), Cmndr RM Williams (Canada), Susan Pares, WD Webber, RC Rider, Colin Baker (UK), Heather and Steve Oxley (Turkey), Bob and Hilda Helling (UK), Andrew and Val White, Christopher Turner, Keith Fothergill (Guernsey), Keith Watson (UK), Jeffrey de Forrestier (Canada), Joan Eriksson (Finland), Robert Bray, Joan Nicholls (UK).

Quotations used in Part 5 are from the *Guide to the Great Siberian Railway 1900*.

A note on prices and a request

In this guide most prices are given in dollars since their value appears to remain reliably constant from year to year: convert at the current exchange rate for the rouble price. Note that although US$ are shown here only roubles are accepted in Russia.

The author and publisher have tried to ensure that this guide is as accurate and up-to-date as possible but things change quickly in Russia. If you notice any changes or omissions please write to Bryn Thomas at Trailblazer Publications (address on p2). A free copy of the next edition will be sent to persons making a significant contribution.

Cover photograph: A rare picture, taken in the early 1970s, of the Trans-Siberian being hauled by a steam engine (© Ron Ziel 2001).

CONTENTS

PART 4: CITY GUIDES AND PLANS

Other Siberian excursions

PART 5: ROUTE GUIDES AND MAPS

Trans-Siberian route

Trans-Mongllan route

Trans-Manchurian route

PART 6: DESTINATIONS AND DEPARTURES

APPENDICES

INDEX

INTRODUCTION

There can be few people who have not, at some time in their lives, wondered what it must be like to travel on the Trans-Siberian Railway – to cross Russia and the wild forests and steppes of Siberia on the world's longest railway journey. The distances spanned by this famous line are immense: almost 6000 miles (a seven-day journey) between Moscow and the Pacific port of Vladivostok (for boat connections to Japan) and just under 5000 miles (five days) between Moscow and Beijing.

Ever since a rail service linking Europe with the Far East was established at the turn of the century, foreign travellers and adventurers have been drawn to this great journey. Most of the early travellers crossed Siberia in the comfort of the carriages of the Belgian Wagon Lits company, which were as luxurious as those of the Venice-Simplon Orient Express of today. Things changed somewhat after the Russian Revolution in 1917 and it became increasingly difficult for foreigners to obtain permits for Siberia. It was not until the 1960s that the situation improved and Westerners began to use the railway again for getting to Japan, taking the boat from Nakhodka (it now leaves from Vladivostok) for the last part of the journey. In the early 1980s, travel restrictions for foreigners visiting China were eased and since then many people have found the Trans-Siberian a cheap and interesting way to get to or from both the Middle Kingdom and Mongolia.

In this jet age, the great advantage of going by rail is that it allows passengers to absorb some of the atmosphere of the country through which they are travelling. On a journey on this train you are guaranteed to meet local people for this is no 'tourist special' but a working service; you may find yourself draining a bottle of vodka with a Russian soldier, discussing politics with a Chinese academic or drinking Russian champagne with a Mongolian trader.

Experimenting with democracy and the market economy, Russia is now undergoing phenomenal changes after years of stagnation. While the ending of the Cold War may have removed some of the mystique of travelling in the former USSR, the fact that Russia is now much more accessible means that there are new travel opportunities right across the country. With foreigners no longer obliged to stay in overpriced Intourist hotels, visiting the country is now cheaper than ever before.

Although travel in Siberia today presents few of the dangers and difficulties that it did earlier this century, a journey on the Trans-Siberian still demands a considerable amount of planning and preparation. The aim of this guide is to help you cut through the red tape when arranging the trip, to give background information on Russia and Siberia and to provide a kilometre-by-kilometre guide to the entire route of the greatest rail adventure – the Trans-Siberian.

Routes and costs

*Best of all, he would tell me of the great train that ran across half the world ... He held me enthralled then, and today, a life-time later, the spell still holds. He told me the train's history, its beginnings ... how a Tzar had said, 'Let the Railway be built!' And it was ... For me, nothing was ever the same again. I had fallen in love with the Traveller's travels. Gradually, I became possessed by love of a horizon and a train which would take me there ...*Lesley Blanch *Journey into the Mind's Eye*

ROUTE OPTIONS

Travellers crossing Siberia have a choice of three routes: the Trans-Siberian, Trans-Manchurian and Trans-Mongolian. The **Trans-Siberian** is the most expensive route as it crosses the entire length of Siberia to the Pacific terminus at Vladivostok. The **Trans-Manchurian** travels through most of Siberia before turning south through Manchuria and ending in Beijing. The **Trans-Mongolian** also terminates in Beijing but travels via Mongolia which gives you the chance to stop off in Ulan Bator.

If you want to travel on to **Japan** after your Trans-Siberian trip you have two options: from Vladivostok there are sea links (summer months only and schedules currently unreliable) and flights, or a more regular passenger ferry service from Shanghai, which is an overnight rail journey from Beijing.

From Beijing after a journey on the Trans-Manchurian or Trans-Mongolian routes you can continue by train round **China**, which has an extensive rail system and also direct rail links into **Vietnam**.

If it's a **long-distance rail-travel record** that you're after begin your journey in Vila Real de Santo Antonio in Portugal, take the Trans-Mongolian route from Moscow to Beijing and continue into Vietnam to Ho Chi Minh City (Saigon) – a journey of 11,155 miles (17,852km).

COSTS

Overall costs

How much you pay for a trip on the world's longest railway line depends on the level of comfort you demand, the number of stops you wish to make along the way and the amount of time you're prepared to put into getting hold of a budget ticket. Although the cheapest tickets for rail travel from Moscow to Beijing or vice versa (and purchased in these cities) currently cost around US$200 (£140), this price does not reflect what you'll end up paying for your trip. There are several major costs to add on: getting to your departure point and getting back at the end of your journey, accommodation in Moscow and Beijing, food etc. If you do want to buy your ticket yourself you'll need to budget for the time you'll spend in these cities while you're making a booking – and it may take time to get a reservation. In the light of this, the independent package deals offered by travel agents can be better value than they might at first appear. Packages on the Trans-Siberian between Moscow and Beijing, including transfers and one night's accommodation in Moscow, cost from £230/US$345.

From **London**, flights to Moscow cost around £150 single. Flights between London and Beijing are around £320. An 'open-jaw' ticket allowing you to fly in to Moscow and out of Beijing is about £370. The cheapest fully inclusive Trans-Siberian holidays cost from around £1300 for a 12-day package including flights to and from London.

From **New York**, flights to Moscow cost US$500-700 depending on the season. Flights between New York and Beijing cost around US$800 one way. The cheapest fully inclusive Trans-Siberian holidays cost from around US$2300 including flights to and from New York.

From **Australia**, single flights to Beijing cost around A$1000 and to Moscow cost A$1600-1800. The cheapest Trans-Manchurian trip costs A$1140 which includes two nights in Moscow. An 11-day Vladivostok to Moscow budget package costs A$795.

If a two-week guided rail tour from Moscow to Vladivostok with comfortable accommodation in private saloon cars pulled partly by old steam locomotives is more your idea of travelling then be prepared to part with US$3995 (see Trans-Siberian Express Company, p26).

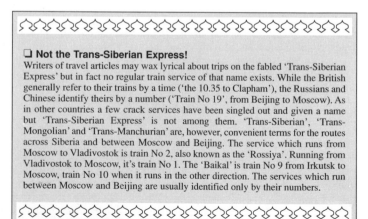

❑ **Not the Trans-Siberian Express!**
Writers of travel articles may wax lyrical about trips on the fabled 'Trans-Siberian Express' but in fact no regular train service of that name exists. While the British generally refer to their trains by a time ('the 10.35 to Clapham'), the Russians and Chinese identify theirs by a number ('Train No 19', from Beijing to Moscow). As in other countries a few crack services have been singled out and given a name but 'Trans-Siberian Express' is not among them. 'Trans-Siberian', 'Trans-Mongolian' and 'Trans-Manchurian' are, however, convenient terms for the routes across Siberia and between Moscow and Beijing. The service which runs from Moscow to Vladivostok is train No 2, also known as the 'Rossiya'. Running from Vladivostok to Moscow, it's train No 1. The 'Baikal' is train No 9 from Irkutsk to Moscow, train No 10 when it runs in the other direction. The services which run between Moscow and Beijing are usually identified only by their numbers.

Travel in Russia – better value, fewer restrictions

Travel in Russia is much better value and far less restricted than it was in the communist era. It is now easier to get a visa (see p18); relatively easy to travel independently; you do not have to deal with Intourist; you don't have to pre-book hotel rooms, and train tickets are easy to buy although long-distance tickets can still be difficult to get.

During the Soviet period, all travel arrangements for foreigners were handled by the monolithic organizations of Intourist (general travel), Sputnik (youth travel) and CCTE (business travel). This enforced division allowed them to charge monopoly prices and restrict travellers' options. These organizations have now been broken up and some replaced by new companies. You'll still see plenty of Intourist hotels and travel desks but it increasingly seems that top hotels are run by foreign companies.

Hotel costs

The price and value of hotel rooms in Russia varies wildly: some hotels have a dual-pricing system and charge foreigners more than Russians. This can be as much as three times the local price so what may be excellent value if you could pay Russian prices becomes absurdly bad value as far as you're concerned. Although 'foreigner' prices are quoted in this book, do not be surprised if they are not the same as what you are offered in the hotel. You will almost certainly be offered the most expensive room first: ask for something cheaper. If, as has recently happened with rail tickets, foreigner prices are abolished you'll get a very pleasant surprise when you check in.

Moscow and St Petersburg are the only places with five star hotels (£220/US$350 or more a night) although there are a number of Trans-Siberian cities which have good four-star hotels, for example Vladivostok and Khabarovsk. Hotel prices in Moscow and St. Petersburg are higher than anywhere else in the country.

Most visitors stay in the former Intourist hotels. A room with attached bathroom will cost £35-65/US$50-100 for a single or £45-70/US$70-120 for a double. Independent travellers go for the cheapest hotels. A basic room with attached bathroom is £7-15/US$10-25 for a single or £8-20/US$12-30 for a double. Breakfast is sometimes included in the price.

Guest-houses have sprung up in Moscow, St Petersburg and Irkutsk and are opening in other places. They charge about £13/US$20 for bed and breakfast. **Homestay** is an option that is available in most Trans-Siberian cities. It costs about £22/US$35 a night including two meals. For more information on accommodation, see p65.

Train classes and prices

Foreigners are offered three levels of train berths. See p118 for more information about each. The prices shown in each category below range from the cheapest ticket bought from the railway ticket office in Moscow or

Beijing to the most expensive ticket offered by a travel agent in the West.
● **First/Soft De luxe/SV, two-berth**: On the **Moscow–Vladivostok route** prices are: £140-600/US$200-900 for the rail trip to Vladivostok. For the **Moscow–Beijing route**, prices are £300-430/US$450-650. De luxe Class is available only on the Trans-Mongolian train and comprises the most luxurious compartments of any regular train crossing Siberia, and the only ones containing showers.
● **First/SV, four-berth**: Available only on the Trans-Mongolian Train Nos 3 & 4, prices for the **Moscow–Beijing route** are £230-310/ US$350-500.
● **Second/Hard/Coupé, four-berth**: Most people find the coupé class perfectly adequate. Prices for the **Moscow–Vladivostok route** are £80-360/ US$120-550. **Moscow–Beijing** is £150-300/US$220-450.

Compartments are not single sex. Foreigners may find themselves sharing with other foreigners if they've booked through a large agency that deals mainly with non-Russians.

BREAKING YOUR JOURNEY

Most people will want to break their journey and stop off along the way. This is a good idea not only because it gives you a chance to get off the train, stretch your legs and, most importantly, have a shower but also because some of the places you pass through are well worth exploring; you won't learn much about life in Siberia by looking through a train window especially if also sharing a compartment with other foreigners. All cities on the Trans-Siberian can be visited with the exception of a few military cities. If booking through an agency, plan your stops carefully; it's too late to decide to break your journey once you have started on your trip. If you travel independently, however, you can just buy train tickets as you go along and stop off whenever and wherever you like.

If your trip starts in **Moscow** (see p151) it's usually necessary to spend one night there but you'd need several days to see just the main sights. A side-trip to **St Petersburg** (p133) is highly recommended. At the other end of the rails, it's worth spending several days in **Beijing** (p296).

Along the routes, Irkutsk and Ulan Bator are the most popular places to stop off at. **Irkutsk** (p228) is the eastern capital of Siberia and 64km from Lake Baikal, the world's deepest freshwater lake. Staying at **Listvyanka** (p243), right by the lake, is highly recommended as is a visit to **Ulan Bator** (p282), the capital of Mongolia. **Ulan Ude** (p251) is worth a stop for the Buddhist monastery nearby. **Khabarovsk** (p263) is surprisingly pleasant and **Yekaterinburg** (p199) is interesting. There's also **Novosibirsk** (p213), the huge capital of Western Siberia, Russia's religious capital at **Sergiev-Posad** (p178), the pleasantly-situated city of **Krasnoyarsk** (p222), the Kremlin at **Rostov-Yaroslavski** (p183) and **Vladivostok** (p272), the eastern railway terminus.

❏ INTERNET RESOURCES

Herbert's Trans-Siberian Site – http://tsr.potjevet.net/
The most comprehensive independent site about the Trans-Sib on the Net, maintained by a true Trans-Sib devotee, Herbert Groot Jebbink.

Trans-Siberian Web Encyclopaedia – www.transsib.ru/Eng/

I.S. Steam Train – http://gamayun.physics.sunysb.edu/RR/
Russian Rail fan's site maintained by Dima Zinoviev.

Clickable Trans-Sib picture collection – www.etrema.com/east2000/
You can even check out what the loos on the train look like on this site.

Jaap Hoogenboom's Trans-Sib Site – http://beam.to/nebu
Personal travelogue with lots of great pictures.

Serg Sigachyov's T-Sib site – www.geocities.com/MotorCity/Speedway/4283/
Lots of Trans-Sib historic memorabilia, pictures of trains, stations etc.

Library of Congress Russian Info – http://lcweb2.loc.gov/frd/cs/rutoc.html
A good place to start: in-depth Russian history, culture, politics etc.

Yahoo! – http://fullcoverage.yahoo.com/Full_Coverage/World/Russia/
Round-up of the latest news stories about Russia culled from the main news-service websites (both Western and Russian).

The Red Book – www.eki.ee/books/redbook/foreword.shtml
Superlative piece of research about the ethnic minority communities of the ex-USSR, with lots about the Siberian native peoples.

Oyubilig's Great Mongol Website – www.mongols.com/index_old.htm
Mongolian traditions, folklore, history and culture.

The Buryatia Page – www.geocities.com/Athens/Oracle/8226/Index.html
Interesting collection of information about Buryat culture; with very good links.

Dazhdbog's Grandchildren – www.ibiblio.org/sergei/
Russian folklore, traditions, culture, myths; many useful links too.

Russia Today – www.russiatoday.com/
Excellent impartial round-up of Russian news and current affairs with analysis.

Russian fonts – http://ourworld.compuserve.com/homepages/PaulGor/
Paul Gorodyansky's page: Using Russian on your Computer.

Famous Russian Paintings - www.museum.ru/museum/paintings/menur3.htm

Museums of Russia – www.museum.ru/defengl.htm

Get Boris Drunk – www.newgrounds.com/assassin/yeltsin/index.html
Feed vodka to an animated Boris Yeltsin to get him progressively more drunk!

Russian Cuisine – www.ruscuisine.com/

Russian Cities On The Web – www.city.ru/
Huge series of links to www-sites about individual cities in Russia.

Fabergé Egg postcards – www.geocities.com/Paris/Rue/4819/pcard.html

Many travel agents have Web sites, which, provided they're kept up to date, can be a useful source of information about their services. See pp23-39.

Neil McGowan (UK & Russia)

When to go

The mode of life which the long dark nights of winter induce, the contrivances of man in his struggle with the climate, the dormant aspect of nature with its thick coverage of dazzling snow and its ice-bound lakes now bearing horses and the heaviest burdens where ships floated and waves rolled, perhaps only a fortnight ago: – all these scenes and peculiar phases of life render a journey to Russia very interesting in winter.
Murray's Handbook for Travellers in Russia, Poland and Finland (1865)

For most people the mention of Siberia evokes a picture of snowy scenes from the film *Dr Zhivago* and if they are not to be disappointed, then winter is probably the best time to go. It is, after all, the most Russian of sea-

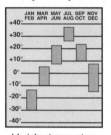

Irkutsk – temperature (max/min °C)

sons, a time of fur coats, sleigh-rides and vodka. In sub-zero temperatures, with the bare birch trees and firs encased in ice, Siberia looks as one imagines it ought to – a bare desolate wasteland. The train, however, is kept well heated. Russian cities, too, look best and feel most 'Russian' under a layer of snow. St Petersburg with its brightly painted Classical architecture is far more attractive in the winter months when the weather is crisp and skies clear. If, however, you want to spend time in any Siberian city, you'll probably find it more enjoyable to go in the late spring, summer or autumn, when there is more to do.

In Siberia, the heaviest snowfalls and coldest temperatures (as low as minus 40°C/F in Krasnoyarsk and some of the other towns the train passes through) occur in December and January. From late January to early April the weather is generally cold and clear. Spring comes late and then

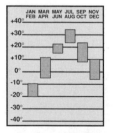

Moscow – temperature (max/min °C)

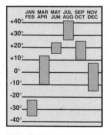

Ulan Bator – temperature (max/min °C)

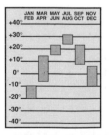

Beijing – temperature (max/min °C)

the warmest months are July and August, when it is warm enough for an invigorating dip in Lake Baikal. The birch and aspen provide a beautiful autumnal display in September and October.

In Moscow the average temperature is 17°C (63°F) in summer and minus 9°C (+16°F) during the winter; there are occasional heavy summer showers.

Tourist season

The tourist season runs from May to the end of September reaching its peak between mid-July and early September. In the low season, between October and April, some companies offer discounts on tours; you'll also find it much easier to get a booking for the train at short notice at this time. During the summer it can be difficult to get a place on the popular Moscow–Beijing route without giving notice of several weeks.

Bookings and visas

ORGANIZED TOURS OR INDIVIDUAL ITINERARIES?

Note that the regulations governing the issuing of Russian visas are particularly susceptible to change. Check the latest situation with your embassy or through the organizations listed on p18-19.

Group tours

Many visitors to Russia travel in organized groups. This is still how the Russian authorities would prefer you to travel. Groups are easier to control and tend to spend more money in the country than the itinerant backpacker. Going with a tour group takes all the hassle out of travelling. Most tours are accompanied by an English-speaking guide from the moment you arrive in Russia right up until you leave the country. Being part of a group also means that because everything is prearranged, there isn't much room for doing your own thing. See pp23-39 for tour companies.

Semi-independent travel

This is currently the most popular way for foreigners to travel on the Trans-Siberian: using a specialist agency who makes the accommodation and train bookings (with or without stops along the way), thereby providing visa support which enables you to get a Russian tourist visa. You are able to choose the number and length of stops and departure dates; in effect you design your own package. Once you're in Russia, you're usually on your own; some agencies, however, also offer guides who meet you at the railway station and will help you organize your time in that city. This is the easiest way to arrange a Trans-Siberian trip and you'll often get good quality accommodation in Moscow as part of the deal. A number of travel agents in the West will make these arrangements, or you can deal directly with one of the locally-based organizations (see p18 and p38-9) that offer packages on the Trans-Siberian.

Fully independent travel

Getting a tourist visa for Russia, one which allows you to wander around freely, is no longer difficult. You must obtain confirmation of hotel booking in Russia with a registered tourist company to present with your visa application. There are various hotels/organizations that can do this for you (see p18). You need only book one night with them to get a one-month tourist visa. Once you have your visa, you can travel wherever you want. Although few Russians outside the largest cities speak English and tourist infrastructure is limited, this shouldn't put you off. Russians are very friendly and you can easily learn some basic Russian to help communication. Travelling independently is not difficult and is the best way to get a true insight into the 'real' Russia and its people.

People may tell you that it's impossible to travel independently but that's no longer true. Nevertheless Russians, in particular, seem to find the idea of foreigners travelling in this way almost incomprehensible; most will assume that you are travelling as part of a tour and seem baffled as to how you can have just made it up as you go along!

ROUTE PLANNING

Main services

For more information see p403 but note that all timetables are subject to change, nowhere more so than in this part of the world. Local times are given below.

No	Name	Leaves	on	at	Arrives	on	at
1	*Rossiya*	Vladivostok	{4-7 trains	15:14	Moscow	Day 7	17:00
2	*Rossiya*	Moscow	{per week	15:26	Vladivostok	Day 7	06:53
3	(via Mongolia)	Beijing	Tue	07:40	Ulan Bator	Thu	13:20
3	(via Mongolia)	Ulan Bator	Thu	13:50	Moscow	Mon	14:10
4	(via Mongolia)	Moscow	Tue	23:42	Ulan Bator	Sun	08:20
4	(via Mongolia)	Ulan Bator	Sun	08:50	Beijing	Mon	15:33
9	*Baikal*	Irkutsk	{4-7 trains	13:55	Moscow	Day 5	15:17
10	*Baikal*	Moscow	{per week	21:29	Irkutsk	Day 5	08:40
19	(via Manchuria)	Beijing	Fri/Sat	23:10	Moscow	Thu/Fri	18:09
20	(via Manchuria)	Moscow	Fri/Sat	22:56	Beijing	Fri/Sat	05:30
23		Beijing	Sat	07:40	Ulan Bator	Sun	13:20
24		Ulan Bator	Thu	09:30	Beijing	Fri	15:33
89		Beijing	Tue/Fri	18:53	Ulan Bator	Thu/Sun	10:45
90		Ulan Bator	Tue/Fri	12:10	Beijing	Thu/Sun	06:20
263		Ulan Bator	Daily	21:35	Irkutsk	Day 3	08:28
264		Irkutsk	Daily	20:10	Ulan Bator	Day 3	06:20

The trains which run across Siberia are not tourist specials but working services used by local people and they're very popular. On most routes they run to capacity, especially in summer. Buying tickets as you go along shouldn't be too difficult as Russians usually seem to leave it to the last minute. If you book a couple of days before you want to travel, you'll probably get what you want on the smaller sections but you'll need more time if you want a ticket for the whole route or a longer section such as Irkutsk–Moscow.

Moscow to Vladivostok

There are many trains that travel the railway between Moscow and Vladivostok but the famous No 1/2 *Rossiya* train would be the top choice for service. There are other very good trains which run between cities along the route such as No 9/10 *Baikal* train (Moscow to Irkutsk) which increases your options if you are making stopovers along the way.

There are occasional sailings from Vladivostok to Japan in the summer months (see p281) but because these are expensive and the schedule unreliable more people wanting to continue to Japan after a trip across Russia are opting for the regular shipping link to Japan from Shanghai (see p36), an overnight rail journey from Beijing.

Moscow to Beijing: Trans-Manchurian or Trans-Mongolian?

You have two choices when travelling by train between Moscow and Beijing: No 3/4 Trans-Mongolian via Ulan Bator (Chinese Train) and the No 19/20 Trans-Manchurian via Harbin (Russian Train).

There are advantages and disadvantages with both. While only the Trans-Mongolian offers de luxe carriages (see p118), the coupé carriages on both routes are identical and this is what most travellers use. The Trans-Manchurian currently departs from Beijing at a more civilized time (in the evening) than the Trans-Mongolian (crack of dawn) but the Trans-Mongolian costs a little less. You need a Mongolian transit visa on the Trans-Mongolian but not on the Trans-Manchurian. The journey time on the Trans-Mongolian is about 12 hours less than on the Trans-Manchurian and you get the chance to stop off in Ulan Bator. There's no difference between the restaurant cars on the two routes as they're supplied by the country through which you're travelling: Russian in Russia and Chinese in China.

Summer is the most difficult time to get bookings for these two routes so make arrangements several months in advance. There are weekly departures in each direction on the both trains, with (most years) an additional Trans-Manchurian service in the summer.

Stopping off in Mongolia

If you're taking the Trans-Mongolian route, breaking your journey in Ulan Bator is highly recommended. It's easy to organize either through a specialist agency or independently.

Side trips
The possibilities for side trips are numerous. These include the Siberian **BAM Railway** (see p131), the **Silk Route** (see p132) and the **Turk-Sib Railway** (see p132) to Kazakhstan. From Beijing it's easy to continue by rail to **Vietnam**, a three-night journey. Travelling to Pyongyang in **North Korea** via Ussurisk, near Vladivostok, may become easier to organize.

From **Blagoveshchensk** (see p360), when the border is also opened to nationalities other than Russians and Chinese you'll be able to cross the river from this Russian town into China. It's rumoured that this may happen shortly; check the latest information with the Chinese embassy.

VISAS

Visas are required by most nationalities visiting Russia, Mongolia and China. Visas for Russia are not the most straightforward to obtain but procedures are becoming simpler. It's now relatively easy to get a Mongolian visa (from some embassies: London, for example) and it's easy to get a Chinese visa. Visa regulations change regularly and even the border guards and police of the country often do not know the latest law. Check with travel agents or embassies.

You'll always need to show your visa when staying at a hotel and whenever you buy a rail ticket.

Visa invitations
If you are going on a package tour your travel agent will organize everything and you will see none of the paperwork. To get a visa to Russia, you need either an invitation or some written document that confirms your accommodation details (usually booked accommodation vouchers). Both of these must state your passport details, and the duration of your stay. You no longer need to list the cities you will visit on your visa, thus making it far easier for independent travellers to visit places on the spur of the moment. Invitations are valid only if they are sent by a registered travel company in Russia. These companies will have a travel company number issued by the country's respective Ministry of Foreign Affairs. The invitations must contain the address of the travel company, and your name, passport data and itinerary.

Sometimes, travel companies will issue an invitation for only the days for which you have paid to stay with them. There are, however, several companies that are willing just to send you the Russian visa invitation once you've booked a night's accommodation and leave the rest to you. These include:

● **Sindbad Travel/St Petersburg Youth Hostel** (☎ +7-812-327 8384, 🖹 +7-812-329 8019, 🖳 sindbad@sindbad.ru/cn, 🖳 www.ryh.ru/visas.htm), ul 3rd Sovetskaya 28, St Petersburg, Russia are recommended. You can also get invitations from their UK partner **Scotts' Tours** (☎ 020-7383 5353, 🖹 020-7383 3709), 141 Whitfield St London W1P 5RY, or from most Hostelling International offices.

● **Andrews Consulting** (☎ 020-7727 2838, 🖹 020-7727 2848, 🖳 london@andrews-consulting.co.uk, 🖳 www.andrews-consulting.ru), 192 Campden Hill Rd, London W8 7TH (nearest tube: Notting Hill Gate). Their main office is in Moscow: (☎ 258 5198, 🖹 258 5199, 🖳 info@ andrews-consulting.ru), ploshchad Novaya 10.

● **Host Families Association (HOFA)** (☎/🖹 +7-812-275 1992, 🖳 alexei@hofak.hop.stu.neva.ru) 5-25 Tavricheskaya, 193015 St Petersburg, Russia. This is a network of academic and professional families offering homestays throughout the country. See p145.

● **Passport Travel** (☎ +61-3-9867 3888, 🖹 +61-3-9867 1055, 🖳 www .russia-rail.com, 🖳 www.travelcentre.com.au), Suite 11, 401 St Kilda Rd, Melbourne, Victoria 3004, Australia.

● **G & R International** (☎ +7-095-374 5731, 🖹 +7-095-374 7506, 🖳 http://grint.tos.ru), Block 6, Office 4, Institute of Youth, ul Yunosti 5/1, Moscow, Russia.

● **Infinity Travel** (☎ +7-095-234 6555, 🖹 +7-095-234 6556, 🖳 www .infinity.ru), Komsomolsky prospekt 13, Moscow.

Visa invitation and in-country registration currently costs approximately:
  £17-26/US$25-40 for one-month single-entry tourist visa invitation
  £17-26/US$25-40 for one-month double-entry tourist visa invitation
  £26-40/US$40-60 for one-month single-entry business visa invitation
  £40-65/US$60-100 for three-month single-entry business visa invitation
  £46-60/US$70-90 for three-month double-entry business visa
  £135-240/US$200-360 for one-year multiple-entry business visa
Additional costs are incurred if you want the visa processed in less than four days. Most of the above companies will take credit cards for online payment.

Russian visa

The Russian visa is normally a three-page passport-sized document rather than a stamp in your passport. This system is a cold-war legacy from when Western countries discriminated against citizens who had visited the Soviet Union and this would be obvious if passport stamps were used. The government is said to be considering putting the visa in your passport but dramatic changes such as this take time. The visa contains all your passport information, entry and exit dates, and the organization that invited you. The Russian embassy requires a completed visa application form, three photos signed on the back, your passport (or photocopy of the first few pages of your passport), and a visa invitation or booked accommodation vouchers. Visas will usually be issued within 10 working days, or less depending on how much you pay.

❏ **Visa tips**
● When applying for a Chinese visa and are asked to list the places you will visit, just write Beijing, Shanghai and Canton. It's not checked and doesn't limit you to those places but is a safer bet than saying your true intentions – Tibet perhaps.
● When you get the Mongolian visa, ensure that it is valid for exit from Mongolia or you'll waste time when there, getting the endorsement to leave.
● Take your visa invitation and three passport photos to Russia with you in case you have to extend your visa or replace it.

Visa costs depend on where you apply, the type of visa you require, the urgency of the issuing of the visa and your nationality. For most nationalities, single entry tourist visas delivered in 5-10 days cost £30-50/ US$45-75; transit visas are marginally cheaper.

Any foreigner visiting Russia for more than three months requires a doctor's certificate proving that they are not HIV/AIDS positive. This system was introduced as a political gimmick to appeal to anti-West forces in Russia.

● **Transit visa** The transit visa is normally given only to those who are in transit through Russia and are not staying overnight in any city. Most Russian embassies issue transit visas for only 72 hours; Russian embassies in China, however, will issue them for up to 10 days which will allow you to travel on the Trans-Siberian, stay in Moscow for one night and then leave. If you are intending to stay anywhere other than Moscow, you will have to get a tourist visa. To get a transit visa you are usually required to show proof such as rail tickets and onward visas that you will be entering and leaving within 72 hours but this rule is not always enforced.

● **Tourist visa** The tourist visa requires an invitation and a hotel booking but to secure the invitation this may be for as little as just one night. You can get a double-entry version.

● **Business visa** This allows you to stay for up to a year and requires an invitation from a registered Russian business. Some of the visa invitation organizations listed on pp18-19 will set you up with a business visa rather than a tourist visa since until recently this was the only way to travel independently around the country.

● **Private visa** This visa is for those who are invited by Russian friends or relatives but it can take three months or more to get. The process involves your Russian friend getting an authorization known as an *izveshchenia* (извещение) from the OViR office in their home town, and mailing the authorization to you. You then need to take the authorization to your Russian embassy which confirms it with OViR back in Russia. You can get a private visa for a stay of only up to three months though extensions are common in Russia. Non-Russian friends in Russia cannot invite you.

Russian visa extension In any country it's always best to arrive with a visa that will cover the length of your trip there, rather than having to go to the trouble of getting it extended.

Provided you have registered your visa (see below), it's possible to get a visa extension but currently not easy. This involves the organization which issued your visa invitation writing an official statement requesting an extension. Sometimes an international train ticket is all the proof you need. The situation and possibility of visa extension changes rapidly.

Russian visa registration All visitors staying in Russia for more than 72 hours must register with the local

> ❏ **Health insurance**
> If you're from Austria, Belgium, Germany, Greece, Spain, Italy, Luxembourg, Netherlands, Portugal, France, Israel, Finland and Estonia, in order to get a Russian visa you are supposed to have health insurance arranged through a company that has an agreement with the Russian company, Ingosstrakh/Rosso. Alternatively, if the organization that issues your visa invitation will offer a written guarantee to cover your medical costs this will be acceptable. For the latest information check with your embassy.

police or OViR within 72 hours of arrival. There may be a government registration fee of US$5. If you are staying at a hotel, registration will be organized by the staff. The company that issued the invitation has to register your visa. If you are late in registering, you may be fined. If you do not register you may be fined at the border when you try to leave.

That's the official line on it all but as with everything else, it doesn't always work like that. You should register within 72 hours if you can but there doesn't seem to be a problem in Siberia if you're late doing so and have a good excuse (you were on a train or if it was a weekend or holiday). After arriving in Chita from Beijing, I dutifully went to register with OViR and was told to wait until I got to Khabarovsk. They didn't seem worried that this would be way past the 72-hour limit. Registering through the company that issued the invitation doesn't always seem essential, though you should definitely try to do so.

Nearly every hotel will hold your passport for a couple of hours after you check in to register you, whether you ask them to do this or not. This is because the law requires them to do so but as far as you're concerned it is necessary to register only once. In the Soviet era, it was important for you to have registration stamps covering every day to indicate your movements. A page full of stamps won't do you any harm, though. Don't forget to pick up your passport from reception.

Mongolian visa

You should get your visa before visiting Mongolia since although visas may be available at the border and the airport in Mongolia you will need to show a letter of invitation to get one there and the visa will cost more than if you get one in advance. To get a visa at a Mongolian embassy, you will need a valid passport, one photo and the visa fee. For a tourist visa for most nationalities the cost is UK£25/US$40 (US$40 cash only at embassies in China and Russia) for a 30-day visa; a letter of invitation is no longer necessary. If you're applying for a visa for a stay of more than 30 days you require a letter of invitation from a Mongolian company or Mongolian citizen. Singaporeans, Israelis, Malaysians and Filipinos are granted a visa-free stay in Mongolia of 14 days.

Transit visas are for stays of 48 hours or less and cost £20/US$30. You do not need an invitation from a Mongolian organization but some embassies may ask to see your visa for the next destination – China or Russia. Some travellers have managed to get a transit visa at the border but since this was expensive and may not always be possible it's not worth the risk.

Tourist visas are issued for up to 90 days and there are single, double and triple entry versions. Confusingly there are also entry visas (US$20) and exit visas (US$20) – you probably need both so the total cost of the visa is US$40. In some embassies there may be a cheaper combined entry and exit visa.

When you pick up your visa double check that it is valid for exit from Mongolia or you'll waste time when you're there getting the endorsement to leave.

If you're staying for **more** than 30 days an official invitation from a Mongolian organization or individual is required. If your trip is booked through a travel company, they will supply the invitation. If you are organizing it yourself, you'll need to get an official letter (with authorizing stamps on it).

Mongolian visa extension Extending your visa once you are in Mongolia can be a trying experience. The Ministry of Foreign Affairs will invariably tell you that it is impossible but be persistent. Everything is possible although it might cost you a few dollars. To do this in Ulan Bator, see p290. A seven-day extension costs US$15 plus US$2 for each additional day. If you overstay your visa the fine is US$75.

Mongolian visa registration If you staying for more than 30 days it is essential to register with the police as soon as possible after arriving in Mongolia and definitely within 10 days of arrival. Visitors who fail to register will be stopped at departure, and fined. For registration in Ulan Bator, see p290.

Chinese visa

The process of getting a visa is straightforward at most Chinese embassies; but if you're entering China via Russia or Mongolia, get a Chinese visa before you reach Moscow as the embassy there is not easy to deal with. Visas are generally given for up to a month but if yo cation form indicates that you will be in the country for less time than this you might be given less. Four week extensions within China are easy to arrange in most cities though easier in the smaller places where there aren't so many tourists.

MAKING A BOOKING IN BRITAIN

Russia has no independent tourist office in Britain although from time to time some travel agent with close Moscow links sets itself up as the 'Official Russian Tourist Office' in an effort to sell more of its own tours. No doubt in response to the numerous questions they receive some of the companies below produce very informative brochures. For the Chinese section of the journey visit the **China National Tourist Office** (☎ 0891-600188: brochure line), 4 Glentworth St, London NW1 5PG, which is open 09.30-17.00, Monday to Friday.

● **The Russia Experience** (☎ 020-8566 8846, ▤ 020-8566 8843, ▣ info@trans-siberian.co.uk), Research House, Fraser Rd, Perivale, Middlesex UB6 7AQ. Recommended specialists in budget and medium-priced travel for individuals. Their innovative system of guides ('buddies') is popular: if there are places you want to visit they'll take you there, if you want to sit in a bar all day and catch up on the latest club news they'll happily sit with you. Homestays can be arranged in most cities, as well as with Siberian villagers and in Mongolian yurts. Their trip from Moscow to Vladivostok costs £299. The company offers a variety of packages, eg Moscow to Beijing including two night's accommodation in Moscow costs from £369. They also offer trekking and rafting in the Altai, trips to Tuva and the Beetroot Bus (see p170) for backpackers. Their website, ▣ www.trans-siberian.co.uk, is informative and fun, too.

● **Regent Holidays** (☎ 0117-921 1711; ▤ 0117-925 4866, ▣ regent@regent-holidays.co.uk, www.regent-holidays.co.uk), 15 John St, Bristol BS1 2HR. Recommended by numerous readers ('The trip was tailor made for us by Regent Holidays who were very efficient.' Dr M Hannan, August 2000), Regent specialize in independent travel to Russia and the CIS, China, Mongolia, Vietnam and North & South Korea but also offer group tours. Moscow–Beijing tickets for either the Trans-Mongolian or the Trans-Manchurian route cost from £357 (£299 for the route from Beijing to Moscow); stopover packages at Lake Baikal and in Irkutsk or Ulan Bator are available. Bookings are accepted from outside the UK. They can arrange visas (allow at least six weeks to obtain all necessary visas), flights, tours and accommodation.

● **China Travel Service and Information Centre** (☎ 020-7388 8838, 🖹 020-7388 8828), 124 Euston Rd, London NW1 2AL. The friendly and helpful staff here can help with tickets from Beijing to Moscow (in this direction only) as well as tours throughout China. Prices ex Beijing are £200/245/300 for hard/soft/soft de luxe class on the Trans-Manchurian or the Trans-Mongolian route; £85/95/110 to Ulan Bator. You'll be given a voucher which you exchange for a confirmed ticket in Beijing.

● **Intourist Travel** (☎ 020-7538 8600, 🖹 020-7538 5967, 🖳 info@in tourist.co.uk, www.intourist.com/uk), Intourist House, 219 Marsh Wall, London E14 9PD; Manchester (☎ 0161-872 4222) Suite 2F, Central Buildings, 211 Deansgate, Manchester M3 3NW. **Tours**: Intourist offers a Trans-Siberian tour with two nights in Moscow, two nights in Irkutsk and four in Beijing, plus flights London–Moscow and Beijing–London from £1379 on the Trans-Manchurian route. The price includes transfers, bed and breakfast in the cities, and city tours. Visas can be arranged. **Independent travel**: Intourist's bookings on the Moscow–Beijing train include transfers and one night's accommodation in Moscow, and meals on the train as far as the Russian border from £355/368 in the low/high season. There's a range of stopover packages and Intourist may be able to book the Vladivostok–Fushiki boat trip if it's running.

● **Adventure Bound/The Imaginative Traveller** (☎ 020-8742 8612, 🖹 020-8742 3045, 🖳 sundowners@imtrav.co.uk, www.sundowners.com), 14 Barley Mow Passage, Chiswick, London W4 4PH, is the UK agent for Sundowners (see p33). This efficient company offers tickets for all the routes (Trans-Siberian, Trans-Mongolian and Trans-Manchurian) for individual travellers, as well as package tours. Moscow–Vladivostok with two night's accommodation in Moscow and one in Vladivostok costs £355. The cheapest Trans-Manchurian trip costs £515 and includes two nights in Moscow. The staff can also arrange flights, visas, and accommodation en route.

● **Progressive Tours** (☎ 020-7262 1676, 🖹 020-7724 6941, 🖳 101535.513@compuserve.com), 12 Porchester Place, Marble Arch, London W2 2BS. Specializes in budget and youth travel to Russia and offers tickets on all routes; Moscow to Beijing from £395 in the low season (Nov-Apr). Various packages are possible. Prices for direct trains (Moscow to Beijing) include one night full board in Moscow, berth on train, transfers, two sightseeing trips, English-speaking guide and meals on board the train until the Russian border. The Trans-Mongolian route costs from £355. The staff can arrange hotels in St Petersburg (from £34) and in Moscow from £40 for a twin room as well as stopovers in various places including Ulan Bator, Novosibirsk, Irkutsk and Ulan Ude and the ferry or flight from Vladivostok to Japan.

● **China Travel Service Ltd** (☎ 020-7836 9911, 🖹 020-7836 3121, 🖥 cts@ctsuk.com, www.ctshorizons.com), 7 Upper St Martin's Lane, London WC2H 9DL. CTS will book individual itineraries across China as well as offering a 22-day tour for £1450 from London to Hong Kong and back with three nights in Beijing and two in Xian, Guilin and Hong Kong. Individual tickets are sold only for the Trans-Mongolian and Trans-Manchurian trains; the cheapest ticket from Beijing to Moscow (rail only) costs £245 (hard class). They can also arrange train travel in China and hotels in Moscow, Irkutsk and Ulan Bator.

● **Steppes East** (☎ 01285-651010, 🖹 01285-885888, 🖥 sales@steppeseast.co.uk, www.steppeseast.co.uk), The Travel House, 51 Castle St, Cirencester, Glos GL7 1QD, has a range of tailor-made individual Trans-Siberian itineraries and tours.

● **STA Travel** (🖥 www.statravel.co.uk) has many branches in Britain including London: 117 Euston Rd, NW1 2SX (☎ 020-7465 0484); 38 Store St, WC1 E7BZ (☎ 020-7580 7733); 86 Old Brompton Rd, SW7 3LQ (☎ 020-7581 4132) and 11 Goodge St, W1P 1FE (☎ 020-7436 7779); Bristol (☎ 0117-929 4399, 🖹 0117-929 4791) 25 Queens Rd; Manchester (☎ 0161-839 7838) 75 Deansgate; Cambridge (☎ 01223-366966) 38 Sidney St; Brighton (☎ 01273-728282), 38/9 North St; Oxford (☎ 01865-792800), 36 George St; Leeds (☎ 0113-244 9212) 88 Vicar Lane; Glasgow (☎ 0141-338 6000, 🖹 0141-338 6022), 184 Byres Rd. A student travel centre which sells tickets for all routes for independent travellers, as well as flights. eg £370 for an open-jaw ticket, London–Moscow then Beijing–London.

● **Voyages Jules Verne** (☎ 020-7616 1000, 🖹 020-7723 8629, 🖥 sales@VJV.co.uk), 21 Dorset Square, London NW1 6QG. The 'Central Kingdom Express' will take you from Moscow to Beijing in the original Pullman carriages of the 'Nostalgic Orient Express'. The 16-day tour costs £2795 including flights from/to London. The train comprises the original carriages of the 1920s together with dining, club and shower cars. There are stops in Moscow, Omsk, Novosibirsk, Irkutsk, Lake Baikal, Ulan Bator and Beijing and for an extra £350 you can start from London on Eurostar to Brussels where you board a sleeper to Moscow.

Other companies in the UK that feature Trans-Siberian trips in their brochures include Bridge the World (☎ 020-7911 0900), Global Village (☎ 020-7692 7770) and Travel Mood (☎ 08700-664545). This last company quotes £873 for London–Sydney using flights and the train.

Budget travellers booking from Britain should note that they can also arrange Trans-Siberian rail tickets through agencies based in Hong Kong (see p38) and Russia (p18-19).

Special interest tours
● **Trans-Siberian Express Company/GW Travel** (☎ 0161-928 9410, 🖹 0161-941 6101, 🖳 mail@gwtravel.co.uk, 🖳 www.gwtravel.co.uk), 6 Old Market Place, Altrincham, Cheshire WA14 4NP, runs distinctly up-market tours chartering its own steam-hauled trains and luxurious carriages that come complete with chefs and attendants. The carriages are your main base while in Russia. A fully-escorted 14-day tour from Moscow via St Petersburg to Vladivostok including city stopovers in Siberia costs £2395. With this company you can charter your own private VIP carriage or even a complete train for a tour anywhere in Russia or the CIS.
● **Intourist** Special interest tours department: ☎ 020-7538 8600.
● **Warwickshire Railway Society** (☎/🖹 01564-826143), 145 Fulford Hall Rd, Tidbury Green, Solihull, West Midlands BN0 1QY, occasionally operates tours on the Trans-Siberian.

Embassies in Britain
● **Russia** (☎ 020-7229 3628, visa information service 0891-171 271), 5 Kensington Palace Gardens, London W8 4QS. Open weekdays, 09.00-12.30 (last entry 11.30). The queues here can be long so it may be worth paying for the visa services offered by most travel agents who deal in Russia (prices for this service vary). Your passport is required, as well as a completed visa application form, a visa invitation from an accredited Russian organization and three passport photos. Note that to be acceptable to the embassy the visa invitation must show that you have accommodation for every one of the nights you will be in Russia. Most of the companies listed on p18-19 that will issue the visa support will state on it that you'll be staying with them for the duration of your trip even though they know you may not be and that this is simply a requirement for you to be able to get the visa. A single-entry visa costs £30 (available in six days), £50 (in 3-5 days), £70 (next day), £80 (same day), £120 (one hour). A multiple-entry visa is £100. For postal applications allow at least three weeks. Note that there's also a Russian consulate in Edinburgh (☎ 0131-225 7098) at 9 Coates Crescent, Edinburgh E13 7RL.
● **China** (☎ 09001-880808 or, between 2 and 4pm, 020-7631 1430, 🖳 www.chinese-embassy.org.uk), 31 Portland Place, London W1B 1TB. Open 09.00-12.00 (Monday to Friday). This is quite easy to obtain yourself; two passport photos are required. A single-entry visa valid for one month from the date of entry and three months from the date of issue costs £30 (£45 for double-entry visa) and takes three working days to issue. Check the dates on the visa before leaving the embassy.
● **Mongolia** (☎ 020-7937 0150), 7 Kensington Court, London W8 5DL. Open 10.00-12.30 (Monday to Friday). A transit visa costs £20 and takes 24 hours to process; rail confirmation is not required. A tourist visa costs £25 and takes 24 hours to process. If you're staying in Mongolia for more

than 30 days you'll need a letter from Zhuulchin or another accredited travel agent in Mongolia. Mongolia also has embassies in Moscow (p168), Irkutsk (p239) and Beijing (p301), along the route of the Trans-Siberian but it's best to get your visa before you leave the UK since the London embassy is easy to deal with.

Getting to Moscow or Beijing from Britain

● **By air:** Flights to Moscow start at around £150 one-way, £240 return; Aeroflot (☎ 020-7355 2233) usually offers the cheapest seats. Beijing is more expensive: at least £300 one way, £460 return. Air China is usually a good bet for cheap seats and can be booked through CTSIC (☎ 020-7388 8838).

● **By rail:** Deutsche Bahn (German Rail: ☎ 08702 435363, 🖹 020-8339 4700) operates a telesales booking service (Monday to Friday 09:00-17:00) and can book a ticket from London to Moscow. The cheapest one-way fare is £213 including sleeper, £260 return and there is a 25 per cent reduction for under 26s on single tickets only. The service is daily and takes a little under 48 hours. Availability, however, is limited particularly for the return journey. Tickets for services to various European cities (but not currently anywhere in Russia) can be booked through Rail Europe (☎ 0990-848848) or Eurostar (☎ 0870-848848).

MAKING A BOOKING IN CONTINENTAL EUROPE

From Belgium

● **Boundless Adventures** (☎ 02-426 40 30, 🖹 02-426 03 60, 🖳 boundless.adventures@joker.be), ave Verdilaan 23/15, 1083 Brussels.

● **Intourist Benelux** (☎ 02-502 4440, 🖹 02-502 7913), 3 rue du Gentilhomme, 1000 Brussels, arranges tickets for the Trans-Mongolian and Manchurian routes, flights, and accommodation en route.

From Bulgaria

● **Sofintour** (☎/🖹 2-876012, 🖹 814928, 🖳 sofintou@bgnet.bg) 24 Bul.al. Stambolijsky 24, 100 Sofia.

From Czech Republic

● **KHKD** (☎/🖹 24 74 90 88), Jaroslav Krenek, na Podkovce 13, CS-147 00 Praha 4.

From Denmark

● **Oriental Tours** (☎ 33-32 75 30, 🖹 33 32 75 31, 🖳 oriental@inet.uni2.dk, www.albatros-travel.dk), Bredgade 58, 1260 Copenhagen K.

● **STA Travel** Fiolstrede 18, Copenhagen 1171, and Holstebro (☎ 97-42 50 00, 🖹 97-41 28 27, Bisgaardsgade 5, DK7500).

● **DSB** (☎ 70 13 14 16) can make Trans-Siberian bookings.

From Finland

● **Kilroy Travels** (☎ 09-680 7811), Kaivokatu 10 D, Helsinki; also in Tampere (☎ 03-223 0995, Hamakata 70) and Turku (☎ 02-273 7500, Eerikinkatu 2). These offices sell tickets for the Trans-Mongolian and the Trans-Manchurian routes and can arrange visas and flights as well as accommodation in Moscow, St Petersburg and Irkutsk.

● **Sindbad Travel/Russian Youth Hostels** (Russia ☎ 812-327 8384, 🖹 812-329 9019, 🖳 sindbad@sindbad.ru), 3 Sozietskaia St, St Petersburg (postal address PO Box 8, SF-53501, Lappeenranta). Sindbad is associated with Russian Youth Hostels (see p145) and will make hostel reservations, provide visa support and sell air and train tickets. Letters are sent to RYH by Finnish post.

● **OY Finnsov Tours Ltd** (☎ 09-694 2011/2511, 🖹 09-694 5534, 🖳 webmaster@finnsov.fi, www.finnsov.fi), Eerikinkatu 3, 00100 Helsinki.

● **STA Travel** (☎ 09-818 3491, 🖹 09-818 3293), Mikonkatu 2D, 2nd Floor, 00100 Helsinki.

From France

● **Nouvelles Frontières** (☎ 08 03 33 33 33, 🖳 www.nouvelles-frontieres.com), 66 Boulevard Saint Michel, and many other branches.

● **Forum Voyages** (☎ 01 53 32 71 72), 11 ave de l'Opéra

● **Office de Tourisme de Chine** (☎ 01 42 96 95 48), 116 ave des Champs Elysées, 75008 Paris.

● **CTS**, 32 rue Vignon, 75009 Paris.

From Germany

● **Travel Service Asia Gmbh** (TSA-Reisen) (☎ 7351-373210; fax 7351-373211, 🖳 TSA-Reisen@T-Online.de, 🖳 www.travel-service-asia.de) Schmelzweg 10, D-88400 Biberach/Riß. Offers a full range of independent journeys and budget tours on Trans-Siberian, Trans-Manchurian and Trans-Mongolian. Worth contacting even if you don't live in Germany (an English brochure is available and the website is in English as well as German). They will arrange visas if you send your passport or will provide visa support if you want to apply in your own country. They deal with Baikal Complex in Irkutsk (see p237) who provide hiking tours round Lake Baikal, with treks on Olkhon Island.

● **Lernidee Reisen** (☎ 030-786 0000; 🖹 030-786 5596, 🖳 team@lernidee-reisen.de, 🖳 www.lernidee-reisen.de), Dudenstrasse 78, 10965 Berlin. Siberian itineraries from this company range from a 2nd-class ticket on the Moscow–Beijing train to stopovers in Mongolia (four days/ three nights including full board, English-speaking guide). Other routes include Moscow to Vladivostok. Homestay and hotel accommodation are offered in several cities.

● **White Nights** (☎ 06221-400337), Dantestrasse 55, 69115 Heidelberg. Agent for budget travel operator based in St Petersburg.

● **Reise-Service Rusland** (☎ 030-201 87285), Taubenstrasse 20, 10117 Berlin, works with Russian Youth Hostels (see p145) and will make hostel reservations, provide visa support and sell air and train tickets.

● **STA Travel** has many branches in Germany some of which include: Hamburg (☎ 040-450 38400), Renzelstrasse 16, 20146 Hamburg; Bonn (☎ 0228-225579), Nassestrasse 11, 53113 Bonn; Berlin (☎ 030-311 0950), Goethestrasse 73, 10625 Berlin; Frankfurt/Main (☎ 069-703035), Bockenheimer Landstrasse 133, 60325 Frankfurt/Main; Mannheim (☎ 0621-10074) L14.11, 68161 Mannheim; Cologne (☎ 0221-442011), Zuelpicher Strasse 178, 50937 Cologne; Heidelberg (☎ 06221-23528), Haupstrasse 139, 69117 Heidelberg; Wuerzburg (☎ 0931-52176), Zwinger 6, 97070 Wuerzburg. A student travel centre which sells tickets for all routes for independent travellers, as well as flights.

● **China Tourist Office** (☎ 069-520135), Ilkenhanstrasse 6, D-60433 Frankfurt/Main. Information office for Germany, Austria, Switzerland and Holland.

● **Mongolia Zhuulchin Foreign Tourism Corporation** (☎ 030-474 2484, 🖹 030-471 8833) 2 Arnold Zweig St, 3R 13189 Berlin. This office accepts bookings from outside Germany.

● **Verein Frankische Reisefreunde** (☎ 0911-513 771), D-90409 Nurnberg, Aussere Bayreuther Strasse 57.

From Hungary
● **Danubius Travels** (Ms Edit Rubos), (☎ 01-117 3652, 🖹 01-117 0210. Budapest 1051, Szervita 8.

From Italy
● **Hans Jurgen Rosenberger** (☎/🖹 045 715 1751), I-37012 Bussolengo (VR), Via E Toti 3.

From the Netherlands
● **Circ Rusland Reizen** (☎ 020-625 3528), Honthorststraat 42, 1071 Amsterdam, can organize train tickets, visas and accommodation. Recommended by readers: 'Very good! It is not too big, more personal, though professional', (Laurens den Dulk, August 2000).

● **VNC Travel** (☎ 030-231 1500, 🖹 030-231 0232, 🖵 www.vnc.nl), Catharijnesingel 70, 3511 GM Utrecht. Can organize trips for independent travellers as well as group tours.

● **Eurocult** (☎ 030-243 96 34, 🖹 030-244 24 75, 🖵 euro.cult@ inter.nl.net, www.xs4all.nl/~eurocult), Wittercrouwenstraat 36, 3512 CV Utrecht. Check its Web site for the latest prices.

● **Global Travel** (☎ 020-696 75 85, 🖹 020-697 35 87, 🖵 golden-trains@wxs.nl), Anne Kooistrahof 15, 1106 WG Amsterdam; can make train reservations in 51 countries – worth contacting even if you don't live in the Netherlands.

● **Tiara Tours** (☎ 076-565 28 79, 🖹 076-560 26 30, 🖳 tiara@ tref.nl, www.tiaratours.nl), Beukenlaan 2, 4834 CR Breda.

From Norway

● **Intourist** (☎ 22 42 28 99, 🖹 22 42 62 01), FR Nansens Plass 8, 0160 Oslo, can arrange tickets for all routes (in either direction) as well as visas, accommodation and flights.

● **Kinareiser** (China Travel Ltd) (☎ 22-110 057, 🖹 22-360 544, 🖳 nihao@kinareise.no), Hegdehaugsveien 10, 0167 Oslo. This company represents Sweden's Eco Tour Production Mongolian adventure trips and also arranges Trans-Siberian trips.

From Poland

● **Intourist Warsawa Ltd** (☎/🖹 22-625 0852, 🖹 22-629 0202, 🖳 war@intourist.com.pl), 10 Novogrodska St, 00-509 Warsaw.

From Russia

Many organizations within Russia can arrange visa support (see pp18-19). For other companies refer to the travel agents in each city (see Part 4: City Guides and Plans).

From Sweden

● **Swedish-Chinese Travel LTD** (☎ 08-108824, 🖹 08-4110888, 🖳 info @svenskkinesiska.se), Sveavagen 31, 103 68 Stockholm. Trans-Siberian specialist.

● **Fram Resor AB** (☎ 08-215934. 🖹 08-214060), Box 64, Kingsgaten 56, 10120 Stockholm.

● **Eco Tour Production/Nomadic Journeys** (☎ 0498 487 105, 🖹 0498 487 115, 🖳 info@nomadicjourneys.com, www.nomadicjourneys.com), Burge i Hablingbo, 620 11 Havdhem, Gotland. One of the best adventure travel agencies operating in Mongolia, they offer treks, horse riding and sports fishing. On a typical trek, luggage and one *ger* (yurt) are loaded onto yak carts and the group is accompanied by a cook, trailfinder and two horses or camels. Also contactable via Nomadic Journeys in Ulan Bator (☎ 328 737, 🖹 321 489, 🖳 mongolia@nomadicjourneys.com).

● **STA Travel** (☎ 046 13 72 05, 🖹 046 13 43 66), Kiliansgatan 17, 5-223 51 Lund, and at Uppsala (☎ 018 601000, 🖹 018 6001001, St Olofsgatan 11).

From Switzerland

● **White Nights** (☎/🖹 031-333 8855), Haldenstrasse 5, 3014 Bern. Agent for St Petersburg budget travel operator.

● **SSR Travel** (part of STA Travel) has many branches in Switzerland some of which include: Basle (☎ 61 284 90 60, 🖹 61 284 90 66, Steinenberg 19, 4001 Basle); Bern (☎ 31 302 03 12, 🖹 31 302 39 93, Falkenplatz 9, 3012 Bern); Fribourg (☎ 26 322 61 62, 🖹 26 322 64 68, rue de Lausanne 35, 1700 Fribourg); Geneva (☎ 22 329 77 33/4, 🖹 22 329

50 62, rue Vignier 3, 1205 Geneva); Lausanne (☎ 21 617 56 27, 🖹 21 616 50 77, boulevard de Grancy 20, 1006 Lausanne); Zurich (☎ 1 260 7050, 1 266 7056, Stadelhofestrasse 22, 8001 Zurich).

From Turkey
● **Intourist** (☎ 212 245 5653, 🖹 212 249 4903, A/S GUMUSSUYU, Miralay Sefik Bey Sok N13-D3, 80090 Taksim, Istanbul.

MAKING A BOOKING IN NORTH AMERICA
From the USA
● **Safaricentre** (☎ 310-546-4411; 🖹 310-546-3188; 🖳 info@safaricentre.com), 3201 N Sepulveda Blvd, Manhattan Beach, CA 90266. Agents for the popular Sundowners Adventure Travel trips (see p33).

● **Intourist USA** (☎ 561-585-5305; 🖹 561-582-1353, toll free ☎ 800-556 5305, 🖳 info@intourist.com), 12 South Dixie Highway, Lake Worth, Florida 33460. Offers Trans-Siberian tours and will also arrange individual itineraries. Homestays are offered in several cities; Moscow and St Petersburg from US$45 and Irkutsk from US$52. Intourist also arranges city tours and visas.

● **White Nights** (☎/🖹 916-979-9381, 🖳 wnights@concourse.net, www.concourse.net/bus/wnights/), 610 La Sierra Drive, Sacramento, CA 95864, is the US agent for the budget operator based in St Petersburg (Russia). Moscow to Vladivostok costs from US$582.

● **Mir Corporation** (☎ 206-624-7289, 800-424-7289, 🖹 206-624-7360, 🖳 mir@igc.apc.org, www.mircorp.com), 85 South Washington St, Suite 210, Seattle, WA 98104. This company has a wide range of individual and small group itineraries with accommodation in homestays or hotels.

● **Asia Voyages** (☎ 415-398-2244, 800-914-9133, 🖹 415-399-0827, 🖳 info@asiavoyages.com, www.asiavoyages.com), 582 Market St, San Francisco, CA 94104. The company markets a range of independent and group tours in Russia, Mongolia and China, and arranges a 21-day trip from Moscow to Beijing.

● **STA** (☎ 415-391-8407), 51 Grant Avenue, San Francisco, CA 94108. STA has many branches in North America, some of which include: Boston (297 Newbury St, Boston, MA 02115, ☎ 617-266-6014), Santa Monica (411 Santa Monica Boulevard, CA 90401, ☎ 310-394-5126), New York (10 Downing St: 6th Avenue and Bleecker), New York, NY 10014, ☎ 212-627-3111, 🖹 212-627-3387), Chicago (429 South Dearborn St, Chicago, Il 60605, ☎ 312-786-9050) and Seattle (4341 University Way NE, Seattle, WA 98105, ☎ 206-633-5000). A student travel centre which sells tickets for all routes for independent travellers.

● **General Tours** (☎ 800-221-2216), 53 Summer St, Keene NH 0343.

● **Russian Travel Bureau Inc** (☎ 800-847-1800, 🖹 212-490-1650, 🖳 russtvl@interserve.com, 🖳 www.russiantravelbureau.com), 225 East 44

Street, New York, NY 10017. Features several Trans-Siberian packages and can also organize individual itineraries.

● **Boojum Expeditions** (☎ 406-587 0125, 🖹 406-585 3474, 🖳 tg@boojum.comt, www.boojum.com), 14543 Kelly Canyon Rd, Bozeman, MT 59715. Organizes horse-riding trips in the Hovsgol region which is the northernmost province of Mongolia and lies on the border with Siberia and Tuva.

Embassies There are **Russian Consulates** in Washington (☎ 202-939-8907, 🖹 202-483-7579, 2641 Tunlaw Rd NW, Washington DC 20008); San Francisco (☎ 415-928-6878, 2790 Green St, CA 94123), New York (☎ 212-348-0926, 11 E 91st St, NY 10128) and Seattle (☎ 206-728-1910, 2323 Westin Building, 201 6th Ave, Seattle, WA 98121.

There are **Chinese Consulates** in New York (☎ 212-330-7400, 520 12th Ave) and Houston (☎ 713-524-0780).

The **Mongolian Embassy** (☎ 202-333-7117) is at 28-33 M Street North West, Washington DC 20001, and also in New York at 6 East 77th St, New York, NY 10021 (☎ 212-861-9460).

The **Belarus Embassy** (☎ 202-986 1604) is at 1619 New Hampshire Ave NW, Washington DC 20009 and there's a consulate in New York (☎ 212-682 5392) at 708 3rd Ave. Note that you will need a transit visa if crossing Belarus by train.

Further information You can get information from the **Russian National Tourist Office** (☎ 212-575 3431), 130 West 42 St, No 412, New York. **China National Tourist Office** (☎ 212-760-9700) is at Suite 6413, 350 5th Avenue, New York, NY 10118 and in Los Angeles (☎ 818-545-7507), 600 West Broadway, Suite 320, Glendale, Los Angeles, CA 91204.

Getting to Russia or China Numerous airlines fly from the US to Russia. Aeroflot is among the cheapest with departures from many US cities. From New York, flights to Moscow cost US$500-700 depending on the season. Flights between New York and Beijing cost around US$800 one way. There are now also weekly flights between Magadan (on the north-east Pacific coast of Russia) and Seattle with a stop in Anchorage. Magadan is linked by air to main cities in Siberia.

From Canada

● **Travel by Rail** (☎ 416-701-0756, 🖹 416-701-0751), 72 Prescott Ave, Toronto, Ontario M6N 3GS. Agents for Sundowners Adventure Travel (p33).

● **Adventure Centre/Westcan Treks** has several branches in Canada and operates a range of Trans-Siberian itineraries. Group tours as well as individual itineraries can be arranged. There are offices in Toronto (☎ 416-922-7584, 🖹 416-922-8136, 🖳 toronto@theadventurecentre.com), 25 Bellair St, Toronto, Ontario M5R 3L3; Vancouver (2911 West 4th

Avenue, Vancouver BC V6K 1R3, ☎ 604-734 1066, 🖳 vancouver@west cantreks.com), Edmonton (8412 109th St, Edmonton, Alberta T6G 1E2, ☎ 780-439 9118, 🖳 edmonton@westcantreks.com) and Calgary (336 14th St NW, Calgary, Alberta T2N 1Z7, ☎ 403-283 6115, 🖳 cal gary@westcantreks.com).

● **Intours Corporation** (☎ 416-766 4720, 🗎 416-766 8507, 🖳 intours @pathcom.com), 2150 Bloor St West, Toronto, Ontario M6 SM8, can organize trips on the Trans-Siberian for individuals or groups.

● **Exotik Tours** (☎ 514-284-3324, 🗎 514-843-5493, 🖳 exotictours @exotictours.com), Suite 806, 1117 Ste-Catherine St West, Montreal, Quebec H3B 1H9. Exotik sells packages for the Trans-Mongolian and Trans-Manchurian routes and arrange stops in Novosibirsk and Irkutsk. Sightseeing tours in Mongolia are available. In addition the staff can arrange scheduled flights and visas for Russia, Mongolia and China.

Embassies in Canada There are **Russian Consulates** in Ottawa (☎ 613-236 6215, 🗎 613-238 6158), 285 Charlotte St, Ottawa, Ontario K1N 8J5, and Montreal (☎ 514-843 5901, 🗎 514-842-2012), 3655 Ave du Musée, Montreal, Quebec H3G 2I1.

The **Chinese Consulate** is in Ottawa (☎ 613-789-3434), 515 St Patrick's St, Ottawa, Ontario K1N 5H3. There are consular representatives in Vancouver (☎ 604-734 0704), 3380 Granville St, Vancouver, BC V6H 3K3; and Toronto (☎ 416 324 6466), 240 St George St, Toronto, Ontario M5R 2P4. The **Belarus Consulate** is in Ottawa (☎ 613-233 9994), Suite 600, 130 Albert St, Ottawa, Ontario K1P 5G4. **Mongolia** does not have an embassy in Canada. You're advised to collect your visa in Beijing or Moscow.

MAKING A BOOKING IN AUSTRALASIA

From Australia

● **Passport Travel** (☎ 03-9867 3888, 🗎 03-9867 1055, 🖳 passport@trav elcentre.com.au, www.travelcentre.com.au), Suite 11, 401 St Kilda Rd, Melbourne, Victoria, 3004. Incorporates Russian Passport 🖳 www.rus-sia-rail.com. The staff can arrange visa invitations and organize group tours for the Trans-Siberian, BAM railway and in Mongolia, and make individual travel arrangements.

● **Sundowners Adventure Travel** (☎ 03-9600 1934, 🗎 9642 5838, 🖳 rail@sundowners.com, 🖳 www.sundowners.com), Suite 15, 600 Lonsdale St, Melbourne, Vic 3000, has been recommended by several readers. Sundowners offers independent or escorted Trans-Siberian, Trans-Mongolian and Trans-Manchurian trips. On their independent trips all bookings on the train and in hotels are tailor made so you travel independently. There's a range of group trips including a 25-day fully escorted rail itinerary from Hong Kong via Xi'an to Beijing, Ulan Bator,

Irkutsk, Moscow and St Petersburg, and a 17-day St Petersburg to Vladivostok trip (seven nights on the train, nine nights in hotels). The itinerary can also include Vietnam by rail from Beijing.

● **Iris Hotels Pty Ltd** (☎ 02-9580 6466; 🖹 02-9580 7256, 💻 iristour @mpx.com.au), PO Box 60, Hurstville, NSW 2220. This Australian-Russian joint venture has offices in both countries but accepts bookings from abroad at the Australian office. The Russian partner is pioneering eye-surgeon Professor SN Fyodorov, whose Mikof Group (MNTK) operates 13 accommodation centres in Russia, each attached to an eye micro-surgery clinic. Aimed at mature travellers in self-formed groups (minimum 12 people) it offers stopovers in Khabarovsk, Irkutsk, Novosibirsk, Yekaterinburg, Moscow and St Petersburg. Kiev and Warsaw options are also available. Staying beside a clinic may sound unusual but you're guaranteed hot water, absolute cleanliness and if you happened to fall ill you couldn't be in better hands.

● **Gateway Travel** (☎ 02-9745 3333, 🖹 02-9745 3237, 💻 sales@russian-gateway.com.au, www.russian-gateway.com.au), 48 The Boulevard, Strathfield NSW 2135.

● **STA** (toll free ☎ 1-300-360-390, 🖹 02-9281 5259), Shop 3, 702-730 Harris St, Ultimo, Sydney NSW 2011. STA has dozens of branches including Adelaide (☎ 08-223 2426) 235 Rundle St; and Canberra (☎ 06-247 8633), 13-15 Garema Place.

● **China Travel Service** (☎ 02 9211 2633, 🖹 02-9281 3595, cts@all.com.au), 757-759 George St, Sydney NSW 2000.

● **Russian Travel Bureau** Sydney (☎ (02-9262 1144 🖹 02-9262 4479, 💻 eetb@ozemail.com.au), Level 5, 75 King St; Melbourne (☎ 03-9600 0299, 🖹 03-9670 1793, 💻 eetbmelb@netlink.com.au), 3rd Floor, 343 Little Collins St; Brisbane (☎ 07-3229 9716), 3rd Floor, 190 Edward St; the agent for Russian Travel Bureau in Perth is Living Travel (☎ 09-322 6812, 💻 living@jazzline.net.au), 5 Mill St. All branches offer semi-independent Trans-Mongolian and Trans-Manchurian trips.

Embassies in Australia The **Russian Embassy** (☎ 06-6295 9033, 6295 9474, 🖹 6295 1847) is at 78 Canberra Ave, Griffith, ACT 2603. There's also a **Russian Consulate** (☎ 02-9327 1866) at 7-9 Fullerton St, Woollahra NSW 2025.

There are **Chinese Consulates** at 539 Elizabeth St, Surry Hills, NSW 2010 (☎ 02-9698 7929), 75-77 Irving Rd, Toorak, Vic 3142 (☎ 03-9822 0607), and 15-17 William St, Perth, WA 6000 (☎ 08-9481 3278). The **Mongolian Consulate** (☎ 02-9319 4797) is at 112/189 Philip St, Waterloo, NSW 2017.

From New Zealand

● **Eurolynx** (☎ 09-379 9717, 💻 www.sundowners.com), 3rd floor, 20 Fort St, Auckland, is the agent for Sundowners Adventure Travel (see p33).

● **Suntravel** (☎ 09-525 3074, 🖹 09-525 3065, 🖳 mail@suntravel.co.nz, www.suntravel.co.nz), PO Box 12-424, 407 Great South Rd, Penrose, Auckland. Specializes in China, Russia and Mongolia with homestay and hotel accommodation.

● **Adventure World** (☎ 09-524 5118, 🖹 09-520 6629, 🖳 discover@ adventureworld.co.nz, www.adventure.world.co.nz), 101 Great South Road, Remuera, PO Box 74008, Auckland.

● **STA** (☎ 09-309 0458), 10 High St, Auckland. STA also has branches at 90 Cashel St, Christchurch (☎ 03-379 9098) and 130 Cuba St, Wellington (☎ 04-385 0561).

● **Innovative Travel** (☎ 03 365 3910, 🖳 innovative.travel@clear.net.nz), Box 21, 247 Christchurch, is the agent for Russian Travel Bureau (see p33).

Embassies in New Zealand   The **Russian Consulate** (☎ 04-476 6113, 🖹 04-476 3843) is at 57 Messines Rd, Karori, Wellington. The **Chinese Consulate** (☎ 04-472 1382) is at 2-6 Glenmore St, Wellington. **Mongolia** and **Belarus** do not have embassies in New Zealand.

MAKING A BOOKING IN SOUTH AFRICA

● **Concorde Travel** (☎ 11-486 1850), 3rd Floor, Killarney Mall, Riviera Rd, Killarney, Johannesburg 2193. Agents for Iris Hotels (see p34).

● **Travelvision** (☎ 11-482 5222, 11-482 6043/4, 🖳 info@tvision.co.nz), 9th Floor, Metal Box Centre, 20 Owl St (postal address PO Box 4779, Johannesburg 2000). Agents for Intourist London (see p24).

● **STA Travel** has many branches in South Africa, some of which include: Cape Town (☎ 21-418 6570, 🖹 21-418 4689, 31 Riebeek St, Cape Town 8000); Johannesburg (☎ 11-482 2666, 🖹 11-482 4667, 12c Seventh St, Melville 2092); Pretoria (☎ 12-342 5292, 🖹 12-342 5291, 1102 Hilda St, Hatfield).

MAKING A BOOKING IN ASIA

From Japan

The friendly and efficient **Euras Tours Inc** (☎ 03-5562 3381, 🖹 03-5562 3380, 🖳 euras.tyo@ ma.neweb.ne.jp), 1-26-8 Higashi-Azabu, Minato-ku, Tokyo 106-1044, will handle bookings for rail journeys to Europe. Euras offers a series of itineraries, combinations of flights and train journeys, and it's possible to fly from Japan (Niigata) to Khabarovsk or to arrange ferry tickets to Vladivostok. Note that the boat does not operate in the winter. It can also organize your journey via Shanghai, Beijing and Ulan Bator. Contact the staff for full details and prices.

● **FKK Air Service** (☎ 0766-222 212, 🖹 0766-227 456), Shimozeki-machi 4-56, Takaoka City, Toyama. Sells boat tickets for the Fushiki to Vladivostok trip. The cheapest ticket is ¥25,200 (US$216) including meals and the port tax at Vladivostok. The schedules vary from year to year: in 2000 the ferry ran each Friday from July to October. Schedules are not usually announced before May which makes advance planning for this route difficult. FKK also sells tickets for flights to Vladivostok.

● **United Orient Shipping Agency Co** (☎ 813-3249 4412), 7th Floor, Rikkokai-sogo Bldg, 32-3 Kita Shinagawa 2-chome, Shinagawa-ku, Tokyo 140. Sells boat tickets for the Niigata/Fushiki to Vladivostok trip.

Alternatively, you could take the boat from **Kobe to Shanghai**, make your own way to Beijing and organize your ticket there. The journey takes two days and although the boat is Chinese-run, the chef is Japanese, there are futons in the cabins and Japanese-style baths. Details of the weekly service and tickets from:

● **Japan-China International Ferry Co Ltd (JIFCO)** (☎ 03-5489 4800, ▤ 03-5489 4788), Daikanyama Pacific Bldg, 10-14 Sarugakucho, Shibuya-ku, Tokyo 150-0033, and Room No 201, Sanai Bldg, 1-8-6, Shinmachi, Nishi-ku, Osaka 550-0013. Services from Kobe or Osaka to Shanghai operate all year, from ¥20,000 (students ¥18,000) one way. Tickets can also be bought from branch offices of Japan Travel Bureau and Kinki Nihon Tourist.

● **STA** Tokyo: 4th Floor, Nukariya Bldg, 1-16-20 Minami-Ikebukuro, Toshima-Ku, Tokyo 171 0022 (☎ 03-5391 2922, ▤ 03-5391 2273); 1st Floor, Star Plaza Aoyama Bldg, 1-10-3 Shibuya, Shibuya-ku, Tokyo 150-0002, (☎ 03-5485 8380, ▤ 03-5485 8373); 2nd Floor, Toko Bldg, 1-5 Yotsuya, Shinjuku-ku, Tokyo 160-0004, (☎ 03-5269 0751, ▤ 03-5269 0759). Osaka: 6th Floor, Honmachi Meidai Bldg, 2-5-5, Azuchi-machi, Chuo-ku, 541-0052 (☎ 06-6262 7066, ▤ 06-6262 7065).

● **Intourist Japan Co Ltd** (☎ 03-3238 9118, ▤ 03-3238 9128), 5F Daihachi Tanaka Bldg, 5-1 Gobancho, Chiyoda-ku, Tokyo 102-0076.

● **Mongol Zhuulchin Tours Co** (☎ 03-3486 7351, ▤ 03-3486 7440, ▭ yermakov@i.bekkoame.ne.jp), 3rd Floor, Dai-2 Kawana Bldg, Shibuya 2-14-6, Shibuya-ku, Tokyo 150-0002. This company is the Tokyo office of Mongolia's Zhuulchin Foreign Tourism Corporation.

● **Japan China Tourist Office** (☎ 03-3433 1461), 6F Hachidai Hamamatsu-cho Bldg, 1-27-13 Hamamatsu-cho, Minato-ku, Tokyo.

● **Russian Embassy** (☎ 03-3583 5982, ▤ 03-3505 0593), 2-1-1 Azabudai, Minato-ku, Tokyo 106-0041; **Consulate** (☎ 06-848 3452, ▤ 06-848 3453), Toyonaka-shi, Nizhimidorigaoka 1-2-2, Osaka-ku.

● **Chinese Embassy** (☎ 03-3403 3381, ▤ 03-3403 3345), 3-4-33, Moto-Azabu, Minato-ku, Tokyo 106-0046.

From China

● **CITS Beijing** (☎ 6512 0507, ▭ wuxx@cits.com.cn, www.ctn.com.cn), West Lobby, Beijing International Hotel, can book rail tickets and it's open Monday to Friday, 08.30-17.00 with a 13.00-14.00 lunch break. The cheapest Trans-Siberian tickets you are likely to get anywhere are sold here, although availability can be difficult in the summer owing to the high demand. Tickets are currently around Y1700 for hard class to Moscow.

● **Monkey Business Infocenter** (☎ 6509 3642, 🖹 6415 8206, 💻 MonkeyChina@compuserve.com, www.monkeyshrine.com) has moved from the Capital Forbidden City Hotel to Sanlitun south 'Bar St': 12 Dong Da Qiao Xie St, Nan San Li Tun, Chao Yang District, 100027 Beijing. It's above the Hidden Tree Belgian beer bar. They can arrange Trans-Siberian tickets (organized through their Hong Kong office), stopovers and accommodation in Moscow as well as excursions in Mongolia. The office is open 10:00-21:00 Monday-Saturday and 16:00-20:00 Sunday. See p38 for further information.

● **STA Travel** (20-8667 1455, 🖹 20-8667 7462), 179 Huan Shi Xi Rd, Guangzhou 510010.

Getting tickets In the summer trains fill up quickly so if you plan to spend some time travelling around China make Beijing your first stop and get your reservations. It may also be possible to reserve a place on the train in Shanghai (ask at the travel bureau in Peace Hotel) and there's also a Russian embassy there (20 Huangpu Lu).

Once you've made your reservation and paid your deposit, do the rounds of the embassies and collect your visas. You'll need US dollars in cash and a stock of passport photos.

Embassies in Beijing You'll need to visit the Russian embassy and, for the Trans-Mongolian route, the Mongolian embassy. If you're continuing through Europe after Moscow most nationalities will need a **transit visa for Belarus**; this regulation was introduced in May 2000. Most European nationalities and Americans don't need a visa for Poland; Canadians, Australians and New Zealanders still do.

If you need visas for the countries you'll be visiting after Moscow it may be better to get all your visas here rather than in Moscow.

Note that **German nationals** are not currently able to get Russian visas in Beijing. Contact Monkey Business (see p38) for the latest information about this. Some **European nationalities** need health insurance (see p21) to qualify for a Russian visa.

● **Russia** (☎ 6532 1267), 4 Dongzhimen Beizhong Jie. Open 09.30-12.00 on weekdays. It's possible to get a **transit visa** (valid for 10 days from your departure date from Beijing) without having to show your ticket out of Russia but this may change so check check with the embassy. There are always long queues here: arrive early and certainly not after 11:00 if you hope to get in that day. You'll need three photos and a photocopy of the personal information pages of your passport; the service costs US$50 (five-day wait), US$80 (three days), or US$120 in one hour. Some nationalities have to pay an additional consular fee (US$45 if you're from the US). If you're stopping off anywhere, or for more than two days in Moscow, you'll need a **tourist visa**, which requires visa support; visa charges for most nationalities are almost the same as for the transit visa.

● **Mongolia** (☎ 6532 1203), 2 Xiushui Beijie, Jianguomenwai. Open 09:00-11:00 and 14:00-16:00 weekdays. Queues are also long here. You'll need one passport photo and US$30 for a transit visa (three days to process); the express service costs US$60 (same day). You won't be allowed to stop off in Mongolia on a transit visa. A tourist visa costs US$40 (US$60 for same-day processing). Monkey Business (see p37) should be able to help with tours and accommodation.

● **Belarus**, Jianguomenwai Compound (near New Zealand embassy). For the mandatory transit visa you must apply in person with your passport, one photo, your Russian visa plus a photocopy of it and US$46. The service takes two days and the embassy is open Monday, Wednesday and Friday, 10:00-12:00.

For more information on **Beijing** and other embassies see p301.

From Hong Kong

Hong Kong can be a good place to arrange a ticket or stopover package on the Trans-Siberian. The agencies here offer a range of services and booking with them from abroad is usually no problem.

Several of the travel agencies in the Nathan Road area can arrange tickets at short notice (two weeks or less). Some will sell you a voucher to exchange at their branch in Beijing for a ticket with reservation. Others sell you an open ticket with a reservation voucher and you must get the ticket endorsed by CITS in Beijing. Getting the reservation is the difficult part so don't accept an open ticket without a reservation voucher. To visit any Russian cities apart from Moscow you'll need tourist visas and for these you need visa support.

● **Monkey Business/Moonsky Star** (☎ 2723 1376, 🖃 2723 6653, 🖳 MonkeyHK@compuserve.com, 🖳 www.monkeyshrine.com), E-Block, 4th Floor, Flat 6, Chungking Mansion, 36-44 Nathan Rd, Kowloon (open 10am-6pm, Monday to Saturday). The Monkeys are André and Patrick, two Belgian brothers who've now put literally thousands of budget travellers on the trains across Siberia. The Hong Kong office sells their packages and in Beijing at their **infocentre** (see p36-7) they make sure everyone gets on the right train. The advantage of travelling with the Monkeys is that they organize everything for you and provide the vital visa support you'll need for stopovers in Russia. They sell a range of individual packages from Beijing to Moscow (from US$345) and stopover packages including Ulan Bator (from US$560), Irkutsk and Listvyanka (from US$790) – the first night's accommodation in Moscow (in a three-star hotel) is included in most packages. In the summer they run a popular six-day Mongolian tour (from US$495). Monkey Business have an itinerary which starts in Beijing and includes five nights in Mongolia, four nights in Irkutsk and Listvyanka, two nights in Yekaterinburg and then on to Moscow (from US$1130).

● **Time Travel Services** (☎ 2366 6222; 🖹 2739 5413, 🖳 timetrvl@hkstar.com), Block A, 16th Floor, Chungking Mansions, 40 Nathan Rd, Kowloon, sells tickets only for both the Trans-Siberian and Trans-Manchurian routes and will email you a brochure.

● **Shoestring Travel** (☎ 2723 2306; 🖹 2721 2085, 🖳 shoetvl@ hkstar.com), Flat A, 4th Floor, Alpha House, 27-33 Nathan Rd, Kowloon, sells tickets from Beijing to Moscow for the Trans-Mongolian and Trans-Manchurian routes as well as flights and visas.

● **Phoenix Services Agency** (☎ 2722 7378; 🖹 2369 8884), Room A, 7th Floor, Milton Mansion, 96 Nathan Rd, Kowloon.

From Malaysia
● **STA Travel** (☎ 3-248 9800, 🖹 3-243 3046), Lot 506, 5th Floor, Plaza Magnum, Kuala Lumpur.

From Singapore
● **STA Travel** (☎ 737 7188, 🖹 737 2591), 33a Cuppage Rd, Cuppage Terrace, Singapore 229458.

From Thailand
● **STA Travel** (☎ 2-236 0262, Wall St Tower Bldg, 33/70 Surawong Rd, (between Thaniya Rd and Patpong), Bangrak, 10500 Bangkok.

What to take

Woollen underwear is the best safeguard against sudden changes in temperature. High goloshes or 'rubber boots' are desirable, as the unpaved streets of the towns are almost impassable in spring and autumn; in winter felt overshoes or 'arctics' are also necessary. A mosquito-veil is desirable in E. Siberia and Manchuria during the summer. It is desirable to carry a revolver in Manchuria and in trips away from the railway. **Karl Baedeker** *Russia with Teheran, Port Arthur and Pekin, 1914,*

The best advice today is to travel as light as possible. Some people recommend that you put out everything you think you'll need and then pack only half of it. Remember that unless you're going on an up-market tour, you'll be carrying your luggage yourself.

Clothes
For summer in Moscow and Siberia pack as for an English summer: thin clothes, a sweater and a raincoat. In every hotel you will be able to get laundry done, often returned the same day, for a few roubles. Take shirts

and tops of a quick-drying cotton/polyester mixture if you are going to wash them yourself.

Winter in Russia and northern China is extremely cold, although trains and most buildings are kept well-heated: inside the train you can be quite warm enough in a thin shirt as you watch Arctic scenes pass by your window. When you're outside, however, a thick winter overcoat is an absolute necessity, as well as gloves and a warm hat. It's easy to buy good quality overcoats/jackets in Beijing for about £30/US$45. If you're travelling in winter and plan to stop off in Siberian cities along the way you might consider taking thermal underwear. Shoes should be strong, light and comfortable; most travellers take sturdy trainers. On the train, Russians discard their shoes and wear flip flops – the type you can wear with socks. This is a good idea and you can buy them at any station or on virtually any street. Russians also wear track-suits throughout the journey whilst the Chinese might resort to pyjamas.

Dress casually; jeans are quite acceptable even for a visit to the Bolshoi Theatre. If you forget anything, clothes are expensive in Japan, cheap but shoddy in Russia, cheap and fashionable in Hong Kong, and very cheap but curiously dated in China.

Luggage

If you're going on one of the more expensive tours which include baggage handling, take a suitcase. Those on individual itineraries have the choice of rucksack (comfortable to carry for long distances but bulky) or shoulder-bag (not so good for longer walks but more compact than the

❏ **Luggage limits**

On my first Trans-Siberian trip from Beijing we had so much luggage that several taxi-drivers refused to take us to the station. Unfortunately all thirteen bags were necessary as we were moving back from Japan. On the train we'd managed to get some of them stowed away in the compartments above the door and under the seats when we were joined by a German woman travelling home after three years in China. Her equally voluminous baggage included two full-size theatrical lanterns which were very fragile. Then the man from Yaroslavl arrived with three trunks. We solved the storage situation by covering the floor between the bottom bunks with luggage and spreading the bedding over it, making a sort of triple bed on which we all lounged comfortably – eating, drinking, reading, playing cards and sleeping for the next six days. Dragging our bags around Moscow, Berlin and Paris was no fun, however. On subsequent journeys I didn't even take a rucksack, only a light 'sausage' bag with a shoulder strap and a small day-pack. Never travel with an ounce more than you absolutely need. Nowadays a 35kg luggage limit in compartments is strictly applied in Beijing and to a lesser extent in Moscow.

rucksack). Unless you are going trekking in Russia or China, a zip-up holdall with a shoulder strap or a frameless backpack are probably the best bet. It's also useful to take along a small daypack for camera, books etc. Since bedding on the train and in hotels is supplied you don't need to take a sleeping-bag even when travelling in winter. However, sheets provided on the train are occasionally still damp from the laundry, so a sleeping sheet (a sheet used inside a sleeping bag) might be worth considering.

Medical supplies

Essential items are: aspirin or paracetamol; lip salve; sunscreen lotion; insect repellent (vital if you're travelling in summer); antiseptic cream and some plasters/bandaids; an anti-AIDS kit containing sterile syringes and swabs for emergency medical treatment. Note that Western brands of tampons and condoms are not always easily available in Russia or China. Bring an extra pair of glasses or contacts lenses if you wear them.

You may want to take along something for an upset stomach ('Arrêt', for example) but use it only in an emergency, as changes in diet often cause slight diarrhoea which stops of its own accord. Avoid rich food, alcohol and strong coffee to give your stomach time to adjust. Paradoxically, a number of travellers have suggested that it's a good idea to take along laxatives. For vaccination requirements, see p48.

General items

A money-belt is essential to safeguard your documents and cash. Wear it underneath your clothing and don't take it off on the train, as compartments are very occasionally broken into. A good pair of sun-glasses is necessary in summer as well as in winter when the sun on the snow is particularly bright. A water bottle (two-litre) which can take boiling water is essential as is a mug (insulated is best), spoon and knife.

The following items are also useful: a few clothes pegs, adhesive tape, ball-point pens, business cards, camera and adequate supplies of film (see p45), flashlight, folding umbrella, games (cards, chess – the Russians are very keen chess players – Scrabble etc), lavatory paper, calculator (for exchange rates), notebook or diary, penknife with corkscrew and can-opener (although there's a bottle opener fixed underneath the table in each compartment on the train), photocopies of passport, visa, air tickets, etc. (keep them in two separate places), sewing-kit, spare passport photographs for visas, string (to use as a washing-line), the addresses of friends and relatives (don't take your address book in case you lose it), tissues (including the wet variety), universal bathplug (Russian basins usually don't have a plug), walkman (batteries are easily found locally), washing powder (liquid 'Travel Soap' is good). Some people take along an electric heating coil for boiling a mug of water when staying in a hotel. A compass is useful when looking at maps and out of the window of the train. Don't forget to take a good book (see p46).

Gifts

Once the sale of a pair of Levis in Moscow could cover your spending money for the entire trip but this is just not the case any more. It is now very hard for foreigners to trade anything on the black market.

Rather than things to trade, what you should bring in abundance is gifts. The Russians are great present givers and there's nothing more embarrassing than being entertained in a Russian home and then being presented with a truckload of souvenirs when you have nothing to offer in return. In the major cities, most Western goods can be purchased; however in Siberia it can be harder. Rather than give something that can be bought locally, bring things that are harder for Russians to get. These include postcards of your country, key rings and baseball caps. Bring a few foreign coins and badges as Russia is full of collectors, although interest in badges (and stamps) seems to be on the wane.

It is essential to make sure that when on the train you have things to share: chocolate biscuits, sweets and other snacks. Don't bother with Twixes, Mars Bars or Snickers bars, as they're all widely available. If you're trying to impress Russians with chocolate it will have to be good since theirs, the Red October brand in particular, can be excellent. Red October's Gold Label bar has been on the market since 1867.

It's also a very good idea to bring things to show people: glossy magazines (as many glamorous pictures of celebrities as possible) and pictures of your family and friends will all be interesting to someone who has never been abroad. The Chinese in particular adore looking at photographs of people.

Provisions

The range of food and drink available on the train is improving and you can now buy numerous things in the dining car that weren't previously available: alcohol, chocolate and biscuits. There's also now a good selection of things to eat available from the hawkers on the platforms at the stations along the way. It's still wise to buy some provisions before you

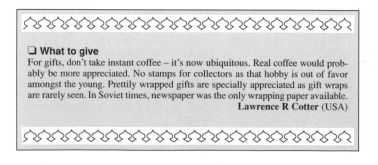

❏ **What to give**
For gifts, don't take instant coffee – it's now ubiquitous. Real coffee would probably be more appreciated. No stamps for collectors as that hobby is out of favor amongst the young. Prettily wrapped gifts are specially appreciated as gift wraps are rarely seen. In Soviet times, newspaper was the only wrapping paper available.
Lawrence R Cotter (USA)

❏ **Platform food – see also p123**

I rather regretted having taken on so many supplies at Moscow before the jour-ney, when I saw how much was on offer at the informal markets en route. Gastronomic offerings available from the hawkers at the various stations on the route included: fresh fruit and vegetables, bread, savoury pastries, pancakes, ice-cream, potatoes and various other hot dishes. Big city stations, however, often have no hawkers at all. **Anthony Kay** (UK)

get on the train, though, especially if you are going the whole way with-out a break. If you are sharing a compartment with Russians, they will probably insist that you share their food, usually bread, tomatoes, cucum-ber, sausage, boiled eggs and sweets. To refuse would be rude but you should obviously offer some of your food as well, though often it will not be accepted as they will see you as their guest.

Some travellers bring rucksacks filled with food, though it's more real-istic to bring just some biscuits and tea-bags or instant coffee (with whiten-er and sugar if required); hot water is always available from the samovar in each carriage. Other popular items include drinking chocolate, beer and vodka (much cheaper on the platform than on the train), dried soups, tinned or fresh fruit, Tang or other fruit-juice powder, peanut butter, Marmite or Vegemite, chocolate, crackers, cheese and pot noodles. If you forget to buy provisions at home there are Western-style supermarkets in both Moscow and Beijing where you can stock up with essentials.

Money – see also p71

Moscow, St Petersburg and Beijing are about the only cities where using ATMs, cashing travellers' cheques and getting credit card cash advances is reasonably straightforward. Most banks will do the exchange for between 2% and 4% commission. In Siberia all of the above are some-times possible but you shouldn't always expect to be able to do any of them easily.

Thus it is best to take as much US$ cash as you feel safe to carry and the rest in travellers' cheques. Always carry just a small amount of money in your pocket and the rest safely under your clothing in a moneybelt (worn in bed at night as well as during the day). Have a second stash hid-den somewhere else for emergencies. Bear in mind that although cash seems more risky than travellers' cheques many Russians carry far larger stashes of money on their person than you will probably have; and note also that you'd be unlikely to get a swift refund or replacement of your travellers' cheques whilst in Russia if they did get stolen. While other currencies may be acceptable (UK£, and, in Vladivostok and Khabarovsk, Japanese yen), everyone in Russia understands the word 'dollar'. The above is also true for Mongolia. In China travellers' cheques are widely accepted but take care when countersigning to ensure the signatures match exactly. Credit cards are accepted in some places and there will usually be at least one bank in each town where you can get a cash advance on your credit card.

For the train, it's important that you bring notes of small denominations like US$1s and US$5s because it can be hard to get the correct change. Make sure your US$ notes are in immaculate condition and not dated before 1996 if possible and certainly not 1991 or before. It's probably best to have plenty of US$20s and US$50s for exchange rather than US$100 notes. People are far more suspicious of US$100s and so the slightest mark may make it worthless in their eyes. Traders and even banks are likely to reject any note if it is torn, badly creased or worn. Because of the circulation of outdated and worthless Russian bank notes, and the small difference in the legal and black markets, exchanging money on the street is not recommended.

In Russia you will have to pay for everything in roubles. Hotels must take roubles even though some may ask you for dollars.

Photographic equipment

Bring more film than you think you'll need, as you'll find there's a lot to photograph. Don't forget to bring some faster film for shots from the train (400 ASA). It's wise to carry all your film in a lead-lined pouch (available from camera shops) if you are going to let them go through Russian X-ray machines at airports.

Most major brands of film are available in Russia cities, but slide or high/low ASA film may be difficult to find outside Moscow and St Petersburg. In the large cities in Siberia and China, you can have your film processed in one hour and the quality is acceptable. In Ulan Bator there seem to be plenty of newly-opened developers with imported machines. Film development is naturally of a high standard in Japan but, unless you request otherwise, prints will be small.

What not to photograph

Taking pictures from the train used to be forbidden but now it's OK, although it would be wise not to get trigger-happy at aerodromes, military installations or other politically sensitive areas. In addition, many Russians still believe it is illegal to take any photos from a train and they may tell you in no uncertain terms to stop.

Remember that in Russia, as in most other countries, it's considered rude to take pictures of strangers, their children or possessions without asking permission. Often people are keen to have their picture taken but you must always ask. This is particularly the case during political demonstrations or rallies: the updater of an earlier edition of this guide got stoned by a group of pensioners outside the White House in September 1993 for trying to get the next cover for *Time* magazine. Beware!

Refrain from photographing touchy subjects such as drunks, queues and beggars. Photography in churches is normally discouraged, and taking a photo of someone in front of an icon is

> ❑ **Window cleaning**
> A squeegie, an instrument used by window-cleaners to remove water, can be easily obtained in a small size for car windows. This tool is an invaluable aid for cleaning the train's windows for photography or, for that matter, just for passengers' viewing.
> **Robert Bray** (UK)

considered disrespectful. A useful phrase is 'Mozhno vas snimat?' (Можно Вас Снимать) meaning simply, 'Can I take a photo of you?' When asking for permission, offer to send them a copy: and keep your word. If travelling in winter always carry your camera inside your pocket or elsewhere near your body as film gets brittle and batteries get sluggish in the intense cold.

Photography from the train

The problem on the train is to find a window that isn't opaque or one that opens. They're usually locked in winter so that no warmth escapes. Opening doors and hanging out will upset the carriage attendants if they catch you; if one carriage's doors are locked try the next, and remember that the kitchen car's doors are always open. Probably the best place for undisturbed photography is right at the end of the train: 'No one seemed to mind if we opened the door in the very last carriage. We got some great shots of the tracks extending for miles behind the train'. (Elizabeth Hehir, The Netherlands).

Background reading

A number of excellent books have been written about the Trans-Siberian, several of which are unfortunately out of print. If they're not in your library they should be available through the inter-library loans system. The following are well worth reading before you go:

● *Journey Into the Mind's Eye* by Lesley Blanch, is a fascinating book: a witty, semi-autobiographical story of the author's romantic obsession with Russia and the Trans-Siberian Railway.

● *To the Great Ocean* by Harmon Tupper (Secker and Warburg, 1965 and out of print) gives an entertaining account of Siberia and the building of the railway.

● *Guide to the Great Siberian Railway 1900* by A I Dmitriev-Mamanov, a reprint (David and Charles 1971 and also out of print) of the guide originally published by the Tsar's government to publicize their new railway. Highly detailed but interesting to look at.

● *Peking to Paris: A Journey across two Continents* by Luigi Barzini tells the story of the Peking to Paris Rally in 1907. The author accompanied the Italian Prince Borghese and his chauffeur in the winning car, a 40 horse-power Itala. Their route took them across Mongolia and Siberia and for some of the journey they actually drove along the railway tracks.

● *The Big Red Train Ride* by Eric Newby. This is a perceptive and entertaining account of the journey he made in the Soviet era, written in Newby's characteristically humorous style.

● *In Siberia* by Colin Thubron was in the best-seller lists throughout 2000, and deserved to be. It's the best modern book for background on Siberia and certainly one you should either read before you go or take with you on the trip. His excellent earlier travelogue, *Among the Russians*, was written after his travels in Soviet times.

● *The Trans-Siberian Railway: A Traveller's Anthology*, edited by Deborah Manley, is well worth taking on the trip for a greater insight into the railway and the journey, as seen through the eyes of travellers from Annette Meakin to Bob Geldof. Now out of print but available in libraries.

● The *Princess of Siberia* is Christine Sutherland's biography of Princess Maria Volkonsky, who followed her husband to Siberia after he'd been exiled for his part in the Decembrists' Uprising. Her house in Irkutsk is now a museum.

● *Stalin's Nose* by Rory Maclean. Maclean explores the former Eastern Bloc in a battered Trabant with his elderly aunt Zita and a pig named Winston. He recounts the histories of some of his more notorious relatives and it serves as a darkly humorous commentary on communism and its demise.

● *Lenin's Tomb* by David Remnick is an historical account of the Gorbachev era to its end.

● *Between the Hammer and the Sickle – across Russia by Cycle* by Simon Vickers is a highly-entertaining account of the author's epic bicycle journey from St Petersburg to Vladivostok in 1990. Out of print but available from libraries.

● *A People's Tragedy – The Russian Revolution 1891-1924*, by Orlando Figes is a scholarly work that brings this turning point in Russia's history to life. Winner of the 1997 NCR Book Award.

● *East of the Sun: The Conquest and Settlement of Siberia* by Benson Bobrick. Published in 1993, this is a clear and readable narrative of the last four centuries of Siberian history.

However well written and accurate, these books are only the impressions of foreign travellers. You will get more of an idea of the Russian mind and soul from their own literature, even from the pre-Revolution classics. If you haven't already read them you might try some of the following:

● Dostoyevsky's thought provoking and atmospheric *Crime and Punishment* (set in the Haymarket in St Petersburg).

● Tolstoy's *War and Peace*.
● Mikhail Bulgakov's weird but fascinating *The Master and Margarita*.
● *Dr Zhivago* by Boris Pasternak (whose grave you can visit in Moscow).
● *The Gulag Archipelago* by Alexander Solzhenitsyn.
● *Memories from the House of the Dead* is a semi-autobiographical account of Dostoyevsky's life as a convict in Omsk.
● *A Day in the Life of Ivan Denisovitch* by Alexander Solzhenitsyn details twenty-four hours in the life of a Siberian convict.

The following guidebooks are recommended:
● *Siberian BAM Guide – rail, rivers and road*, by Athol Yates and Nicholas Zvegintzov is a comprehensive guide for travellers in the NE Siberian BAM zone, including the 3400km long BAM (Baikal-Amur Mainline) railway in Eastern Siberia and good coverage of the northern end of Lake Baikal and Lena River routes. Now in its second edition.
● *Lonely Planet Russia, Ukraine & Belarus* is very comprehensive. Other areas of interest to Trans-Siberian travellers that are covered by Lonely Planet include: Mongolia, North-East Asia, China, Tibet, Japan, Hong Kong, Korea, Western Europe, Eastern Europe, the Baltic States, Poland, Hungary and Scandinavia. Their phrasebooks are also useful.
● *Trekking in Russia & Central Asia* by Frith Maier has coverage of parts of Siberia but is now out of print.
● *The Insider's Guide to Russia*, by Gleb Uspensky, is filled with anecdotes and insights that only a native can provide.
● *Holy Russia* by Fitzroy Maclean is probably the best historical summary (with walking tours) for the traveller.

For further rail travels in Russia there's *Russia by Rail including Belarus and Ukraine* by Athol Yates covering 50 cities and 300 towns along major rail lines. Trailblazer publishes guides to rail travel in **China**, **Japan**, **Vietnam** and several other countries – see p432 for more information.
    For information on locomotives, *Soviet Locomotive Types – The Union Legacy*, by AJ Heywood and IDC Button is invaluable. It's co-published by Luddenden Press (UK) and Frank Stenvalls (Sweden).

Health precautions and inoculations

No vaccinations are listed as official requirements for Western tourists visiting Russia, China, Mongolia or Japan. Some may be advisable, however, for certain areas (see below). If you plan to spend more than three months in Russia evidence of a recent negative AIDS test is required.

❑ **Drinking water**
It's best to stick to mineral water or boiled water in **Russia** although the tap water is safe to drink in some cities. Avoid it in St Petersburg since the water here can cause a nasty form of diarrhoea (giardia), particularly in summer. In Irkutsk and Listvyanka you can drink the tap water, which comes directly from Lake Baikal.

   Drink only boiled or bottled water in **Mongolia** and **China**; boiled water (in a thermos) is provided on trains and in hotels. Tap water is safe in **Japan** and **Hong Kong**.

   On the **train** getting boiled water is no problem as each carriage is equipped with a samovar (*batchok* – see p117).

Russia now has the highest incidence of AIDS infection in the world, 90% of it drug related. Since the 1990s there has been a worrying decline in public health in Russia: an outbreak of diphtheria in 1993, a rise in tuberculosis particularly amongst prison inmates and the reappearance of diseases such as anthrax and bubonic plague. Vaccination services are available in London at **Trailfinders** (☎ 020-7938 3999) at 194 Kensington High St, and at **British Airways Travel Clinic** (☎ 020-7439 9584) at 156 Regent St. **Nomad Travellers' Store & Medical Centre** (☎ 020-8889 7014) at 3-4 Turnpike Lane (Wellington Tce), London N8 0PX offers travel medical advice, inoculations and supplies.

   In the USA, the **Center for Disease Control and Prevention** (☎ 404-332 4559) in Atlanta is the best place to call for health information. If you have a fax an automated service is provided on the above number to fax you back the latest health information for the countries you are visiting.

   You should have **health insurance**, available from any travel agent, wherever you are travelling. The UK has a reciprocal health care agreement with 40 countries, including Russia but not China or Mongolia. Treatment in Russian hospitals is free as long as you collect Form E111 from a UK post office before you go; given the state of most Russian hospitals, however, you're advised to go to a private clinic if you get ill and arrange proper health insurance before you leave the UK. Some other nationalities will need health insurance before they can get a Russian visa (see p21).

INOCULATIONS

● **Diphtheria** Check that you were given the initial vaccine as a child and a booster within the last ten years. The World Health Organization recommends a combined booster dose of tetanus-diphtheria toxoid.

● **Tetanus** A booster is advisable if you haven't had one in the last 10 years: if you then cut yourself badly in Russia you won't need another.

● **Infectious hepatitis** Those travelling on a tight budget who will be eating in the cheaper restaurants run the risk of catching infectious hepatitis, a disease of the liver that drains you of energy and can last from three to eight weeks. It's spread by infected water or food, or by using utensils handled by an infected person. Gamma globulin injections give a certain amount of protection and are effective for 3-6 months. A more recent vaccine, Havrix, lasts twice that time (and up to 10 years if a further booster is given).

> ❑ **Mongolian scam**
> In 2000 a Mongolian company was approaching foreigners on the train at the border requesting US$10 for what they said was mandatory insurance cover for a visit to the country. Those who paid up were presented with an official-looking document from the Mongol Daatgal National Insurance & Reinsurance Co. Don't fall for this one!

● **Malaria** If you plan to go to the south of China you may need to take **anti-malarial tablets**. In parts of China, the parasite (carried by the *Anopheles* mosquito) that causes malaria is resistant to chloroquine, so you may need to take two kinds of tablet. Start taking the tablets one week before you go and continue for six weeks after you leave the malarial zone. If you're going to be in a malarial area you'd be foolish not to take the tablets: the disease is dangerous and on the increase. Contact one of the organizations above for up-to-date advice.

● **Other** Ensure you've had recent **typhoid**, **polio** and **BCG** (tuberculosis) boosters. Most people are vaccinated against these diseases in childhood. If you're planning to go off the beaten track it's advisable to have a vaccination against **meningococcal meningitis**. Those going on a long trek in Siberia may want to consider a vaccination against **tick borne encephalitis**. It's also worth considering a pre-exposure **rabies** vaccination course.

MEDICAL SERVICES

Those travelling with tour groups will be with guides who can contact doctors to sort out medical problems. Serious problems can be expensive but you'll get the best treatment possible from doctors used to dealing with foreigners. If you're travelling independently and require medical assistance contact an up-market hotel for help. In Moscow or St Petersburg the best places to go in an emergency are the US Medical Centres. If you are in St Petersburg, Moscow, Yekaterinburg, Novosibirsk, Irkutsk or Khabarovsk, medical assistance is available at the clinics beside MNTK-Iris hotels.

Large hotels in China usually have a doctor in residence and in Beijing, Shanghai and Canton there are special hospitals for foreigners. Take supplies of any prescription medicine you may need. Medical facilities in Mongolia are very limited and some medicine is unavailable.

RUSSIA

Facts about the country

GEOGRAPHICAL BACKGROUND

The Russian Federation includes over 75 per cent of the former UŞSR. It is still the largest country in the world, incorporating 17,175,000 square km (over 6.5 million square miles) and stretching from well into the Arctic Circle right down to the northern Caucasus in the south, and from the Black Sea in the west to the Bering Straits in the east, only a few miles from Alaska. Russia is twice as big as the USA; the UK could fit into this vast country some 69 times.

Climate

Much of the country is situated in far northern latitudes. Moscow is on the same latitude as Edinburgh, St Petersburg is almost as far north as Anchorage in Alaska. Winters are extremely cold, and temperatures as low as -68°C (-90°F) have been recorded in Oymyakon in Siberia. It is not only the extremes of latitude which cause the severe winters: the physical make-up of the country is as much to blame. Most of the land is an open plain stretching up across Siberia to the Arctic. While there is higher ground in the south there are no mountains in the north to shield it from the cold Arctic air which blows down to fill this plain. To the west are the Urals, the low range which divides Europe and Asia. The Himalayan and Pamir ranges beyond the southern borders stop warm tropical air from reaching the Siberian and Russian plains. Thus blocked off, the plains warm rapidly in summer and become very cold in winter. Olekminsk, in north-east Siberia, holds the record for the place with the greatest temperature range in the world: from -60°C (-87°F) in winter to a record summer high of 45°C (113°F). Along the route of the Trans-Siberian, however, summers are rather more mild.

Transport and communications

Railways remain the principal transport system for both passengers and goods, and there are some 87,500km of track in the country. The heaviest traffic on the entire system and in the world is on certain stretches of the Trans-Siberian, with trains passing every few minutes. Although Russia's **road network** is comparatively well-developed (624,000km), few people own cars which means that, as well as the 47% of freight, 31% of all passengers also travel by rail.

The **rivers** of Russia have always been of vital importance as a communication network across the country. Some of these rivers are huge and are navigable by ocean-going ships for considerable distances. Harsh winters preclude year-round navigation and **air travel** is gradually taking over.

Landscape zones: flora and fauna

The main landscape zones of interest to the Trans-Siberian traveller are as follows:

● **European Russia** West of the Urals the flora and fauna are similar to that found in the rest of northern Europe. Trees include oak, elm, hazel, ash, apple, aspen, spruce, lime and maple.

● **North Siberia and the Arctic regions** The *tundra* zone (short grass, mosses and lichens) covers the tree-less area in the far north. Soil is poor and much of it permanently frozen. In fact *permafrost* affects over 40% of Russia and extends down into southern Siberia, where it causes building problems for architects and engineers. In this desolate northern zone the wildlife includes reindeer, arctic fox, wolf, lemming and vole. Bird life is more numerous: ptarmigan, snow-bunting, Iceland falcon and snow-owl as well as many kinds of migratory water and marsh fowl.

● **The Siberian plain** Much of this area is covered with *taiga* (pronounced 'tiger') meaning thick forest. To the north the trees are stunted and windblown; in the south they grow into dark impenetrable forests. More than 30% of all the world's trees grow in this taiga zone. These include larch, pine and silver fir, intermingled with birch, aspen and maple. Willow and poplar line the rivers and streams. Much of the taiga forest along the route of the Trans-Siberian has been cleared and replaced with fields of wheat or sun-flowers. Parts of this region are affected by permafrost and in places rails and roads sink, and houses, trees and telegraph poles keel over drunkenly. Fauna includes species once common in Europe: bear, badger, wolverine, polecat, ermine, sable, squirrel, weasel, otter, wolf, fox, lynx, beaver, several types of rodent, musk deer, roebuck, reindeer and elk.

● **East Siberia and Trans-Baikal** Much of the flora and fauna of this region is unique including, in Lake Baikal, such rarities as the world's only fresh-water seals. Amongst the ubiquitous larch and pine there grows a type of birch with dark bark, *Betula daurica*. Towards the south and into China and Mongolia, the forests give way to open grassy areas known as *steppes*. The black earth (*chernozem*) of the northern steppes is quite fertile and some areas are under cultivation.

● **The Far Eastern territories: the Amur region** Along the Amur River the flora and fauna are similar to that found in northern China and it is here that the rare Amur tiger (see p366) is found. European flora makes a reappearance in the Far Eastern region including such trees as cork, walnut and acacia.

HISTORICAL OUTLINE

The first Russians

Artefacts recently uncovered in Siberia (see p87) suggest that human history in Russia may stretch back much further than had previously been believed: 500,000 or more years. Around the thirteenth millennium BC there were Stone Age nomads living beside Lake Baikal.

By the second millennium BC when fairly advanced civilizations had emerged here, European Russia was inhabited by Ural-Altaic and Indo-European peoples. In the sixth century BC the Scythians (whose magnificent goldwork may be seen in the Hermitage) settled in southern Russia, near the Black Sea.

Through the early centuries of the first millennium AD trade routes developed between Scandinavia, Russia and Byzantium, following the Dnieper River. Centres of trade grew up along the route (Novgorod, Kiev, Smolensk, Chernigov) and by the sixth century AD the towns were populated by Slavic tribes known as the Rus (hence 'Russian').

The year 830 saw the first of the Varangian (Viking) invasions and in 862 Novgorod fell to the Varangian chief, Rurik, Russia's first sovereign.

Vladimir and Christian Russia

The great Tsar Vladimir (978-1015) ruled Russia from Kiev and was responsible for the conversion of the country to Christianity. At the time the Slavs worshipped a range of pagan gods and it is said that in his search for a new religion Vladimir invited bids from the Muslims, the Jews and the Christians. Since Islam and the consumption of vodka were not compatible and Judaism did not make for a unified nation, he chose Christianity as the state religion and had himself baptized at Constantinople in 988 AD. It was at his order that the mass conversion of all the Russian people began, with whole towns being baptized simultaneously.

The eleventh century was marked by continual feuding between his heirs. It was at this time that the northern principalities of Vladimir and Suzdal were founded.

The Mongol invasion and the rise of Muscovy

Between 1220 and 1230, the Golden Horde brought a sudden halt to economic progress in Russia, burning towns and putting the local population to the sword.

By 1249 Kiev was under their control and the Russians moved north, establishing a new political centre at Muscovy (Moscow). All Russian principalities were obliged to pay tribute to the Mongol khans but Muscovy was the first to challenge their authority. Over the next three centuries Moscow gained control of the other Russian principalities and shook off the Mongol yoke.

❏ **An English Tsarina for Ivan Bazilovitch?**
In Elizabethan times there were diplomatic and trading links between England and Muscovy whose emissaries and merchants came to London "dripping pearls and vermin" while Englishmen went to Moscow. Indeed the Tsar had occasion to complain of the behaviour of some of them thereby eliciting a tactful letter from the Queen.

Elizabeth's diplomatic skills brought about a peace between Ivan Bazilovitch and John, king of Sweden, and the former was so grateful to her that "imagining she might stand his friend in a matter more interesting to his personal happiness, he made humble suit to her majesty to send him a wife out of England". The Queen chose Anne, sister of the Earl of Huntingdon and of royal Plantagenet blood, but the lady was not willing to risk "the barbarous laws of Muscovy which allowed the sovereign to put away his czarina as soon as he was tired of her and wanted something new in the conjugal department. The czar was dissatisfied and did not long survive his disappointment", dying in 1584. He is better known to history as Ivan the Terrible and his reputation may well have affected the Queen's thinking when she sorely tried Tsar Boris Godunov's patience with her diplomatic procrastination over his attempts to get an English bride for one of his sons.

(Sources: *The Letters of Queen Elizabeth*, ed. Harrison; *Lives of the Queens of England*, Agnes Strickland, Camden's Annals).   **Patricia Major**

Ivan the Terrible (1530-84)

When Ivan the Terrible came to the throne he declared himself Tsar of All the Russias and by his successful military campaigns extended the borders of the young country. He was as wild and blood-thirsty as his name suggests and in a fit of anger in 1582 he struck his favourite son with a metal staff, fatally injuring him (a scene used by Ilya Repin as the subject of one of his greatest paintings). Ivan was succeeded by his mentally-retarded son, Fyodor, but the real power was with the regent, Boris Godunov. Godunov later became the Tsar and ruled from 1598 to 1605. The early part of the seventeenth century was marked by dynastic feuding which ended with the election of Michael Romanov (1613-45), the first of a long line that lasted until the Revolution in 1917.

Peter the Great and the Westernization of Russia

Peter (1672-1725) well deserved his soubriquet 'the Great' for it was due to his policy of Westernization that Russia emerged from centuries of isolation and backwardness into the eighteenth century. He founded St Petersburg in 1703 as a 'window open on the West' and made it his capital in 1712. During his reign there were wars with Sweden and Turkey.

Territorial gains included the Baltic provinces and the southern and western shores of the Caspian.

The extravagant building programme in St Petersburg continued under Catherine the Great (1762-96). While her generals were taking the Black Sea steppes, the Ukraine and parts of Poland for Russia, Catherine conducted extensive campaigns of a more romantic nature with a series of favourites in her elegant capital.

Alexander I and the Napoleonic Wars

In Russia during the nineteenth century, the political pendulum swung back and forth between conservatism and enlightenment. The mad Tsar Paul I came to the throne in 1796 but was murdered five years later. He was succeeded by his son Alexander I (1801-25) who was said to have had a hand in the sudden demise of his father. In the course of Alexander's reign, he abolished the secret police, lifted the laws of censorship and would have freed the serfs had the aristocracy not objected so strongly to the idea. In 1812 Napoleon invaded Russia, and Moscow was burnt to the ground (by the inhabitants, not by the French) before he was pushed back over the border.

Growing unrest among the peasants

Nicholas I's reign began with the first Russian Revolution, the Decembrists' uprising (see p134), and ended, after he had reversed most of Alexander's enlightened policies, with the Crimean War against the English and the French in 1853-6. Nicholas was succeeded by Alexander II (1855-81) who was known as the Tsar Liberator, for it was he who freed the serfs. His reward was his assassination by a student in St Petersburg in 1881. He was succeeded by the strong Tsar Alexander III, during whose reign work began on the Trans-Siberian Railway.

Nicholas II: last of the Tsars

The dice were heavily loaded against this unfortunate Tsar. Nicholas inherited a vast empire and a restless population that was beginning to discover its own power. In 1905 his army and navy suffered a most humiliating defeat at the hands of the Japanese. Just when his country needed him most, as strikes and riots swept through the cities in the first few years of this century, Nicholas's attention was drawn into his own family crisis. It was discovered that the heir to the throne, Alexis, was suffering from haemophilia. The Siberian monk, Rasputin, ingratiated himself into the court circle through his ability to exert a calming influence over the Tsarevich. His influence over other members of the royal family, including the Tsar, was not so beneficial.

October 1917: the Russian Revolution

After the riots in 1905, Nicholas agreed to allow the formation of a national parliament (Duma) but its elected members had no real power.

Reforms came too slowly for the people and morale fell further when, during the First World War, Russia suffered heavy losses. By March 1917 the Tsar had lost all control and was forced to abdicate in favour of a provisional government led by Alexander Kerensky. The Revolution that abruptly changed the course of Russian history took place in October 1917, when the reins of government were seized by Lenin and his Bolshevik Party. Nicholas and his family were taken to Siberia where they were murdered (see p199). Civil war raged across the country and it was not until 1920 that the Bolsheviks brought the lands of Russia under their control, forming the Union of Soviet Socialist Republics.

The Stalin era

After the death of Lenin in 1924, control of the country passed to Stalin and it was under his leadership that the USSR was transformed from a backward agricultural country into an industrial world power. The cost to the people was tremendous and most of those who were unwilling to swim with the current were jailed for their 'political' crimes. During the Great Terror in the 1930s, millions were sentenced to work camps, which provided much of the labour for ambitious building projects.

During the Second World War the USSR played a vital part in the defeat of the Nazis and extended its influence to the East European countries that took on Communist governments after the war.

Khrushchev, Brezhnev, Andropov and Chernenko

After Stalin's death in 1953, Khrushchev became Party Secretary and attempted to ease the strict regulations which governed Soviet society. In 1962 his installation of missiles in Cuba almost led to war with the USA. Khrushchev was forced to resign in 1964, blamed for the failure of the country's economy and for his clumsy foreign policy. He was replaced by Brezhnev who continued the USSR's policy of adopting friendly 'buffer' states along the Iron Curtain by ordering the invasion of Afghanistan in 1979 'at the invitation of the leaders of the country'. When Brezhnev died in 1982, he was replaced by the former head of the KGB, Yuri Andropov. He died in 1984 and was succeeded by the elderly Chernenko, who managed a mere thirteen months in office before becoming the chief participant in yet another state funeral.

Gorbachev and the end of the Cold War

Mikhail Gorbachev, the youngest Soviet premier since Stalin, was elected in 1985 and quickly initiated a process of change categorized under the terms *glasnost* (openness) and *perestroika* (restructuring). The West credits him with bringing about the end of the Cold War (he received the Nobel Prize in 1990) but it would be misguided to think that he was the sole architect of the changes that took place in the USSR: it was widely acknowledged before he came to power that things had gone seriously wrong. Gorbachev launched a series of bold reforms: Soviet troops were pulled out of Afghanistan, Eastern Europe and Mongolia, political dissidents were freed, laws on religion relaxed and press censorship lifted. These changes displeased many of the Soviet 'old guard,' and on 19 August 1991, a group of senior military and political figures staged a coup. Gorbachev was isolated at his Crimean villa and Vice President Yanaev took over, declaring a state of emergency. Other politicians, including the President of the Russian Republic, Boris Yeltsin, denounced the coup and rallied popular support. There were general strikes and, after a very limited skirmish in Moscow (three casualties), the coup committee was put to flight.

The collapse of the USSR

Because most levels of the Communist Party had been compromised in the failed coup attempt, it was soon seen as corrupt and ineffectual. Gorbachev resigned his position as Chairman in late August and the Party was abolished five days later. The Communist Party's collapse heralded the demise of the republic it had created, and Gorbachev commenced a desperate struggle to stop this happening. His reforms, however, had already sparked nationalist uprisings in the Baltic republics, Armenia and Azerbaijan. Despite his suggestions for loose 'federations' of Russian states, by the end of 1991 the USSR had split into 15 independent republics. Having lost almost all his support, Gorbachev resigned and was relieved by Yeltsin.

Yeltsin vs the Congress of Deputies

Yeltsin's plans for economic reforms were thwarted at every turn by the Congress of People's Deputies (parliament). Members of Congress, elected before the collapse of communism, were well aware that by voting for reforms they were, in effect, removing themselves from office. In the Western press this struggle was described as the fight between the reformists (Yeltsin and his followers) and the hard-liners (Vice President Alexander Rutskoi, Congress's Speaker Ruslan Khasbulatov, and the rest of Congress). Yeltsin's hard-won referendum in April 1993 gave him a majority of 58% but this didn't give him a mandate to overrule parliament.

On 22 September 1993, Yeltsin suddenly dissolved parliament and declared presidential rule. (Some have suggested that this swift action was to avert another coup attempt). The Congress denounced his action, stripped him of all powers and swore in Rutskoi as President. The Constitutional Court ruled that, having acted illegally, Yeltsin could now be impeached. Khasbulatov accused him of effecting a 'state coup' and appealed for a national strike. The deciding factor in the confrontation between parliament and president was the question of whom the military would support. Rutskoi, an Afghan war veteran with a keen military following, ordered troops to march on Moscow. They never did, but some 5000 supporters surrounded the White House. Inside, the Congress voted to impeach Yeltsin, who retaliated by severing their telephone lines. The White House vigil turned into a siege; electricity lines were cut and the building surrounded by troops faithful to Yeltsin.

On 3 October a crowd of 10,000 communist supporters converged on the White House where Rutskoi exhorted the people to seize the Kremlin and other strategic locations around the city. All through the night there were confrontations as rioters attacked the mayor's office, the Tass news service building and the main TV station. At dawn on 4 October Yeltsin's troops stormed the White House. Fighting went on for most of the day but by the evening the building, charred and battered, was taken. By the end of the week, when order had been restored, 171 people had been killed.

Zhirinovsky and Chechnya

The state elections, held in December 1993, supported Yeltsin's draft constitution, which outlined Russia's new democratic architecture. Although the immediate threat was seen to have been the constitution's rejection (Yeltsin warned that this might lead to civil war), the election revealed a new problem in the form of the Liberal Democrat Party. Its leader, Vladimir Zhirinovsky, espoused some extremely sinister policies. Particularly worrying were his comments about reuniting the former USSR, his racist jibes and his aim to re-establish a Russian empire reaching 'from Murmansk to Madras'. In a move to demonstrate Yeltsin's strong leadership, to warn other republics considering separation and to regain control over oil industry in the region, Yeltsin ordered Russian troops into the breakaway Russian republic of Chechnya in November 1994. This military solution to a political problem was doomed to failure. By the time a truce was signed in mid-1996, over 80,000 Russian and Chechen soldiers and civilians had died, with a decision on the status of Chechnya being put off until November 2001.

1996 presidential elections

Zhirinovsky's star had fallen by the start of the 1996 election and for some time it appeared that the winner would be the communist leader, Genardi Zyuganov. At the start of the campaign, Yeltsin was written off as a contender with under 20% of the primary vote. At the end of the first round of voting, however, Yeltsin had proved his enormous campaign ability winning first place with a fistful of electoral bribes, strict control of the media, and the backing of the nation's richest businesses. Interestingly, Gorbachev polled less than 3% of the vote. The popular General Alexander Lebed posed a last minute threat having polled over 15% of the primary vote. Courted by Yeltsin and Zyuganov he finally supported Yeltsin in return for appointment as chairman of the powerful National Security Council. This tipped the election scales in Yeltsin's favour.

Immediately after Yeltsin's victory, he disappeared from public view and it soon became obvious that the campaign had taken a serious toll of the hard-drinking president. For nearly four months until his heart bypass operation in November 1996, Russia was leaderless and power plays were the only decisions being made in the Kremlin. In early 1997, Yeltsin regained control of the Kremlin and by the end of the year, some progress had been made. Inflation was under control and the rouble had been stabilized. Unfortunately in 1998 the Asian economic crisis spoiled Russia's success and it experienced a huge drop in oil exports followed by the withdrawal of foreign investors.

Putin's rise to presidency

In August 1999, Yeltsin fired the fourth of his prime ministers in 18 months and installed Vldimir Putin, an ex-KGB officer.

A series of terrorist attacks in major Russian cities including Moscow in September 1999 (and August 2000) were blamed on Chechen terrorists and the conflict in the Caucasus republic flared up once again. Many of the same mistakes seem to have been made and the aim, whether official or not, is to deal with Chechnya once and for all.

On New Year's Eve 1999 Yeltsin resigned, much to everyone's surprise, handing over power to Putin, his prime minister. In March 2000 Putin won the presidential elections with a narrow margin of 52.5% of the vote. He pledged to clean up Russia and transform it into a 'rich, strong and civilized country'. His past career as a KGB spy have left him with dangerous authoritarian tendencies and he has shown himself to be no friend of free speech. Putin has signed decrees allowing email and Internet usage to be monitored, reporters and press barons have been hounded and, most worrying, the Duma has approved his new law giving him the right to introduce a state of emergency and close down political parties when or if ever he sees fit to do so. On the positive side he has overhauled the tax system making it simpler to operate and harder to evade, and he is committed to protecting property rights and a liberalized economy. Most Russians seem to believe that if an authoritarian approach is what is needed to bring order and prosperity to their country then so be it but they, and the West, worry that he may take things too far and send Russia spiralling back into a police state.

ECONOMY

Russia has vast natural resources and in this sense it is an extremely rich country. It has the world's largest reserves of natural gas as well as deposits of oil, coal, iron ore, manganese, asbestos, lead, gold, silver and copper that will continue to be extracted long after most other countries have exhausted their supplies. The forested regions in Russia cover an area almost four times the size of the Amazon basin. Yet, owing to gross economic mismanagement under communism and continuing corruption since the privatization of state industries, the country is experiencing severe financial hardship and has been receiving Western aid since 1990.

Privatization

Mass privatization started in the early 1990s and in an attempt to create public approval of the process in October 1992 every citizen received vouchers worth 10,000 roubles (about US$60 at time of issue). The vouchers could be sold for cash or exchanged for shares in the growing number of private companies. Although the idea of buying and selling stocks caught on, there was some confusion over how exactly the market works. Western economic advisers were often asked such questions as 'If I own part of the company, why can't I take the computer home?'

Despite the fact that over 150,000 organizations were privatized, it is now obvious that privatization did nothing to benefit the average Russian. The country's valuable raw materials and viable industries were mostly sold at closed auctions to officially-preferred banks and tycoons, while economically unviable factories and collective farms were purchased by their workers. Consequently a relatively small number of well-connected business people pocketed Russia's wealth while millions of workers were lumbered with worthless investments.

Hyperinflation

When the markets for most commodities, previously artificially regulated, were freed on 2 January 1992, prices immediately soared by 300-400%. Inflation was already being fuelled by a law passed in 1990, allowing possession of hard currency, which led to a rush for dollars. Another factor adding to inflation was that in some instances the debts of former Communist Bloc countries to Russia were payable in roubles. These countries reserved their right to print Russian banknotes and simply set their presses running, releasing their own debts but fuelling the Russian problem. In an effort to limit the amount of Russian currency on the streets, a law passed in August 1993 withdrew all old rouble notes, replacing them with new ones. By late 1993, inflation was still running at around 25% per month. Following a year of tight monetary policy, the monthly inflation rate was a mere 2% a month by the end of 1996.

This did not last long and the rouble soon started to dive again reaching 6000 to US$1 towards the end of 1997. People desperately tried to change their rouble savings into dollars before they became worthless. In August 1998 Yeltsin took the decision to devalue the currency: three zeros were knocked off to make the exchange rate six roubles to the dollar; new banknotes were printed and strict rules governing the access to foreign currencies were introduced. It did not solve the problem immediately and the rate dropped from six to fifty roubles to the dollar. Since that low point it has crept back up to 25 roubles to US$1 in late 1999 and 27.8 roubles to US$1 in January 2001.

Economic future

The rise in the world price of oil was a considerable help to the Russian economy in 2000 and GDP rose by 4%. Putin has brought in a much-needed reform of the tax system. In 1996, only 16% of Russian enterprises paid their taxes in full and on time and only 14 regions out of Russia's 75 paid their tax bills in full. For most people there's now a flat tax rate of 13% with 1% set aside for welfare; corporation taxes have been simplified, too, the idea being that if taxes are low and fair people will pay. It is estimated that over the last decade taxes amounting to US$150 billion have not been collected.

The enormous backlog of wages is gradually being addressed and government coffers are slightly fuller. On paper, things do seem to be getting better very slowly but ask any person in the street and you'll find that real life for the vast majority of Russian people is just as tough as ever.

THE PEOPLE

Russia is the sixth most populous nation in the world with 146.4 million people (about half the population of the former USSR), though this figure is declining at a rate of about a million a year. Of these, a high proportion (82%) are actually Russian. The rest belong to any one of nearly 100 ethnic minorities, most commonly Tartar (4%) and Ukrainian (3%). In the former USSR it was always unwise to refer to people as 'Russian' because of the vast number of other republics they might have come from. With the establishment of independence for many of these states you must be even more careful: Kazakhs or Ukrainians, for example, will not appreciate being called Russians.

Russia is divided up into *oblasts* (the basic administrative unit), *krays* (smaller territories) and *autonomous republics* (containing ethnic minority groups such as the Buryats in Siberia). Siberia forms part of the Russian Federation and exists only as a geographical, not a political, unit.

Government

Russia moved briskly down the political path from autocracy to 'socialist state', with a period of a few months in 1917 when it was a republic. From November 1917 until August 1991 the country was in the hands of the Communist Party, and until September 1993 it was run by the Congress of People's Deputies. This 1068-seat forum was elected from throughout the USSR. At its head sat the Supreme Soviet, the legislative body, elected from Congress. Since only Party members could stand for election in Congress, only Party members could ever run the country.

The confirmation of the new Russian Constitution in December 1993 means that the country is now governed by a European-style two-tier parliament very similar to that of France. The head of state is the Russian president, currently Vladimir Putin.

Despite the theory, Russia is far from democratic. The power of the country is vested in a few hundred chief executives of huge corporations who picked up enormous wealth through the corrupt privatization of the state enterprises under communism. These people now monopolize the media, gas and oil, military production and banking sectors, in effect controlling the entire Russian state. Seven of these tycoons bankrolled the 1996 Yeltsin re-election and were rewarded with powerful government positions. With these oligarchic, criminal and monopolistic power merchants securely lodged in the Kremlin, true democracy is a long way off. Under the autocratic control of Putin the situation has not changed.

Education and social welfare

Education and health care are provided free for the entire population but standards for both are now falling. School is compulsory between the ages of seven and seventeen with the result that Russia has a literacy rate of 98%. Although funding for research is currently at an all-time low, until a few years ago the country used to plough 5% of its national income directly into scientific research in its 900 universities and institutes. Russia's present inability to maintain its scientists has led to a brain drain; certain states in the Middle East are very keen for Russian scientists to help them with their nuclear programmes. The national health care programme is likewise suffering through lack of funds. Russia has produced some of the world's leading surgeons yet recent outbreaks of diseases extinct in the developed world have demonstrated that health services here were never comprehensive. The most publicized epidemic in the last few years has been diphtheria: hundreds of Russians who should have been inoculated at birth have died.

On re-election in July 1996, Yeltsin promised that, to counteract the downside of the market reforms, the government would give higher priority to social reform and raising the living standards of ordinary Russians. These reforms saw real incomes fall by about 40% between 1991 and 1996, unemployment reach 6.6 million, and in 1996 nearly 26% of Russian households existed below the poverty level, considered to be US$70 a month. The average salary in 1996 was US$1800 (£1100) and the average pension was US$60 a month. By 1998, the average salary had risen to around US$4000 (£2600) though the number of Russians living below the poverty line has risen slightly to 28.6%. The country's external debt, US$38 million in 1987 under the communists, has now rocketed to US$164 billion.

The new government programme aims to stabilize living standards, gradually reduce poverty and stop mass unemployment, and to create the conditions for real growth in incomes and the end to poverty. Even the most optimistic Russian believes that this programme has virtually no chance of success.

Religion

Russia was a pagan nation until 988 when Tsar Vladimir ordered the mass conversion of the country to Christianity. The state religion adopted was that of the Greek Orthodox Eastern Church (Russian Orthodox) rather than Roman Catholicism. After the Revolution, religion was suppressed until the late 1930s when Stalin, recognizing the importance of the Church's patriotism in time of war, restored Orthodoxy to respectability. This policy was reversed shortly after the war and many of the country's churches, synagogues and mosques were closed down. Labour camps were filled with religious dissidents, particularly under Khrushchev.

Gorbachev's attitude towards religion was more relaxed and the Freedom of Conscience law, passed in 1990, took religion off the black-list. In 1991 Yeltsin even legalized Christmas: Russian Christmas Day, celebrated on 7 January, is now an official public holiday again. Numerous churches have been restored to cater for the country's estimated 50 million Orthodox believers. In 1997 the Cathedral of Christ the Saviour, demolished by Stalin to make way for a swimming-pool was rebuilt in Moscow (see p164). The new cathedral was the setting for a magnificent service on 20 August 2000 in which Tsar Nicholas II and his family, the arch victims of communism and the revolution, were made saints in an elaborate canonization ceremony.

As well as Russian Orthodox Christians there are also about 1.4 million Roman Catholics. Numbers of Christian sects are growing. Sects as diverse as the so-called 'Old Believers' (who split from the Orthodox church in the 17th century), Scientology and Jehovah's Witnesses are attempting to find converts here. This has worried some Russians, and on 14 June 1993 the Supreme Soviet passed an amendment to the 1990 Freedom of Conscience law banning foreign organizations from recruiting by 'independent' religious activities without permission.

Religious freedoms have also brought a growth in animism and Shamanism, particularly in Siberia.

Although numbers of Moslems in the country have fallen with the independence of the Central Asian Republics, there are still about 11 million Moslems in Russia.

Russian Jews, historically subject to the most cruel discrimination, have been less trusting of the greater religious freedoms. Their position has been made even less comfortable recently by the growth of Neo-Nazi groups in the country and the canonization of the last tsar who was a confirmed anti-Semite. In 1990 more than 200,000 moved to Israel, pouring in at a rate of up to 3000 per day. By 1998 over 500,000 had left but there are still large Jewish communities in Moscow and St Petersburg.

In Buryatia, the centre of Russian Buddhism, many of the monasteries have reopened. Since all are a long way off the tourist track, they have not been kept in good repair as museums, unlike churches in European Russia.

Practical information for the visitor

DOCUMENTS, TICKETS AND VOUCHERS

(Also see Part 1: Planning Your Trip.) One 19th-century English traveller left his passport and tickets behind in London and yet still managed to travel across Siberia carrying no other document than a pass to the Reading Room at the British Library. Entry requirements for foreigners are somewhat stricter nowadays.

The essential documents are your passport, Russian visa (currently supplied as a separate document but there are plans to stamp it in your passport as most other countries do) and a visa for the first country that you'll be entering after Russia. If any organization you are travelling with (eg Intourist) has issued you with vouchers to exchange for hotel accommodation or train tickets, don't forget these.

It's worth bringing some additional identification (eg driver's licence) as your passport will be taken by the hotel when you check in so that they can register you with the authorities (OViR). Don't forget, as many travellers do, to get your passport back before you leave the hotel. Note that **all visas must be registered within three days of your arrival in the country**. Failure to do so will make leaving the country difficult without paying a fine (as high as US$400 in one case!) and make extending a visa almost impossible.

If you want to rent self-drive cars in Russia you'll need an international driving licence (available from your country's automobile club).

International student cards are useful for discounts. Part of the IS card is written in Russian, too, which might impress someone.

Note that if you're arriving from Africa or South America you may be required to show a yellow fever vaccination certificate.

CROSSING THE BORDER

Customs declaration form

At the Russian border you will be given a Customs Declaration Form on which you must declare the total amount of money you are carrying if it exceeds US$1500 (cash and travellers' cheques) and list the number of pieces of luggage you have. You must keep this form until you leave, when it may be checked; note that on departure you must fill out another identical form. Customs used to require documentation of all currency exchange transactions and, referring to the form, they would deduct these from the money you had declared on entry to check that you had not been exchanging money on the black market. Although this is no longer the case you should still keep records of your exchange transactions. The authorities seem to have little time or incentive to check these forms nowadays.

China also requires visitors to fill in a customs form. Don't give away or sell anything you have listed on the form or you may be expected to account for it later. If anything is stolen, get a letter from the local Public Security Bureau (police station) to that effect. Make a photocopy to give to customs, as the original must go to your travel insurance company if you want to claim compensation.

Customs allowances: entering or leaving the country

Russia's customs laws are being reformed: check current regulations before arrival. You should not, however, have any problems bringing in items for personal use or consumption and a litre of spirits or wine. Russian currency may not legally be brought into or taken out of the country.

When leaving the country note that you need a special permit to export 'cultural treasures', a term used to include almost anything that looks old or valuable. Paintings, gold and silver items made before 1968, military medals and coins attract the attention of customs officials and may be confiscated or charged at 100% or more duty if you do not have a permit from the Ministry of Culture.

Border crossing procedure

The border crossing procedure in the train takes anything from two to seven hours. The first step is for customs officers of the country you are leaving to check your passports and visas, and collect customs forms. Remove all loose papers from your passport and make sure you get it back. The compartments are then searched by border guards looking for stowaways before the train crosses the border and the entire procedure is run through again. As rails in Russia and Mongolia are set to a wider gauge than those in

---

❑ **Border etiquette**

While it's never a good idea to act smart in front of border guards this is perhaps nowhere more true than in Russia. A disturbing study reported by the Russian ITAR-TASS news service states that about 60% of Russia's border guards are so unstable they shouldn't be allowed to carry guns. The study, which was released two days after a guard in eastern Siberia killed five of his colleagues on a shooting rampage, was based on tests conducted by doctors, psychologists and lawyers following a series of similar shootouts by border guards over the previous two years.

China and most of Europe, the bogies have to be changed at the borders. The carriages are lifted individually, the bogies being rolled out and replaced. If you do not want to stay on the train as the bogies are being changed, you can wait at the border station. If you do get off, the carriage attendants won't normally let you get back on before the official boarding time which is when the train returns to the station to pick up the passengers. Don't leave valuables behind. Bear in mind that during the entire border crossing procedure, the train's lavatories remain locked. This is not purely for security reasons since changing the bogies requires workers operating beneath the train.

WHERE TO STAY

There's now a wide range of places to stay in Russia: everything from B&Bs (homestays) to luxurious hotels of an international standard. Generally, though, Russian hotels are of gargantuan proportions and about as architecturally interesting as the average multi-storey car park. Moscow's Hotel Rossiya, once the world's largest hotel, with 3200 rooms and beds for 6000 guests, fell to second place in 1990 with the opening of the 4032-room Excalibur Hotel in Las Vegas. This having been said, some of the old hotels in Moscow and St Petersburg have now been restored to a very high standard.

Note that hotels often operate a two-tier pricing system with the higher price for foreign 'guests'. Except in the up-market hotels, it's actually very difficult to pin down hotel prices: the price they quote seems to vary widely from month to month.

Main types of accommodation

Top hotels Many are owned by large Western chains such as Marriott, Radisson and Novotel. While they look glitzy like international hotels everywhere, the service still has a touch of Soviet reticence about it. Their restaurants are normally excellent, they have banking facilities, room service and shops, and their staff are motivated. These hotels are mostly found in Moscow and St Petersburg and prices are what you would expect in the West – £100-250/ US$150-400 per night.

Standard hotels These are mostly the solid old Intourist hotels. They have all the tourist facilities of restaurants, banks and shops. Their rooms were once good but lack of maintenance and interest have resulted in their becoming a bit run down. In Moscow and St Petersburg, standard hotel rooms cost £35-100/US$50-150 and in other cities they're much cheaper: £10-25/US$15-40.

Basic hotels Once impossible for foreigners to stay in, these places are usually clean if basically equipped. Basic hotels normally have a restaurant but no shops, foreign exchange or room service. The rooms are simple with a TV and fridge; about 50% will have a bathroom. You will generally be offered one with a bathroom and as long as you don't look too closely, the rooms are generally adequate. The best rooms are called *lyuks* (meaning 'luxury') and most hotels have at least one such room. *Lyuks* is a relative term and it just means that it is the best of all the rooms in that one hotel. Basic hotel rooms range from £6-14/US$10-20.

Very basic hotels/hostels These come in many forms; some are quite good and others lousy. They're often attached to an industrial enterprise or a market to accommodate visiting workers or farmers. Sometimes foreigners are refused a room at these hotels because staff feel that this isn't quite the sort of place a foreigner should stay in and they'll direct you to the local Intourist hotel. If you have been refused, be persistent or return later when the reception staff have been changed. These hotels will often not even have a restaurant or café. Very few rooms will have an attached bathroom and rooms will have up to four beds. At most stations there's a Rest Room (Komnata Otdykha Комната отдыха) where you can stay overnight with a ticket for a train the next morning. Rooms at very basic hotels cost from £1.20-6/US$2-10.

Other types of accommodation
Youth hostels A few cities in Russia, including Moscow, St Petersburg and Irkutsk, have youth hostels. Standards are surprisingly high and about what you would expect in the West; dormitory beds cost about £10 US$15 a night including breakfast. Information on these can be obtained from Russian Youth Hostel Association (🖳 www.hostelling-russia.ru).

Holiday homes (Dom Otdykha Дом отдыха) In the Soviet era these were holiday destinations for city dwellers. They were like country hotels and offered meals and some organized activities. Today the ones that still operate are mostly run down and often do not have even a restaurant. A few are excellent and remain the holiday choice of the country's élite.

Sanatoriums (Sanitorti Санитори) are similar to holiday homes with the addition of a sauna, therapeutic services and mud or spring pools. You do not have to be sick to stay at one and many locals visit them once a year as they believe that this will keep them healthy for another year.

Homestays can be organized in most cities on the Trans-Siberian route; they cost £15-30/$20-40 a night, often including meals. Host Families Association, Bed and Breakfast in Russia (HOFA), (☎ 275 1992, 535 7824, 🖳 alexei@hofak.hop.stu.neva.ru), is one company to contact. Also see 'Part 1: Planning your trip' and the 'Bookings' section for your country. To minimize possible misunderstandings agree on an upper limit as to how much you can afford to pay for food if this is not included; each day establish set times for your meals. Also it is customary to supplement the household catering when you visit the markets by buying food, fruit or goods that they may not normally have. You must expect to pay for additional services such as organizing theatre tickets, sightseeing and taxis.

At some railway stations you'll be approached by locals wanting to put you up in their houses for about £5/US$7.50 per night. Look at the place before agreeing and don't allow yourself to be persuaded if you don't trust them or feel in any way uncomfortable.

Checking in at a hotel

Checking in is never the swift procedure it should be. After the receptionist has kept you waiting for a while, serving other customers and occasionally glancing at you, you'll be relieved of your passport and money and handed a small pass-card. You'll have to present this to the *dezhurnaya* (floor attendant) on your floor in exchange for your room key; in some of the up-market hotels, however, you may actually be given your key by the receptionist. The dezhurnaya, very often an elderly female busybody, seems to spend most of her time drinking tea in a little den, gossiping to her friends and keeping an eagle eye on all that goes on her floor. She's usually very friendly when she realizes that you are foreign and, as with the provodniks on the trains, it is very wise to keep on good terms with the dezhurnaya (see p72). She can arrange to get laundry done and can provide boiling water or mineral water.

Most hotels have a check out time of midday but you can always pay for just a couple of extra hours or a half day if your train leaves in the evening.

Bedrooms

In some of the older hotels the rooms are vast and comfortable but they're rather smaller in the more modern places. Mid-range hotels are generally furnished in the worst possible taste that often verges on the schizophrenic: pink roses on the wallpaper matched with purple nylon curtains. Beds are often too short, usually of orthopaedic hardness or so old that every spring ends up digging into you. Bedding consists of blankets in a duvet cover.

There's usually an internal phone and wake-up calls may be arranged at the reception desk; these seem to be reliable and often the dezhurnaya will knock on your door as well to make sure. You may get phone calls in the evening to your room from women offering various 'personal services'!

Bathrooms

Things are improving but it's still true to say that except in the smarter hotels, bathrooms are often equipped with broken fittings and dripping taps, lavatories have dislocated seats and baths and basins lack plugs. Don't forget to take a universal bathplug, soap and loo paper, although more hotels now provide these essentials. Hot water in your bathroom may take a long time to come through: up to 10 minutes. During summer you may find that your hotel doesn't even have hot water. This is because it's centrally supplied and each year the water has to be turned off so that the pipes can be cleaned. This means that for a four-week period (eight weeks in some Siberian cities – Ulan Ude for example) every building in the city will be without hot water. The only exceptions are the expensive hotels which have their own independent hot water systems. If you don't have hot water don't expect a discount on your bill.

TOURS

While guided tours allow you to cover a lot of ground quickly, you can easily get around by yourself in all the cities in this book. You'll learn far more on the buses and metro than you will inside a tour bus. There are some tours that are worth going on, though, and these are mentioned in the relevant city section of this book.

If you fancy a tour of Moscow, St Petersburg and some of the Golden Ring cities there's now a backpacker tour bus: the Beetroot Bus (☎ UK 020-8566 8846, ▭ www.beetroot.org).

LOCAL TRANSPORT

If you are booking an independent trip through an agency, you may be encouraged to purchase 'transfers' so that you will be met at the airport or station and taken to your hotel. The prices charged for this service can be high (£20-35/US$30-50) but it can sometimes be worthwhile. If you are planning to take a taxi from the airport when you arrive, you may prefer to arrange a transfer in advance, if only to keep yourself out of the hands of the taxi mafia.

Taxis

Virtually every car in Russia is a taxi: stand in the street with your arm outstretched, someone will pull over and ask where you want to go. Negotiate a price and get in. It's illegal but if drivers are going your way it makes perfect sense for them to take along paying passengers. While this may be very convenient, it could also be dangerous, as you have no idea of the driver's intentions. For this reason, women travelling alone would be unwise to hitch rides and no one should get into a car that has more than one occupant. Don't put your luggage into the boot or your driver could simply pull away when you get out to retrieve it. Russians seem to delight in worrying about crime and if you ask them they'll tell you numerous stories about unwary passengers being driven into the countryside and robbed.

Official taxis are safer but more difficult to find. You'll recognize them by the chequerboard pattern on the door and the green 'for hire' light. Although they have meters, few use them. You should agree on a price before you get in since once the driver realizes you're a foreigner, he'll bump it up accordingly. Ask a local beforehand what the taxi trip should cost and don't be afraid to haggle. Even if you haven't a clue, at least get the price down a bit. You'll find that taxi drivers stick together and one won't offer you a lower price than the others. You're more likely to be charged local rates if you don't pick up taxis outside big hotels or major tourist spots.

Metro

The metro is a very cheap way to get around with a flat fare of about US$0.20 (£0.13) and trains every few minutes. In Moscow it's worth using the metro just to see the stations, which are more like subterranean stately homes, with ornate ceilings, gilded statues and enormous chandeliers.

Be careful not to fall over getting on the escalators: they move twice as fast as those in the West. Russian metro systems were built deeper underground than their Western counterparts, perhaps to act as shelters in the event of aerial bombing. Because they're so far down, escalators need to be extremely long as well as swift. The world's longest escalator is, in fact, in St Petersburg (Ploshchad Lenina), and has 729 steps, rising 59 metres.

In the street, metro stations are indicated by a large blue or red 'M'. Lines are named after their terminal stations, as on the Paris metro. One peculiarity you'll notice is that where two lines intersect the station is given two names, one for each line. As trains move off from the station, the next station is announced. The counter above the end of each tunnel indicates how long it's been since the last train. In Siberia, there are metros in Novosibirsk and Yekaterinburg.

Buses

In all cities there's a bus service (fixed fare and often very crowded) and usually also trolley-buses and trams. Some buses have conductors, some ticket machines and in others tickets are purchased from the driver in strips or booklets. If there's no conductor you must punch the ticket yourself, using one of the punches by the windows. If the bus is crowded and you can't reach, pass your ticket to someone near the machine and they'll do it for you. Occasionally, inspectors impose on the spot fines for those without punched tickets.

Domestic flights

Domestic flights usually involve long delays and far too much sitting around in airports. Safety standards are not high: if you must fly use one of the larger carriers such as Aeroflot or Transaero. Getting airline tickets in Russia is now considerably easier than getting tickets for some trains because most Russians can't afford to fly. Nearly all up-market hotels have air ticket booking offices.

Boat

Most of the cities you will visit are built on rivers and short trips on the water are usually possible. In St Petersburg the most interesting way to reach Petrodvorets is by hydrofoil. You can also get to Lake Baikal by boat up the Angara from Irkutsk. There are many long-distance boat trips you could do: there is, for example, a four-day trip up the Yenisei from Krasnoyarsk to Dudinka.

Car rental

In St Petersburg and Moscow and some other cities, it is possible to rent self-drive cars. Charges are from US$50 a day and you will need an international driving licence.

ELECTRICITY

In almost all Russian cities electricity is 220v, 50 cycles AC. Sockets require a continental-type plug or adaptor. In some places the voltage is 127v so you should enquire at the reception desk before using your own appliances. Sockets for electric razors are provided on trains.

TIME

Russia spans ten time zones and on the Trans-Siberian you will be adjusting your watch an hour almost every day. Russian railways run on Moscow time and timetables do not list local time. It can be disconcerting to cross the border from China at breakfast-time to be informed by station clocks that it is really only 02:00.

Moscow Time (MT) is four hours ahead of Greenwich Mean Time when the country runs on 'summer time': from the last Saturday in March to the last Saturday in September. Outside that period MT = GMT+3; Siberian time zones are listed throughout the route guide and the main cities are in the following zones: Novosibirsk (MT+3), Irkutsk (MT+5), Khabarovsk (MT+7), Vladivostok (MT+7).

MONEY

(See also pp43-4). The rouble is the basic unit of Russian currency. This is divided into 100 kopecks which come in 1, 10 and 50 coins. Notes in circulation are 5, 10, 50, 100, 500 roubles. There are 1, 2 and 5 rouble coins. Following the devaluation of the currency in 1998 when the rouble's value was reduced by a factor of 1000 the old notes for thousands of roubles ceased to be legal tender. The use of US dollars is illegal in Russia with the exception of a few sectors of the economy such as airline tickets and payment for visas. Up-market hotels and restaurants may quote prices in US$ but they will want to be paid in roubles.

Some Russians still change their roubles to dollars for security although with the rouble becoming steadier they are gaining confidence in their own currency. Note that in this guide most prices are given in dollars since their value appears to remain reliably constant from year to year: convert at the current exchange rate for the rouble price.

UK pounds are easy to exchange into roubles in Moscow and St Petersburg but in Siberia US$ are a better bet. The Euro,

> ❏ **Exchange rates**
> To get the latest rates of exchange visit www.oan da.com/convert/classic.
>
> | US$1 | R27.97 |
> | UK£1 | R41.09 |
> | Euro1 | R25.05 |
> | China Y1 | R3.38 |
> | Mong T1 | R0.025 |

when it comes out in 2002, is unlikely to become accepted quickly in Russia: Eurolanders should bring US$. In St Petersburg you can also exchange the Swedish kroner and Finnish marks, while in the Russian Far East you can exchange Japanese yen. Note that travellers' cheques aren't always easy to exchange outside the biggest cities so you should bring your money as a mixture of US$ and travellers' cheques.

Which dollar bills to bring

Bills should be new enough to have the vertical watermark stripe, which can be seen by holding the bills up to the light. The newly designed US$100 bills, issued since 1996, provide increased protection against counterfeiting. Soiled or torn bills are not accepted, nor are any which have writing or ink stamps on them.

Exchanging dollars for roubles

You'll never have any problem finding somewhere to change money as there are hundreds of official currency exchange offices (*Obmen Valyuty*) in hotels, banks, stores and kiosks in most cities. Keep currency exchange receipts as you may have to show them to customs on departure if you are carrying more that US$1500 into or out of the country. In banks, the difference in the buying and selling rate is about 2-4%. At currency exchange offices the rates may vary according to supply and demand and whether banks are open. Out of hours you will get a worse deal than during bank hours.

Credit/debit cards and ATMs

Credit cards are accepted in up-market hotels and some restaurants. Their usage became severely restricted after the devaluation of the rouble but places are starting to accept them again. In larger cities you'll find banks with ATMs in which you can use your own bank's debit (cash) card and access your account if one of the symbols on your card matches one on the machine (Cirrus, Plus, Maestro etc). You can almost always use a credit card (Visa/MasterCard) in an ATM but check the rates your credit card company will charge before you leave home.

The black market

With little difference between the bank rate and the black market rate the risks involved in changing money this way far outweigh the benefits. There's also no advantage to be gained from 'speculation': bringing in articles from the West to sell in Russia. Most Western goods can now be bought locally.

Tipping

Soviet policy outlawed tipping. It was seen as nothing less than bribery: the thin end of the corruption wedge. Glasnost soon changed all this, though, and you'll find that certain people (waiters etc) have come to accept the practice. It's really up to you, though, and Russians generally don't.

If you've arranged a price with a taxi driver there's no need to add a tip. In restaurants you should tip whatever you feel is deserved, up to a maximum of 10% in the better restaurants. Porters expect about US$1 and guides US$5-10 per day.

If you want to thank your carriage attendant on the train or your hotel floor attendant, a good way of doing so is with a small gift, preferably something that is obviously imported. Scented soap, perfume or any particularly exotic Western food product will all go down well. Note that with most foreign items now available in Russia people are much more brand conscious than they were in Soviet days.

POST AND TELECOMMUNICATIONS

Post

Outbound airmail to the UK and USA takes about three weeks and is reliable. Inbound mail is less reliable and can take more than three weeks. Be warned that letters are likely to be opened in transit by thieves looking for money, so don't send anything valuable or important. To send a parcel from Russia, you have to go to a post office where it will be wrapped and sealed with a wax stamp.

Addresses on international mail into and out of Russia may be written in English and in standard Western format. The usual order of writing an address within Russia is the following and all should be in Russian:

> Six-digit postal code of the city or town
> City or town
> Street name
> Name of addressee
> followed below by the return address.

For international mail write the name of the country in Cyrillic:

UK: **Великобритания**, USA: **США**
Canada: **Канада**, Germany: **Германия**
Australia: **Австралия**, New Zealand: **Новая Зеландия**

If you have something urgent or valuable to send out of Russia you should use one of the courier companies such as DHL that now have branches in Russia.

Email

Internet access is becoming more widespread in Russia. There are Internet cafés in most cities covered in this book (see city guide chapter for addresses) and new ones opening every month; you can check the locations of new ones at www.cybercafes.com; costs at these places are about US$2 per hour. It's worth setting up an email account with hotmail or yahoo before you get to Russia.

Phone

The Russian phone system has greatly improved and it's now relatively easy to dial into or out of the country. To make an international call dial 8 then wait for the tone before dialling 10 followed by your country code and number.

To call from a street phone (*Taksofon*), you need a prepaid phone card or, in an older payphone, a token. Both are available from metro stations and kiosks.

You can also make calls from telephone offices, usually part of the post office. Leave a deposit with the cashier who will assign you a booth from which you make your call. Pay the balance after the call.

The best hotels in most large Russian cities also have credit card or debit card phones in their foyers. The cards are often unique to each hotel and only available there. These sorts of calls are very expensive.

Fax

The main city post offices often have fax machines and a typical international fax costs about £3/US$5 a minute.

MAGAZINES AND NEWSPAPERS IN ENGLISH

The two papers well worth looking out for are the daily *Moscow Times* and the bi-weekly *St Petersburg Times* available in their respective cities. They're both free and can be found in the hotels, hostels and supermarkets which foreigners frequent. There's also the *Moscow Tribune*, less widely available.

Western news magazines such as *Time* and *Newsweek* are available at top hotels.

PUBLIC HOLIDAYS
National holidays

If a holiday falls on Thursday, then Friday and Saturday may also be holidays. If a holiday falls on Saturday or Sunday, then Monday will be a holiday.

❏ RUSSIAN CUSTOMS AND ETIQUETTE

Customs
● A bottle of wine, cake, box of candy or bouquet of flowers are traditional gifts if you're invited to dinner in someone's home. A small gift for any children is always appropriate. If you bring flowers, make sure the number of flowers is uneven; even numbers of flowers are for funerals.

● Do not shake hands or kiss across the threshold of the doorstep; this is traditionally bad luck.

● Take off your gloves when shaking hands.

● Be prepared to remove your shoes upon entering a home. You will be given a pair of slippers (*tapki*) to help keep the apartment clean.

● Do not cross your legs with the ankle on the knee. It's impolite to show people the soles of your shoes. When in the metro or sitting on a bus, don't let your feet even come close to the seat or another passenger.

● Smoking is common and accepted in Russia.

● Be prepared to accept all alcohol and food offered when visiting friends, and this can be quite a lot. Refusing a drink or a toast is a serious breach of etiquette. An open bottle must be finished.

● Be prepared to give toasts at dinners, etc. Be careful, the vodka can catch up with you.

● Dress for the theatre. Check your coat and any large bags at the garderobe.

● Be careful how you admire something in a home. Your host may offer it to you to take away.

● Russian men still expect women to act in a traditional manner. You're not supposed to be assertive in public, carry heavy bags if walking with a man, open doors, uncork bottles or pay for yourself in social situations. A woman alone in a restaurant or hotel risks being taken for a prostitute.

● Dress casually for dinner in someone's home. In cold weather, wear a hat or babushkas will lecture you on your foolishness!

● In a Russian Orthodox church, women should cover their heads with a scarf or hat and wear a skirt. Men should remove their hats.

● Putting your thumb between your first two fingers is a very rude gesture.

Superstitions
Russians are still remarkably superstitious; many of the following were once also common in Europe:

● Never light a cigarette from a candle. It will bring you bad luck.

● Do not whistle inside or you will whistle away your money.

● Never pour wine back handed, it means you will also pour away your money.

● A black cat crossing your path is bad luck.

● If you're a woman and find yourself sitting on the corner of a table you'll be single for the next seven years.

● If you spill salt at the table you will be plagued by bad luck unless you throw three pinches over your left shoulder immediately.

● If someone gives good wishes, or you talk about your good fortune, you must spit three times over your left shoulder and touch (knock on) wood to keep your good fortune.

● 1 January: New Year's Day
● 7 January: Russian Orthodox Christmas Day
● 13 January: New Years Day according to the old Julian calendar
● 15 February: Defenders of the Motherland Day
● 8 March: International Women's Day
● Late April/early May Russian Orthodox Easter
● 1 May: Day of Spring and Labour (formerly May Day or the International Working People's Solidarity Day). The next working day is also a holiday.
● 9 May: Victory Day, to commemorate the end of World War II (known in Russia as the 1941-45 Great Patriotic War)
● 12 June: Independence Day for Russia
● 7 and 8 November: Formerly the Anniversary of the Communist October Revolution and now called Grief Day or The Day Of Reconciliation
● 12 December: Constitution Day

School and university holidays
Schools start 1 September and finish 31 May with a week's vacation in November, two weeks in January at the New Year and one week in March. Universities usually start on 1 September and finish on 25 June with the winter break from 25 January to 8 February.

FESTIVALS

Annual arts festivals in Moscow include Moscow Stars (5-15 May) and Russian Winter (25 December to 5 January).

The most interesting festival is St Petersburg's White Nights, held around the summer solstice, when the sun does not set. The days are separated by only a few hours of silvery light: a combined dusk and dawn. Theatres and concert halls save their best performances for this time and a festival is also held at Petrodvorets.

FOOD AND DRINK

There's rather more to Russian cuisine than borscht and chicken Kiev but if you're eating most of your meals on the train, you won't have much of a chance to discover this. You will probably leave with the idea that Russian cooking is of the school dinner variety, with large hunks of meat, piles of potatoes and one vegetable (the interminable cabbage), followed by tinned fruit or ice-cream. On the whole, Russian food can be bland. You will, however, occasionally be surprised by the delicious food which seems to appear in the most unlikely restaurants.

Food is no problem if you have money. Even in remote Siberia, you can now get a Mars bar although it may be expensive. Although there are

❑ **Caviare**
The roe of the sturgeon is becoming more expensive as the fish itself becomes
gets rarer. Four species are acknowledged to produce the best caviare: beluga,
sterlet, osetra and sevruga, all from the Caspian and Black Seas. To produce its
characteristic flavour (preferably not too 'fishy') a complicated process is
involved. First the female fish is stunned with a mallet. Her belly is slit open and
the roe sacs removed. The eggs are washed and put through strainers to grade
them into batches of a similar size. The master-taster then samples the roe and
decides how much salt to add for preservation.

Processed caviare varies in colour (black, red or golden) and also in the size
of the roe. It is eaten either with brown bread or served with sour cream in *blinis* (thin pancakes). You can get it in most tourist hotels and on the train.

A recent report from the World Wide Fund for Nature warns that the sturgeon
is on the brink of extinction because of aggressive fishing by Russia. The report
says up to 90% of caviare is now obtained illegally and the Russian authorities
are doing nothing because of corruption.

food shortages in some parts of the country, Westerners are well catered
for. A substantial breakfast will provide you with enough energy to tackle
even the heaviest sight-seeing schedule. The first meal of the day consists
of fruit juice (good if it's apple), cheese, eggs, sausage, bread, jam and
kefir (thin, sour yoghurt).

Lunch and dinner will be of similarly large size, consisting of at least
three courses. Meat dishes can be good but there is still a shortage of fresh
fruit and vegetables except at the best hotels.

Zakuski
Russian hors d'oeuvres (*zakuski*), consist of some or all of the following:
cold meat, sausages, salmon, pickled herring, paté, tomato salads, sturgeon and caviare. Large quantities of vodka are drunk with zakuski.

Soups
Soups are usually watery but good, meals in themselves with a stack of
brown bread. Best known is *borscht*: beetroot soup which often includes
other vegetables (potatoes, cabbage and onion), chopped ham and a swirl
of sour cream (*smetane*).

Cabbage soup or *shchi* is the traditional soup of the proletariat and
was a favourite of Nicholas II, who is said to have enjoyed only plain
peasant cooking (to the great disappointment of his French chef).
Akroshka is a chilled soup made from meat, vegetables and *kvas* (thin
beer). *Rassolnik* is a soup of pickled vegetables.

❏ You don't eat meat?!

Vegetarian cooking isn't widely understood in Russia, and with the exception of one or two Hare Krishna-style Asian restaurants there are no real vegetarian restaurants. As a vegetarian you can eat in Russian restaurants if you choose your dishes carefully but don't rely on the waiter's imagination or assistance!

Amongst the **appetizers**, *shchi* (cabbage soup) is often meatless, suluguni cheese is very similar to Greek halloumi and usually served grilled; carrot, tomato and cucumber salads are also possibles.

Main courses are harder; one option is to order a double portion of a starter found in almost every Russian restaurant: *Julienne*, also known as *griby v smetane* – wild mushrooms baked in cream sauce. Omelette is another option, if a horribly predictable one. Perversely, you can often do better in cheap cafés than in fine restaurants because meatless food is regarded as too down-market by posher places. Items to look for in cafés are *piroshkie* (dough-pastries with fillings like onion, cabbage or carrot), *vatrushkie* (cream-cheese pastries), and *vareniki* (cheese-filled dumplings). You can almost always find *blini* or *oladi* (different kinds of Russian pancakes) served with either sour cream or jam. In Georgian restaurants, *lobio* (spicy bean stew) is a vegetarian mainstay, a few Georgian places also serve *achma* (a kind of cream sauce lasagne) – combined with *khachapuri* cheesebreads and some salads, this is about as good as it gets.

Neil McGowan (The Russia Experience, UK & Russia)

Fish

Fish common in Russia include herring, halibut, salmon and sturgeon. These last two may be served with a creamy sauce of vegetables. In Irkutsk you should try *omul*, the famous Lake Baikal fish, which has a delicious, delicate flavour.

Meat

The most famous Russian main course is chicken Kiev (fried breast of chicken filled with garlic and butter). Almost as famous is *boeuf stroganov*, a beef stew made with sour cream and mushrooms, and named after the wealthy merchant family who financed the first Siberian explorations in the 1580s. Other regional specialities that you are likely to encounter include *shashlik* (mutton kebabs) and *pilov* (rice with spiced meat) from Central Asia, chicken *tabaka* (with garlic sauce) from Georgia, and (to be avoided at all costs) *salo* which is pig's fat preserved with salt, from the Ukraine and said to be good for hangovers. From Siberia comes *pelmeni*, small dumplings filled with meat and served in a soup or as a main course. If you're expecting a rump steak when you order *bifstek* you'll be disappointed: it's just a compressed lump of minced meat, usually swimming in grease and grey in colour.

Puddings

Very often the choice is limited to ice-cream (*morozhenoye* – always good, safe, and available everywhere) and fruit compôte (a disappointing fruit salad of a few pieces of tinned fruit floating in a large dish of syrup). You may, however, be offered *blinis* with sour cream and fruit jam which are always delicious; *vareniki* (sweet dumplings filled with cheese or fruit) or rice pudding. Unless you are staying in one of the more expensive hotels there won't be much fresh fruit on offer although it is now easily available from street vendors.

Bread

Russian bread, served with every meal, is wholesome and filling. Tourist literature claims that over one hundred different types are baked in Moscow. Communist 'bread technology' was said to be so much in demand in the West that Soviet experts were allegedly recruited to build a brown bread factory in Finland.

Drinks

Non alcoholic Most popular is tea, traditionally served black with a spoonful of jam or sugar. Milk is not always available so you may want to take along some whitener. The Russians have been brewing coffee since Peter the Great introduced it in the 17th century but standards have dropped since then; take a jar of instant with you. Bottled mineral water is available everywhere but it often tastes rather too strongly of all those natural minerals that are supposed to be so good for you and is usually carbonated.

There are several varieties of bottled fruit juice (*sok*), of which apple seems to be the most consistently good. The Pepsi and Coca Cola companies fought bitterly over distribution in the USSR and during the 1980s Pepsi was awarded sole rights. Now both are widely obtainable, as are other Western soft drinks like Sprite.

Alcoholic Vodka predominates, of course, and Russians will be disgusted if you do anything other than drink it straight. The spirit originated in Poland (although some say that it was brought back from Holland by Peter the Great) and means 'little water', something of an understatement. If you tire of the original product, there's a wide range of flavoured vodkas to sample: lemon, cherry, blackberry or pepper.

Be warned that the standard vodka measure in Russia is the *sto gram*, one hundred grams; in the UK it's 25 grams. Vodka should be served ice cold and drained in one from single shot glasses. You must keep up if you are male but as a woman you might drop out after a couple of shots. It can be easy enough to drink but it will quickly catch up with you. You may be asked to give a toast and you should take this seriously – a short speech about your subject is enough. Note that a shot of vodka ought to be followed immediately by zakuski (see above): 'Only drunkards drink without food', is a popular saying in Russia. Another saying goes: 'Drinking vodka without beer is like throwing money to the wind'. If someone flicks their throat with their forefinger, it often means 'Would you like a drink'. It's considered impolite to refuse.

There's also wine although most tend to be rather sweet for the Western palate but Georgian wines are worth trying. Russian champagne is surprisingly good and very cheap. Beer is widely available and popular. It's cheap and sold everywhere. A good brand is Baltika which comes in nine different types – No 3 with the blue label is one of the best.

You should also try *kvas* (a fermented mixture of stale brown bread, yeast, malt sugar and water). A popular drink sold on the streets during the summer from yellow tankers, its alcohol content is so low it's hardly noticeable at all.

BUYING YOUR OWN FOOD

The once sparse self-serve Soviet supermarkets *(universam)* have rapidly modernized their facilities and improved the quality and selection of

❏ **Food and drink prices**

Many food stores have been privatized and now set their own prices. Only a few products such as bread, milk, and eggs are still subsidized and regulated. Some examples of current prices:

Hot dog	US$0.30
Georgian cheese bread	US$0.20
McDonald's Big Mac (US$2 in Moscow)	US$1.10
Large loaf of tasty white bread	US$0.15
Sweet cake	US$0.08
Russian 'Edam' style cheese (1kg)	US$3.20
Large jar of Nutella spread	US$3.00
Cheapest bottle of Russian beer (330ml)	US$0.30
Good Russian beer 330ml	US$0.80
Imported small can of Heineken	US$1.00
Cheapest vodka (500ml)	US$1.00
Moskovskaya vodka (500ml)	US$2.00
Gzhel Crystal vodka (500ml)	US$30.00
Georgian red wine (1l)	US$2.80
Sekt Russian champagne	US$3.70

When you buy vodka check the seal on the bottle to make sure it hasn't been diluted. It's wise to go for the bigger brands as there are reports of the smaller distilleries cutting costs to produce low grade alcohol which has resulted in blindness and death amongst some drinkers.

goods. Canned and packaged goods, juices, pots, tableware, soap, paper products, dry goods, as well as meat, bread, fruits and vegetables can be found here. *Produkty* stores sell a limited range of fresh vegetables, fruit, bread, meat, eggs and manufactured products. Western-style supermarkets in the larger cities have wide ranges of products both imported and local.

A *gastronome* is a delicatessen; a *dieta* sells food for those on special diets, such as diabetics.

Markets (*rynok*) range from small groups of old people selling garden produce around the metro exits to large, covered markets with dozens of stalls selling everything from honey to dried mushrooms and meat to imported pineapples.

WHERE TO EAT

It used to be very difficult to get a good meal in Russia. Because all restaurants were state-run, waiters had no incentive to serve you, chefs couldn't be bothered to cook for you and you considered yourself lucky if you managed to bribe your way to a table. All that's changed now and there are restaurants that are as good as in any Western city; not surprisingly prices in the top places equal those in the West.

The cheapest places to eat are the **self-service cafés** (*stolovnaya*) found in most shopping streets where you can get a filling but stodgy meal for less than a pound or around U\$1. In most cities there are Western **fast-food chains** such as McDonald's (highly recommended for their clean loos) and Russian derivatives such as Russkoe Bistro. In larger cities, particularly in Moscow and St Petersburg, **cafés** are good places to get a more interesting and still reasonably cheap meal.

In **restaurants**, service varies wildly; sometimes it's an effort to get anyone to realize why you have been sitting there for the last ten minutes trying to get their attention but at other times there will be a friendly English-speaking waiter or waitress who can't do enough to help you. Russians rarely dine out and so when they do it's always a big occasion. When they go to a restaurant, they go in large groups and like to make a meal last the evening. Staff do their best to ensure no dish arrives too quickly and give you more than enough time to try to interpret the menu. While you wait for your food a dance-band entertains with folk-songs and Western hits from the sixties at so high a volume that you can't ignore it; there may even be a cabaret show (of sorts). If you get invited to join a

---

(**Opposite**) **Top:** Each carriage is staffed by a *provodnitsa* (female attendant) or a *provodnik* (male attendant). **Bottom:** The *Rossiya* is the name the Russians give to the train which crosses Siberia from Moscow 9289km to Vladivostok. (Photos © Tatyana Pozar-Burgar).

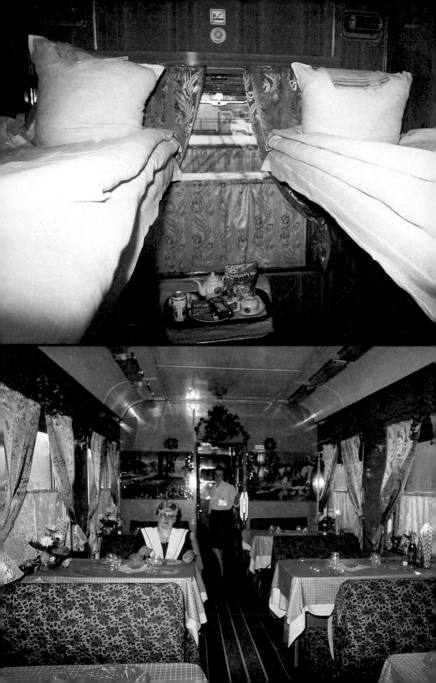

Russian party, a visit to a restaurant can be a very entertaining and often drunken affair. Note that tsarist traditions die hard: if a man wishes to invite a woman from another table to dance he will ask permission of the men at her table before she joins him on the dance-floor.

In some up-market restaurants you may find a cover charge and charges for entertainment of about 10% added to your bill. Sometimes they'll just round up the total by about this amount to save the bother of doing an accurate calculation.

WHAT TO DO IN THE EVENING

Nightlife in Moscow and St Petersburg is now as good as you'll get in any big city in the West. It really helps to have Russian friends who will show you the best places. In these cities there are lots of night clubs, discos and bars. In the smaller cities, your major night life options are the hotel bars and discos which often stay open late, casinos which you may find difficult to get into and want to leave as soon as you do, and cultural activities such as opera, theatre, ballet or circus. Performances usually start early: between 18:00 and 19:00. Don't be late as the ushers may not let you in until half time.

As you might imagine, things are rather quieter in the evenings in Siberia.

Ballet

Many of the world's greatest dancers were Russians from the Bolshoi and Kirov companies. Some defected to the West including Rudolf Nureyev (Kirov), Russia's most famous ballet star, who was 'shaken out' of his mother's womb on the Trans-Siberian as it was rattling along towards Lake Baikal.

Don't miss the chance of a night at the magnificent Bolshoi Theatre; the season runs from September to May. Note that many touring groups dance at the Bolshoi so it may not be the famous company you see.

Opera and theatre

In the past, opera was encouraged more than theatre as it was seen as politically neutral. Glasnost, however, encouraged playwrights to produce drama that reflected Russian life as it is, rather than as the government would like people to see it. This has led to a number of successful new theatre groups opening in Moscow and St Petersburg. There are also several puppet theatres which are highly recommended.

(Opposite) Top: Russian Railways compartment (see p118). **Bottom:** Dining car. (Photos: © Tatyana Pozar-Burgar)

Cinema and television

In the 1980s the Soviet film industry also benefited from the greater freedoms that came with glasnost. In early 1987, one of the most successful and controversial films was *Is It Easy To Be Young?*, which was deeply critical of the Soviet war in Afghanistan. In the 1990s the pessimism of the people towards life is reflected in films made in the country. *Little Vera* (1990) is the story of a provincial girl who sinks into small-time prostitution and finally drowns herself. Gorbachev walked out of it saying he disapproved of the sex scenes. In *Executioner* (1991) a female journalist takes on the mafia in St Petersburg and loses. By the end of the 1990s, however, far fewer films were being made in Russia as state sponsorship of the arts has been cut back considerably.

Nowadays Western and American movies are everywhere. There are cinemas in every town and shows start early in the evening. There is a thriving black market in bootlegged American movies; don't be surprised to find *Titanic* showing in your restaurant car.

Russian television has evolved fast in the last few years; news and current affairs programmes are now of quite high quality. In hotel rooms you'll sometimes have satellite channels which are a break from the garish games shows. Moscow time rules the airwaves so owing to the time difference children's programmes shown at 16:00 in Moscow, come on at 23:00 in Vladivostok!

Rock concerts and sports matches

Rock concerts and various sports fixtures are invariably held in stadiums. These are usually well worth attending and very safe as the arenas are swarming with police and soldiers to keep the order. Football is very popular as well as ice hockey in the winter. Tennis is also becoming popular after the successes of Kafelnikov.

SHOPPING

Shopping was an incredibly complicated and frustrating affair in the USSR. Shops were crowded and if they weren't this was a sign that there was nothing worth buying in them. The common view on market reform is that while twenty years ago there wasn't much in the stores, at least everyone could afford what there was. Now the shelves are overflowing with goods but no one has the money to buy them. This is the chief reason for the nostalgia for the old days. The situation, one hopes, will improve as wages increase. Despite the fact that the majority of Russian shoppers tend to flock to the stores with the lowest prices, you are unlikely to see food queues. Having said this, Russians still carry around their *avoska* (a 'just in case' bag) and are quick to notice a queue forming, joining it even before they know what it is for in the hope that they may snap up a bargain.

For foreigners shopping is no problem at all: you only have to wander into the main street to see the wide variety of goods on sale and if you walk into the electronics section of a department store you'll find quality merchandise on a par with anything available in the West. Whereas previously this was all sold for hard currency, now it's for roubles; the change still doesn't mean that ordinary people can afford it, though.

Making a purchase

Although many shops have the same system for shopping as in shops in the West, the procedure for purchasing something in others (in bakeries and bookshops, for example) is rather more complicated and exactly the same as the outmoded purchasing process used in the department stores of New Delhi. First you must decide what you want to buy and find out the price (the assistant may write this down on a ticket for you). Then go to the cash desk (where an abacus may be used to calculate the purchase price of the goods you want) and pay, getting a receipt. This must then be taken back to the first counter and exchanged for your purchases.

Department stores

Department stores (*univermag*) sell a variety of manufactured goods such as clothing, linens, toys, homewares and shoes.

No visit to Moscow would be complete without a visit to GUM, the largest department store in Russia. It comprises an enormous collection of arcades, now taken over by up-market chains and boutiques from the West and is housed in an impressive glass-roofed building, rather like a giant greenhouse. There is another department store chain: TsUM, which has branches in Moscow and most of the larger cities.

Kiosks

Outdoor kiosks are shops in small booths on the sidewalks, squares, markets and around the metros and stations. They often remain open late and a few are open 24 hours. Most sell telephone cards, alcohol, drinks and cigarettes, while others also specialize in newspapers, ticket sales, lotto, milk, souvenirs, fruit and vegetables, bootleg cassettes and CDs and clothing. It is better not to buy vodka from kiosks as dishonest operators may pass off watered-down industrial alcohol or home-brew as genuine factory vodka.

Opening hours

Large department stores are open from 09:00 to 20:00 Monday to Saturday. Smaller stores have a wide range of opening times, anywhere from 08:00 to 11:00, closing between 20:00 and 23:00, with an hour's lunch-break either from 13:00 to 14:00 or 14:00 to 15:00. Most shops are closed on Sundays. Many modern shops and large department stores now work without a lunch-break.

WHAT TO BUY

Handicrafts

These include the attractively decorated black lacquer *palekh* boxes (icon-painters started making them when religious art lost popularity after the Revolution); enamelled bowls and ornaments; embroidered blouses and tablecloths from the Ukraine; large black printed scarves; guitars and *balalaikas*; lace tablecloths and handkerchiefs; jewellery and gemstones from Siberia and the Urals and painted wooden ornaments, including the ubiquitous *matrioshka* dolls which fit one inside the other. Modern variations on the matrioshka doll include leaders of the former USSR, the Beatles and even South Park cartoon characters.

Old communist memorabilia has long been removed from the shops but is still sold to tourists and makes interesting souvenirs. There is much military memorabilia on sale: anything from hats and hip flasks to diving suits and medals. Check what you're buying carefully as it might not be genuine and don't declare any of it when you leave Russia. This is equally true with the old bank notes you can buy.

Beware of buying paintings, especially if they are expensive, as duty of 100% or more may be imposed on them when you leave the country. If you are going to buy one, make it a small one so that it will fit into your bag easily. If the painting looks old and as if it might be really valuable, it may well be confiscated by customs officials unless you have a permit from the Ministry of Culture. Customs officials always make a point of looking at paintings when you leave the country.

Books

You'll find few English-language books in the shops but up-market hotels usually have a small selection of novels in their gift shops. If you haven't already got one, it's well worth buying an English-Russian/Russian-English dictionary to supplement your phrase book. Dictionaries can be found in most bookshops for under US$2.

Russian-language art books are worth buying for their reproductions and they can be very cheap. There are branches of Dom Knigi (House of Books) in Moscow, St Petersburg and most other large cities.

Tapes, CDs and CD Roms

Pirated tapes and CD's of both Russian and current Western music are available everywhere: US$1 for a tape, US$2 for a CD. The quality is very good, even for CDs.

Currently very popular amongst teenage Russian girls is the group, Ruki Vehr; Chai-F is a long-running rock band. Alla Pugacheva is an older female singer who's had a wide following for many years, particularly from over-40s women. CD Roms are widely available containing pirated computer software. Virtually any application is available but you need to know what you are looking for; many have an English 'set up' option on them. They can be very cheap (around US$5) but, of course, you never know what viruses they may contain.

❑ **Safety tips for Trans-Siberian travellers**

There are many stories of crimes on railways. The majority are exaggerations, distortions or complete fabrications. The most outrageous story in recent years was the so-called 'Sleeping Gas Incident' on a Moscow–St Petersburg train. This story involved an entire carriage supposedly being put to sleep by gas and everyone being robbed. After a week of international media coverage, the Russian journalist who wrote the story admitted that it was fictitious but she still maintained that she did lose her purse when she was asleep!

Crime does exist on railways but a few simple precautions will substantially reduce your chances of anything untoward happening to you.

● Lock the cabin from the inside when you are asleep, by using both the normal door handle lock and the flick-down lock – your Russian companions will do this anyway. Put your bags under the sleeping bench or in the space above the door, depending on which berth you are in. It is not really necessary to lock your bags, but don't leave them lying around either. Dress down on trains and always carry valuables on your body. The railways are currently installing a new type of lock on coupé doors in trains which they claim is not openable from the outside.

● Some people padlock their bags to the compartment wall but this is unnecessary. It is a good idea always to leave someone in the cabin to look after the luggage. If everyone has to leave, ask the *provodnik* (conductor) to lock your cabin. Although valuables can be left in a small safe that is located in the chief provodnik's cabin, this is not recommended.

● Carry only a small amount of roubles and US$ in your wallet. Don't show large amounts of money, especially hard currency. Large amounts of money and important documents should always be carried in a money belt under your clothing. Even sleep with it on.

● Carry only non-essential goods in bags over your shoulder.

● Have a pocket torch/flashlight handy as many entrance halls and stairways have no lights. This is really important in winter when it gets dark very early.

● Never get into a taxi carrying anyone other than the driver. Look at the driver and condition of the car. If in doubt, wave the taxi on. Taxis ordered by phone or through organized services at hotels are often a better bet.

● Change money only at kiosks and banks.

● Watch out for street urchins and gipsy children as they are the most visible and aggressive thieves. Unless you ignore them they'll swarm around you like bees, begging and even grabbing your legs or arms to distract you. Before you realize it, they'll have opened your bag or pulled out your wallet. Their 'controller' is often a dishevelled woman beggar with a small infant in her arms. If you're approached, don't look at them but walk away quickly. If you look like becoming a victim, go into a shop or towards a group of Russians who will usually send them packing.

Clothes

There is a huge market for fake sports clothes and there are now also dozens of trendy foreign fashion shops in the biggest cities. Russian or old Soviet military clothing is a popular buy for foreigners but this should be concealed as you leave the country or it may be confiscated.

CRIME

Russia is as safe a place for tourists to visit as London or New York: there's much the same amount of petty crime about. It can, however, be a dangerous place if you're involved in business.

On 19 December 2000 gunmen opened fire on the car of Moscow's deputy mayor just after he had brokered a deal to open the city's first Formula One racetrack. Deputy Mayor Josif Ordzhonikidze was seriously injured becoming yet another statistic to confirm that doing business in Russia is still dangerous despite Putin's pledge to firmly establish 'the dictatorship of the law'. There are believed to be over 8000 gangs operating in the country, many of whom, using 'heavies' recruited from the army, extort money from businesses. Protection payments are demanded of the proprietors. Restaurant owners must pay up or face their properties being set on fire. Taxi-drivers have been threatened with having their cars damaged or families attacked. There are even occasional shoot-outs between rival gangs in the streets of Moscow and St Petersburg. St Petersburg is believed to be the most dangerous city in which to operate a business, followed by Moscow and then Krasnoyarsk. It seems that it's not the local councils but the mafia who now run Russia's cities.

Crimes against tourists were almost unimaginable in the communist era when the streets of Moscow were far safer than those of New York but now a new branch of the police force has had to be set up especially to protect foreigners. The situation is not as bad as in some other European or American cities but you shouldn't wander around late at night, especially in Moscow or St Petersburg. The mafia really aren't interested in tourists; they deal in far more money than they could get from you.

Be sensible about your safety: as a Russian woman warned me, 'Where there is big crime, there will also be small crime'. Don't dress too ostentatiously or wear expensive watches or jewellery. Watch out for pickpockets. Travellers have reported that petty pilfering from hotel rooms has increased quite considerably over the last few years. Don't take valuables with you to Russia. A money-belt for your passport, travellers' cheques and foreign currency is essential. Read the warnings on p85 for Trans-Siberian travellers.

The foreign media has exaggerated the dangers of the mafia as far as tourists are concerned – only bad news sells. After visiting Russia you will remember, more than anything else, just how friendly and genuine the people were to you.

Historical outline

EARLY HISTORY

Prehistory: the first Siberians

Discoveries at Dering Yuryakh, by the Lena River 100km south of Yakutsk, have indicated that man has lived in Siberia for far longer than had previously been thought. Archaeologist Yuri Mochanov, who led the excavations here in the 1980s and 90s, believes that the thousands of stone tools he found embedded in geological stratum dating back over two million years suggests human habitation stretching back this far, which would place the site on a par with Professor Leakey's discoveries in East Africa. It's a highly controversial theory as it would mean that initial human evolution also occurred outside Africa. Western archaeologists who have studied the material believe, however, that it cannot be more than 500,000 years old; that would still give the Siberians an impressively long history.

There is evidence of rather more recent human life in the Lake Baikal area. In the 13th millennium BC, Stone Age nomads were roaming round the shores of the lake, hunting mammoths and carving their tusks into the tubby fertility goddesses that can been seen in the museums of Irkutsk today. Several of these sites in the Baikal area have been discovered and the railway passes through one at the village of Malta, 45 miles west of Irkutsk, where a camp dating back to this early period has been excavated.

By the Neolithic Age (twelfth to fifth millennia BC) there is far more archaeological evidence and it shows that the nomadic tribes had reached the Arctic Circle and moved into North America through Alaska. These northern tribes trained dogs to pull their sledges but were left behind technologically, remaining in the Stone Age until Russian colonists arrived in the mid-seventeenth century.

In the south, however, several Bronze Age cultures emerged around the central parts of the Yenisei River. Afanassevskaya, south of Krasnoyarsk, has given its name to the culture of the people who lived in this area in the second millennium BC. They made pottery and decorated it with a herring-bone pattern.

The first evidence of permanent buildings has been found near Achinsk, where the Andronovo people built huge log cabins in the first millennium BC. Excavations of sites of the Karassuk culture, also dated to the first millennium BC, have yielded Chinese artifacts, indicating trade between these two peoples.

Early civilizations
The Iron Age sites show evidence of more complex and organized societies. The clear air of the Altai Mountains has preserved the contents of numerous graves of the Tagar Culture which existed here in the second century BC. Their leaders were embalmed and buried like Egyptian pharaohs with all that they might need in the afterlife. In their burial mounds archaeologists have found perfectly preserved woollen blankets, decorated leather saddles and the complete skeletons of horses, probably buried alive when their master died.

The Huns moved into the region south of Lake Baikal in the third century BC where the Buryats, their descendants, now live. Their move west continued slowly over the next five centuries when their infamous leader Attila, the 'Scourge of God', having pillaged his way across Europe, reached Paris where he was defeated in 452 AD.

The ancestors of the Kyrgyz people were the Tashtyks from west Siberia, who built large houses of clay (one found near Abakan even has an underfloor central heating system), moulded the features of their dead in clay death masks and decorated their bodies with elaborate tattoos. The tiny republic of Kyrgyzstan, south of Kazakhstan, is all that remains of a once mighty empire that stretched from Samarkand to Manchuria in the twelfth century AD. In the following century, the Kyrgyz were taken over by the rapidly advancing Mongols. Genghis Khan's Mongol empire grew to become the largest empire ever, including the Tartars of South Russia, and the peoples of North Asia, Mongolia and China.

The first Russian expeditions to Siberia
In mediaeval times, Siberia was known to Russians only as a distant land of valuable fur-bearing animals. There were occasional expeditions from Novgorod in the fifteenth century. These became more frequent in the sixteenth century, once the lands of South Russia had been released from the grip of the Mongols by Tsar Ivan the Terrible who seized Kazan and Astrakhan, opening the way to Siberia. Yediger, the leader of a small Siberian kingdom just over the Urals, realized his vulnerability and sent Ivan a large tribute of furs, declaring himself a vassal of the Tsar.

Yediger's son, Kuchum, was of a more independent mind and, having murdered his father, he put an end to the annual tribute of furs, proclaiming himself Tsar of Siberia. Since Ivan's armies were occupied on his western frontiers, he allowed the powerful Stroganov family to raise a private army to annex the rebel lands. In 1574 he granted them a twenty-year lease on the land over the Urals as far east as the Tobol River, the centre of Kuchum's kingdom.

Yermak: the founder of Siberia

The Stroganovs' army was a wild bunch of mercenaries led by ex-pirate Yermak, the man now recognized as the founder of Siberia. They crossed the Urals and challenged Kuchum, gaining control of his lands after a struggle that was surprisingly long, since the Russians were armed with muskets, the enemy with swords and bows and arrows. On 5 November 1581, Yermak raised the Russian flag in Isker (near modern Tobolsk) and sent the Tsar a tribute of over 2500 furs. In return Ivan pardoned him for his past crimes, sent him a fur-lined cape that had once graced the royal shoulders and a magnificent suit of armour. Over the next few years Yermak was constantly harassed by Kuchum. On 16 August 1584, the enemy ambushed them when they were asleep on an island in the Irtysh. The story goes that Yermak drowned in the river, dragged under by the weight of the armour given him by the Tsar. His name lives on as the top brand of Russian rucksack.

The quest for furs

Over the next fifty years Cossack forces moved rapidly across Siberia, establishing *ostrogs* (military outposts) as they went and gathering tributes of fur for the Tsar. Tyumen was founded in 1586, Tomsk in 1604, Krasnoyarsk in 1628, Yakutsk in 1633 and by 1639 the Cossacks had crossed the width of the country reaching the east coast. Like the Spanish Conquistadors in South America they dealt roughly with the native tribes they met, who were no match for their muskets and cannon. The prize they lusted after was not gold, as it was for the Spaniards in Peru and for later Russian adventurers in Siberia, but furs. In the days before fur farms certain pelts were worth far more than they are today and from the proceeds of a season's trapping in Siberia a man could buy and stock a large farm with cattle and sheep; the chances that such a man would be successful in finding his way into or out of the dark, swampy forests of the taiga were not very high but quite a few did.

Khabarov and the Amur

In 1650, a Russian fur merchant named Khabarov set out from Yakutsk to explore the Amur region in what is now the Far Eastern Territories. He found the local tribes extremely hostile as the Russians' reputation for rape and pillage had spread before him. The land was fertile and rich in fur-bearing animals and Khabarov and his men committed such atrocities that the news reached the ears of the Tsar, who ordered him back to the capital to explain himself. Bearing gifts of fur, he convinced the Tsar that he had won valuable new lands which would enrich his empire. The local tribes, however, appealed to the Manchus, their southern neighbours, who sent an army to help them fight off the Russians. The Tsar's men were gradually beaten back but periodic fighting went on until 1689, when the Russians were forced out of Manchuria and the Amur by the Treaty of Nerchinsk.

Eighteenth-century explorers

Peter the Great became Tsar in 1696 and initiated a new era of exploration in the Far East. By the following year the explorer, Atlassov, had claimed Kamchatka for Russia. In 1719 the first scientific expedition set out for Siberia. Peter commissioned the Danish seaman, Vitus Bering, to try to find a northern sea-passage to Kamchatka and the Sea of Okhotsk (unaware that the route had been discovered by Deshnev 80 years before). However, the Tsar did not live to see Bering set out in 1725.

Between 1733 and 1743 another scientific expedition, comprising naval officers, topographers, geodesic surveyors, naturalists and astronomers, made detailed charts of Russians lands in the Far East. Fur traders reached the Aleutian Islands and the first colony in Alaska (on Kodiak Island) was founded in 1784 by Gregory Shelekhov. (His grave is in the cemetery of the Znamensky Convent in Irkutsk.) The Russian colony of Alaska was sold to the United States in 1868 for the bargain price of two cents an acre.

THE NINETEENTH CENTURY

There were two developments in Siberia in the nineteenth century which had a tremendous effect upon its history. First, the practice of sentencing criminals to a life of exile or hard labour in Siberia was increased to provide labour for the mines and to establish communities around the military outposts. The exile system, which caused a great deal of human misery, (see below) greatly increased the population in this vast and empty region. Secondly, and of far greater importance was the building of the Trans-Siberian Railway in the 1890s (described in a later section).

Colonization

By the end of the eighteenth century, the population of Siberia was estimated to be about one and a half million people, most of whom belonged to nomadic native tribes. The policy of populating the region through the exile system swelled the numbers of settlers but criminals did not make the best colonists. As a result, voluntary emigration from overcrowded European Russia was encouraged by the government. Peasant settlers could escape the bonds of serfdom by crossing the Urals but Siberia's reputation as a place of exile was not much of an incentive to move.

As the railway penetrated Siberia, the transport of colonists was facilitated. Tsar Alexander's emigration representatives were sent to many thickly-populated regions in European Russia in the 1880s. They offered prospective colonists incentives including a reduced rail fare (six roubles for the 1200-mile journey) and a free allotment of twenty-seven acres of land. Prices in Siberia were high for most things and colonists could expect get up to 100 per cent more than in European Russia for produce grown on this land. Many peasants left Europe for Siberia after the great famine of 1890-91.

Further exploration and expansion

Throughout the century scientists and explorers continued to make expeditions to Siberia, recording their discoveries in the region. In 1829, an expedition led by the German scientist, Baron von Humboldt, who had become famous for his scientific explorations in South America, investigated the geological structure of the Altai plateau in southern Siberia.

In 1840 the estuary of the Amur was discovered and colonization encouraged after Count Muraviev-Amursky, Governor General of Eastern Siberia, had annexed the entire Amur territory for Russia. This was in flagrant violation of the Russo-Chinese Treaty of Nerchinsk, which had been signed in 1689. However, the Chinese were in no position to argue, being threatened by the French and English as well as by internal troubles in Peking. By the Treaty of Peking (1860) they ceded the territory north of the Amur to Russia, and also the land east of the Ussuri, including the valuable Pacific port of Vladivostok.

THE EXILE SYSTEM

The word 'Siberia' meant only one thing in Victorian England and nineteenth-century Russia: an inhospitable land of exiled murderers and other evil criminals who paid for their sins by working in the infamous salt mines. To a great extent this was a true picture of Siberia except that the prisoners were mining gold, silver and coal rather than salt. Some of the first exiles sent over the Urals did indeed work in salt mines which may be why people associated Siberia with salt.

By the year 1900, over one million people had been exiled and made the long march over the Urals to the squalid and overcrowded prisons of Siberia.

George Kennan

In 1891 a book entitled *Siberia and the Exile System*, written by George Kennan, was published in America. It exposed the truly horrific conditions under which prisoners were kept in Siberia and aroused public opinion in both America and Britain. Kennan was a journalist working for the *New York Century Magazine*. He knew Siberia well, having previously spent two years there. He was then unaware, however, of quite how badly the convicts were treated and in a series of lectures before the American Geographical Society he defended the Tsarist government and the exile system.

When his editor commissioned him to investigate the system more thoroughly, the bureaucrats in St Petersburg were happy to give him the letters of introduction which allowed him to venture into the very worst of the prisons and to meet the governors and convicts. The government hoped, no doubt, that Kennan would champion their cause. Such had been the case with the Rev Dr Henry Landsell who had travelled in Siberia in 1879. In his account of the journey, *Through Siberia*, he wrote that 'on the whole, if a Russian exile behaves himself decently well, he may in Siberia be more comfortable than in many, and as comfortable as in most of the prisons of the world.' After the year he spent visiting Siberian prisons, Kennan could not agree with Landsell and the inhumanity of the exile system, the convict mines and the terrible conditions in the overcrowded prisons were all revealed in his book.

The first exiles
The earliest mention of exile in Russian documents of law is in 1648. In the seventeenth century, exile was used as a way of getting rid of criminals who had already been punished. In Kennan's words: 'The Russian criminal code of that age was almost incredibly cruel and barbarous. Men were impaled on sharp stakes, hanged and beheaded by the hundred for crimes that would not now be regarded as criminal in any civilized country in the world, while lesser offenders were flogged with the knut (a whip of leather and metal thongs, which could break a man's back with a single blow) and bastinado (cane), branded with hot irons, mutilated by amputation of one or more of their limbs, deprived of their tongues, and suspended in the air by hooks passed under two of their ribs until they died a lingering and miserable death.' Those who survived these ordeals were too mutilated to be of any use so they were then driven out of their villages to the lands beyond the Urals.

Exile as a punishment: the convict mines
With the discovery of valuable minerals in Siberia and the shortage of labourers available to mine them, the government began to use criminals to work them. Exile was thus developed into a form of punishment and extended to cover a range of crimes including desertion, assault with intent to kill and vagrancy (when the vagrant was of no use to the army or the community). It was also the punishment for offences that now seem nothing short of ridiculous. According to Kennan, exile became the punishment for fortune-telling, prize-fighting, snuff-taking (the snuff-taker was not only banished to Siberia but also had the septum between his nostrils torn out) and driving with reins. (The old Russian driver had been accustomed to ride his horse or run beside it – using reins was regarded as too Western, too European.)

Abolition of the death penalty
In the eighteenth century demand for labour for the mines continued to grow and the list of crimes punishable by exile was further extended to include drunkenness and wife-beating, the cutting down of trees by serfs, begging with a pretence to being in distress, and setting fire to property accidentally.

In 1753, the death penalty was abolished (for all crimes except an attempt on the life of the Tsar) and replaced by exile with hard labour. No

The Siberian Boundary Post (circa 1880) In this melancholy scene, friends and relatives bid exiled prisoners farewell by the brick pillar that marked the western border of Siberia, on the Great Post Road.

attention was given to the treatment of exiles en route, they were simply herded like animals over the Urals, many dying on the way. The system was chaotically corrupt and disorganized, with hardened murderers being set free in Siberia while people convicted of relatively insignificant offences perished down the mines.

Reorganization in the nineteenth century

In the nineteenth century the system became more organized but no less corrupt. In 1817 a series of *étapes* (exile stations) was built along the way to provide overnight shelter for the marching parties. They were nothing more than crude log cabins with wooden sleeping platforms. Forwarding prisons were established at Tyumen and Tomsk from where prisoners were sent to their final place of exile. From Tyumen, convicts travelled by barge in specially designed cages to Tomsk. From here some would be directed on to Krasnoyarsk or else to Irkutsk, a 1040-mile, three-month march away. The prisoners would be sent from these large centres to smaller prisons, penal colonies and to the mines. The most infamous mines were on the island of Sakhalin, off the east coast, where convicts dug for coal; the mines at Kara, which Kennan states were producing an annual average of 3600 pounds of pure gold in the late nineteenth century; and the silver mines of Nerchinsk.

Records were started in 1823 and between this date and 1887, when Kennan consulted the books in Tomsk, 772,979 prisoners had passed through on their way to Siberia. They comprised *katorzhniki* (hard labour convicts) who were distinguishable by their half-shaved heads; *poselentsi* (penal colonists); *silni* (persons simply banished and allowed to return to European Russia after serving their sentence), and *dobrovolni* (women and children voluntarily accompanying their husbands or fathers). Until the 1850s convicts and penal colonists would be branded on the cheek with a letter to indicate the nature of their crime. More than half of those who crossed the Urals had had no proper trial but were exiled by 'administrative process'. As Kennan states: 'Every village commune has the right to banish any of its members who, through bad conduct or general worthlessness, have proved themselves obnoxious to their fellow citizens.'

Life in the cells

The first prison Kennan was shown round on his trip in 1887 was the Tyumen forwarding prison. He records the experience thus: 'As we entered the cell, the convicts, with a sudden jingling of chains, sprang to their feet, removed their caps and stood in a dense throng around the *nari* (wooden sleeping platforms).... "The prison" said the warden, "is terribly overcrowded. This cell for example is only 35 feet long by 25 wide, and has air space for 35, or at most 40 men. How many men slept here last night?" he inquired, turning to the prisoners. "A hundred and sixty, your high nobility", shouted half a dozen hoarse voices.....I looked around the cell. There was practically no ventilation and the air was so poisoned and foul that I could hardly force myself to breathe it in.'

The hospital cells

None of these dreadful experiences could prepare Kennan for the hospital cells, filled with prisoners suffering from typhus, scurvy, pneumonia, smallpox, diphtheria, dysentery and syphilis. He wrote afterwards: 'Never before in my life had I seen faces so white, haggard, and ghastly as those that lay on the gray pillows in the hospital cells....As I breathed that heavy, stifling atmosphere, poisoned with the breaths of syphilitic and fever-stricken patients, loaded and saturated with the odor of excrement, disease germs, exhalations from unclean human bodies, and foulness inconceivable, it seemed to me that over the hospital doors should be written "All hope abandon, ye who enter here".'

From the records he discovered that almost thirty per cent of the patients in the prison hospital died each year. This he compared with 3.8 per cent for French prisons of the time, two per cent for American and 1.4 per cent for English prisons.

Corruption

As well as the grossly inhuman conditions he saw in the prisons, Kennan found that the whole exile system was riddled with corruption. Bribes were regularly accepted by warders and other officials. One provincial administrator boasted that his governor, the Governor of Tobolsk, was so careless that he could get him to sign any document he was given. As a wager he wrote out The Lord's Prayer on an official form and placed it before the Governor who blindly signed it. The government in St Petersburg was too far away to know what was going on in the lands beyond the Urals.

Many high-ranking officials in Siberia were so tightly bound by bureaucratic ties that change was impossible, even if they desired it. An officer in the Tomsk prison confided in Kennan: 'I would gladly resign tomorrow if I could see the (exile) system abolished. It is disastrous to Siberia, it is ruinous to the criminal, and it causes an immense amount of misery; but what can be done? If we say anything to our superiors in St Petersburg, they strike us in the face; and they strike hard – it hurts!'

Political exiles

Life for the so-called 'politicals' and 'nihilists', banished to prevent them infecting European Russians with their criticisms of the autocratic political system that was choking the country to death, was generally better than that of other prisoners. Many came from rich aristocratic families and, once out of prison, life for them continued in much the same way as it had west of the Urals. The most famous political exiles were the 'Decembrists': the men who took part in the unsuccessful coup in 1825. Many

(**Above**) Political exiles (circa 1880), many of whom came from aristocratic families, were free to adopt whatever lifestyle they could afford within the confines of Siberia, once they had completed their prison sentences.

were accompanied into exile by their wives. Some of the houses in which they lived are now preserved as *dom* (house) museums in Irkutsk (see p234). Kennan secretly visited many of the politicals in Siberia and was convinced that they did not deserve being exiled. He wrote later: 'If such men are in exile in a lonely Siberian village on the frontier of Mongolia, instead of being at home in the service of the state – so much the worse for the state.' A few politicals were sentenced to exile with the native Yakut tribe within the Arctic Circle. Escape was impossible and life with a Stone Age tribe must have seemed unbearable for cultured aristocrats who had until recently been part of the St Petersburg court circle.

Temporary abolition of the exile system

The exile system was abolished in 1900. However corrupt the system and inhuman the conditions in these early Siberian prisons, worse was to come only thirty years later. Under Stalin's regime, vast concentration camps (in European Russia as well as in Siberia) were set up to provide a huge slave-labour force to build roads, railways and factories in the 1930s and 40s. Prisoners were grossly overworked and undernourished. The mortality rate in some of these camps is said to have been as high as thirty per cent. Reports of the number of people sentenced to these slave labour camps range from between three million and twenty million. Some reports place the death toll up to the late 1950s as high as eighteen million.

(**Opposite**) **Top:** The house of Decembrist, Maria Volkonsky, the 'Princess of Siberia', in Irkutsk is now a museum. **Bottom:** Convict monument, Krasnoyarsk © Nick Hill.

Early travellers

VICTORIAN ADVENTURERS

This was the great age of the gentleman (and gentlewoman) adventurer. These upper-class travellers spent the greater part of their lives exploring the lesser-known regions of the world, writing long and usually highly-readable accounts of their adventures and encounters with the 'natives'. Siberia attracted almost as many of this brave breed as did Africa and India. Once they had travelled across the great Siberian plain using the normal forms of transport of the time (carriage and sledge) they resorted to such new-fangled inventions as the bicycle (R.L. Jefferson in 1896), the train (from 1900) and then the car (the Italian Prince Borghese in an Itala in 1907). Some even crossed the country entirely on foot.

THE GREAT SIBERIAN POST ROAD

Before the railway was built, there was but one way for convicts, colonists and adventurers to cross this region: a rough track known as the Great Siberian Post Road or *Trakt*. Posting stations were set up at approximately 25 mile intervals along the route, where travellers could rent horses and drivers. Murray, in his *Handbook for Russia, Poland and Finland* (1865 edition) told his travellers: 'Three kinds of conveyances are available: the *telega*, or cart without springs, which has to be changed at every station, and for which a charge of about 8d is made at every stage; the *kibitka* or cart (in winter a sledge) with a hood; and the *tarantass*, a kind of carriage on wooden springs which admits of the traveller lying down full length and which can be made very comfortable at night. The two latter vehicles have to be purchased at Perm, if the *telega*, or postal conveyance be not accepted. A *tarantass* may be bought from £12 to £15.'

George Kennan called the Imperial Russian Post System 'the most perfectly organized horse express service in the world'.

The discomforts of Siberian travel

Since a visit to Siberia could rarely be completed in a single season, most travellers experienced the different modes of transport used in summer and winter. They found the sledge more comfortable than the tarantass and indeed no nineteenth-century travelogue would be complete without

(Opposite): There are still some traditional wooden buildings to be seen in Siberian cities, such as this house in the back streets of Novosibirsk © Nick Hill.

(**Above**) Until the building of the Trans-Siberian, the Great Post Road formed the life-line for hundreds of tiny communities such as this. (**Below**) There were few bridges on the Road – crossing frozen rivers and lakes was treacherous in early winter and spring.

a detailed description of this unique vehicle. The tarantass had a large boat-shaped body and travellers stored their belongings on the floor, covering them with straw and mattresses on top of which they lay. Although this may sound comfortable, when experienced at speed over atrocious roads and for great distances, by contemporary accounts it was not. S.S.Hill wrote in 1854: 'The worst of the inconveniences arose from the deep ruts which were everywhere...and

> ❏ **Travel by tarantass**
> Kate Marsden, a nurse travelling in 1894, recalled the agony of days spent in a tarantass in the following way: 'Your limbs ache, your muscles ache, your head aches, and, worst of all, your inside aches terribly. "Tarantass rheumatism" internal and external, chronic, or rather perpetual, is the complaint.'

from the necessity of galloping down the declivities to force the carriage upon the bridges. And often our carriage fell with such force against the bridges that it was unsafe to retain our accustomed reclining position...'

The yamshchiki

The driver (*yamshchik*) of the tarantass or sledge, was invariably drunk. He had to be bribed with vodka to make good time between the post stations and Murray's 1865 guide-book thoughtfully includes in its 'Useful Russian Phrases' section, the words 'Dam na vodki' ('I will give you drink money'). Accidents were commonplace and R.L. Jefferson (on a trip without his bicycle in 1895) wrote that his yamshchik became so inebriated that he fell off the sledge and died. The same fate befell one of Kate Marsden's sledge-drivers who had gone to sleep with the reins tied around his wrists. She wrote: 'And there was the poor fellow being tossed to and fro amongst the legs of the horses, which, now terrified, tore down the hill like mad creatures.... In a few minutes there was a fearful crash. We had come into collision with another tarantass and the six horses and the two tarantasses were mixed up in a chaotic mass'.

The horses

Sledges and tarantasses were pulled by a *troika*, a group of three horses. These were small furry specimens, 'not much larger than the average English donkey', noted R.L.Jefferson. They were hired between post stations and usually belonged to the yamshchik.

S.S.Hill was shocked at the way in which these animals were treated. He remarked: 'The Arab is the friend of his horse. The Russian or Siberian peasant is his severe master who exacts every grain of his strength by blows accompanied with curses....lodges him badly or not at all, cares little how he feeds him, and never cleans him or clips a hair of his body from the hour of his birth to that of his death.' Horses were worked literally until they died. R.L.Jefferson recalls that two of his animals dropped dead in harness and had to be cut free.

❑ **Dangers**
Travel in Siberia was not only uncomfortable, it was also dangerous. Wolves and bears roamed the forests and when food was scarce would attack a horse or man (although you were safe in a tarantass). In the Amur region lived the world's largest tiger, the Amur tiger. Just as wild as these animals, and probably more dangerous, were the *brodyagi*, escaped convicts in search of money and a passport to readmit them to Europe.

Dirt and disease

As well as the discomfort of the 'conveyance' and the dangers along the Trakt, travellers were warned about the dirt and disease they could encounter. R.L.Jefferson wrote: 'No wonder that Siberia is looked upon by the traveller with abhorrence. Apart from its inhabitants, no one can say that Siberia is not a land of beauty, plenty and promise; but it is the nature of its inhabitants which make it the terrible place it is. The independence, the filth and general want of comfort which characterize every effort of the community, serve to make a visit to any Siberian centre a thing to be remembered for many years and an experience not desirable to repeat.'

Hotel rooms were universally squalid. Kate Marsden gives the following advice to anyone entering a hotel bedroom in Siberia: 'Have your pocket handkerchief ready...and place it close to your nostrils the moment the door is opened. The hinges creak and your first greeting is a gust of hot, foetid air.'

Insects

Especially in the summer months, travellers were plagued by flies and mosquitoes. Kate Marsden wrote: 'After a few days the body swells from their bites into a form that can neither be imagined nor described. They attack your eyes and your face, so that you would hardly be recognized by your dearest friend.'

At night, travellers who had stopped in the dirty hotels or posting stations were kept awake by lice, bed-bugs and a variety of other insects with which the bedding was infested. R.L.Jefferson met a man who never travelled without four saucers and a can of kerosene. In the hotel room at night he would put a saucer filled with kerosene under each bed-leg, to stop the bugs reaching him in bed. However, Jefferson noted that: 'With a sagacity which one would hardly credit so small an insect, it would make a detour by getting up the wall on to the ceiling, and then, having accurately poised, drop down upon the victim – no doubt to his extreme discomfort.'

Bovril and Jaeger underwear: essential provisions

R.L.Jefferson (see 'Jefferson's Bicycle Jaunts', opposite) never travelled without a large supply of Bovril and a change of Jaeger 'Cellular' underwear – 'capital stuff for lightness and durability' he wrote after one long ride on his Imperial Rover bicycle. Kate Marsden shared his enthusiasm for Dr Jaeger's undergarments: 'without which it would have been quite impossible to go through all the changes of climate; and to remain for weeks together without changing my clothes', she wrote. On the subject of provisions for the trip, Murray recommended taking along basic foodstuffs. Miss Marsden packed into her tarantass 'a few boxes of sardines, biscuits, some bread, tea and one or two other trifles which included forty pounds of plum pudding'.

S.S.HILL'S *TRAVELS IN SIBERIA*

This account of Hill's Siberian adventures was the result of a journey made in the early 1850s to Irkutsk and then Yakutsk (now in the Far Eastern Territories). Armed with a pistol loaded with goose-shot (for the law forbade a foreigner to shoot at a Russian, even in self defence), he travelled by tarantass and existed on *shchi* (soup) and tea for most of the time. He makes some interesting observations upon the culinary habits of the Siberians he met along the way.

He records that on one occasion, when settling down to a bowl of shchi after a long winter's journey 'we found the taste of our accustomed dish, however, today peculiar'. He was made aware of the main ingredient of their soup later, 'by the yamshchik pointing out to us the marks of the axe upon the frozen carcass of a horse lying within a quarter of a verst of the site of our feast'. In some places even tea and shchi were unavailable and they could find only cedar nuts ('a favourite food article with the peasants of Eastern Siberia'). He ate better in Irkutsk, where, at a dinner party, he was treated to *comba* fish, six feet in length and served whole. 'I confess I never before saw so enormous an animal served or cooked whole save once, an ox roasted at a 'mop' in Worcestershire', he wrote later. He was shocked by the behaviour of the ladies at the table, who, when bored, displayed 'a very droll habit of rolling the damp crumb of rye bread... into pills'. He remarks with surprise that in Siberian society 'a glass of milk terminates the dinner'.

JEFFERSON'S BICYCLE JAUNTS

R.L.Jefferson was also an enthusiastic cyclist and he made several journeys to Siberia in the 1890s. A year after bicycling from London to Constantinople and back, he set out again from Kennington Oval for Moscow on his Imperial Rover bicycle. Twelve hours out of Moscow, a speeding tarantass knocked him down, squashing the back wheel of his 'machine'. Repairs took a few days but he still managed to set a cycling speed record of just under fifty days for the 4281-mile journey from London to Moscow and back.

His next ride was to the decaying capital of the Khanate of Khiva, now in Uzbekistan. The 6000-mile journey took him across the Kyrgyz ↄ̌

❏ KATE MARSDEN VISITS SIBERIAN LEPERS

Miss Marsden was a nurse with a definite mission in Siberia. In the 1880s she learnt, through travellers' accounts, of the numerous leper colonies to the north of Yakutsk. There were rumours of a special herb found there, that could alleviate the symptoms of the disease. After an audience with Queen Victoria, during which she was given useful letters of introduction, she travelled to Moscow. She arrived, in mid-winter, wearing her thin cotton nurse's uniform and a white bonnet, which she immediately exchanged for thick Russian clothes.

Crossing Siberia

When she had met the Empress Marya, who gave her a thousand roubles for her relief fund, she started on her long sledge ride. It was not a dignified send-off – 'three muscular policemen attempted to lift me into the sledge; but their combined strength was futile under the load'. She got aboard eventually and was soon experiencing the extreme discomfort of Siberian travel. She said it made her feel more like 'a battered old log of mahogany than a gently nurtured English-woman'.

Distributing tea, sugar and copies of the Gospels to convicts in the marching parties she encountered along the Post Road, she reached Irkutsk in the summer. She boarded a leaky barge on the Lena River, north of Lake Baikal and drifted down to Yakutsk, sitting on the sacks of potatoes with which the boat was filled. Of this part of the journey she wrote: 'Fortunately we had only about 3,000 miles of this but 3,000 miles were enough'.

Her goal was still a 2,000 mile ride away when she reached Yakutsk. Although she had never been on a horse before, this brave woman arranged an escort of fifteen men and rode with them through insect-infested swamps and across a fiery plain, below which the earth was in a constant state of combustion, until she reached the settlement of Viluisk.

The Lepers of Viluisk

On her arrival, the local priest informed her that 'On the whole of the earth you will not find men in so miserable a condition as the Smedni Viluisk lepers'. She found them dressed in rags, living in hovels and barely existing on a diet of rotten fish. This was in an area where, in winter, some of the lowest temperatures in the world have been recorded. Unfortunately she did not find the herb that was rumoured to exist there but left all the more convinced that finances must be raised for a hospital.

Although she managed to raise 25,000 roubles towards the enterprise, her task was not made any easier by several individuals who took exception to her breezy style of writing, accusing her of having undertaken the journey for her own fame and fortune. Some even suggested that the journey was a fiction invented so that Miss Marsden could collect charitable sums for her own use. In the end she was forced to sue one of her attackers who wrote a letter to *The Times* describing her journey as 'only a little pleasure trip'. Nevertheless she achieved her aim: a hospital opened in Viluisk in 1897. It still stands and her name is still remembered in this remote corner of Russia.

ↄ̌

Steppes in south-west Siberia, along the coast of the Aral Sea and over the Karakum Desert. When the bicycle's wheels sank up to their axles in the sand he had the Rover lashed to the back of a camel for the rest of the journey. While in Central Asia he lived on a diet of boiled mutton and *koumis* (fermented mares' milk). He travelled in a camel-hair suit (Jaeger, of course) and top boots, with a white cork helmet to complete the outfit.

Across Siberia

Jefferson made two more trips to Siberia. In *Across Siberia by Bicycle* (1896), he wrote that he left Moscow and 'sleeping the night in some woodman's hut, subsisting on occasional lumps of black bread, bitten to desperation by fearful insects, and tormented out of my life during the day by swarms of mosquitoes, I arrived in Perm jaded and disgusted'. He then cycled over the Urals and through the mud of the Great Post Road to Yekaterinburg. Here he was entertained by the Yekaterinburg Cyclists' Club whom he described as 'friends of the wheel – jolly good fellows all'.

Declaring that 'from a cyclist's point of view, Russian roads cannot be recommended', he abandoned his Rover in 1897 for the adventure described in *Roughing it in Siberia*. With three chums, he travelled by sledge from Krasnoyarsk up the frozen Yenisei ('jerking about like peas in a frying pan') to the gold mines in Minusinsk district, spending several weeks prospecting in the Syansk Mountains.

Building the railway

The first railway to be built in Russia was Tsar Nicholas I's private line (opened in 1836) which ran from his summer palace at Tsarkoye Selo (Pushkin) to Pavlovsk and later to St Petersburg, a distance of 14 miles. The Tsar was said to have been most impressed with this new form of transport and over the next 30 years several lines were laid in European Russia, linking the main cities and towns. Siberia, however, was really too far away to deserve serious consideration since most people went there only if they were forced to as exiles. As far as the Tsar was concerned, traditional methods of transport kept him supplied with all the gold and furs he needed.

PLANS FOR A TRANS-SIBERIAN RAILWAY

Horse-powered Trans-Siberian Express?

The earliest plans for long-distance railways in Siberia came from a number of foreigners. Most books which include a history of the Trans-Siberian give a passing mention to an English engineer, if only because of his wildly eccentric ideas and his unfortunate name. Thus a Mr Dull has gone down in history as the man who seriously suggested the building of a line from Perm across Siberia to the Pacific, with carriages being pulled by wild horses (of which there were a great many in the region at the time). He is said to have formally proposed his plan to the Ministry of Ways of Communication, who turned it down.

The Englishman's name was, in fact, not Dull but Duff and it's not only his name that has been distorted through time. His descendants (John Howell and William Lawrie) have requested that the story be set straight. Thomas Duff was an enterprising adventurer who went out to China to seek his fortune in the 1850s. He returned to England via Siberia, spending some time in St Petersburg with wealthy aristocratic friends. Here he was introduced to the Minister of Ways of Communication and it was probably during their conversation that he remarked on the vast numbers of wild horses he had encountered on his journey. Could they not be put to some use? Perhaps they might be trained to pull the trains that people were saying would soon run across Siberia. It is unlikely that this remark was intended to be serious but it has gone down in history as a formal proposal for a horse-powered Trans-Siberian Express.

More serious proposals

At around this time the American Perry McDonough Collins was exploring the Amur river, having persuaded the US government to appoint him as their commercial agent in the region. He had been given an enthusiastic welcome by Count Amurski Muravyev, the Governor-General of Siberia, before setting off to descend the Amur in a small boat. Collins envisaged a trade link between America and Siberia with vessels sailing up the Amur and Shilka rivers to Chita, where a railway link would shuttle goods to and from Irkutsk. He sent his plans for the building and financing of such a line to the government but these too were rejected. Collins' next venture, a telegraph link between America and Russia, also failed but not before he had made himself a considerable fortune.

It took a further twenty years for the government to become interested enough in the idea of a railway in Siberia to send surveyors to investigate the feasibility of such a project. Plans were considered for the building of lines to link the great Siberian rivers, so that future travellers could cross Siberia in relative comfort by a combination of rail and ship. European lines were extended from Perm over the Urals, reaching Yekaterinburg in 1878.

Tsar Alexander III : the railway's founder

In 1881 Alexander III became Tsar and in 1886 gave the Trans-Siberian project his official sanction with the words: 'I have read many reports of the Governors-General of Siberia and must own with grief and shame that until now the government has done scarcely anything towards satisfying the needs of this rich, but neglected country! It is time, high time!'

He was thus able to add 'Most August Founder of The Great Siberian Railway' to his many other titles. He rightly saw the railway as both the key to developing the land beyond the Urals and also as the means to transport his troops to the Amur region which was being threatened by the Chinese. When the commission looking into the building of the new line declared that the country did not have the money to pay for it, the Tsar solved the problem simply by forming a new committee, dismissing the first.

THE DECISION TO BUILD

The new commission took note of the petitions from Count Ignatyev and Baron Korf, the Governors-General of Irkutsk and the Amur territories, respectively. They proposed rail links between Tomsk and Irkutsk, Lake Baikal and Sretensk (where passengers could board ships for the journey down the Shilka and Amur Rivers to the coast) and for the Ussuri line to Vladivostok. Baron Korf considered that it was imperative for the Ussuri line to be built as soon as possible if the valuable port of Vladivostok was not to be cut off by the advancing Chinese. The Tsar took note and declared: 'I hope the Ministry will practically prove the possibility of the quick and cheap construction of the line'.

Surveys were commissioned and detailed plans prepared. In 1891 it was announced that the Trans-Siberian Railway would indeed be built and work would start immediately. It was, however, to be constructed as cheaply as possible using thinner rails, shorter sleepers and timber (rather than stone) for the smaller bridges.

The route

The railway committee decided that the great project should be divided into several sections with work commencing simultaneously on a number of them. The West Siberian Railway would run from Chelyabinsk (the railway over the Urals reached this town in 1892) to the Ob River where the settlement of Novo Nikolayevsk (now Novosibirsk) was being built. The Mid-Siberian Railway would link the Ob to Irkutsk, the capital of Eastern Siberia. Passengers would cross Lake Baikal on ferries to Mysovaya, the start of the Transbaikal Railway to Sretensk. From here they would continue to use the Shilka and Amur River for the journey to Khabarovsk, until the Amur Railway could be built between these towns. The Ussuri Railway would link Khabarovsk with Vladivostok.

There were also plans for a shortcut from the Transbaikal area to Vladivostok, across Manchuria. This would be known as the East Chinese Railway.

Nicholas lays the foundation stone

After the decision to start work, the Tsar wrote the following letter to his son, the Tsarevich, who had just reached Vladivostok at the end of a tour around the world: 'Having given the order to build a continuous line of railway across Siberia, which is to unite the rich Siberian provinces with the railway system of the interior, I entrust you to declare My will, upon your entering the Russian dominions after your inspection of the foreign countries of the East. At the same time I desire you to lay the first stone at Vladivostok for the construction of the Ussuri line forming part of the Siberian Railway...'

On 31 May 1891, Nicholas carried out his father's wishes, filling a wheelbarrow with earth and emptying it onto what was to become part of the embankment for the Ussuri Railway. He then laid the foundation stone for the station.

RAILWAY CONSTRUCTION: PHASE 1 (1891-1901)

● **The Ussuri, West Siberian & Mid-Siberian Railways (1891-98)** Work started on the Ussuri line (Vladivostok to Khabarovsk) some time after the inauguration ceremony and proceeded slowly. In July 1892, the construction of the West Siberian (Chelyabinsk to the west bank of the Ob River) was begun. In July 1893 work started on the Mid-Siberian (east bank of the Ob to Irkutsk).

The West Siberian reached Omsk in 1894 and was completed when the rails reached the Ob in October 1895. The Ussuri Railway was completed in 1897 and in the following year the final rails of the Mid-Siberian were laid and Irkutsk was linked to Moscow and St Petersburg.

● **The Transbaikal Railway (1895-1900)** The rail link between the Lake Baikal port of Mysovaya and Sretensk on the Shilka River was begun in 1895. In spite of a flood which swept away part of the track in 1897, the line was completed by the beginning of 1900.

Passengers could now travel to Irkutsk by train, take the ferry across Lake Baikal and the train again from Mysovaya to Srtensk, where steamers would take them to Khabarovsk.

● **The East Chinese Railway (1897-1901)** Surveys showed that the proposed Amur Railway between Sretensk and Khabarovsk would be expensive to build because of the mountainous region it would have to pass through and the large supplies of explosives required to deal with the permafrost. In 1894 the Russian government granted China a generous loan to help pay off China's debts to Japan. In exchange for this financial help, a secret treaty was signed between Russia and China allowing the former to build and control a rail link between the Transbaikal region and Vladivostok, across the Chinese territory of Manchuria. Every difficulty encountered in building railways in Siberia (severe winters, mountains, rivers, floods, disease and bandits) was part of the construction of the East Chinese Railway, begun in 1897 and opened to light traffic in 1901.

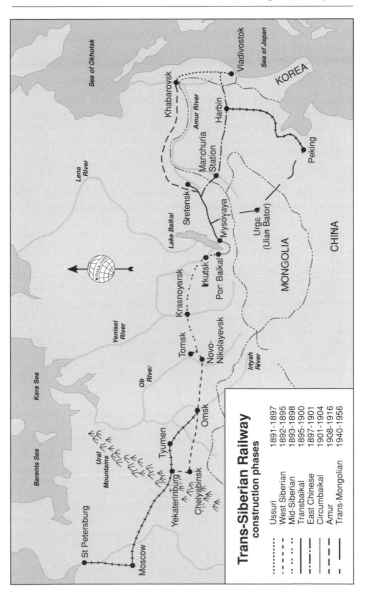

Trans-Siberian Railway
construction phases

Ussuri	1891-1897
West Siberian	1892-1895
Mid-Siberian	1893-1898
Transbaikal	1895-1900
East Chinese	1897-1901
Circumbaikal	1901-1904
Amur	1908-1916
Trans-Mongolian	1940-1956

The labour force

The greater part of the Trans-Siberian Railway was built without heavy machinery by men with nothing more than wooden shovels. They nevertheless managed to lay up to two and a half miles of rail on a good day. Most of the labour force had to be imported as the local peasants were already fully employed on the land. They came not only from European Russia but also from as far away as Italy and Turkey. Chinese coolies were employed on the Ussuri Railway but overseers found them unreliable and terrified of the Amur tigers with which the area was infested.

The government soon turned to the prisons to relieve the shortage of labour and gangs of convicts were put to work on the lines. They were paid 25 kopecks (a quarter of a rouble) a day and had their sentences reduced – eight months on the railways counted for a year in prison. The 1500 convicts employed on the Mid-Siberian worked hard but those brought in from Sakhalin Island to work on the Ussuri line ran riot and terrorized the inhabitants of Vladivostok.

Shortage of materials

On many parts of the Siberian Plain engineers discovered that although there were vast forests of trees, none of them was suitable for using as sleepers (ties). Timber had to be imported over great distances. Rails came from European Russia and some even from Britain. They were either shipped via the Kara Sea (a southern part of the Arctic Ocean) and up the Yenisei River to Krasnoyarsk or else right around the continent by boat to Vladivostok (which took two months). From here, when work started on the Transbaikal line in 1895, materials had to be shipped up the Ussuri, Amur and Shilka Rivers to Sretensk (over 1000 miles). Horses and carts were scarce in Siberia and these, too, had to be brought in from Europe.

Difficult terrain

When the railway between St Petersburg and Moscow was being planned, the Tsar took ruler and pencil and drew a straight line between the two cities, declaring that this was the route to be followed, with almost every town by-passed. For the Trans-Siberian, Alexander ordered that it be built as cheaply as possible which is why in some places the route twists and turns so that expensive tunnelling might be avoided. There were few problems in laying foundations for the rails across the open steppe land of the Siberian plain but cutting through the almost impenetrable forests of the taiga proved extremely difficult. Much of this area was not only thickly forested but swampy in summer and frozen in winter until July. Consequently the building season lasted no more than four months in most places.

In eastern Siberia parts of the ground were locked in permafrost and, even in mid-summer, had to be dynamited or warmed with fires before rails could be laid. The most difficult terrain was the short line around the southern end of Lake Baikal, the Circumbaikal Loop, which required over 200 trestles and bridges and 33 tunnels.

Conditions

For the workers who laboured in Siberia, conditions were hardly the most enjoyable. All were far from home, living in isolated log cabins that were not much cleaner or more comfortable than the squalid prison in Tyumen, graphically described by George Kennan in *Siberia and the Exile System*. Winters were very long and extremely cold. The brief summer brought relief from the cold but the added discomfort of plagues of black flies and mosquitoes in the swamps of the taiga. There were numerous outbreaks of disease. Workers on the East Chinese Railway were struck first by an outbreak of bubonic plague in 1899 and cholera in 1902. In many places the horses were wiped out by Siberian anthrax.

There were other dangers in addition to disease. In Manchuria and the Amur and Ussuri regions, the forests were filled with Amur tigers for whom the occasional railway labourer no doubt made a pleasant snack. In Manchuria construction camps were frequently raided by *hunghutzes* (bandits) who roamed around the country in gangs of up to seven hundred men. As a result, the Russian government was obliged to allocate considerable sums of money and men to the policing of the region.

There were several set-backs that no one could have foreseen. In July 1897 severe flooding swept away or damaged over two hundred miles of track near Lake Baikal on the Transbaikal line, also destroying settlements and livestock. Damage was estimated at six million roubles. In other areas landslides were caused by torrential rainfall.

RAILWAY CONSTRUCTION: PHASE 2 (1898-1916)

Reconstruction

As the first trains began to travel over the newly-laid tracks, the short-sightedness of the policy of building the railway as cheaply as possible soon became clear. Many of the materials used in its construction were either sub-standard or unsuitable to the conditions they were expected to withstand. The rails were under half the weight of those used in North America and fashioned of iron of an inferior quality. They soon bent and buckled and needed replacing. The ballast under the sleepers was far thinner than that put down on the major railways of Europe. As a result, the ride in the carriages was bumpy and uncomfortable and speed had to be kept down to 13mph for passenger trains, 8mph for freight. Foreign engineers proclaimed the whole system unsafe and were proved correct by the frequent derailments which took place.

In 1895 Prince Khilkov became Minister of Ways of Communication. On a tour of inspection along the West and Mid-Siberian lines he quickly realized that a massive rebuilding programme would have to be put into operation. Extra trains were also needed to transport the hundreds of thousands of emigrants who were now flooding over the Urals. In 1899 100 million roubles were allocated for repairs, work which would have been unnecessary had sufficient funds been made available from the start.

● **The Circumbaikal Loop Line (1901-1904)** In 1901 work began on the 260km Circumbaikal Loop line around Lake Baikal's southern shores. The initial project had been shelved in 1893, since the terrain was considered too difficult. Passengers used the ferry service across the lake but it was soon found that the ships couldn't cope with the increased traffic. The situation became critical at the start of the Russo-Japanese war in 1904, when troops and machinery being sent to the East by rail were delayed at the lake. Construction of the new line continued as fast as possible and by the end of the year the final section of the Trans-Siberian was opened. Passengers were at last able to travel from Calais to Vladivostok entirely by train.

● **The Amur Railway (1907-1916)** The original plans for a railway from Sretensk to Khabarovsk along the Shilka and Amur Rivers were abandoned because the route would entail expensive engineering work. After the Russo-Japanese war in 1904-5, the government realized that there was a danger of Japan taking control of Manchuria and the East Chinese Railway. This was the only rail-link to Russia's naval base at Vladivostok. It was therefore decided that the Amur Railway must indeed be built. Work began at Kuenga in 1908. There were the usual problems of insects, disease and permafrost but with the rest of the railway operational, it was easier to transport men and materials to the Amur area. When the bridge over the Amur at Khabarovsk was finished in 1916, the Trans-Siberian Railway was at last complete. Over 1000 million roubles had been spent on building all the sections (including the East Chinese line) since 1891.

THE FIRST RAIL TRAVELLERS

Rail service begins

As each of the sectors of the Trans-Siberian was completed, a rail service was begun. To say that there were teething troubles would be a gross understatement; there was a shortage of engines and carriages, most of the system operated without a timetable and there were frequent delays and derailments along the shoddily-constructed line. Nevertheless, to attract foreign travellers, luxury trains and 'Expresses' were introduced. Those run by the government were known as Russian State Expresses while another service was operated by the Belgian 'Compagnie Internationale des Wagons-Lits'. In 1900 the Ministry of Ways of Communication published their *Guide to The Great Siberian Railway* in English.

❏ **The Paris Exhibition**

The Russian government was keen to show off to the world the country's great engineering feat and at the Paris 'Exposition Universelle' of 1900, a comprehensive Trans-Siberian exhibit was staged. Amongst photographs and maps of Siberia, with Kyrgyz, Buryat and Goldi robes and artifacts, there were several carriages to be operated by the Wagons-Lits Company on the Great Siberian Railway. They were furnished in the most sumptuous style, with just four spacious compartments in the sleeping carriages, each with a connecting lavatory. The other carriages contained a smoking-room done up in Chinese style, a library and music-room complete with piano.

In the two restaurant cars, decorated with mahogany panelling and heavy curtains, visitors to the exhibition could dine on the luxurious fare that was promised on the journey itself. To give diners the feeling of crossing Siberia, a length of canvas on which was painted a Siberian panorama of wide steppes, thick taiga and little villages of log cabins, could be seen through the windows. In order to complete the illusion that the train was actually chugging across the Great Siberian Plain, the painted panorama was made to move past the windows by mechanical means.

Visitors were intrigued and impressed and more than a few soon set off on the epic trip. The reality, they were to discover, was a little different from what they experienced at the exhibition.

Early rail travellers

When R.L.Jefferson set out to investigate the Minusinsk gold-mining region in 1897, he was able to take the train (travelling this time without his bicycle but no doubt taking along a good supply of Bovril and Jaeger underwear) as far as Krasnoyarsk.

The first English woman to travel the entire length of this route was Annette Meakin, who took her aged mother for company on the journey made in 1900. They travelled via Paris to see the Siberian display at the Paris Exhibition. Having crossed Siberia, they went by ship to Japan and then to North America, crossing that continent by train, too. Having circumnavigated the globe by rail, Miss Meakin recorded her experiences in the book she called *A Ribbon of Iron*. Two years later, in 1902, Michael Myres Shoemaker took *The Great Siberian Railway from St Petersburg to Pekin* (the name of his account of the journey). He wrote enthusiastically: 'This Railway will take its place amongst the most important works of the world .... Russia is awakening at last and moving forward.'

It is interesting to compare the descriptions these travellers give of the trains they took, with the carriages displayed at the Paris Exhibition as well as with the service operated today by Russian Railways.

The carriages

Advertising brochures informed prospective Trans-Siberian travellers, in gushing prose, that the carriages in which they were to be conveyed would be of a standard equal to those used by European royalty. In addition to the luxurious sleeping compartments and dining cars shown at the Paris Exhibition, there would be a bathroom with marble bath-tub, a gymnasium equipped with a stationary bicycle and other exercising machines, a fire-proof safe, a hair-dressing salon and a dark-room equipped with all the chemicals a photographer would need. The carriages would be lit by electric lighting, individually heated in winter and cooled by under-floor ice-boxes in summer.

Although more than a few of those luxurious appointments, which they had seen in the carriages of the Siberian exhibit in Paris, were missing on their train, Annette Meakin and her mother found their accommodation entirely satisfactory. The ride was not so comfortable for the Meakins from Mysovaya on the Transbaikal Railway. Only fourth class carriages were provided and they were forced to take their travelling rugs and picnic hamper to the luggage van, where they spent the next four days.

Travelling in 1902, Michael Myres Shoemaker was very impressed with the bathing arrangements on the train and wrote: 'I have just discovered that there is a fine bathroom in the restaurant car, large and tiled, with all sorts of sprays, plunges and douches. This bath has its separate attendant and all the bath towels you may demand.' He was less enthusiastic about his travelling companions, a French Consul and family whose fox terrier 'promptly domesticated itself in my compartment'.

The restaurant car

At the Paris Exhibition visitors were led to believe that a good part of the enjoyment of travelling on the Trans-Siberian would be the cordon bleu cuisine served in the restaurant car. It was claimed that the kitchens were even equipped with water tanks filled with live fish. The waiters would be multi-lingual and a truly international service was promised.

Travellers found the above description to be something of an exaggeration. Annette Meakin reported the existence of a Bechstein piano and a library of Russian novels in the restaurant car. Shoemaker wrote: 'The restaurant car is just like all those on the trains of Europe. There is a piano, generally used to hold dirty dishes. There are three very stupid waiters who speak nothing save Russian. The food is very poor.'

Travellers were warned by their guide-books that there were occasional food shortages on the trains and advised to take along a picnic hamper. The Meakins found theirs invaluable on their four-day jaunt in the luggage van. In fact, for the first few years after the service began, there had been no restaurant cars. R.L.Jefferson wrote that at meal-times, the train would stop at a convenient station and all passengers (and the engine-driver) would get off for a meal at the station.

> ❏ Travelling in 1901, John Foster Fraser reports, in *The Real Siberia*, that locals did good business on the platforms selling 'dumplings with hashed meat and seasoning inside... huge loaves of new made bread, bottles of beer, pails of milk, apples, grapes, and fifty other things'. This is still true today.

The church car

Behind the baggage car was a peculiar carriage known as the church car. It was a Russian Orthodox Church on wheels, complete with icons and candelabra inside, church bells and a cross on the roof, and a peripatetic priest who dispensed blessings along the way. This carriage was detached at stations and settlements where churches had not yet been built and services were conducted for railway workers and their families.

Transport of emigrants

While foreign visitors discussed whether or not their accommodation was all that the Siberian exhibit in Paris had led them to believe, emigrants travelled in the unenviable conditions described by R.L.Jefferson: 'The emigrants' train is simply one of the cattle trucks, each car being marked on the side "Forty men or eight horses". There are no seats or lights provided, and into each of these pens forty men, women and children have to herd over a dreary journey of fourteen or fifteen days...They have to provide their own food but at every station a large samovar is kept boiling in order to provide them with hot water for their tea.'

By the end of the century they were crossing the Urals to Siberia at the rate of about a quarter of a million peasants each year.

Stations

Little wooden station buildings mushroomed along the railway. Russian stations were traditionally given a class number from one to five. Of the stations listed in the official *Guide to the Great Siberian Railway*, none was of the first class and the majority were no more than fifth class. Beside most stations there towered a water-tank to supply the steam engines. Many of these towers, their eaves decorated with ornate fretwork, can still be seen today. Most of the larger stations also had their own churches and resident priests. If the train did not have a church car, stops would be made for lengthy services at these railside churches, especially on the eve of an important saint's day.

R.L.Jefferson found that in the early years of the railways, the arrival and departure of every train at a Siberian station was quite an event, being 'attended with an amount of excitement that it is hard to associate with the usually stolid Russian. Particularly is this so in Eastern Russia where railways are new and interesting.' A man 'performs a terrific tintinabulation on a large suspended bell. All the conductors blow whistles.' Jefferson goes on to explain that none of the passengers was allowed out of the train until the engine driver had got down and shaken hands with the station-master and his staff.

Delays

Because the original line was so badly laid, the ride in the carriages was rough and uncomfortable and speed had to be kept down. There were frequent derailments and long delays. Annette Meakin complained: 'We stopped at a great many stations; indeed on some parts of the route we seemed to get into a chronic state of stopping'. 'All day long at a dog trot,' wrote Shoemaker, 'Certainly no more than ten miles an hour.' Over some sections the train went so slowly passengers could get out and pick flowers as they walked along beside it. Still, the delays did give one time to catch up on current affairs, as Miss Meakin observes when her train was delayed for four hours ('a mere nothing in Siberia') at Taiga. She writes: 'As we sat waiting in the station the good news was brought that Mafeking had been relieved.'

Bridges

Although the rails were badly laid and of poor quality, the bridges that were made of stone were built to such a high standard that many are still in use today. They were largely the work of Italian masons, who laboured throughout the winter months, the bridge-building season, since no work could be done on the snow-covered line. Many labourers caught hypothermia while they worked in temperatures as low as -40°C, dropping to their death on the ice below.

If a bridge was not finished in the winter when the railway lines reached it, engineers had had the brilliant idea of laying rails across the ice. The sleepers were literally frozen onto the surface of the river by large amounts of water being poured over them. When R.L.Jefferson's train reached the track laid across the Chulim River, passengers were made to get out and walk, in case the train proved too great a weight for the ice to bear. He wrote: 'As it passed us we felt the ice quiver, and heard innumerable cracks, like the reports of pistols in the distance, but the train got across the centre safely.'

Breakdowns

These were all too frequent. A wait of twenty-four hours for a new engine was not regarded as a long delay. Annette Meakin recorded the following incident: 'Outside Kainsk the train stopped. "The engine has smashed up," said a jolly Russian sailor in broken English. "She is sixty years old and was made in Glasgow. She is no use any more"....The poor old engine was now towed to her last berth....I had whipped out my "Kodak" and taken her photograph, thinking of Turner's "Fighting Temeraire".'

Cost of the journey

The *Guide to the Great Siberian Railway* informed its readers that, for the journey from London to Shanghai: 'The conveyance by the Siberian Railway will be over twice as quick and two and a half times cheaper than that now existing' (the sea passage via the Suez Canal). The cost of a first class ticket for the sixteen-day journey was to be 319 roubles. From Moscow to Vladivostok the price was 114 roubles.

THE RAILWAY IN THE TWENTIETH CENTURY

After the Revolution

'When the trains stop, that will be the end,' announced Lenin and the trains continued to run, the Trans-Siberian included, throughout those troubled times.

When the new Bolshevik government pulled out of the First World War in early 1918, a Czech force of 50,000 well armed men found themselves marooned in Russia, German forces preventing them getting back to western Europe. Receiving permission to leave Russia via Vladivostok, they set off on the Trans-Siberian. Their passage was not a smooth one for the Bolsheviks suspected that the Czechs would join the White Russian resistance movement while the Czechs suspected that the Bolsheviks were not going to allow them to leave. Violence erupted, several Czechs were arrested and the rest of the legion decided they would shoot their way out of Russia. They took over the Trans-Siberian line from the Urals to Lake Baikal and travelled the railway in armour-plated carriages.

The Civil War in Siberia (1918-20)

At this time Siberia was divided amongst a number of forces, all fighting against the Bolsheviks but not as a combined unit. Many of the leaders were nothing more than gangsters. East Siberia and Manchuria were controlled by the evil Ataman Semenov, half-Russian, half-Buryat and supported by the Japanese. He charged around Transbaikalia murdering whole villages and, to alleviate the boredom of these mass executions, a different method of death was adopted each day. Then there was Baron General von Ungern Sternberg, one of the White Russian commanders whose cruelty rivalled that of Semenov. The Americans, French, English and Japanese all brought troops into Siberia to evacuate the Czech legions and to help Admiral Kolchak, the Supreme Ruler of the White

Government which was based at Omsk. Kolchak, however, failed to win the support of the people in the Siberian towns, his troops were undisciplined and in November 1919 he lost Omsk to the Bolsheviks. He was executed in Irkutsk in early 1920 and the Allies abandoned the White Russian cause. The Japanese gave up Vladivostok in 1922 and all Siberia was then in Communist hands.

Reconstruction

After the Civil War, the Soviet Union set about rebuilding its battered economy. High on the priority list was the repair of the Trans-Siberian line, so that raw materials like iron ore could be transported to European Russia. The First Five Year Plan (1928) set ambitious goals for the expansion of industry and agriculture. It also included new railway projects, the double-tracking of the Trans-Siberian and the building of the Turk-Sib, the line between Turkestan and Novosibirsk. Work began on two giant industrial complexes known as the Ural-Kuznetsk Combine. Iron ore from the Urals was taken by rail to the Kuznetsk in Siberia, where it was exchanged for coal to take back to the Ural blast furnaces. For all these giant projects an enormous, controllable labour force was needed and this was to a large extent provided by prisoners from the corrective labour camps.

The Second World War

Siberia played an important backstage role in the Great Patriotic War as Russians call the Second World War. Many factories were moved from European Russia to Siberia and the populations of cities such as Novosibirsk rose dramatically. The Trans-Siberian's part was a vital one and loads of coal and food were continuously despatched over the Urals to Europe throughout the war years.

The Trans-Siberian today

THE TRAIN

Engines

If you imagined you would be hauled across Siberia by a puffing steam locomotive you will be sadly disappointed. Soviet Railways (SZD), now Russian Railways (RZD), began converting the system to electricity in 1927 (now 3kV dc or, more commonly, 25kV ac 50Hz) and the Trans-Siberian line is now almost entirely electrified. Only 353km in the Far Eastern Region, from Bikin to Sibirtsevo, have yet to be electrified. Passenger engines are usually Czech Skoda ChS2's (line voltage 3kV dc;

max output 4620kW; max speed 160kph; weight 126 tonnes) and ChS4T's (25kV 50 Hz; 5200kW; 180kph; 126 tonnes) or Russian-built VL10's, VL60's and VL65's type. On the Moscow–St Petersburg route the latest Czech-built engines are used: the CS200 (3kV dc; 8400kW; 200kph; 157 tonnes) and the CS7 developed from it. The most common freight engines are the large VL80S and the newer VL85.

Where electrification has yet to be completed (Bikin–Sibirtsevo on the Far Eastern Railway in East Siberia), diesel rather than steam engines are used. They are usually Russian-built 2TE10L/M/V types (with overhanging windscreens) or sometimes a 2M62U or 3M62U twin or triple-unit. If you're continuing on the Trans-Mongolian or Trans-Manchurian routes to Beijing, it is quite likely that a steam loco will be hitched to your carriages at the China border, at least for shunting duties. Although steam engines have officially been phased out in Russia, there were still 5900 on the books in 1992, many lining the tracks in remote sidings along the way. Their numbers are shrinking fast now as they are sold off to Western Europe and China for scrap and parts. See below for identification information and class numbers.

Carriages and carriage attendants

Most of the carriages now used are of East German origin, solidly-built, warm in winter and each staffed by an **attendant** (*provodnitsa* (female), *provodnik* (male) in Russian, *fuwuyuen* in Chinese), whose 'den' is situated at one end of the carriage. Their duties include collecting your tickets, letting down the carriage steps at stations, coming round with the vacuum-cleaner and providing you with tea (good but without milk) or coffee (utterly disgusting). You pay for what you've drunk on your trip (around US$0.10 a glass) just before you reach your destination. The attendant also maintains the **samovar** which is opposite the attendant's compartment at one end of the carriage, and provides a continuous supply of boiling water for drinks.

There are doors at both ends of the carriages and if you're a **smoker** the only place where you're allowed to indulge your habit is in this area between the carriages (unheated in winter). Travellers on some trains, Nos 3/4 in particular, have reported that if there are a lot of smokers on board

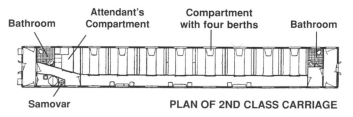

Bathroom   Attendant's Compartment   Compartment with four berths   Bathroom

Samovar   **PLAN OF 2ND CLASS CARRIAGE**

❏ **Thermal differences**
Many travellers say the carriages are very warm – I far from agree and often found them chilly. However, as a Scandinavian I, like the Americans, also found it cold in Poland, while the Continental Europeans found the temperature on board just fine and the Britons complained about it being too warm! **Matz Lonnedal Risberg** (Norway)

this rule is waived. The no-smoking rule doesn't seem to be applied strictly in the dining car, either.

Carriages are heated in winter and air-conditioned in summer. In order for the air-conditioning to operate properly all windows is the carriage must be kept shut, since the system works on the pressure difference between the inside and outside of the carriage and takes about an hour to get going. The initial instinct (and certainly that of the Russian passengers) is to open all the windows, and the carriage attendant wages a constant battle with everyone to keep them closed. Music (either radio or cassettes) is piped to the compartments from the attendant's den; the knob above the window controls the volume though in some compartments it can't be turned off completely. This can be annoying if you don't happen to share the same obscure taste in music as your carriage attendant.

Compartments

On the Trans-Siberian and Trans-Manchurian, there are two main classes of compartments – SV and coupé. On the Trans-Mongolian Train Nos 3 & 4, there are three main classes of compartments – de luxe, SV and coupé. The reason for the difference is that Train Nos 3 & 4 are Chinese made carriages and have a slightly different layout to the Russian ones.

● **De luxe First Class (Trans-Mongolian Train Nos 3 and 4 only)** The closest you can get to luxury accommodation while crossing Siberia on standard services, these two-berth compartments have attached bathrooms with rudimentary hand-held showers (the only showers on any of the trains but there's no shower cubicle and water pressure is very weak), wider bunks, wood panelling, a wind-down window, armchair and plush carpet.

● **First Class/SV/Soft** On Russian trains, SV is a two-berth compartment which may or may not have a washbasin. On the Trans-Mongolian Train No 3 and 4, SV is a four-berth compartment of an identical layout to the coupé compartment but 16cm wider. As you pay significantly more for this compartment compared to a coupé, it is not good value.

● **Second Class/Coupé/Hard/Tourist** These four-berth cabins are the most popular with travellers as they are reasonably comfortable and cheap. They are called *kupé* in Russia.

● **Third Class/Platskartny** is not really recommended; it's a cheap but rough way of travelling. Platskartny carriages are open plan with doorless compartments containing four bunks in tiers of two with another bunk opposite, beside the corridor. While these are adequate for a day or two, do not even contemplate them for the Trans-Siberian.

Bedding is provided and sheets are supposed to be changed every three days. You may have to pay anything up to US$1 for the sealed bag containing the clean sheets and pillow case. You may also receive a small towel and toiletries for free on the better trains. In newer carriages, it is possible to move the lower bed up to 10cm away from the wall giving a wider sleeping area.

> ❏ **Varied baggage**
> If you're travelling on local trains between smaller stations in Siberia be prepared to share your compartment with almost any form of luggage – animate or inanimate. Since not many people can afford to run a car the train is their primary means of transport.
> I have had to politely move over in order to accommodate bicycles, televisions, car windscreens and even several sacks of leeches.
> **Nick Hill** (UK)

Luggage

Each passenger can take up to 35kg of luggage with them for free on the Trans-Siberian. In Beijing, this limit is rigidly enforced as your baggage is weighed before you are allowed onto the platform.

You can take additional luggage totalling up to 75kg into your compartment providing you pay excess baggage (about US$11 per 10kg). If you are departing from Moscow, go to the station early on the day of departure and pay the excess luggage fee. You will be asked to show the receipt before boarding the train.

If you are departing from Beijing, bring the excess baggage to the Luggage Shipment Office the day before departure. This office is located on the right hand side of the main station and is open 8:00-10:30 and 11:20-18:15. Bring your passport, ticket and customs entry declaration. The Mongolian traders who use the trains seem to manage to get around these luggage limits, however.

Luggage in the carriage can be stored in the box under the seat (57x 134x24cm), in the free space next to the box under the seat (57x28x24cm) and in the space above the door (33x 190x67cm).

Bathroom

Sadly the marble bath-tub (ingeniously designed so that the water would not spill as the train rounded a corner) and the copious supplies of hot water and towels that Michael Myres Shoemaker enthused over on his trip in 1902 are no more. The lack of proper bathing facilities is usually the biggest grumble from people who have done the trip. Apart from the de luxe First Class compartments of the Trans-Mongolian, which have shower-heads fitted to the basins in the attached bathrooms, there are no showers on the train – a ridiculous oversight. With most of the rail sys-

❏ **Carriage keys**
On our train (No 6) there were a large number of Mongolian traders who proved to be very entertaining. They had managed to obtain a carriage key so that they could unlock the loo door after it had been locked. They would always oblige us with a quick unlock when we asked. We did notice that this carriage key looked familiar and it may be worth advising British travellers to try taking their British Gas meter cupboard key with them since it looks as if it is identical.

Andrew Wingham (UK)

tem now electrified there is a cheap power source for heated shower units but no doubt it will be years before they are installed.

Today, in every carriage there's a 'bathroom' at each end. This small cubicle contains a stainless steel basin and a lavatory, with or without a seat. To flush the lavatory, fully depress the foot pedal, hold it down and lean back out of the way, as the contents have a nasty habit of going the wrong way if the train is moving fast. Sometimes, however, the carriage attendants will keep the bathroom next to their compartment locked for their personal use. Complaining about this is unlikely to achieve anything but a strategic friendly gift might gain you access.

The taps on the basin are operated by pushing up the little lever located under the tap outlet. You should get hot water by turning the left hand wheel above the sink (the right hand wheel controls the cold water). However the flow of hot water depends on the whim of the attendant who may not want to switch the system on. Don't forget to bring along a **universal plug** (or a squash ball) for the basin, **soap**, a **sponge** or **flannel** and **lavatory paper**.

There's a socket for an electric razor but you may need to ask the attendant to turn the power on. Don't try to charge video camera batteries from these sockets: one traveller reported blowing the fuses attempting this.

There are two ways to have a shower in these bathrooms. Either fill the basin and use a mug to scoop out the water and pour it over yourself,

❏ If you'd like a shower when travelling in Second Class it may be worth bringing along a length of garden hose or a similar tube (say one metre long) and an attachment for the tap (such as the rubber type used in the UK). This seems to be what the provodnitzas use, and it will also enable you to hose down the toilets.

Edward Wilson (UK)

or fit a flexible shower hose over the tap nozzle. Some attendants carry these hoses and you may be able to rent one from them. Don't worry about splashing water around as there is a drain in the floor.

The bathrooms are generally kept clean and are often locked for up to 20 minutes before (and after) the big stations. Sometimes they never seem to be locked at all, even when the train has stopped at a station.

Restaurant cars

One of the myths that has sprung up amongst prospective travellers is that you'll get better food if you take the Chinese (Trans-Mongolian) train. As is the custom with international rail travel, restaurant cars belonging to the country through which the train is travelling are attached to the train at the border. Regardless of which train you're on, when you're travelling through China you'll be eating in a restaurant car supplied by Chinese Railways; at the border with Mongolia this will be replaced by a Mongolian restaurant car; while the same train is on Russian territory meals will be provided by a restaurant car from Russian Railways.

Note that on the Trans-Mongolian train there is usually no restaurant car service between the Russian border and Ulan Bator.

● **Russian restaurant car** The food was never much to write home about and financial hardship in Russia has not made things any better but it's true to say that the quality of the food seems to vary widely between one Russian restaurant car and the next. Rather than cooking, staff seem more interested in buying and selling produce at stations along the way.

On entering the restaurant car (having averted your eyes from the grubby kitchen to preserve your appetite) you

❑ **Getting better service**
The only relevant information about Russian restaurant cars is that the food seems to vary much between one Russian restaurant car and the next, as every Russian restaurant car is its own private enterprise, and I've experienced everything from excellent to disaster. I've found out that a very good way to obtain a good relationship with the staff is simply to be a regular customer and learn a few Russian words. **Matz Lonnedal Risberg** (Norway)

The food you're served in the Russian restaurant car seems to depend entirely on your relationship with the staff. I thought greasy lumps of compressed beef with fried eggs and rice were *de rigueur* until a trip with a flamboyantly friendly Australian/Ukrainian lady, who made a point of introducing herself and her friends to the staff of each car. Not only did she discover that the waiters and cooks were all invariably distant relatives or old family friends but the food was spectacular. Excellent *pelmeni*, tasty Stroganov: the cooks all rustled up their 'specials' for the crazy Australian and her entourage. Over at the adjacent tables, meanwhile, glum Russians tucked into greasy chunks of beef with eggs on top.
Dominic Streatfeild-James (UK)

may be presented with the menu, almost invariably in Russian and often running to ten pages or more. The only dishes available will be indicated by a pencilled-in price or added in an almost indecipherable scrawl. The choice includes egg or tomato salad (the white sauce is not mayonnaise but sour cream, actually rather good), *shchi* (thick cabbage soup with meat), *solyanka* (meat soup, thick and nourishing), meat-balls and mash or macaroni, smoked *teshka* fish (like hunks of smoked salmon), *skum-*

bria fish (usually fried and quite good), beef Stroganov, the ever present *bifstek*, boiled chicken or duck, tea and coffee, and occasionally cakes. Piles of bread and various fizzy drinks (*napitok*) and fruit juice (*sok*) are also on sale. A main course will cost about US$2 but the portions are rather small; and a whole meal should come to less that US$5. There are usually two people serving, each with their own half of the restaurant car (one won't serve you if you're in the other section). Small gifts or tips given early on in the trip will help encourage attentive service.

The trend towards free trade means that the restaurant car staff can now sell all sorts of goodies on the side. Banned for several years, alcohol is now sold on the train. You should be able to get chilled Russian champagne (US$6), vodka, caviare (overpriced compared to prices in Moscow), chocolate bars and cartons of fruit juice. Some restaurant cars even show videos, charging passengers an entry fee to watch bootleg copies of American movies.

Note that you can pay only in roubles; US$ are not accepted.

● **Mongolian restaurant car** With luck you'll get one of the smart new Mongolian restaurant cars. Generally the main differences between the Mongolian and the Russian restaurant cars are that in the Mongolian car you're likely to get a menu in English and nearly everything comes with mutton. If you are travelling on train Nos 3/4, 89/90 or 23/24, you may have to pay in US$ unless you can change some hard currency into togrogs with the Mongolian traders. Take lots of small denomination US bills as staff never have any change. Sometimes they also accept Chinese currency.

Delicacies include main course with roast potatoes, main course with rice, main course with noodles and main course with cabbage; all priced from US$3-5. For breakfast they can do you a one-egg omelette with onions for US$2. Tea is US$0.50 and coffee US$1; a Pepsi costs US$1. Some Mongolian cars have extensive stocks of duty-free goods and even souvenirs, post cards and stamps. Mongolian beer is recommended.

Train Nos 5/6 and 263/264 rarely have a restaurant carriage inside Mongolia.

● **Chinese restaurant car** Travellers tend to agree that the food in the Chinese car is the best, and there's a bit more choice. It's altogether a better run car than the other two. It's full every evening which is a good sign. For US$3 you'll get a breakfast of eggs, bread, jam and tea. Lunch and supper consist of tomato salad (US$2), cold chicken or sauté chicken with hot sauce and peanuts (US$3), fish (US$2.50), sweet and sour pork (US$3), sauté beef or egg plant with dried shrimp. Drinks include beer (US$0.50), cola (US$1) and mineral water (US$1).

● **Food at the stations** At many of the stops along the Trans-Siberian locals turn out on the station platform to sell all manner of foodstuffs: fruit, vegetables and whole cooked meals (cabbage rolls, freshly-boiled potatoes with dill, pancakes filled with goat's cheese, boiled eggs and fresh bread). 'Buying provisions this way is more fun and varied than the staple rice and fish or meat in the restaurant car; Dmitri Gorokhov (Russia)'.

Note that some travellers have reported upset stomachs after eating platform food so you should take care with salads, cold meats and fish and anything that looks as if it has been sitting around for too long. Generally, if the food is hot you should be fine; and all fruit should be washed.

□ **Platform food**
What you can buy at stations very much depends upon the season in which you're travelling and where the train stops. 'We stocked up really well in Moscow and I'm glad that we did as we only had two station stops where people were selling things. Maybe our train (No 6) went through stations such as these in the middle of the night but we had fellow travellers who had not brought much food who would have been very hungry were it not for the Mongolian traders selling pot noodles.'
Angela Hollingsworth (UK)

It is worth stressing the abundance and variety of food on sale at many stations, especially rural ones, during stops. If you see something you want, buy it: the next stop might be a city, where sellers will not appear on the platforms, or rows of babushkas with prams full of raspberries might be replaced by a monotonous offering of, say, fish. Regulars knew what to expect at each stop.
Howard Dymock (UK)

LIFE ON THE TRAIN

Most people imagine they'll get bored on so long a journey but you may be surprised at how quickly the time flies. Don't overdo the number of books you bring: *War and Peace,* all 1444 pages of it, is a frequent choice, although I know of only one person who actually managed to finish it on the trip. There are so many other things to do apart from reading. You can have monosyllabic conversations with inquisitive Russians, meet the other Westerners on the train, play cards or chess, visit the restaurant car or hop off at the stations for a little exercise.

'Time passes very pleasantly on such a train', as Annette Meakin wrote in 1900. It is surprising how the time drifts by and even though you do very little, you won't be bored. Having said that, the Russian man who bought the Tetris electronic game at the Manzhouli Friendship Store quickly became everyone's best friend.

❏ Local travellers

Unlike the Orient Express, most trains that cross Siberia are working trains, not tourist specials. Russian passengers are extremely friendly and genuinely interested in foreign travellers. Sharing her compartment with three Russians, a winter traveller writes: 'Inside the carriage there's interest on both sides. Great concern all round about my travelling unaccompanied and questions as to the whereabouts of my parents. Much shaking of heads and 'tutting'. There's plenty for me to find out. The thin man (with cold eyes that have gradually thawed over the last two days) has five children and is going to Moscow to get stomach medicine for one of them (or for himself?). The large motherly babushka in the corner who has been so kind to me is an artist, going to visit her son (or is the son an artist?). The fourth member of the compartment played chess with me last night, totally baffled by my tactics (there weren't any) so that we ended with a stalemate. He hasn't offered again. So much can be achieved with not a word of language in common.'

Heather Oxley (Turkey)

The Trans-Siberian time warp

During his trip on the Great Siberian Railway in 1902, Michael Myres Shoemaker wrote: 'There is an odd state of affairs as regards time over here. Though Irkutsk is 2,400 miles from St Petersburg, the trains all run on the time of the latter city, therefore arriving in Irkutsk at 5pm when the sun would make it 9pm. The confusion en route is amusing; one never knows when to go to bed or when to eat. Today I should make it now about 8.30 – these clocks say 10.30 and some of these people are eating their luncheon.'

You will be pleased to know that this is something that hasn't changed, although the system now operates on Moscow time (same as St Petersburg time). Crossing the border from China after breakfast, the first Russian station clock you see tells you that it's actually 01:00 hours. All timetables quote Moscow time. The restaurant car, however, runs on local time. Passing through up to seven time-zones, things can get rather confusing. The answer is to ignore Moscow time and reset your watch as you cross into new time zones (details in the Route Guide). A watch that can show the time in two zones might be useful, otherwise just add or subtract the appropriate number of hours every time you consult the timetable in the carriage corridor.

Stops

Getting enough exercise on so long a journey can be a problem and most people make full use of the brief stops: 'We even managed to persuade our carriage attendant (never seen out of her pink woolen hat) to take part in our efforts to keep fit on the platforms. However, if your attendant indicates that you shouldn't get off at a stop, take her advice. At some stops another train pulls in between the platform and yours, making it almost impossible for you to get back on board.' Jane Bull (UK). Always carry your passport and valuables with you in case you miss your train.

Traders' trains

The growth of free trade in Russia led to some Trans-Siberian routes becoming monopolized by Chinese, Mongolian and Russian shuttle traders in the mid-1990s. Excess baggage charges, and a reduction in the duty-free allowance from US$2000 to US$1000 has now stemmed the flow but you may still find yourself sharing a compartment on the Trans-Mongolian route with a trader and anything from pile of imitation Adidas trainers to several thousand yellow plastic ducks. Sometimes the carriage attendant will be in on the smuggling and will stash the traders' wares in his compartment until the police have gone. Other traders flout the laws by dividing their purchases in half and swapping one half for half of a friend's items. This way, neither goes over the limit for each type of object, but between them they have gone over both limits. One traveller recalled how everyone in the carriage was asked by a Mongolian trader to wear one of his leather jackets as they went through customs to avoid being caught. One can't imagine the customs officials were particularly impressed when all the passengers turned up in the same leather jackets. The traders are often the target of robbers.

RAIL TICKETS

Prices

Despite recent price rises, overnight rail tickets in Russia are still considerably cheaper than in the West. A coupé ticket for a 24-hour journey costs around US$15. Supply varies and the authorities' response appears to be to raise prices when demand seems to be exceeding supply. In September 2000 reports suggested that a price rise of 30 per cent was imminent.

The ticket price comprises a **booking fee** (about US$2), the **class of ticket** and the **distance** travelled. The most popular ticket is the four-berth coupé ticket. The two-berth SV ticket is about $1\frac{1}{2}$ to 2 times the cost of a coupé ticket. Tickets on special, more comfortable services, called *firmenny* trains, cost about 1.2 to 1.5 times that of non-firmenny tickets.

The requirement that foreigners had to purchase only more expensive 'foreigner tickets' and not the tickets available to Russians was abolished in 2000. In case foreigner tickets (which used to cost between 15 and 50 per cent more than local prices) are re-introduced, it's worth knowing that foreigners could anyway always legally buy Russian tickets from those stations which did not sell foreigner tickets, such as small stations but they sometimes had difficulty in persuading carriage attendants to accept them without being made to pay the difference. They would issue a receipt which you kept to show the ticket inspector if one got on your train. Some rail personnel may not be aware that foreigners do not now have to pay a higher price for domestic tickets. A recent traveller wrote: 'I travelled with a Russian friend, who obtained the rail tickets himself in Moscow, using a photocopy of my passport...I was assured that foreigner prices have just been abolished, but there was much discussion with the provodnitsas when my ticket was taken and it had become clear that I was foreign (and the only one on the train). A small gift to the two attendants of some English cosmetics immediately removed any further questioning.' Howard Dymock (UK).

Stations in Moscow will issue tickets up to 45 days in advance; large stations in the rest of the country issue them up to 30 days in advance. Locals can hold reservations until ten days before departure without paying, at which point any unsold tickets are released and resold.

Getting off in the middle of a journey

It is possible to break your journey once on any ticket, however it is not really worth the effort. You have to get the station master to validate your ticket within 30 minutes of arriving. Secondly you have to re-book a berth for the onward journey which will often only be done by the chief ticket officer. If you don't speak Russian, don't even attempt this.

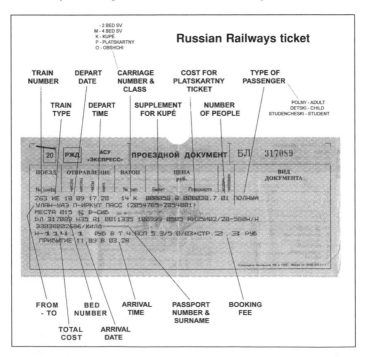

❏ BUYING A TICKET

When buying a ticket within Russia, you will probably be buying it either for travelling the same day or a couple of days later. In either situation, it is easy to go to the station, find the correct window, buy your ticket and be out again fairly quickly. If you don't speak Russian see the ticket buying form overleaf.

Which train?

You can check the timetable which is displayed in the booking hall. It states the train's number, time of departure and the days on which it travels.
● The train number indicates which way it is heading. If the number is even it means that it is going to the east or north and if odd, the train is heading west or south.
● The time given on timetables is invariably Moscow Time. Across a network covering eight time zones (the country is 11 zones), this is the only way the system could work. The clock in the booking hall is normally set to Moscow Time. Some station clocks (eg Khabarovsk) have two hour hands, black for Local Time and red for Moscow Time.
● Most trains depart every day, some, however, run on odd numbered days (1st, 3rd, 5th etc) and some on even days.
It's simplest to tell the ticket clerk roughly what time of day you want to go and they'll find the right train for you.

Which ticket window?

At railway stations there are several ticket windows, known as *kassa*. If it's not obvious where to queue, go to the 'administrator' window and you'll either be sold a ticket or told where to get one. Check to see what time your kassa closes if there is a queue, but it's rarely long. Larger stations may have an Intourist window. Often it will not be marked as Intourist and instead say in Russian Иностранцы (*inostrantsy* meaning *foreigner*).

Which ticket?

When you get to the window you'll need to tell them the train number; date of departure, class of cabin: Л (l = two-berth *SV*), M (M = four-berth *SV*), K (K = *coupé*), П (P = *platskartny*), O (O = *obshchi*); and your destination. You can do this either verbally or have it written down (see overleaf). There are several types of tickets for long-distance trains but the most common is the long paper computer-printed ticket (see opposite). It contains not only information about the train but also your name so don't buy someone else's ticket from them. Ticket sellers will often only sell you as many tickets as you have passports. This system was introduced to stop speculators from buying tickets and reselling them for a profit when the train is all sold out. The only way for a ticket to be legally renamed once it is bought is for the ticket selling staff to overstamp the original name with an official stamp and write your name on it. In the Soviet era, a rail ticket would be sold only to foreigners if the destination was written on their visa. With the change in visa regulations, this is no longer the case.

On the train, the conductor tears off a portion of the ticket which prevents it from being used again. If the ticket is for a train that originates elsewhere, the berth number is given only once you board the train.

TICKET BUYING FOR NON-RUSSIAN SPEAKERS

If you can't speak enough Russian to buy a ticket write what you need on a piece of paper as shown below. The clerk will usually write down a suggested train number and departure time and hand it back to you. Say *Da* (Yes) and you'll get the ticket. Check that the time the clerk writes down is Moscow Time by pointing to it and saying *Moskovskoe vremya*?

For more complex enquiries use the form opposite. If there's a long queue, however, it would be better to transcribe the question you need answered from the page opposite onto a piece of paper rather than trying to get the clerk to look through the whole page.

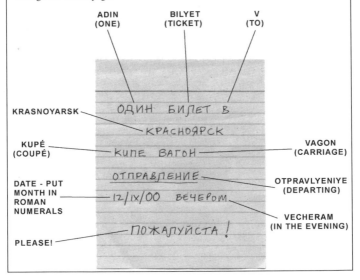

ADIN (ONE) · BILYET (TICKET) · V (TO)

KRASNOYARSK — ОДИН БИЛЕТ В КРАСНОЯРСК

KUPÉ (COUPÉ) — КУПЕ ВАГОН — VAGON (CARRIAGE)

ОТПРАВЛЕНИЕ — OTPRAVLYENIYE (DEPARTING)

DATE - PUT MONTH IN ROMAN NUMERALS — 12/IX/00 ВЕЧЕРОМ — VECHERAM (IN THE EVENING)

PLEASE! — ПОЖАЛУЙСТА !

STEAM LOCOMOTIVES IN SIBERIA

In 1956, the USSR stopped producing steam engines, and the official policy was to phase out these locomotives by 1970. As with most official plans in the country, this one overran a little and a second official end of steam was announced for the end of 1987, when the number of locos stood at over 6000. Some of these have been sold as scrap to Germany and Korea but many are still stored as a 'strategic reserve' in remote sidings and used very occasionally for shunting work – there are some to be seen along the Trans-Siberian line (see Route Guide for locations). In Northern China, there are large numbers still at work.

In 1836, the first locomotive was delivered in St Petersburg, a Hackworth 2-2-2, to pull the Tsar's private carriages over the fourteen

TRAIN INFORMATION AND TICKET BUYING FORM

Please help me. I don't speak Russian.
  Please read the question I point to and
  write the answer.

Будте любезны, помогите мне.
  Я не говорю по-русски.
  прочтите вопросы на которые я
  укажу, и напишите ответ.

MT = Moscow Time
* = Circle your choice
Q = question/A = answer

MT = Московское Время
* = Я показал свой выбор
Воп. = вопрос/Отв. = ответ

Information

Q. When is the next train with spare
  SV* coupé* platskartny* tickets
  to ....?
A. It departs at .... : .... (MT) and
  is Train No. ....

Информация

Воп. Когда следующий поезд со
  свободными местами (СВ*
  купе* плацкарт*) до ....?
Отв. Поезд отправляется в
  ...:...(МВ) и номер у поезда ....

Q. Are there SV* coupé* platskartny*
  tickets to .... on
  Train No. ....?
A. Yes No

Воп. Есть свободные места
  (СВ *купе* плацкарт*) до
  .... в поезде номер ....?
Отв. Да Нет

Q. When does the train depart and
  arrive?
A. It departs at .... : .... and arrives
  .... at ...   · ...... (MT).

Воп. Когда поезд отправляется и
  прибывает?
Отв. Поезд отправляется в .... :....
  и прибывает в .... : .... (МВ).

Q. How much is a SV* coupé*
  platskartny* ticket?
A. It costs .... roubles.

Воп. Сколько стоит билет в СВ*
  купе* плацкарт*?
Отв. Билет стоит ...... рублей.

Q. Which ticket window should I go to?
A. Ticket window No. ....

Воп. К какой кассе мне подойти?
Отв. Касса номер ....

Q. What platform does train No. ....
  leave from?
A. Platform No. ....

Воп. С какой платформы
  отправляется поезд номер ....?
Отв. Платформа номер ....

Buying tickets

Q. May I buy ...... SV* coupé*
  platskartny* tickets to ....
  on Train No. ....departing on ....?
  (Use DD/MM/YY format, eg 31/12/00.)
A. Yes, it costs .... roubles.
A. No.

Покупка билетов

Воп. Можно купить .. (СВ* купе*
  плацкарт*) билет до ....
  на поезд номер .... который
  отправляется до ....?
Отв. Да. билет стоит ...... рублей.
Отв. Нет.

Q. Why can't I buy a ticket?
A. There is no train.
A. The train is fully booked.
A. You have to buy a ticket at window
  No. ....
A. You can only buy a ticket .... hours
  before the train arrives.

Воп. Почему я не могу купить билет?
Отв. Нет поезда.
Отв. Нет мест.
Отв. Вы должны купить билет в
  кассе номер...........
Отв. Вы можете купить билет за
  ... часов до прибытия поезда.

Thank you for your help.

Большое спасибо за помощь.

miles of six-foot gauge track to his palace at Tsarskoye Selo. The Russians have always been (and still are) conservative by nature when it comes to buying or building engines. Usually large numbers of a few standard locomotives have been ordered so there's not much of a range to be seen today. They seem to be uniformly large, standing up to 17 feet high, and larger than British locos (partly because the Russian gauge is $3^{1}/_{2}$ inches wider than that used in Britain). They are numbered separately by classes, not in a single series and not by railway regions. If variations of the class have been built, they are given an additional letter to follow the main class letter. Thus, for example, the first type of 0-10-0 freight locomotive was Class E and those of this class built in Germany were Class Eg. Classes you may see in Siberia should include some of the following (Roman alphabet class letters given in brackets; * = very rare):

● **Class O (O)** The first freight trains on the Trans-Siberian route were pulled by these long-boilered 0-8-0 locos (55 tons) which date back to 1889. The 'O' in the class name stands for *Osnovnoi Tip* meaning 'basic type'. Although production ceased in 1923, as late as 1958 there were 1500 of these locomotives still at work.

● **Class C (S)*** 2-6-2 (75 tons) A highly successful passenger engine. 'S' stands for *Sormovo*, where these locos were built from 1911. **Class Cy (Su)** ('u' for usileny, meaning 'strengthened') was developed from the former class and in production from 1926-51.

● **Class E (Ye)** 2-10-0 (imported from the USA in 1914). There were 1500 Ye 2-10-0s imported.

● **Class Эу/Эм/Эр (Eu/Em/Er)*** (subclasses of the old type (E) 0-10-0, 80 tons, built in Russia from 1926-52. The old type E was also produced in Germany and Sweden, as Esh and Eg subclasses.

● **Class Ea (YeA)*** 2-10-0 (90 tons) Over 2000 were built in the USA between 1944 and 1947 and shipped across the Pacific.

● **Class Л (L)** 2-10-0 (103 tons) About 4130 were built between 1945-56.

● **Class П36 (P36)** 4-8-4 (133 tons) 251 were built between 1950 and 1956 – the last express passenger type built for Soviet railways. 'Skyliner'-style, fitted with large smoke-deflectors, and painted green with a cream stripe. Preserved examples at Sharya, Taiga, Sibirtsevo, Skovorodino, Belogorsk, Mogzon, and Chernyshevsk

The classes **Class O, C/Cy, E (O, S/Su, YE)** have all disappeared from the steam dumps but you will see the occasional one on a plinth.

For more information refer to the comprehensive *Soviet Locomotive Types – The Union Legacy* by AJ Heywood and IDC Button (1995, Frank Stenvalls/Luddenden Press).

As one might expect there's a good deal of information about Russian trains on the Internet. A good place to start is **www.transsib.ru/Eng/** – the Trans-Siberian Railway Web Encyclopedia.

OTHER RAILWAY LINES IN SIBERIA

BAM – a second Trans-Siberian

In the 1930s another Herculean undertaking was begun on the railways in Russia. The project was named the Baikal-Amur-Magistral (BAM): a second Trans-Siberian railway, 3140km long, running parallel but to the north of the existing line. It was to run through the rich mining districts of northern Siberia, providing an east-west communications back-up to the main line. Work began in Taishet and the track reached Ust Kut on the Lena River before the project was officially abandoned at the end of the war. Much of the 700km of track that had been laid was torn up to replace war-damaged lines in the west. Construction continued in secret, using slave labour until the gulags were closed in 1954.

In 1976 it was announced that work on the BAM was recommencing. Incentives were offered to labourers to collect the 100,000 strong workforce needed for so large a project. For eight years they laboured heroically, dynamiting their way through the permafrost which covers almost half the route, across a region where temperatures fall as low as -60°C in winter. In October 1984 it was announced that the way was open from Taishet to Komsomolsk-na-Amur. Although track-laying had been completed, only the eastern half was operational (from Komsomolsk to BAM station, where traffic joined the old Trans-Siberian route).

By 1991 the whole system was still not fully operational, the main obstacle being the Severomuisk Tunnel, bypassed by an unsatisfactory detour with a 1 in 25 gradient. It took from 1981 to 1991 to drill eight of the ten miles of this tunnel in the most difficult of conditions. Many were already questioning the point of a railway that was beginning to look like a white elephant. Work has more or less stopped now; the main sections of the line are complete but traffic is infrequent. The BAM was built to compete with shipping routes for the transfer of freight but the cost has been tremendous: there has been considerable ecological damage and there is little money left for the extraction of the minerals that was the other reason for the building of the railway. It is possible to travel along the BAM route starting near the north of Lake Baikal and ending up at Khabarovsk. You can find full details about the BAM and travel in the BAM region in the recently-updated *Siberian BAM Guide – rail, rivers and road*, by Athol Yates and Nicholas Zvegintzov (also from Trailblazer).

AYaM and Little BAM

The **AYaM** or Amuro-Yakutskaya Magistral is the Amur-Yakutsk Mainline which will eventually run from Tynda on the BAM north to Yakutsk. The project was scheduled for completion at the same time as the BAM but the line has now only reached Tommot, and passenger services operate only as far as Aldan. The final 456km section from Tommot to Yakutsk is unlikely to be completed for several years. The

Little BAM is the 180km rail link that runs between the Trans-Siberian at Bamovskaya and Tynda, the start of the AYaM.

Sakhalin Railway
The island of Sakhalin (north of Japan) is currently linked to the Russian mainland by rail ferries operating between Vanino and Kholmsk. Steam specials are occasionally run on the island's 3ft 6in-gauge rail system.

Turkestan-Siberia (Turksib) Railway
The Turksib links Novosibirsk on the Trans-Siberian with Almaty in Kazakhstan, a journey of 1678km. It was constructed in the 1930s to make it easier to transport grain from Siberia and cotton from Turkestan between these two regions. For more information visit the website – **http://turksib.com**.

Second Asia-Europe Land Bridge
In September 1990 the rail link between Urumqi in north-west China and the border with Kazakhstan was completed, opening a new rail route between east Asia and Europe via the Central Asian Republics. The Chinese built this new link to create the shortest rail route (2000km shorter than the Trans-Siberian) between countries on the western Pacific coast and the eastern Atlantic coast, enabling freight to be transported faster and more cheaply than by ship. With the breakup of the Soviet Union it has not really taken off in the way that the Chinese authorities had hoped but it does mean that it's now possible to travel along the old Silk Route by rail, through the old Central Asian capitals of Khiva, Bukhara and Samarkand, and the Chinese cities of Dunhuang, Luoyang and Xi'an. For the adventurous, the trip represents a unique travel opportunity. Full details are given in *Silk Route by Rail* by Dominic Streatfeild-James (also from Trailblazer).

Third Asia-Europe Land Bridge
The 295km railway linking Turkmenistan and Iran was officially opened on 13 May 1996. The US$216 million railway links land-locked Central Asia with the Persian Gulf and, via Turkey, the Mediterranean. In addition the railway connects Central Asia to the Istanbul–Beijing railway. Work on the Meshhed (Iran)–Sarakhs–Tedzhen (Turkmenistan) railway started in 1992. It has the as yet unrealized potential to become a new silk route connecting Southern Europe and the Far East, cutting the travel time by up to 10 days.

In November 2000, however, this new line still did not feature in railway timetables and remained closed to foreigners. If you do come this way by train, to cross this border currently the only way is to take the weekly Turkmen Airlines flight between Mashhad (Iran) and Ashgabat (Turkmenistan).

St Petersburg
Санкт-Петербург

In 2003 St Petersburg will celebrate only its 300th anniversary: it's a young city compared to Moscow and yet there is probably as much, if not more, to see here. Many visitors prefer this northern city, perhaps because it is of more manageable proportions than the sprawling capital. It is certainly more beautiful, having been laid out in 18th-century Classical style by Peter the Great on a grand scale. A trip to St Petersburg is well worth it if only for a visit to the Hermitage Museum, one of the world's most spectacular collections of European art, partly housed in the fabulously ornate Winter Palace.

You can visit Manchester's twin city by taking a side-trip from Moscow on the overnight train and staying a night or two but you really need at least four days to do justice to the sights. Other options are to route your Trans-Siberian journey through St Petersburg by starting (or ending) your trip in Helsinki (200km from St Petersburg) or to travel directly between St Petersburg and Warsaw, bypassing Moscow.

'Peter', as the locals call their city, is especially attractive in winter, when the snow shows up the brightly painted façades of the buildings. In summer, the most important cultural festival in Russia, 'White Nights', is held here in the last week of June. Whatever season you choose, St Petersburg with its grand architecture and emerging café culture is a fascinating place to visit.

HISTORY

Window on Europe

Peter the Great decided to build his new capital here to give Russia a 'window on Europe'. He felt that his country was becoming introverted and backward with its capital isolated from the West. The building of this European capital, St Petersburg, was the first step in Peter's crusade for Russia's modernization. The site selected for the new capital was particularly inhospitable: the marshy estuary of the River Neva. Work began in May 1703 and in 1712 the capital was moved here from Moscow. St Petersburg grew quickly and stylishly, for Peter employed the finest Italian architects for the palaces and many other important buildings.

Cultural and revolutionary centre

St Petersburg soon developed into the cultural heart of Russia and in the nineteenth century became one of the great centres of Europe; there gathered composers such as Tchaikovsky, Glinka, Mussorgsky, Rimsky-Korsakov and Shostakovich and writers like Gorky, Pushkin, Turgenev and Dostoyevsky. It was the birth place of new ideas and among them inevitably were revolutionary ideals. On 14 December 1825, these were translated into action for the first time in Russia's history, when a group of revolutionaries from the nobility (the 'Decembrists') refused to swear allegiance to Nicholas I and led their troops into Senate Square. Quickly disarmed, they were exiled to Siberia.

The Revolutions of 1905 and 1917

The second 'revolution' took place in 1905 when, on 22 January (Bloody Sunday), the Tsar's troops fired on a crowd that had marched to the Winter Palace to ask his help in improving working conditions. Ninety-two people were killed and several hundred wounded but more tragic for the country was the fact that the people's faith in their Tsar was finally shattered. Strikes and civil disorder followed and on 25 October 1917, a cannon shot from the cruiser *Aurora* provided the signal for the start of the Revolution proper.

Leningrad: 'Hero City'

In 1914 Tsar Nicholas II changed the city's name to the more Russian-sounding Petrograd; following Lenin's death ten years later, it was renamed Leningrad. In 1945 it was awarded the title, 'Hero City', for its stand against the Germans during the Second World War. From September 1941 to January 1943 the city was besieged and bombarded with an average of 250 shells per day. In fact most of the 641,803 inhabitants who died during the blockade died of starvation. During the winter of 1941/2 the daily bread ration was reduced to 250g for labourers and 125g for everyone else. People ate dogs, cats and rats; they chewed paper and glue to dull the hunger pains and made coffee from acorns. The streets were littered with piles of frozen corpses waiting until the ground was soft enough for mass graves to be dug.

St Petersburg today

The city has been almost entirely rebuilt since the war but fortunately the planners opted for restoration of many of the historic buildings rather than replacement. Throughout its short history, the city has always been at the forefront of change in the country. In June 1991, after a heated public debate, 55 per cent of Leningrad's citizens voted to change the city's name back to St Petersburg. Anatoly Sobchak, mayor during this period, did much to attract foreign investment to the city and St Petersburg has been more successful than Moscow in this respect.

The modern city is still in something of a state of flux, however: a shortage of housing means that many inhabitants still live in communal flats, and there is serious pollution caused by the industrial plants on the city's outskirts.

In 1998 the city made its peace with its former ruler when the bones of the last Tsar and his family were buried in the Peter and Paul Cathedral, beside Peter the Great and his successors.

In the run up to the anniversary in 2003 St Petersburg is undergoing something of a makeover, albeit a cosmetic one. The buildings of Nevsky Prospekt are being painted and there are plans to pedestrianise some of the surrounding streets.

WHAT TO SEE

The Hermitage Museum

Bigger than the British Museum or the Louvre, this museum surpasses both in the lavishness of its setting and the comprehensiveness of its collection of paintings. It comprises two huge buildings, the **Winter Palace** and the **Hermitage**. The Winter Palace, designed by the Italian architect, Rastrelli, was completed in 1762. The dozens of rooms and halls contained within its Baroque exterior were decorated in the reign of Catherine the Great who favoured the Classical style. Catherine ordered the building of the Hermitage, next door to her palace, as a place of retreat where she could contemplate the art collection she had begun.

In Soviet times the collection continued to benefit from the patronage of the rulers both in government handouts and also from the large numbers of visitors it received: over four million people per year. In 1999 there were only 1.7 million visitors so it appears that the citizens would rather spend their money on Nike trainers and all the other Western goodies available in the city's shops; and in the New Russia, the funds from the government have dried up too. The museum is almost bankrupt. (*Continued on p140*).

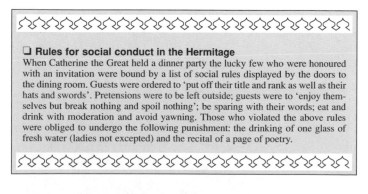

❏ **Rules for social conduct in the Hermitage**
When Catherine the Great held a dinner party the lucky few who were honoured with an invitation were bound by a list of social rules displayed by the doors to the dining room. Guests were ordered to 'put off their title and rank as well as their hats and swords'. Pretensions were to be left outside; guests were to 'enjoy themselves but break nothing and spoil nothing'; be sparing with their words; eat and drink with moderation and avoid yawning. Those who violated the above rules were obliged to undergo the following punishment: the drinking of one glass of fresh water (ladies not excepted) and the recital of a page of poetry.

St Petersburg
Санкт-Петербург

0 APPROX SCALE 500m

METRO STATIONS

A Gorkovskaya — Горьковская
B Ploshchad Lenina — Площадь Ленина
C Nevsky Prospekt — Невский Проспект
D Gostiny Dvor — Гостиный Двор
E Pl. Sadovaya/Sennaya — Площадь Садовая/Сенная
F Mayakovskaya — Маяковская
G Ploshchad Vosstaniya — Площадь Восстания
H Pl. Aleksandra Nevskovo — Площадь Александра Невского
J Chernyshevskaya — Чернышевская
K Vladimirskaya Ploshchad Vladimirskaya Площадь

6 Peter and Paul Fortress Петропавловская Крепость
7 Peter the Great's Log Cabin Домик Петра
8 Cruiser *Aurora* Аврора
10 Finland Station Финляндский Вокзал
13 Decembrists' Square Площадь Декабристов
13 Admiralty Адмиралтейство
14 Winter Palace/Hermitage Зимний Дворец/Эрмитаж
15 Central Post Office Главпочтамт
16 St P'burg Trvl Co Ст. Петербургская Компания Путешествий
17 St Isaac's Cathedral Исаакиевский Собор
20 Air Terminal Агентство Воздушных
21 Former General Staff Building Здание Главного Штаба
22 Telephone Office Центральнй Переговорный Пункт
25 Yusupovsky Palace Юсуповский Дворец
26 Mariinski Palace Мариинский Дворец
27 Kazan Cathedral Казанский Собор
28 Pushkin House Дом Пушкина
29 Rail Ticket Office Центральные Железнодорожные Кассы
31 Gostiny Dvor Универмаг Гостиный Двор
32 ATM Банк
33 Theatre Tickets Kiosk Театр билет киоск
37 Church of Resurrection Церковь Воскресения Христова
38 Russian State Museum Русский Государственный Музей
39 Anichkov Palace Аничков Дворец
40 US Consulate Консульство США
42 Central OVIR ОВиР
43 Cathedral of the Transfiguration of Our Saviour Собор
44 Argl a Book Shop Англия книга магазин
45 Maly Theatre Малый Театр
53 Arctic Museum Музей Арктика
54 Dostoevsky House-Museum Музей Ф.М. Достоевского
55 Moscow Station Московский Вокзал

HOTELS AND RESTAURANTS
1 To Restaurant Kalinka (200m) Ресторан Калинка
4 To Troitsky Most Café (200m) Кафе Тройцкий Мост
9 Hotel St Petersburg Гостиница Санкт-Петербург
11 Holiday Hostel Гостиница Holiday
18 Tandoor Indian Restaurant Индийский Ресторан Тандур
19 Astoria Hotel & Hôtel d'Angleterre Гостиница Астория
23 Café Literaturnoe Кафе Литературное
24 Pizza Hut Пицца Хат
30 Café Idiot Кафе
32 Grillmaster & ATM
34 Valhall
35 McDonald's Restaurant Макдоналдс
36 Grand Hotel Europe Гостиница Гранд
41 Laima Ресторан Laima
46 Mollie's Irish Bar Молис Ирландский Бар
47 Jazz Club
48 Aphrodite Restaurant Ресторан Афролита
49 KFC/Pizza Hut Пицца Хат
50 Nevsky Palace Hotel Гостиница Невский Дворец
51 Bahlsen Bakery
52 Baskin Robbins Ice Cream
56 Hotel Oktyabrskaya Гостиница Октябрьская
58 HI St Petersburg Hostel and Sindbad Travel
59 Hotel Moskva Гостиница Москва

OTHER
2 Literature Museum/Geological Museum Музей Русской
   Литературы/Карпинский Геологический Музей
3 Naval Museum Военно-Морской Музей
   & Anthropology Museum Музей Антропологии
5 Artillery Museum Артиллерийский Музей

❑ A walk down Nevsky Prospekt

Nevsky Prospekt has been the main shopping street and most fashionable place to be seen in St Petersburg since the foundation of the city. A walk along this grand street, past palaces and churches, over canals and beside faded buildings is a walk through the history of the city itself. Nevsky Prospekt starts near the Admiralty Building and, as you walk south-east from here, you can identify the buildings by the numbers beside the doors.

Where to eat There are numerous cafés, bars and restaurants so you can stop for a rest when you want. To name but a few there's *Nevski 40* (Russian-German) at No 40, *Baskin Robbins* at No 79, *Pizza Hut* at No 96, *Balsen* at No 142 and *Zolotaya Rybka* (good fish dishes) at No 166.

No 7 Gogol wrote *The Government Inspector* here in the 1830s.

No 9 This building was modelled on the Doges' Palace in Venice, for the Swedish banker, Wawelberg. Now it's the **Airline Ticket Office**.

No 14 Note the blue and white sign here which dates from the Siege of Leningrad in WWII and advises pedestrians to walk on the other side of the street during shelling.

No 17 This impressive building, designed by Rastrelli and built in 1754, was once the palace of the wealthy Stroganov family. Although they are more famous for the beef stew named after them, it was the Stroganovs who initiated the conquest and colonization of Siberia by sending their private army to the Urals in the 1570s.

No 18 The *Café Literaturnoe* was Pushkin's favourite café. Worth seeing but it's now packed with tourists. It charges an entry fee which includes high class entertainment such as violin concerts.

No 20 The former **Dutch Church**, built in 1837.

No 24 Once the showrooms of the court jewellers Fabergé (creators of the golden Easter eggs now on display in the Kremlin).

No 28 The former showrooms of the Singer Sewing Machine Company with their trademark (a glass globe) still on the roof. Now it's home to **Dom Knigi Bookstore**, the largest bookshop in the city.

Kazan Cathedral was designed by Voronikhin and completed in 1811. Prince Peter Kropotkin, writing in 1911, called it 'an ugly imitation on a smaller scale of St Peter's in Rome'.The large, domed cathedral is approached by a semi-circular colonnade. There is a statue at each end of the colonnade. The one on the left is Mikhail Kutuzov who prayed here before leading an army to fight Napoleon. After the victory over the French in 1812, the cathedral became a monument to Russia's military glory.

KAZAN CATHEDRAL

In an act of supreme tastelessness, the Soviets turned it into a Museum of Atheism. Part of the cathedral still houses exhibits on the history of religion, the rest has been returned to the Orthodox Church.

Looking north along the Griboyedova Canal, you'll see the onion-domed **Church of the Resurrection** (also known as the Church of the Resurrection

Built on Spilt Blood) which is reminiscent of St Basil's in Moscow. It was built on the spot where Alexander II was assassinated in 1881.

No 31 This building housed the City Duma (Municipal Council) in Tsarist times. The tower was used as a fire-lookout. The little portico around the corner is a **Theatre Booking Office**. Foreigners may buy tickets here. Opposite the Duma, is ul Brodskovo which runs north into Arts Square (Plosh-chad Iskustvo) which is where the **Russian Museum** is located. The museum was the former Mikhailovsky Palace and now houses over 300,000 paintings, drawings and sculptures. Well worth seeing, it is open 10:00-18:00, closed Tuesday, admission US$5. The **Maly Theatre** and the **St Petersburg State Philharmonia** are situated near the museum. The **Grand Hotel Europe** is a short distance down ul Brodskovo 32.

No 32 In the **Church of St Catherine,** Stanislaw Poniatowski, the last king of Poland and one of the lovers of Catherine the Great, is buried. Local artists sell their sketches and watercolours outside.

No 41 St Petersburg Tourist Information Centre (☎ 311 2943) opened here in 2000.

Gostiny Dvor, the city's largest department store, fills the whole of the next block (south side). It's been renovated and is a good place to buy souvenirs. **Passazh Department Store** is on the opposite side of the street. Passazh was the city's first privately owned department store and has a range of goods similar to any large Western department store. There is a large **supermarket** in the basement.

From the street, you can see a **statue of Catherine the Great**, surrounded by her lovers (or 'associates' as some guides coyly put it) and other famous people of the time. In the park behind the statues is the Pushkin Theatre.

No 56 Eliseyevsky Gastronome was a delicatessen that rivalled the Food Hall at Harrods in Tsarist days when it was presided over by Mr Eliseyev. After the Revolution it became Gastronom Number One and the ornate showcases of its sumptuous interior were heaped with jars of boiled vegetables. It is a wonderful example of classic St Petersburg interior design. Exotic Western fare is now on offer.

The building on the south side of the street beside the Fontanka Canal is known as the **Anichkov Palace**, after the nearby **Anichkov Bridge** with its famous equestrian statues.

No 82 Art Gallery of the Master's Guild (Gildiya Masterov) offers a good range of graphics, tapestries, ceramics, batik, jewellery and glassware by well-known artists. Open 11:00-16:00 weekdays.

Continuing east along the Nevsky Prospekt, it's one km from here to Ploshchad Vosstaniya where **Moskovsky railway station** (for trains to Moscow) is situated.

From Ploshchad Vosstaniya it's a further 700m to the end of the avenue at Ploshchad Aleksandra Nevskovo. The interesting **Alexander Nevsky Monastery** with seven churches in the grounds is situated here across the square from the **Hotel Moskva**.

MOSKOVSKY RAILWAY STATION

(*Continued from p135*). The solution to the Hermitage Museum's problems has been to develop links with other museums outside Russia so that more of its collection can be put on show to earn the funds so desperately needed. A branch was opened in 2000 in London – the Hermitage Rooms at Somerset House, and an agreement has also been signed with the Guggenheim in New York. There are also plans for a permanent gallery in Amsterdam.

Nothing beats seeing this collection in the galleries of the Hermitage and the Winter Palace but it's so large it would be impossible to see more than a small part of it in one visit. There are nearly three million works of art in its collection and to walk through each of the 300 galleries you'd cover a total distance of almost 25km! You could plan your visit in advance on the Internet: **www.hermitagemuseum.org**. The museum comprises the following departments:

● **The History of Russian Culture**

● **Ancient History** The highlight here is the exquisite Scythian goldwork exhibited in the Golden Rooms Special Collection. You're allowed in only if you are with a tour group or if you book in advance (US$10).

● **Central Asian Department**

● **The Middle East, China and Japan**

● **Ancient Greece and Rome**

● **European Art** This is the section that draws the tourists. There are works by Leonardo da Vinci, Raphael and Michelangelo (Halls 207-30); El Greco, Velazquez, Murillo and Goya (Halls 239-40); Van Dyck, Rembrandt and Rubens (Halls 245-54). French artists are well represented in Halls 143-6 and 272 to 289, and the Impressionists can be seen in Halls 317-345. The works of Reynolds, Gainsborough and other English artists are displayed in Halls 298-300.

The setting for these masterpieces could not be more magnificent: grand marble halls with gilded columns, mosaic floors and vast crystal chandeliers. As the place is so big, it may be worthwhile getting a guided tour one day and coming back the next day to wander at your leisure.

While the museum is open 10:30-18:00 (17:00 on Sunday), closed Monday, the front doors close at 17:30. Entrance is US$10, or free with a student card. (It's US$0.50 for Russians). You pay extra to use cameras (US$3) and video cameras (US$10). No tripods or flashes allowed.

Decembrists' Square

This square was the scene of the uprising by the group of officers on 14 December 1825 (see p95-6). They came to be known as the Decembrists and were sent to Siberia for their treachery,

The **Bronze Horseman**, a monument to Peter the Great, stands in the square. The statue was commissioned by Catherine II and the work carried out by the French sculptor, Falconet, in 1782.

St Isaac's Cathedral

South of Decembrists' Square is St Isaac's Cathedral (built between 1819 and 1859) with its vast gilded dome and ornate interior. In pre-Revolutionary days, the Cathedral would be packed with up to 14,000 people for major celebrations like Easter and St Isaac's birthday.

Reconsecrated in 1990 services are held here only at major Christian festivals but it's possible to view the spectacular interior daily except Wednesday from 11:00 to 19:00. There's an US$8 admission charge to the church. No photography is allowed. For another US$3.50 you can climb part of the way up the dome for a great view over the city.

Nevsky Prospekt

For a description of this famous St Petersburg street that is the heart of the city see p138.

Peter and Paul Fortress

In 1703 work began on this fortress, situated on an island in the very heart of the city. It was used as a maximum security prison until 1921, when it was turned into a museum. If you're here at midday don't be surprised by the sound of a cannon. It's the daily noonday cannon that St Petersburgers check their watches by. At the centre of the fortress is the **Peter and Paul Cathedral**, with its soaring, needle-like spire (122m). It now serves as a mausoleum for Peter the Great and his successors and is crammed with their ornate tombs. In July 1998 the remains of Nicholas II, Russia's last monarch, and his family who were killed in 1917 in Yekaterinburg were reburied here. The cathedral is open daily except Wednesday, and the fortress is open 10:00-18:00, closed Wednesday and last Tuesday of the month. Entry is US$3 for foreigners, US$0.50 for Russians.

Leaving the fortress, crossing the bridge and walking east along the river you will come to a small brick building amongst the trees in a square. This outer shell protects **Peter the Great's Log Cabin**, the earliest surviving building in the city, built in 1703, and now preserved as an interesting little museum (US$0.50, open 10:00-17:00, closed Tuesday).

Other sights

Since the city boasts over 60 museums, it is impossible to give details of more than a few in a guide of this type. Others include museums of social history (the **Cruiser *Aurora*** from which the signal for the Revolution was fired); literary museums (homes of **Dostoyevsky** and **Pushkin**) and scientific museums: the history of rail transport at the **Railway Museum**; the **Museum of the Arctic and Antarctic** and the **Natural History Museum**, where a fully preserved baby mammoth dug out of the Siberian permafrost, is on display. You can even visit the city's prison, **Kresty Prison**, near Finland Station. From its barred windows some of its 10,000 inmates communicate with family and friends in the street outside using sign language.

ST PETERSBURG METRO PLAN (ROMAN SCRIPT)

PRACTICAL INFORMATION
Arrival
● **By air** There are two airports: **Pulkovo II** (20km south of the city) for international and some domestic flights (bus or very frequent minibus No 13 from Moskovskaya metro station takes about 10 mins) and **Pulkovo I** for domestic flights (bus No 39 from Moskovskaya metro station). A taxi could cost up to US$50 but you should be able to get this down to US$30. A private car will do the journey out to the airport for US$5. You should get to the airport two full hours ahead of scheduled take-off, since baggage and passport control queues can be long.

What with getting to and from the airports and the usual delays, it's better to take the train from Moscow to St Petersburg rather than fly.

● **By train** There are five railway stations in St Petersburg. The three most important are: **Finland** (metro station: Ploshchad Lenina) for trains to and from Helsinki; **Moscow** (metro: Ploshchad Vosstaniya) for Moscow trains; and **Warsaw** (metro: Frunzenskaya) for trains to Warsaw, Berlin and other Western cities.

Local transport
In this city of canals and rivers, the 'Venice of the North', you might expect the local transportation system to be dominated by gondolas or punts but it's just like any other city in Russia.

There's a good metro system; although not as impressive as Moscow's

The St Petersburg area code is ☎ 812. From outside Russia dial +7-812.

ST PETERSBURG METRO PLAN (CYRILLIC SCRIPT)

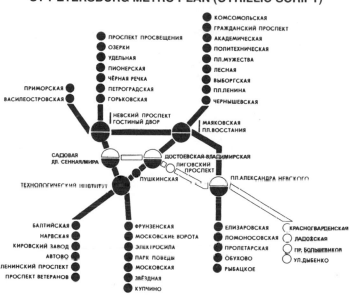

КОМСОМОЛЬСКАЯ
ГРАЖДАНСКИЙ ПРОСПЕКТ
АКАДЕМИЧЕСКАЯ
ПОЛИТЕХНИЧЕСКАЯ
ПЛ.МУЖЕСТВА
ЛЕСНАЯ
ВЫБОРГСКАЯ
ПЛ.ЛЕНИНА
ЧЕРНЫШЕВСКАЯ

ПРОСПЕКТ ПРОСВЕЩЕНИЯ
ОЗЕРКИ
УДЕЛЬНАЯ
ПИОНЕРСКАЯ
ЧЁРНАЯ РЕЧКА
ПЕТРОГРАДСКАЯ
ГОРЬКОВСКАЯ

ПРИМОРСКАЯ
ВАСИЛЕОСТРОВСКАЯ

НЕВСКИЙ ПРОСПЕКТ
ГОСТИНЫЙ ДВОР

МАЯКОВСКАЯ
ПЛ.ВОССТАНИЯ

САДОВАЯ
ПЛ. СЕННАЯ/МИРА

ДОСТОЕВСКАЯ-ВЛАДИМИРСКАЯ
ЛИГОВСКИЙ ПРОСПЕКТ

ТЕХНОЛОГИЧЕСКИЙ ИНСТИТУТ
ПУШКИНСКАЯ
ПЛ.АЛЕКСАНДРА НЕВСКОГО

БАЛТИЙСКАЯ
НАРВСКАЯ
КИРОВСКИЙ ЗАВОД
АВТОВО
ЛЕНИНСКИЙ ПРОСПЕКТ
ПРОСПЕКТ ВЕТЕРАНОВ

ФРУНЗЕНСКАЯ
МОСКОВСКИЕ ВОРОТА
ЭЛЕКТРОСИЛА
ПАРК ПОБЕДЫ
МОСКОВСКАЯ
ЗВЁЗДНАЯ
КУПЧИНО

ЕЛИЗАРОВСКАЯ
ЛОМОНОСОВСКАЯ
ПРОЛЕТАРСКАЯ
ОБУХОВО
РЫБАЦКОЕ

КРАСНОГВАРДЕЙСКАЯ
ЛАДОЖСКАЯ
ПР. БОЛЬШЕВИКОВ
УЛ.ДЫБЕНКО

metro, it's the quickest way around the city. Some of the stations have automatic safety doors; be aware that it may make finding the station you need confusing. Stay alert and count the stops. A few of the metro stations rival Moscow's in their Baroque décor and trains run from 05:35 to 00:30. As well as the metro there are buses, trams and trolley-buses.

Fares have just risen to US$0.20 on the metro, and US$0.13 on trolley-buses, buses and trams. For buses and taxis to and from the airport (see p142).

Orientation and services
St Petersburg stands at the mouth of the Neva, where the river meets the Baltic Sea's Gulf of Finland. The centre of the city is the 4km Nevsky Prospekt with the Hermitage Museum and the city's top hotels at its north-western end.

The new **St Petersburg Tourist Information Centre** (☎ 311 2943) is at 41 Nevsky Prospekt. **Sindbad Travel** (☎ 327 8384, 🖻 329 8019, 🖳 sindbad @sindbad.ru, www.sindbad.ru/en) at ul 3rd Sovetskaya 28, offers train and plane tickets, visa support, city tours, theatre tickets and information for hostelling in Russia, the Baltic States and worldwide. They sell and service all student and youth air tickets on all international carriers. **Dyum Tourist Agency** (☎ 279 0037) is at Nevsky Prospekt 86, inside House of Actors ('Dom Actyor'). The friendly staff will assist you any way they can. **American Express** has a travel agency in the Hotel Grand Europe.

There are a number of useful guides to St Petersburg including *The Traveller's Yellow Pages Saint Petersburg* (US$8) which is revised twice a year, *Where in St Petersburg*, and the entertaining and informative, locally-produced guide *The Fresh Guide to St Petersburg*. For current information on events around St

Petersburg you can pick up one of the local English-language newspapers. These are free and available in most hotels, hostels and Western supermarkets on and around Nevsky Prospekt. The *Saint Petersburg Times* (part of the *Moscow Times* group) is published twice weekly, while other regular papers include *Neva News* and *Pulse St Petersburg*.

Visas and extensions If St Petersburg is your first stop in Russia, remember that you are meant to register your visa within three working days. Your hotel should do this for you. To get a visa extension, you need to visit the Visa and Registration Department (OViR) with your passport, visa, proof of hotel reservations, official letter of extension and a translator if you don't speak Russian. The **Central OViR office** (☎ 278 3486) is at ul Saltkova-Shchedrina 4 (metro Chernishevskaya).

As the visa extension situation changes from month to month, contact your sponsor, hotel or hostel, rather than trekking down to OViR for the latest rules

Diplomatic representation China (☎ 114 6230), nab Griboyedova Kanala 134; **Czech Republic** (☎ 271 0459, 🖹 271 4615), ul Tverskaya 5; **Estonia** (☎ 233 5548, 🖹 233 5309), ul Bolshaya Monetnaya 14; **Finland** (☎ 273 7321, 272 4256 (visas), 🖹 272 1421), ul Chaykovskovo 71; **Germany** (☎ 273 5598, 279 3207, 🖹 279 3242), ul Furshtadtskaya 39; **Hungary** (☎ 312 6753, 312 6458, 🖹 312 6432), ul Marata 15; **Latvia** (☎ 315 1774, 230 3974, 🖹 554 3619), ul Galernaya 69; **Lithuania** (☎ 314 5857), ul Gorokhovaya 4;

Poland (☎ 274 4318, 274 4170, 🖹 274 4318), ul 5th Sovetskaya 12; **Sweden** (☎ 218 3526, 213 4191 (visas), 🖹 213 7198), ul 10th Liniya 11; **UK** (☎ 119 6036, 325 6166, 325 6036, 🖹 325 6037), pl Protetarski Diktatury 5; **USA** (☎ 274 8689, 274 8568, 🖹 110 6479), ul Furshtadtskaya 15.

Communications Most **payphones** use pre-paid cards available from metro token kiosks. in some older phones you can even use metro tokens.

You can make **long-distance calls** at the Central Telephone Office at Bolshaya Morskaya 3 where there's also the city's cheapest **Internet access** – from US$2 per hour. There are numerous other places around town with Internet access at higher rates.

Tours Independent sightseeing is easy, but if it's a tour you want, the **St Petersburg Travel Company**, formerly Intourist, (☎ 315 5129, 100 Nevsky Prospekt) operates the following half-day tours: the **Hermitage** (about US$23), **Peter and Paul Fortress** (US$23) and a **city tour** (US$16). There are also architecture tours, metro station tours and excursions to **Petrodvorets** (US$28), or to **Pushkin** and **Pavlovsk** (US$40).

Peter's Tours (☎ 329 8018, 🖳 pkozyrev@hotmail.com) leads recommended walking tours daily from the HI St Petersburg Hostel.

Between May and September, sightseeing **boats** leave from the Hermitage and Decembrists' Piers. Unfortunately most commentaries are in Russian so check first before paying.

(Opposite) Top: Looking through the arches of the General Staff Building across Palace Square to the Winter Palace. **Bottom left:** St Peter and St Paul Cathedral, where the last Tsar and his family were finally buried in July 1998. (Photo © Tatyana Pozar-Burgar). **Bottom right:** The Church of the Resurrection, built in the style of St Basil's in Moscow (Photo © Tatyana Pozar-Burgar).

Where to stay

Budget accommodation The *HI St Petersburg Hostel* (☎ 329 8018, 🖹 329 8019, 🖳 ryh@ryh.ru 🖳 www.ryh.ru), at ul 3rd Sovetskaya 28, was the first hostel to open in St Petersburg. A bed in a four-bed dormitory costs US$15 summer (US$12 winter) including breakfast with an international hostel card. Without a card it's US$19 (US$15 in winter). The building is clean and well-organized and it's an excellent place to meet other travellers and pick up the latest travel information. English-language movies are shown nightly. Ticket bookings are handled here at reasonable rates via Sindbad Travel, as are visa invitations and extensions (they can only help extend your visa if you have booked it through them). As the hostel is well known, in summer it is often full. If making a booking via Moscow's Travellers Guest House, hold on to your receipt. Communication between the two hostels is unreliable. To get to the hostel from Moscow train station, turn right onto Staraya Nevsky, then left at the first traffic lights onto pro Suvorovky (a Philips Electronics Store is on the left), then right at the second traffic light into ul 3rd Sovetskaya.

If you are arriving from Finland, *Holiday Hostel* (☎ 327 1070, 🖹 327 1033, 🖳 info@hostel.spb.su, www.hostel.spb.ru) at ul Mikhaylova 1 is very convenient. It is a five-minute walk from Findlandsky station and metro Ploshchad Lenina. Bed and (hot) breakfast costs US$19 in a double room and US$15 in a 3/5-bed room in summer, US$14/12 respectively in winter. With an HI or ISIC card there's a US$1 discount. It's beautifully located on the waterfront and despite being next door to Kresty Prison this is a fairly peaceful area. It seems to get very mixed reviews from travellers – some love it. The entrance is via the Zdorovyak fast-food café, owned by the Holiday Hostel. The hostel has a useful website: www.hostel.spb.ru.

A number of international companies organize **homestays** in St Petersburg. You can try e-mailing **homestay @nb.sp b.ru** who are recommended and offer homestays for around $20 plus visa support and registration for around US$50. Homestays and visas can also be organized through the *Host Families Association, Bed and Breakfast in Russia (HOFA)*,(☎ 275 1992, 535 7824, 🖳 alexei@hofak.hop.stu.neva.ru), ul Tavricheskaya 5, kv 25 and start at US$30/50 a night for a single/double. You will stay with an English-speaking host and prices go up to US$85/120 for deluxe singles/doubles which include transfers, all meals, guided tours (walking and by car) and ticket booking.

Sometimes at Moskovsky Station you can find people offering a room for overnight stays for around US$10 but you should be cautious when pursuing these options.

Midrange hotels Hotels in St Petersburg attract combined taxes of 25% (Russian Federation tax 20% and sales tax 5%) and these have been included in the prices where appropriate. Many of the hotels offer discounts at weekends (Friday and Saturday nights) which can be up to 30%; always ask about these. All rooms in this category have attached bathroom.

A good deal is the very well located *Hotel Oktyabrskaya* (☎ 277 6330) at Ligovsky Prospekt 10 (metro Ploshchad Vosstaniya). Old but comfortable, rooms start from US$30 for a single, and US$35

(Opposite) Top: This preserved Class Su steam engine stands by the platform at Ulan Ude station (see p251). **Bottom:** In the cemetery at Moscow's Novodevichy Convent (see p164) there are some quite extraordinary gravestones.

for a double room. They have cheaper rooms at their annexe, the *Filial* which is opposite Moscovsky station

The *Hotel Rossiya* (☎ 294 6322), at ul Chernysevskovo 11, is a big Soviet-era hotel. It is about 3km south of the city centre near the metro station, Park Pobedy. Prices go from US$30 for a single and US$50 for a double. There's luggage storage and a sauna. To reach the hotel walk along ul Chernysevskovo in the *opposite* direction to the obelisk and look out for the statue of Chernysevsky.

Hotel St Petersburg (☎ 542 9411, 📋 248 8002 🖳 postmaster@spbhotel.s pb.ru), at Nab Pirogovskaya 5/2, is only a five-minute walk from Finlandsky railway station (metro Ploshchad Lenina). Its rooms start at US$81 for a single and US$101 for a double, and the front ones have a majestic view of the Neva River.

The *Hotel Moskva* is a large place that's often used by groups. It's right by the Alexander Nevskogo metro, at the far end of Nevsky Prospekt. Rooms cost US$100/130 for a single/double: not good value.

Up-market hotels All rooms in this category have attached bathrooms. The two most centrally located hotels offer luxury facilities at seriously luxurious prices.

The *Grand Hotel Europe* (☎ 329 6000, 📋 329 6001, 🖳 res@ghe.spb.ru), at 1/7 Nevsky Prospekt, is reputed to be the best hotel in the country; singles start at US$354 and there are doubles from US$400. The Imperial Suite goes for a mere US$2700 a night. The hotel has four restaurants (breakfast costs US$26), and several bars.

The *Astoria Hotel* (☎ 210 5757, 🖳 front@Astoria.spb.ru, www.rfhotels.com) ul Bolshaya Morskaya 39, built in 1913 and furnished in beautiful Art Nouveau style, is now a Finnish/Russian joint venture. It's opposite St Isaac's Cathedral and prices are from US$300 for a single and US$360 for a double. Good tours can be arranged from here. Next door is the *Hôtel D'Angleterre* which has the same

telephone numbers and address as the Astoria but is slightly cheaper at US$260/ US$310 for a single/double.

The *Nevsky Palace Hotel* (☎ 275 2001, 📋 310 7323), a five-star place owned by Sheraton Hotels, is at the other end of Nevsky Prospekt (No 57). A standard room costs US$400 (single or double occupancy).

The Finnish-built *Pulkhovskaya Hotel* (☎ 264 5122, 264 5022, 📋 264 6396) is at Ploshchad Pobedy 1, (metro: Moskovskaya five minutes' walk) with comfortable and clean rooms starting from US$150 for a single and US$175 for a double including breakfast. Its restaurants offer Russian and Finnish cuisine.

Where to eat
There are lots of fast food restaurants but try the Russian places before resorting to McD's. *Laima*, on Kanala Griboedova (near Nevsky Prospekt) does filling meals for around US$2.50. There's a German *Grillmaster* at Nevsky Prospekt 46, *Kentucky Fried Chicken* at Nevsky Prospekt 96 and *McDonald's* at Bolshaya Morskaya 11 and other locations around the city.

Café Idiot, at Naberezhnaya Reki Moyki 82, is a vegetarian place that's popular with foreigners: ex-pats and tourists alike. Most dishes are around US$4 and you can always find someone to play backgammon or chess with while Louis Armstrong croons in the background.

Another good vegetarian choice is *Troitsky Most Café*, at ul Malaya Posadskaya 2; open 24 hours. The food's good and cheap but the décor's awful.

The *Metekhi Café* at ul Belinskovo 3 isn't exclusively veggie but it has some

---

❏ **Drinking water**
Avoid St Petersburg's tap water, even to brush your teeth with as it can cause giardia, a particularly nasty infection which leads to diarrhoea, stomach cramps and nausea. Buy bottled water and peel all fruit.

great vegetarian options. Even better is another Georgian restaurant, the *Tbilisi* (☎ 232 9391) ul Sitninskaya 10. The shashlik is excellent and even though the place looks expensive the food isn't although drinks are pricey.

The *Pizza House* at ul Podolskaya 23 offers 13 types of Finnish (thin crust) pizza, salad and beer; and a delivery service (☎ 316 2666, open 12:30-23:00). *Pizza Hut* is on the corner of nab Moyki Reki and ul Gorokhovaya (open 11:00-21:00).

Tandoor (☎ 312 3886), is a good Indian restaurant conveniently located at pro Voznesensky 2. Main dishes are around US$15; there's a wide selection of vegetarian dishes which are cheaper.

Russkie Bliny Café ☎ 279 0559), ul Furmanova 13, is renowned for its traditional *bliny* pancakes served in a relaxed atmosphere where patrons share wooden tables.

St Petersburg's first cybercafé, the *Tetris Internet Café* (☎ 164 8759) is at ul Chernyakhovskovo 33, open daily 12:00 24:00. It costs from US$2.50 per hour and is near Ligovsky Prospekt metro.

The city's top restaurants charge anything from US$20 to US$50 plus for a meal. Recommended places include the *Aphrodite* (☎ 275 7620) Nevsky Prospekt 86 for seafood; the *Imperial* (☎ 234 1742) pro Kamenovstrovsky 53 for good Russian food, and the *Europe Restaurant* (☎ 113 8066) at the Grand Hotel Europe, where the Bacchanalian Sunday brunch (12:00 to 15:00), with live jazz, is popular. The restaurants at the *Nevsky Palace Hotel* are also among the city's best *Kalinka* (☎ 213 3751, 218 2866) is one of St Petersburg's top restaurants with very good traditional Russian cuisine and folk music. It's on Sezdovskaya liniya 9.

The *Café Literaturnoe* (☎ 312 8543), where Pushkin had his last meal before his fatal duel, is at Nevsky Prospekt 18. Always packed with tourists, it offers classical music and traditional Russian fare. It's best to make a reservation here .

Bars There are dozens of bars in St Petersburg and most offer a relaxed and convivial evening of good spirits, music, and pub food.

The *Jazz Club* (☎ 164 5683), Zagorodny Prospekt 27 is an internationally-famous club open 19:00-23:00

There are also several pleasant Irish bars: the long-running *Mollie's Irish Bar*, ul Rubinshteyna 36 (open 11:00-03:00), and *Shamrock Irish Bar*, ul Dekabristov 27 (12:00-01:00) are both popular. *Valhall* at Nevsky Prospekt 24 is a Viking theme bar with live music some nights.

Nightlife

St Petersburg is probably the most interesting city in Russia for nightlife. Everything from sitting around in cafés and bars to a night out at the ballet. For current information on events around St Petersburg, pick up one of the local English-language newspapers listed on p144 or look for the posters around the city. There are always good listings in *Pulse* magazine.

Ask at the service bureau for a programme of **ballet** (Kirov at the Mariinsky Theatre, Maly), **opera, concerts** and the **circus**. For the top shows you have to pay grossly-inflated 'foreigner prices' for tickets (Kirov US$50, Maly US$20). They keep an eye out for Westerner imposters at the theatres (!) so you probably won't get away with paying Russian prices unless you look and speak like a Russian. You can buy tickets from the Theatre Booking Office off Nevsky Prospekt (see p139). Touts sell tickets outside the theatre just before curtain up.

There are more than 30 casinos in St Petersburg. The best are the **Eldorado** at the Hotel Kareliya, ul Tukhachevskovo 7/2 (open 20:00-05:00), and **Nevskaya Melody**, nab Sverdlovskaya 62.

Moving on

By air Most European airlines have offices in St Petersburg. There are daily

---

The St Petersburg area code is ☎ 812. From outside Russia dial +7-812.

❏ **Bridge raising**

If you plan to be out late on the opposite side of the river to your hotel, remember that the metro trains across the river stop running at 00:30, and the bridges open up for ships at around 02:00 for up to two hours. The length of times varies depending on traffic but if you have to wait the river front is the perfect place to watch the sun rise.

---

international flights from London, Berlin, Helsinki, Prague and Warsaw and regular weekly flights to most other European capitals. All international flights land at Pulkovo-2 while domestic flights land at Pulkovo-1. For information on getting to the airports, see p142.

Air tickets for within Russia can be obtained from Aeroflot offices or the **Central Agency of Air Communications** (☎ 314 6963) at pro Nevsky 7/9 or at pro Kamennoostrovsky 27. Both offices are open weekdays from 08:00-19:00 and weekends 08:00-18:00. **Transaero** (☎ 279 6463) is at pro Liteynyy 48.

By rail Check **departure times** and arrive half an hour before the train is due to leave. If you don't know the stations, give yourself extra time to find the right platform as the sheer size of the stations can be daunting. Long-distance and suburban trains may depart from the same station. Russian trains rarely depart late and have been known to roll out of the station a few minutes ahead of schedule.

Printed intercity **train schedules** are available at all stations and if you can speak Russian, you can call for railway information on ☎ 168 0111 (general), ☎ 162 3344 (domestic) and ☎ 274 2092 (international).

● **Tickets** Tickets for **same day departure** can be purchased only at the station of departure at the 'same-day window' (*sutochnaya*) or Intourist window. Last minute tickets can sometimes be obtained from speculators, but at a high price. It is also risky because of the name-on-ticket/passport rule (see p127).

Advance tickets for departures from the following day up to 45 days in advance can be purchased at the Central Railroad Ticket Office (*Tsentralnye Zheleznodorozhnye Kassy*) at nab Kanala Griboyedova 24. The closest metro is Nevsky Prospekt. The office is open 08:00-20:00 on Monday to Saturday and 08:00-16:00 on Sundays. They sell tickets for all long-distance and international train routes but not suburban rail tickets. Foreigners can purchase tickets in the Intourist hall to the left of the entrance. You can also buy the tickets at the station from which your train departs (both Finland and Moscow stations have Intourist windows). Note that you can't buy a ticket without your passport.

If you do not want to go to the hassle of buying tickets yourself, you can get them from most hotel service desks (who add a sizeable commission) or from Sindbad Travel (who add a smaller one).

● **International trains** Foreigners pay six times the Russian price for international rail tickets.

If you plan to return to Europe by train from here, you will have to pass through one or more of Latvia, Lithuania, Estonia and Belarus. See pp398-401 for the visa requirements of each country. You will be able to get all your visas in St Petersburg with the exception of the Belorusian one. Note that if you're only crossing Belorus on the train and not stopping you don't need a transit visa providing you have a valid Russian visa when leaving Russia.

Train No 25 to Berlin via Warsaw goes through the Baltic states avoiding Belarus, train No 57 goes to Warsaw via Belarus, and train No 183 goes to Prague via Belarus and Ukraine.

Some international trains and journey times from St Petersburg are as follows:

Berlin (32 hours, train No 25), Budapest (44 hours), Warsaw (22 hours, train No 57), Prague (48 hours, train No 183), Helsinki (8 hours), Riga (12 hours), Tallinn (9 hours), Vilnius (13 hours).

By bus If you've had enough of trains and planes, several companies operate buses to Helsinki for around US$40 for the eight-hour trip, **Finnord Bus Agency**

❏ Moscow to St Petersburg by train

There are about 20 trains a day between Moscow and St Petersburg. If you buy the ticket yourself, a berth in a two-berth cabin (SV) costs US$45-60 and in a four-berth cabin (coupé) it's US$20-30 on the better trains. On a day train (eg Nos 23/24), you could do the trip for around US$10. The 650km line is Russia's busiest and most prestigious railway. Consequently, high standards are maintained, both in terms of carriage conditions and service. When the line was opened in 1851, the average travel time was 25 hours. Today most of the overnight trains take eight hours, with the once a week, high speed ER-200 train taking just five hours. This compares to over 10 hours if you travel by car.

Most travellers prefer an overnight journey as it saves accommodation costs and maximizes daytime sightseeing. Service is excellent compared to some other Russian trains. You are given a lunch box on daytime trains or breakfast box on overnight trains if you are in first class. The dining cars are usually open all night and security guards patrol the corridors throughout the night. The best overnight trains are Nos 1/2 (*Red Arrow*), 3/4 and 5/6 (*Nikolaevsky Express*).

Origin	Name	No	Jny time	Dep	Arr	Destination
Moscow	*Krasnaya Strela*	2	8hrs30	23:55	08:25	St Petersburg
Moscow	*Express*	4	8hrs30	23:59	08:29	St Petersburg
Moscow	*Nikolaevsky Exp*	6	8hrs45	23:10	07:55	St Petersburg
Moscow		14	8hrs30	20:26	05:00	St Petersburg
Moscow	*Yunost*	24	8hrs 34	12:16	29:50	St Petersburg
Moscow	*Smena*	26	8hrs15	23:00	07:05	St Petersburg
Moscow	*ER200*	158*	4hrs59	12:11	17:09	St Petersburg
Moscow	*Avrora*	160	6hrs15	17:20	23:35	St Petersburg
St Petersburg	*Krasnaya Strela*	1	8hrs30	23:55	08:25	Moscow
St Petersburg	*Express*	3	8hrs29	23:59	08:30	Moscow
St Petersburg	*Nikolaevsky Exp*	5	7hrs10	23:35	07:47	Moscow
St Petersburg		13	9hrs23	21:55	06:03	Moscow
St Petersburg	*Yunost*	23	8hrs 36	13:05	21:41	Moscow
St Petersburg	*Smena*	25	8hrs05	23:10	07:15	Moscow
St Petersburg	*ER200*	157¶	4hrs59	12:15	17:08	Moscow
St Petersburg	*Avrora*	159	6hrs15	15:55	22:10	Moscow

* Friday only   ¶ Thursday only

(☎ 314 8951, 📄 314 7058) at ul Italianskaya 37, operates a coach service to Helsinki departing at 15:40 and gives student discounts. Another option is the **St Petersburg Express Bus Service** which offers a daily bus from Hotel Astoria. Sovavto also offers daily departures to Helsinki from the Grand Hotel Europe at 8:45, arriving at 15:45.

Sovavto also has regular departures for the routes: St Petersburg–Helsinki–Turku–St Petersburg, and St Petersburg–Vyborg–Lappeenranta–Yvyas

kyulya–St Petersburg. Tickets can be purchased from several hotels, including the Pulkovskaya, Astoria, Grand Hotel Europe, and Saint Petersburg, and also from Sovavto offices (☎ 264 5125) at pl Pobedy 1 and pro Kamennoostrovski 39.

By ship Baltic Shipping Company discontinued its ferry services to St Petersburg from Stockholm, Helsinki and Riga several years ago. Check with Sindbad Travel to find out if the services have been reinstated.

EXCURSIONS FROM ST PETERSBURG

Thirty kilometres west of the city lies **Petrodvorets** (Peterhof), built as Peter the Great's Versailles by the sea. It is most famous for its spectacular fountains, with the gilded figures which appear in all the tourist literature. Open daily (though the main palace is closed on Monday) from 09:00 to 21:00. In the summer you can get there by hydrofoil from Hermitage Pier (several boats each hour, US$15 each way). Much cheaper is the bus (US$0.40) from outside the Baltic station in St Petersburg.

At **Pushkin** (25km outside St Petersburg) is the Catherine Palace (closed Tuesday) that was the home of the Imperial family. Set in a beautiful park, it was formerly known as Tsarskoye Selo (the Tsar's village). The Catherine Palace was looted by the Germans in WWII and its famous Amber Room has been under renovation for the last 21 years; it should be complete in 2003. The original amber panels disappeared during the German retreat and have never been found. The room has been called the largest piece of jewellery in the world, and is valued at US$142 million.

Four km south of here is **Pavlovsk**, built by Catherine the Great for her son Paul. Pavlovsk is closed Fridays. Trains for Pushkin and Pavlovsk leave from Vitebsky railway station (metro: Pushkinskaya). **Lomonosov (Oranienbaum) Palace** with its beautiful park attracts far fewer tourists than the above three and is a peaceful place to visit. It is closed Tuesday and in winter. Trains leave from Baltiisky railway station (metro: Baltiiskaya).

Moscow
Москва

All railway lines in Russia lead to the capital, so you'll be spending some time here, even if it's just a quick visit to Red Square as you change stations. Moscow is worth much more than that, however. Almost all the resounding changes that have taken place in the country over the past decade have been initiated here and if you're looking for the pulse of the new Russia it's here that you will find it.

Moscow's historic sights alone make it a fascinating place to explore; bank on a minimum of three days here to see the main attractions. Finding a place to stay, whatever your budget, is not a problem and the metro makes getting around easy.

HISTORY

The archaeological record shows that Moscow has been inhabited since Neolithic times. However, the first written mention of the city was not until 1147, when Prince Yuri Dolguruky was said to have founded the city by building a fort on a site beside the Moskva River, in the principality of Vladimir. The settlement which grew up around the wooden fort soon developed into a major trading centre.

The Mongols

Disaster struck the Russian principalities in the early thirteenth century in the form of the Mongol invasion. Moscow was razed to the ground in 1238 and for the next two and a half centuries was obliged to pay an annual tribute to the Mongol Khan. During this time the principality of Muscovy (of which Moscow was capital) emerged as the most important state in Russia. In 1326, Moscow became the seat of the Russian Orthodox Church. Prince Dimitri Donskoi strengthened the city's defences and built a stone wall around the Kremlin. In 1380 he defeated a Mongol-Tatar army at Kulikovo but it was not until 1476 that tributes to the Khan ceased.

The years of growth

The reign of Ivan III (Ivan the Great: 1462-1505) was a period of intensive construction in the city. Italian architects were commissioned to redesign the Kremlin, and many of the cathedrals and churches date from this period. Prosperity continued into the 16th century under Ivan IV (Ivan the Terrible) and it was at this time that St Basil's Cathedral was built.

The early seventeenth century was a time of civil disorder, and a peasant uprising culminated in the invasion of Moscow by Polish and Lithuanian forces. When they were driven out in 1612 the city was yet again burnt to the ground. Rebuilt in stone, Moscow became the most important trading city in Russia by the end of the century. It remained a major economic and cultural centre even when Peter the Great transferred the capital of Russia to St Petersburg in 1712.

The final sacking of the city occurred in 1812 when Napoleon invaded Russia. As much of the damage was probably caused by retreating Muscovites as by the French armies but three quarters of the buildings were destroyed. Recovery was swift and trade increased after the abolition of serfdom in 1861.

Revolution

Towards the end of the century Moscow became a revolutionary centre and its factories were hit by a series of strikes and riots. Michael Myres Shoemaker, who was here in 1903, wrote in *The Great Siberian Railway from St Petersburg to Peking*: 'Up to the present day the dissatisfaction has arisen from the middle classes especially the students, but now for the first time in Russia's history it is spreading downward to the peasants... but it will be a century at least before that vast inert mass awakens to life.' In 1905 there was an armed uprising and twelve years later 'that vast inert mass' had stormed the Kremlin and established Soviet power in the city. The civil war saw terrible food shortages and great loss of life.

The capital once more

In March 1918 Lenin transferred the government back to Moscow. In the years between the two world wars the city embarked on an ambitious programme of industrial development and the population doubled to four million by 1939. During the Second World War many of the factories in the European part of the USSR were relocated to the other side of the Urals, which turned out to be sensible move. By October 1941, the German army had surrounded the city and the two-month Siege of Moscow had begun.

Moscow was rebuilt following the war and grew in size, grandeur and power. However by the late 1980s, the city's clean appearance and services had started to collapse under Gorbachev's reforms and the breakdown of communist power. The few years following the 1991 disintegration of the Soviet Union was a time when little worked in the city and road, buildings and public utilities were continually on the verge of complete collapse.

Moscow today

The only thing that can be said with certainty about Moscow is that the changes that have transformed it over the last ten years are not about to stop now. On the one hand the restructuring here seems to be part of a beneficial transition to a market economy: new hotels spring up, restaurants open and shops flourish. On the other hand it's impossible to ignore the widespread poverty: old women in the streets stand for hours trying to hawk their few belongings, ragged war veterans sleep in the subways and everywhere, it seems, there are beggars. The fact that the new generation of foreign shops, bars and restaurants offer all the latest in Western luxuries highlights the contrasts. Many Muscovites can only afford to window-shop in such places and few can afford to eat in the restaurants. Crime, ranging from petty pilfering to gang warfare on the streets has increased and many businesses are forced to pay protection money to local 'mafia' gangs. There is also a chronic shortage of housing which has worsened with the arrival of thousands of ethnic Russians from the other CIS republics.

All the negative press, some of it undeserved, has been partly responsible for a tourist slump in the city: from six million visitors in 1990 to only about a million in 2000. You should certainly not be put off by it: Moscow is a fascinating place to visit and the first few years of the 21st century an exciting time to be here.

In an effort to reassure prospective visitors the city government plans to introduce 300 Tourist Police in 2001 who will be 'trained to smile'. Putin's plan to get the tourists back involves building a US$300 million 'Kremlin Center' next to St Basil's. There will be an icon auction house and a diamond showroom. Can you wait?

WHAT TO SEE

Red Square
This wide cobbled square, Krasnaya Ploshchad in Russian, extends across the area beside the north-eastern wall of the Kremlin. The main sights around the square are St Basil's Cathedral, Lenin's Mausoleum, the GUM Department Store and the Kremlin.

Lenin's Mausoleum
Built onto the side of the Kremlin in 1930, the red granite mausoleum and its mummified occupant are something of an embarrassment to the current regime. Tourists still queue up to file past the once-revered corpse, laid out in its dark suit and tie. Lenin currently receives visitors from 10:00 to 13:00, but not on Monday or Friday. There's no entry charge.

The mausoleum was the centre of a cult that flourished for almost 70 years. The cubist design is the work of A.V.Shchusev who envisaged the cube, like the pyramid, as a symbol of eternity and it was his plan that every Soviet home would have its own little cube to the memory of the dead leader. Until the early 1990s, no Soviet town was without a Lenin statue, and no public office lacked a Lenin portrait. (*Continued on p160*)

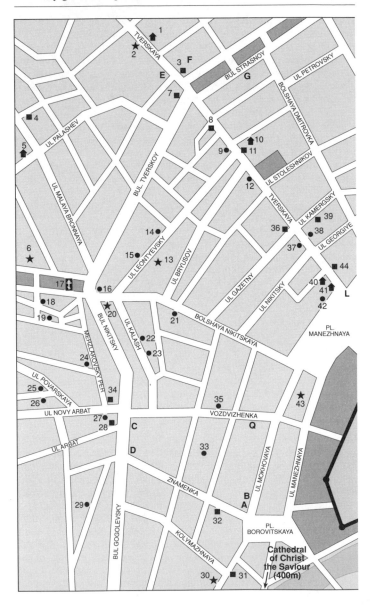

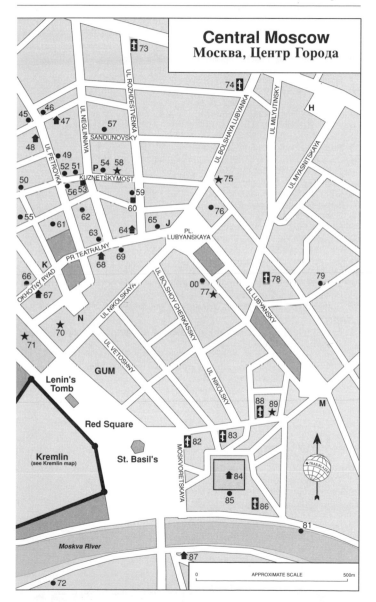

Central Moscow
Москва, Центр Города

UL ROZHDESTVENKA

UL NEGLINNAYA

SANDUNOVSKY

UL PETROVKA

KUZNETSKYMOST

UL BOLSHAYA LUBYANKA

UL MILYUTINSKY

UL MYASNITSKAYA

H

P

PL. LUBYANSKAYA

J

K

PR TEATRALNY

OKHOTNY RYAD

UL LUBYANSKY

UL NIKOLSKAYA

UL BOLSHOY CHERKASSKY

N

UL VETOSHNY

GUM

Lenin's Tomb

Red Square

Kremlin
(see Kremlin map)

St. Basil's

UL NIKOLSKY

M

MOSKVORETSKAYA

TRAB.PLAZA

Moskva River

APPROXIMATE SCALE

0   500m

HOTELS AND RESTAURANTS
1 Marriott Grand Hotel Гостиница Марриотт Гранд
3 Russkoe Bistroe/Yolki Polki Restaurants Ресторан Руссое/Елки Палки
4 Margarita Café Кафе Маргарита
5 Marco Polo-Preshya Hotel Гостинца Марко Поло-Пресня
7 McDonald's Restaurant Макдоналдс
8 Mesto Vstrechi Restaurant Ресторан Место Встречий
10 Tsentralnaya Hotel Гостиница Центральная
11 Pizza Hut Restaurant Пицца Хат
28 Praga Restaurant Ресторан Прага
31 Patio Pizza Патио Пицца
32 Rosie O'Grady's Pub Бар Рози Огрэдис
34 Dioscuria Restaurant Ресторан Дюскурия
36 McDonald's Restaurant Макдоналдс
39 Tibet Kitchen Ресторан Тибетская Кухня
40 Intourist Hotel Гостиница Интурист
41 National Hotel Гостиница Националь
47 Budapest Hotel Гостиница Будапешт
48 Marriott Royal Hotel Гостиница Марриотт Роял
53 Juggernaut Restaurant Ресторан Джэганот
60 Pizzeria Пиццерия
64 Savoy Hotel Гостиница Савой
67 Moskva Hotel Гостиница Москва
68 Metropol Hotel Гостиница Метрополь
84 Rossiya Hotel Гостиница Россия
87 Hotel Kempinski-Baltschug Гостиница Кемпинский-Балчуг

OTHER
2 Museum of Contemporary Russian History (Russian Revolutions)
     Музей Революции
6 Gorky House Museum Дом-Музей Горького
9 Moscow Drama Theatre Московсий Драмитический Театр
12 Moscow City Government Building Мэрия
13 Museum of Folk Art Музей народного искусства
14 Azerbaijan Embassy Посольство Азербайджана
15 Ukraine Embassy Посольство Украины
16 ITAR-TASS news agency ИТАР-ТАСС
17 Grand Ascension Church Большая Вознесеная Цекровь
18 Georgia Embassy Посольство Грузии
19 Tajikistan Embassy Посольство Таджикистана
20 Mayakovsky House-Museum Дом-Музей Маяковского
21 Tchaikovsky Conservatory Консерватория имени Чайковского
22 Estonia Embassy Посольство Эстонии
23 Netherlands Embassy Посольство Нидерландов
24 USA & Canada Institute Институт США и Канады
25 Norway Embassy Посольство Норвегии
26 Belgium Embassy Посольство Бельгии
27 Irish Arbat Department Store Ирландский Дом
29 Turkmen Embassy Посольство Туркменистана
30 Pushkin Museum of Fine Arts
     Музей Изобразительных Искусств имени А С Пушкина
33 Russian State Library Российская Государственная Библиотека

35 Military Department Store Воинторг
37 Central Post Office Центральный Телеграф
38 Finnair & Malev Airline Offices Finnair Malev Авиа Касса
42 Intourist Travel Agency Интурист
43 Central Exhibition Hall Центральный Выставочный Зал
44 Transaero Трансаэро
45 Intourtrans Travel Agency Интуртранс
46 Aeroflot Airlines Office Касса Аэрофлотаа
49 Petrovsky Passazh Department Store Универмаг Петровский Пассаж
50 SAS Airline Office SAS Авиакасса
51 JAL Airline Office JAL Авиакасса
52 Atlas Map Shop Магазин Атлас
54 Moldova Embassy Посольство Молдавии
55 Operetta Theatre Театр Оперетты
56 Air China Airline Office Air China Авиакасса
57 Sandunovskaya Baths Бани Сандуновские
58 Artists' Union Gallery Выставочный Зал
59 City Excursion Bureau Московское Городское Экскурсконное Бюро
61 Bolshoi Theatre Большой Театр
62 TsUM Department Store ЦУМ
63 Maly Theatre Малый Театр
65 Detskiy Mir Children's Department Store Универмаг Детский Мир
66 State Duma Parliament House Государственная Дума
69 Arkadia Jazz Club Джаз Клуб Аркадия
70 Former Lenin Museum Бывший Центральный Музей Ленина
71 State History Museum Государственный Исторический Музей
72 British Embassy Британское Посольство
73 Nativity of Our Lady Cathedral Рождественский Собор
74 Church of Vladimir Mother of God Церковь Владимирской Богоматери
75 KGB Museum Музей КГБ
76 Former KGB Headquarters Лубянка
77 Moscow City History Museum Музей Истории Города Москвы
78 St Nicholas Church Никольская церковь
79 Belarus Embassy Посольство Белоруссии
80 Andrew's Consulting Travel Agency
81 Boat Landing Пристань
82 St Barbara's Church Церковь Святово Варвары
83 Monastery of the Sign Belltower Колокольня Знаменского Монастыря
85 Central Concert Hall Центральный Концертный Зал
86 Church of St Anne's Conception Церковь Святой Зачатия Анны
88 St George's Church Церковь Святово Святово Георгия
89 17th Century Art Museum Художественний музей 17 века

METRO STATIONS Станция Метро

A Borovitskaya Боровитска
B Biblioteka im Lenina
   Библиотека имени Ленинаz
C Arbatskaya 1 Арбатская
D Arbatskaya 2 Арбатская
E Tverskaya Тверская
F Pushkinskaya Пушкинская
G Chekhovskaya Чеховская
H Turgenevskaya Тургеневская

J Lubyanka Лубянка
K Teatralnaya Театральная
L Okhotny Ryad Охотный Ряд
M Kitai-Gorod Китай-Город
N Ploshchad Revolyutsi
   Площадь Революции
P Kuznetsky Most
   Кузнецкий Мост
Q Aleksandrovski Sad
   Александровский Сад

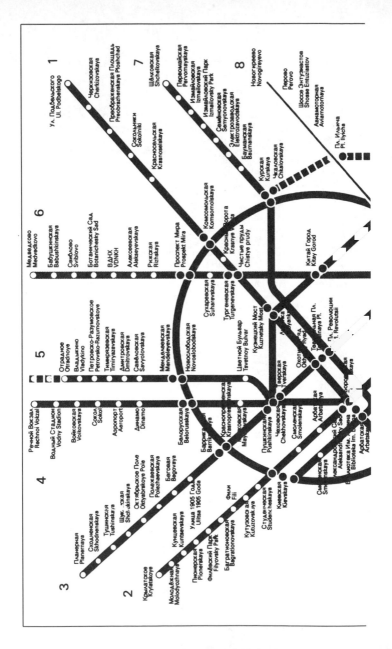

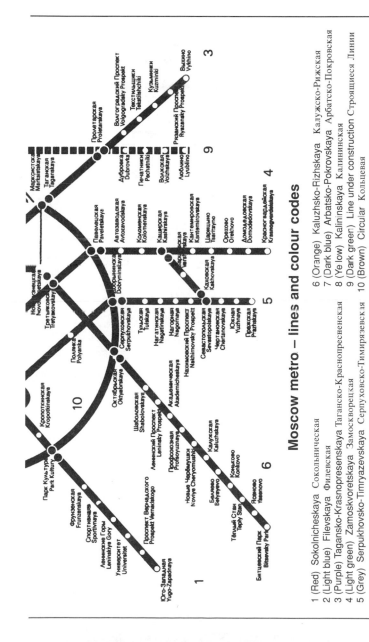

Moscow metro – lines and colour codes

1 (Red) Sokolnicheskaya Сокольническая
2 (Light blue) Filevskaya Филевская
3 (Purple) Tagansko-Krasnopresenskaya Таганско-Краснопресненская
4 (Light green) Zamoskvoretskaya Замоскворецкая
5 (Grey) Serpukhovsko-Timryazevskaya Серпуховско-Тимирязевская

6 (Orange) Kaluzhsko-Rizhskaya Калужско-Рижская
7 (Dark blue) Arbatsko-Pokrovskaya Арбатско-Покровская
8 (Yellow) Kalininskaya Калининская
9 (Dark green) Line under construction Строящиеся Линии
10 (Brown) Circular Кольцевая

❏ **Mummification for the masses**
The Centre for Biological Researches, responsible for the preservation of Lenin's body, recently announced the offer of full mummification services to anyone for a mere US$300,000.

Previous clients are a testimony to their considerable skill. An independent team of embalmers recently inspected Lenin's corpse and declared it to be in perfect condition. After his death on 21 January 1924, an autopsy was carried out and a full report published in *Pravda*. The public were treated to a list of weights and measurements of most of the internal organs of their dead leader (his brain weighed 1340g – far larger than average). Then the embalmers began their work. One wonders if the decision the Central Executive Committee took in 1924 to preserve Lenin's body had anything to do with Howard Carter's discovery of the Pharaoh Tuthankamun 14 months earlier.

In 1997 Lenin was put back on display after a three-month cosmetic makeover. In December 2000 he was freshened up again. The debate over what to do with him continues with liberal politicians suggesting that Russia should bury its past and Communists arguing that to move Lenin now would be a denial of the country's history. Meanwhile the former leader continues to be an excellent advertisement for the services of the Centre for Biological Researches. Dr Zbarsky, who headed the original team of embalmers, boasted that Lenin's body would remain unchanged indefinitely. This claim is reiterated by Dr Yuri Denisov-Nikolsky, who hopes to attract rich American corpses.

(*Continued from p153*) There are plans to move Lenin's body to the family plot in St Petersburg. Behind the mausoleum are the graves of other communist heroes, including Brezhnev and Stalin, and these will be moved to Novodevichy Cemetery. The fate of the building itself is uncertain. Campaigners want it demolished and replaced with the statue of Kuzma Minin and Prince Pozharsky, famed for saving Moscow during the 'Times of Troubles' in the early 17th century; this statue originally stood on the spot but is now in front of St Basil's.

St Basil's Cathedral
Also known as the Church of the Saviour and nicknamed the Pineapple Church by Victorian travellers, this whimsical architectural creation is as much a symbol of Moscow as Tower Bridge is of London. Commissioned by Ivan the Terrible, it was completed in 1561 and so pleased with the result was the Tsar that he had the architect's eyes put out so that he would never be able to produce anything to equal or surpass it.

(**Opposite**) St Basil's Cathedral on Red Square is Moscow's most famous landmark.

Apparently the architect went on to produce other buildings, so perhaps this is a tall story but it's a good one fitting the Tsar's character perfectly. St Basil's is a quite incredible building, with its nine brightly-painted, dissimilar domes and the stone-work decorated with intricate patterns more usually found on the wooden buildings of the time.

For many years a museum, it has been returned to the Church. There are entry charges, however: US$3.20 (half price for students). Opening hours are 10:00-17:00 (11:00-16:00 November-April) and it's closed every Tuesday and the first Monday of each month.

GUM

The remarkable glass-roofed GUM building (pronounced 'goom') was constructed in 1894 as a shopping mall where individual traders could set up their stalls. It was nationalized after the Revolution and turned into a huge state store, a monument to Soviet shortages, but following the market reforms the Western chains have moved in. You can now buy anything from a Benetton sweater to the latest compact disc but most Muscovites, and many tourists can afford only to browse.

State History Museum

Reopened in 1997 this museum is at the north end of Red Square. The extensive collections cover the history of the country up to the present. It's open 10:30-19:00 daily except Tuesday; entry is US$2.50.

The Tomb of the Unknown Soldier

It is traditional for bridal couples to visit this monument in the Aleksandrovski Gardens on their wedding day, to be photographed beside the eternal flame. Beneath the marble lies the body of one of the soldiers who helped to stop the German advance on Moscow in 1941.

The Kremlin

The heart of Moscow and the seat of the Russian government, the Kremlin is, in fact, a large walled castle. Although the site has been continuously occupied for at least the last 800 years, the walls and many of the cathedrals date from the fifteenth century. There are 20 towers, the most famous being the **Saviour Tower** above Red Square. Russian officials drive through its gate to work. The Kremlin's main entrance and ticket office is in **Kutafya Tower**, on the opposite side to Red Square. Note that you may not take large bags or rucksacks in, and that you won't get past the guards if you are wearing shorts.

You buy a ticket to the Kremlin grounds (US$8, or US$5 for students) and then additional tickets for each major museum or group of churches.

(Opposite) Russian Orthodox priests outside St Basil's Cathedral, Moscow.

All the tickets can be bought at the Kutafya Tower or the ticket office in the Aleksandrovski Park. Check large bags into the left luggage office under the Kutafya Tower. As tours for some of the museums start at particular times, your tickets may have a time printed on them. To prevent disappointment, you can always buy your tickets a few days ahead. You can also buy tickets for the individual museums and churches at their respective doors. The Kremlin grounds are open 10:00-17:00, closed Thursday.

Cathedral Square
In the centre of the Kremlin is a square around which stand four cathedrals and the **Bell Tower** of Ivan the Great (81m/263ft high), which Napoleon attempted to blow up in 1812. Beneath the tower stands the **Tsar Bell**, at 200 tons the heaviest in the world. The piece of the bell that stands beside it broke off during the fire of 1737. Nearby is the largest calibre **cannon** in the world.

The **Cathedral of the Assumption**, the work of an Italian, was completed in 1479 and was the traditional place of coronation for Russia's tsars. During the last coronation, on 26 May 1896, something happened that was taken by those who saw it as a bad omen: as Nicholas II walked up the steps to the altar, the chain of the Order of St Anthony fell from his shoulders to the floor. Inside are three thrones; the wooden one to the right as you enter belonged to Ivan the Terrible.

The **Cathedral of the Archangel Mikhael** (1505-09) looks classically Russian from the outside but the hand of its Italian architect Alevisio Novi can be seen in the light interior. Forty-six tsars (including Ivan the Great and Ivan the Terrible) are buried here. The smaller **Cathedral of the Annunciation** (1484-89), the private chapel of the tsars, was the work of Russian architects and contains icons by the great master, Andrei Rublyev. The **Church of the Deposition of the Robe** (1484-5) was designed as a private chapel for the clergy. The Patriarch worshipped in the **Church of the 12 Apostles** next door to his residence.

Other buildings The **Great Kremlin Palace**, now a government building, is not usually open to visitors. Total renovation, to restore the palace to its pre-communist era finery was completed in 1999: 'Put it back as it was before', said Yeltsin; and they did, for a mere US$800 million.

One wall of the Italian-designed **Faceted Chamber** (so-called because of its façade of pointed stone blocks) faces Cathedral Square. The **Golden Tsarina Palace** or Terem Palace has a striking red and white tiled roof. The seat of Russian government is the modern **Palace of Congress**. The **Armoury** should not be missed (entry is US$11, or US$6 for students) as it contains a dazzling display of various tsars' jewellery and regalia, weapons and armour. Of special interest to Trans-Siberian passengers is the ornate **Great Siberian Easter Egg** (probably the finest of the 56 famous

Moscow – The Kremlin   **Москва – Кремль**

Legend:
1 War Memorial
2 Kutafya Tower
3 Trinity Tower
4 Palace of Congresses
5 Church of the Twelve Apostles
6 Church of the Deposition of the Virgin's Robe
7 Cathedral of the Assumption
8 Tsar Cannon
9 Bell Tower of Ivan III
10 Tsar Bell
11 Cathedral of the Archangel
12 Cathedral of the Annunciation
13 Faceted Palace
14 Saviour Cathedral
15 Terem Palace
16 Grand Kremlin Palace
17 Armoury
18 Potochny Palace
19 Arsenal
20 Senate
21 Supreme Soviet
22 Spassky Tower
23 Ticket Kiosks
24 Patriach's Palace

Imperial Easter Eggs made by Carl Fabergé), which contains a clockwork model of the train, complete with gold and platinum engine (with a ruby for the headlight), five gold coaches and a church-car (Hall III).

Tretyakov Art Gallery

The best collection of icons and sculpture in Russia is housed here. There are icons painted by Andrei Rublyev; *Christ's First Appearance to the People* which took Alexander Ivanov 20 years to complete; and two halls devoted to the great Russian masters, Ilya Repin and Vasily Surikov. The gallery is at 10 Lavrushinsky Perelok, (Metro: Tretyakovskaya). The museum (☎ 230 7788) is at pro Lavrushinski 12, costs US$8 or US$4 for students and is open daily (except Mon) 10:00 to 18:30.

Pushkin Museum of Fine Arts

Most interesting for its large collection of Impressionist paintings including many famous canvases (Manet's *Déjeuner sur l'Herbe,* for example, and Monet's *Boulevard des Capucines*). There are also galleries of

Egyptian antiquities and Old Masters. Well worth a visit, the gallery (☎ 203 9578) is at ul Volkhonka 12 (metro: Kropotkinskaya) and is open daily (except Mon) 10:00 to 17:00. It's US$5 or US$2.50 for students.

Cathedral of Christ the Saviour

CATHEDRAL OF
CHRIST THE SAVIOUR

The original church here was a 19th century cathedral that was blown up by Stalin to make way for an enormous open-air heated swimming-pool. To replace the original building was the brainchild of mayor Yuri Luzhkov and that was achieved in 1997. Prince Charles certainly wouldn't like this brash repro carbuncle. Go for the views from the roof. The cathedral lies between the river and ul Volkhonka.

Old Arbat Street (Stari Arbat)

This pedestrianised shopping street is popular with tourists. There are buskers, street artists and swarms of souvenir sellers hawking everything from matrioshkas to pirated CDs. Bargain hard and watch for pickpockets.

Sandunovskaya Baths

If you've just stepped off a Trans-Sib train, a traditional Russian bath in the oldest public banya in the city is an invigorating and interesting experience. On Sandunovsky per (off ul Petrovka), they're beautifully decorated in the Classical style. Open daily 08:00-22:00 (closed Tuesday); entry is US$10.

Novodevichy Convent

This beautiful sixteenth-century walled convent is well worth visiting. Dating back to the sixteenth century it has been used at various times as a fortress (it held out against the Poles during a siege in 1610) and a prison (it was here that Peter the Great banished his sister Sophia, among others). Although Napoleon tried to blow it up in 1812 it remained undamaged: one brave nun rushed in and extinguished the fuses to the powder kegs at the last minute. The **cathedral** is famous for its frescoes and highly ornate, multi-tiered iconostasis (the backdrop to the altar). It also contains a small museum. Novodevichy is open 08:00-18:00 daily but closed Tuesday and the first Monday of the month. (Nearest metro: Sportivnaya).

Behind the convent is the **cemetery**. As well as graves of many influential people (including Khrushchev, Chekhov and Prokofiev), there are some outlandish gravestones: one soldier lies under a model tank. Stalin, Gagarin and Brezhnev will probably be moved here from Red Square.

Other museums, galleries and churches in Moscow

There is simply not room in a guide-book of this type to give details of more than a few of Moscow's 150 museums and exhibitions. However a few of the best are the **Andrei Rublyov Ancient Russian Culture and Art Museum** (☎ 278 1467), pl Andronyevskaya 10, open 11:00-18:00, closed Wednesday and last Friday of each month, entry US$3; **Museum of Cosmonauts** (☎ 286 3714), ul 1st Ostankinskaya 41/9; **Borodino Battle Field Panorama** (☎ 148 1965), pro Kutuzovski 38, open 10:30-20:00, open Saturday to Thursday; **Federal Counterintelligence Service (KGB) Museum** (☎ 224 1982), ul Lubyanka 12/1s; and **Former Political Prisoners Museum** (☎ 925 0144), ul Chaplyghina 15. There are other museums devoted to Gorky, Tolstoy, Dostoyevsky, Pushkin, Chekhov, Gogol, Glinka, Bulgakov and Lermontov.

❏ **The Moscow metro and the secret metro**

Construction of the metro began in the early 1930s and it was planned that the first line would be opened on May Day 1935. In late April 1935, Stalin was invited to inspect the system but his train tour came to an unexpected halt for 30 minutes following a signal failure. Expecting imprisonment or worse, the engineers nearly collapsed with relief when Stalin simply suggested that it might be better to fix all the problems and delay the opening until 15 May. The honour of driving the first metro train, which consisted of local copies of the 1932 New York carriages, went to the strangely named Ivan Ivanovich Ivanov.

As well as transporting passengers, the metro served as a bomb shelter in 1941 and 1942. Male Moscovites slept on wooden platforms assembled every evening in the tunnels while women and children slept on camp stretchers on the platforms. Following the start of the Cold War, the metro was modified to contain fall out shelters and evidence of both the World War and Cold War preparations can still be seen today. These include large recessed blast doors at the entrances of the metros on ground level, collapsible platform edges which become steps, and large storerooms on the platforms for medical supplies.

A second, 'secret' metro was finished in 1967 which would enable government leaders to flee Moscow in the face of a nuclear attack. The 30km line runs from the former Central Communist Headquarters building on Staraya Square (near metro station Kitai-Gorod) to the government's underground bunker complex in the Ramenki region (near metro station Universitet) to the government's airport, Vnukovo-2. Closed to the public, the line is said to be still operational.

Over the next few years, new N5 metro carriages from Moscow's Mytishchi railway factory are being phased in. They are significantly quieter, smoother and safer with automatic fire quenchers and extensive use of fireproof material.

It is interesting to note that while women drive many of Moscow's buses and trams, until recently only men were train drivers. The reason for this is the belief that men better handle the stress of suicidal passengers who jump into the path of the oncoming metro trains.

Moscow Metro Museum (☎ 222 7309, Khamovnicheski val 35, metro: Sportivnaya) part of Sportivnaya metro station, contains maps, models and documents about the history of Moscow's public transport and metro from the early 19th century. Open 11:00-18:00 Mon, 9:00-16:00 Tue to Fri. Booking advisable.

❑ Star City

A half-day trip to Russia's Star City (Zvezdny Gorodok), 30km from Moscow, is a must if you are interested in outer space. This is the centre responsible for controlling all manned spacecraft and space station activities. This city of about 20,000 people is a smaller version of the US Johnson Space Center in Houston and is responsible for controlling all manned spacecraft and space station activities. It is also the main training ground for cosmonauts and contains Soyuz, Prognoz, and Salyut rocket simulators. Other interesting places to visit include the Star City Museum, the Space Station Simulators Hall where mock-ups of all MIR space station modules are kept, the Neutral Buoyancy Simulator, and the main centrifuge with 18-metre arm to imitate g-forces during take off. The area is also home to several military space research institutes so be discreet when taking photos. The town around Zvezdny Gorodok is called Kaliningrad (Калининград). The stations that service Kaliningrad are Podlipki (Подлипки) and Bolshevo (Болшево). Zvezdny Gorodok has a sister-city relationship with Nassau Bay, Texas. To organize a visit to the Gagarin Training Center, contact Anton Nemchimov at the Youth Space Academy at Baumann Technical Institute in Moscow (☎ (095) 263 6994, 🖹 (095) 262 6511) and mark it Box 4462 for Youth Space Center, email: ipjakk@redline.ru, http://ysc.sm.bmstu.ru/).

AROUND MOSCOW

A visit to the cathedrals and churches of **Sergiev Posad** (formerly Zagorsk, see p178), 75km from Moscow, is the most interesting day trip. Until 1988, it was the seat of the Russian Orthodox Church and today, it is still the site of one of the most important seminaries in the country.

About 80km from Moscow is **Abramtsevo Estate (Абрамцево)**, one of the most important centres of Russian culture in the second half of the 19th century. Today it's a museum and well worth a day trip. The estate was originally known as *Obromkovo Pustosh* when the current wooden house was built in the 1770s. Bought in 1843 by the Slavophile writer Sergei Aksakov it became the regular haunt of eminent Russian writers and actors including Gogol and Turgenev. In 1870, the estate was purchased by the railway tycoon and art connoisseur, Savva Mamontov. It was then turned into a colony for artists who shared a belief in the greatness of Russian native art and architecture but were concerned that it faced extinction by rapid industrialization – ironic considering the estate's patron.

From Moscow, take a suburban train from Yaroslavski station bound for either Sergiev Posad (Сергиев Посад) or Aleksandrov (Александров), both to the north of Abramtsevo. Get off at Abramtsevo. This trip takes 70 minutes. It's a 15-minute walk from the station.

PRACTICAL INFORMATION
Orientation
At the very centre of the city are the Kremlin, Red Square and St Basil's Cathedral. The most conveniently placed (and generally expensive) hotels are in this area. The metro system is efficient, however, so it's not vital or financially sensible to stay at a hotel right on Red Square.

There are no tourist offices. Most large hotels have a service bureau which offers a range of standard tours.

Arriving in Moscow
By air There are five airports: Sheremetyevo 2 for international flights and Sheremetyevo 1, Domodedovo, Vnukovo and Bykovo for domestic flights.

Sheremetyevo 2 International Airport is 35km from the city centre. Buses from just across the parking lot here will ferry you to or from the metro stations Rechnoi Vokzal (bus No 551) or Planernaya (bus No 517), departing every half hour (06.00-23.00).

Faster and a little more expensive are the minibuses (US$0.35) which run between Rechnoi Vokzal and Sheremetyevo 1 stopping at Sheremetyevo 2 on the way.

Taxis charge US$40-50 to the city centre; for your own safety take an official cab rather than just any car whose driver offers you a lift.

By train There are nine railway stations, the four you are most likely to use being: **Belorusski** (metro: Belorusskaya), for trains to and from Western Europe (note that the station is sometimes called Smolenski); **Leningradski** (metro: Komsomolskaya) for Helsinki and St Petersburg; and, next door to it, **Yaroslavlski** (metro: Komsomolskaya) for Trans-Siberian trains (except No 26 to Novosibirsk via Kazan, which leaves from Kazanski) and **Kazanski**, opposite Leningradski, for trains to Central Asia. **Kievski** (metro: Kievskaya) is for trains to Budapest; note that departures require a Ukrainian visa. See p176 for information on **leaving Moscow.**

Local transport
Metro The palatial metro system (see map pp158-9), a tourist attraction in itself, is the best way to travel around Moscow.

The metro uses magnetic cards which can be purchased in denominations of 1, 2, 5, 10 and 20 rides, with a small discount for 10 and 20 rides. One ride costs US$0.18 – currently five roubles. Buy the tickets inside the metro station building, near the entry barriers. You can travel any distance and change trains as often as you want without exiting. Trains arrive every minute in peak hours and you have to wait a maximum of five minutes even at midnight. All stations open from 06:00 to 01:00. During peak hours, from 07:00 to 10:00 and 15:00 to 19:00, trains are very crowded.

When you leave a station, a recorded message announces the name of the next station, warns you not to lean against the doors, and following the terrorist campaign during the Chechnya war, reminds you not to forget your luggage.

Bus and **tram** services are comprehensive but overcrowded. Tickets cost US$0.10. Virtually any Russian car will be a **taxi** but don't get in if there are already passengers. Self-drive **hire cars** (from hotel service bureaux) might be worth considering for some of the sights outside the city but are not recommended for city sightseeing.

There's a pleasant **river trip** (US$1.10) which leaves from the Kiev River Terminal (near Kievskaya metro station) and passes Lenin Hills and Gorky Park on its way towards the Kremlin. The 1½-hour trip ends at the Novospassky Bridge terminal which is about 2km past the Kremlin.

Services
Diplomatic representation Australia (☎ 956 6070) per Kropotkinski 13; **Austria** (☎ 201 7317) per Starokonyushenni 1; **Belarus** (embassy ☎ 924

7031, visa 924 7095, general 🕮 928 6403) ul Maroseka 17/6; **Belgium** (☎ 291 6027) ul Malaya Molchanovka 7; **Canada** (☎ 956 6666) per Starokonyushenni 23; **China** (☎ 143 1540, 143 1543 (visa)) ul Druzhby 6, (metro Universitet). Open weekdays 09:00-11.30. Service here is extremely slow. It is best to arrive at least by 07:00 in order to get a place (some will be here by 05:00). If there are more than 20 people in front of you in the queue you are unlikely to get in that day. Most travellers think it's worth paying the extra US$20 on-the-spot express fee so that they don't have to return and go through the queuing process again; **Czech Republic** (☎ 251 0540) ul Yuliusa Fuchika 12/14, (metro Mayakovskaya); **Denmark** (☎ 201 7860) per Prechistenski 9; **Estonia** (☎ 290 5013) mal Kislovskiy per 5, (metro Arbatskaya); **Finland** (☎ 246 4027) per Kropotkinski 15/17; **France** (☎ 236 0003) ul Bolshaya Yakimanka 45; **Georgia** (☎ 241 9767) ul Arbat 42; **Germany** (☎ 956 1080) ul Mosfilmovskaya 56; consulate (☎ 936 2401), pro Leninsky 94A; **Hungary** (☎ 146 8611) ul Mosfilmovskaya 62, (metro Kievskaya); **Ireland** (☎ 288 4101, 230 2763) per Grokholski 5; **Israel** (☎ 238 2732, 230 6700) ul Bolshaya Ordynka 56; **Italy** (☎ 241 1533) per Denezhny 5; **Japan** (☎ 291 8500) per Kalashny 12; **Kazakhstan** (☎ 208 9852, 927 1836) bul Chistoprudny 3A; **Kyrgyzstan** ul Bolshaya Ordynka 64, (metro Dobryninskaya). Visa available on the spot. US$70 and one photo. Open 14:00-16:00; **Latvia** (☎ 925 2707) ul Chaplygina 3, (metro Chistye Prudy); **Lithuania** (☎ 291 1501) per Borisoglebski 10, (metro Arbatskaya); **Moldova** (☎ 928 5405) ul Kuznetsky Most 18; **Mongolia** (☎ 290 6792) per Borisoglebski 11; consulate (☎ 244 7867), per Spasoskovski 7, (metro Smolenskaya). Open weekdays 10:00-12:00, 15:00-17:00; **Netherlands** (☎ 291 2999) per Kalashny 6; **New Zealand** (☎ 956 3579) ul Povarskaya 44; **Norway** (☎ 290 3872) ul Povarskaya 7; **Poland** (☎ 255 0017, 254 3621 (visa) ul Klimashkina 4, (metro Barrikadnaya); **Slovakia** (☎ 251 0540, 251 1070) ul Yuliusa Fuchika 12/14; **South Africa** (☎ 230 6869) per Bolshoi Strochenovski 22/25; **UK** (☎ 956 7400) nab Sofiyskaya 14; **Ukraine** (☎ 229 3422, 229 1079, 229 3442, 🕮 229 3542) ul Leontevskiy per 18, (metro Pushkinskaya); **USA** (☎ 230 0076) bul Novinski 19/23.

❏ **The Penthouse at Miami Beach**
Not quite what you might expect the British Embassy in Moscow to look like but, when you see it, the Russian description of the newly-opened building beside the Moskva River seems spot on. There are large areas of glass, balconies and a wavy roof that looks as if it would be more at home on a clubhouse by a beach. Rather than gilt portraits of dignitaries there's modern art on the walls of the entrance lobby, bright carpets and comfy sofas.

Everyone agrees that it's impressive, and the light airy architecture was chosen to give a more encouraging first impression of Britain than the high walls, drab waiting-rooms and long queues that one usually associates with embassies.

Designed by Ahrends Burton & Koralek it was built by Ove Arup. Despite all the openness, it was thought better to import all the materials for the central section so as to avoid the problems that befell the Americans when they contracted out the reconstruction of the US Embassy to the Russians – and then found the bricks bristling with listening devices!

Local publications The two best English-language newspapers are the daily *Moscow Times* (www.moscow-times.com) and *Moscow Tribune*. These can be picked up free from most hotels and Western supermarkets. The Moscow Times has a travel section at the weekend and a good 'what's on' guide on Friday.

Medical The **European Medical Centre** at per 2nd Tverskoi-Yamskoi 10 offers medical (☎ 956 7999), dental and emergency services; as does the **American Medical Centre** (☎ 956 3366) at the same address.

There is a **dental clinic** (☎ 488 8279) at the Pullman Iris Hotel, shosse Korovinskoye 10.

Pharmacies include **Farmakon** (☎ 292 0301) at ul 4th Tverskaya-Yamskaya 2/11; **Eczacibasi** (☎ 928 9189) at per Telegrafny 5/4 or at ul Maroseyka 2/15; and the **American Medical Centre** (above).

Money Many of Moscow's banks have **ATMs** so you can use your bank card to access your account or to get credit card advances. Commissions vary from bank to bank. You can check inside the bank before you use their ATM.

Hard currency used to be the number one requirement for travellers in Moscow but there's less demand for it now. Locals may approach you for dollars, however, offering slightly better rates than the banks.

Travellers' cheques are more widely accepted but are time-consuming to cash.

American Express, on ul Sadovo Kudrinskaya 21A (metro Maykovskaya) will change only their own cheques. There's an ATM for American Express cards. It's open weekdays 9:00-17:00, Saturday 9:00-13:00.

Russian visa extensions The availability of visa extensions is ever changing, as is the advice you will be given by anyone you ask. The travel agencies listed on p170 can be helpful for the latest information. The best advice is to plan so

you won't need an extension, or if you think you might, make enquiries well in advance. Don't assume that you will definitely get an extension.

UViR (as OViR, the state visa office, is known in Moscow) is at ul Pokrovka 42 (formerly ul Chernishevskogo) which is near metro Kurskaya and Krasnye Vorota. It is open Monday, Tuesday, Thursday and Friday from 10:00 to 13:00 and 15:00 to 18:00 (17:00 on Friday). It is also open on Saturday from 10:00 to 13:00 but only for emergencies. The visa extension situation changes from month to month but five-day extensions are currently available if you have a day to spend getting the right documents, including tickets to prove when you are leaving. Longer extensions or a second extension are not so straightforward and are often refused.

To get an extension, take your passport, ticket out of the country and visa to Room No 1 on the ground floor. You need to fill in a form and hand it in. You will then be given a chit to take to the nearby Sberegatelny Bank (Savings Bank) about 30m west of UViR on the other side of the street. The bank (ul Pokrovka 31) is open weekdays 8:30-14:00 and 15:00-19:30. At the bank, you must show your chit, fill in another form and pay the fee in roubles. You will get a receipt back and take this back to UViR and your visa will be stamped with an extension.

Because of the complications that sometimes occur, it is advisable to take a Russian speaker or a letter from the organization which gave you your visa invitation saying that they will provide for you.

As the extension starts from the date of your application, go to UViR only a few days before your visa expires. If you have difficulty, contact one of the specialist visa agencies listed in the classified section of the *Moscow Times* and *Moscow Tribune* newspapers.

Telecommunications The Central Post and Telegraph Office (ul Tverskaya) is the best place for phone calls, faxes and email. Rates are listed in English and they also have some English-speaking staff.

Pay **phones** use cards sold from most kiosks. You can get instructions on the phone by pressing the button with the flag on it.

There are numerous places to access the **Internet** in Moscow. Note that these places seem to close almost as fast as they open so it may be worth phoning first.

● **Internet café at RGGU** (☎ 250 6169, 🖵 cafe@rsuh.ru), Russian State University for the Humanities (RGGU), 1st floor, ul Chayanova 15 (metro: Novoslobodskaya). Charges US$1 per hour; open daily 10:00-20:00.

● **Image.ru** (☎ 737 3700 ext 146, 🖵 cafe@image.ru), ul Novoslobodskaya 16 (metro: Mendeleevskaya) is a small internet café at the computer centre serving beer and other drinks. They charge US$1.50 per hour; open daily 09:00-21:00.

● **IRPO Cybercafé** (☎ 152 7331, 🖵 www.irpo.ru/cafe), Cherniachovskogo 9

● **Nice** (☎ 253 3234, 🖵 webmaster @nice.ru), 2 claims to be open 24 hours and charges US$1-2 per hour.

● **Agmar Multimedia** (☎ 245 8496, 🖵 mdm@agmar.ru), Komsomolsky prospekt 28 (metro: Frunzenskaya) charge US$2 per hour and have 20 computers; open daily 10:00-22:00.

Tours Tours of the main sights can be arranged in any of the up-market hotels or at the Intourist office (☎ 292 1278), at ul Mokhovaya 13. Intourist offers: **Armoury and Kremlin** (four hours, US$25, not Thursday), **city sightseeing** (three hours, US$20, daily), **Kremlin grounds tour** (two hours, US$10, not Thursday), **Pushkin Fine Arts Museum** (three hours, US$15, not Monday), **Tretyakov Art Gallery** (four hours, US$20 not Mon), a **metro tour** and tours to many museums.

You could also try **Patriarshy Dom Tours** (☎ 795 0927 🖵 alanskaya@co.ru) who run English-language.

Cheaper tours are offered by guides who hang around at the Tomb of the Unknown Soldier; if they are registered they will have ID cards to prove it.

It's worth enquiring about the **KGB**

Tour that is occasionally offered by Intourist and Patriarshy Dom Tours. If this is running you'll be treated to demonstrations of miniature cameras, microdots, bugging techniques and more at the **Federal Counterintelligence Service (KGB) Museum**. You cannot visit this museum except on a tour.

If you're looking for a backpacker tour bus, Russia now has the **Beetroot Bus** (☎ 453 4368) which takes in the sights of Moscow, Kostroma, Rybinsk, Vologda, St Petersburg, Novgorod and Valdai – two weeks for US$720, one week for US$370, including accommodation, breakfast and guide.

Travel agencies

● **G & R International** (☎ 374 5731, 📄 374 7366, 🖵 grtour@online.ru 🖵 http://grint.tos.ru), Block 6, Office 38 & 39, Institute of Youth, ul Yunosti 5/1. To get there take the metro to Vykhino, then catch bus Nos 196 or 197 to the stop Institut Molodyozh.

● **Andrew's Consulting** (☎ 258 5198, 📄 258 5199, 🖵 info@andrews-consulting.ru, www.andrews-consulting.ru), 5th floor, ploshchad Novaya 10. It's very centrally-located: the nearest metro is Lubyanka.

● **Infinity Travel** (☎ 234 6555, 📄 234 6556, 🖵 info@infinity.ru, www.infinity.ru) Komsomolsky prospekt 13, metro: Park Kultury.

Where to stay

Accommodation in Moscow attracts a 24% surcharge and this is included in the prices below for a fairer comparison.

Budget accommodation *G&R Hostel Asia* (☎ 378 0001, 📄 378 2866, 🖵 grtour@online.ru) occupies the 13th to 15th floors of Hotel Asia, ul Zelenodolskaya 2/3, in the south-east of the city. Dorm beds cost US$16 in two- or three-bedded rooms with one bathroom shared between two rooms. There are also single/double rooms for US$20/25 (US$36/US$40 with attached bath). There are free transfers to any railway station if you stay

at the hotel, which is about 100m from metro Ryazansky Prospekt.

TGH Travellers Guest House Moscow (☎ 971 4059 or 280 8562, 🗎 280 7686, 🖳 tgh @star travel.ru) on the 10th floor at ul Bolshaya Pereyaslavskaya 50, is a magnet for the city's budget travellers; it's an excellent place to pick up the latest travel tips, although some people may find it just too much of a scene. A bed in a five-bed room costs US$18, with shared bathroom single rooms are US$36 and double rooms US$48. A double with bathroom attached is US$54. There's a café, bar, kitchen, laundry facilities and a travel agency. (If booking accommodation here for St Petersburg make sure you retain your receipt). Trolleybus No 14 from Leningradski Station takes you right past TGHM. To get there by metro: from Prospekt Mira metro station walk north for 10 minutes. Take the third turning on the right (pereulok Banniy) at the end of which you'll see four tall chimneys. This leads to a T-junction; turn left and the building is the first tall one on your right.

Prakash Guest House (☎/🗎 334 2598, 🖳 ralekc@misa.ru), is at ul Profsoyuznaya 83. It's about 10 minutes' walk from Belyaevo metro. Several blocks are numbered 83: you want the one with the children's park in front of it. Walk round the left side of it and Prakash is through the unlikely-looking door to the right of Simplex: there's no sign whatsoever. A single costs US$30 and a double US$40 and they sometimes have cheaper dormitory accommodation. The friendly Indian owner cooks Indian food as well and you can sometimes get meals here.

Hotel Molodezhnaya (☎ 977 3155, 🗎 956 1078) is a monster of a place built for the 1980 Olympics, at shosse Dmitrovskoe 27. They charge US$18 for a single or US$22 for a double but these prices may rise as the place is about to be renovated. It's a 10-minute walk from

Timiryazevskaya metro station and easily visible from the station itself.

At Kibalicha 7 is a small ***Hostel*** (☎ 975 3501 🗎 975 2175, 🖳 aztour@onl ine.ru) near the metro station VDNKh. Phone first to get directions and check that there is space. A bed in a small dormitory costs US$7 (without breakfast). Including breakfast, accommodation in a single/double costs US$13/22. The hostel also offers a range of reasonably priced tours.

Several old rather grim Soviet-era hotels offer reasonably cheap accommodation, although prices charged to foreigners seem to vary wildly from year to year. ***Hotel Tsentralnaya*** (☎ 229 8957), ul Tverskaya 10, currently charges US$20/$25 for a single/double with shared bath. The nearest metro is Tverskaya. ***Hotel Kievskaya*** (☎ 240 1234), ul Kievskaya 2, (metro Kievskaya) is similarly priced. You could also try the vast ***Hotel Sputnik*** (☎ 938 7106), pro Leninski 38, US$30/40 for a single/double with attached bath. Nearest metro is Leninski Prospekt. None of these places is anything to write home about.

Homestays are possible from US$30 per day. Check out the ads in the *Moscow Times* or contact ***HOFA***, see p18.

Mid-range accommodation
Prices in this category also seem to vary widely from month to month. Phone ahead to check.

The ***AST Gof Hotel*** (☎ 142 2117, 🗎 142 2384) is a comfortable three-star hotel on ul Bolshaya Filyovskaya, right opposite Fili park. Bagrationovskaya metro station is just around the corner. A single room with attached shower is US$72, a double costs US$104. Breakfast is included. There's a bank nearby and a large market opposite the metro station.

The huge ***Hotel Moskva*** (☎ 960 2020, 🗎 928 5938), on Okhotni Ryad 2, is well located and costs from US$60/75 for a single/double. Some rooms have views of the Kremlin and it's not a bad place. The closest metro station is Okhotny Ryad. The even bigger *Hotel Rossiya* (☎ 232 5000, 🖹 298 5544), at ul Varvarka 6 (formerly ul Razina), is the world's second biggest hotel and only a step from Red Square. It's now pretty shoddy and way overpriced at US$95/120 for singles/doubles. The closest metro station is Katai-Gorod. There have been numerous reports of petty pilfering from rooms.

Hotel Aeropolis (☎ 151 0442), formerly Aeroflot, on pro Leningradsky 37, has been refurbished recently and charges US$75 for a double. The hotel is between metros Dynamo and Aeroport and convenient if you're in transit between airports. The hotel boasts a 24-hour restaurant, bar, sauna and laundry.

Hotel Izmaulovo (☎ 166 4127, 🖹 166 7486), at Izmaulovski Sosshe 71 is a giant Soviet-era hotel divided into six blocks, with Intourist having an office in Block D. Rooms cost US$60/75 for a single/double. However, it's a nice place once you get inside. The closest metro station is Izmaulovski Park.

At US$60 per person in a double room, the *MNTK budget guesthouse* (☎ 483 0460, 🖹 485 5954), at bulvar Beskudnikovski 59A, is good value. It's right next door to the Hotel Pullman/Sofitel Iris so it's easy to find.

The grand *Hotel Ukraina* (☎ 243 3030, 🖹 243 3092), pro Kutuzovski 2/1 (metro Kievskaya) has been partly renovated and is a good three-star option. They charge US$120/160 for singles/doubles including breakfast. You may be able to get a better price for the unrenovated rooms.

The *Hotel Intourist* (☎ 956 8400, 🖹 956 8450), at ul Tverskaya 3/5, is a popular choice since it's very close to Red Square but it's starting to look very tired now. Prices start from US$105 for a single and US$120 for a double. The closest metro station is Okhoti Ryad. In 2000 there were rumours that the Hyatt group were about to purchase the hotel and knock it down but so far nothing's come of that.

Up-market hotels Note that the **24%**

taxes have been included in the prices given here. When you check hotel prices you will usually be quoted the price without tax. You should also check if breakfast is included: in the top places it will cost US$28.70 including tax. The best deals are at weekends when hotels popular with business clients during the week will drop their prices, sometimes by up to 40%: always ask.

The US hotel Marriott hotel group now has several hotels in Moscow; you can get detailed information about them from the hotel website at www.marriotthotels.com. Charges are per room not per person and the closer the hotel is to the centre, the higher the room charges. The *Marriott Tverskaya Hotel* (☎ 258 3000, 🖹 258 3099), at 34 1st Tverskaya-Yamskaya, charges from US$240 per room. *Marriott Grand Hotel* (☎ 935 8500, 🖹 935 8501), is at ul Tverskaya 26; rooms are US$310. *Marriott Moscow Royal* (☎ 937 1000, 🖹 937 1001), is well run and very centrally located at ul Petrovka 11/20; room charges are US$346.

Hotel Savoy (☎ 929 8590, 🖹 230 2186, 🖳 infa-hotel@mtu-net.ru) at ul Rozhdestvenka 3, is close to Red Square, and charges from US$186 for a single and US$236 for a double, (metro Lubyanka). You can often get good deals here.

Hotel Radisson Slavyanskaya (☎ 941 8020, 🖹 941 8000, 🖳 reserv@mosbusiness.ru) at nab Berezhkovsaya 2, charges from US$221 a room (single or double occupancy) and breakfast is included. There's a swimming-pool, shopping mall and cinema here, too. The closest metro station is Kievskaya.

Hotel Aerostar (☎ 213 9000, 🖹 213 9001, 🖳 aerostar1@co.ru, www.aerostar.ru), at 37 Leningradsky Prospekt (seven km from the centre of town towards the airport), has single rooms from US$199 and doubles from US$240. A buffet breakfast is included.

Also quite distant from the centre is *Hotel Pullman/Sofitel Iris* (☎ 203 0131) at 10 Korovinskoye shosse, with swimming-pool and single rooms from

US$260. It's convenient for the airport.

Hotel Metropol (☎ 927 6000, 🖹 927 6010, 🖳 metropol@metmos.ru), close to Red Square at Teatralni proezd 1, is as much a historic monument as a hotel for it was here that Rasputin is said to have dined, and Lenin to have made several speeches. Its beautiful Art Nouveau interior featured in the film *Dr Zhivago*. Rooms cost from US$260/297 for a single/double room to US$3100 for the presidential suite. It offers an exotic level of comfort but service can be patchy.

It's a short walk to the Kremlin and Red Square from the **Hotel National** (☎ 258 7000, 🖹 258 7100), a beautiful period hotel at 15/1 Mokhovaya that's very well run and now part of the international Le Meridien/Forte group. Prices start at US$334 for a single or US$446 for a double.

Now probably the best hotel in Moscow is the **Hotel Kempinski Baltschug** (☎ 230 6500, 🖹 230 6502, 🖳 reservation.mos@kempinski.com, hotel website: www.kempinski-moscow.com), ul Balchug 1. The service at this German-run hotel is impeccable and the location beside the river affords superb views across to the Kremlin. Facilities are all you would expect in a hotel of this class, with marble bath-tubs and satellite telephones. Rooms range from US$496 to US$2350. Buffet meals are priced as follows: breakfast US$28.70, brunch US$41, lunch US$35, dinner US$48 (all including tax). Former guests include Helmut Kohl, Tina Turner and Sting.

Where to eat

The restaurant scene in Moscow is changing very fast with new places opening daily. You can now eat very well in Moscow. The following recommendations were provided by local resident and epicurean, Neil McGowan:

Some Moscow restaurants put a cover charge on your bill as well as a service charge. These extras can mount up to US$10 or more. As they won't be printed on the menu, ask before you order if there will be any extra charges on top of the food cost. The way to make your budget go further in Moscow is to eat your main meal at lunchtime. Almost all restaurants offer a 'business-lunch' deal Mon-Fri between US$3-10, offering savings of up to 50% off the same dishes ordered à la carte.

If you aren't sure what you want to eat and want to browse in lots of different places to get a feel for them, **Arbat** is the best street to check out. It's a long thoroughfare and the most interesting prospects are at the Smolenskaya Metro end, the so-called Vostochny Kvartal (oriental quarter). There's a mixture of Turkish, Greek, Georgian, Armenian cafés – ownership seems to change quite frequently, so it's best to go and look yourself. In this area there's also *Pancho Villa's* Mexican restaurant at Arbat 44 (☎ 241 9853) which serves fantastic breakfasts in addition to their lunchtime/evening menu, and *Rioni* (budget Georgian) at the mid-point of the street. At the far end (Arbatskaya plosh-chad) of both the street and the price scale is the *Praga Restaurant*, recognized as one of Moscow's élite dining establishments for the ultra-rich.

● **Russian** There are branches of *Yolki-Palki* all over Moscow; the largest being adjacent to Tverskaya metro. They're rustic-style theme restaurants with a buffet of tasty salads for US$8 and a wide selection of main courses and drinks. The food is always reliable if a bit mass produced. Count on US$10-15 per person. The name roughly translates as "bleedin' 'ell!"– a favourite cuss of Russian villagers.

Mesto Vstrechi (☎ 229 2373) 9/8 Maly Gnezdnikovsky per, is on the corner with Tverskaya, (metro: Pushkinskaya). Basement pub-style restaurant popular with young professionals. Business lunch for US$3 includes a beer! Mainly Russian food.

Taras Bulva Korchma (☎ 200 6082) Ul Petrovka 30/7 (metro: Chekhovskaya) offers hearty Ukrainian dishes at wallet-friendly prices. Interior is a bit cutesy-folky but service is good. Expect to spend around US$8-12 for a meal.

Ryby Glaz (☎ 261 1148) Ul Novoryazanskaya (metro: Komsomolskaya) is an ideal summer-time place, a pub in a park, with Russian home-cooking favourites and range of speciality beers, including their own brew. Business lunch is US$3 with a beer. In the evening an average meal will cost US$6-10 per person.

For a celebratory dinner try *Red Square* (☎ 925 3600) at Krasnaya ploshchad 1 (metro: Okhotny Ryad). Super traditional Russian cuisine in the smartest address in Moscow. A meal will cost around US$30 per person.

For a true gourmet experience *Oblomov* (☎ 255 9290) Ul 1905 goda, Dom 2 (metro: Ul 1905) is highly recommended. There's a different menu for each day of the month. The US$56 per person price may seem high but it includes everything on your bill in this palatial 19th century restaurant.

● **Budget and fast food** Moscow has seen a fast-food explosion in the past few years and you can get hot-dogs, burgers, shwarma-kebab, pancakes and snacks of all kinds at stands gathered around most metro stations, for very low prices. *Rostiks* serve reliable chicken and sandwiches.

In summer, the latest trend is 'summer cafés' – which spring up on any spare patch of ground, serving beer, pizza and snacks at rock-bottom prices.

For ultra-convenient central fast food the *Food Court* on the bottom level of Manzhnaya Shopping Centre (adjacent to Red Square, entrance opposite the Hotel Moskva or directly from Metro Okhotny Ryad Stn) has everything you want. Around 10 concessions including Russian, Italian, Japanese, Korean and Pizza, low prices and clean loos too. *Russkoe Bistro* has branches all over Moscow, notably on ul Petrovka behind the department store, where you can sit outside in summer. Super-cheap Russian

café food – pies, pastries, soups etc. Branches on major railway stations, too. Main disadvantage: none of their outlets has lavatories.

McDonald's – branches all over Moscow, most centrally at the junction of Gazetny perulok and Tverskaya. There are other branches at ul Arbat 50 near metro Smolenskaya, prospekt Mira close to metro Prospekt Mira, Sokolniki near metro Sokolniki, and pl Pushkina 29 near metro Pushkinskaya.

● **Georgian** *Guriya* (☎ 246 0378) Komsomol'sky prospekt 7/3 (metro: Park Kultury). The favourite ethnic food in Russia is Georgian and Guriya offers some of the best. Delicious mediterranean-style food at low prices attract the crowds, so go early. Khachapuri (cheesebreads) are a favourite. A meal will cost about US$12 per person.

Dioscuria (☎ 290 6908) is another great Georgian place, slightly more upscale than Guriya, and featuring some Abkhaz dishes, too (cheesebreads here are egg-topped). There's a good range of Georgian wines: try Saperavi or Kindzmarauli (reds) or Tsinandali (white). Expect to pay around US$15 per person. It's at Merzlyakovsky pereulok 2 and the entrance is through the arch of the post office on ul Novy Arbat, opposite Praga Restaurant.

● **International** *Moosehead* (☎ 230 7333) is at Bolshaya Polyanka 54 (metro: Dobryninskaya). Tex-Mex doesn't get cheaper than this in Moscow. There's a good range of beers, too. Budget around US$9-12 per person.

For your US diner favourites at moderate prices visit *American Bar & Grill* (☎ 251 7999) 1-ya Tverskaya Yamskaya, (metro: Mayakovskaya). Attentive US-style service, with the chance to avoid American beer by ordering Russian instead. Attracts lots of young Americans in Moscow and costs around US$12-15 for a meal.

The Moscow area code is ☎ 095. From outside Russia dial +7-095.

B B King (☎ 299 8206) Sadovaya-Samotyochnaya ul 4/2 (metro: Tsvetnoy Boulevard). Authentic cajun cooking comes to Moscow! Jambalaya and gumbo jockey for positions on a packed menu – great business lunch deals too. Around US$20 per person.

Tibet Kitchen (☎ 923 2422) Kamergersky per 5/6 (M Okhotny Ryad) offers a very wide choice of near authentic Tibetan and Nepalese food in a calm and cosy atmosphere. There are lots of vegetarian choices. Around US$20 per person. Lousy coffee but you can finish-up at **Zen Coffee**, two doors down the street, where caffeine doesn't come better. At the same address is **Café des Artistes** (☎ 292 0673) Kamergerksy per 5/6. Bistro European menu with a French accent, higher prices in the evening but business lunch at US$12 is a bargain. This is a major hangout for media types.

Drago (☎ 923 0492) Myasnitskaya 13 (metro: Chistie Prudi) serves up Serbian food in hearty-sized portions. The US$6 business lunch will have you letting your belt out and includes a drink, too.

Soleil Express (☎ 725 6474) Sadovaya-Samotechnaya 24/27 (metro: Tsvetnoy Boulevard) is a Parisian-style brasserie with light meals, sandwiches, baguettes and excellent coffee.

Juggernaut (☎ 928 3580) Kuznetsky Most 11 (metro: Kuznetsky Most) is a vegetarian Indian restaurant in the hypertrendy Kuznetsky Most area. It's hard to spend more than US$6 on a meal here.

Mei Amici (☎ 251 1116) 1-ya Tverskaya Yamskaya 22 (metro: Mayakovskaya). Italian restaurant offering reasonably-priced Italian classic cuisine, and great-value pizzas; this is one of the few places in Moscow for Italian-style pizza. About US$12 per person.

Nightlife

Even more than St Petersburg, Moscow really is where it's at in Russia for nightlife. It's all a very far cry from those evenings back in the communist era when the choice was either the ballet or the circus – and so to bed. Now you can have as wild a time as in any Western city. Anything goes – Lenin must be spinning in his mausoleum.

For **bars**, ex-pats and visitors seem to favour the **American Bar & Grill** (☎ 251 7999) 1-ya Tverskaya Yamskaya, (metro: Mayakovskaya), and **Moosehead** (☎ 230 7333), at Bolshaya Polyanka 54 (metro: Dobry-ninskaya), a popular Canadian bar and restaurant with a good range of beers. Both these places do good meals (see 'Where to eat', above). **Rosie o'Grady's** ul Znamenka 9 (metro: Borovitskaya) is, as you would expect, an Irish theme pub and there's no better place for a pint of Guinness. **B B King** (☎ 299 8206) Sadovaya-Samot-yochnaya ul 4/2 (metro: Tsvetnoy Boulevard) often has live jazz and blues.

For the **club scene** see the Entertainment section of the *Moscow Times*. Get your Russian friends to ring the club before you go so that you can get an idea of their clientele. Don't be put off by the Kalashnikov toting bouncers.

The season at the fabulous **Bolshoi Theatre** (☎ 292 0050), ul Theatralni, runs from October to June and there are alternating programmes of ballet and opera. Many of the world's greatest dancers are Russian or were trained here and, despite deflections to other companies the Bolshoi is still brilliant; nevertheless ensure that it is the Bolshoi Ballet that you will be seeing and not a company visiting while they are on tour. To watch classical ballet here is an experience made more magical by the ambience of the 145-year-old theatre. Recent renovations should be completed by now but check that the evening's performance will actually be in the theatre and not in the temporary venue nearby. Tickets are easy to come by for US$50 (or more for star performances): try the service bureau in your hotel. There's a ticket office at the theatre but all tickets are usually bought up in advance by touts. If you want a cheap ticket, stand around outside the theatre before the performance and they'll find you. They'll access your gullibility and quote prices of US$10-40. Barter and remember that the later you leave it before the performance the more anxious they'll be to get rid of their tickets. Check the date and time of the performance on the ticket before you pay.

For ballet or opera on a budget, equally good (some would say better) performances can be seen at two other auditoria: the **Kremlin Palace of Congresses** and the **Stanislavsky Musical Theatre**. The Kremlin Palace of Congresses is inside the Kremlin and in the evening you can enter the Kremlin grounds only if you're already holding a ticket. Tickets are available at any city theatre-kiosk, such as the one at Teatralnaya metro station. Tickets for both cost US$2-6 and like the Bolshoi they can sometimes be closed in summer. This does seem to be changing, though, with out-of-town touring companies playing at this time.

There are two permanent circuses in Moscow. The **New Circus** (metro: Universitet) is more spectacular and the **Old Circus** (metro: Tsvetnoye Blvd) has a more traditional show. In both cases the human performers are generally excellent but Western visitors tend to be somewhat dismayed by the animal acts. Tickets are readily available and cost US$2-5.

What to buy
Most foreigners end up buying their matrioshkas, ceramic boxes and furry hats from street sellers, although you'll need to check quality first and then bargain hard.

The best market is at **Ismailovsky Park** at a weekend: you'll find everything from stolen icons to Stalin pictures. It's easy to get to as you go to metro Ismailovsky Park and then just need to follow the crowds to the market, which is about a five-minute walk away. Some of the market is just clothing and shoes but if you head towards the recently built old-style wooden buildings, you'll find the part of the market aimed at tourists.

The main areas for general shopping in Moscow are Novy Arbat and ul Tverskaya.

Moving on
By air For tickets try the travel agents on p170 as well as the airlines direct.

Aeroflot has numerous branches around the city – ul Petrovka 20 (☎ 150 3883) and ul Korovy Val 7 (☎ 156 8019) among them. **Transaero** (☎ 241 4800, 241 7676, 292 7526), is at Hotel Moskva, ul Okhotny Ryad 2.

The other main airlines are **Air China** (☎ 292 3387), ul Kuznetsky Most 1/8; **Air France** (☎ 234 3894), ul Korovy Val 7; **Alitalia** (☎ 923 9840), ul Pushechnaya 7; **ANA**-All Nippon Airways (☎ 253 1546) nab Krasnopresnenskaya 12, office 1405; **British Airways** (☎ 258 2492), Krasnopresnenskaya 12, office 1905; **Delta Airlines** (258 1168), Krasnopresnenskaya 12, office 1102a; **Finnair** (☎ 292 8788), ul Kuznetski Most 3; **JAL** (☎ 921 6448), ul Kuznetski Most 3; **KLM** (☎ 258 3600, 956 1666), ul Usacheva 33; **LOT** (☎ 238 0003), ul Korovy Val 7, office 5; **Lufthansa** (☎ 737 6400), pro Olympiyski 18/1; **MIAT**-Mongolian Airlines (☎ 241 0754), per Spasopeskovsky 7/1; **SAS** (☎ 925 4747), ul Kuznetski Most 3; and **Swissair** (☎ 258 1888), Krasnopresnenskaya 12, office 2005.

From Moscow's four local airports, there are frequent flights to St Petersburg, and many cities in Siberia including Yekaterinburg, Irkutsk, Khaba-rovsk, Novosibirsk, Ulan Ude and Vladivostok: all daily. Fares have risen considerably in the last six months. Sample prices: St Petersburg (US$60-80), Irkutsk (US$180-220) and Vladivostok (US$280-340).

By rail Trains from Siberia arrive either at Yaroslavski or Kazanski stations (both at pl Komsomolskaya). For Moscow and St Petersburg trains, see p149.

● **Getting railway tickets and information** You can buy tickets at railway stations, the Transport Agency, Central Railway Booking Agency and resellers (who will add their own mark-up). Railway information can be obtained on ☎ 266 9000-9. It's probably easiest and certainly cheapest to buy your ticket from the railway station. Railway stations sell tickets only for trains that depart from their station. In some there may still be an Intourist window to help foreigners.

The Central Railway Booking Agency has four offices around the city, all open 08:00-13:00 and 14:00- 19:00:

● **Tsentralnoe Zheleznodorozhnoe Agentstvo** (Central Railway Booking Agency), beside the Yaroslavski station (☎ 266 0004, metro Komsomolskaya) is the easiest place to buy your own Trans-Siberian ticket. The only sign indicating which windows to queue up in front of is in Russian: 'Иностранцы'. It may be also worth trying window 2 for tickets to destinations within the ex-USSR and windows 5 to 8 for other destinations. You can also try the **Transport Agency** (*Transagentsevo*), also beside Yaroslavski station.

● **Tsentralnoe Zheleznodorozhnoe Agentstvo** ul Maly Kharitonevsky 6/11 (formerly ul Griboedova) (☎ 262 9605, 262

7935, 262 0604). The closest metros are Chistye Prudy and Krasnaya Vorota. For tickets to ex-USSR destinations, go to windows 1 to 3 in Hall 1 of Building (Korpus) 1. Tickets will be sold for departures on the following day up to 10 days. For tickets to other countries, go to windows 7 and 8 on the ground floor of Building 2. Tickets will be sold for departures on the following day up to 30 days ahead.

● **Tsentralnoe Zheleznodorozhnoe Agentstvo** pro Leningradskaya 1, (☎ 262 3342). The closest metro is Belorusskaya. To get to it from the Belorussia Station, cross the railway bridge and it's on the corner of pro Leningradskaya and ul Nizhnyaya. Enter from the lane on the west side of pro Leningradskaya. From windows 9 and 10 tickets are sold for departures on the following day up to 30 days.

● **Tsentralnoe Zheleznodorozhnoe Agentstvo** ul Mozhayski val 4/6, (☎ 240 0505). The closest metro is Kievskaya which is about 1km away.

❏ **Luggage lockers (Автоматические Камеры Хранения)**

It's worth explaining how to use the combination-lock luggage lockers, called *avtomaticheskie kamery khranenia*, at stations because they're not as straightforward as they look. To store luggage, get a token from the supervisor, and choose a locker within view of the supervisor. On the inside of the door is a set of four combination locks. Select a combination of three numbers and one Cyrillic character. Write the combination and the locker number down immediately. Put in the token and close the door and twirl around the knobs on the outside of the locker. To get your luggage out, set the combination on the knobs and wait two seconds until you hear the electric lock click back. Some lockers require you to put in a second token before the electric lock clicks back. If there is a problem call the supervisor. (Bribes are not necessary). They can open any locker but first you must describe what your luggage looks like. The supervisor can open up to three lockers at once for you. If you want more opened because you have forgotten which locker you put your luggage in, the supervisor has to call a militia officer. After finding your things, you pay a small fine, fill in a form and show the supervisor your passport. Don't forget to write down the code – never rely on your memory as the opening process can take an hour and you may miss your train. You can only leave luggage in the lockers until 23:59 of the next day before it is cleared. The coin-operated lockers function 24 hours a day but are closed several times a day for breaks of up to 30 minutes.

Sergiev Posad
Сергиев Посад

Sergiev-Posad, known as **Zagorsk** in the communist period, is the most popular tourist attraction in the Golden Ring (see p310) and a must for even those who are 'all churched out'. The city contains Russia's religious capital: the Exalted Trinity Monastery of St Sergius (Troitse-Sergiyeva Lavra). Entering the white-walled, 600-year-old monastery is like taking a step back into mediaeval Russia with long-bearded monks in traditional black robes and tall *klobuki* hats, and continuous chanting emanating from lamp-lit, incense-filled churches.

HISTORY

The monastery was founded in 1340 by Sergius of Radonezh (1321-1391) who became the patron saint of Russia. The power of Sergius's monastery grew quickly because he was closely allied to Moscow's princes and actively worked for the unification of Russian lands by building a ring of 23 similar monastery-fortresses around Moscow. The friendship between Moscow's ruler, Grand Prince Dmitry Donskoi, and Sergius was so strong that when Dmitry asked for the church's blessing in 1380 before he left to fight the Tatar-Mongols at Kulikovo, Sergius himself delivered the service. While the resultant victory had already indicated to Sergius's followers that he had God's ear, 17 years after his death it became obvious that Sergius also had divine protection. The 'proof' of this appeared in 1408 when the Tatar-Mongols levelled the monastery and the only thing that survived unscathed was Sergius's corpse.

Between 1540 and 1550, the monastery was ringed with a massive stone wall and 12 defensive towers. Never again was the complex to fall, not even after an 18-month siege by 20,000 Poles against 1500 defenders in 1608. Both Ivan the Terrible and Peter the Great hid here after fleeing plotting princes in Moscow. Besides its military function, the monastery was a great centre of learning. It became famous for its *sergievski* style, hand-copied books adorned with gold and vermilion letters. Several of these books are on display in the monastery's museum. It is also believed that Russia's first printer, Ivan Fedorov, studied here.

During the 18th century the monastery's spiritual power grew considerably. In 1744, it was elevated to a *lavra* monastery which meant that it was a 'most exalted monastery'. At the time, there were only four lavra monasteries in Russia with the other three being the Kievo-Pechorskaya in Kiev, the Aleksandro-Nevskaya in St Petersburg and Pochayevsko-Uspenskaya in Volyn. In 1749 a Theological College was opened at Sergiev-Posad and in 1814 an Ecclesiastical Academy was created.

Two years after the communists came to power, the monastery was closed down and it was reopened only in 1946 after Stalin fulfilled his side of a pact with the Orthodox Church for their support during WWII. The monastery was the seat of the Patriarch of Russia until 1988 when this was moved to Danilovsky Monastery in Moscow.

WHAT TO SEE

Exalted Trinity Monastery of St Sergius
The monastery is spread over six hectares and ringed by a white-washed, 1km long wall which is up to 15m thick. Of the 13 defensive towers, note the Duck Tower: the metal duck on its spire was put there for the young Peter the Great to use for archery practice.

Many of the churches are open for services but you may be turned away if you are wearing shorts or have bare shoulders. Photography is forbidden inside the monastery unless you pay a fee at the entrance. You should never take photos with a flash, as this damages the icons, nor have your photo taken in front of an icon as this is considered disrespectful.

The monastery grounds are open 10:00-18:00 daily and entry is free. For the monastery's three museums (open 10:00-17:00, closed Mondays, and the last Friday of each month) you have to buy tickets from the kiosk at the north end of the Art Museum. There are separate tickets (US$2-5) for each museum, and the Art Museum has specific entry times on the tickets.

About 200m from the monastery on the road to Moscow are two churches. Both the **Church of St Pareskeva Pyatnitsa** and the **Church of the Presentation of the Mother of God** were built in 1547 which was the year Ivan the Terrible was crowned Tsar. On the opposite side of the road is the attractive **Pyatnitsa Well Chapel**. One of the most popular photographs of Sergiev Posad is taken from just across the river with Pyatnitsa Well Chapel in the foreground and the Church of the Presentation of the Mother of God and the monastery in the background. You enter the monastery via the Red Gate which leads to the Holy Gates, above which is the **Church of St John the Baptist**. The church was paid for by the wealthy Stroganov family in 1693.

The sky-blue and gold-starred, five cupola **Assumption Cathedral** is the heart of the monastery. It was consecrated in 1585 in honour of Ivan the Terrible's victory over the Mongols near Astrakhan and Kazan and was the church in which many of the Tsars were baptized. Outside the western door is the **tomb of Tsar Boris Godunov**, his wife and two of their children.

The **Chapel over the Well** was built over a sacred spring which is claimed to have appeared during the Polish siege of 1608. Pilgrims fill up drinking bottles with holy water here. The **Bell-tower** is the monastery's

HOTELS AND RESTAURANTS
  1 Hotel Druzhba (Zagorsk) Гостиница Дружба/Загорск
  2 Café Zagorsk Кафе Загорск
  6 McDonald's Макдоналадс
 33 Café Minutka Кафе Минутка
 34 Restaurant Russky Dvorik
     Ресторан Русский Дворик
 39 Restaurant Zolotoe Koltso
     Ресторан Золотое Колцо

TRINITY CATHEDRAL

OTHER
  3 Market Рынок
  4 Church
  5 Stables Конный Двор
  7 Inkom Bank Инком Банк
  8 Lenin Bust
  9 Duck Tower Уточья Башня
 10 Pilgrim Gate Tower Каличья Воротная Башня
 11 Bathhouse Баня
 12 Tsar's Palace Царские Дворец
 13 History Museum in Hospital & Church of Saints Zosima & Savvaty
     Исторический Музей (Больничные палаты) и Церковь Зосимы и Савватия
 14 Smolensk Church Смоленская Церковь
 15 Bell-tower Колокольня
 16 Assumption/Dormition Cathedral Успенский Собор
 17 Holy Gates & John the Baptist Gate Church
     Святые Ворота и Надвратная Церковь Иоанна Предтечи
 18 Museum Ticket Kiosk Касса
 19 Art Museum in former Treasurer's Wing
     Художественный Музей (Казначейский Корпус)
 20 Chapel above the Well Надкладезная Часовня
 21 Old Art Museum in the Vestry
     Музей Древнерусского Прикладного Искусства (Ризница)
 22 Trinity Cathedral Троицкий Собор
 23 Descent of the Holy Spirit Church Духовская Церковь
 24 St Micah's Church Михеевская Церковь
 25 Refectory & St Sergius's Church
     Трапезная Палата и Церковь Святого Сергия
 26 Metropolitan's Chambers Митрополичьи Палаты
 27 Former Hospital of the Trinity Monastery of St Sergei
     Больница-Богадельня Троице-Сергиевой Лавры
 28 Water Gate/Tower Водяные Ворота/Башня
 29 St Paraskeva Pyatnitsa Church Пятницкая Церковь
 30 Presentation of the Mother of God Church Введенская Церковь
 31 Krasnogorskaya Chapel Красногорская Часовня
 32 Sber Bank Сбер Банк
 35 Chapel over St Paraskeva Pyatnitsa's Well Часовня Пятницкого Колодца
 36 War Memorial Война памятник
 37 Elijah the Prophet's Church Ильинская Церковь
 38 Toy Museum Музей Игрушки
 40 Ascension Church Вознесенская Церковь
 41 Bus Station Автовокзал 42 Railway Station Железнодорожний Вокзал
 43 Dormition Church Успенская Церковь

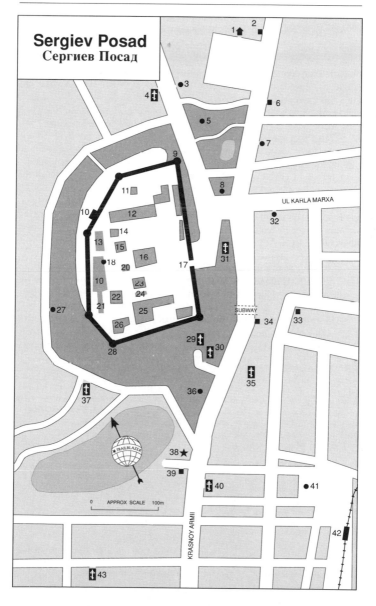

Sergiev Posad
Сергиев Посад

tallest building, 93m high. Construction began in 1740 and took 30 years.

The **Refectory and Church of St Sergius** was built from 1686 to 1693 and served as a dining hall for pilgrims. You can't miss this red, blue, green and yellow chequered building with its carved columns. Outside the refectory is the squat **Church of St Sergius** crowned with a single golden dome. The **Church of the Descent of the Holy Spirit** contains the grave of the first Bishop of Russian Alaska.

Trinity Cathedral is the most sacred place in the monastery as it is on the site of the original wooden church built by St Sergius. It contains St Sergius's corpse in a dull silver sarcophagus donated by Ivan the Terrible. Built in 1422 in honour of St Sergius's canonization, the cathedral contains 42 icons by Andrei Rublev, Russia's most famous painter.

Church of Our Lady of Smolensk was built to house the icon of the same name in 1745. Decorated in baroque style, it resembles a rotunda .

The **Old Art Museum** contains one of Russia's richest collections of religious art as well as gifts presented to the monastery. As the gifts are displayed in the order they were given, it is interesting to see how tastes changed over the centuries. The **Art Museum** contains Russian handicrafts from the 14th century to the present. The **History Museum** is in the former hospital. Nearby, you can climb **Pilgrim Gate Tower** and walk along the wall.

The **Tsar's Palace** was built at the end of the 17th century to be the residence of the visiting Tsar Alexei and his entourage of over 500 people. It now houses a Theological College and Ecclesiastical Academy.

The large, peach and white **Dormition Church** is interesting. It's taken years to fully restore it. Inside you can see photos of the state it was in before work started and also photos taken during the restoration process.

PRACTICAL INFORMATION

Sergiev-Posad has always been associated with carved wooden toys as St Sergius used to give them to children. Locally produced *matryaskhas* are distinctive as they are painted with gouache and covered with varnish. Before you buy one, visit the **Toy Museum** so that you see the variety available.

Where to stay

Hotel Druzhba, also still called Hotel Zagorsk, is on pl Sovetskaya. It's a typical huge concrete structure with single rooms costing US$28 and doubles at US$45 with attached bathroom and a decent breakfast included. The rooms are large but spartan and getting shabby. There's a tourist office, a money changer (offering bad rates) and a souvenir shop.

Where to eat

Restaurant Russky Dvorik is opposite the Monastery and usually full of tourists. The *Restaurant Zolotoe Koltso* (also known as the Restaurant Golden Ring) is popular with tour groups and has a café downstairs.

The restaurant at the *Hotel Druzhba* is good but the music and floor show is completely over the top, as usual. *Café Zagorsk* round the side of the Hotel Druzhba is a good place for a quiet drink and a snack.

There is a branch of *McDonald's* on ul Krasnoy Armii.

Getting there

About two trains an hour run out here from Moscow's Yaraslavl station. It's US$0.45 for the 95 minute trip.

Rostov-Yaroslavski
Ростов-Ярославский

Also known as **Rostov-Veliki**, this is one of the most attractive Golden Ring cities to visit. Packed with interesting places it's a small city in a beautiful location beside scenic Lake Nero. Rostov-Yaroslavski has a wonderfully sleepy atmosphere; and the added attraction of being able to stay right in the kremlin itself makes it well worth a visit.

Founded in 862, Rostov-Yaroslavski played a major role in the formation of Russia and at one time was as big as the mighty capitals of Kiev and Novgorod. Yuri Dolgoruky, who founded Moscow in 1147, gave Rostov the honourable and rare title of *veliki,* meaning great. Rostov-Veliki soon became an independent principality.

Rebuilt after the Tatar-Mongol sacking, Rostov-Veliki continued to have political importance for two more centuries until the local prince sold the remainder of his hereditary domain to Moscow's Grand Prince Ivan III in 1474. The city remained an important ecclesiastical centre as it was the religious capital of northern Russia and home to the senior religious leader called the Metropolitan. In the 17th century, however, the Metropolitan was moved to the larger city of Yaroslavl. No longer called Rostov the Great, the city became known as Rostov-Yaroslavski, rapidly became a backwater and has remained one ever since.

Much of Russia's lousy coffee originates here as Rostov-Yaroslavski boasts a factory for roasting chicory roots which are often substituted for or added to coffee beans.

WHAT TO SEE

CATHEDRAL OF THE ASSUMPTION

Cathedral of the Assumption

The cathedral, just north of the kremlin, is a 16th century, 60m high, five-domed building with white stone friezes decorating the outside. The cathedral contains the tomb of the canonized Bishop Leontius who was martyred by Rostov's pagans in 1071 during his Christianity drive. The Metropolitan Ion is also buried here. The **bell-tower** contains superb examples of 17th-century Russian bells, the largest weighing 32 tons. There are 13 bells in all and they can be heard up to twenty kilometres away. They're rung at 13:00 on Saturday and Sunday.

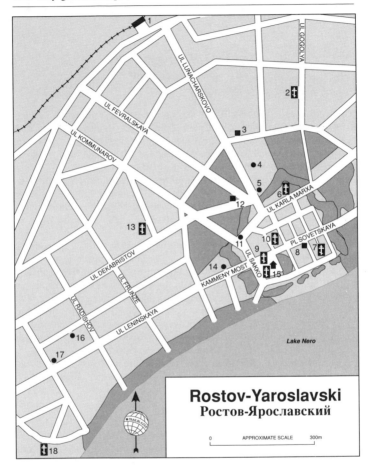

The Rostov Kremlin

The white-walled Rostov Kremlin is one of the most photogenic in the country. It is spread over two hectares, has six churches and is ringed by 11 towers. The kremlin was founded in 1162 by Prince Andrei Bogolybusky, son of Yuri Dolgoruky; all traces of the original buildings disappeared in the 17th century when the kremlin was rebuilt.

Despite its mighty 12m high and 2m thick walls and towers, this reconstructed kremlin is actually an imitation fortress. All the elements of real fortifications are missing. The ambitious 17th-century Metropolitan,

Ion Sisoyevich, wanted a residence to reflect his importance. After the 17th century when the Metropolitan was moved to nearby Yaroslavl, the kremlin became derelict. Today most of the buildings have been restored to their 16th- and 17th-century condition, though work still continues.

The central part of the kremlin contains five churches. The religious part of each church occupies only the 2nd floor as the ground floor was left for animal husbandry, storage and accommodation.

The kremlin grounds are always open as the gate on the eastern wall is never locked. The kremlin's **main entrance** is on its western side through the **St John the Divine Gateway Church** built in 1683, which has a richly decorated façade. The ticket office is in this building and charges US$1.20 for entrance to everywhere in the kremlin. The museums are normally open 10:00-17:00 and are staffed by the usual plethora of babushkas, each insisting on adding another tear to your disintegrating ticket.

The entrance to the kremlin's northern part from the central part is through the **Resurrection of Christ Gate Church** built in 1670. This church has a stone iconostasis instead of the traditional wooden one.

The **Transfiguration of the Saviour above the Cellars Church** is one of the gems of the kremlin as it was the private church of the Metropolitan. It is quite austere from the outside but its interior is lavish. This church is the tallest in the kremlin and has a single dome. The **White Chamber** next door was designed as a sumptuous dining hall; it now houses a museum for local Rostov crafts.

The **Church of the Virgin Hodegetria** was erected 20 years after the death of Metropolitan Ion and has a Moscow baroque interior. It now contains an exhibition of church vestments.

❏ **Finift**
Rostov-Yaroslavski's most famous handicraft is *finift* multi-coloured enamel work. This craft originated in Byzantium: the name derives from the Greek *fingitis* meaning colourful and shiny. Finift was used to decorate icons, sacred utensils and bible covers, as well as in portraits of people. The enamel's greatest advantages are that it cannot be damaged by water and does not fade with time.

The process of making the enamel is extremely complex and involves oxidizing various metals to produce different colours. Iron produces yellow, orange-red and brown, copper produces green and blue, tin produces a non-transparent white, and gold with tin produces a cold ruby red.

Finift has been produced here since the 12th century and the Rostov Finift Factory has been operating since the 18th century. While there are no regular tours of the Rostov Finift Factory, you can organize one through Intourist or by talking to the factory's director (☎ 352 29).

The building housing the **Prince's Chambers** is the oldest here, dating from the the 16th century. It's claustrophobic with small dark passages, narrow doors and slit windows filled with slivers of mica. This is a good place to get an impression of the daily life of 16th-century Russian nobility.

The **Metropolitan's House** is now a museum and has a large collection of stone carvings, wooden sculptures, and 14th and 15th-century doors from local churches. The **Red Chamber**, built as a residence for visiting tsars and their large retinue, is now the hostel of the International Youth Tourism Centre.

Other places of interest
In front of the eastern entrance of the kremlin is the **Saviour on the Market Place Church**. It was built in the late 1600s and is now a library. The name comes from the rows of shops and stalls around the church that have stood there for centuries.

Beside the church is the Arcade built in the 1830s and on the opposite side of the street is the Traders' Row. In 2000 there was extensive restoration work going on in this area and it will probably continue for some time.

The neoclassical **St Nicholas in the Field Church** on ul Gogola was built in 1813 and has recently been well restored. It has a golden iconostasis with finift enamel decorations and icons from the 15th to 19th centuries. This was one of two main churches in Rostov that conducted services during the communist era (the other was the **Church of the Tolg Virgin**).

The single-domed **Church of St Isidore the Blessed**, ul Karla Marxa, dates from the 16th century and was originally called Ascension Church. It is hidden partly by the old Kremlin walls and seems out of use.

In front of the kremlin's main gate on the western side, ul Kamenny Most, are the **Metropolitan's Horse Stables**. It was planned to demolish this nondescript two-storey building recently. After the plaster was knocked off the walls, however, it was discovered that the building was part of a 300-year-old complex which included stables, rooms for tack, sledges and carriages, and quarters for grooms, coachmen and watchmen.

It's worth walking to the **St Jacob Monastery**. Although it seems almost deserted, it is still functioning and you might glimpse a monk walking silently between the buildings. There is shop that stocks a wide range of icons in the main church and a courtyard of beautifully scented flowers.

If you walk through an archway between houses on pl Sovetskaya into a courtyard you will come upon the **Church of the Virgin Birth**. It's a big church but out of use at the moment. The babushkas in the court yard will tell you it's 'ne rabota', then rattle on for ages; you may not understand a word but it's well meant.

PRACTICAL INFORMATION
Services
Intourist (☎ 312 44) is located in the kremlin.

There are two small **markets** in town. One just outside the old Kremlin walls on ul Belinskovo and the other on ul October where you can buy all sorts of things from fruit to a three-piece suite.

You can hire rowing boats at the **river station** near the kremlin.

Where to stay
One of the most appealing places to stay in all of Russia is in the *Rostov Kremlin*. The former servants' quarters have been turned into a basic hotel run by the International Tourist Centre (☎ 318 54). The rooms cost from US$3 for a single or US$5 for a double. The cheaper rooms have no bathroom but the location is amazing.

Where to eat
As well as the delicious cakes in the *café* in the International Tourist Centre, you can get a good three-course meal at *Restaurant Teremok*. It looks pretty awful from the outside and not so much better inside but it's always busy, the food is good and it's absurdly cheap. Three courses will cost a little over US$1. Open 12:00-24:00.

The *Restaurant Slavansky* on pl Sovetskaya is a new place and recommended. There is a large restaurant and a dark bar in another room. The salads are particularly good and three courses will cost around US$3; drinks are extra.

Getting there
Rostov is about 60km from Yaroslavl and there are trains and buses almost every hour. From Moscow, Rostov is five hours by train (US$2.50).

To get from the railway station to the kremlin and the main bus station, take bus No 6. To get from the main bus station to St Jacob Monastery, take bus Nos 1 or 2; for St Avraamy Monastery, take bus No 1.

Yaroslavl
Ярославль

Yaroslav's old central section and the tree-lined streets and squares make this one of the most attractive cities in Russia. In many ways, the buildings in this old section surpass those of Moscow as they have not suffered as much from the ravages of war and rapid industrialization.

Yaroslavl is the Volga River's oldest city, founded in 1010 by Grand Prince Yaroslav the Wise. With the expansion of river trade from the 16th century, Yaroslavl became the second most populous city after Moscow. Until the opening of the Moscow-Volga River Canal in 1937, which gave Moscow direct access to the Volga, Yaroslavl was Moscow's main port.

WHAT TO SEE

Transfiguration of Our Saviour Monastery

This attractive white monastery was founded in the 12th century but the oldest building to be seen today dates from 1516 when the wooden walls were replaced with stone and brick. As it was considered impregnable, part of the tsar's treasury was stored here, protected by a garrison.

The **Transfiguration of Our Saviour Cathedral** occupies central place in the monastery. This three-domed cathedral was built in 1516 after the original building was destroyed in a fire in 1501 and is currently being renovated. Sixteenth-century frescoes include depictions of John the Baptist on the eastern wall, Christ Pantokrator on the cupola in the central dome, and the Last Judgement on the western wall.

The **Refectory** was built in the 16th century. On the second floor a single mighty pillar supports the vaults, creating a large open dining area. It's now a history museum. The **Nativity Church**, which is also known as the Refectory Church, became a natural history museum in the communist era but may now be returned to the church.

Climb the **bell tower** for a panoramic view of the city. There are four flights of stairs, each getting narrower and you'll end up standing on the wooden roof. Directly above you is the main bell which was cast in 1738. The bell-tower's clock was installed in 1624 after being brought from the Saviour (Spassky) Tower in the Moscow Kremlin.

The **Monks' Cell Block** consists of four buildings and was built at the end of the 17th century. It now contains a large museum of Old Russia which includes icons, handicrafts, weapons, armour and books.

Entry into the grounds (open daily) is free; entry to each museum and exhibition (open 10:00-17:00 daily except Monday) costs US$0.50.

Around the monastery

This area is rich in churches and other historic buildings. Directly opposite the monastery on the Moscow Highway is the **Epiphany Church**.
The five-domed church was completed in 1693 and has nine large windows which make the interior extraordinarily light. It is an excellent example of the Yaroslavl school of architecture with its glazed tiles and festive decorations. Most of the church has been restored save for the dangerously-leaning tower near the entrance. It's open 10:00-17:00, closed Tuesday.

THE EPIPHANY TOWER

The **House of Ivanov**, ul Chaikovskovo 4, is a typical two-storey residence of a well-to-do town dweller built at the end of the 17th century. The ground floor was used for storage and the sleeping and living rooms are upstairs.

The **Church of St Nicholas on the Waters**, ul Chaikovskovo 1, was built from 1665 to 1672 in red brick and has marvellous glazed bands around the altar windows. The five green onion-domes complement the red brick and make for an impressive sight.

The white **Church of the Tikhvin Virgin** next door is a small church dwarfed by its neighbour but specially designed for winter worship as it can be heated. It has extensive glazed-tile work on its exterior.

The Volga River Embankment

A stroll down the landscaped high right bank of the Volga River from the river station to the Metropolitan's Chambers is an enjoyable way of exploring this area. At the end of ul Pervomaiskaya is the **river station**: one section is for long-distance hydrofoils and, slightly downstream, there's another for local passenger ferries.

The tent-roofed **Nativity Church**, ul Kedrova 1, built over nine years starting in 1635 consists of two buildings and is famous as being the first church to use glazed tiles for external decoration. This practice was soon adopted everywhere and led to the development of the Yaroslavl Architecture style (see p193). The names of those involved in the building of the church have been inscribed on the tiles and if you look closely, you can still see them. Unfortunately, this church is in desperate need of restoration and much of the tilework is disappearing.

St Nicholas-Nadeyina Church, per Narodny 2a, was funded by the wealthy merchant, Nadey Sveshnikov, hence its name. The Annunciation Chapel here was built for Nadey's private use so that he could pray in the company of only his closest friends. It has an interesting iconostasis framed in ornamental lead. The church is now a museum (entry US$0.40), open 1 May to 30 September, 10:00-17:00, closed Sunday and Monday.

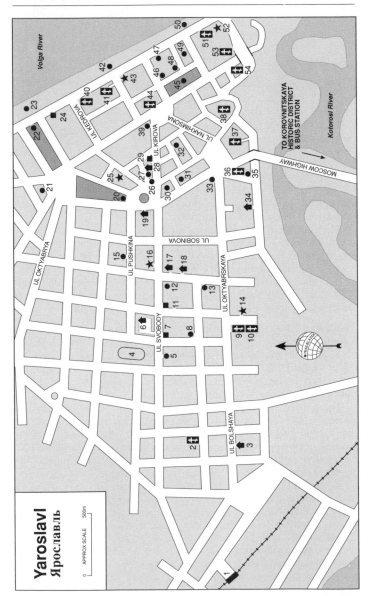

Yaroslavl
Ярославль

0 APPROX SCALE 500m

Volga River

Kotorosl River

TO KOROVNITSKAYA
HISTORIC DISTRICT
& BUS STATION

MOSCOW HIGHWAY

UL KEDROVA

UL OKTYABRYA

UL PUSHKINA

UL SVOBODY

UL BOLSHAYA

UL NAKHIMSONA

UL KIROVA

UL SOBINOVA

UL OKTYABRSKAYA

OTHER (cont)

25 Planetarium Планетарий
26 Book Store Дом Книги
27 Philharmonic Hall Филармония
30 Vlasyevskaya Tower Власьевская Башня
31 Arcade Гостиный Двор
32 Market Рынок
33 Post Office Почтами
35 Descent of Holy Spirit Consistorium Духовная Консистория
36 Epiphany Church Церковь Богоявления
37 Transfiguration of our Saviour Monastery
   Спасо-Преображенский Монастырь
38 Church of St Michael the Archangel
   Церковь Михаила-Архангелск
39 Government Offices Присутственные Места
40 Church of the Nativity Церковь Рождества Христова
41 Church of St Nicholas-Naden
   Церковь Цвятого Николы Надеина
42 Provincial Governor's Rotunda-Pavilion Павильон
43 Art Museum Художественный Музей
44 Church of Elijah the Prophet Церковь Ильы Пророка
45 Chelyuskirtsev Park Парк Челюскинцев
46 House of Matrev Дом Матреева
47 Physicians Society House Дом Врачов
48 House of the Vakhrameevs Дом Вахрамеевых
49 Medical Institute Медицинский Институт
50 Volga Tower Волжская Башня
51 Church of Patriarch Tikhon Церковь Патриарха Тихона
52 Metropolitan's Chamber Митрополичьи Палаты
53 Church of St Nicholas in Log Town
   Церковь Святого Николы
54 Church of Saviour in the Town Церковь Спаса

HOTELS AND RESTAURANTS

3 Hotel Kotorosl Гостиница Которосль
6 Hotel Stariy Gorod Гостиница Старйи Город
7 McDonald's Макдоналдс
11 Restaurant Vlasyevsky Ресторан Власьевскйи
17 Hotel Vest Гостиница Вест
18 Hotel Yuta Гостиница Юта
19 Hotel Yaroslavl Гостиница Ярославль
24 Café Lira Кафе Лира
28 Hotel Volga Гостиница Волга
29 Restaurant Rus Ресторан Русь
34 Hotel Yubileynaya Гостиница Юбилейная

OTHER

1 Yaroslavl Main Station Уарослав-Главный Вокзал
2 Church of Vladimir Mother of God
   Церковь Владимирскои Богоматери
4 Stadium Стадион
5 Circus Цирк
8 Bell-tower of St Nicholas Колокольня Николы
9 Church of St Nicholas on the Waters
   Церковь Святого Николы
10 Church of Tikhvin Virgin Церковь Тихвинской Богоматери
12 Youth and Puppet Theatres Театры Юного Зрителя и Кукол
13 Seminary Духовная Семинрия
14 House of Ivanov Дом Иванова
15 Airlines Office
16 House of Nikin Дом Никина
20 Volkov's Theatre Драматический Театр имени Волкова
21 University Университет
22 Nekrasov Monument Памятник Некрасову
23 River Station Речной Вокзал

The **Art Museum** is housed in the former governor's residence and it contains European works of art and furniture from the 15th to 19th century watched over by a friendly retired English teacher. Rooms of Russian art cover the 18th-20th centuries. You'll have to dodge around the art students practising there but a visit makes an interesting break from all the churches. Located at nab Volzhskaya 23, entry is US$1 and it's open 10:00-18:00, closed Friday.

The **Volga Tower**, also known as the Arsenal Tower, sits on the river bank at nab Volzhskaya 7. It is one of two towers which remain from the former Yaroslavl Kremlin. This citadel consisted of earth ramparts with wooden fortress walls and stone towers. This tower was finished in 1668 and is now a naval club.

The **Metropolitan's Chamber**, nab Volzhskaya 1, was built in the 1680s for the Metropolitan of the nearby city of Rostov-Yaroslavski. The two-storey building is now one of the country's richest museums of **old Russian Art**. While Yaroslavl's most revered icon, *The Sign of the Virgin,* painted in about 1218, now sits in Moscow's Tretyakov Gallery, the museum contains a number of other notable icons. Particularly interesting are the 13th and 14th centuries Mongolian icons. Entry is US$1, the museum is open 10:00-17:30, closed Monday.

Yaroslavl centre

The centre of the city is Soviet Square (pl Sovetskaya). On the east side of the square is the Church of St Elijah the Prophet and on the north side is a government office building of circa 1780.

The imposing **Church of St Elijah the Prophet** is well worth seeing for its superb 17th-century frescoes, still in excellent condition. The church was commissioned by one of the richest and most influential Russian merchant dynasties, the Shripins. It's now a museum and is open from 1 May to 30 September, from 10:00 to 18:00, closed Wednesday.

The **Vlasyevskaya Tower**, ul Pervomaiskaya 21, is the second of the two towers that remain from Yaroslavl's original kremlin. It's also known as the Sign (Znamenskaya) Tower and flower sellers gather underneath it everyday.

The **Volkov Drama Theatre**, pl Volkova, was built in 1911 and is named after Fedor Volkov (1729-1763) who is considered the founder of Russian national theatre. He inherited his stepfather's factories in Yaroslavl which enabled him to organize his own private theatre company before moving on to bigger and better things. Amongst his claims to fame was that he organized the first staging of *Hamlet* in Russia. The theatre is currently being restored and the finished parts look beautiful.

The Yaroslavl area code is ☎ 0852. From outside Russia dial +7-852.

Although the Rostov Finift Enamel factory is based in the nearby city of Rostov-Yaroslavski, the **factory shop** is here at ul Kirova 13, next to the Hotel Volga. It has a great range of *finift* enamel gifts.

The **planetarium** is on ul Trefoleva and open 10:00-18:00. It is frequently used for teaching local school groups.

Korovnitskaya Sloboda Historic District

Korovnitskaya Sloboda, which means 'cattle breeding settlement on the outskirts of town', sits on the right bank of the Kotorosl River as it flows into the Volga River. The district's focal point is the **Church of St John Chrysostom**, nab Portovaya 2, which was built from 1649 to 1654. It has four domes and two tent-shaped side chapels which makes it appealingly symmetrical. As it was built at the height of the decorative arts in Yaroslavl, its ornamentation is very elaborate. The **Church of Vladimir Mother of God**, surrounded by apartment blocks is very similar in style but significantly smaller. It's in a very poor state now and seems closed.

The most obvious building in this historic area is the pointed 37m high **bell-tower** which carries the nickname of the Candle of Yaroslavl. There isn't much left of it except the brickwork now.

Church of St John the Baptist

In the Tolchkovski district, once famous for its leather work, this impressive 15-domed church (1671-87) is considered the architectural pinnacle of Yaroslavl. From a distance it looks as if it is trimmed in lace and carved of wood but this deception is created by carved and patterned bricks. It consists of two side chapels, unusual in that they are practically as tall as the church and each is crowned with five domes. Inside is a mass of frescoes – reputedly more than in any other church in Russia. The church is open daily 10:00-18:00 except Tuesday.

You can see this church from the train as you cross over the Kotorosl River.

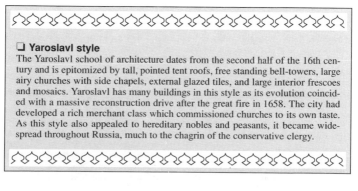

❏ Yaroslavl style
The Yaroslavl school of architecture dates from the second half of the 16th century and is epitomized by tall, pointed tent roofs, free standing bell-towers, large airy churches with side chapels, external glazed tiles, and large interior frescoes and mosaics. Yaroslavl has many buildings in this style as its evolution coincided with a massive reconstruction drive after the great fire in 1658. The city had developed a rich merchant class which commissioned churches to its own taste. As this style also appealed to hereditary nobles and peasants, it became widespread throughout Russia, much to the chagrin of the conservative clergy.

PRACTICAL INFORMATION
Orientation and services
There are two railway stations. **Yaroslavl-Glavny** (*Yaroslavl-Main*) is on the north side of the Kotorosl River and **Yaroslavl-Moskovski** is on the south side. All trains to Yaroslavl go through Yaroslavl-Glavny while only those trains travelling along the east and west line (such as from Ivanovo and St Petersburg) go through Yaroslavl-Moskovski.

To get from the station to pl Volkova (for Hotel Yaroslavl), catch trolley-bus No 1. From the station to Hotel Kotorosl, take tram No 3.

Aeroflot is at ul Svobody 20. The airport is to the north and its closest railway station is Molot (Мотол) on the line to St Petersburg. Bus No 140 from pl Sovetskaya runs to the airport.

You can change money and travellers' cheques at **Sberbank** which is on the pedestrianized section of ul Kirova. Black market money changers hang around outside.

For a virtual tour of the city's churches and other sights visit http://cnit 2.uni yar.ac.ru/yaros/wwe00039.htm.

In the summer there are various **river trips** leaving from the river station. Tolga, 30 minutes along the Konstantinovo route, is worth visiting.

Where to stay
Homestays are available in Yaroslavl through *HOFA*, see p18.

Hotel Yuta (☎ 218 793), ul Respublikanskaya 79, looks newish but the rooms are fast becoming tatty. It's still reasonable value: a single with attached bathroom costs US$15; there are doubles for US$20. The basic *Hotel Volga* (☎ 229 131), ul Kirova 10, formerly known as the Bristol Hotel, is in a fine location. It's US$12 for a single or from US$18 for a double with shared bath. Rooms with attached bath cost US$22/32.

Hotel Kotorosl (☎ 212 415), ul Bolshaya Oktyabrskaya 87, has recently been renovated and is now a good choice although it is 2km from the centre. They charge US$15-55 for a single and US$26-60 for a double. *Hotel Stariy Gorod* (☎

320 488/321 327), ul Svobody 46, is a curious place tucked away at the back of a courtyard – see map. It's very quiet and is run by a friendly and helpful woman. It costs US$24 for a single, US$30 for a double. Rooms have bathroom attached.

The *Hotel Yaroslavl* (☎ 221 275), ul Ushinskovo 40, and with an entrance also at ul 2 Svobody, has been undergoing major renovation work. When it reopens it will probably be one of the top hotels in Yaroslavl. It's in a prime location so worth considering.

Currently the best option is the *Hotel Yubileynaya* (☎ 726 565, 730 704, ▤/☎ 726 565, ▱ www.hotel.yaroslavl.ru), nab Kotoroslennaya 11A, at US$35/55 (foreigner price) for a single/double room with attached bath. There are views over the river.

Where to eat
McDonald's has arrived in Yaroslavl and is very popular. You can't miss the giant M emblem erected with the company's usual sensitivity not far from the war memorial. There are several other cheap places to eat nearby along ul Svobody.

The *Restaurant Vlasevski* is a good place on the corner of ul Svobody and ul Tchaikovskogo. Downstairs is a café and upstairs is the restaurant serving a variety of dishes for around US$3.50. The food is tasty and the portions are generous. Other places to eat are *Restaurant Staroe Mesto*, and *Restaurant Volga* at the River Station.

The up-market *Restaurant Rus* is at the end of the pedestrianised section of ul Kirova and serves traditional Russian food. It's probably the best that Yaroslavl currently has to offer. There's a cheaper version, *Café Rus*, near Hotel Volga.

Moving on
There are about 20 trains a day to Moscow (five hours).

The bus station is about 2km south of the city. There are buses to many destinations including about six buses a day to Rostov-Yaroslavski (US$1, 90 minutes).

In the summer from the river station it's possible to get a boat along the Volga to Moscow. The trip takes 40 hours.

Vyatka (Kirov)
Вятка (Киров)

Vyatka was founded in 1181 on the banks of the Vyatka River and was originally named Klynov. It developed into a fur-trading centre entirely dependent on the river for transport and communication with the rest of the country. In the eighteenth century it fell under the rule of Moscow and was renamed Vyatka, soon gaining a reputation as a place of exile.

In 1934 its name was changed once more, this time to Kirov, in honour of the communist leader assassinated earlier in the same year. Kirov was at one time so close to Stalin that most people assumed that he would eventually succeed him as General Secretary of the Party. However, in the 1930s he broke away and it is more than likely that Stalin had a hand in his murder. His death served as the excuse for Stalin's Great Purge in the mid-1930s during which several million people died in labour camps.

Modern Vyatka, still sometimes referred to as Kirov, is a large industrial and administrative centre with a population of 491,000. It's not of great interest but there's enough to keep you occupied for a day and the river front is attractive.

❏ Vyatka to Vyelikoryetskaya Pilgrimage

Every year on 3 June, 1000-odd worshippers take part in the Russian Orthodox Church's longest procession: a 170-kilometre trek starting from Vyatka and ending in Vyelikoryetskaya village. At the head of the procession is carried the icon of St Nikolai, the miracle curer.

According to religious lore, a peasant in 1383 found this icon up a tree surrounded by candles on the outskirts of Vyelikoryetskaya. The villagers agreed to house the icon in Klynov (as Vyatka was then known) providing that it was brought back to the village in the yearly procession. This condition has been met every year since then, even during the communist era when the icon was hidden, the tree in Vyelikoryetskaya chopped down and the devout had to pretend that they were out strolling.

Today the procession is gaining popularity as more people seek the miracles that they believe result from participating. Everyone is welcome but you must bring your own blanket, food and drink for three days of walking.

WHAT TO SEE

Russia's answer to Joseph Conrad was AC Grin (1880-1932) who was born 35km away at Slobodskoi. Grin's adventure novels set in mysterious places are still popular today and his works are on display in the **AC Grin Museum**, ul Volodarskovo 44, open 10:00-18:00, closed Monday.

Other museums include the **Museum of Aviation and Space**, ul Engelsa, open 10:00-18:00, closed Monday; the **Museum of Vyatka Local Handicrafts**, ul Drelevskovo 4B, which has a large collection of Dymkovo clay toys, and the large **United Historical Archive and Literary Museum**, ul Lenina 82.

The **Exhibition Hall of the Kirov Region**, ul Gertsina, open 10:00-16:00, closed Monday, exhibits works of local artists and each month has a different exhibition. The staff are very helpful and some speak English.

The **Assumption Cathedral** at the Trifon Monastery dates from the late 17th century.

PRACTICAL INFORMATION
Orientation and services

Vyatka is spread out and has no real main street which means that you need to do a lot of walking to get around.

Russian Railways still refers to the town as Kirov. To get from Kirov-1 railway station to the Hotel Administratsi Oblast and Drama Theatre, take bus No 23 from in front of Detski Mir department store. To get from Kirov-1 railway station to the Hotel Vyatka, take trolley bus Nos 2, 3 or 6 also from Detski Mir.

Intourist (☎ 90 949), ul Volodarskovo 127, offers tours of the city (3 hours), the Trifon Monastery (1 hour), and the **Bakulev Museum of Heart Surgery** in the nearby town of Slobodskoi (2 hours), as well as a four-day **rafting trip** down the Velikaya River. **Aeroflot** (☎ 44 472, 25 287), is at ul Gorkovo 56.

For Internet access go to **InetCafé** (☎ 624 984, 🖳 www.inetcafe.vyatka.ru) at ul Svobody 67. For US$2 you get one hour's access and a cup of tea.

Where to stay

Hotel Vyatka (☎ 648 396), pr Oktyabrski 145, charges US$30/70 for a single/double room. *Hotel Administratsi Oblast* (☎ 691 018), ul Gertsena 49, has single rooms for US$25. *Motel Kolos* (☎ 679 324), ul Bolshoe Bolshevikov has beds in the dormitory for US$6 and single rooms for US$30.

Where to eat

The best restaurant is the *Rossiya*, ul Lenina 80 which is near the M E Saltykov-Shchedrin House Museum. There is a restaurant in the *Hotel Vyatka* and three canteens near the puppet theatre.

Moving on

You can buy tickets only for trains departing the same day at the station; for advance bookings, you need to go to the Advance Railway Ticket Booking Office.

On the fastest trains it's fifteen hours to Moscow and eight hours to Perm.

The Vyatka area code is ☎ 8332. From outside Russia dial +7-8332.

Perm
Пермь

The city of Perm, Pasternak's Yuryatin in *Dr Zhivago*, is the gateway to Siberia. Lying in the foothills of the Ural Mountains it's an industrial city of over one million people and the focus of the region. The surrounding area is good for hiking and skiing. Some operators now offer white-water rafting trips.

Perm dates back to 1723 when construction of the Egoshikhinski copper foundry began. It was started by VN Tatichev who was one of the close associates of Peter the Great. The location on two major trading rivers ensured that Perm grew as not only an industrial but also a trading city. Salt caravans arrived along the Kama River while wheat, honey and metal products from the Urals travelled along the Chusovi River. The arrival of the railway in 1878, the discovery of oil in the region, and the transfer of factories from European Russia during WWII all boosted the local economy further.

The city's most familiar product is the Kama bicycle which, while rarely seen on the streets of Russian cities, is still widely used in the country. Nearly all of Russia's domestic 'phones are made here but Perm's most specialized products are the first stage motors for the Proton Heavy Lift rockets.

Despite its industries, Perm has a long history of culture and scholarship. This can mostly be attributed to the revolutionaries, intellectuals and political prisoners who were exiled here in the 19th century. Perm had the first university in the Urals and its most famous student was Alexander Popov (1859-1905) who, according to Russian historians, invented the wireless. He first demonstrated his invention in 1895, the same year that Marconi also proved his concept. Popov was born in nearby Krasnoturinsk.

From 1940 to 1957 Perm was called Molotov after the disgraced Soviet Foreign Minister who signed the 1939 Ribbentrop-Molotov Pact, dividing up Poland with the Nazis.

WHAT TO SEE

The most interesting part of town is the old quarter around Perm 1 station. Old churches here include the baroque **Cathedral of Peter and Paul** (1757-1765 with a 19th-century belfry) and the Empire-style **Cathedral of the Saviour of the Transfiguration Monastery** (1798-1832). There are also numerous examples of eclectic and art nouveau styles of which the old building of Perm 2 station is one. The river station is near Perm 1.

Perm Art Gallery, pr Komsomolski 2, is one of the largest in Russia. Its collection of wooden sculptures is interesting and includes a figure of Jesus with Mongolian features. It's open 11:00-18:00, closed Monday. The city also boasts a **terrarium** in Gorky Park, a **planetarium**, and a **Museum of Local Studies**.

About 45km out of town near the village of **Khokhlovka** is an open-air ethnographic museum which has a collection of 16-20th century buildings. This museum is open all year around.

About 100km from Perm are the fabulous **Kungur Ice Caves**, some of the biggest in the Urals region with a total length of 5.6km including 58 grottos, 60 lakes, and hundreds of stalactites and stalagmites. About 1.3km of the caves are open to the public and fitted with electric lights. Take warm clothes. There are several direct trains a day from Perm (two hours) to Kungur and the caves are 6km from the town.

PRACTICAL INFORMATION
Orientation and services

The town extends for 80km along the Kama River with the centre being around Perm 1 station on the left (eastern) bank. At the southern end of Perm, also on the left bank, is Perm 2 which is the station at which the Trans-Siberian stops. There are suburban trains that run the 5km between Perm 2 and Perm 1.

The city has two airports: Bolshoe Savino Airport which handles most traffic and is 20km to the west, and the older Bakharevka Airport which is 10km to the south in the suburb of Balatovo.

JSC Permtourist (☎ 348 703, 🖹 342 609, 🖳 www.nevod.ru/Permtourist), is at the Hotel Ural, which is part of the same company. Another recommended travel agency is **Galakon** (☎ 338 087, 🖹 341 568), ul Kuibysheva 14. They offer boat trips along the Kama and Chisovaya Rivers, and day trips to the Kungur ice caves.

Aeroflot (☎ 334 668) is at ul Krisanova 19 and you can also buy tickets from the Ural and Prikamiye Hotels.

You can access the Internet at the **post office** which is near the corner of ul Lenina/Glavny and ul Popova.

Where to stay

The best place to stay is the large *Ural Hotel* (☎ 344 417, 🖹 349 217, 🖳 www.nevod.ru/Permtourist), ul Lenina 58. There are basic double rooms for US$15 but first they'll offer you the smarter rooms for US$40/60 for a single/double. They also have a business centre and travel agency. *Hotel Prikamiye* (☎ 348 662), ul Komsomolskaya 27, is not bad and has singles for US$14, doubles for US$18.

At the Kungur Ice Caves (see above), the *Hotel Stalagmit* (contact through Ural Hotel) has double rooms from US$10.

Where to eat

All the hotels have restaurants. At the Ural Hotel there's a *restaurant* on the 7th floor and the *Grot Bar* (better than it sounds) in the basement.

Probably the best place to eat is the *European* (☎ 338 716), ul Lenina 72b. Main dishes cost US$15-20.

Moving on

There are flights to Frankfurt as well as many places in Russia. By rail it's 7hrs to Yekaterinburg and 28hrs to Novosibirsk.

The Perm area code is ☎ 3422. From outside Russia dial +7-3422.

Yekaterinburg
Екатеринбург

Yekaterinburg's role in shaping Russian history has been both immense and paradoxical: ushering in the Socialist era in 1918 with the murder of the Romanov family, providing the setting for the 1960's 'U2 Affair' (effectively a caricature of the Cold War itself), and giving the country Boris Yeltsin, who played a key role in dismantling the Soviet myth. The city seems to act as Russia's litmus paper: as a harbinger of whatever is to come.

Its historical significance alone justifies a visit and while there is not much to see here in real terms, the wealth of pre-Stalinist architecture makes a change from other Siberian cities, harking back to the days before the Revolution, when Yekaterinburg was already the centre of a rich mining region. From 1924 to 1992 the city was known as Sverdlovsk, the name that Russian Railways still uses for it on their timetables.

HISTORY

The earliest settlers in the area were the 'Old Believers', religious dissidents fleeing the reforms of the Russian Orthodox Church in 1672. They created the *Shartash* township here and were the first to discover that the area was rich in iron ore. This discovery was the key to later development: Peter the Great, in the process of fighting the Great Northern War against Sweden, gave instructions for new sources of iron to be found, and the first ironworks were established here just as the war ended in 1721. A fortress was built a year later and the town was officially founded in 1723. The city was named Yekaterinburg in honour of Peter's new wife, Catherine. The railway reached the town in 1888 bringing foreign travellers on their way to Siberia.

The murder of the Romanovs

The Romanov family was moved from Tobolsk to Yekaterinburg in May 1918 and imprisoned in a house belonging to a rich merchant, Ipatev. Here they spent the last two months of their lives being tormented by the guards, who openly referred to Nicholas as the 'Blood Drinker' and scrawled lewd pictures on the walls depicting the Tsarina with Rasputin.

Several attempts were made to save the royal family, and eventually the Bolshevik government, deciding that the Tsar was too great a threat to its security, ordered his elimination. Shortly before midnight on 16 July, Nicholas, Alexandra, their four daughters and their haemophiliac son,

Alexis, were taken down to the cellar where they were shot and bayonet-ted to death. The bodies were then taken to the Four Brothers Mine, 40km outside the city, where the guards spent three days destroying the evidence. The corpses were dismembered, doused with petrol and burned.

A week later the White Army took Yekaterinburg and their suspicions were immediately aroused by the sight of the blood-spattered walls of the cellar. In the garden they found the Tsarevich's spaniel, Joy, neglected and half starved. However, it was not until the following January that investigators were led to the mineshaft, where they found fragments of bone and pieces of jewellery that had once belonged to members of the Imperial Family. They also found the body of Jimmy, Anastasia's dog, which the murderers had callously flung down the mineshaft without bothering to kill it first. All the evidence was identified by the Tsarevich's tutor, Pierre Gilliard. At first the Bolsheviks would not admit to more than the 'execution' of Nicholas, accusing a group of counter-revolutionaries of the murders of his family. Five of them were tried, 'found guilty' and

❏ The road to Romanov sainthood

The story behind the discovery of the Romanov remains is almost as bizarre as that of their 'disappearance'. In July 1991 it was announced that parts of nine bodies had been found and that these were almost certainly those of the Imperial Family. Perhaps the most intriguing aspect of the discovery was the fact that three of the skulls, including that of the Tsar himself, had been placed in a wooden box. In fact the bodies had been discovered some 20 years before by a local detective novel writer named Geli Ryabov. He deduced, by the skulls' immaculate dental work, that these were indeed the bodies of the Royal Family, but reburied them for fear of persecution by the secret police.

In December 1992, testing at the Forensic Science Service laboratory in Aldermaston matched DNA samples from the bodies with DNA taken from a blood sample from Prince Philip, Duke of Edinburgh, (Tsarina Alexandra's sister was Philip's maternal grandmother).

The state burial of the royal remains was delayed for several years following a disagreement between surviving members of the Romanov family who wanted the bones to be returned to Yekaterinburg as a memorial to the millions killed by the Communists, and the government who favoured burial in St Petersburg. On 19 August 1998 the remains of the royal family were finally interred in the Romanov vault in the cathedral in St Petersburg (see p141) in a service attended by the then president, Boris Yeltsin. He made the first official apology: 'The massacre of the Tsar was one of the most shameful pages of our history....We are all guilty. It is impossible to lie to ourselves by justifying the senseless cruelty on political grounds'.

On 20 August 2000, at a special ceremony in Moscow's Cathedral of Christ the Saviour, Patriarch Alexi II canonised the Tsar, the royal family and hundreds of priests who died as 'zealots of faith and piety' during the Communist era.

executed. However, in 1919 after the death of Party official Yacob Sverdlov, it was acknowledged that it was, in fact, he who had arranged the massacre. In his honour the town was renamed Sverdlovsk.

The U2 Affair
The next time the town became the focus of world attention was in May 1960 when the American U2 pilot, Gary Powers, was shot down in this area (see p320). He survived the crash, parachuting into the arms of the Soviets and confirming that he had been spying. The ensuing confrontation led to the collapse of the Summit conference in Paris.

The city today
Yekaterinburg is now one of Russia's most important industrial cities, with a population of nearly 1½ million. The city's most famous son is, of course, Boris Yeltsin: coup-buster, economic reformer, referendum winner, dissolver of parliament and former Russian President.

Industries include heavy engineering, chemical production with 200 complexes and a transport hub with seven radiating railway lines. It is educationally rich with more than 200 schools, 50 technical schools and 14 higher education institutions. It also has over 600 libraries, including the Belinski Library which has more than 15 million books and was founded in 1899. The city used to focus on armaments research and production but munitions factories, including the vast 'Pentagon' building in the eastern part of the town, are now being closed down. The area's biggest employer, Uralmash, which makes machine tools, has cut its 40,000 workforce by 65%. There has been some foreign investment, however, the three biggest investors being Coca Cola, Pepsi and the mobile phone company, USWest.

If Yekaterinburg is an indicator of the state of affairs in Russia, things don't look too good: I asked if anything important had happened here recently and was told only that there had been 'a number of mafia funerals'. Local mafia gangs hold a lot of power here: Yekaterinburg is a transit point on the 'heroin route' between Asia and Europe. Unless you're also involved in this trade you'll be all right.

WHAT TO SEE

The Romanov Memorial
The site of the murder of the Imperial family is 500m north of prospekt Glavny and currently marked by a **white metal cross** and a **plaque** inscribed with the names of the Romanov family. Yeltsin had the original building (Ipatev House) demolished in 1976. A **memorial church** is being built on the site. Also here is a small wooden **chapel** dedicated to St Elizabeth (Elizabeth Fyodorov) originally built in the late 1980s but burnt down more than once by anti-monarchists. Elizabeth was Alexander II's

HOTELS AND RESTAURANTS

2 Hotel Sverdlovsk Гостиница Свердловск
3 Restaurant Kosmos Ресторан Космос
8 Café Karavella Кафе Каравелла
15 Hotel Iset Гостиница Исет
16 Hotel Bolshoi Ural Гостиница Большой Урал
17 Restaurant Okean Ресторан Океан
19 Food Store Гастроном Централный
21 Teatralnoe Restaurant & Café Pizza Театрално Ресторан + Кафе Пицца
25 Hotel Tsentralnaya Гостиница Центральная
29 Hotel Magister Гостиница Магистр
32 Restaurant Harbin Ресторан Харбин
33 Atrium Palace Hotel Гостиница Атрум Дворец

OTHER

1 Yekaterinburg Railway Station Вокзал
4 Romanov Memorial (Ipatev House) Белый Крест (Быв. Дом Ипатьева)
5 Former Estate of Rastorguev-Kharitonov (1794-1836)
   Быв. Усадьба Расторгуева-Харитонова
6 Monument to the Ural's Komsomol Young Communists
   Памятник Комсомолу Урала
7 Ascension Cathedral Церковь Вознесения
9 Central Post Office Почтамт
10 ATM Банк
11 Cinema Кино
12 Sverdlov Statue Памятник Свердлову
13 Afghan War Memorial Афган Война памятник
14 Military Museum in the House of Officers (U2)
   Музей «Боевая Слава Урала»
18 Opera & Ballet Theatre Театр Оперы и Балета
20 Most Bank & ATM Мост-Банк
22 Puppet Theatre Театр Кукол
23 Sputnik Travel Спутник
24 British & US Consulates Консулъство Британское/США
26 Popov's Radio Museum Музей радио имени Попова
27 Museum of Decorative Arts Музей Изобразительных Искусств
28 Museum of Local History Краеведческий Музей
30 To Bus Station Автовокзал
31 Circus Цирк

MAP KEY

♠	Hotel	✝	Church or Cathedral
■	Restaurant	⬛	Buddhist Temple
✳	Museum	⬕	Synagogue
●	Other	◖	Mosque

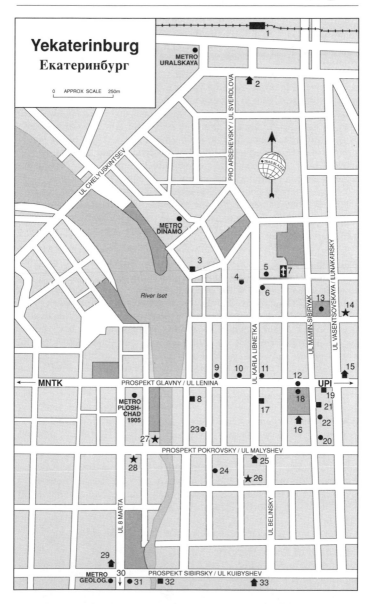

Yekaterinburg
Екатеринбург

0   APPROX SCALE   250m

METRO URALSKAYA

PRO ARSENEVSKY / UL SVERDLOVA

UL CHELYUSKINTSEV

METRO DINAMO

River Iset

UL KARLA LIBNETKA

UL MAMIN-SIBIRYAK

UL VASENTSOVSKAYA / LUNAKARSKY

←— MNTK

PROSPEKT GLAVNY / UL LENINA

UPI

METRO PLOSH-CHAD 1905

PROSPEKT POKROVSKY / UL MALYSHEV

UL 8 MARTA

UL BELINSKY

METRO GEOLOG.

PROSPEKT SIBIRSKY / UL KUIBYSHEV

sister-in-law and following the Romanov murders was thrown down a mineshaft and left to die. Local villagers claimed to have heard her miserable wailings for two days as she prayed for the souls of her attackers who, when they realized that she was still alive, piped poisonous gas into the well and then filled the hole with earth.

The grand building opposite the Romanov site now houses the headquarters of the Children's Movement. It was commissioned by one of Yekaterinburg's wealthy merchants, Rastoguiev, and legend holds that he was so rich that he used to mint his own gold coins in the basement. Apparently he was a cruel man: having bailed an architect out of jail, he offered to buy the man's freedom if he designed him a beautiful enough house. The architect laboured hard to complete his side of the bargain but, when Rastoguiev did not keep his promise, hanged himself.

Next door to this building is **Ascension Cathedral**, impressive from the outside but containing nothing of particular note. It was closed following the Revolution, its treasures removed and its murals painted over.

Military Museum

The remains of Gary Powers' U2 aircraft are exhibited in the Military Museum at the House of Officers (Dom Officerov) near the city centre but staff here are sometimes unwilling to let foreigners in or occasionally seem to be ignorant of the fact that the plane is even here at all. The exhibit itself is impressive but what was state-of-the-art espionage equipment in 1960 is today only the remains of an old aeroplane. Pride of place goes to the U2 camera which so impressed Nikita Khrushchev: 'It must be said that the camera is not a bad one,' he said, 'the photographs are very accurate. But I must say that our cameras take better pictures and are more accurate'. The House of Officers is easily recognizable by the massive armoury outside, and around the back is a collection of Soviet military hardware including a couple of fighter planes, a helicopter, a long line of tanks and the cosmonauts' re-entry capsule from the rocket Soyuz. The Military Museum (☎ 552 106), to the right of the House of Officers, is open 10:00-16:00, Tuesday to Saturday (closes at 15:00 on Saturday).

Museum of Decorative Arts

There's a fine collection of nineteenth-century iron sculpture here, a gallery of Russian paintings, including works by Ivanov and Tarakanova, a portrait of PA Stroganov (of Beef Stroganov fame), and a famous painting of Christ by Polenov. Pride of place goes to the iron pavilion, which won first prize in the Paris Exposition in 1900. It's very impressive but you can't but wonder what it's for. Open daily 09:00-17:00.

Museum of Local History

The museum of local history (☎ 511 819) is at ul Malysheva 46, relocated from the old museum in Alexander Nevsky Cathedral. There are interesting displays on 19th-century Yekaterinburg, the revolution and the murder of the Romanovs and the discovery of their remains. It's well worth a visit and is open daily from 11:00 to 17:00.

Other things to see in Yekaterinburg

The **Ural Geology Museum** (☎ 223 109) at ul Kuibysheva 30 is good; try to track down the curator, who speaks perfect English and seems to enjoy showing visitors around. It is open 11:00-18:00, closed at weekends. Other museums include the **Literary Quarter Museum**, ul Tolmacheva 41 and **Popov's Radio Museum**, ul Rozy Lyuksemburg 9, also a Planetarium: open 11:00-18:00, closed Monday and Tuesday.

There is a number of interesting buildings in the city including the classical-style **Mining Office** (1737-1739), and the former estate of **Rastorguev-Kharitonov** (1794-1824) ul Karla Libknehkta 44 (opposite the Romanov memorial site). At the eastern end of pro Lenina/Glavny is **UPI**, the Urals Polytechnical Institute, an impressive building which often features on postcards. In fact it was recently redesignated a university but the old name has stuck. The building beside it with the cannons outside is the city's military college.

The **Opera and Ballet Theatre** (☎ 558 057) at prospekt Glavny 46a is the third most important in Russia after Moscow and St Petersburg. The **Puppet Theatre** on ul Mamin-Sibiryak is newly opened.

In the square opposite the House of Officers is a powerful **Afghan war memorial**. The pose of the soldier is very different from most that you see at war memorials around Russia and is an interesting insight as to how people feel about the war.

At ul Mamin-Sibiryak 189 there is a depressing **zoo** which looks more like a prison.

Excursions from Yekaterinburg

● **Europe/Asia marker** About 40km to the west along the main road to Moscow (Novi Moscovski Trakt) the German scientists, Humboldt and Roze, decided the border between Europe and Asia in 1829 while doing barometric surveying along the Trakt. The original marker was destroyed in the 1920s and replaced with a concrete obelisk faced with granite. Intourist runs trips to this obelisk. There's a another marker beside the railway line, 36km to the west at Vershina (Вершина).

● **Museum of wooden architecture** It's a long way away (120km to the north) and not as good as the one outside Irkutsk but bus No 31 from the railway station will get you here. The most interesting building is the old church. Closed since the Revolution, craftsmen began its restoration recently and were surprised to find many of the carved floor tiles missing. As work proceeded, the lost tiles began to show up, brought in by pensioners who had long ago removed pieces of their church as mementos. Incredibly, all the tiles have now been returned.

PRACTICAL INFORMATION
Orientation and services

The main street, prospekt Lenina (now renamed prospekt Glavny), runs from east to west through the city and is bisected by the River Iset. The point where the road and the river cross is more or less the city centre and most of the hotels, restaurants and sights are within walking distance of it.

For local information and maps look for the *City Guide* (US$2) in hotels and other places frequented by foreigners.

Travel agents include Intourist, (☎ 518 434, 🖃 518 230), prospekt Lenina 40; Sputnik (☎ 513 743, 519 157, 🖃 513 483), ul Pushkina 5; Miklukho-Maklay (☎ 237 596, 🖃 518 087), ul Shaumyana 100; Globe Tour (☎ 589 819, 🖃 516 455), ul Dzerzhinski 2.

Aeroflot (☎ 299 298) is at ul Bolshakova 99A. **Lufthansa** (☎ 598 300) and **Transaero** at ul Pushkina 5.

For **rail tickets**, you have to go to the second floor of the **Central Railway Ticket Booking Office** located in a newish building on the west side of the main railway station.

There's an ATM at **Most Bank**, 145 ul Mamin-Sibiryak. You can also cash travellers' cheques here.

The **Central Post Office**, at pro Lenina 51, has all the usual services plus **Internet** access for US$1.60 per hour.

There's a **Mongolian Consulate** (☎ 445 453) at ul Furmanova 45, a **British Consulate** (☎ 564 931, 🖃 592 901, 🖳 brit @sky.ru) at ul Gogolya 15A, and a **US Consulate** (☎ 564 619, 🖃 564 515, 🖳 usc gyekat@gin.ru) also at ul Gogolya 15A.

THE MODERNIST POST OFFICE

Local transport

Yekaterinburg has a good bus and trolley-bus system, and also a rather limited metro. To get to the centre from the station, take bus Nos 1, 13, 21, 23, 31 or trolley-bus Nos 1, 3, 5, 9, 12. From the station to Hotel Tsentralnaya, take trolley-bus Nos 1, 5, 9 down ul Karla Libknekhta. For Hotel Iset and Hotel Bolshoi Ural, take tram Nos 27 and 29 which go down ul Lunacharskovo, then pro Lenina. For MNTK Iris, take bus No 41 westward from the junction of pro Lenina and ul Karla Libknetka. This bus passes the hotel about 500m from its terminus.

To get to the airport, catch a bus from the Air Station (Aerovokzal) beside the Aeroflot office at ul Bolshakova 99A.

Where to stay

All hotels in this section have attached bathrooms.

Hotel Eurasia (☎ 578 028) on prospekt Lenina 40 is a busy place and has a wide variety of rooms starting from US$8/14 for a single/double. There is an Intourist office on the 4th floor. It's also possible to stay very cheaply at the railway station *rest rooms*.

Directly opposite the railway station is the vast *Hotel Sverdlovsk* (☎ 536 261), ul Chelyuskintsev 106, which is a conventional, Intourist-style place, partly renovated in 1999. the rooms cost US$28 for a single and US$40 for a double. Occasionally they have some cheaper rooms: it's worth enquiring.

Hotel Bolshoi Ural (☎ 556 896), ul Krasnoarmeiskaya 1, is right next door to a 'secret' weapons technology plant and offers an interesting insight into how hotels were run years ago. Still, the people are friendly enough and it costs from US$15/25 for a single/double.

Hotel Iset (☎ 556 943), prospekt Lenina 69/1, has singles from US$30 and doubles from US$60. It's much better than it looks and is a quiet place. It was built to resemble a hammer and sickle from above. The sickle, which one imagines would be the tricky bit, turned out well but the hammer never really quite happened. It's unclear what the three stars above the door refer to.

Hotel Tsentralnaya (☎ 551 109) on ul Malisheva 74, is worth trying and has singles for US$32 and doubles for US$64. There are also a few cheaper rooms. It's friendly enough and is popular with business people.

Also very popular with business visitors is *Hotel Magister* (☎ 224 206, 🖹 225 674), ul 8 Marta 50. The well-appointed rooms have kitchenettes, and many of the residents stay here long term so you should book well in advance. Single rooms are US$110, doubles cost from US$135. Breakfast is included.

MNTK-Iris (☎ 289 145, 🖹 286 292), ul Bardina 4, is a 20-30 minute bus ride from the city centre. To get here, take bus No 18, which starts opposite UPI and stops right outside the building (it's on the right). The spotless rooms start from US$70.

The top place to stay is the *Atrium Palace Hotel* (☎ 556 076, 🖹 555 136) at the World Trade Centre at prospekt Sibirsky 44. There are rooms from US$200 to US$700.

Homestays can be organized by the Moscow based *G&R International* for US$23 including breakfast. Another company that can arrange a homestay in Yekaterinburg is *HOFA*. For contact information, see p18.

Where to eat
The *Kosmos* is a trendy ex-Party restaurant with reasonable food, a casino and a large, gaudy plastic rainbow sign. They serve standard Russian/European fare. The pelmeni at *Hotel Iset* is good, although the place is a bit dingy and service can be casual.

The *Restaurant Teatralnoe* (ul Mamin-Sibiryak opposite the Opera and Ballet Theatre) is recommended although it serves rather small portions so you need to fill up on bread. Mushrooms in sour cream cost US$5, meat soup is US$4 and shashlik costs US$8. Also in the building is the *Kafe Pizza* where you'll get a pizza of sorts, ice-cream and a shake for US$5. *Café Karavella* on ul Gorkogo is a small place good for a quiet drink.

The *Astoria* (☎ 510 161), at Malyshev 28, is a small smart restaurant that is among the city's best. Main dishes cost US$10-15, service is quite good and it's popular amongst business people. Nearby is *Irlandsky Dvorik*, an Irish pub and restaurant. It often gets busy in the evenings here.

The *Harbin* (☎ 617 571), at ul Kuibysheva 38 in the south of the city, is located in a flamboyant Chinese-style building that you can't miss. There's hardly a chopstick in sight and the service can be poor but the food is surprisingly good. Around US$25 will get you a set four-course meal for one which will probably be more than enough for two. The restaurant is very near the circus. To get here take tram Nos 4, 14, 26 or 34 from the city centre to the stop on ul Belinskogo, or trolley-bus Nos 1, 5 or 9 from the railway station.

Moving on
By rail Yekaterinburg is 22 hours from Novosibirsk and 30 hours from Moscow. Note that if you travel to Moscow on the train known as the Ural, the route goes via Kazan and uses Moscow's Kazanski station.

There are numerous rail services to Tyumen (five hours) and Omsk (twelve hours).

By air The main airport is 16km south of the city. There are several flights a week to **Frankfurt** on Lufthansa and daily flights on Transaero and Aeroflot to **Moscow** and **Irkutsk**. You can also fly to St Petersburg, Novosibirsk, Vladivostok, Krasnoyarsk, Almaty and Tashkent from Yekaterinburg.

The Yekaterinburg area code is ☎ 3432. From outside Russia dial +7-3432.

Tyumen
Тюмень

The only city in Asia to have hosted a European cup, Tyumen is the booming oil capital of Western Siberia and its wealth is illustrated by the expensive goods in the shops.

Founded in 1586, Tyumen's location on a major trading river, the Tura, made it an important transit point for goods between Siberia and China. It was also a major transit point for settlers and convicts destined for Siberia and the Russian Far East. By 1900, over one million convicts had tramped through Tyumen. During WWII, many of European Russia's people, treasures and factories were relocated to Siberia. The greatest treasure to be transferred from Moscow to Tyumen during this time was Lenin's corpse. For years he rested secretly in a building of the Agricultural Institute, tended by a team of specialists.

Prior to the drilling of the first well in the region in 1960, Tyumen was just a dusty backwater of 150,000 inhabitants. Since then its population has grown to over 500,000. The importance of oil to the city can be seen in the two giant crude oil pipelines running through it. Tyumen is a pleasant enough place and certainly feels more affluent than many other Siberian cities.

WHAT TO SEE

All museums in Tyumen are closed on Monday and Tuesday. The most interesting buildings are in the area known as the **History Museum Complex** at ul Kommunisticheskaya 10, open 09:30-17:00. The complex includes displays on local history and Siberian religious history, Trinity Cathedral built in 1616, the Church of Saints Peter and Paul, and the walls of the monastery. This monastery is unusual in Siberia as it was one of only a few built from stone.

Particularly interesting is the wooden **Household Goods and Architecture Museum** which was formerly the Blyukher Museum (ul Respubliki). The wooden house was built in 1804 and its owners included the 1830s Tyumen mayor, Ikonikov. The **House-Museum of Masharov**, ul Lenina 24, provides an insight into the life and times of a wealthy 19th-century factory owner. Specialist museums include the **Fire Technology Museum** on ul Gorkovo, and the **Geology, Oil and Gas Museum** (☎ 227 426) on ul Respubliki 42. The city park is the local Hari Krishna hangout. Bookstores sell old Tsarist coins: don't declare them at customs when you leave Russia as it's illegal to export them.

1 History Museum Complex (Saints Peter & Paul Church & Cathedral of Trinity Monastery Музей Истории Города (Петропавловская Церковь и Троицкий Собор Троицкого Мужского Монастыря)
2 Elevation of the Cross Church Крестовоздвиженская Церковь
3 Remains of the Kremlin Walls Остатки Земляных Валов быв. Кремля
4 Local Studies Museum Краеведческий Музей
5 Church of Mikhaila Maleina Церковь Михаила Малеина
6 House-Museum of Masharov Дом-музей Машарова
7 Household Goods & Architecture Museum
8 University Университет
9 Puppet Theatre Театр Кукол
10 Cathedral of Holy Cross Знаменский Собор
11 Church of the Saviour Спасская Церковь
12 Philharmonic Hall Филармония
13 Sputnik Travel Agency Спутник
14 Credo Bank Кредо Банк
15 Drama Theatre Театр Драмы
16 Circus Цирк
17 Pizza Tyumen Пицца Тюмень
18 Police Station Милиция
19 Café Chebureki Кафе Чебуреки
20 City Park Парк
21 Tsentralni Stadium Стадион Центральный
22 Parliament House Дом Советов
23 Central Square Центральная Площадь
24 Central Post Office Почтамт
25 Bakery Булочная
26 Hotel Prometei Гостиница Прометей
27 Hotel Quality Tyumen Гостиница Тюмень
28 Department Store Умивермаг
29 Market Рынок
30 Restaurant Slavutich Ресторан Слабутич
31 Friday's Fast Food Фрайдис Ресторан
32 Art Gallery Картинная Галерея
33 Fire Technology Museum Музей
34 Old Cemetery Старое Кладбище
35 Geology Museum Музей Геология
36 Hotel Zapsibgazprom Гостиница Запсибгазпром
37 Book Shop Дом Книги
38 Hotel Vostok Гостиница Восток
39 Aeroflot Касса Аэрофлота

PRACTICAL INFORMATION
Orientation and services
From the train station, all buses and trolley-buses take you along ul Pervomaiskaya, then either down ul Respubliki or ul Lenina.

Travel agencies include **Intourist** (☎ 322 782), ul Melnikite 93, and **Sputnik** (☎ 240 721), ul Respubliki 19. **Aeroflot** (☎ 223 252, 262 946) is at ul Respubliki 156, and you can get information about flights from the airport (☎ 232 124).

Credit card **cash advances** can be obtained from the exchange office in Hotel Prometei and the Credo Bank office at ul Pervomaiskaya 8.

You can get more information about the city on the website of local telecommunications company Sibtel: 🖳 www .sibtel.ru/English/win/histori/htm.

Where to stay
The cheapest accommodation is also the worst. The *Komnata Otdikha* (☎ 292 073), at the station, charges US$6 a single room, US$10 a double room, and US$12 a triple. Bathrooms are in the corridor. The entrance to the Komnata Otdikha is on the street in the front of the station.

The *Hotel Vostok* (☎ 225 205), ul Respubliki 159, is a huge characterless place with singles from US$12 and doubles from US$25; all rooms have bathroom attached. To get to Hotel Vostok from the Central Square on ul Respubliki, take trolley-bus 14. To walk will take you half an hour.

Hotel Prometei (☎ 251 423), ul Sovetskaya 20, charges US$30/60 for a single/double – more than double the price that the Russians pay. It looks shabby from the outside but the rooms inside have been renovated, unfortunately with the drab appearance of a portakabin.

The *Hotel Zapsibgazprom*, on the corner of ul Respubliki down by the Geology Museum, is a quiet place with rooms from US$25-70. All rooms have bathroom attached.

Opened in 1995, the 230-room *Hotel Quality/Kvaliti Tyumen* (☎ 394 040, 🖹 394 050), ul Ordzhonikidze 46, is the top hotel. It's very well run and often full of business people. If you were allowed to pay the Russian prices it would be a bargain. Foreigners pay US$95 for singles and US$105 for doubles. There's a sauna, gym and excellent restaurants.

Where to eat
A very popular fast-food place is *Fridays* on the corner of ul Ordzhonikidze and ul Respubliki. The food is nothing special but it's only US$2 for a meal and a drink. Another good place for snacks is the *Pizza Tyumen* (☎ 261 868), ul Lenina 61 (opposite the city park) which has a good range of fast food such as pizza (US$1), pelmini (US$1) and salad (US$1). In summer, the patio upstairs is open and becomes the *Café Letnee*.

Restaurant Slavutich (☎ 465 013, ul Respubliki 62) is Tyumen's best Russian restaurant with friendly service and large portions. It has a wide range of meals including assorted salads (US$2), *varenki* (potato filled dumplings) (US$3), stuffed tomatoes (US$2) and soups (US$2). In the evenings the restaurant is popular with wealthy locals who all seem to want a turn on the piano, singing old folk songs.

Restaurant Tyumen (☎ 394 040) at Hotel Quality is one of the top places in town. Main dishes cost US$8-12. Many of the guests at the Hotel Prometei next door walk across in the evening to eat here.

Moving on
Tyumen is about halfway between Moscow and Irkutsk, each about 41 hours away by rail.

It's just under 7 hours to Omsk and 17 hours to Novosibirsk.

The Tyumen area code is ☎ 3452. From outside Russia dial +7-3452.

Omsk
Омск

Omsk is the second largest city in Siberia founded in 1719 when a small fortress was set up on the west bank of the Om. This was the military headquarters of the Cossack regiments in Siberia. The fortress had been considerably enlarged and included a large *ostrog* (prison). It was here that Dostoyevsky did four years hard labour for political crimes in 1849. His unenviable experiences were recorded in *Buried Alive in Siberia*. He was twice flogged, once for complaining about a lump of dirt in his soup; the second time he saved the life of a drowning prisoner, ignoring a guard who ordered that the man be left to drown. Dostoyevsky received so severe a flogging for this charitable act that he almost died and had to spend six weeks in the hospital.

During the Civil War, Omsk was the capital of the White Russian government of Admiral Kolchak, until November 1919 when the Red Army entered and took the city. The population grew fast after the war and now more than a million people live here. Textiles, food, agricultural machinery and timber-products are the main industries. There is also an important petro-chemical industry here, supplied by a pipeline from the Ural-Volga oil region.

Omsk has a sister city relationship with Milwaukee, Wisconsin.

WHAT TO SEE

Omsk prides itself on having numerous parks and there isn't really a lot to see here unless you're into museums of the 'Former Home of Unknown Artist and Obscure Soviet Poet' variety. The **Dostoyevsky Museum** (☎ 242 965), ul Dostoevskovo, is fairly interesting, however. The **Military Museum**, ul Taube 7, has displays on WW1, WW2, the Afghanistan and Chechnya conflicts. Most museums are closed on Monday. Near the junction of the Om and Irtysh Rivers are the ramparts and the **Tobolsk Gate** of the old Omsk Fortress.

Tobolsk
Probably the most interesting thing to do in the area is to take a trip 235km north to the historic town of Tobolsk. This was the capital of Siberia until 1824 and some of the old buildings survive. Tobolsk Kremlin sits high above the river; the Bishop's Chambers, Gostiny Dvor and the bell-tower are also worth seeing and there are daily hydrofoil trips along the Irtysh River.

Getting to Tobolsk   You can reach Tobolsk by train from Omsk via Tyumen. The fastest train is the No 273N which leaves Omsk at 15:16 (17:16 local time), reaches Tyumen at 05:15 next morning and arrives in Tobolsk at 10:42. For the journey back, train No 273E leaves Tobolsk at 12:15, reaches Tyumen at 17:55 and gets to Omsk at 07:50 next morning. If you've more time, the boat from Tyumen can be a pleasant way to reach Tobolsk.

River trips

There are two river stations in Omsk. Long-distance vessels, such as those for Tobolsk, leave from the **Long-Distance River Station**. The timetable and ticket office are in the large station building.

Tourist trips along the Irtysh River depart from the **Excursion River Station**. Tickets and timetables are available from the kiosk under the Lenin bridge. A one-hour trip costs about US$3. The river is navigable from late May to September.

PRACTICAL INFORMATION
Orientation and services

Most of the hotels and museums are located in the city centre which is about 2¹/₂km from the station at the junction of the Om and Irtysh rivers.

If you need a travel agency, **Intourist** (☎ 311 490) is at pr Karla Marxa 4, and **Turist** (☎ 250 624) at ul Gagarina 2. The main office of **Aeroflot** (☎ 223 252, 262 946) is at ul Respubliki 156.

For more information about Omsk and pictures of the city visit Omsk-On-Line at ⌨ www.univer.omsk.su/omsk.

Where to stay

Only the very basic *Hotel Avtomobilist* (☎ 411 700), pro Karla Marxa 43, and the standard *Hotel Omsk* (☎ 310 721), Irtyshskaya nab 30, are within walking distance (but only just) of the railway station. Bus Nos 11, 24, 60 and trolley-bus Nos 3, 4 and 7 run this way.

The best of the hotels located in downtown Omsk is the *Hotel Mayak* (☎ 315 431), ul Lermontova 2. There are single rooms for US$50, doubles for US$75, and executive suites consisting of two large rooms from US$100. It has very clean rooms and rather kitch Russian décor. They offer student discounts.

Other good choices are the *Hotel Tourist* (☎ 316 414), ul Tito 2: double room US$40 with bathroom, de luxe single US$70; and the *Hotel Sibir* (formerly Hotel Evropa) (☎ 312 571), ul Lenina 22: single US$40, double de luxe room US$80.

Moving on

By rail it's 9¹/₂ hours to Novosibirsk. For suggested rail services between Omsk and Tyumen and Tobolsk see above.

The Omsk area code is ☎ 3812. From outside Russia dial +7-3812.

Novosibirsk
Новосибирск

With a population of over 1.4 million people, this is the largest city in Siberia and its industrial centre but, of the cities along the Trans-Siberian that foreigners usually visit, Novosibirsk has the least to offer the tourist; it's a relatively young city and has few buildings of historic interest. But it's a pleasant enough place for a day or two and the huge scale of some parts of the centre is amazing. 'Space', writes Colin Thubron in *In Siberia*, 'in the end, may be all you remember of Novosibirsk'.

You can visit the enormous opera house, the museums and the nearby town of Akademgorodok, the Scientists' City where hundreds of scientists live in a purpose-built town beside a lake. Winters here are particularly harsh, with temperatures falling as low as minus 35°C. Novosibirsk is the starting point of the Turksib railway line (see p132); travellers can catch a train from here to Almaty in Kazakhstan and then continue west into China.

HISTORY

Novosibirsk didn't exist before the Trans-Siberian was built and its spectacular growth this century is largely due to the railway. In 1891 it was decided that a railway bridge over the Ob should be built here and in 1893, a small settlement on the river bank sprang up to house the bridge builders. The town was named Novo-Nikolayevsk in honour of the accession of the new Tsar.

By 1900 over 15,000 people lived here and the numbers grew as railway and water-borne trade developed. As far as tourists were concerned, there was only one reason for getting off the Trans-Siberian in Novo-Nikolayevsk, as Baedeker's 1914 *Guide to Russia* points out: 'It is a favourite starting point for sportsmen in pursuit of the wapiti, mountain sheep, ibex and other big game on the north slopes of the Altai'. The town suffered badly during the Civil War when 30,000 people lost their lives. During the first four months of 1920 a further 60,000 died of typhus. In 1925 Novo-Nikolayevsk was re-christened Novosibirsk ('New Siberia').

Between 1926 and 1939 the population increased greatly as the city's iron-making furnaces were built and fed with coal from the nearby Kuznetsk Basin and iron ore from the Urals. In the early 1930s, the 900-mile Turksib Railway was completed linking Novosibirsk with Turkestan in former Soviet Central Asia, via Semipalatinsk and Almaty. Grain from

HOTELS AND RESTAURANTS

2 Hotel Novosibirsk Гостиница Новосибирск
3 Hotel & Stolovar Гостиница + Столовая
8 Restaurant Sobek Ресторан Собек
14 Hotel Sibir, Intourist & American Business Centre Гостиница Сибирь
16 Allegro Fast Food Аллегро
17 Stolovar Столовая
18 New York Pizza New York Пицца
19 Irish Pub
20 Zolotoye Kolos Булочная «Золотой Колос»
26 Grill Master
27 Hotel Tsentralnaya/Restaurant Druzhba Гостиница Центральная
    Ресторан Дружба
31 Hotel Sapfir Гостиница Сапфир
39 To Hotel Ob/River Station Гостиница Обь/Речной Вокзал

OTHER

1 Central Railway Station Железнодорожний Вокзал
4 Cathedral of the Ascension/Circus Вознесенский Собор/Цирк
5 Aeroflot Касса Аэрофлота
6 Inkom Bank Инком Банк
7 Sputnik Travel Спутник
9 Market Рынок
10 Banya Баня
11 Museum of Local Studies Краеведческий Музей
12 TsUM Department Store ЦУМ
13 House-Museum of Kirov Дом-Музей Кирова
15 Puppet Theatre Театр Кукол
21 Sibirski Bank Сибирский Банк
22 Tsentralny Dom Knigi Bookstore Центральный Дом Книги
23 Medical Institute Медицинский Институт
24 Museum of Local Studies Extension (see 11 above) Музей
25 Opera & Ballet Theatre Театр Оперы и Балета
28 Central Post Office Почтамт
29 Long-distance Telephone Office & Internet Междугородний
    Переговорный Пункт + Интернет
30 Steam Engine Паровоз
32 Synagogue
33 Cinema Кино
34 Chapel of St Nicholas Часовня Святителя Николая
35 German Consulate Консольство Германии
36 Transaero
37 Bus Station Автовокзал
38 Oktyabrski Commercial Port Октябрьский Порт

METRO STATIONS Станция Метро

A Ploshchad Garina-Mikailovskovo Площадь Гарина-Михайловского
B Ploshchad Lenina Пл Ленина
C Ploshchad Gagarinskaya Пл Гагаринская
D Krasny Prospekt Красный Проспект
E Ploshchad Oktyabrskaya Октябьская
F Rechnoi Vokzal Речной Вокзал

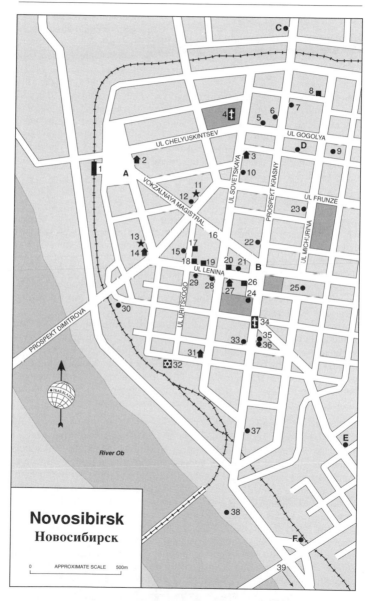

UL CHELYUSKINTSEV

UL GOGOLYA

UL SOVETSKAYA

PROSPEKT KRASNY

VOKZALNAYA MAGISTRAL

UL FRUNZE

UL MICHURINA

UL LENINA

UL URITSKOGO

PROSPEKT DIMITROVA

River Ob

Novosibirsk
Новосибирск

0   APPROXIMATE SCALE   500m

NOVOSIBIRSK RAILWAY STATION – SIBERIA'S LARGEST

the lands around Novosibirsk could then easily be exchanged for cotton, which grew best in Central Asia. The building of this railway, the jewel in the new government's first Five Year Plan, was filmed and is still shown today as a fascinating early example of documentary film. During World War II large numbers of civilians and complete factories were moved here from European Russia, and the city has been growing ever since. It's now the busiest river port in the area and the major industrial centre in Siberia, many people being employed in engineering or metallurgy factories.

WHAT TO SEE

Lenin Square and the Opera House

This is the centre of the city and the square is dominated by the vast **Opera House**, one of the largest in the world, with its silver dome. It was completed in 1945, when most of the builders had been sent off to join the war effort. Its completion is seen as all the more heroic in that it was to some extent due to the city's women and children, who helped the few remaining builders. You get tickets from the kiosk on the left side of the theatre or book seats by phoning ☎ 223 866.

In the middle of the square is a **statue of Lenin**, his coat blowing behind him in the cold Siberian wind, a rather more artistic representation of the man than the many others produced. He is flanked by three soldiers on his right and by two 'Peace' figures on his left, who look as if they are directing the traffic that flows around the great square. In the winter there are troika rides here, and people build ice-sculptures. The low building above the metro station is the oldest stone structure in the city.

Museum of Local Studies

The Museum of Local Studies (☎ 218 630) has two branches: ul Vokzalnaya Magistral 11 and prospekt Krasny 21. The bulk of this collection is housed at the former address, in the ground floor (entrance at the side) of the block right behind TsUM. It's an interesting museum, although you will need a guide to explain the significance of some of the historical exhibits. There's a display showing life before the Revolution including a Singer sewing machine, a rusty British Norton motorbike (built in 1909) and an early piece of rail (stamped 'Birmingham 1899'). There's also a special section recording the troubled times during the civil war, when the city was occupied by the White Russians and then the Bolsheviks, before being devastated by an outbreak of typhus in 1920. The extensive display of Siberian flora and fauna includes some of the 50 species of mammals, 30 species of fish and 30 species of birds that are found only in Novosibirsk oblast. There's also a collection of Siberian trees and grasses, a geological display and the skeleton of a mammoth. The labels on the natural history exhibits are in Latin as well as Russian: for a translation see pp411-3. Entry is US$0.50 and the museum is open from 10:00-18:00 daily except Monday and Tuesday.

Other things to see
Alexander Nevsky Cathedral, at the south end of Krasny Prospekt near the river, is now fully restored and is well worth a visit. Closer to the centre of town, however, is the tiny **Chapel of St Nicholas**, reached from underneath via the subway, opened during the 1993 centenary celebrations and built on the spot that is said to mark the exact centre of the country. The original church here was destroyed after the Revolution.

The **Dom Museum Kirov** is devoted to Kirov, a rising Communist Party leader who was assassinated in 1934 on Stalin's orders. It is overshadowed by the Sibir Hotel next door, in an attractive log cabin, one of the few that have survived. In the neighbouring apartment block there is a small exhibition of local handicrafts, mainly wood-carvings. There is a good **Art Gallery**, pr Krasnyi 5 (near the regional administration building, on Sverdlovsk Square. It is open 11:00-18:30, closed Tuesday.

PRACTICAL INFORMATION
Orientation and services
The fifth largest city in Russia, Novosibirsk was designed on a grand scale. Krasny Prospekt, its main street, extends for over ten kilometres. The mighty River Ob bisects the city, leaving the main hotels, sights and the railway station on the east bank. Although there were plans to rid the city of its Communist era street names, the signs are still in place.

Recommended local travel agents include the adventure travel company, **Sibalp** (☎ 495 922, 🖹 541 374, 🖳 sibalp@online.nsk.su), ul Nemirovicha-Danchenko 155/1, kv 47, who offer tours of the Altai region and can arrange climbing and rafting expeditions; **Magic Tours** (☎ 204 252), pro Krasny 62 (specialists in the Altai); and **Tourist Guide Union** (☎ 297 561, 🖹 239 529), ul Lenina 30/2 (specialists in sports). **Intourist** (☎ 237 870) is in Hotel Sibir at ul Lenina 21.

You can use the **Internet** at the telephone office for US$0.80 an hour. On the Internet Resources of Novosibirsk site at 🖳 www.nsc.ru/lans/resources.html there's a range of links to sites associated with the city, even including a live web cam. Many of the sites are in Russian.

Money can be exchanged at most banks and at the Central Post Office on ul Lenina. Sibirski Bank, ul Lenina, offers Visa card cash advances.

Novosibirsk University offers reasonably priced **Russian language courses**. Contact Gwendolin Fricker, KASSI Language, Novosibirsk University, ☎ 352 653, 🖹 397 124, 🖳 admin@kassi.ns u.nsk.su, 🖳 http://www.cnit.nsk.su/univ er/english/kassi.htm.

There is a **banya** on ul Sovetskaya which costs only US$0.80 and is open 12:00-21:00. As everyone else does, you should buy your bunches of leaves from the men outside before going into the banya.

Local transport
On foot, Lenin Square is about twenty minutes from the railway station, straight

down Vokzalnaya (Station) Magistral. Novosibirsk has a good **metro** system (some stations lined with Siberian marble). To get to Lenin Square (metro: Ploshchad Lenina) from the station (metro: Ploshchad Garina-Mikhailovskovo), go one stop to Sibirskaya/Krasny Prospekt, change to the Studentskaya line and it's one stop to Ploshchad Lenina.

There are two airports: the international **Tolmachovo airport**, 23km from the city's centre on the western bank, and the domestic **Sverny airport**, 6km to the north of the centre. Buses No 122 and 111 run between the two via the railway station and bus station.

Near the metro station of Rechnoi Vokzal (meaning 'river station') is the **river boat station** and the **long-distance bus station**.

To get to Akademgorodok, see p221.

Tours

The travel desks at most hotels offer a morning tour of the city as well as tours to the sights and museums described below for about US$25. Tours to Akademgorodok usually include a visit to the geological museum and a boat-trip on the Ob Dam in summer. They will also arrange tickets for the circus (closed in summer) and for opera and ballet at the Opera House.

You can organize your own boat trip from the landing stage near Rechnoi Vokzal metro station to Korablik Island, which is popular with Novosibirskians for swimming and sunbathing from May to September.

Where to stay

The *railway station rest rooms* are on the ground floor at the station. Accommodation ranges from US$6 for a bed in a shared room and there are single and double rooms, too. You need to show a ticket for onward travel.

The *Hotel Novosibirsk* (☎ 201 120) is well located right opposite the railway

station at Vokzalnaya Magistral 1. It's a typical Soviet place even down to the off-hand receptionists; they might tell you they are full, in which case hang around for a few minutes, then ask again and they'll probably find a room, unless they really are full! Single rooms with attached bath cost US$15-25 and double rooms are US$30-50. Breakfast is included, whether you'll want it or not is another matter.

While *Hotel Tsentralnaya* (☎ 227 660) is right in the city centre on ul Lenina 3; it's now looking quite shabby. There are singles for US$25 and doubles for US$35 and they sometimes have cheaper rooms.

Hotel Ob (☎ 667 401), ul Obnaya 49 is about 3km south of the city's centre on the banks of the Ob River; it's next to the River Station and near Rechnoi Vokzal metro station. Singles start from US$35 and double rooms from US$45.

By far the most up-market place in the centre is the *Hotel Sibir* (☎ 231 215), ul Lenina 21, a Polish/Russian joint venture and Intourist's standard pad. Rooms are US$80 single, US$140 double including breakfast. The rooms are clean and well maintained. There's a classy souvenir shop in the foyer, several bars and a business centre.

The excellent *MNTK-Iris* is some way from the centre of town to the west of the river, at ul Kolkhidskaya 10 (☎ 410 155, 🖹 403 73); double rooms with attached bathroom cost US$80 including breakfast. There are reductions for singles. To get there, take bus Nos 2 or 37 from pl Stanislavskaya.

For *homestays* contact the agencies listed on p18.

Where to eat

There are numerous fast-food places in the centre including *New York Pizza & Traveler's Coffee* on the corner of ul Lenina and ul Uritskogo. It's owned by an American and the pizzas are good. You'll

---

The Novosibirsk area code is ☎ 3832. From outside Russia dial +7-3832.

get a slice of pizza and a drink for around US$1. There are several other branches around town. *Allegro Food* is also a chain, with one branch next to Hotel Novosibirsk. It's always busy and serves OK chicken for US$1. There's also a branch of *Grill Master* on Ul Lenina.

There is a *stolovar* on ul Sovetskaya just up past the banya. The food's pretty basic but very cheap and the people who work here are friendly.

There is a surprisingly good snack bar in *TsUM* where the pastries are excellent and the coffee thoroughly drinkable.

Zolotoye Kolos is a recommended bakery opposite the Hotel Tsentralny and a good place to stock up for the Trans-Siberian trip as it sells a range of bottled and tinned foods.

The canteen at ul Lenina 9 is now the first *Irish Pub* in Siberia – is Ireland really like this?!

A night at the *Sobek* (☎ 205 867), ul Dostoevsky 19, a Korean restaurant, can be exciting. It's an intimate little place that's packed with racketeers and mafia men. The food's not bad, about US$5 per person, drinks and live ammunition are extra.

A reasonable choice is the *Hotel Sibir*. In the restaurant downstairs, service is good, as is the food, but it tends to fill up with leather-jacketed, shell-suited 'businessmen' in the evenings. Directly above it, the second floor restaurant is better and often has live music. Expect to pay US$20 without drinks; if you want wine it's best to buy it in the kiosk outside the restaurant.

Entertainment
Good places for a drink and live music in the evening are the *New York Times* (☎ 227 809, ul Lenina 12), where there's a band most nights, kicking off at 21:00; and *Pub 501* (ul Lenina 20).

Novosibirsk boasts numerous theatres and cultural groups beside the Opera House. These include the **Chaldony Song and Dance Company** (☎ 418 889), ul Zabaluyeva 47; the **Circus** (☎ 237 584), ul Sovetskaya 11; the **Puppet**

Theatre (☎ 221 202), ul Revolyutsi 6; the **Siberian Dixieland Jazz Band** (☎ 235 642), ul Kirova 3; the **Siberian Russian Folk Chorus** (☎ 202 269), ul Krasnoyarskaya 117; and the **Symphony and Chamber Orchestras Halls** (☎ 224 880), ul Spartaka 11.

What to buy
There are the usual souvenir shops in the hotels. The main street for shopping is Vokzalnaya Magistral. The market is one block east of Krasny Prospekt.

The Tsentralny Dom Knigi Bookstore, on pl Lenina, has a good selection of maps and dictionaries.

TsUM Department Store next door to the Museum of Local Studies is surprisingly well stocked. There is also a large department store complex next to Hotel Novosibirsk.

Moving on
By rail You can buy tickets at the station and also at the Central Railway Office at ul Sovetskaya 50.

On the Trans-Siberian line Novosibirsk is 50 hours from Moscow, $9^{1}/_{2}$ hours from Omsk, 32 hours from Irkutsk and $4^{1}/_{2}$ days from Vladivostok.

On the Turk-Sib railway, Novosibirsk is 33 hours from Almaty and 68 hours from Tashkent.

By air Most international flights and long-distance domestic flights use **Tolmachovo airport**, 23km from the city centre; other domestic air traffic uses **Sverny airport**, 6km to the north of the centre.

Airlines here include: **Olympia-Reisen-Sibir** (☎ 185 015 ⌨ olympia@ olympia.nsk.su), ul Pyatovo Goda 83; **Sibir Aviation** (☎ 669 078, ▤ 227 572); **Lufthansa** (at the airport: ☎ 696 377, ▤ 227 151), and **Transaero** (☎ 231 917, ▤ 230 321) at prospekt Krasny 28. Transaero is the agent for many well known foreign airlines.

There are daily flights to Moscow (four hours), for about US$100; less on the smaller airlines like Sibir Aviation.

EXCURSIONS FROM NOVOSIBIRSK

River Cruises The Ob River which flows through Novosibirsk is the busiest river in Siberia. The most popular trip is the 65-minute round trip from the river station to Korablik Island. Most passengers get off here as it is a favourite swimming spot. The ferry travels this route three times a day from May to September. To get to the river station, take the metro to the Rechnoi Vokzal station and you can see it from the exit.

Akademgorodok Academic City (Академгородок)

Akademgorodok, 30km from Novosibirsk, was established in the 1950s as a university and research centre for scientists and it soon grew into an élite township of over 30,000 of the Soviet Union's top intellectuals and their families. In this pleasant sylvan setting, the researchers and students grappled with scientific problems with a two-fold aim: to push ahead of the West in the arms race and to harness the wealth of Siberia for the good of the USSR. As with its Olympic athletes, the Soviet Union believed in training its academics from a very early age, spiriting them away from home to attend special boarding schools for the gifted in Akademgorodok. Compared to the ordinary citizen they were well looked after here, pampered with little luxuries in the shops that were hard to find elsewhere. As government funding is reduced to a mere trickle, the utopian dream is now over and many scientists have been lured abroad but the university still has a good reputation.

It is, however, well worth a visit. Akademgorodok's forest setting beside a lake offers a relaxing opportunity to get away from polluted Novosibirsk. There's little to see and the town has a rather melancholic atmosphere now with its badly maintained buildings but it can still give you some idea of the Soviet utopian dream of a City of Scientists.

The **Geological Museum** in the Institute of Geology and Geophysics is open to tours only. You could follow one in or just say, 'Moozay' to the doorman, and you may be let into the museum which is straight ahead, up the stairs. The overpowering mineral wealth of Siberia is displayed here, including the purple mineral chaorite, found only in this part of the world.

After looking round Akademgorodok you can walk through the birch forest and over the railway-track to the beaches of the **Ob Dam**. It was created by the building of the Novo-Sibirskaya power station, Siberia's first large hydroelectric project. This is a good place to swim as the water is surprisingly warm. It is 18°C for 2-3 months a year and reaches 22°C for about one month, usually July. In winter, **cross-country skiers** converge on Akademgorodok as it is the site of some good tracks maintained by the Alik Tulskii ski centre.

Where to stay/eat *Hotel Zolotaya Dolina* (☎ 3832-356 609), ul Ilicha 10, charges US$25 for a single and US$40 for a double room. It has a good *restaurant*. For cheap food try the *café* on the first floor of the **Torgovi Centre** nearby. In the same street is a **bookshop** which has a small selection of maps, posters and books in English.

Getting there To get to Akademgorodok, from Novosibirsk take a **train** from the suburban station located south of the Central Railway Station to Obskoe More (Обское Море). The terminus for the train to Obskoe More is Bredek (Бредек) and a timetable can be found at the entrance to the suburban station on the street. Expect a slow 50-minute trip. Trains run hourly from 06:02 to 23:17. To get to Akademgorodok from Obskoe More station, walk 100m away from the Ob Dam, cross over shosse Berdskoe, which runs parallel to the railway line, and continue on any of the dirt paths through the park. In about 10 minutes you reach the bus station and if you keep going, you get to the Torgovi Centre and Hotel Zolotaya Dolina.

There are several **buses** from Novosibirsk. Catch bus Nos 8 or 22 from in front of Rechnoi Vokzal metro station, or Nos 2 or 8 from in front of Studentskaya metro station. Number 15 minibuses go every 15-20 mins from outside the railway station and cost about US$0.50.

A **taxi** from Novosibirsk costs about US$20 one way but you may be able to beat them down.

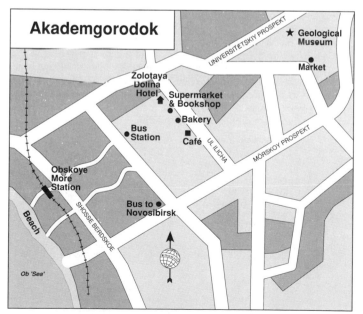

Krasnoyarsk
Красноярск

Krasnoyarsk is a major industrial centre, producing one quarter of Russia's aluminium, almost a quarter of its refrigerators and millions of truck and car tyres a year. As a result air pollution can be bad at times but Krasnoyarsk is nevertheless worth a visit. The city centre is quite attractive and with hills on the outskirts, Krasnoyarsk is certainly more pleasantly located than some other large Siberian cities, Novosibirsk, for example.

Russian settlement dates back to 1628 when a fort was built. Long since disappeared, it was situated on a hill overlooking the river and was first known as Krasny Yar meaning 'beautiful steep bank'. By 1900, the population was 27,000 and the town boasted 20 churches and two cathedrals, a synagogue, 26 schools, a railway technical college and a botanical garden reputed to be the finest in Siberia.

RL Jefferson visited Krasnoyarsk in 1897 and was impressed: 'Its situation cannot fail to elicit admiration – the tall mountains rear up around it.' Most of the townsfolk he met here were ex-convicts. So used were they to their own kind, that they were particularly suspicious of anyone who lacked a criminal record. He was told of a certain merchant in the city who found it difficult to do business, never having been behind bars. To remedy the situation he travelled all the way to St Petersburg and deliberately committed a crime that was punishable by exile to Siberia. After a short sentence in Irkutsk he returned to his business in Krasnoyarsk and 'got on famously' thereafter.

❏ Travelling intellectuals at the turn of the 20th century were advised to visit the library of Krasnoyarsk merchant, Yudin. This bibliophile assembled a collection of 100,000 volumes, including almost every publication ever issued in Siberia. At the end of the 19th century, while sentenced to exile in Krasnoyarsk, Lenin spent several months working in this library.

In 1906 Yudin sold his valuable collection to the Library of Congress, for just US$40,000 even though it was valued at US$114,000. He did this 'with the sole idea of establishing closer relations between the two nations,' he wrote to the Congressional Librarian.

During the Second World War, many factories were evacuated from European Russia and rebuilt here. The city grew as a trading centre and during the Soviet's early five-year plans, underwent massive industrialization to become Siberia's third largest city, with a population of just under one million.

The current local governor is ex-army hardliner, Alexander Lebed. In the 1996 presidential elections he challenged Yeltsin but finally stood down and supported him, earning Yeltsin's backing in his own election campaign in Krasnoyarsk.

WHAT TO SEE

The terraced hill around the old part of town is an interesting place for a walk. Restoration should now be complete at the **Annunciation Cathedral**, which is worth visiting; it's on ul Lenina. The old **Catholic Church**, which contains an organ, is near the central park.

The tiny **Chapel of St Parasceva Pyatnitsa** stands above the city and there are good views from here. It takes about 40 minutes to reach the chapel from Hotel Krasnoyarsk.

There are several museums including the **Surikov Art Museum** (☎ 272 558), ul Parizhskoi Kommuny 20, open 10:00-18:00 (closed Monday), and the **Museum of Local Studies**, ul Dubrovinskovo 84, which has recently been renovated. The House Museum of V I Lenin, who stayed here for

STALINIST-GOTHIC
RIVER STATION
KRASNOYARSK

all of two months in 1897 is now the **Literature Museum**, and the **SS Nikolai Steamship**, the ship on which Lenin sailed to exile in Shushenkoe, is now a bar and disco. What would he think?!

PRACTICAL INFORMATION
Orientation and services

Krasnoyarsk is divided into two sections, separated by the Yenisei River. The **north bank** is a mass of terraces and is bounded on the north by a steep hill known as Karaulnaya Mountain and on the west by the forested Gremiachinskaya Ridge. The railway station, museums and hotels are located on this side. Just south of the station is the academic area (another Akademgorodok). The **south bank** is relatively flat and is mostly factories and multi-storey apartment blocks.

Intourist (☎ 273 715) is in Hotel Krasnoyarsk and offers a range of tours.

In the same hotel is the friendly and helpful **Dula Tour** (☎ 274 325, 🖳 274 591, 🖳 dula@dionis.kts.ru, www.dula.kts.ru). The staff speak good English and can arrange tours, boat tickets and will help with any other travel requests. Sample prices are US$15 for a city tour, US$36 for a tour to Stolby and US$25 to Divnogorsk. **Krasnoyarskturist** (☎ .361 810, 361 470) has a branch at Hotel Turist and owns and operates 14 hotels and tourist camps throughout the kray. They offer rafting, riding, skiing and river cruises.

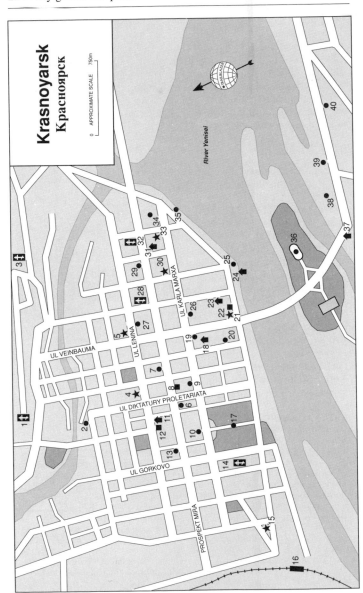

HOTELS AND RESTAURANTS

8 Café Shakhmatnoe Кафе Шахматное
11 Hotel Sever Гостиница Север
12 Rosso Italian Restaurant Ресторан Россо
18 Hotel Krasnoyarsk Гостиница Красноярск
22 Café Kofenya Кафе Кофиня
23 Hotel Enisei Гостиница Енисей
24 Hotel-Boat Mikhail Godinko Гостиница Пароход
31 Hotel Oktyabrskaya Гостиница Октябрьская
37 Hotel Turist Гостиница Турист

OTHER

1 Chapel of St Parasceva Pyatnitsa
   Часовня Святой Великомученницы Парескевы Пятницы
2 Market Рынок
3 Trinity Church Троицкая Церковь
4 House-Museum of Surikov Дом-Музей В И Сурикова
5 Literature Museum Литературный Музей
6 Sinto Bank Синто Банк
7 Book Shop Книжный Мир
9 TsUM Department Store ЦУМ
10 Lenin Statue Ленин
13 Aeroflot Office Агентство Аэрофлота
14 Catholic Church Католическая Церковь
15 Palace of Culture of the Combine Harvester Builders (!)
   Дворец Культуры Комбайностроителей
16 Railway Station Железнодорожный Вокзал
17 Central Park Центральный Парк Культуры и Отдыха

OTHER (cont)

19 Bus Station Автовокзал
20 Opera & Ballet Theatre Театр Оперы и Балета
21 Museum of Local Studies
   Краеведческий Музей
25 River Station
   Речной Вокзал
26 City Administration Building
   Здание Городской Администрации
27 Central Post Office Почтамт
28 Intercession Church
   Покровская Церковь
29 Avtobaz Bank Автобазбанк
30 Surikov Art Museum
   Художественный Музей В И Сурикова
32 Annunciation Cathedral
   Благовещенский Собор
33 Art Gallery Художественная Галерея
34 Main Concert Hall
   Большой Концертный Зал
35 SS Nikolai Steamship
   Пароход «Св. Николай»
36 Stadium Lenin Komsomol
   Центральный Стадион имени Ленинского Комсомола
38 Concert & Dance Theatre
   Концертно-Танцевальный Зал
39 Monument to the Tsarist Convict Route
   Памятник Кандальный Путь
40 Circus Цирк

There's an **ATM** at Most Bank, ul Bograda 15. Visa and MasterCard cash advances are available from Inkombank at pro Mira 106, Avtovazbank at pro Mira 39 and Sinto Bank at pro Mira 87.

For more information on Krasnoyarsk, the online **Krasnoyarsk City Guide** is at http://tlcom.krs.ru (go to the English version on this site).

Local transport

For the airport catch bus No 135 from the bus station (US$0.50) or take a taxi (US$20). To get from the station to Hotel Krasnoyarsk, take trolley bus No 2 and get off at the bus station. To get to Hotel Turist from the bus station, take any tram along ul Veinbauma.

Where to stay

HOFA offer homestays in Krasnoyarsk, see p18.

There's accommodation on the water in the *Mikhail Godinko*, a boat moored down by the river station. They charge only US$7 for a single or US$14 for a double but the cabins are small and bathrooms are shared. There are also some more up-market double cabins with attached bathrooms.

The *Hotel Enisei* (☎ 278 262), ul Dubrovinskovo 80, is pretty basic and charges US$15/28 for a single/double. The *Hotel Sever* (☎ 224 114) on the corner of ul Lenina and ul Dzerzhinskogo is also basic but it's adequate and charges US$10-20 for a single and US$15-30 for a double.

Hotel Turist (☎ 361 470), ul Matrossova 2, has a swimming pool but is poorly located across the river. A single room with attached bath costs US$20-35 and doubles are US$40-60.

The best value hotel is the large, standard *Hotel Krasnoyarsk* (☎ 273 769), ul Uritskovo 94, charging US$30-45 for a single and US$45-60 for a double. All rooms have a bathroom attached.

Intourist groups usually stay at the 103-room *Hotel Oktyabrskaya* (☎ 271 916 🖳 october@krsk.ru, http://tlcom.krs.ru/october), ul Mira 15, with rooms from US$40 for a single and US$60 for a double unless you're Russian in which case you'll pay around a third of that. Rooms have bathroom attached, breakfast is included and there's even a casino.

Where to eat

While all the hotels have restaurants, the best is *Hotel Krasnoyarsk* as it has a range: three cafés, a restaurant and a bar. You can get a reasonable meal for US$10 in the restaurant. Another good choice is *Café Shakhmatnoe* (pro Mira 85).

Quite possibly the best pizza in Siberia is served at the *Rosso* Italian restaurant. You can buy the pizza by the slice. The restaurant can be found next door to the Hotel Sever on ul Lenina.

The attractive *Café Kofeinya* on ul Dubrovinskogo, between the Hotel Yenisei and the Museum of Local Studies is a good place. Their roast chicken is recommended.

SS Nikolai Steamship, the ship on which Lenin sailed into exile in Shushenkoe, has now been turned into a bar and disco. It's open daily from 14:00 to 02:00.

Moving on

By rail Krasnoyarsk is 65 hours from Moscow and 20 hours from Irkutsk.

By river The Yenisei River is a major communications link and passenger ferries sail nearly 2000km along it from Krasnoyarsk. For three months in the summer, you can take a boat all the way north to Dudinka or even Dikson at the mouth of the Arctic Ocean. The trip takes around 4-5 days. Tickets are available from the River Station.

Contact the **Yenisei Steamship Line** (☎ 274 845 🖺 236 567), on the second floor of the river station for more information.

The Krasnoyarsk area code is ☎ 3912. From outside Russia dial +7-3912.

By air Krasnoyarsk's main **airport** (Emelyanovo) is 40km north of the railway station. There are daily flights to Moscow (5 hours) and several flights a week to Novosibirsk, Yekaterinburg, Khabarovsk and Yakutsk. There are also occasional charter flights to Hanover.

In the city are offices for **Aeroflot** (☎ 222 156, ul Matrosova 4) and **Krasnoyarsk Airlines** (☎ 236 366, 🖹 234 896).

EXCURSIONS AROUND KRASNOYARSK

Stolby Nature Sanctuary (Заповедные Столбы)

An excursion to this 17,000 hectare recreational area is probably the most pleasant thing to do in Krasnoyarsk. It's a few kilometres upstream of the Yenisei River and there are over 100 large rock pillars, some up to 100m high, that look like people and have been given fanciful names like The Grandfather and The Woman.

Getting there To get to Stolby take the **suburban train** to Ovsyanka (Овсянка), 5km from the city or to Turbaza (Турбаза). Or you could take **bus** No 7 from pl Predmostnaya (Площадь Пред-мостная) and get off at the Turbaza (Турбаза) stop but it is still a good 5km uphill walk to the first of the pillars. If you stay on the bus until the village of Bazaikha (Базайха), a few stops further on, you can take a **chair lift** (if it is working) to the top and walk to the pillars from there. Another option is to take a tour (see p223).

Divnogorsk (Дивногорск)

About 30km away on the railway past Stolby Nature Sanctuary is the town of Divnogorsk and the Yenisei Hydroelectric Dam.

The 100m high hydroelectric dam is technically interesting as it has a large moving basin to transport ships over the dam. The basin is about 5m by 15m and after the ship above the dam enters it, the basin's doors close, and the entire basin and enclosed ship move up to the top of the dam on a cog-railway. The basin is then rotated and lowered the 100m on the other side of the dam to river level. You can see this unusual system operating until late October when the river freezes over.

Where to stay You can stay at the *Hotel Biryusa*, ul Naberezhnaya, which charges US$30 for a double.

Getting there **Hydrofoils** travel between Krasnoyarsk's River Station and Divnogorsk from 1 May to 31 August and depart every two hours. The trip takes about 45 minutes and costs US$5 for a return ticket.

There are also **buses** from the long-distance bus station behind Hotel Krasnoyarsk which take about an hour and a half, or you can catch a suburban **train** (three times a day).

Travel agents in Krasnoyarsk (see p223) will arrange tours to Divnogorsk.

Irkutsk
Иркутск

If you make only one stop on the Trans-Siberian, it should be Irkutsk. In this city, which was once known as the 'Paris of Siberia', you'll find the people rather more friendly and relaxed than the people in European Russia. Along many of the streets you can still see the cosy-looking log cabins (eaves and windows decorated with intricate fretwork) which are typical of the Siberian style of domestic architecture.

Sixty-four kilometres from Irkutsk is Lake Baikal, set amongst some of the world's most beautiful countryside. Trekking, camping, boat excursions, diving and riding are just a few of the pursuits that are now available in this outdoor paradise.

HISTORY
Military outpost
Irkutsk was founded as a military outpost in 1652 by Ivan Pakhobov, a tax-collector who had come to encourage the local Buryat tribesmen to pay their fur tribute. By 1686 a church had been built and a small town established on the banks of the Angara. Tea caravans from China passed through Irkutsk, fur-traders sold their pelts here and the town quickly developed into a centre for trade in Siberia.

By the beginning of the nineteenth century, Irkutsk was recognized as the administrative capital of Siberia. The Governor, who lived in the elegant white building that still stands by the river (opposite the obelisk), presided over an area twenty times the size of France. Being the capital of Siberia, it was the destination of many exiled nobles from Western Russia. The most celebrated exiles were the Decembrists, who had attempted a coup in St Petersburg in 1825. The houses in which some of them lived are now museums.

Boom town
With the discovery of gold in the area in the early 1800s, 'Gold Fever' hit Irkutsk. Fortunes were made in a day and lost overnight in the gambling dens. By the end of the century, in spite of a great fire in 1879 which destroyed 75 per cent of the houses, the city had become the financial and cultural centre of Siberia. Its cosmopolitan population included fur traders, tea merchants, gold prospectors, exiles and ex-convicts. Those prospectors who were lucky became exceedingly rich, some amassing personal fortunes that would be equivalent to £70 or £80 million today.

❏ How to get on in society

Travelling along the Trans-Siberian at the end of the 19th century, John Foster Fraser spent several days in Irkutsk. Recording his observations on the social order in the city he wrote, 'To do things in the proper way and be correct and Western is, of course, the ambition of Irkutsk. So there is quite a social code. The old millionaires, who for forty years found Irkutsk society – such as it was before the coming of the railway – quite satisfied with a red shirt and a pair of greased top boots, are now "out of it". A millionaire only becomes a gentleman when he tucks in his shirt and wears his trousers outside and not inside his boots. It is etiquette to put on a black coat between the hours of ten in the morning and noon. No matter how sultry the evening is, if you go for the usual promenade and not wear a black overcoat you proclaim you are unacquainted with the ways of good society. As to wealth, there is but one standard in Irkutsk. A man is known by his furs, and his wife by her furs and pearls'.

In Irkutsk Fraser was unimpressed by the standards of hygiene exhibited by all classes of society and declared that '.certainly the Russian is as sparing with water as though it were holy oil from Jerusalem'.

John Foster Fraser, *The Real Siberia* (1902)

Often no more than illiterate adventurers or ex-convicts, they spent their money on lavish houses, French tutors for their children and clothes from the Paris fashion houses for their wives.

By far the most exciting occasion in the Irkutskian social calendar for 1891 was the visit of the Tsarevich (later Nicholas II) who stayed only a day but still had time to visit the museum, gold-smelting laboratory and the monastery, to consecrate and open the new pontoon bridge over the Angara (replaced only in 1936), to review the troops and to attend a ball.

The first rail travellers arrive

On 16 August 1898 Irkutsk was linked by rail to Europe with the arrival of the first Trans-Siberian Express. The train brought more European tourists than had dared venture into Siberia in the days when travelling meant weeks of discomfort bumping along the Trakt (the Post Road) in a wooden tarantass (carriage). Their guide books warned them of the dangers that awaited them in Irkutsk. Bradshaw's *Through Routes to the Capitals of the World* (1903) had this to say about the town: 'The streets are not paved or lighted; the sidewalks are merely boards on crosspieces over the open sewers. In summer it is almost impassable owing to the mud, or unbearable owing to the dust. The police are few, escaped criminals and ticket-of-leave criminals many. In Irkutsk and all towns east of it, the stranger should not walk after dark; if a carriage cannot be got as is often the case, the only way is to walk noisily along the planked walk;

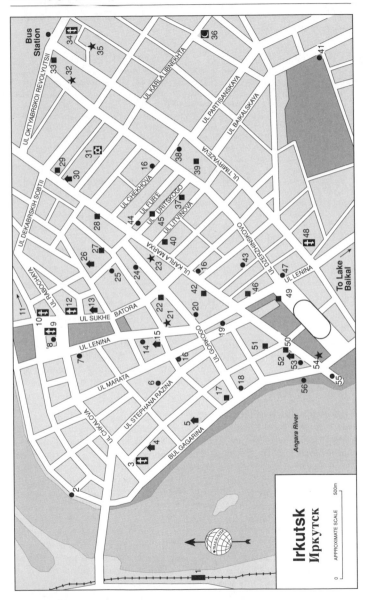

Irkutsk
Иркутск

APPROXIMATE SCALE

0   500m

HOTELS AND RESTAURANTS

- 4 Hotel Agat Гостиница Агат
- 5 Hotel Intourist Гостиница Иркутск-Интурист
- 13 Hotel Angara Гостиница Ангара
- 14 Site of Hotel Sibir Быв. Гостиница Сибирь
- 15 Hotel Rus Гостиница Русь
- 17 Café Bagira & Alfa Bank Кафе Багира + Алфа Банк
- 22 Café Blinaya Кафе Блиная
- 26 Hotel Arena Гостиница Арена
- 27 Restaurant Aura & Circus Ресторан Аура и Цирк
- 28 Niva Bakery Пекарня Нива
- 29 Beer Bar U Shveika Бар
- 30 Hotel Kech Гостиница Кэч
- 37 Café Vernisazh Кафе Вернисаж
- 39 Restaurant & Bar Tsentralny Ресторан + Бар Центральный
- 40 Café Snezhinka Кафе Снужинка
- 45 Belgrad Restaurant-Bar Ресторан-Бар Белград
- 46 Café Karlson Кафе Карлсон
- 47 Café Teatralnoe Театр + Кафе
- 49 Fikhtelberg Restaurant Ресторан Казино Фихтельберг
- 50 Bar Efimich Бар
- 51 Restaurant Drakon Ресторан Дракон
- 52 Hotel Retro Гостиница Ретро

OTHER

- 1 Railway Station Железнодорожний Вокзал
- 2 River Station Речной Вокзал
- 3 Planetarium/Trinity Church Планетарий в Троитской Церкви
- 6 Central Post Office Почтамт
- 7 Pl. Kirova (Kirov Sq) bus stop Остановка «Пл. Кирова»
- 8 Government Headquarters Дом Правительства
- 9 Church of Our Saviour Краеведческий Музей-Спасская Церковь
- 10 Epiphany Cathedral Богоявленский Собор
- 11 To Znamensky Monastery Знаменский Монастырь
- 12 Polish Catholic Cathedral Органный Зал-Польский Костёл
- 16 Internet Интернет-Кафе
- 17 Alfa-Bank Алфа-Банк
- 18 Transaero Авиакомпания Трансаэро
- 19 Inkom Bank (for travellers' cheques) ИнкомБанк
- 20 Inkom Bank (for Visa card cash advances) Инком Банк
- 21 Art Museum Художественный Музей
- 23 Exhibition Hall Выставочный Зал Художественного Музея
- 24 Aeroflot & Air Baikal Касса Аэрофлота и Air Baikal
- 25 Central Telegraph Office Центральнный Телеграф
- 27 Circus Цирк
- 31 Synagogue Синагога
- 32 Trubetskoi House Музей-усадьба Трубецкого
- 33 Titanic Nightclub Клуб-Титаньк
- 34 Church of the Transfiguration Преображенская Церковь
- 35 Maria Volkonsky's House Музей-усадьба Волконского
- 36 Mosque Мечеть
- 38 Market Рынок
- 41 Aistenok Puppet Theatre Театр Кукол Аистенока
- 42 Stratosfera Nightclub Клуб-Стратосфера
- 43 Mongolian Consulate Кунсульство Монголии
- 44 Sberbank Сбер-Банк
- 47 Theatre & Café Teatralnoe Театр + Кафе
- 48 Church of the Elevation of the Cross Крестовдвиженская Церковь
- 53 White House/Irkutsk University Белый Дом/Университет
- 54 Regional Museum Краеведческий Музей
- 55 Trans-Sib Monument Обелиск Транссибирской
- 56 Gagarin Pier Причал Гагарина

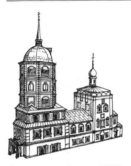

CHURCH OF OUR SAVIOUR (1706)

be careful in making crossings, and do not stop, or the immense mongrel mastiffs turned loose into the streets as guards will attack. To walk in the middle of the road is to court attack from the garrotters with which Siberian towns abound.' The dangers that Bradshaw warned his travellers against were no exaggeration for at the time the average number of reported murders per year in Irkutsk was over 400, out of a population of barely 50,000.

Irkutsk today

Today's Irkutskians are rather better behaved, although as everywhere in Russia, mafia-related crime is on the increase. A city of over half a million, Irkutsk is still one of the largest suppliers of furs to the world markets, although engineering is now the main industry.

In the 2000 elections Putin polled just over 50% of votes in Irkutsk oblast. On the campaign trail in February 2000 he had visited Irkutsk where he highlighted the problems of the region: 'The economic successes of the oblast are modest...More than four million people live in extreme poverty'. He added that he wanted to encourage the creation of large companies able not only to extract the region's mineral resources but also to develop and sell them on Russian and world markets. It's now more than a decade since the dawn of the market economy in Russia but the dream of what could happen when its full effect is applied to Siberia has yet to come true.

WHAT TO SEE

Cathedrals and War Memorial

In Irkutsk in 1900 there were two cathedrals: the splendid Cathedral of Our Lady of Kazan, bigger than Kazan Cathedral in St Petersburg, was damaged during the Civil War. It was demolished and now the ugly bulk of the **Central Government Headquarters** stands in its place, opposite the **WWII Memorial**; the second cathedral, the **Cathedral of the Epiphany** (1724), is across the road. In the great fire of 1879 it was badly damaged and the heat was so intense that it melted one of the 12-ton bells. It used to contain an icon museum but is now a practising church again. The icons have been relocated to the Art Museum.

Church of Our Saviour

This boat-shaped church contains the **Museum of Local Studies**. There are some interesting frescoes on the exterior which depict, from left to right, Buryats being baptized, Christ being baptized and the local bishop,

Innocenti, being canonized. The museum inside contains a small display of stuffed local animals. Upstairs there's an interesting religious history display including the robes, rattle of human bones and feathered head-dress of a shaman (see below); masks and robes used in Tibetan Buddhist mystery plays; prayer wheels and Buddhist texts from the monasteries south of Irkutsk. Up a very narrow staircase is a small exhibition of bells. Open 10:00-18:00, daily except Tuesday. Entry is US$2 and there's a camera charge of US$2.

Polish Catholic Church

Opposite the Church of Our Saviour is a church with a tall steeple, the Catholic Church. It is the only neo-Gothic church in Siberia and was built in 1883 by exiled Poles. Services are held on Sundays for the descendants of Poles exiled to Siberia. During summer there are usually organ concerts held on Sundays and Wednesdays, starting around 19:30.

Regional Museum

This museum of local history, situated beside the river just south of the Hotel Intourist, has some interesting exhibits. Upstairs is a 'local achieve-

❏ Shamanism

Shamanism is a primitive form of religion centred around the shaman, a medium and healer. Although the concept of the shaman is fairly common throughout the world, the word itself originally derives from the Tungus tribes of Siberia.

Wearing spectacular robes, the shaman beats a drum and goes into a trance in order to communicate with the spirits. From them the shaman discovers the cause of an illness, the reason for the failure of the crops, or is warned of some approaching disaster. Commonly, spirits are thought to select their shamans before they are born and brand them with distinguishing features: an extra finger or toe or a large birthmark. During their adolescence they may be 'tortured' by the spirits with an illness of some kind until they agree to act as shaman. Some shamans may be physically weak, epileptic, mentally disordered; through their spiritual power they gain authority and perform rituals.

'Shamanism played an extremely negative role in the history of the Siberian peoples... In status, activity and interests, the shamans were hand in glove with the ruling cliques of the indigenous populations', wrote the Marxist anthropologists M.G.Levin and L.P.Potapov, in *The Peoples of Siberia*. Other anthropologists have been less severe, noting that shamanism gave those with mental and physical disorders a place in society at a time when most other societies shunned the handicapped.

In the spirit of freedom of religious expression in Russia today shamanism is undergoing something of a revival. The Republic of Tuva, west of Irkutsk is the modern centre of Shamanism.

ments' gallery including a model of part of the BAM railway. Above the stairs is a panorama showing the Great Irkutsk Fire of 1879. The ethnographic galleries are downstairs and exhibits include flints and bones from the archaeological site of Malta, just outside Irkutsk where evidence of human habitation has been found dating back 24,000 years; the inside of a settler's house from earlier this century with carved wooden sideboard and HMV gramophone and 78rpm records; a set of robes worn by a shaman, together with his antlers and drum; photographs showing what life was like for past inhabitants and the convicts; and also a most peculiar article of clothing: a suit made completely of fish skins, the standard summer costume of the Goldi tribe who lived in the Far Eastern Territories. The museum (☎ 333 449), ul Karla Marxa, is open 10:00-16:00, not Monday. Entry is US$2.50. There are discounts for student card holders.

Other places of worship

At the turn of the century, Irkutsk boasted fifty-eight places of worship. This fell to only three or four after the Revolution but many are now reopening.

Znamensky Monastery (Apparition of the Virgin), with its turquoise domes, lies to the north-east of the city, over the bridge and is well worth a visit. Services are held here regularly. The frescoes inside are impressive but recent restoration has left the interior looking rather modern. The casket containing the body of **St Innokent**, the Siberian missionary who died here in 1731, was returned to Irkutsk in the 1990s but may be moved to the cathedral when restoration there is complete. It is said that his body is incorruptible and has been the source of many miracles.

Beside the church are the graves of Yekaterina Trubetskoi (see opposite) and also Gregory Shelekhov, who founded the colony of Alaska in 1784 (sold to the USA in 1868). His grave is marked by an obelisk decorated with cartographic instruments. To get here, take trolley-bus No 3 from the south end of pl Kirova.

It's also interesting to visit the old **synagogue**, ul Karla Libknekhta 23, a large blue building, the lower storey of which has been converted into a factory. Enter through the door on left with the three stars above it. There is also a **mosque** at ul Karla Libknekhta 86.

Art museum

Comprising works by eighteenth and nineteenth-century Russian, German, Flemish, French, Italian and English painters, the collection was begun by Vladimir Sukachev in the 1870s and 'donated' to the city after the Revolution. There are, however, the inevitable modern Soviet masterpieces: A A Plastov's *Supper of Tractor Operators* and A V Moravov's *Calculating of Working Days*, for example. The gallery devoted to nineteenth-century local scenes is particularly interesting and in the gallery of

Western Art (XV–XIX centuries) you will find a small canvas with the label 'Landsir 1802-73' which is *The Family of Dogs* by Sir Edwin Landseer, who designed the lions in Trafalgar Square.

The Art Museum (☎ 244 336), ul Lenina 5, is open 10:00-18:00, closed Tuesday; entry is US$3.50.

Trubetskoi house

The wooden house once occupied by Sergei and Yekaterina Trubetskoi and other nobles involved in an unsuccessful coup in 1825 is preserved as a museum, kept as it was when the exiles lived here. In the cellar there is an interesting display of old photographs showing life in the Nerchinsk silver mines and a prison cell in Chita. There is also a picture of Maria Volkonsky (see below) and her child. At ul Dzerzhinskovo 64 (☎ 275 773), it's open 10:00-18:00, closed Tuesday. Entry is US$2.50. ('With thermopane windows it would be a great place'. Louis Wozniak (USA): Visitors' book in this museum.)

Maria Volkonsky's house

The large and attractive blue and white house of this famous Decembrist who followed her husband into Siberian exile is open to the public. If you've read Caroline Sutherland's *The Princess of Siberia* then you must visit Maria Volkonsky's house. It is a grand old building but it's a pity it's so sparsely furnished as it doesn't have the lived-in feel of the other house museums. Displays include Maria's clothes, letters, furniture, and church robes of 18th and 19th centuries. In the yard there are several wooden buildings and a well. At per Volkhonskovo 10 (☎ 277 818), it is open 10:00-18:00, closed Monday. Entry is US$3.50.

Angara steamship

The *Angara*, commissioned in 1899, was partially assembled in England and then sent to Irkutsk in pieces by train. Until the completion of the Circumbaikal line she ferried rail passengers across the lake, together with her bigger sister, the *Baikal*. Following the line's completion in 1904, the *Angara* performed a series of menial tasks before being abandoned, partially submerged, in 1958. The boat was restored and became the Museum of Nautical Navigation. In 1995, the ship was again converted and this time became the office of a local newspaper. Unfortunately you can't currently wander around the vessel although there are plans to reopen part of the collection so it may be worth asking. Trolley-bus No 5 passes this way.

Other sights

In the summer, touring companies perform in the imposing **Drama Theatre**, built at the turn of the century, in ul Karla Marxa. There are also **boat trips** (1-2hrs) along the river to the dam and power station. They leave daily from the Gagarin Pier near the **Trans-Siberian Builder's Monument**. This statue has Yermak and Count Muravyev-Amursky on its sides and the double-headed Imperial eagle on the railings surrounding it. The building beside the obelisk may look like a mini Sydney Opera House but its main use is for dog shows. You can take a pony ride from here as well.

In the **Fur Distribution Centre**, on the southern outskirts of the city, visitors are shown some of the 18 varieties of mink and also the pelts of the Barguzinsk sable, which sell for over US$750 each. It's open to tours only, and only between October and May.

Also worth a visit is the **House of Artists** (Dom Khudozhnikov) at ul Karla Marxa 38, which has the occasional exhibition.

RIVER CRUISES

Rivers are navigable from mid May to September. There are three river stations in Irkutsk, each for a different destination. Scenic cruises depart from Gagarin Pier which is at the intersection of bul Gagarina and ul Gorkovo. Boats travel upstream to the Angara Hydroelectric Power Station dam and departures for the eighty-minute return trip leave every hour. Tickets can be bought at the pier. For long-distance boats and boats to Lake Baikal see p240 and p243.

PRACTICAL INFORMATION
Orientation

Irkutsk railway station is on the west bank of the river; the city centre and the tourist hotels are on the east. The city centre is along two intersected main streets: ul Lenina and ul Karla Marxa. Ul Lenina runs north-south from the administrative and public transport centre of pl Kirova, while the main shopping and museum street of ul Karla Marxa runs east-west.

Any bus heading north from the railway station should take you over the bridge; from here all the main hotels are within walking distance.

Services
Information On the Internet a good starting place is 🖳 **www.icc.ru** which has links to numerous other Irkutsk-related sites such as the **Irkutsk Electronic Yellow Pages** which can be found at 🖳 www.icc.ru/fed/yellow.html. You can even

check the temperature at 🖳 http://cavs .irk.ru/termall.htm.

Locally, you can get good **maps** from the Hotel Intourist, and Sibtorg Bookshop at ul Karla Marxa 24.

Irkutsk State Teachers' Training Institute of Foreign Languages (☎ 333 246, 🖷 333 244), Room 201/203, ul Lenina 8, has **Russian language courses** lasting anything from a week to four years. The cost is US$350 per month tuition and US$60 a month for accommodation.

Communications **Faxes** can be sent from the Central Telegraph Office and the Central Post Office, both open daily 08:00-20:00. For **courier services**, DHL (☎ 290 307) is at Hotel Intourist.

There is an **Internet** connection at the Central Telegraph Office which costs US$1 per hour. There is only one com-

---

The Irkutsk area code is ☎ 3952. From outside Russia dial +7-3952.

puter though and the queue can be long. One of the **Internet cafés** may be better: ul Marata 38 (US$2/hour, open 24 hours) and ul Chekhova 19 (US$2/ hour, open 10:00-19:00).

Banks There's an **ATM** inside the Alfa-Bank at ul Gagarina 38, open 10:00-19:00. You can also cash travellers' cheques here and get advances on credit cards.

Other banks with exchange facilities include Inkombank on ul Lenina, and Sberbank at ul Fur'e 2.

You can exchange only US$ cash at Hotel Intourist (open 24 hours) and at the office on the 2nd floor at the central market (daily, 09:00-18:00).

Travel agents A reliable budget agency is **Baikal Complex** (☎ 359 205 464 /62, 🖷 432 060, 432 322 (marked attn Baikalcomplex), 🖳 youry@baikal .irku tsk.su, www.icc.ru/baikalcom plex), PO Box 3598, Irkutsk-29. It's run by the friendly Yuri Nemirorsky.

Another helpful tour operator is Alexander (Sasha) Medvedev whose company, **AquaEco** (☎ 334 290), is based at ul Karla Libknekhta 12.

You could also try **Baikal House** (☎ 335 378, 🖷 335 378), ul Karla Marxa 3113; **Sputnik** (☎ 341 727), ul Dzerzhinskovo 48, which organizes both local and Mongolian trips; and **Maria Travel** (☎ 341 486), ul Kievskaya 2, kv 211, 🖳 maria@pop.irk.ru.

Intourist (☎ 290 161) runs over-priced tours from the Hotel Intourist.

Tours

The travel agents listed above run similar tour programmes which include city tours, day trips and **adventure tours** such as hiking, skiing and trekking. They also offer two-day trips along the **Circumbaikal Railway Line**. See p344 for information on this trip.

Also on offer is **scuba diving** (US$55, PADI or BSAC certificate required), **horse riding** (US$10 per hour), and a four-day trip to **Olkhon Island** (200km north in Lake Baikal) costing about US$60 a day

per person. You stay in the wooden hotel (no hot water) in Khuzhir village, and visit several Buryat sacred sites and a Stalin era gulag camp.

Mirage (☎ 461 921, 464 943 🖳 miraj@irk.ru) run trips in their boat, *Mirage*. Operated by Igor Sher and recommended by two readers the maximum group size is six people, meals are said to be superb and there are hot showers available on board. Their programme includes day trips for fishing and also a ten-day cruise around Lake Baikal for US$914 per person.

Local transport

Since most of the sights, restaurants and shops are within walking distance of the hotels, this is the most pleasant and interesting way to get around.

There's no metro but the usual bus service operates. Bus No 20 runs between the station and the airport down ul Lenina. Trams 1 and 2 go from the station over the bridge and into the centre of town. Tram No 4 goes out to the airport (25 minutes) and back from ul Lenina, near the Art Museum.

The shared minibuses (*mikriki*) which run on fixed routes are even more useful: you can see what the other passengers pay (about US$0.25 per km).

Where to stay

Baikal Complex, HOFA and G&R International (see p18 and p236-7) are among some of the companies offering *homestays* in Irkutsk, Listvyanka and Bolshie Koty for US$20-30 per person including meals. You may also be approached on the station platform by people offering rooms in their houses for US$5-10. Don't agree to anything without seeing the place and the family first.

Two cheap hotels in the town are the *Hotel Agat* (☎ 297 325), ul 5 Armi, 12 which charges US$8/15 for singles/doubles and the *Hotel Kech* (☎ 335 972), ul Karla Marxa 34, which is very basic but clean and friendly, with singles for US$7. Bathrooms in both these places are shared.

Near the circus is *Hotel Arena* (☎ 344 642), ul Zhelyabova 8a. It looks much better inside than out; rooms cost US$15-28 for a single and US$20-35 for a double. Bathrooms are shared.

The *Hotel Angara* (☎ 293 616), ul Sukhe-Batora 7, is in a good location and always busy; a bus service along the never-ending corridors might be an idea. Single rooms with attached shower are US$15-40 and doubles US$28-50; there are also some more pricey rooms. They'll offer you the top rooms first. A buffet breakfast which is remarkably good is included. A bit more expensive but worth it is the *Hotel Rus* (☎ 343 715), ul Sverdlova 19. Prices for singles are US$30-50 and it's US$40-70 for doubles room, all including breakfast and attached bathrooms. It has a good restaurant and the whole place is well run.

For budget travellers by far the best choice is the *American House* (☎ 432 689), ul Ostrovski 19, a very relaxed place with friendly proprietors who speak a little English. It has three single rooms, two double rooms and overflow areas. Bed and breakfast costs US$15-20. From the railway station, you have to either take a taxi or walk as no public transport goes past it. On foot (15 minutes) leave the station and cross the road. An opening between the row of kiosks takes you to some stairs. At the top of the stairs, a dirt road leads between apartment blocks to a large dirt road. This goes up a very steep hill and near the top on the left is a newly-built brick church. Opposite, on the right, is ul Ostrovski. Ask locals for 'Americansky Dom' if you can't find it. Coming from the centre of Irkutsk, bus No 11 from in front of Hotel Angara takes you across the river, and along ul Mayakovskovo, before turning left into ul Chaikovskovo. Get off at the first stop along this street which is on the corner of the dirt road leading to the railway station. Walk down the street for about 20m and you will see the church on the right; turn left down ul Ostrovski.

On the western side of the river is *MNTK-Iris* (☎ 462 569, 🖹 461 762) at ul

Lermontova 337. Immaculate rooms start from US$45 for one person or US$55 for two. There's a sauna and café. Take trolley-buses Nos 1, 2 or 7 from pl Kirova or trolley-bus No 6 from the airport.

Hotel Intourist (☎ 290 171, 🖹 277 872), bul Gagarina 44, is good but seems overpriced when compared to Irkutsk's other hotels. Singles start from US$117 and double rooms from US$133. The price includes breakfast and the hotel offers a wide range of tourist services.

The comfortable *Hotel Retro* (☎ 333 981), ul Karla Marxa 1, has a high wall round it and big iron gates. You may have trouble getting the security guards to open the gates unless you drive a new Mercedes or have mafia connections. Rooms cost around US$200.

Hotel Sibir, ul Lenina 8, was destroyed by fire in the summer of 1995.

Where to eat

One local delicacy worth looking out for on restaurant menus is the delicious *omul*, from Lake Baikal.

The *Café Karlson*, ul Lenina, is decorated in a fairy-tale style and is quiet and friendly. They serve good snacks. There's a *Pizzeria* (☎ 340 373) at ul Karla Marxa 45. Delicious blinis are served at *Café Blinaya* which is on the corner of ul Sukhe Batora and ul Sverdlova.

Between Transaero and Alpha Bank on bul Gagarina is *Café Bagira*. They have a good selection and some of it is laid out on tables so it's easy to point to and order if you don't speak much Russian. Other good cheap cafés include the popular *Café Teatralnoe*, ul Lenina 23, open 12:00-04:00, and the *Café Belgrad*, ul Uritskogo 7, which offers Yugoslav dishes for around US$5. This is also a good place for a drink.

Café Vernisazh, ul Uritskogo 16, serves tasty Russian food. Count on around US$10 for a meal. *Café Snezhinka*, ul Litvinova 2 also serves good Russian dishes and is similarly priced. It's open until 02:00.

An excellent restaurant serving traditional Siberian meals is *Restaurant Rus* in

Hotel Rus (☎ 277 315), ul Sverdlova 19. A three-course meal costs US$10-15. The food in the restaurant in the *Hotel Angara* is good. Even the live singer isn't too bad. A three-course meal is around US$10.

The best oriental food is at the *Chinese Restaurant Drakon*, ul 5th Armii 67, but it's difficult to get in for dinner without a reservation.

The *Restaurant Aura* (☎ 336 139), on the first floor of the circus building, offers authentic Siberian fare: their pelmeni are recommended. A meal without drinks will cost about US$10. The drawback is the nightly cabaret act (striptease at weekends): an entry fee will indicate that there's a show in progress.

The *Fikhtelberg Casino Restaurant* (☎ 336 101), on ul Lenina 46, is good for steaks. Unfortunately there's a house band, and it gets rather hot and stuffy here on summer evenings. For a wide range of food, try the two restaurants in the *Hotel Intourist*. Choices consist of the expensive Chinese Peking Restaurant that's usually full in the evenings and the Russian Irkutsk Restaurant. Both serve reasonable food but service can be very slow unless you're with a group.

Self-caterers should visit the *central market*. The best bread in town comes from *Niva Bakery*, ul Karla Marxa, and you can also get a good cup of coffee here.

Entertainment

This is Siberia not New York but Irkutsk is at least livelier in the evenings than it was in the communist era.

For bars, try the *Belgrad* (see Where to eat), *Bar Efimich* (ul Karla Marxa 5), *Beer Bar U Shveika* (ul Karla Marxa 34), and *Bar Tsentralni* (ul Litvinova 17). There are also bars in the larger hotels such as the *Intourist*.

There are several nightclubs: the one at the Intourist Hotel is the *Butterfly*;

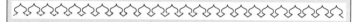

❑ Getting to Mongolia

Irkutsk has a Mongolian Consulate, travel agents specializing in Mongolian travel and daily trains to Mongolia.

The **Mongolian Consulate** (☎ 342 447, 242 370, 🖹 342 445), ul Lapina 11, is open 09:00-13:00 weekdays. A transit visa good for 10 days in the country is available in only 45 minutes for US$30 here or in three to four days for US$15; bring two passport photographs and your ticket out of Mongolia. To get a tourist visa, you may still need an invitation, although other Mongolian embassies are no longer insisting on this (see Irkutsk travel agents that offer Monglian services), US$40 and two photos. Processing takes three to four days or for US$60 a faster service is possible. Getting a Mongolian visa can be difficult if you do not speak Russian or Mongolian so using a local travel agent is advisable.

Travel agents that can organize train tickets, accommodation and tours to Mongolia include Baikal Complex, Intourist and Sputnik. Baikal Complex offers the cheapest deals.

To buy **train tickets** from Irkutsk to Mongolia, go to the International Ticket Office on the first floor of the Irkutsk railway station. To get to the ticket office, you have to go through the waiting hall. You normally will have to pay to enter the waiting hall, but if you say that you want to buy an international ticket, you will probably get in for free. Train No 264 leaves daily for Ulan Bator at 20:10 local time. Ask for wagon 15 which is the best carriage. A coupé ticket should cost around US$70.

there's also *Titanic*, ul Oktyabrskoi Revolyutsii 25, and *Stratosfera*, ul Karla Marxa 15. Entry to Stratosfera is US$2.50 and there's a bowling alley here, too.

Irkutsk also has a **circus** and the **Aistenok Puppet Theatre** (☎ 270 666) is at ul 1st Sovetskaya 1.

Concerts are given at the **Philharmonic Hall** (☎ 345 873), ul Dzershinskovo 2, and there are organ recitals at the Polish Catholic Church.

What to buy

The heart of the city is the **market**, which extends for several hundred metres behind the main shopping street, ul Karla Marxa. It's not hard to find: long before you see it you'll hear the many bootleg cassette dealers demonstrating their 'latest' releases. Good quality CDs sell for about US$2. Other stalls sell everything from Sindy dolls and Snickers bars to sports shoes and switchblades. The **Detsky Mir Children's Store** is the best proper shop in the market area. You can buy Kodak film here, or have your photographs processed in an hour. The best local bookshops are **Military Books**, ul Uritskovo 15; **Rodnik Books**, ul Litvinova 1, and **Sibtorg**, ul Karla Marxa 24. Next to Sibtorg is an **art shop** which sells semi-precious gems such as chaorite which are found only in the Baikal area.

Moving on

By rail Irkutsk is 86 hours from Moscow by rail, 31 hours from Novosibirsk, 20 hours from Krasnoyarsk, 8 hours from Ulan Ude, 36 hours to Ulan Bator and 72 hours from Vladivostok.

Although there's now no difference in price between tickets bought by Russians and those bought by foreigners, the foreigner's window at the railway station may still be open. It's the kassa on the far right of the line and is staffed by friendly English-speaking staff.

By bus For Listvyanka see p243.

By river Boats for **Lake Baikal** and **Listvyanka** depart from the Hydrofoil Pier (☎ 238 072), above the Angara Dam which is 5km upstream (to the south) of Irkutsk. Bus No 16 runs there from pl Kirova; the trip takes 45 minutes.

From the Hydrofoil Pier there are also hydrofoils to **Nizhneangarsk** (12 hours) via **Severobaikalsk** four times a week, **Ust Barguzin** (Monday), **Bukhta Peschannaya** (three per week) and **Bolshie Koty** (three per day).

Hydrofoils for **Bratsk** (12 hours, three per week) via **Angarsk** depart from the River Station at the base of the bridge over the Angara. When you cross this bridge from the railway station, you can see it on the left. To get to it from pl Kirova, walk down ul Chkalova which runs to the bridge. Avoid this area after dark as it's notoriously dangerous.

By air There are international flights to Ulan Bator, Niigata (Japan) and Sheyang (China). Transaero operates flights to Frankfurt for US$600 with a change of plane in Moscow (two flights per week). They occasionally have deals on flights from Irkutsk to London via Moscow for US$450.

Transero (☎ 330 891) is at bul Gagarina 38. **Aeroflot** (☎ 276 917) is at ul Gorkovo 29; and next door is the new airline, **Air Baikal** which operates a Boeing 757 on the Moscow–Irkutsk route (US$180) and also has a service to Khabarovsk (US$100).

Tickets for any airline can also be purchased from the Flight Ticket Office (☎ 293 415) in Hotel Angara.

(Opposite) Top: The body of St Innokent, the Siberian missionary who died in 1731, now lies in the church at Znamensky Monastery, Irkutsk (see p234). The church has recently been restored. **Bottom:** Looking across Yaroslavl (see p188) from the bell tower of the Transfiguration of our Saviour Monastery. (Photo © Nick Hill).

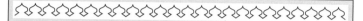

❏ **Life-enhancing waters**

Guides never fail to recount the superstition concerning the power of Baikal water. Dip your hands in, they say, and you will live a year longer than you otherwise would. Dip your feet in too and this will be extended to five years. Brave the icy waters for a swim and, if the shock doesn't kill you instantly, you'll be around for twenty-five extra years.

A world record was set in here in 1991, as a team of relay swimmers managed to cross the width of the lake in 17 hours. Even these intrepid athletes had trouble, though: because of the extreme cold, the longest period any one of them could spend in the water at one time was 30 minutes.

Lake Baikal
Озеро Байкал

The world's deepest lake

Sixty-four kilometres (forty miles) south of Irkutsk, Lake Baikal is 1637 metres (5371 feet) deep and is estimated to contain more than 20,000 cubic km of water, roughly 20 per cent of the world's freshwater supplies. If all the rest of the world's drinking water ran out tomorrow, Lake Baikal could supply the entire population of the planet for the next 40 years.

Known as the 'Blue Eye of Siberia' it is also the world's oldest lake, formed almost 50 million years ago. It is among the largest lakes on the planet, being about 400 miles long and between 20 and 40 miles wide. The water is incredibly clear and, except around Baikalsk and the Selenga delta, completely safe to drink owing to the filtering action of numerous types of sponge which live in its depths, along with hundreds of other species found nowhere else.

Holy Sea

Russian colonists called Baikal the 'Holy Sea' since there were so many local myths and legends surrounding it. The Buryats believed that the evil spirit Begdozi lived on Olkhon Island in the middle of the lake, though the Evenki shamans held that this was the home of the sea god, Dianda. It is hardly surprising that these primitive tribes were impressed by the

---

(Opposite) Lake Baikal: the view down to Port Baikal from the hill above Listvyanka.

strange power of the lake for at times sudden violent storms spring up, lashing the coast with waves up to seven feet high. It freezes to a depth of about ten feet for four months of the year, from late December. The Angara is the only river that flows out of the lake and since the dam and hydroelectric power station were built on the Angara in 1959, the water-level of the lake has been slowly rising.

Environmental threats

The remoteness of the lake kept it safe from the threat of environmental damage until the building of the Trans-Siberian at the end of the last century. Damage to the environment is increasing, with the building of new towns on the northern shores for the construction of the BAM line, and also owing to industrial waste from Ulan Ude (the Selenga River flows past this city into the lake via one of the world's last large wetlands, the Selenga delta). The most famous campaigner for the protection of the lake is author Valentin Rasputin. Demonstrations in Irkutsk in 1987 resulted in filtration equipment being installed in the wood pulp mill at Baikalsk on the edge of the lake but current reports suggest that it is inefficient and that pollution is continuing. A coastal protection zone was established around the edge of the entire lake in 1987 but campaigners bemoan the fact that the government's anti-pollution laws have no teeth. They believe that the lake should be placed under the independent protection of UNESCO. For more information, contact **Greenpeace's Baikal Campaign** Coordinator, Roman Pukalov in Moscow at ▤ (095) 251 9088 or by ▤ gpmoscow@glas.apc.org.

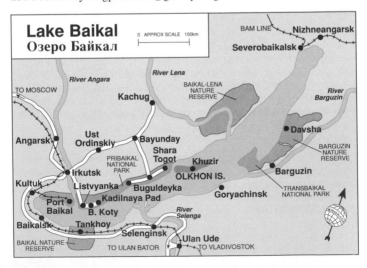

Lake Baikal / Озеро Байкал

GETTING TO LAKE BAIKAL

The two ways of getting from Irkutsk to Lake Baikal are by boat (see p240) or by bus. Buses depart from Irkutsk's long-distance bus station on ul Oktyabrskoi Revolutsii. The trip takes about 90 minutes. During summer, buses depart from Irkutsk at 9:00, 14:30, 16:30 and 19:00 and from Listvyanka at 7:00, 11:50, 16:45 and 18:00. The bus will stop on request virtually anywhere with major stops at the Open Air Museum, Baikal Ecological Museum, Listvyanka village and Listvyanka pier.

Open Air Museum

On the road between Irkutsk and Listvyanka is the Museum of Wooden Architecture (☎ 145 249), an interesting collection of reconstructed, traditional wooden houses. It is located at the km47 marker from Irkutsk, which is the km23 marker from Listvyanka – ask the bus driver for the 'moozay'. There is a large farmhouse, a bathroom with a vast wooden tub and, a short way along a path, a water-mill and a post-house, complete with the Imperial crest on its roof-top. When the only way to cross Siberia was by road and river, fresh horses and simple accommodation were available from post-houses. The museum is open only in the summer but you can wander round outside in spring and autumn.

LISTVYANKA

Listvyanka is an attractive village of wooden houses beside Lake Baikal. There's a shop, two small cafés and the jetty. The Baikal Ecological Museum and the Hotel Baikal-Intourist above it are about one km before the village on the road from Irkutsk. Behind the Intourist Hotel is a hill that gives a good view over the water to the Khamar Daban Mountains. The half-hour hike up is well worth it. At the top there's a little shelter and a tree decorated with paper ribbons that people have tied to it for good luck, a very old Siberian superstition.

Baikal Ecological Museum

The Baikal Ecological Museum (formerly the Limnological Museum, ☎ 460 324), has a number of fascinating displays of the unique marine life and animals in the Baikal area. Entry is US$2.

Over 80 per cent of the species in Lake Baikal cannot be found anywhere else in the world. These include 1085 types of algae, 250 mosses, 450 lichens, 1500 vascular plants, 255 small crustaceans, 83 gastropods, 86 worms and 52 fish. The exceptionally high oxygen levels in the lake create the ideal environment for many creatures which have long since become extinct elsewhere. These include the freshwater seals, found only here and until recently threatened with extinction by the Buryats who turned them into overcoats. They are now a protected species, listed in the *Red Book of Endangered Species*, and currently number about 60,000. A unique Baikal fish is the tiny *golomyanka* which, composed almost entirely of transparent fat, lives at depths up to 1½km. Surprisingly, it gives birth to its young alive and fully formed. The museum also contains a model of the *Angara*, some examples of the tasty *omul*, and a collection of the sponges which keep the water so clean. The colonists' wives discovered that they were also very useful for polishing the samovar.

Listvyanka Church
A pleasant ten-minute walk through the village takes you to a tiny church in which an old woman sells cheap-looking icons. Although the village is worth seeing, one feels that this church has been part of the Intourist 'milk-run' for a long time. 'No smoking on the territory of the Church', warns a sign in English. Concessions to tourists have their advantages: five-star lavatories are thoughtfully located behind the building.

Shaman Rock
In the stretch of water between the Baikal Ecological Museum and Port Baikal it's just possible to make out the top of a rock sticking out of the water. The legend relating to its origin is as follows: Old Man Baikal had 336 sons (the number of rivers which flow into the lake) and one daughter, the beautiful but headstrong Angara. She enraged him by refusing to marry the weak and feeble Irkut, preferring the mighty Yenisei (Russia's longest river). The old man chained her up but one stormy night she slipped her bonds and fled north to her lover. As she ran her furious father hurled a huge boulder after her. She got away but the rock remains to this day, a small point showing above the water. The level of the lake has since risen and very little of Shaman Rock is now visible.

Where to stay
Near the Baikal Ecological Museum is the pleasant ***Hotel Baikal-Intourist*** (☎ 3952-290 391) where most tours stop for lunch. Rooms are

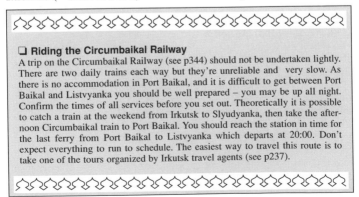

❏ **Riding the Circumbaikal Railway**
A trip on the Circumbaikal Railway (see p344) should not be undertaken lightly. There are two daily trains each way but they're unreliable and very slow. As there is no accommodation in Port Baikal, and it is difficult to get between Port Baikal and Listvyanka you should be well prepared – you may be up all night. Confirm the times of all services before you set out. Theoretically it is possible to catch a train at the weekend from Irkutsk to Slyudyanka, then take the afternoon Circumbaikal train to Port Baikal. You should reach the station in time for the last ferry from Port Baikal to Listvyanka which departs at 20:00. Don't expect everything to run to schedule. The easiest way to travel this route is to take one of the tours organized by Irkutsk travel agents (see p237).

priced at US$117/133 for a single/double. Various services are offered here including bike hire (US$6 per day), skiing, sleigh rides, boat trips and riding. There is an expensive sauna, too.

Several travel agencies in Irkutsk (see p237) offer *homestays* in the Listvyanka area. Baikal Complex charges US$29 a night including meals.

You can also stay at the *Sand Bay Holiday Home* (Turbasa Bukhta Peschanaya) about 80km north of Listvyanka on the shores of Lake Baikal by booking it at Turbasa Bukhta Peschanaya's office (☎ 243 515) in Irkutsk ul Karla Marxa 22, kv 17.

Where to eat

The restaurant in *Hotel Baikal-Intourist* is excellent; try their omul soup. The only other places to eat are two *cafés* in Listvyanka village. During summer, you can always pick up freshly smoked or barbecued omul from local traders on the jetty.

Banya

There is a banya in Listvyanka which is cheaper than the one at the Hotel Baikal-Intourist. If you follow the main road past the museum and then the white monument, you will see a telegraph pole with a white sign fixed to it (Баня). The banya is next to the river which you can run into to cool off. It costs US$6.

PORT BAIKAL

Across the water from Listvyanka is the attractive village of Port Baikal. Before 1904, the western end of the Trans-Siberian terminated here and passengers had to cross the lake by steamer to Mysovaya which is where

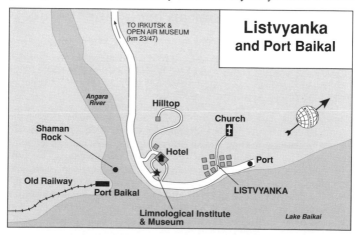

Listvyanka and Port Baikal

the eastern end of the Trans-Siberian finished. The largest steamer was a 290-foot ice-breaker, *Baikal*, which transported the carriages from the train on her deck. She was built by the English firm of Sir W G Armstrong, Whitworth and Co. in Newcastle, UK, delivered by train in kit-form and she sank in 1919 during the Civil War. Her sister ship, the smaller *Angara*, supplied by the same firm, survived (see p235).

Four ferries a day run between Port Baikal and Listvyanka from May to December. The first leaves Port Baikal at 06:30 and Listvyanka at 07:00, and the last leaves Port Baikal at 20:00 and Listvyanka at 20:30. A hydrofoil also runs from Port Baikal and Listvyanka all the way along Lake Baikal to Severobaikalsk (see p240).

Travel agents in Irkutsk organize trips to Port Baikal along the old Circumbaikal Railway (see p246).

BOLSHIE KOTY

Bolshie Koty is a small village north of Listvyanka. Its main attraction is Irkutsk University's Limnological Institute where the students do their practical work. Gold used to be extracted from the Bolshie Koty River and the rusting dredges can still be seen 1km beyond the village. Baikal Complex organizes trips here, offering *homestays* (US$20).

Three hydrofoils a day link Irkutsk with Listvyanka and Bolshie Koty. If you miss the hydrofoil back, you'll have to walk the 18km to Listvyanka along a dirt track along the lake. Note that in some seasons parts of the track may become submerged. Ask locals before setting out.

Other Siberian excursions

The excursions mentioned below are covered in detail in the new *Siberian BAM Guide – rail, rivers & road*, also from Trailblazer (see p431).

BRATSK (Братск)

Three hundred miles north of Irkutsk lies one of the largest dams in the world. The enormous hydroelectric power station at Bratsk, the second largest in Russia after the one at Krasnoyarsk, is the chief attraction of this town. Originally founded in 1631, it was never more than a tiny village until construction of the dam started in 1955. It reputedly produces an enormous $4^{1}/_{2}$ million kW which is a great deal but not as much as the Raul Leoni power station in Venezuela which currently holds the world's title, producing 10.3 million kW. Despite being one of the top ten most polluted cities in Russia, Bratsk is still awe-inspiring considering the massive achievement of constructing a modern city, a giant dam and massive industrial enterprises in just two decades. Bratsk is on the BAM line but unless you're stopping off on this line, or unless you're especially interested in power stations, there seems little reason to come here.

Orientation and hotels

Bratsk is not one town but a ring of connected settlements around the man-made Bratsk Sea, which is a large reservoir created by the Bratsk dam. From the south in a counter-clockwise direction, the towns are Novobratsk Port (Порт Новобратск), Bratsk More (Братское море), Bratsk Tsentralny (Центральный район) which is the administration centre, Padun (Падун), Energetik (Энергетик) on the dam's west bank and Gidrostroitel (Гидростроитель) on the east bank.

The station of Padunskie Porogi services the suburbs of Padun and Energetik. This station is the closest to Hotel Turist. Padun is the most attractive part of Bratsk as it has a pleasant promenade with an old log watchtower and the city's only church. Bratsk airport is to the north of Padunskie Porogi and can be reached by a 40-minute bus trip from the station.

The best accommodation is the standard *Hotel Taiga* (☎ 39531-413 979), ul Mira 35, US$50 for a single room, US$60 for a double. Intourist is on the second floor. Other choices are the standard *Hotel Turist* (☎ 39531-378 743), Energetik, ul Naymushina 28, with rooms from US$30, and the basic *Hotel Bratsk* (☎ 39531-438 436), ul Deputatskaya 32: US$24-46 for a single room.

What to see

The top site is the impressive **Bratsk Hydroelectric Station** and the dam. Bus Nos 4, 102, 103, 104, and 107 run along the dam, and you can also visit the powerhouse. On the outskirts of Angara Village there's an open-air **ethnographic museum** containing an Evenki camp, a watchtower and a fort. There's a history museum at ul Komsomolskaya 38.

Getting to Bratsk

From Irkutsk, you could take the hydrofoil (US$10 one way), which leaves Irkutsk at 08.30, arriving in Bratsk at 20.50. On the return journey it leaves at 07.50 arriving at 20.40 in Irkutsk. Hydrofoils travel three times a week from May to September. There are daily trains between Bratsk and Irkutsk and the trip takes 18 hours.

SEVEROBAIKALSK (Северобайкальск)

Severobaikalsk is the capital of the northern end of Lake Baikal on the BAM railway. The town provides excellent access to the North Baikal attractions, which include trekking and mountaineering in the Baikal Mountains, indigenous villages, a Stalin era gulag, downhill skiing, sailing around the north end of the lake and seal-watching.

Orientation and hotels

Everything in Severobaikalsk is within walking distance, with the exception of the port from which the hydrofoil departs. To get to the port, take Bus No 1 from the central bus station in front of the railway station. Bus No 3 goes past the BAM railway museum and near Hotel Sever.

BAMTour (☎/📠 30139-21560, 🖳 rashit.yahin@usa.net, 671717 Severobaikalsk, ul. Oktyabrya 16-2) is a recommended company organizing tours on the BAM and in the north Lake Baikal region. It's run by Rashit Yakhin who worked on the railway in the early 1970s.

The best place to stay is at the excellent *BAM Railway Cottages*, a 10-minute walk from the station, and with a view of the coast. Booking is done via BAMTour and costs US$15 a night per person.

What to see

Railway places of interest are the **BAM Museum**, ul Mira 2, open 10:00-18:00 closed Monday, and the **BAM Art Museum**, ul Druzhba.

Akikan Gulag (Акикана ГУЛаг) was a mica mining camp that operated in the late 1930s. The residue of those terrible years consists of several collapsed wooden and stone buildings, towers and barbed wire fences. The camp is a two-hour walk from Kholodnoe (60 minutes by bus or train from Severobaikalsk); BAMTour can provide guides.

Getting to Severobaikalsk

The easiest way to get between Severobaikalsk and Irkutsk is by hydrofoil (see p240). You can also get there by train from Taishet on the Trans-Siberian. Unfortunately there is no direct Severobaikalsk–Irkutsk train: change at Taishet or Bratsk.

NIZHNEANGARSK (Нижнеангарск)

Nizhneangarsk is 40km east of Severobaikalsk, wedged on a narrow strip between Lake Baikal and steep mountains. The 20km-long town has a large port for a small fishing fleet. The harbour was built for the construction of the BAM but the railway arrived before it was needed. Despite being the regional power, Nizhneangarsk is smaller than neighbouring Severobaikalsk.

The town is pleasant to stroll around with its mainly wooden buildings. Despite most of it being built since the mid 1970s, Nizhneangarsk is not dominated by multi-storey concrete flats and prefabricated buildings. Even the two-storey City Council building is wooden. An architectural oddity is the wooden boat rental and water rescue station on the lake's edge. The fish-processing factory can be visited and gives an interesting insight into Russian methods and working conditions. The plant makes delicious smoked or salted *omul*.

Nizhneangarsk is linked to Irkutsk by hydrofoil (see p240).

YAKUTSK

This is the capital of Sakha, the vast Yakut Republic (see p358). Lying only 600km south of the Arctic Circle, it is one of the world's coldest cities (average temperature in January is minus 32°C) although summers are pleasantly mild (plus 19°C in July). It is also one of Siberia's oldest settlements, founded in 1632 on the banks of the mighty Lena River as a base for exploration and a trading centre for gold and furs. There is little left of historic interest in this polluted city, but it is worth visiting for the excursions on the Lena and to see the effects of permafrost. All the buildings here have to be built on massive stilts or they would sink into the ground as the heat from them melts the permafrost.

Only about 30 per cent of the people are ethnic Yakuts, the majority of the rest being Russians and Ukrainians. Like other minority groups in Russia the Yakuts are now making themselves heard in Moscow. In 1991 an agreement was signed between the presidents of Russia and Sakha, giving the latter a certain degree of autonomy within the Russian Federation and more local control over the proceeds of gold and diamond mining in their immensely mineral-rich region.

Getting to Yakutsk

Until the rail link is finished (which will be many years from now as there is still 800km to cover) the only way in is by plane from Irkutsk, Moscow or several other cities. Local airline agencies are located at ul Ordzhonikidze 8 (☎ 420 204, 425 139). A new airport was built by the Canadians in 1995 after the last one was burned down.

Where to stay

An inexpensive hotel is the basic *Hotel Yakutsk* (☎ 250 700), ul Oktyabrskaya 20/1. A single room costs US$35. *Hotel Sterkh* (☎ 242 701) pro Lenin 8 is a better choice with singles from US$60.

The Canadian-built *Hotel Ontario* (☎ 422 066, 🖹 259 438), Viliusky trakt 6, has 12 rooms from US$40 for a single. It is in a quiet location in a park zone about 20 minutes out of the city centre. The best hotel is the *Hotel Tygyn Darkhan* (formerly the President Hotel), (☎ 435 109, 🖹 435 004), ul Ammosov 9. Recently renovated by a Swiss company, it's in the heart of the city. It has 46 rooms, from US$100 to US$200. The restaurant here is excellent but very pricey.

What to see

The most interesting place to visit in Yakutsk is the **Permafrost Institute**. You are taken 12 metres underground to see part of the old river bed, where the temperature never varies from -5°C. Permafrost is said to affect

The Yakutsk area code is ☎ 4112. From outside Russia dial +7-4112.

25 per cent of the planet and 50 per cent of Russia. Outside the Institute is a model of the baby mammoth (now in St Petersburg Natural History Museum) that was found preserved in permafrost.

The **State Museum of the History and Culture of the Peoples of the North**, housed in what was formerly the Bishop's Palace, is one of the oldest museums in Siberia. It is said to include over 140,000 items illustrating Yakut flora, fauna and anthropology. Outside is part of the old wooden fort. The **Museum of Yakut Music and Folklore**, at ul Kirova 8, has an interesting display about Yakut shamanism. There's also the **Yakut Literature Museum** in a large yurt and the **Geological Museum**, crammed full of all the geological wealth of Yakutia. Tours can be arranged to reindeer-breeding farms.

Excursions on the Lena River

The geological formations known as the **Lena Pillars** have fascinated travellers here since the 17th century. About 140km upriver from Yakutsk, the rock of the cliffs alongside the river has been eroded away into delicate shapes of a reddish brown colour.

Two-day cruises to the Lena Pillars leave each Friday evening in the summer. Tickets cost from US$200 and are available from LenaRechFlot (☎/🖷 422 762, 425 761, ul Dzerzhinskogo 2). From the landing spot it takes about an hour's strenuous climb to reach the top for a magnificent view of the river and the pillar-like cliffs. Tour groups are sometimes taken on day trips by hydrofoil to the Lena Pillars from Yakutsk, leaving early in the morning and getting back after dark.

On the way to the Lena Pillars you pass the archaeological site of **Dering Yuryakh** (see p87).

The luxury cruise ships *M/S Demyan Bedny* and *M/S Mikhail Svetlov* do 7-10 day trips along the Lena River starting from Yakutsk, passing the Lena Pillars and continuing to the river port of **Lensk**. It's also possible to make a trip down the Lena from Yakutsk to Tiksi on the Arctic Ocean. For more information contact LenaRechFlot.

Ulan Ude
Улан Уде

Ulan Ude is well worth a stop if only to visit the **Ivolginsky Datsan** (35km outside the city), the centre of Buddhism in Russia. Rail enthusiasts may also be interested in a visit to the **locomotive repair workshops**. The people of Ulan Ude are very friendly and hospitable and the place has a relaxed atmosphere, with quite a few traditional Siberian wooden buildings still standing.

HISTORY

Military outpost

In 1668 a military outpost was set up here in the valley between the Khamar Daban and Tsaga Daban mountain ranges. Strategically located beside the Selenga and Ude rivers, it was named Verkhneudinsk. A cathedral was built in 1745 and the town became a key trading centre on the route of the tea caravans from China. The railway reached the town in 1900 and in 1949 the branch line to Mongolia was opened.

Ulan Ude today

Capital of the Buryat Republic, Ulan Ude is now a pleasant city of nearly 400,000 people (only 21% of whom are Buryats, the rest mainly Russians). Local industries include the large railway repair workshop and locomotive plant, food processing, helicopter assembly and glass making.

Buildings here require firm foundations since the city is in an earthquake zone. The most recent 'quake, measuring 9.5 on the Richter scale, was in 1959 but because its epicentre was directly beneath Lake Baikal nobody in Ulan Ude was killed. The military bases in the area kept Ulan Ude off-limits to foreigners until the thaw in East-West relations. In 1990, Princess Anne led the tourists in with the first royal visit to Russia since the Tsar's execution. A local official declared that her visit was probably the most exciting thing to have happened since Genghis Khan swept through on his way to Moscow in 1239.

WHAT TO SEE

Giant Lenin Head

The pl Sovetov is dominated by the sinister bulk of **Lenin's head**, the biggest in the world; standing in front of him you feel like Dorothy meeting the Wizard of Oz.

HOTELS AND RESTAURANTS

2 Hotel Odon Гостиница Одон
4 Hotel Geser Гостиница Гэсэр
12 Hotel Baikal Гостиница Байкал
13 Café Buterbrodnya Кафе Бутербродня
14 Hotel Buryatia & Mongolian Consulate
      Гостиница Бурятия и Кулсульство Монголии
17 Hotel Barguzin Гостиница Баргузин
19 Letnee Café Кафе Летнйи

OTHER

1 Railway Station Железнодорожний Вокзал
3 To Open-air Museum
5 Central Post Office Почтамт
6 Buryat Teaching Institute Бурятский Педагогический Институт
7 Giant Head of Lenin (Main Square) Бюст Ленина
8 Western-style supermarket
9 Philharmonic Hall Филармония
10 Opera and Ballet Theatre Театр Оперы и Балета
11 Airlines Office
15 History Museum Музей Истории
16 Bus Station Автовокзал
18 Nature Museum Музей Природы
20 T-34 Tank Monument Памятник-монумент «Танк Т-34»
21 Troitskaya Church Церковь Троицы
22 Buryat Drama Theatre Бурятский Театр Драмы
23 Arcade Гостиный Двор
24 Market Рынок
25 Virgin Hodegetria Cathedral Одигитриевский Собор
26 River Station Речной Вокзал

History Museum

This collection was greatly enriched by the recent transfer (which should now be complete) of a fantastic collection of items relating to Lamaism (Tibetan Buddhism) and the spiritual culture of the Buryats which was being stored in the Virgin Hodegetria Cathedral. Assembled from monasteries closed after the Revolution, the collection includes Buddha figures; the robes of a Buryat shaman; musical instruments (conches and horns and a beautiful guitar with a carved horse's head); a large collection of masks used in Buddhist mystery plays; and a valuable collection of Tibetan *thangkas* (paintings). As well as healing thangkas used by monks practising traditional medicine, there's a unique *Atlas of Tibetan Medicine*. Local Russian history is also covered: there are icons dating back to the 17th century and day-to-day objects from the houses of the rich traders of Kyakhta. The History Museum, at ul Profsoyuznaya 29, is open 10:00-17:30 daily except Monday. Entry is US$5.

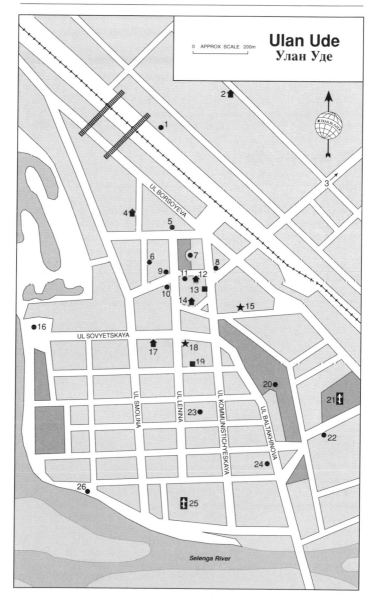

Ulan Ude
Улан Уде

Natural History Museum

Some of the interesting displays here include a Lake Baikal panorama with flora and fauna (ask an attendant to turn on the 'authentic Siberian' soundtrack for you) and a model of the mini-submarine Pisces XI which reached a depth of 1410m in the lake in 1977; there are two large galleries of local wildlife including eagles, wolves, bears and reindeer. Since one of the world's few remaining wetlands is the Selenga Delta on the edge of Lake Baikal, there is also a comprehensive display of local birds. Labels are in Cyrillic and Latin (see pp411-3). It's open 10:00-17:00, closed Monday and Tuesday. Entry is US$1.

Open-Air Ethnographic Museum

One of the best of the numerous open-air museums in the country, this collection of reconstructed buildings is about 6km north of Ulan Ude. Exhibits include a Bronze Age stone circle; Evenki camp with birchwood wigwam, a shaman's hut with wooden carvings outside it; birds on poles, animals and fish. There is a dreadful zoo with camels standing in the mud, bears in tiny cages and disconsolate reindeer (the more people complain to the guides about this the better). The Buryat area contains *gers* (yurts) of felt and wood and also a log cabin in which there are silk robes and day-to-day items. There are also houses of Kazakhs, Cossacks and 17th-century Orthodox Christians, built around large brick ovens with sleeping platforms above them. Except in mid-summer it gets very cold walking round here; bring warm clothing.

It's open 10:00-17:00 daily in summer. There's no longer a bus right to the museum but bus No 8 drops you at a T-junction from which it's a 20-minute walk. This bus passes a new monastery where there's a homeo-pathic shop and a restaurant where you can get tasty Buryat meat *pozi* (dumplings) and delicious *ponchike* (jam-filled doughnuts).

Locomotive Works

Ulan Ude's railway factory is definitely worth a visit even if you are not interested in trains. The conditions under which people work are surpris-ing, as is the age of most of the equipment. The factory was founded in 1932 to repair locomotives and passenger carriages and from 1938 to 1956 it built large SO series freight steam locomotives. After a massive refit in 1959, the factory concentrated on rebuilding electric locomotives and passenger carriages. Today it repairs VL60 and VL80 locomotives and passenger carriages. Intourist organizes visits to the factory.

There's a preserved SO17 on the right-hand side of the road to the Open-Air Ethnographic Museum.

Other sights

It's worth spending some time wandering around the town as there are still quite a few interesting buildings to be seen here. The **Virgin**

Hodegetria Cathedral, which was built from 1745 to 1785, is being renovated very slowly. For many years it was used as a storeroom by the History Museum (which has an interesting display of photographs showing the cathedral in happier days). The streets around the cathedral are lined with picturesque old wooden buildings, some now being restored.

The attractive **Troitskaya Church**, built in 1798, was closed during the communist era but has now reopened and renovation continues; new bells were added in 1993. As at many Russian churches, begging babushkas crowd around the entrance.

The **Opera and Ballet Theatre** has excellent socialist paintings and murals inside but the doormen won't be keen to let you wander round without a ticket for a performance. The theatre was built by some of the 18,000

OPERA AND BALLET THEATRE

Japanese prisoners of war who were interned in the Buryat Republic between 1945 and 1948.

The **Geological Museum**, ul Lenina 57, is open 10:00-16:00, on Tuesday and Friday only.

IVOLGINSKY DATSAN (MONASTERY)

The centre of Russian Buddhism stands on a wide plain 35km outside the city and it's a fascinating place to visit. Before the Revolution there were hundreds of similar monasteries in the area with the largest and most important at Selenginsk. Almost all were closed and the monks sent to the gulags in the 1930s but when Stalin sanctioned greater religious tolerance in the 1940s, astrologers selected this site for a new monastery and it was built in 1946. There are now 30 lamas, some of them very elderly but novices still join each year and most spend up to five years studying in Ulan Bator. Tibetan Buddhism is practised here and the Dalai Lama has visited the Datsan five times.

Getting there
Bus No 104 from Ulan Ude's Central Bus Station passes the Datsan and goes as far as Kalenovo village. There are three departures a day and the trip takes 45 minutes. Another not very convenient option is to catch bus No 130 which runs past Ivolga village. From here walk straight ahead out of the village, then turn right after about 3km, and from here you can see the Datsan.

Visiting the Datsan
As you walk around the Datsan don't forget that you should walk clockwise around objects of Buddhist veneration (prayer wheels, temples and stupas); hats must be taken off inside the buildings. Visitors are shown round by a monk. Be sure to make a donation.

The **largest temple**, a three-storey building constructed in 1971, burnt down four months after completion, with the loss of numerous valuable *thangkas* (paintings). It was rebuilt in just seven months. Inside, its joyous technicolour decoration seems rather out of place in grey Russia: golden dragons slide down the sixteen wooden columns supporting the upper galleries (where there is a library of Tantric texts), and hundreds of incarnations of the Buddha line one wall. Easy to recognize is Manla, with the dark blue face, the Buddha of Tibetan medicine. The largest thangka hanging above the incarnations is of the founder of this Gelukpa (Yellow Hat) sect. Juniper wood is burnt and food and money offered to the incarnations.

Beside this is a smaller stupa, and the **green temple** behind it is the oldest building in the complex, constructed in 1946. The octagonal white building houses a model of **Paradise** (*Devashin*) and a library of several hundred Tibetan and Mongolian texts, each wrapped in silk. In the big **white stupa** nearby are the ashes of the most famous former head lama of the Datsan, Sherapov, who died in 1961. There is even a **Bo tree** growing very successfully in its own greenhouse from seeds brought in 1956 from Delhi. Visiting Buddhists stay in the 'hotel' and students now come from all over the region to study Buddhism here.

Snacks are available at the kiosk outside, which is where the buses go from. You could also try hitching a ride back in a tour bus.

PRACTICAL INFORMATION
Orientation and services

To reach the centre of town from the railway station, cross the line via the pedestrian bridge. It takes about 15 minutes to walk to pl Lenina. The main hotels and the Intourist office are all in this area.

The helpful **Buryat-Intourist** office is in the Hotel Geser (☎ 216 954) and **Sputnik** Travel (☎ 210 834) is at pr Pobedy 9.

There's a **Mongolian Consulate** at ul Profsouznay, 16.

You can send **emails** at the post office or from the office at Hotel Geser.

Local transport

Most places, except the Datsan and the Open-air museum, are within walking distance. Buses No 7 or 10 from in front of the station run along pl Sovetov and past Hotel Baikal. Bus No 7 terminates at the central bus station and bus No 10 continues to the airport. Bus No 35 travels between the airport and pl Sovetov.

Taxis congregate in the usual places: outside the hotels and by the railway and bus stations but are not in great supply.

Tours Buryat-Intourist offers tours to all of the major sights. The resurgence of Buddhism in the area has resulted in the reopening, reconstruction, or construction of a large number of Buddhist temples and monasteries. Intourist is quite willing to take you to any of them, the closest being **Ivolginsky Datsan**: US$30 on a group tour. A day trip to **Tamcha Datsan** which is 150 km away costs US$80 for a car or US$20 if you go as part of a group

---

(Opposite): The ashes of Sherapov, former head lama of Ivolginsky, are contained in this stupa at the Datsan.

The Ulan Ude area code is ☎ 3012. From outside Russia dial +7-3012.

on a bus tour. A visit to **Atsagat Temple**, 50km away, costs US$50 for a car or US$12 on a group tour. Other tours go to **Lake Baikal**, some of the old cities along the tea route to China (**Kyakhta, Novoselenginsk** etc), or to remote villages with interesting ethnic roots (**Bolshoi Kunali**). There is also a tour of the **locomotive museum and workshops** for US$26.

Where to stay

There are numerous cheap hotels in Ulan Ude but none is particularly good.

The *Hotel Barguzin* (☎ 219 58) at ul Sovetskaya 28 charges US$15/30 for a single/double. It has friendly staff and an aging stuffed bear in the foyer but the place is looking a bit tired nowadays. The *Hotel Baikal* (☎ 213 718) at ul Erbanova 12, on the main square is similarly priced and similarly scruffy. Less pleasant and on the wrong side of the tracks is the *Hotel Odon* (☎ 343 480) at ul Gagarina 43 which charges just US$12 for a double.

The *Hotel Buryatia* (☎ 211 835) at pr Pobedy is the most expensive hotel but nothing special. They charge US$40/65 for a single/double with attached bathrooms and also have a few cheaper rooms.

The old Communist Party hotel, the *Hotel Geser* (☎ 218 151) at ul Ranzhurova 12, is probably the best place to stay. Service is good; the rooms are comfortable and they cost US$30-35 for a single with attached bathroom and US$45-55 for a double.

Where to eat

On the corner where ul Lenina and ul Kalandarishvili meet is the *Letnee Café* – inside a ger tent. Run by friendly people, it's a pleasant place and a range of snacks is served.

Hotel Buryatia has some tasty dishes and rather reluctant service. It costs around US$6 for three courses. In the restaurant every night there's a disco which can be entertaining.

The *Hotel Barguzin* restaurant is on the second floor and is also good. Next door to the Hotel Barguzin is the *Restaurant Turistsky* which is fine, though sometimes a bit noisy.

Restaurant Baikal at ul Erbanova 8, serves typically bland meals.

The food at the main restaurant at the *Hotel Geser* is good and the service efficient but there's usually a live band in the evening. There's also a buffet (open late) down the hall

What to buy

There is a **Buryat Crafts Store** in the Arcade. Other good places to pick up souvenirs are **Art Store**, ul Lenina 33, **Podarki Gift Shop**, ul Lenina 40, and **Yantar Amber Jewellery Store**, ul Lenina 40.

Interesting Siberian alcohol is brewed at ul Novokuznetskaya 1. Under the brand name 'Crystal', it comes in a range of colours and it's worth buying a bottle just for the label which states 'The smell of Siberian taiga which you'd never visited gives you a happy recollection of last summer'. Sounds rather like a crossword clue.

Moving on

Ulan Ude is a 45-minute flight, or a seven and a half hour train journey from Irkutsk.

Aeroflot (☎ 212 248) is at ul Erbanova 14. **Buryat Avia** has offices in Hotel Geser and Hotel Buryatia. **Transaero** has an office in the Hotel Buryatia.

(Opposite) Top: Lake Baikal in winter. **Bottom:** View over Vladivostok from Eagle's Nest Hill, reached on the funicular railway – see p276. (Photo © Nick Hill).

Chita
Чита

Chita is the junction of the Trans-Siberian and the Trans-Manchurian railway lines. The city was closed to foreigners until the late 1980s as it was the military centre for the sometimes tense Siberian/Chinese border. There's just about enough to keep you occupied for a day here: a Decembrists museum, a museum full of military hardware and an interesting Army Officers' Club where non-members are welcome.

HISTORY

Founded in 1653, Chita became a *sloboda* (tax-exempt settlement) in 1690, populated by Cossacks and trappers. It was famous in the 1800s when it became the place of exile for many revolutionary Decembrists. George Kennan was here in 1887 and wrote: 'Among the exiles of Chita were some of the brightest, most cultivated, most sympathetic men and women we had met in Eastern Siberia.'

By 1900 more than 11,000 people lived here. There were nine churches, a cathedral, a nunnery, a synagogue, thirteen schools and even a telephone system. Soviet power was established in the city on 16 February 1918 but by 26 August the city was captured by the White Army. On 22 October, however, it was firmly back in the hands of the Soviets.

OLD WOODEN HOUSE IN CHITA

Chita is now the major industrial and cultural centre of Eastern Siberia and still of military importance. The numerous army buildings around the city look much like ordinary office buildings but have their foyers hidden from the streets with armed guards just inside the door.

WHAT TO SEE

The **Army Officers' Club**, ul Lenina 80, is well worth a visit. On the second floor, opposite the bar, is the entertainment room with eight full-size billiard tables, and this is surrounded by chess tables with another balcony above, also full of tables. Despite the fact that few people speak, the noise level is unbelievable as each chess player punches his time clock every 30 seconds. The bar is open 12:00-23:00 every day except Monday and there is a popular disco here every weekend. The **Military Museum** is next door, open 10:00-18:00 Wednesday, Thursday and Friday, and 10:00-17:00 at weekends.

The **Decembrists Museum** (☎ 34803) is housed in the former Archangel Michael Church, ul Dekabristov 3b. It's open 10:00-18:00, closed Monday.

The **Art Museum** is housed in a modern-looking building on ul Chealova, above an MFI-type shop. The exhibitions are interesting; entry is US$0.20 and it's open 09:00-17:00.

The **Museum of Local Studies** is currently closed for major repairs.

PRACTICAL INFORMATION
Orientation and services
The railway station is only a short walk away from the centre of the town and most hotels. The central bus station is in front of the railway station and the airport is 13km east of the city (bus Nos 4 or 14 from pl Lenina).

Intourist (☎ 31246) is at ul Lenina 56. **Chitakurort Services** (☎ 32379), ul Angarskaya 15, can give you information about the numerous health spas in the region. **Aeroflot** (☎ 34381) is at ul Leningradskaya 36.

If you are interested in traditional medicine you should visit the **Centre of Eastern Medicine** (☎ 66520). It's housed in a grand old building at ul Lenina 109.

There is internet access for US$2 per hour at **Jin Internet** just round the corner from the City Administration building.

Where to stay
The best of the cheapies is the *Hotel Dauriya* (☎ 62365), ul Profsoyuznaya 17, which charges US$8 for a single and US$15 for a double. Prices may rise when renovation is complete, however. There's also the centrally located *Hotel Zabaikalsk* (☎ 64520), ul Leningradskaya 36, which charges US$10/17 for a single/double. The usual selection of services downstairs includes a tattoo parlour.

In the middle price range (rooms with bathrooms attached for around US$20-30 for a single and US$30-50 for a double) there's the *Hotel Obkomovskaya* (☎ 65270), ul Profsoyuznaya 18, which has a good café downstairs; *Hotel Turist* (☎ 65270), ul Babushkina 42, with a snooker hall below; and out of town on the way to the airport, the *Krasni Drakon Motel* (☎ 11973), ul Magistralnaya. To get to this last place take bus No 14 and tell the driver 'motel' so you're let out at the stop just before it.

Where to eat
The best of the inner-city restaurants is *Café Tsyplyata Tabaka* at ul Ostrovskovo 20, which does excellent roast chicken. It's easy to miss as the sign isn't obvious. *Restaurant Moran* at ul Bogomyakova 23, claims to be a Korean restaurant but everything seems to be Russian.

The most expensive restaurant in town is the *Restaurant Krasni Drakon* at the motel of the same name. Bookings (☎ 14288) are recommended as it is a long trip there.

Moving on
By rail Chita is 19 hours from Khabarovsk and 34 hours from Irkutsk.

The Chita area code is ☎ 30222. From outside Russia dial +7-30222.

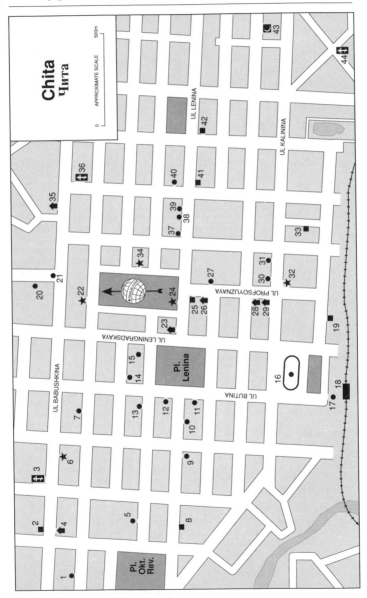

HOTELS AND RESTAURANTS

2 Restaurant Moran Ресторан Моран
4 Hotel Kommohalnaya
   Гостиница Коммунальная
8 Café Bar Кафе или Бар
19 Café Bar Кафе или Бар
23 Hotel Zabaikale Гостиница Забайкалье
25 Café Sibir Кафе Сибирь
26 Hotel Ingoda Гостиница Ингода
28 Hotel Obkomovskaya
   Обкомовеная Гостиница
29 Hotel Dauriya Гостиница Даурия
33 Café Кафе
35 Hotel Turist Гостиница Турист
41 Restaurant Argol Ресторан Аргол
42 Café Tsyplyata Tabaka Кафе Цыплята Табака

OTHER

1 Market Рынок
3 Old Church Старая Церковь
5 Old Market Старый Рынок
6 Teaching Institute & Lenin Museum
   Педагогический Институт и Музей Ленина
7 Stamp Shop Филателия
9 Book Shop Дом Книги
10 Centre of Eastern Medicine Центр Восточной Медицины
11 Central Post Office Почтамт
12 City Administration Дом Советов
13 Jin Internet Джин Интернет

OTHER (cont)

14 Aeroflot Office Касса Аэрофлота
15 Delfin Swimming Pool Бассейн «Дельфин»
16 Stadium Trud Стадион «Труд»
17 Bus Station Автовокзал
18 Railway Station Железнодорожний Вокзал
20 Medical Institute Медицинский Институт
21 Tank Moniument Танк Памятник
22 Art Museum Художественный Музей
24 Military Museum & Officers' Club
   Музей Истории Войск и Дом Офицеров
27 Drama Theatre
   Драматический Театр
30 Sputnik Спутник
31 Book Shop Дом Книги
32 Museum of Minerals
   Минералогический Музей
34 Museum of Local Studies
   Краеведческий Музей
36 Church
37 Shumov Palace & Site of future Museum of Local Studies
   Дворец Шумова и Будущий Краеведческий Музей
38 Art Shop Художественный Магазин
39 Intourist Интурист
40 OViR
43 Tatar Mosque
   Татарская Мечеть
44 Decembrists Museum in Archangel Michael Church
   Музей Декабристов Михайло-Архангельской Церкови

Birobidzhan
Биробиджан

Birobidzhan is the capital of the so-called Jewish Autonomous Region, a remote site selected in 1928 as the 'homeland' for Soviet Jews. An effective propaganda campaign and starvation in Eastern Europe encouraged 41,000 Soviet Jews to move here in the 1930s. Jewish schools and synagogues were established and a considerable effort was made to give the city a Jewish feel. This included providing street signs in Hebrew, making Hebrew the official language of the region and establishing Russia's only Hebrew paper, the *Birbobidzhaner Stern*.

It soon became obvious, however, that this was no Promised Land. Conditions in the region are extremely harsh with winter lows of minus 40°C and things were made worse for the Jewish settlers by a resurgence of religious repression in 1937 with the closure of the synagogues and the banning of Hebrew and Yiddish. By 1938 60% of the Jewish population had left.

In the 1950s the town developed into an agricultural and industrial centre. Birobidzhan's most famous export was the rice combine harvester made at the Dalselmash factory on the western outskirts of the town. With the economic downturn this is now on the brink of closure. Many Jewish people have moved to Israel and today less than 6% of the population have Jewish ancestry.

Birobidzhan is not a 'must see' but could make an interesting day trip from Khabarovsk, 180km east.

WHAT TO SEE

The **Museum of Local Studies**, ul Lenina 24, is open 09:00-17:50, closed Mondays. The **Art Museum** is on ul Pionerskaya. The **synagogue** is on the eastern outskirts of town, ul Maya-kovskovo 11; take bus Nos 5, 16 or 22 eastward from Hotel Vostok. There's a **beach** on the Bira River which is packed at summer weekends. To get there, keep walking down ul Gorky until you reach the river and you'll see it on the left beside Park Kultury. It is only 800m past the Art Museum.

PRACTICAL INFORMATION

Everything is within walking distance of the station.

The town's only travel agent is **Intour-Birobidzhan** (☎ 42145-61573), ul Sholom-Aleikhema 55.

The only hotel is the standard *Hotel Vostok* (☎ 42145-65330), ul Sholom-Aleikhema 1. They charge US$35 for a single and US$50 a double. There's a restaurant here and several in the town.

Khabarovsk
Хабаровск

Khabarovsk is a relaxed provincial city of 610,000 people, pleasantly situated beside the Amur River.

It's well worth stopping here for a day or two. In summer, holiday crowds flock to the sandy river banks, giving the place the atmosphere of a friendly English seaside resort; (but for some reason sunbathing in Russia is often done standing up). It's bitterly cold here in winter and when the river freezes, people drive their cars onto it and fish through holes chopped in the two-foot thick ice.

Apart from the river, the other sights include an interesting Museum of Local History, a Military Museum and the arboretum, which was founded over one hundred years ago to supply the numerous parks and gardens in the city.

HISTORY

In 1858 a military settlement was founded here by Count Muravev-Amurski, the Governor-General of East Siberia who did much to advance Russia's interests in the Far East. It was named Khabarovka, in honour of the Cossack explorer who conquered the Amur region in the 17th century, and whose statue now stands in the square in front of the railway station.

By 1883 the town was known as Khabarovsk and the following year, when the Far Eastern Territories were made a region separate from Eastern Siberia, it became the administrative capital and home of the governor-general of the area.

Until the railway arrived, the town was just a trading and military post picturesquely situated on three hills on the banks of the Amur River, where it is joined by its tributary, the Ussuri. It was a junction for passengers who arrived by steamer from west Siberia, along the Shilka and Amur rivers. Here they would transfer to another ship for the voyage down the Amur and Ussuri to Vladivostok.

From 1875 onwards several plans were submitted for the building of the Ussuri Railway, which now runs along the great river between Khabarovsk and Vladivostok. Work began in 1893 and on 3 September 1897 a train completed the first journey between these two towns. A railway technical school was opened in the following year on the street that is now named ul Karla Marxa.

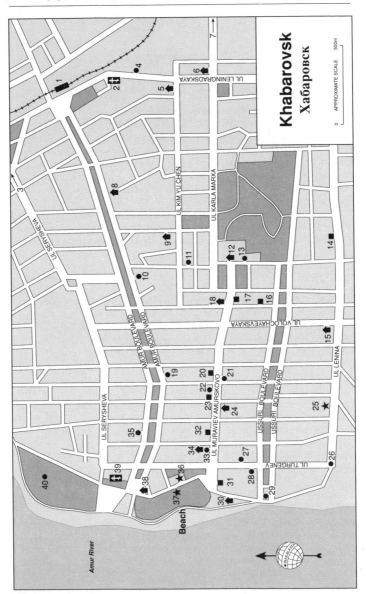

Khabarovsk
Хабаровск

0   APPROXIMATE SCALE   500m

HOTELS AND RESTAURANTS

5 Hotel Zarya Гостиница Заря
6 Hotel Turist Гостиница Турист
8 Hotel Mayak Гостиница Маяк
9 Hotel Amethyst Гостиница Аметист
12 Hotel Tsentralnaya Гостиница Центральная
14 Restaurant Okean Ресторан Океан
15 Hotel Amur Гостиница Амур
16 Pizzeria Пицца
17 Café Kasam Кафе Касам
18 Hotel Lyudmila Гостиница Людмила
20 Café Dauria & Cinema Кафе Даурия и Кино
23 Bistro Erofe Бистро Ерофе
24 Hotel Dalny Vostok Гостиница Дальний Восток
30 Hotel Parus & Restaurant Гостиница Парус + ресторан
31 Syangan Restaurant Ресторан Сянган
32 Restaurant Rus Ресторан Русь
34 Hotel Sapporo Гостиница Саппоро
38 Hotel Intourist Гостиница Интурист

OTHER

1 Railway Station Железнодорожний Вокзал
2 Church Церковь
3 To Bus Station Автовокзал
4 Advance Purchase Rail Ticket Office
   Предварительная Железнодорожная Касса
7 To War Cemetery

OTHER (cont)

10 Market Рынок
11 Japanese Consulate Кулсульство Японии
13 Internet Интернет
19 International Airlines Office Касса Аэрофлота
21 Central Post Office Почтамт
22 Tairy Remesla Art Store
   Художественный Магазин Тайны Ремесла
25 Geological Museum Геологический Музей
26 Victory Monument Слава Памятник
27 Eurasia Trans Inc
   Предприятие Eurasia
28 United States Foreign Office
   Американский Торговый Центр
29 River Station Речной Вокзал
33 ATM
35 Domestic Airlines Office Касса Аэрофлота
36 Military Museum Музей Истории Краснознаменного
   Дальневосточного Военного Округа
37 Museum of Local Studies Краеведческий Музей
39 Church of St Innocent Иннокентьевская Церковь
40 Sports centre & Open-air Pool
   Спорт центр + Открытный Бассейн

Early visitors

As more of the sections of the Trans-Siberian Railway were built, greater numbers of foreign travellers arrived in Khabarovsk. The *1900 Guide to the Great Siberian Railway* did not encourage them to stay long, reporting that: 'The conditions of life in Khabarovsk are not attractive, on account of the absence of comfortable dwellings, and the expensiveness of some products and of most necessary articles ... Imported colonial goods are sold at a high price and only fish is very cheap.' Tourists at the time were also advised against trying Mr Khlebnikov's locally produced wine, made from the wild vines that grow in the area because: 'it is of inferior quality and without any flavour'. Recommended sights included the wooden triumphal arch (now demolished) erected in commemoration of the visit of the Tsarevich Nicholas in 1891 and the bronze statue of Count Muravev-Amurski on the promontory above the river. After the Revolution, the Count was traded in for an image from the Lenin Statue Factory but Muravev-Amurski has now reappeared in front of the railway station.

The city today

The railway brought more trade than tourists, and though it suffered during the Civil War, the town quickly grew into the modern city it is today. Few of the old wooden cabins remain but there are some attractive stone buildings from Imperial times. It is the capital of Khabarovsk Territory and one of the regions with the richest mineral deposits in Russia, although the land is little more than a gigantic swampy forest. Khabarovsk is now a major industrial centre involved in engineering, petroleum refining and timber-working.

In the last few years the Japanese and South Koreans have moved in, opening factories and businesses. Most of the city's foreign visitors now come from these two countries.

WHAT TO SEE

Museum of Local History

The museum, based on the extensive collection of Baron Korff, a former governor-general of the Amur region, was opened in 1894. In 1897 it was moved into the three-storey building in which it is now housed. With donations made by hunters and explorers over the last 90 years, the collection has grown into an impressive display of local history, flora and fauna. Labels are in Cyrillic and Latin (see p411-3).

Among the animals in the galleries on the ground floor are two Amur tigers. Also known as the Siberian or Manchurian tiger (*Felis/Panthera tigris altaica*), this is the largest member of the cat family and can weigh up to 350kg, about twice the average weight of an African lion. In the same gallery are various fur-bearing animals including the large sea-otter or Kamchatka beaver (*Enhydra lutris*) from which come the highest-priced pelts in the world. Before protection of the animal began in the early 1900s single pelts were selling for over US$2000.

The upper galleries are devoted to local history and ethnography. The area was inhabited by several tribes at the time of the Revolution. The Goldi and Orochi lived near the mouth of the Ussuri; the Olchi and the Giliak beside the Amur. All tribes had their *shamans* and some of their robes and equipment are on display as well as a suit made entirely from fish-skins. The skin of a common fish, the *keta*, was used not only for clothing but also for tents, sails and boots. There's also a display of early settlers' furniture, samovars and other utensils, including some bread baked by the original colonists.

The museum is at ul Shevchenko 11; open 10:00-18:00, closed Monday.

Military Museum

Fifty metres up the street from the Museum of Local History, this museum provides a record of military activity here since the city was founded.

There are numerous pictures of Russian soldiers, as well as photographs of British, French, Italians and Americans in Vladivostok in 1918. The museum's walls are decorated with medals and old weapons, including a weather-beaten Winchester rifle and a few Smith and Wesson pistols. There's a small display on Mongolia including a picture of Lenin and Sukhe Bator sharing a joke. Upstairs is a large quantity of

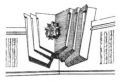

THE MEMORIAL OF GLORY
KHABAROVSK

WWII memorabilia. Behind the building there's a row of armoured vehicles and tanks, a Mig fighter plane and a train carriage used by the commander of the Russian Far East military forces in the 1930s. Entry is US$2; it's open 10:00-17:00, closed Monday.

Geological Museum

The Geological Museum, on the corner of ul Lenina and ul Pushkina, contains a well laid-out display of local minerals. You've heard how rich Siberia is in natural resources: now come and see what they actually look like. Paradoxically, pride of place goes to some rocks from the moon, small fragments under a microscope. Open 10:00-18:00 (not Monday), entry is US$0.50.

Arboretum

Founded long before the railway arrived in Khabarovsk, the arboretum is an interesting place to visit. Originally set up to provide trees and shrubs for the new town's parks, it now claims to have a specimen of every plant species found in the Far Eastern Territories. The arboretum is located at ul Volochaevskaya, and open 9:00-18:00 weekdays. Take bus No 1 to the corner of ul Volochaevskaya and ul Lenina, then bus No 25 to the Ussurisky stop.

Other sights and things to do

The **Amur River** is a focus of interest in both winter and summer. In the winter when it freezes locals drill holes through the ice and set up little tents to sit in while they fish. In the summer the beaches along the banks become crowded with swimmers. The water is certainly not crystal clear but it's refreshing on a hot summer's day; you should, however, watch out for the strong current. There are also boat trips on the river.

There are regular services at the **church** on ul Leningradskaya, the interior of which is beautifully decorated.

The excellent **sauna** (☎ 331 729), ul Moskovskaya 7, is very popular with foreigners. The sauna also includes a pool, billiards room and a restaurant. Bookings are not necessary; a visit costs US$10.

PRACTICAL INFORMATION
Orientation and services

Khabarovsk is a large city; the railway station and the Hotel Intourist are about 3-4kms apart, a half-hour walk. The Intourist-Khabarovsk office is at this hotel and many of the tourist sights are within walking distance of it.

The main street is ul Karla Marxa which becomes ul Muraveva-Amurskovo as it goes around the city's central square, pl Lenina.

Banks Several of the banks now have ATMs. The one near Hotel Sapporo on Ul Muraveva-Amurskovo is convenient. There's a Sberbank on Amur Boulevard near the railway station.

Communications It is possible to use the **Internet** in the telegraph office (near Hotel Tsentralnaya) for US$0.60 an hour. It's open 10:00-21:45.

Consulates The **Japanese Consulate** (☎ 326 907, satellite ☎ 50985-21 002, 🖹 327 212, 🖳 consul@japan.khv.ru) is at ul Pushkina 38/A, open Monday to Friday, 9:00-12:30, 14:00-17:30 for visas.

The **Chinese Consulate** (☎ 348 537, 🖹 348 537) is at Lenin Stadium, Southern Korpus, open 9:30-12:00 Monday, Wednesday and Friday for visas.

The USA foreign trade mission (☎ 337 923, 336 923) is at ul Turgeneva 69.

Travel agents There are numerous travel agencies here including **Intourist-Khabarovsk** (☎ 399 919, 399 308) at the Hotel Intourist; **Dalni Vostok Company** (☎ 388 079, 🖹 338 679); and **Michael Travel Agency** (☎ 334 992).

Local transport

There's no metro but there are regular **bus, trolley-bus** and **tram** services. From the station, bus No 1 travels down ul Karla Marxa and ul Muraveva-Amurskovo and then back to the station along ul Lenina. Bus No 2 from the station runs down ul Serysheva (which is parallel to bul Amurski) and back up to the station via ul Karla Marxa and ul Muraveva-Amurskovo. Trolley-bus No 1 runs between the airport and pl Komsomolskaya.

Boats along the Amur River operate from May to October. Both local ferries and long-distance hydrofoils depart from the river station at ul Shevchenko 1. The boats go as far as Nikolaevsk in one direction and Amurzet in the other. While Intourist can organize tickets for a trip it's easy enough to do this yourself.

Tours
Intourist-Khabarovsk (☎ 399 919) at the Hotel Intourist are friendly and helpful. They offer the following tours: **city tour** (2¹/₂hrs by car: US$35); **museum tours** (US$10); the **arboretum** (1hr: US$20); **Nanai village folk show** (4hrs: US$75) which includes a visit to see the **petroglyphs** (rock carvings) nearby. They will also arrange **boat trips**, with a folk group performing on deck, and they may sell tickets for the **Drama Theatre**, the **Musical Comedy Theatre** and the **circus** but are likely to suggest that you buy them directly from the theatre. Note that these are all closed on Mondays and that tickets must be booked before 13:00 on the day you wish to go to a performance.

Where to stay
You can organize a *homestay* in Khabarovsk through HOFA or any of the other agencies on p18.

The basic *Hotel Mayak* (☎ 330 935), ul Kooperativnaya 11, is in a standard apartment block behind some shops. They're somewhat reluctant to take foreigners and may charge what they think you will pay – anything from US$5 to US$20 per person – for a room with shared bathroom.

The most centrally located hotel and the best value is the *Hotel Tsentralnaya* (☎ 336 731), ul Pushkina 52. Comfortable rooms cost US$12-28 for a single and US$25-45 for a double with attached bath.

The old *Hotel Turist* (☎ 370 417), ul Karla Marxa 67, is popular with Chinese tour groups and has a good WI-style cake stall in the foyer. There's a range of rooms and they cost US$15-30 for a single and US$20-50 for a double. The best have fridges and attached bathrooms.

Hotel Amur (☎ 335 043, ▤ 221 223), ul Lenina 29, is newly renovated and charges US$25/40 for a single/double with attached bath.

MNTK-Iris Hotel (☎ 399 401, ▤ 352 121) is situated a fair way away from the centre of town, at ul Tikhookeanskaya 211. The rooms, however, are spotlessly clean and comfortable; they cost US$45/ US$60 for a single/double and they also have some more expensive suites. To get to MNTK take tram No 5 from the station; the trip takes 45 minutes.

Mar Kuel Apartment Hotel, at perulok Derzhinski 3, has studio apartments with kitchen for US$80. (Note that this is not ulitsa Derzhinski but a small road between ul Derzhinski and ul Zaparina toward the Amur River from ul Lenina).

The *Hotel Amethyst* (☎ 334 699, ▤ 334 699), ul Tolstovo 5a, has singles for US$55-70 and doubles for US$80-120.

The main tourist hotel is the *Hotel Intourist* (☎ 399 317) at per Arseneva 7 which is expensive at US$95/120 for a single/double but is, however, well organized and pleasant. There's a number of good shops on the ground floor, an excellent restaurant on the eleventh, and the helpful service bureau on the second offers a wide range of excursions. Aeroflot and Asiana also have offices here. In its brochure, the hotel is described as 'a twelve storey modern style building with a clear-cut architectural silhouette' – basically just another modernist block, painted white.

There is an ever increasing number of excellent hotels and these are popular with business travellers. You're advised to book in advance, but you might be lucky if you just turn up. *Hotel Parus* (☎ 324 414, 327 270, ▤ 327 609) at ul Shchevchenko 5 has single rooms for US$90 and doubles for US$120. There is a business centre in the hotel and the restaurant serves European food which is reputed to be the best in town. *Hotel Sapporo* (☎ 236 745, ▤ 226 075) at ul Komsomolskaya 79 caters for Japanese business people and tour groups, charging US$110/140 for a single/double room.

Hotel Dalny Vostok (☎ 335 093), ul Muravieva-Amurskovo 18, is in an excellent location but is being refurbished.

The Khabarovsk area code is ☎ 4212. From outside Russia dial +7-4212.

❏ **Excursions from Khabarovsk**

Khabarovsk is an ideal base from which to start trips into the Siberian outback. Intourist-Khabarovsk (☎ 4212-399 308, 399 319; 🖹 4212-338 774) offers special interest tours to various distant and not so distant regions. Some of the excursions and tours currently being offered are listed below but as the region opens up to tourism many other places will become available.

Sakhalin is an island just off the East Siberian coast. The main attraction here is the great variety of wildlife which foreigners may explore, photograph, study, ride horses amongst, or kill. The most popular tours are the fishing trips and bird watching trips. Vanino, from where you catch a ferry to Sakhalin Island, is on the **BAM Railway**.

Other destinations in Eastern Siberia and the Far Eastern Territories that can be visited from Khabarovsk include **Yakutsk** (see p249), **Kamchatka** (for fishing and hunting and adventure tours; approximately US$1600 for 10 days), **Perelk** in the Arctic Circle (to see the Northern Lights) and **Magadan** (a former gulag centre).

These destinations are covered in detail in the new *Siberian BAM Guide – rail, rivers & road*, also from Trailblazer (see p431).

Where to eat

A great find is the small *Pizzeria* at ul Dzerzhinskovo 36. There is a sign for the place but it's inside an unassuming entrance. Service is quick and the pizzas (US$1-2) are good.

Café Kasam sells good coffee and cakes and is at the top of ul Muraveva-Amurskovo.

Further down the same street is the *Café Dauria*, good for a quick snack. *Bistro Erofe* nearby sells coffee and good pizza for US$0.50.

There are various cafés along the river side which are pleasant places for a drink and a snack.

On Komsomolskaya Square, you could join the tour groups downstairs in the new *Syangan* Chinese restaurant.

If you're staying at MNTK-Iris, the closest restaurant is the *Kitayski Samovar* (Chinese Samovar). Despite being only 50m from the main road, it's difficult to locate. Take tram No 5 to Avtodorozhny Technikum.

The Japanese restaurant, *Unikhab* (☎ 399 315), on the top storey of Hotel Intourist, is reliable but expensive. For some reason the floor here slopes to the right on the southern side of the building, promoting a somewhat unsteady feeling even before the vodka appears but the food more than makes up for this.

The *Sapporo Restaurant* (☎ 236 745) on ul Muraveva-Amurskovo 3 is the best place to eat. There's a choice of three areas to eat here: they serve Russian cuisine on the first two floors and sushi and other Japanese food on the third. It's expensive and an ATM has been thoughtfully positioned in the wall just outside the restaurant to ensure that you will have enough roubles ready when the bill comes!

Entertainment

Khabarovsk doesn't offer much in terms of nightlife but gamblers may be interested in **Casino Tourist** (☎ 370 473). Located in the Hotel Tourist, ul Karla

Marxa 67, it's the ideal place for an encounter with the city's petty criminals.

Most of the locals seem to dress up in the evenings and walk along the busy ul Muraveva-Amurskovo or sit in the open-air cafés along this road and people-watch. There is quite a Western atmosphere to this part of town and it's difficult to believe that China is less than 30 kilometres away.

What to buy

Interesting local products include ginseng and a special blend of vodka and herbs known as *aralievaya vodka*.

The attractive, tree-lined ul Muraveva-Amurskovo is the place to go shopping, although the shops close from 14:00 to 15:00 for lunch. The best souvenir shops are the **Tainy Remesla** art store, Muraveva-Amurskovo 17; **Art Salon**, ul Muraveva-Amurskovo 19; and **Art Shop**, ul Karla Marxa 15. **Hotel Intourist** also has a good selection.

The best clothing and electronics market is the open-air **Vyborgskaya Market**, otherwise known as the Oriental Bazaar. Trolley-bus No 1 runs to ul Vyborgskaya where you catch a cab for 3km to the market.

Moving on

By rail Khabarovsk is 13 hours from Vladivostok and 59 hours from Irkutsk. There are also links to Tynda and the BAM railway from Khabarovsk.

The advance purchase rail **ticket office** is at ul Leningradskaya 56 (☎ 383 164). You can also get tickets through the travel agency **Eurasia Trans Inc** (☎ 226 067, ▤ 332 726) at ul Turgeneva 64.

By air The airport is 8km east of the city centre. Departure tax is US$25. **Aeroflot** (☎ 335 346) is at bul Amursky 18. This office is for international and domestic departures and includes counters for **DAL Avia** (for flights to Harbin, Seoul and Singapore) and **Asiana Airlines** (South Korea).

Other airlines include **Alaska Airlines** (☎ 378 804); **Chosonminhang Airlines** of North Korea (at airport ☎ 373 204); Japan Airlines **JAL** (at airport ☎ 370 686); and **Chinese Northern Airlines** (☎ 373 440).

By river Hydrofoils run between Khabarovsk and Nikolaeyevsk via Komsomolsk in the summer. There are also hydrofoils to Fuyuan in China.

Vladivostok
Владивосток

Vladivostok, eastern terminus of the Trans-Siberian line and home of the Pacific Fleet, was off-limits until 1990. Soviet citizens needed special permits to visit and foreigners, with a few notable exceptions (Gerald Ford, 1975), required nothing short of divine intervention.

Ferries link Vladivostok with several ports in Japan and Korea, operating mainly in the summer and to irregular schedules. The weather never seems to be very good here ('Torrential rain for three whole days while we were there', Howard Dymock, UK), and there's a local saying that goes, 'It rains only twice in June: once for 13 days and then for 14!'. Nevertheless whether you're coming from the east or heading west it's well worth stopping off to explore one of the former USSR's major Cold War secrets and to enjoy the seaside town atmosphere. Just don't forget your umbrella.

HISTORY

This region has been inhabited for many thousands of years, certainly back at least to the second millennium BC; inhabitants were, however, largely nomadic so few relics remain. Eastern chronicles reveal that this area was considered part of the Chinese empire at a very early stage but also that it was so remote and conditions so harsh that they left it well alone.

The Russians arrive
In the mid-19th century the Russians were concentrating on expanding their territory eastwards at China's expense. At the head of the exploratory missions was Count Muravyev-Amurski who, in 1859, chose the site for a harbour here from his steamer, the *Amerika*. A year later a party of forty soldiers landed to secure the region. The port was named Vladivostok, or 'Rule the East'.

In 1861 the first shipments of soldiers arrived to protect Russia's new eastern frontier and settlers were not far behind. It soon became apparent just how important a find this city was: one of the few deep water ports on the east coast, Vladivostok's coastline remains unfrozen for longer than other parts of Siberia, being inaccessible for only 72 days per year on average compared with Nakhodka's 98. The city's strategic location resulted in the movement of the Russian eastern naval base here in 1872 from Nikolaevsk-na-Amur (where the water remains frozen for an impressive 190 days per year).

Conflict in the east

In 1904 the Russo-Japanese war broke out. Vladivostok was heavily bombarded during the fighting and trade virtually ceased but while large parts of the port were destroyed, the war was ultimately to prove beneficial: peace settlements with Japan left Vladivostok as Russia's prime east coast port although Japan gained Port Arthur and parts of Sakhalin Island.

During the First World War the city served as the chief entry point for supplies and ammunition from the USA. At the same time, foreign troops (British, Japanese, American, Canadian and Italian) flooded in to support the White Russians' struggle against the Bolsheviks. The most notorious foreign 'visitors' were the Czech legions which had fought their way east all the way from the Ukraine in a desperate bid for freedom (see p115). Many of their graves, and those of other foreigners, can still be found in the cemetery here.

Ultimately, as it became clear that the Bolsheviks were gaining the upper hand, the foreign forces departed. Most troops had left by 1920 although some Japanese stayed on until October 1922. Finally, on 25 October, the city was 'liberated' and Soviet power established, prompting Lenin's famous comment about Vladivostok, 'It's a long way away. But it's ours'.

The Soviet period

The Soviet period was good for the city. Money poured in, along with orders to develop the port and build more ships. In the last days of the Great Patriotic War Vladivostok assumed a key role as the centre of operations from which the fight against the Japanese in Manchuria was co-ordinated. Twenty-five ships from here were sunk in four years and some 30,000 sailors perished.

The city was then sealed off completely from the outside world as the Cold War set in, and the Pacific Fleet expanded fast. The West heard little more of this protected port until 1986 when Gorbachev made his 'Vladivostok Initiative' speech, in which he highlighted a grand new plan for Soviet economics and military commitments in the Far East. Echoing Peter the Great, he announced that Vladivostok was to become 'A wide open window on the East'.

Vladivostok today

The city is keen to establish itself as a major player on the Pacific Rim. There are even periodic murmurs of a movement whereby the entire Primorsky region would become an independent economic zone; undoubtedly it is an area of enormous potential and not surprisingly it has attracted mafia gangs from all over Russia who deal in every commodity imaginable. Don't let this put you off; the criminal underworld isn't interested in small fry such as tourists.

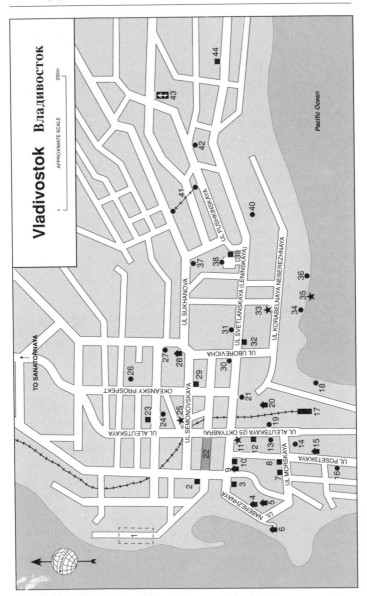

HOTELS AND RESTAURANTS

2 Café Elite Кафе Елите
3 Restaurant Okean Ресторан Океан
4 Hotel Ekvator Гостиница Екватор
5 Hotel Vladivostok Гостиница Владивосток
6 Hotel Amurski Zaliv & Casino
   Гостиница Амурский Залив и Казино
7 Café Nostalgia and Art Shop Кафе Ностальгия
8 Restaurant Morambom Ресторан Морамбом
9 Hotel Versailles & Casino Гостиница Версаленс и Казино
10 Green Crocodile Bar
12 Café Ldinka Кафе Льдинк
15 Hotel Primorje Гостиница Приморье
20 Hotel Malaya Venezia Гостиница Малая Венеция
23 Pizzaland
28 Hyundai Hotel Гостиница Хундай
29 Restaurant Hare Krishna Ресторан Кришна
32 Magic Burger Кафе Мажик Бургер
39 Restaurant Zhemchuzhina Ресторан Жемчужина
44 Restaurant Nagasaki Ресторан Нагасакий

OTHER

1 Oceanarium Океанариум
11 Museum of Local Studies Краеведческий Музей
13 House of the Brynner Family Быв. Дом Бриннера
14 Central Post Office & Internet Почтамт + Интернет
16 Airlines Office Касса Аэрофлота
17 Railway Station Железнодорожный Вокзал
18 Sea Ferry Terminal (Morskoi Vokzal) Морской Вокзал

OTHER (cont)

19 Picture Gallery Картинная Галерея
21 Victory of Soviet Power Monument
   Памятник «Борцам за Власть Советов»
22 Market Рынок
24 Japanese Consulate Кулсульство Японии
25 Pacific Fleet Military Museum/Border Guard Museum
   Музей Тихоокеанского Флота/Музей «Пограничников»
26 Market Рынок
27 Australian Consulate Кулсульство Австралии
30 GUM Department Store ГУМ
31 Book Shop Дом Книги
33 Submarine Museum & Navy Memorials
   Мемориальный Комплекс «Боевая Слава
   Краснознаменного Тихоокеанского Флота»
34 125th Anniversary of Vladivostok Monument
   Обелиск в Честь 125-летия Основания
   Города Владивостока
35 *Krasni Vympel* Ship Museum
   Пароход «Красный Вымпел»
36 Local Ferry Terminal
   Морской Вокзал Прибрежных Сообщений
37 Lucky Tour
38 Drama Theatre Драматический Театр
40 Admiral Nevelski Monument
   Памятник Адмиралу Невельскому
41 Funicular Railway Фуникулёр
42 USA Consulate Консульство США
43 Catholic Church Католический Костёл

WHAT TO SEE

The Pacific Fleet

Don't miss this unique opportunity to see some of the world's finest naval technology, although owing to a lack of funds it's beginning to look a little weatherbeaten now. Locals will tell you that it's all right to take photographs but telephoto lenses and hundreds of pictures of radar sites might arouse suspicion; caution is advised. A good place to watch the ships is from the Eagle's Nest Hill (*Orlinoye Gnezdo*). To get to the top, take the **funicular** railway from near the old church (which formerly housed the Pacific Fleet Museum: see below).

Arsenev History Museum

This is the biggest and best of Vladivostok's museums, recalling the history of both the city and the region and named after a local writer. The wildlife display is interesting: local sea life, an Ussuri leopard, a large Amur tiger and a couple of moose locking antlers in the corner. There's a display of the belongings of the early settlers, the robes of a Tungus shaman and the safe from the first bank here, stuffed with old rouble notes. Upstairs there's a small Yul Brynner exhibition (his family lived here before the Revolution), naval memorabilia and local art (the wood carvings are particularly attractive). The museum is at ul Svetlanskaya 20, and is open 10:00-17:00, closed Monday. Entry is US$1.60.

Pacific Fleet Military Museum & Border Guard Museum

The Pacific Fleet Military Museum has interesting displays with miscellaneous items from various conflicts: muskets, model ships, propaganda posters, a flame-thrower, an ejector seat and the twisted propeller and gun from a ditched fighter plane. The Border Guard Museum collection details the history of protecting the nearby frontier with China. Both displays are at the same address: ul Semyononvska 18 and open 10:00-17:00, closed Sunday and Monday. Entry is US$1.60.

Submarine Museum

On the waterfront and next to the eternal flame is an old S56 submarine, housing a display covering the history of submarines in Vladivostok. There are early uniforms, ships' instruments, pictures of the earliest submarine (1865) and the first flotillas (1906). The display is largely made up of old photographs, although you can also see some of the gifts made to submarine commanders from foreign hosts including, strangely enough, the key to the Freedom of the City of San Diego and (Tom Cruise fans, take note) a USN Fighter Weapons School Top Gun shield. Open 10:00-18:00; it's officially closed from Sunday to Tuesday although you may be able to get them to open up also on those days. Entry is US$1.60.

Krasnie Vimpel

Although marginally less interesting than the Submarine Museum, the first ship in the Soviet Pacific Fleet is moored just opposite and can also be visited. The *Krasnie Vimpel* was launched on 24 January 1923. Displays include lots of photographs of early crew members, medals, uniforms and various other pieces of salty memorabilia. Some of the machinery is preserved down below. If you're interested in buying bits and pieces of naval uniforms (belt buckles, cap badges etc) the sailors who run the museum may be able to help out. The museum, at nab Korabelnaya, is open 09:30-17:45, closed Sunday, Monday and Tuesday.

Other things to see

The **Primorskaya Art Museum** (open 10:00-18:00 daily, not Monday) at ul Aleutskaya 12 is worth a visit. There's a lot to see in here, most of the art having been donated by the Tretyakov Gallery in Moscow. Almost directly opposite, at No 15, is the **Brynner House**. You can't get inside the former residence of Yul Brynner's family but it's a real pilgrimage for some. In the well-tended **Naval Cemetery** are the graves of the Russians and people from other countries who died fighting the Communists in 1919-20. Unfortunately it's a fair way away, on the hill overlooking the Zolotoi Rog Bay, so you would be wise to take a car.

VLADIVOSTOK RAILWAY STATION

The **Oceanarium** is interesting, with displays of stuffed birds and marine life and many species of live fish in tanks.

Vladivostok Railway Station, recently repainted, is one of the city's most impressive buildings. The current building was constructed in 1911-12.

PRACTICAL INFORMATION
Orientation and services

Vladivostok is built along the Muravyev Peninsula, which stretches south-west into the Sea of Japan. Scattered around it is a series of islands, of which Russia Island remains the most important. It's still very much off-limits and protected by ferocious guard dogs so don't try any sightseeing there.

The focal point of the city is **Zolotoi Rog** (Golden Horn) Bay, so called because of its resemblance to the Golden Horn of Istanbul, and it's here that most of the ferries, warships and fishing boats dock. The **railway station** is conveniently located on the waterfront, ideal if you're transferring directly to the **ferry terminal** (*morskoi vokzal*). Opposite this is pl Lenina and between the square and the station is ul Aleutskaya (previously known as 25 Oktabrya). The central hotels are within walking distance of the station, to the east. Everything, in fact, is within walking distance but Vladivostok is quite a hilly place so distances can seem longer.

Note that the **Central Bus Station** is not at all central, being near Vtoraya Rechka suburban railway station.

Information *Vladivostok: Your Essential Guide* (Azulay US$6.50), is useful if you're here for any length of time. It's on sale at Vlad Motor Inn, and they might have a copy at the Nostalgia Art Salon. *Vladivostok News,* on the internet at http://vn.vladnews.ru, is a good source of local information. It's updated twice weekly.

The **American Business Center** (☎ 300 093, 🖷 300 092, 🖳 abcvlad@sovam .com) is at the US embassy (ul Pushkinskaya 32).

The top hotels, such as the Hyundai, all have their own business centres offering everything from email to full secretarial services.

Banks There's an **ATM** which takes all major cards at the business centre by the post office.

Communications The **central post office** is on ul Aleutskaya, near the railway station.

There are several places where you can access the **Internet**. Most convenient is probably the business centre by the post office which charges US$2 per hour. You could also try Vladivostok Cybercafé (☎ 269 135, 🖳 cybercafe@ vladivostok.com) on ul Uborevicha. Phone for directions first.

Travel agents **Lucky Tour** (☎ 267 800, 🖳 lucky@online.vladivostok.ru) is helpful and can be found at ul Sukhanova 20. There's also **Intourist** (☎ 256 210, 🖷 258 839), pr Okeanski 90; and **ACFES Tour Centre** (☎ 319 000) in the Hotel Acfes Seiyo, pr 100th Vladivostoka 103. **Sputnik** at ul Partizanski 2 can be contacted at 🖳 sputnik@online.marine.su or www.marine.su/sputnik.

For adventure travel try **Primoski Klub Travel Service** (☎ 318 037 or 320 632), 4th floor, ul Russkaya 17, Vtoraya Rechka, or **Dal'intourist** (☎ 222 949, 🖳 taiga@dalint.marine.su), ul Admirala Fokina 1.

Tours All the sights are within easy walking distance so there's not really any need for a tour. If, however, you want to

see something further away contact one of the travel agencies above.

Boat trips around the harbour are highly recommended: the chance to take pictures of Russian nuclear submarines doesn't arise that often. One-hour ferry cruises around Vladivostok's harbours and straits leave from Sportivnaya Gavan Pier approximately every hour between 11:00 and 16:00 in summer. A tour guide will give a history of sights (in Russian) including Russia Island, Skryplev Strait, Tokarevski Hill and the lighthouse at the end of Egersheld. The boat has a bar and the trip costs US$2.

Local transport
The **airport** is 30km outside Vladivostok near Artem-Primorski railway station. A taxi to Vladivostok railway station costs about US$50.

Bus No 101 runs from the airport to the central bus station (not actually very central as it's 9km to the north of Vladivostok railway station and just in front of Vtoraya Rechka railway station). There are regular suburban trains between Vtoraya Rechka and Vladivostok railway stations.

The cheapest way to get from the airport to Vladivostok is also the most time consuming. Take bus No 7 to Artem-Primorski railway station and get on a local train heading west. Get off at the fourth stop (Amurski Zaliv) and change trains for Vladivostok.

The **railway station** is a delightful two-storey building, recently repainted. To leave the station walk up to the top floor which is at street level. To get to the Hotel Pensionat and Vlad Motor Inn, take the suburban train six stops to the station Sanatornaya (Санаторная). Behind the station is a modern **sea ferry terminal**.

There are numerous daily ferries from the **local ferry station** opposite the Submarine Museum. Destinations include the popular swimming spots of Russia Island, Popov Island, Reiniky Island, Cape Peshanaya, and Slavyanka Beach (two hydrofoils a day).

Diplomatic representation

● **US Consulate** (☎ 300 070, 📄 300 091), ul Pushkinskaya 32; American citizen services 14:30-16:00 weekdays.

● **Australian Consulate** (☎ 427 464), Krasnogo Znameni Pr., 42; open 9:00-17:00 weekdays.

● **Japanese Consulate** (☎ 267 481, satellite ☎ 509-851 1001), ul Verkhne-portovaya 46; open 10:00-12:00 weekdays except Wed.

● **South Korean Consulate** (☎ 227 318), ul Aleutskaya 45, 5th floor; open 9:00-18:00 weekdays.

● **Indian Consulate** (☎ 228 110, 📄 228 666), ul Aleutskaya 14; open 9:30-12:00 for visas.

● **Philippines Consulate** (☎ 221 351), ul Aleutskaya 14; open 9:00-17:00 weekdays.

Where to stay

Hotel prices in Vladivostok seem to vary wildly from month to month depending on demand. Take the following prices as a rough guide only. Don't expect there to be hot water unless you're in one of the top hotels and even then it may be available only between specified hours. Note that there are often power and heating shortages in parts of Vladivostok and the surrounding oblast.

HOFA can arrange homestays in Vladivostok, see pp18-19.

The cheapest place to stay in Vladivostok is the *Hotel Malaya Venezia* which is wedged in down by the railway tracks, just behind the station. It's a motel-style place and the rooms cost only US$6. Bring your earplugs as the walls are thin.

The following hotel rooms all have attached bathrooms. The friendly *Hotel Amurski Zaliv* (☎ 267 102) at ul Naberezhnaya 9, is down a steep road opposite the Hotel Vladivostok. It's a bit of a maze but the cheaper rooms are well worth it at US$10/18 for a single/double. They also have smarter rooms for US$40/85. There

are two restaurants, one of which serves good Georgian food.

Near the station, *Hotel Primorje* (☎ 414 266), ul Posetskaya 20, is a recommended place with rooms from US$12-45 for a single and US$18-50 for a double. There is a swimming pool at this hotel.

Hotel Vladivostok (☎ 222 208), up on the hill at ul Naberezhnaya 10 is more expensive and the standards here are almost Western. It's where a lot of Chinese tour groups stay and costs from US$26 for singles and US$52 for doubles. There are various bars and a restaurant which are aimed at the Chinese tour groups. Just around the corner from the Vladivostok but in a less desirable state is the *Hotel Ekvator* (☎ 410 673) at ul Naberezhnaya 20. The surly staff will charge you US$15 for a 'luks' single or US$28 for a 'luks' double. Neither could be considered 'luks'-orious.

One of the top hotels is the Japanese-owned *Hotel Versailles* (☎ 265 124, 📧 versal@mail.primorye.ru) Svetlanskaya 10. Rooms are luxurious and cost between US$150 and US$230. The other top hotel and probably the best, is the *Hotel Hyundai* (402 233, 📄 407 008) set up on the junction where ul Semenov-skaya, ul Sukhanova and ul Uborevicha meet. It's a fairly new place which offers a quite bewildering range of services and includes the Vladivostok Business Centre. This would explain to some extent the wide price range (US$190 to US$1000).

Located about 20 km to the north of Vladivostok around the station Sanatornaya (*sanatorium*) is the *Vlad Motor Inn* (☎ 331 351, satellite ☎ 509-851 5111, 📄 509-851 5116, 📧 vmi.res@gin.global-one.ru, 📧 www.vlad-inn.ru) ul Vosmaya 11, is a Canadian/Russian joint-venture, well-run and recommended. A double here costs US$165 including taxes. A US$10 breakfast is included.

The Vladivostok area code is ☎ 4232. From outside Russia dial +7-4232.

Where to eat

The best restaurant within easy reach of the railway station is *Café Nostalgia*. They serve genuinely good coffee (most unusual in Russia) and the tiny restaurant next door is clean and offers good Russian dishes: zakuski for about US$2 and main courses for US$4-6. Right next door, through the ornate Oriental doorway, is the Korean *Restaurant Morambom* (☎ 227 725) which is probably better known for being difficult to get into than for its good food. It's expensive and you will need to book.

The cheapest meal in town seems to be at the *Magic Burger*, a McDonald's wanna-be at ul Svetlanskaya 42. Service is reasonably fast although you might have to queue to get in; burgers cost less than US$1.

The *shashlik stall* in the basement of the Hotel Vladivostok is another good place for a quick meal.

There's excellent vegetarian food at the *Hare Krishna Restaurant*. It is at pro Okeanski 10/12, open 10:00-19:00 weekdays. You'll get three courses for US$3 in a most serene atmosphere.

Pizzaland at ul Verkhneportovaya 40 is a popular place serving exactly what you would expect.

Down by the waterfront there are several *cafés* serving drinks and various snacks all day. You can buy prawns, crabs and other seafood here for US$3-6 and beer to go with them.

In *Hotel Amurski Zaliv* there is an excellent Georgian restaurant with main courses costing US$2-5. It's well worth a visit.

Up-market restaurants include the Russian-Japanese *Restaurant Nagasaki* (☎ 269 748), at ul Svetlanskaya 115 and recognizable by the bright orange mosaic on the doorway; the Japanese *Sakura Restaurant* (☎ 260 305) in Hotel Vladivostok; and the seafood *Okean Restaurant* (☎ 268 186) at Naberezhnaya 3 which is cheaper than these other two. Main dishes are US$6-9.

The city's other top restaurants are further away, in the Sanatornaya district.

The *Vlad Motor Inn* serves de luxe hamburgers that actually taste like de luxe hamburgers, for US$6, and some of the biggest steaks you'll ever see for US$20. Their Kamchatka crabs are another speciality. Main courses range from US$13-25 and are North American. Book in advance and wear reasonably smart dress when dining here. Begin the night with an unforgettable cocktail (US$6) from the bar. Up the block in the Hotel Pensionat is the excellent and cheaper *Captain Cook Restaurant* (☎ 215 341), an Australian/Russian joint venture. The steaks (US$9-12) are recommended.

Restaurant Volna (☎ 219 340) on top of the sea ferry terminal, offers splendid views but it usually caters only for pre-booked groups. In the evenings this place becomes a popular disco.

What to buy

The best souvenirs in town are sold in the **Nostalgia Café and Art Saloon**, ul 1st Morskaya 6/25. Many of the things here are expensive but they do seem to be of a high standard. The gift shops in the **Art Museum** at ul Aleutskaya 12, open 10:00-18:00, closed Sunday and Monday, or the **Arsenev History Museum** are worth a look. **GUM**, on ul Svetlanskaya 33, also has quite a good range but many of its goods are now imported from Japan.

It is best not to buy **vodka** here as there are a number of fake brands on sale that contain more than the legal amount of fusel oil, a by-product of the fermenting process, that will give you very much more than a nasty hangover. These include Avrora, Baren Chezzy, Russkaya, Piezo, Krom and Korona.

Entertainment

There's a smart bar at the **Hotel Hyundai**. Rather less salubrious places of entertainment include the **Green Crocodile Bar**, just a few doors down from the Hotel Versailles; **Casino Amurski Zaliv** at the Hotel Amurski Zaliv, ul Naberezhnaya 9 and **Casino Versailles** at the Hotel Versailles.

Films in English are organized by ACTR and IREX educational organizations (☎ 223 798) on Thursday at 18:00 at ul Svetlanskaya 150.

Roller blades and skates can be hired on the deck at the Okean Cinema for US$2 an hour between 10:00 and 20:00. Rowing boats (US$2 an hour) can be hired near the barge which doubles as a disco in summer.

Moving on

By air The new international air terminal building opened in 1999.

Vladivostok has international air links with Niigata, Osaka, Tokyo, Seoul, Pusan, Bangkok, Ancorage and Seattle. There are also flights to many Siberian cities.

Airlines in the Primorsky Agency of Aviation Companies offices (☎ 260 880) at ul Posetskaya 17, include Transaero, Korean Air, British Airways, Aeroflot and fourteen other 'babyflots'.

Sample fares are Moscow (US$330), Seoul (US$280), Osaka (US$255), Niigata (US$220). Alaska Airlines no longer fly here.

By train Both long-distance and local train tickets are available from the **central railway station** (☎ 210 440). At the station local tickets are sold upstairs and long-distance tickets downstairs.

Significant fare increases are due in early 2001. On the *Rossiya* to Moscow, expect to pay US$170-220 for an SV ticket, US$70-120 for a coupé.

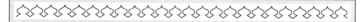

❑ Vladivostok–Japan/Korea ferries

A weekly ferry plies between Vladivostok and Japan between early April and late October. In past years it has run in the summer months only, usually from late June to early October and, things being as they are in Russia, there's more than a chance that it may go back to the shorter season. It departs weekly from Vladivostok and travels to Fushiki (or sometimes Niigata). The trip takes about 45 hours. Ferries leaving Japan at 16:00 on Friday arrive in Vladivostok at 09:30 on Sunday, and leaving Vladivostok at 15:00 on Monday reach Japan at 09:00 on Wednesday. There are also very occasional ferries to Pusan in Korea. Contact the agencies listed below for schedules.

Depending on the season, the price for the Vladivostok–Fushiki trip ranges from about US$280 to US$360 for the cheapest ticket in a third class four-berth cabin: October being the cheapest time. This fare includes port tax at Vladivostok of US$10 and all meals. There is a 10 per cent discount for round trips and a luggage limit of 100kg per person. For second class (also four-berth but on a higher deck) a ticket costs an extra US$30-50. First class (two berths in the cabin) is about twice the price of third class.

The ships are currently operated by **FESCO** (☎ 411 432, 🖹 413 037, 🖳 uef@fesco.ru, 🖳 www.fesco.ru), ul Aleutskaya 15, Vladivostok and a Cypriot company, Vladistar Shipping. For more information and bookings contact:
● **United Orient Shipping and Agency Co**, (☎ (813) 3249 4412, 🖹 (813) 3740 2085), Level 7 Rikkokai-sogo Building, 2-32-3 Kita-Shinagawa, Shinagawa-ku, Tokyo 140.
● **Biznes Intur Servis** (☎ 497 393, 🖹 497 391), Morskoi Vokzal, Vladivostok, have an office in the sea ferry terminal.

Ulan Bator
Ulaanbaatar

The world's coldest capital is a fascinating place to visit even if it does, at first sight, look like just another Soviet-style city. Things are changing fast here now though, as the free market takes hold and many more foreigners are visiting the country than ever before.

Ulan Bator (population: 600,000) sits in a basin surrounded by four mountains: Bogd Uul, Songino Khairkhan, Chingeltei and Bayanzurkh, all part of the beautiful Khentii range, the southernmost boundary of the great Siberian taiga. The city experiences great climatic extremes; the temperature ranges from -49°C (-46°F) in winter to 38°C (93°F) in summer. The average annual precipitation is only 236mm and there are on average 283 sunny days in the year. Ulan Bator is 1350 metres above sea level.

Among the industrial suburbs and concrete tower blocks there are vibrant splashes of colour in the temples and old palaces. The Mongolian people are charming and cheerful (Luigi Barzini, driving across the country in 1907, was amazed at their high spirits; the nomads he encountered galloped alongside his car roaring with laughter).

The best time to visit Ulan Bator is during the **Naadam Festival**, usually held between 11 and 13 July. The festival involves the three traditional Mongolian sports of horse riding, wrestling and archery.

HISTORY
Home of the Living Buddha
For much of its 350-year existence the town was little more than a semi-nomadic settlement. From 1639 to 1778, it moved some 30 times, like a migrating *ger* (yurt) city. The Da Khure Lamasery was built here in 1639 and this was the abode of the 'Living Buddha' or Dalai Lama, one of the three incarnations of the Buddha, the other two being in Tibet and Peking. The Dalai Lama at Da Khure was usually a child who died, or rather was murdered, shortly before reaching puberty, since it was believed that the soul of a deity could dwell only in the body of a child.

From 1639 to 1706 the town was known as Örgöö, from the Mongolian word for palace. From 1706 to 1911 it was Ikh Khuree or Da Khure to the Mongolians and Urga to foreigners.

Independence
When Mongolia declared itself independent of China in 1911, the city was renamed Niislel Khurehe, and by this time it had become a large trad-

ing centre on the route between China and Russia. There were, in fact, three separate cities here: the Chinese, the Russian and the Mongolian. The Chinese and Russian cities were engaged in the tea and silk trades but the Mongolian city's concern was the salvation (or rather the liberation) of souls. There was a population of 30,000 Buddhist monks in the lamaseries here.

Ulan Bator today

After the Communist Party came to power in 1921, the capital was renamed Ulan Bator, meaning 'Red Hero'. With considerable help from the USSR, the city was redesigned and the architectural origins of the austere tower blocks and municipal buildings are recognizably Soviet. In the mid 1990s, the city experienced a private sector boom with new buildings springing up everywhere and shops and restaurants opening. As in Russia, most of this money came from Communist-era power brokers who quickly took control of privatized state assets.

In 1999-2000 Mongolia was hit by severe weather conditions: a serious drought followed by an extremely cold winter. This led to food shortages but the capital escaped the worst of these. What it did not escape was the shortage of petrol caused by the rise in oil prices and this is something that may affect visitors, too.

WHAT TO SEE

Sühbaatar Square

A mounted statue of Sühbaatar in heroic pose stands in the centre of this large square, opposite his mausoleum (modelled on Lenin's Mausoleum in Red Square). His preserved body does not receive visitors but newly-weds queue up to have their photos taken at the foot of his statue, more out of tradition than inclination. In 1990 the square was the scene of the pro-democracy demonstrations that led to the first free elections.

Gandan (Gandantegchinlen) Monastery

Mongolia once had 700 monasteries but virtually all were destroyed in the communist crackdown at the end of the 1930s. More than 14,000 monks were killed and tens of thousands forced to give up their vows. Following the pro-democracy movement in 1990, restrictions were eased allowing some monasteries to reopen and Gandan to operate less as a showpiece for tourists.

GANDAN MONASTERY

The original monastery on this site was built in 1785 but destroyed. The first group of new buildings here was put up in 1938 and as well as the main temple there are stupas, a library and accommodation for the monks. Powdered juniper, to be thrown into the big burner outside the temple as an offering, is dispensed in a side building. Many of the buildings have been recently renovated.

It's best to visit the monastery in the morning; watch out for pickpockets when concentrating on the ceremony, and don't wander round this district after dark.

Bogd Khan Palace and Museum

This is a wonderful old place, full of ghosts and rather like Beijing's Forbidden City on a smaller scale. Exploring the palace one gets the impression that the owners walked out a few years ago, leaving it in the hands of rather relaxed caretakers who have forgotten to mow the lawn. Entered through a gateway guarded by four fierce-looking incarnations, the palace comprises two courtyards with small pavilions on each side. There are exhibits of *thangkas* (Buddhist paintings), musical instruments and Buddha figures, as well as the day-to-day furnishings of the buildings. Unfortunately there are very few labels telling you what's what.

❏ **Street names**
Finding your way around Ulan Bator is considerably complicated by the fact that not only are Russian names being changed for Mongolian ones but the script used is now Mongolian rather than Cyrillic. The way words are transliterated into English is also different: you're now likely to see Ulan Bator written as Ulaanbaatar. Below is a table of equivalent street names. In Mongolian a street is a *gudamj*, and an avenue is an *örgön chölöö* (meaning 'wide space').

Russian	Mongolian	English
Prospekt Lenina	Chinggis Khaan Örgön Chölöö	Ghengis Khan Ave
Ikh Toirog	Ikh Toiruu	Big Ring Rd
Ulitsa Stalina	Natsagdori Gudamj	Stalin St
Prospekt Mira	Enkhtaivany Örgön Chölöö	Peace Ave
Ul 40-letiya Oktyabrya	Zamchid Gudamj	40th Year October
Ulitsa Brezhneva	Khatanbaatar Magsa Iav Gudamj	Brezhnev St
Ulitsa Gagarina	Amarsanaa Gudamj	Gagarin St
Ulitsa Gorkovo	Ard-Ayush Örgön Chölöö	Gorky St
Ulitsa Konstitutsi	Zanabazar Gudamj	Constitution St
Ulitsa Khasbatora	Khuvsgal Gudamj	Khuvsgal St
Ulitsa Oktyabrskaya	Khudaldaany Gudamj	October St
Baga Toirou	Baga Toiruu	Small Ring Rd
Ul Obedinennykh Natsi	Negdsen Undestnii Gudamj	United Nations St
Ulitsa Universitetskaya	Ikh Surguul Gudamj	University St
Sukhe Bator	Sühbaatar	Sukhe Bator Sq
Prospekt Karla Marxa	Karl Marxyn Örgön Chölöö	Karl Marx Ave
Ulitsa Irkutskaya	Eldiv-Ochir Gudamj	Irkutsk St
Ulitsa Zaluuchuudyn	Zaluuchuudyn Örgön Chölöö	Sambu St

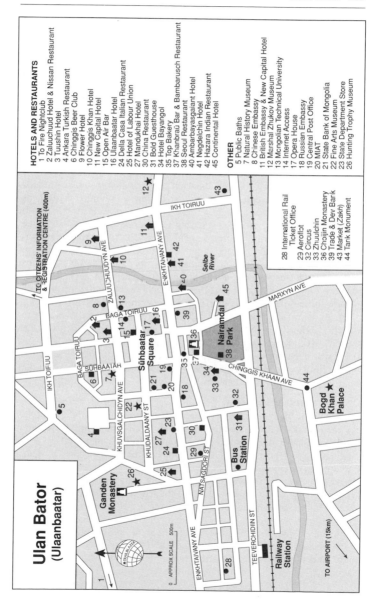

Ulan Bator
(Ulaanbaatar)

APPROX SCALE 500m

0

HOTELS AND RESTAURANTS
1 To Fire Nightclub
2 Zaluuchud Hotel & Nissan Restaurant
3 Tuushin Hotel
4 Ankara Turkish Restaurant
6 Chinggis Beer Club
9 Flower Hotel
10 Chinggis Khan Hotel
11 New Capital Hotel
15 Open Air Bar
16 Ulaanbaatar Hotel
24 Della Casa Italian Restaurant
25 Hotel of Labour Union
27 Mandukhai Hotel
30 China Restaurant
31 Bold Guesthouse
34 Hotel Bayangol
35 Top Bakery
37 Khanbräu Bar & Bambarusch Restaurant
38 Seoul Restaurant
40 Ambarbayasgalant Hotel
41 Negdelchin Hotel
42 Hazara Indian Restaurant
45 Continental Hotel

OTHER
5 Public Baths
7 Natural History Museum
8 Chinese Embassy
11 British Embassy & New Capital Hotel
12 Marshal Zhukov Museum
13 Mongolian Technical University
14 Internet Access
17 Opera House
18 Russian Embassy
19 Central Post Office
20 MIAT
21 State Bank of Mongolia
22 Fine Arts Museum
23 State Department Store
26 Hunting Trophy Museum
28 International Rail Ticket Office
29 Aeroflot
32 Circus
33 Zhuulchin
36 Chojin Monastery
39 Trade & Dev Bank
43 Market (Zakh)
44 Tank Monument

TO CITIZENS' INFORMATION & REGISTRATION CENTRE (400m)

IKH TOIRUU

ZALUUCHUUDYN AVE

ENKHTAIVANY AVE

Selbe River

BAGA TOIRUU

IKH TOIRUU

BAGA TOIRUU

Sühbaatar Square

SÜHBAATAR

KHUVSGALCHIDYN ST

KHUDALDAANY ST

MARXYN AVE

Nairamdal Park

CHINGGIS KHAAN AVE

NATSAGDORJ ST

Bus Station

Ganden Monastery

ENKHTAIVANY AVE

TEEVERCHIDIIN ST

Railway Station

TO AIRPORT (15km)

Bogd Khan Palace

The Bogd Khan museum is beside the palace complex and exhibits include Bogd Khan's throne, fur-lined robes and crown, and his luxurious ger (the exterior covered with the skins of 150 snow leopards and containing stove and portable altar). His collection of stuffed animals is also displayed somewhat haphazardly: a moth-eaten lion sharing the same quarters as a grubby polar bear. Outside is an interesting display of palanquins and carriages. It's open from 10:00 to 18:00 (only until 16:00 on Tuesday and Wednesday) and closed Thursday and the last Wednesday of each month. Entry is US$1 plus US$5 for a camera permit. To get here take any bus heading south from the Bayangol Hotel and get off when you see the tank memorial (five minutes).

Natural History Museum

Mongolia is well known for its dinosaur graveyards and some of the discoveries made in the country are on display here, including several fossilized nests of dinosaurs' eggs. These come in a fascinating range of shapes: cannon balls, ostrich-eggs, even Cornish pasties. Also worth seeing are the displays of stuffed animals arranged in quite imaginative panoramas of the Gobi and the mountains in the west. Here are many of the animals in the *Red Book* for endangered species including the snow leopard, wild Bactrian camel, Gobi bear, khulan (wild ass), red wolf, northern otter, snow griffon and Przewalski's horse. On the top floor are displays of national dress (smelling strongly of moth-balls).

A notice on the door warns: 'Closed last Monday of the month for cleaning'. Hardly surprising that the displays are rather dusty. Open Monday 10:00-16:00 (but not last Monday of the month); closed Tuesday; other days open 10:00-18:00. Entry is US$0.60 plus about US$10 for using cameras and US$20 for video cameras. Each section of the museum has different camera charges.

Choijin Lama Monastery

Preserved for many years as a museum of religion, this temple complex has been handed back to the monks in the new spirit of religious freedom. It was the former home of Luvsan Haidav Choijin Lama, the brother of the 8th Bogdo Gegen (Bogd Khan). Both of them were born Tibetans. The brightly-coloured temple buildings are set amongst overgrown grassy gardens and house a large collection of ornate masks for Buddhist mystery plays. Take a close look at the golden seated Buddha figure, not a statue but the mummified body of a lama, encased in gold. In the northern pavilion you may also want to take a close look at the statues, which graphically depict Tantric rituals involving complex sexual positions.

Open daily (except Tuesday) 10:00-17:00, entry is US$2. Immediately to the south of the museum is a statue of the Mongolian writer Natsagorj.

Fine Arts Museum

The museum includes a comprehensive display of thangkas, one more than 15m long. There are copies of prehistoric cave paintings, robes and masks from Buddhist Tsan dances and a gallery of modern paper-cutting art. Open 10:00-17:00. Entry is US$0.70.

Other museums and sights

Many of the city's smaller, less significant museums have been closed down, a fact which seems to have disappointed few visitors. A few will reopen after renovation or their displays may eventually be moved to other museums. It is no longer possible to visit the museum in Sühbaatar's bungalow or the Lenin Museum which has recently suffered the humiliation of being turned into a shopping centre. The huge Lenin head is still in place looming down on shoppers.

The **Marshal Zhukov Museum** is still open, since there is no museum for Zhukov in Russia; otherwise it would probably close. The small building is filled with military and Soviet memorabilia including Zhukov's pipe and shoes. The man who runs it sometimes dresses up in the marshal's old uniform.

The former Revolutionary Museum is now the **Museum of Mongolian National History**, open 10:00 17:00, closed Wednesday.

The **Hunting Trophy Museum** near Gandan Monastery focuses on a highly controversial issue: the lucrative industry the Mongolians have set up selling hunting packages to foreign tourists. It's open 09:00-17:00 daily except Monday, but closes at 14:00 at weekends.

Nairamdal Park is where locals go to relax and it has a boating lake, ferris wheel, camel rides and model dinosaurs.

PRACTICAL INFORMATION
Orientation

From Ulan Bator railway station to Sühbaatar Square is about 1½km.

Although Ulan Bator is relatively safe compared to some cities in the West, crime is on the increase. Don't wander round the streets alone after dark although hassle from drunks is probably the most trouble you'll get. Take particular care at the railway station, where **pickpockets** and **bag-slitters** operate on the crowded platforms. The post office and on buses have also been reported as prime locations for petty theft of this kind.

Information

The *Mongol Messenger* (US$1) is a good local newspaper, published weekly and available from Ulaanbaatar Hotel among other places. There's also a new freebie, *UB Guide*, available at hotels.

There are several useful **websites** with information on Mongolia. As well as the paper version, the *Mongol Messenger* is available online: 🖳 www.mongolnet.mn/mglmsg/index/html. Also try 🖳 www.ulaanbaatar.net which has local business listings, some good information on Mongolian food with step by step directions for how to make the recipes, weather reports and TV schedules. The US embassy's website, 🖳 www.us-mongolia.com, has business listings and general information about the country; an update is expected soon.

❏ Visiting Mongolia

Visas Although visas are available at the border and the airport in Mongolia you may need to show a letter of invitation to get one there and the visa will cost more than if you get one in advance. **Get your visa before trying to enter Mongolia.** At Mongolian embassies the fee for a tourist visa for most nationalities is UK£25/US$40 (US$40 cash only at embassies in China and Russia) for a 30-day visa; a letter of invitation is no longer necessary. One passport photo is required. If you're applying for a visa for a stay of more than 30 days you require a letter of invitation from a Mongolian company or Mongolian citizen. Singaporeans, Israelis, Malaysians and Filipinos are granted a visa-free stay in Mongolia of 14 days.For more information see Part 1: Planning your trip.

Individual travel vs package tours While individual travel around Mongolia is perfectly possible, the difficulties with language, accommodation, food and organizing travel make joining a group or making one up an option that many travellers go for, especially if time is limited. If you are visiting only Ulan Bator, you can get by on your own but it's not so easy outside the capital. It is possible to organize personal tours once you arrive in Ulan Bator but you must be sure to check what you are getting for your money.

Travel agents in Ulan Bator Zhuulchin/**Juulchin** (☎ 312 095, 🖹 320 246, 🖳 jlncorp@magicnet.mn), the former state-owned organization, still has enormous clout and charges as if it were a monopoly. **Shuren** (☎ 455 745, 🖹 450 718, shuren@magicnet.mn), local agent for Monkey Business and The Russia Experience, is reliable; it can arrange various trekking, riding and jeep trips all over Mongolia for individuals or groups. They're also building a new hotel in UB. **Nomadic Journeys** (☎ 328 737, 🖹 321 489, 🖳 mongolia@nomadicjourneys.com), is also good. As well as providing a number of local tours, it runs Eco Tour Productions' trekking, riding and fishing trips. **Blue Sky Travel** (☎ 312 067 🖹 312067 🖳 blueskytrav@yahoo.com 🖳 www.travel2mongolia .mn), has been recommended by several readers. **Khuvsgul Lodge** (☎ 310 852, 🖹 315 655, 🖳 boojum@magicnet.mn) runs local tours for US operation, Boojum Expeditions. **Karakorum Expeditions** (☎ 315 655, 🖳 info@gomongolia.com 🖳 www.gomongolia.com), is also recommended. **Nassan** (☎ 323 528, 🖳 nassan2037@yahoo.com) has many tour options and can arrange travel for individuals. **Hovsgol Travel** (☎ 687 826, Mob: 99116227 🖹 687 826, 🖳 hovsgol_travel@mongol.net, www.ulaanbaatar.net/hovsgoltravel/ind ex.html), has a wide range of tours.

Local transport

There are **buses** and **trolley-buses** in Ulan Bator (tickets cost the togrog equivalent of US$0.20) but you may prefer to walk as most of the sights are in the city's centre. Watch for pickpockets on buses.

To get a **taxi**, simply put out your hand by the side of the road and a motorist will usually stop. Point to the odometer to show the driver that you expect to pay the prevailing Mongolian rate of US$0.60 per kilometre. Given the current fuel shortages and price rises it's worth asking locals beforehand what the current rate is. **Official taxis** with meters are also available but they're not in great

(Opposite) Top: Mongolians have long been famous for their riding skills. Riding holidays for visitors are easy to organize but you should bring your own hard hat with you if you're worried about falling off. **Bottom:** On excursions from Ulan Bator accommodation is often in gers (yurts). (Photos © Nick Hill).

supply. You'll usually find them outside the top hotels.

It's now possible to rent **bicycles** in Ulan Bator. Try Bike Mongolia (☎ 327 423) or Suren (☎ 453 347). Note that Mongolian dogs like nothing better than to chase a foreigner on bicycle.

Services
Post and telecommunications The **Central Post Office** is on Sühbaatar Square but it's better to buy those wonderful Mongolian stamps from the hotels since they often have a greater range.

The most reliable **courier company** is DHL, at Ulaanbaatar Hotel.

International telephone calls are expensive but can now be made from cardphones in many of the hotels, as well as from the post office and from the 24-hour, AT&T direct call telephone in the lobby of the Flower Hotel.

Hotels will send **faxes** but you should check charges first as some are very high.

There are now several **Internet cafés** in town and going online seems to be swift and reliable. Most charge around US$1.50 per hour. Epsilon Internet Café at Baga Toiruu 13 is open from 10:00 to 22:00 everyday. You can also use the Internet by the post office and at Ulaanbataar Hotel.

Currency and banks The togrogs (tugrik, MNT) is the Mongolian unit of currency; there are currently MNT-1097 togrogs to US$1, MNT-1596 to UK£1, MNT-962 to the Euro and MNT-132 to Y1 (China).

Many hotels and banks will change travellers' cheques, exchange hard currency for togrogs, and sell and buy togrogs. The best place to do this is at the new Trade and Development Bank (opposite the Ulaanbaatar Hotel), though the Chinggis Khaan Hotel and Flower Hotel also offer this service. The commission on exchanging travellers' cheques into US$

> ❏ **Prices in this section**
> Note that prices in this section are quoted in US$ but must usually be paid for in Mongolian togrogs. From year to year, as the togrog exchange rate rises against the dollar, the dollar value seems to stay relatively constant. Convert the US$ price given in this section to togrogs at the going rate and that should be approximately the right price to pay in local currency.

cash is 2% and into togrogs 0%. The post office changes cash only. The **black market** and official rates are now almost identical so the only reason to use the black market is for convenience. You can find it in the old cinema on Baga Toiruu St and you can also get roubles and yuan. The usual caveats about counting money carefully and being aware that there is always a certain risk in changing money this way apply. Fresh US$ bills printed after 1996 are what they want, preferably US$50s or US$100s.

You can get a **cash advance** on Visa and MasterCard in the State Bank of Mongolia, and at several of the biggest hotels for a 4% commission. American Express cash advances attract no commission. When **ATMs** arrive in Ulan Bator the first bank to have one will no doubt be the Trade and Development Bank. Don't hold your breath.

Diplomatic representation Embassies and consulates in Ulan Bator are listed below. Note that there's no longer a Polish embassy here.
● **Belarus** (☎ 452 017).
● **China** (☎ 320 940), Zaluuchuudyn St, open 8:30-11:30 Monday, Wednesday and Friday; a tourist visa costs US$30 processed in a week, US$50 processed in three days and it's US$60 for a same-day

---

(Opposite) Top: Bogd Khan Palace (see p284) was the last Mongolian king's winter residence in Ulan Bator. **Bottom:** Detail from a beam at Bogd Khan Palace.

visa. Travel agents charge around US$6 to get your visa for you.

● **Germany** (☎ 323 325), 7 Negdsen Undestnii St.

● **India** (☎ 329 524), 10 Zaluuchuudyn.

● **Japan** (☎ 320 777), 12 Zaluuchuudyn.

● **Russia** (☎ 327 071), 6A Enkhtaivany Avenue; open 14:00-15:00 for visas. The process isn't straightforward and if at all possible get your Russian visa in Beijing instead. Three photographs are required: a visa costs US$30-$95 depending on how quickly you want it and you have to go to the consulate in person. Note that they don't accept fax copies of the invitation or vouchers. It's best to get them faxed directly to the consulate. There are several guest houses in Ulan Bator who now offer help for travellers to get a Russian visa. Bold Guest House (☎ 9919 6232) has been recommended.

● **South Korea** (☎ 321 548), 10 Karl Marxyn St.

● **UK** (☎ 458 133, 458 238, ▤ 458 036, ☐ britemb@magicnet.mn) Enkhtaivany Ave, open 9:00-13:00, 14:00-18:00 weekdays.

● **USA** (☎ 329 095, ▤ 320 776) Ikh Toiruu, open 9:00-13:00, 14:00-18:00 weekdays.

Medical The first non-government hospital in Ulan Bator, the Yonsei Friendship Hospital (☎ 310 945), opened in 1994. It is sponsored by the Yonsei University of Korea and various Christian missionary groups.

For those seeking a traditional cure, the Institute for Mongolian Traditional Medicine is at the Manba Datsan. To get to it take bus Nos 5, 9, 10, 20 or 21 or trolley 8.

Radio and TV Cable TV (MTV, CNN etc) is available in hotels.

BBC World Service radio broadcasts locally 24 hours a day, on FM103.1.

Visa extensions and registration It's no longer necessary to register with the police on arrival in Ulan Bator unless you are staying for more than 30 days. To register go to the **Citizens' Information and Registration Centre**, which is hard to find as it doesn't have a street address or look like a police station. It is located about 800 metres up the road which starts opposite the northern end of Eldev-Ochir St. It's on the third floor, on the right, at the end of a hall. It's wise to take a Mongolian speaker with you.

Where to stay

Budget accommodation There are budget guest houses opening up frequently and many offer visa services, trips to the countryside, and onward tickets. Their touts will meet you at the railway station. Some offer accommodation in gers, others offer homestays with families. Prices are around US$5, sometimes less. Make sure what is in the price (check whether this includes breakfast) and don't agree to anything before having a look.

Idre's Guest House (☎ 329 137, ☐ idre9@hotmail.com) has four centrally-located apartments which they use for guest accommodation. A bed in one of these is US$4. They also organize trips to the countryside and Gobi, visa extensions and train tickets. The address of the apartments is Khudaldaany gudamj 41, House 41, Door 3, (opposite Trade and Development Bank).

Bold Guest House (☎ 323 498, ☐ Bold777@hotmail.com) is located at Door 70, Floor 2, Entrance 5, Building 14b, V District (near the circus). They charge US$5 per person for dormitory accommodation and arrange visas, tours and train tickets.

Zaluuchuud Hotel (☎ 324 594), 27 Baga Toyruu Rd, is quite a pleasant place. They have a range of rooms and they charge US$10 for a bed in a four-bedded room and US$32-45 for a double.

Much less pleasant though better located and with spartan rooms for less than US$5 is the *Hotel of Labour Union* (Partizan St). There's no sign outside and no hot water inside.

The *Negdelchin Hotel* (☎ 367 209) is located at 25A/1 Enkhtaivany Ave and offers clean, basic rooms at US$12 for a single, US$18 for a double. The *Mandukhai Hotel* (☎ 322 204), 19/2 Enkhtaivany Ave, is centrally located but somewhat overpriced. Rooms range from US$13 to US$60.

Mid-range and up-market hotels

All hotel rooms in this section have attached bathrooms.

The *New Capital Hotel* (☎ 458 235, 🖹 458 281) on Enkhtaivany Ave charges US$30 for a single and US$40 for a double. It is situated near the British embassy.

Tuushin Hotel (☎ 328 594, 🖹 325 903, 🖳 www.ulaanbaatar.net/tuushinhotel, is conveniently located just off Sühbaatar Square. There are singles for US$40 and doubles for US$80-130. There's a sauna, billiard table and travel agency.

Flower Hotel (☎ 458 330, 🖹 458 330), formerly the Altai, at 19/2 Khukh Tengger Ave, is further from the centre but good value at US$44 for a single room or US$70 95 for a double room. Renovations should now be complete.

The Soviet-styled *Ulaanbaatar Hotel* (☎ 325 368, 🖹 324 485) is the most popular haunt for foreigners and ex-pats, who refer to it as the 'UB'. It's very well located, on Sühbaatar Square. A single is US$60 and doubles range from US$130 to US$190. Rates include breakfast; credit cards are accepted.

Partly refurbished, the 418-bed *Bayangol Hotel* (☎ 326 781, 🖹 326 880) 7 Chinggis Khaan Ave, charges US$73 for a single. Doubles cost US$102-180. Breakfast is included. Some rooms are much better than others so you should look at a room before renting it. The hotel accepts credit cards.

At the top of this price range is the *Continental Hotel* (☎ 323 829, 🖹 329 630, 🖳 www.ulaanbaatar.net/continentalhotel/mapt.html), opposite Nairamdal Park, which should now be up and running. It's an impressive-looking place with a grand pillared entrance, there's a

sauna, and even a heated garage to keep your jeep cosy when the temperature plummets below minus 20ºC in winter.

Chinggis Khaan Hotel, (☎ 313 380, 🖹 312 788), 8 Khukh Tengger Ave is the city's smartest place to stay. A single room is US$80 and double range from US$130 to US$180 including breakfast. There's a casino, pricey Western restaurant and business centre.

Where to eat

Mutton features on every menu but the range of food available is certainly much wider than it was a few years back. Chicken is a luxury food, imported from China.

If you're a vegetarian you're advised to bring some supplies with you as Mongolians have never thought much of veggies: some are even convinced that eating vegetables is not healthy!

Mongolian beer is quite good: there's Khan Brau brewed here under licence from Germany and also Chinggis Khan.

The best hotel restaurants are in the *Ulaanbaatar, Bayangol* and *Chinggis Khaan* hotels. Most of the larger hotels have two restaurants; one usually cheaper than the other.

The *Della Cassa* Italian restaurant on Enkhtaivany Ave is well worth a visit. There is a wide choice of pizzas and pasta. Two main courses and drinks cost around US$10. You can also get a great pepper steak in the *Chinggis Beer Club*, on Sühbaatar St.

Curry has come to UB. The *Hazara Indian Restaurant* offers delicious North Indian cuisine and is highly recommended. Open 12:00-14:30 and 18:00-22:00, it's at 16 Enkhtaivany Ave, next to the Negdelchin Hotel.

The *Khanbraü Bar and Bambarusch Restaurant* on Chinggis Khan Ave is popular with ex-pats and rich Mongolians. It is always busy and serves great ice creams but the prices are relatively high. They brew several of their beers at the restaurant.

There is a very good Japanese restaurant called *Hanamasa* across from the Geser Temple on Ih Toiruu Rd. There's a buffet: all you can eat for US$8. Similar in style is the *Seoul Korean Restaurant*, in Nairamdal Park. A meal costs about US$12 and if you are there by about 18:00 there's a performance by the Tumen Eh folklore ensemble.

Right next door to the Zaluuchuud Hotel is the *Nissan Restaurant*, serving mutton stews, cold zakuski, potatoes and pasta. The food is reasonable and very good value.

The *China Restaurant* is on the first floor of the building with the ornate Chinese doorway on Natsagdori St. It serves authentic dishes.

You can find delicious Turkish food at the *Ankara Doner* restaurant on Khuvsgalchidyn Ave in the cinema building. A very filling meal will cost around US$3.

Nightlife

There has been a radical change to evening activities in Mongolia over the last few years and the city seems to be developing something of a taste for decadence.

Fire Nightclub is very popular every night, best on Friday. It's out in Microdistrict 3 so you should get a taxi. It shuts around 03:00 and you can follow others on to another club.

The **Chinggis Beer Club** is a popular place open until 01:00 every night.

Open until 03:00, with a great view of the city, is the **Black Wolf** bar at the top of the tall building next to the Palace of Culture. There is also a pleasant **open air bar** set into the corner of the Palace of Culture. It's open every night. There are many other bars to choose from: **Money Train**, **White House** and **Carlsberg Club** have all been recommended.

Ex-pats seem to favour the bar at the **Bayangol Hotel**.

More traditional activities include a visit to a ballet or opera in the **State Opera and Ballet Theatre** on Sühbaatar Square; inquire at reception in your hotel for tickets and times, or buy tickets from the box office on the night. The Song and Dance Show which is on several times a week at the **Drama Theatre** is worth seeing for some excellent traditional dancing. There's also a **circus**, not usually open in the summer.

Public baths

No hot water in your hotel? Can't face the prospect of another day without soap, shampoo and disinfectant? Then the public bath is the place for you. Entry is US$2.50 and for this you get the use of a sauna, a good hot shower and a towel and slippers. See map on p285 for location.

What to buy

Things to buy include leather goods, cashmere shawls and sweaters, sheepskin, carpets, jewellery, dinosaur cards and models. The country is also noted for its wonderfully bizarre, oversize **postage stamps** with naïve representations of cars and trains. So many are needed for airmail postage that there is little room left on the postcard for a message.

The city **market** (*zakh*), recently relocated to a site on the corner of Ikh Toiruu and Teeverchidiin, is fascinating. You can buy anything from a cowbell to a camel and, of course, heaps of imported Russian and Chinese goods fresh off the train. You can benefit from tough economic times by picking up traditional coats, clothes, hats, silks, thangkas, statuettes, daggers and silver buttons. It's open Wednesday, Thursday, Saturday and Sunday. Watch out for bag-slitters and pickpockets – they are unbelievably dextrous.

Less exciting but more convenient is the **State Department Store**. Here you can buy simple Mongolian toys and souvenirs or a even pair of black riding boots if you are lucky. As these boots are normally custom made, don't be surprised if they sell you a pair and tell you to come back in a few weeks to pick them up. The boots are worn by men as part of their *del*, the national costume. You will also find fur-lined winter and cotton summer Mongolian hats here. There's a bakery selling bread and cakes. There's a **book-shop** opposite the department store.

Moving on

By rail   Rail tickets for **travel within Mongolia** are booked at the new office just to the east of the station.

International trains must be booked at the Railway Ticket Booking Office (see map) just north of the station. The office is open 09:00-14:00 weekdays and until 13:00 on Saturday. Zhuulchin can organize tickets for you but add a service charge of about 5%.

For train departure times see the timetables on pp405-8. Note that with an international student card you can get a discount of 20% on a rail ticket.

By air   Ulan Bator's **Buyant Ukhaa International Airport** has been upgraded considerably in the last few years. Departure tax is US$15.

Mongolian Airlines MIAT (☎ 322 273, www.miat.com.mn) has services to Seoul, Beijing, Almaty, Irkutsk, Osaka, Hohhot, Berlin, Frankfurt and Moscow. MIAT is a lot more reliable than it used to be and most flights go on time nowadays. **Aeroflot** (☎ 320 720) has a weekly Moscow–Ulan Bator flight. **Air China** (☎ 452 548) has twice weekly Beijing–Ulan Bator services arriving and leaving Ulan Bator on Monday and Wednesday. **Korean Airlines** (☎ 326 643) has a weekly Seoul–Ulan Bator flight. For tickets try Air Trans (☎ 310 061) at the Youth Cultural Centre. Sample prices are: Berlin (US$680) Moscow (US$350), Irkutsk (US$90) and Beijing (US$220).

Excursions from Ulan Bator

ULAN BATOR AREA

To really see Mongolia you must get out into the countryside. There's no better antidote to the polluted city than a night or two camping in a ger and a few days trekking or riding.

If you're using the services of a **travel agency** (see p288) for an excursion make absolutely sure of what the tour will entail so you know what you'll be getting for your money. Several readers have written to say that they thought the 'excursion' they went on was a rip-off. One paid US$100 to be told by the tour guide that he didn't really know where to go and it all looked the same anyway! Ask travellers who've just been on excursions for the latest recommendations. If you're renting a **jeep** for an out of town expedition for several days it's recommended that you check the odometer reading at stops as well as at the beginning and end of the trip: some operators are not above altering it so as to be able to charge you for more kilometres.

Entry to all **national parks** in Mongolia now costs US$1 per foreigner and US$3 per vehicle.

For the practical details of exploring beyond Ulan Bator, get a copy of Lonely Planet's *Mongolia* and their excellent *Mongolian phrasebook*.

Ger encampments

Most groups of travellers are shipped off to **Terelj**, 80km from Ulan Bator, where they sleep out under the stars, drink mare's milk for breakfast and sit around campfires lulled by the sound of gently sizzling mutton kebabs. There are two types of accommodation here: *gers* and *hotels*. Zhuulchin and a number of other companies offer trips to Terelj. There's no public transport so you'll have to come with a tour group or by car (US$50).

The smaller ger encampments are rather less touristy although the atmosphere at them often depends as much on your fellow visitors as on the place itself. They're usually linked to just one travel agency in Ulan Bator, through which you should book. Two such places are **Jalnan Meadows/Khan Khentii Ger Camp** used by Nomadic Journeys and **Elstei Ger Camp** used by Shuren. You can rent horses from locals here.

Stars Observatory

A few kilometres west of Ulan Bator is a delightful place called the Stars Observatory. It can be reached on a day trip or with an overnight stay. At the observatory there are two attractive old buildings, one a cheap *hotel* and the other the observatory. The observatory is open weekdays and at night the staff will let you look through the telescope. The view of the city is also worth the trip. To get there, catch bus 14 going west from the central bus station. Ask to get off at the first left turn on the main highway after the bus gets out of town. Cross the road and walk south-west toward the big railway bridge over the river. Continue south-west across the field for half an hour until you get to a dirt road which goes all the way to the observatory.

Bogd Uul Nature Reserve and Manzshir Monastery

This unique mountain region, directly south of Ulan Bator, was proclaimed a protected area in 1778 although conservation of Bogd Uul, which means Holy Mountain, actually began in the 12th century; Khan Turil declared the mountains sacred and prohibited logging and hunting on them. Most of the trees are larch. Rolling, hilly, steppe grasslands stretch to the south. Clouds hang over the mountains in summer, and there are frequent thunderstorms. Snow is abundant in winter. A total of 65,000 hectares of Bogd Uul is a biosphere reserve. The area contains 116 species of birds, including 20 endangered species. Other species in the area include musk deer, ibex, roe-deer, hare and native sable.

The highest peak in Bogd Uul is Tsetsee Gun (2268m). It is possible to hike over the ridge to the ruins of the ancient **Manzshir Monastery** and the museum on the southern slope of Bogd Uul. It's well worth visiting the museum to get an idea of the devastation caused in 1937. A German photographer visited in 1926 and took some amazing photos of the monastery which are now on display in the museum. Entry is US$1.50.

Not far from the monastery you can stay at *Undur Dov Resort*, which has about 40 gers.

FURTHER AFIELD

Hustain Nuruu Reserve

About 110 km west of Ulan Bator is the Hustain Nuruu Reserve, dedicated to the reintroduction and preservation of the last truly wild horse, known in the West as Przewalski's horse, and in Mongolia as the *takhi*. Desertification, hunting, cross breeding and competition with domestic livestock resulted in its extinction in the wild by 1969. At that time, the world population was down to 161 animals in zoos. A carefully monitored breeding programme has resulted in the population increasing to several hundred. It is possible to organize a visit to the reserve but you will have to do it well in advance. Contact the Project Manager, Foundation for the Preservation and Protection of the Przewalski's Horse, PO Box 1160, Central Post Office, Ulan Bator 11. Accommodation consists of basic *guest gers*.

Karakorum (Harhorin)

This ruined city now scattered round the modern town of Harhorin, 370km from Ulan Bator, was the capital of the Mongolian Empire in the 13th century. Today its centrepiece is the **Erdene Zuu Monastery** which was built in 1586 and was the first Buddhist centre in Mongolia. At its height, the monastery housed 1000 monks in 100 temples. During the Stalinist purges of the 1930s, the monastery was badly damaged but it is once again functioning and open to visitors. Entry to the monastery costs US$3.

Travel agents offer three-day package trips which are the easiest way to get here. To do the trip yourself by bus you will need to book in advance at the central bus station in Ulan Bator. The trip takes nine hours and the halfway stop is at the little village of Sansar. Remember to take your own food and water. In Harhorin, you can stay in the *Hangayin Hotel*, next to the movie theatre. A room costs US$10 and the hotel has a restaurant. There are also four tourist *ger camps* in and around Harhorin.

The Gobi

The Gobi stretches for almost 4000km along the border of Mongolia and China. Only about three per cent of the Gobi is true desert; it's said to contain some 33 different ecosystems as well as gazelles, the rare Argali sheep, Asiatic wild ass, wild Bactrian camel, snow leopard and ibex. The site of an ancient inland sea, the Gobi is also a treasure chest of fossilized dinosaur bones and eggs.

Nestled between the beautiful peaks of the Gurvansaikhan (Three Beauties) Mountains towering 3km above the surrounding steppe, is Yol Am Valley. The canyon shelters glaciers which remain frozen in its shadow even on the hottest summer days. Camping is not allowed in the **Gurvansaikhan National Park** but there are plenty of tourist *ger camps* nearby. Most travel companies organize three-day flying trips to the Gobi from Ulan Bator.

Beijing

Both the Trans-Manchurian and Trans-Mongolian routes, by far the most popular with travellers crossing Siberia, start or finish in Beijing, so you'll probably be spending some time here. The city is well worth exploring, budget accommodation is cheap and most travellers stay for at least three or four days.

HISTORY
Early history
Remains of China's oldest known inhabitant, Peking Man, were unearthed some 50km to the south of present-day Beijing in 1921, proving that life in this region dates back at least to 500,000 BC. Chinese records go back only as far as the Zhou dynasty (12th century BC to 771 BC) but indicate that by this period this region was acknowledged as the country's capital.

The city and its environs were to remain at the heart of Chinese culture and politics, although the role of capital was often lost to other cities, including Xi'an (where the Terracotta Army now draws the tourists) and Luoyang. Beijing's strength, however, lay in its proximity to China's northern frontiers: by ruling from here emperors could keep a close eye on military developments to the north, where 'barbarians' were constantly threatening invasion.

Despite the construction of the Great Wall (a continuous process dating from the second century BC) Genghis Khan marched in in 1215, sacked the city and then proceeded to rebuild it as his capital; the Mongols called this Khanbalik (City of the Khan). It was at this stage that the first Westerners visited, including Marco Polo, who liked the place so much that he stayed for 17 years.

The Mongol collapse; further developments
The Mongol empire fell in 1368 and the Chinese shifted their capital to Nanjing. Following a coup led by the son of the first Ming emperor, the government was moved back here and the city renamed Beijing (Northern Capital). The Manchurian invasion in 1644 established the final Chinese dynasty, the Qing, which was to rule from here until the abdication of Pu Yi, the 'Last Emperor', in 1912. Although the early years of Qing dynasty rule were successful, corruption, opium and foreign intervention soon undermined Chinese authority and there were major rebellions in the city in the late 19th century.

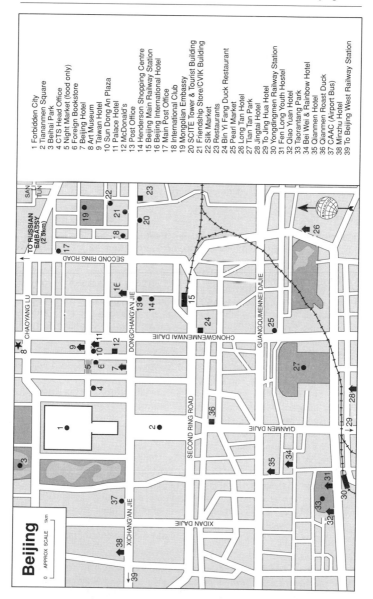

1 Forbidden City
2 Tiananmen Square
3 Beihai Park
4 CTS Head Office
5 Night Market (food only)
6 Foreign Bookstore
7 Beijing Hotel
8 Art Museum
9 Taiwan Hotel
10 Sun Dong An Plaza
11 Palace Hotel
12 McDonald's
13 Post Office
14 Henderson Shopping Centre
15 Beijing Main Railway Station
16 Beijing International Hotel
17 Main Post Office
18 International Club
19 Mongolian Embassy
20 SCITE Tower & Tourist Building
21 Friendship Store/CVIK Building
22 Silk Market
23 Restaurants
24 Bin Yi Fang Duck Restaurant
25 Pearl Market
26 Long Tan Hotel
27 Tian Tan Park
28 Jingtai Hotel
29 To Jing Hua Hotel
30 Yongdingmen Railway Station
31 Fen Long Youth Hostel
32 Qiao Yuan Hotel
33 Taorantang Park
34 Bei Wei & Rainbow Hotel
35 Qianmen Hotel
36 Qianmen Roast Duck
37 CAAC (Airport Bus)
38 Minzhu Hotel
39 To Beijing West Railway Station

The Civil War and beyond

The Kuomintang, under Chiang Kai Shek, relocated China's capital to Nanjing in 1928, although following the Communist victory it was moved back here in 1949. In October of that year, Chairman Mao declared the foundation of the People's Republic of China in Beijing. The city has hardly been quiet in the meantime: every major movement in the country since then, notably the mass conventions of the Cultural Revolution and the Democracy rallies (culminating in the Tiananmen Square Incident of 1989, when over 2000 civilians were killed), has had its roots here.

As the capital roars into the 21st century the economy is booming and Beijing is aiming to show the city off to the world by hosting the 2008 Olympics. A US$430 million National Grand Theatre is to be constructed just to the west of Tiananmen Square.

WHAT TO SEE

Tiananmen Square and the Forbidden City

Just as Red Square is the best place to start a tour of Moscow, so is Tiananmen Square for a trip around Beijing. In the centre is **Chairman Mao's Mausoleum** (open 08.30-11.30 daily) in which, after joining a long queue which moves surprisingly fast, you can see the great man himself. Leave bags at the nearby kiosks (Y1). To the east is the **National Museum of Chinese History**, which also houses the **Museum of the Chinese Revolution**. Both are worth a morning exploring if you have the time, and are open 09.30-15.30, closed Mon. Entry is Y10; the taped tour costs an extra Y40. Opposite the museums on the other side of the square is the Great Hall of the People, used for meetings of the National People's Congress and containing an impressive 10,000 seat auditorium.

To the north of the square is the **Imperial Palace** , better known as the Forbidden City, entered through **Tiananmen Gate**. This enclosure comprising over 178 acres and 1000 buildings takes at least a day to explore to get even a bare impression; there's so much to see here that really you need much longer.

The palace was erected by the Ming emperor Yong Le in the early 15th century and since then has been the home of the last 24 emperors, up until the abdication of Pu Yi in 1912. The best way to get around is to hire a cassette tour at the main gate and have everything explained to you by Roger Moore. It's a good idea to wander round again afterwards, soaking up the atmosphere. The palace is open 08.30-16.30 daily but ticket offices close at 15.30. Entrance is Y55 and the cassette tour costs Y30.

The Great Wall

China's most famous attraction makes an ideal day trip from Beijing. Most tourists visit the Wall at Badaling but it's less crowded at Mutianyu.

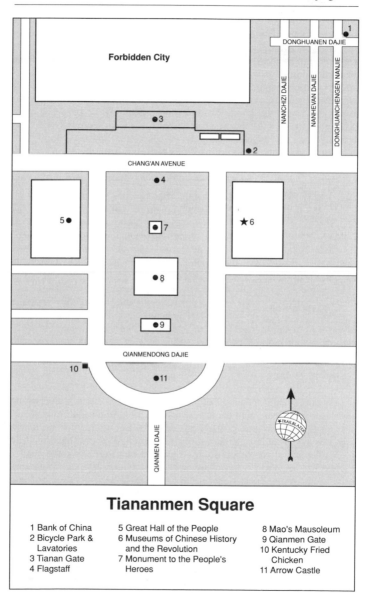

Tiananmen Square

1 Bank of China
2 Bicycle Park & Lavatories
3 Tianan Gate
4 Flagstaff

5 Great Hall of the People
6 Museums of Chinese History and the Revolution
7 Monument to the People's Heroes

8 Mao's Mausoleum
9 Qianmen Gate
10 Kentucky Fried Chicken
11 Arrow Castle

The Wall itself was not built in one massive construction project as many believe; in fact the original scheme under Emperor Shih Huang (first century BC) was simply to join extant stretches of individual defensive walls together. It was hoped that the resulting fortification would protect China from marauding foreigners but this was not the case. It's currently responsible for drawing more foreigners to China than ever, as those who visit at **Badaling** or **Mutianyu** will see. It's possible to get to Badaling independently by train (the Trans-Siberian route passes by – see p380) from Xizhimen station but otherwise you'll have to go with a tour group. The travel agency at the Qiao Yuan Hotel (☎ Mob: 139 0112 3938) runs popular trips to another section of the Wall: **Simatai.** It's a great trip for Y50 but quite tiring. To get to the least touristy section, **Jinshanling**, you'll need to hire a minivan.

TIAN TAN
THE TEMPLE OF HEAVEN

Tian Tan – the Temple of Heaven

This is the site from which China's emperors conducted the country's most important religious rituals, upon which depended the wellbeing of the population. Sights worth noting here include the Hall of Abstinence, the marble circular altar, the Imperial Vault of Heaven (where a whisper towards the surface on one side is perfectly audible around the opposite side). The most famous building of the complex is the Hall of Prayer for Good Harvests, to the north, built entirely without the use of glue or nails. The temple in Tian Tan Park is open from 08.30 to 19.00 and entry to the park is Y1.50, Y30 for a tourist ticket.

Summer Palace

The palace (summer retreat of the Imperial family since 1750) covers an area about four times the size of the Forbidden City. Virtually everything in the grounds apart from the lake dates back only to the start of this century, as there has been repeated destruction by foreigners: the entire area was razed in 1860 as retribution for the Opium Wars and then again in 1900 after the Boxer Rebellion. It's a great place to explore slowly and if the weather is good it's well worth spending a whole day here wandering around the Royal Residence, the Dragon King Temple, the Long Corridor, the Tower of Buddhist Virtue and the lake.

Entry is Y40 and it's open 08:00-19:00. Bus number 808 (air-con) from Tiananmen to the Summer Palace costs Y25.

Chinese Opera

There are numerous performances all over Beijing. The one at the theatre inside Qianmen Hotel is recommended; there are hour-long performances at 19:30 each evening. The cheapest ticket at Y30 gives a good view.

PRACTICAL INFORMATION
Orientation and services

Although Beijing is a large city, finding your way around is not too difficult owing to the fact that most streets head either north-south or east-west. The streets are, however, very crowded.

Trans-Siberian trains still use the main railway station, Beijing Dza. Many other trains arrive and depart from Beijing's smart new West (Xizhan) station, said to be the largest station in Asia.

Local transport The metro system is helpful but stations are not always where you need them. Buses and trolleybuses are cheap but very crowded; **watch out for bag-slitters and pickpockets**. Most travellers join the rest of the city's population on two wheels; there are many places that rent out bikes. Taxis are easiest to get outside hotels. They're metered and reasonable value when shared.

Diplomatic representation See p356 for more information on the **Mongolian, Belarus** and **Russian** embassies in Beijing. Note that to cross Belarus you now need a Belarusian transit visa.

Australia (☎ 6532 2331) 21 Dongzhimenwai Dajie, Sanlitun; **Belarus** Jianguomenwai compound (near NZ embassy); **Canada** (☎ 6532 3536) 19 Dongzhimenwai Dajie, Sanlitun; **Czech Republic** (☎ 6532 1531) Ritan Lu, Jianguomenwai; **Germany** (☎ 6532 2161) 5 Dongzhimenwai Dajie; **Hungary** (☎ 6532 1431) 10 Dongzhimenwai Dajie, Sanlitun; **Mongolia** (☎ 6532 1203) 2 Xiushui Beijie Jianguomenwai; **Netherlands** (☎ 6532 1131) 1-15-2, Ta Yuan Office Building; **New Zealand** (☎ 6532 2732) 1 Dong Er Jie, Ritan Lu; **Poland** (☎ 6532 1235) 1 Ritan Lu, Jianguomenwai; **Russian Federation** (☎ 6532 1267) 4 Dongzhimen Beizhong Jie; **Slovakia** (☎ 6532 1531) Ritan Lu, Jianguomenwai; **Sweden** (☎ 6532 3331) 3 Dongzhimenwai Dajie; **Ukraine** (☎ 6532 4014) Sanlitun Dong 6 Jie; **UK** (☎ 6532 1961) 11 Guanghua Lu; **USA** (☎ 6532 3831) 3 Xiushui Beijie, Jianguomenwai.

Services CITS, China International Travel Service, has representatives in many of the larger hotels in Beijing. **CITS China head office** (☎ 6512 0507, 🖳 wuxx@cits.com.cn, www.ctn.com.cn) is in the West Lobby of the Beijing International Hotel and sells Trans-Sib tickets. Also try the CITS branch at the **Beijing Tourist Building** which is by the SCITE Tower which is about 1km east of the Beijing International Hotel. Another option for rail tickets is the **CTS head office** (☎ 6559 9957) is at 52 Donghuamen Street, Dongcheng District.

CAAC (☎ 6601 7755) is on the western side of Chang'an Ave at 15 Fuxingmen Dajie, and there's an efficient bus service (Y10) to the airport from the stop just across the street.

The main **post office** is on Chaoyangmennan Dajie, the street that runs north off Jianguomen Dajie on the east side of the Beijing International Hotel where you can also use the **Internet** for Y18 per hour. There's also a post office opposite the Beijing International Hotel. More and more places are getting Internet access so you should have no difficulty picking up your email.

Beijing Zhuulchin Office (☎ 6456 1225 🖷 6507 7397), Golden Bride Mansion, East Door, A1, Jianguomenwai Dajie represents Mongolia's Zhuulchin Foreign Tourism Corporation.

The **Public Security Bureau (PSB**: for visa extensions) (☎ 8401 5292) has moved to No 2 Andingmendongdajie, on the north-east corner of the second ring road in a huge new building by the flyover. It's best to get the metro to Yong He Gong and leaving the station turn right onto the main road. Walk straight ahead for 15 minutes to reach the PSB building. It's closed at weekends and 12:30-13:30 daily.

The office for Trans-Sib specialists **Monkey Business** (☎ 6509 3642 www.monkeyshrine.com) has moved from the Capital Forbidden City Hotel to Sanlitun south 'Bar St': 12 Dong Da Qiao Xie St, above the Hidden Tree Belgian beer bar. The office is open 10:00-21:00 Mon-Sat and 16:00-20:00 Sun.

Banks and currency The unit of currency is the yuan (Y) which is divided into 10 jiao or 100 fen. In December 2000 there were Y8.27 to US$1, Y12 to £1. For many years there were two types of yuan circulating in China, Renminbi (RMB) used by the majority of the population, and Foreign Exchange Certificates (FEC) used by tourists, diplomats and the few Chinese who could get hold of them. FEC have been phased out and the humble RMB is legal tender everywhere.

If you need hard currency the CITIC Industrial Bank will change travellers' cheques into US$ and allow credit card withdrawals in US$. There's a branch next to the Friendship Store.

American Express has an office in the China World Trade Centre.

Medical The best place to go if you need a doctor, dentist or emergency treatment is the International Medical Centre (☎ 6465 1561) which is next to the Kempinski Hotel.

Tours There are tours on offer from most of the larger hotels to all the major sights but you can easily visit the Forbidden City, the Temple of Heaven and Beijing's other tourist attractions independently. It is, however, probably worth joining a tour to see the Great Wall and the Ming Tombs. Mr John (☎ Mob: 139 0112 3938) at the Qiao Yuan Hotel has been recommended.

Where to stay
Budget accommodation The standard backpackers' haunt is the *Jing Hua Hostel* (☎ 6722 2211) on Nansanhuan Xi Lu (about 1¹/₂km south-west of the Jingtai Hotel). The dormitories are the best value: beds cost Y25 in a 20-bed dorm, Y35 in a four-bed and Y50 in a triple. There are also doubles with attached bathroom from Y150 to Y480. There's a travel agency, internet access for Y30 per half hour and you can rent bikes from the restaurant next door.

Qiao Yuan Hotel (☎ 6303 8861), near Yongdingmen railway station, has dorm beds for Y25 and doubles for Y140-290. There's a good travel agency here that offers day trips to the Great Wall. Check the noticeboard here for details.

Another budget option is the clean and friendly *Jingtai Hotel* (☎ 6722 4675), Anlelin Lu, south of Tian Tin Park. There are doubles from Y150 with bath attached. Bus No 40 will drop you off at the end of Anlelin Lu and it's only a five-minute walk from there.

Mid-range hotels The following hotel rooms all have attached bathrooms.

Well located west of Tian Tan Park, the *Bei Wei Hotel* (☎ 6301 2266) at 13 Xinling Lu, has singles/doubles for Y150/Y188. Beside it is the *Rainbow Hotel* with rooms for Y349/579. In the same area is *Qiamen Hotel* (☎ 6301 6688) on Hufang Lu, with singles/doubles for Y725/848.

Long Tan Hotel (☎ 6771 1602) on Panjiayuan Nan Li, charges Y280 for a double room and Y370 for a superior room but is not very conveniently located. Bus No 63 runs this way.

Up-market hotels Note that a 15% tax is applicable. Despite the high prices don't be shy about asking for a discount. If business is slow you may get one.

Taiwan Hotel (☎ 6513 6688 ext:8011), 5 Jinyn Hutong Wanguijing Dajie, has rooms from US$70 to US$180.

Minzhu Hotel (☎ 6601 4466), on Fuxingmen Dajie charges US$80 for a double.

Palace Hotel (☎ 6512 8899, 🖳 tph@peninsula.com), Chongwenmenwai Dajie, has doubles from US$290 but a 50% discount may bring this down to US$145.

The *Beijing International Hotel* (☎ 6512 6688, 🖳 bih@ht.rol.cn.net), 9 Jianguomennei Dajie, has rooms from US$120 to US$1000. CTS and CITS are based in this hotel.

At the famous *Beijing Hotel* (☎ 6513 7766 🖳 business@chinabeijinghotel.com.cn) rooms cost from US$180 to US$320. For a night in the best suite here you must be prepared to part with US$3900. Being close to Tiananmen Square it's perfectly located.

Where to eat

There's no shortage of places to eat and the best thing to do is to simply give yourself time to wander around the city and see what you come across; you'll never go hungry.

Peking Duck is, of course, the local speciality and there are numerous restaurants to sample it at: good places include the *Qianmen Quanjude Roast Duck Restaurant* at 32 Qianmen Dajie and *Bian Yi Fang Restaurant* on Chong-wenmen-wei Dajie near the railway station.

Cheap food is easy to find in Beijing: try any backstreet for noodles or dumplings. There's a big, cheap *night market* on Donghuamen Dajie, just to the east of the Forbidden City. The stalls sell food from all over China. Spicy-food fans usually head for the *Sichuan Restaurant* in Xirongxian Alley, just to the other side of the City.

You'll find numerous places to eat in the Chaoyang District and around *Sanlitun* ('Bar Street'). Sanlitun is lined with café bars and always busy. In summer you can sit outside. *Serve the People*, just off Sanlitun Nan, is recommended for its Thai cuisine. At 12 Dong Da Qiao Xie St, the *Hidden Tree* has a pleasant garden and serves a range of food and bar snacks to go with their Belgian beer. Opposite the Zhaolong Hotel is *1001 Nights*, a Syrian restaurant with a pleasant terrace; there's even belly dancing some evenings. *Mediterraneo* is another place in this area that's been recommended, with pasta and a range of tapas. Also try *The Den*, next to the City Hotel, Gongti Bei Lu, where there's a popular Sunday brunch.

The *Vegetarian Restaurant* at 158 Qianmen Dajie continues to be recommended.

The Western fast food chains have been here in force for many years. *McDonald's* is on Chang'an Ave and in around 40 other locations, *Kentucky Fried Chicken* is on Tiananmen Square, and *Pizza Hut* has several branches (there's one on Dongzhimenwai and another south of Tiananmen Square on Zhushikou).

For cakes, pastries and croissants go to *La Vie de France* (beside the Friendship Store and also on the SW corner of Tiananmen Sq) or *Deli France* in the Sun Dong Plaza.

Nightlife

The nightlife in Beijing is varied and goes on late. Check out *Beijing Beat* and *Metro*

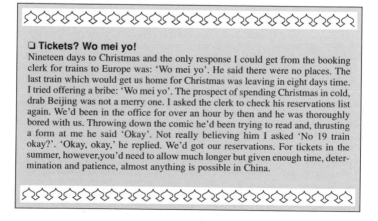

❏ Tickets? Wo mei yo!
Nineteen days to Christmas and the only response I could get from the booking clerk for trains to Europe was: 'Wo mei yo'. He said there were no places. The last train which would get us home for Christmas was leaving in eight days time. I tried offering a bribe: 'Wo mei yo'. The prospect of spending Christmas in cold, drab Beijing was not a merry one. I asked the clerk to check his reservations list again. We'd been in the office for over an hour by then and he was thoroughly bored with us. Throwing down the comic he'd been trying to read and, thrusting a form at me he said 'Okay'. Not really believing him I asked 'No 19 train okay?'. 'Okay, okay,' he replied. We'd got our reservations. For tickets in the summer, however, you'd need to allow much longer but given enough time, determination and patience, almost anything is possible in China.

which list what's on. **Sanlitun** 'Bar Street' is the place to start. In this area you'll find *Minder Café* with live music, *Frank's Place*, the *Hidden Tree* (see Where to eat) and lots of other less salubrious drinking places.

The Den, by City Hotel, Gongti Bei Lu, is popular with students and ex-pats and gets very busy after midnight on Saturday nights. At 44 Guanghua Lu is the *John Bull Pub*.

The ubiquitous Irish-theme pubs have even reached Beijing: *P J O'Reilly's Irish Pub* is in the Henderson Shopping Centre. The *Haidan* area near the university is worth checking out. There's no shortage of bars and it's easy enough to just walk around until you find one that you like the look of.

What to buy
The **Friendship Store** on Jianguomen Dajie (Chang'an Ave) has a wide range of souvenirs. Nearby is the CVIK Plaza with a good **supermarket** in the basement that's useful for Trans-Sib provisions.

For a more challenging time, visit the shops in the **Wangfujing district** directly east of the Forbidden City. Another good place is the **Qianmen district**, where you're likely to have to fight your way through the crowds; bartering is in order here. At 190 Qiamen Dajie is the **Army Store** where you can buy thick winter coats. **Museum St** (a small side street SW of Tiananmen Sq) is quite touristy but there's a good range of souvenirs here.

The **silk market**, a few hundred metres east of the Friendship Store, is also a good place for shopping but you must bargain hard.

Moving on
By air Many major airlines maintain offices in Beijing, so it's usually not difficult finding a seat; the problem is that it can be expensive. Most airline offices are in the SCITE Tower opposite the Friendship Store. The small office directly on your left as you enter offers a good range of flights. Sample prices include London (Y4200), New York (Y4300), Singapore (Y3400), Tokyo (Y3500), Hong Kong (Y2800) and Guangzhou (Y1380).

If you want to fly the first leg of your Trans-Siberian journey, MIAT (☎ 6501 8888, ext 807; Room 807, Jing Guang World Hotel, Hujialou, Chaoyanou) charges Y2040 for Beijing–Ulan Bator. Siberian Airlines are in the Beijing International Hotel and fly to Novosibirsk on Wednesdays.

The airport is 28km from the city centre. Buses for the airport (Y10) leave every half-hour from the International Hotel and across the street from the CAAC office.

By rail **Domestic tickets** can be bought from the station at the foreigners' ticket office on the ground floor. Alternatively CITS or your hotel will book a ticket for you for a small fee, saving you the queuing. From Beijing West station, the train to Hong Kong goes every other day, takes 28 hours and costs US$70 for hard sleeper.

International tickets must be booked either at CITS (Beijing International Hotel), or from a registered ticket agency (see pp35-6). If you've just arrived on the Trans-Siberian and feel like clocking up a few more km by rail, follow the Silk Route back to Europe (see p132).

(Opposite) Top: The Moscow-Beijing railway line passes under the Great Wall at Badaling. **Bottom:** Tiananmen Gate, Beijing, the main entrance gate to the Forbidden City (photo © Nick Hill).

(Overleaf): A tour guide models traditional Halkh Mongolian clothing at the Elstei Ger Camp, Mongolia. It's available for sale from the shop behind her and a very necessary lesson in how to put on the different layers is provided free of charge. Notice any similarities between this and what the Princess wore in the latest *Star Wars* sequel?! (Photo © Nick Hill).

Using this guide

This route guide has been set out to draw your attention to points of interest and to enable you to locate your position along the Trans-Siberian line. On the maps, stations are indicated in Russian and English and their distance from Moscow is given in the text. Note that on the maps there is an orientation symbol (**M**), indicating the direction towards Moscow.

Stations and points of interest are identified in the text by a kilometre number. Note that in some cases this is approximate so start looking out for the point of interest a few kilometres before its stated position. Where something of interest is on only one side of the track, it is identified by the letters **N** (north or left-hand side of the train, going east from Moscow) or **S** (south or right-hand side) after the kilometre number. The altitude of major towns and cities is given in metres and feet beside the station name. Time zones are indicated through the text (MT = Moscow Time). See inside back cover for **key map and time zones**.

Kilometre posts

These are located on the southern side of the track. They are sometimes placed so close to the train that they're difficult to see. The technique is either to hang out of the window (dangerous) or press your face close to

the glass and look along the train until a kilometre post flashes by. The distance from Moscow is on the west side of the post and the distance to Moscow on the other. Note that the distances given on train timetables do not always correspond to the distances shown on the kilometre posts and may vary by up to 10km. If you notice any inaccuracies in the distances as shown in this book please write to the author.

Station name boards

These are almost as difficult to catch sight of as the kilometre posts since they are usually placed only on the station building and not along the platforms as in most other countries. Rail traffic on the line is heavy and even if your carriage does pull up opposite the station building you may have your view of it obscured by another train.

Points of interest and stations in this guide are identified by the nearest kilometre post visible from the train.

Stops

Where the train stops at a station the length of the stop is indicated by:

● (1-5 mins)　　●● (6-12 mins)　　●●● (13-20 mins)

Carriage attendants will tell you the precise amount of time as this may be reduced if the train is running late. Don't stray too far from the train as, except in China, it moves off without a signal or whistle and passengers are occasionally left behind. Three of us, our carriage attendant included, were once almost left in sub-zero temperatures on the platform of some tiny Siberian station, when the train left five minutes ahead of schedule.

Time zones

The trains run on Moscow time (MT). **Siberian time zones** are listed throughout the route guide and the main cities are in the following zones: Novosibirsk (MT+3), Irkutsk (MT+5), Khabarovsk (MT+7), Vladivostok (MT+7). **Moscow Time** is four hours ahead of Greenwich Mean Time when the country runs on 'summer time': from the last Saturday in March to the last Saturday in September. Outside that period MT = GMT+3. Note that **China** operates one time zone, GMT+8, for the whole country and for the whole year. **Mongolian time** is GMT+8.

❏ Speed calculations

Using the kilometre posts and a watch, it's possible to calculate how quickly, or more usually how slowly, the train is going. Note the time that elapses between one post and the next and consult the table below.

'The speed of the train throughout the journey varied dramatically and we found that on a number of occasions we were travelling in excess of 80mph, admittedly at times speed dropped to very low values for very great distances' (Andrew Wingham, UK). The average speed of the train over the seven-day journey between Moscow and Vladivostok is actually only 69kph (43mph).

Seconds	kph	mph	Seconds	kph	mph
24	150	93	52	69	43
26	138	86	54	66	41
28	129	80	56	64	40
30	120	75	60	60	37
32	113	70	64	56	35
34	106	66	68	53	33
36	100	62	72	50	31
38	95	59	78	46	28
40	90	56	84	43	27
42	86	53	92	39	24
44	82	51	100	36	22
46	78	49	120	30	18
48	75	47	150	24	15
50	72	45	180	20	12

TRANS-SIBERIAN ROUTE

Km0: Moscow Москва
Yaroslavski Station Ярославский вокзал
Most Trans-Siberian trains depart from Moscow's
Yaroslavski station, pl Komsomolskaya 5.
However, there are a few trains that go part of the
way along the Trans-Siberian and terminate in
central Siberian cities, such as Krasnoyarsk (train
Nos 56 & 90), Omsk (No 48), Tomsk (No 38 &
118) and Tyumen (No 60), and **these depart
from Kazanski Station nearby**.

If you're arriving from Siberia and leaving
Moscow by train the same day, you may need to
take the metro or a taxi to one of Moscow's nine
other stations. If your journey starts from
Moscow, make sure you get to the station early as
trains invariably leave on time. Yaroslavski station and Kazanski station are on Komsomol
Square (metro: **Komsomolskaya Ploshchad**).
Yaroslavski station is very distinctive; it was built
in 1902 as a stylized reproduction of an old
Russian *terem* (fort), its walls decorated with
coloured tiles. Trains have destination plates
fixed to their sides but any railway official will
point you in the right direction if you show them
your ticket.

Km13: Los Лось
Just after this station, the
train crosses over the Moscow Ring Road. This
road marks the city's metropolitan border and in
order to stop the lavatories being used in urban
areas loo doors remain bolted until this point.

Km15: Taininskaya Таининская
A monu-
ment to Russia's last tsar, Nicholas II, was recently unveiled here, bearing the plaque, 'To Tsar
Nikolai II from the Russian people with repen-
tance'.

Km18: Mytishchi Мытищи
(pop: 154,000) is
famous for three factories. The railway carriage
factory, **Metrovagonmash**, has manufactured all
the Soviet Union's metro cars and is building
Russia's new N5 metro carriages that can be seen

currently in Moscow's metro. While there is a museum at the factory, the best metro museum is in Moscow (see p165).

The **Mytishchinsky Monument Factory**, the source of many of those ponderous Lenin statues that still litter parts of the country, has at last been forced to develop a new line. It now churns out the kind of 'art' banned in the Soviet era: religious statues, memorials to Stalin's purges and busts of mafia heads. Some of its former achievements displayed in Moscow include the giant Lenin in front of Oktyabrskaya metro station, Moscow's founder, Yuri Dolgoruky, on horseback on pl Tverskaya and the Karl Marx across from the Bolshoi Theatre.

Production has also slowed at the **armoured vehicle factory**, one of Russia's three major tank factories, with the other two being in the Siberian cities of Kurgan and Omsk.

The smoking factories and suburban blocks of flats are now left behind and you roll through forests of pine, birch and oak. Amongst the trees there are picturesque wooden dachas where many of Moscow's residents spend their weekends. You pass through little stations with long, white-washed picket fences.

Km30: Pushkino Пушкино This town (pop: 75,600) was founded in 1499 as a resting place for clergy on the road between Moscow and the monastery town of Sergiev-Posad. With the arrival of the railway in 1862,

---

❏ **Dacha**

A dacha is much more than a country cottage or holiday home: it provides its city-dwelling owners with somewhere to grow vegetables, a base for mushroom and wild berry collecting operations as well as providing a place to relax away from the urban environment. Growing fruit and vegetables and collecting mushrooms and berries are not just pastimes for Russians but provide a means of survival during lean years and a supplement to their winter diet during better times. People also pick mushrooms and berries to sell in street markets in the cities. Russians are generally very knowledgeable about preserving techniques, food value and homeopathic remedies.

As one approaches a city on the train, the dacha colonies become larger and more frequent. Each privately-owned house will be set on a large wood-fenced lot. The design of the house is very eclectic: small greenhouses abound and many properties have a sauna building. The earth closet of classic design is at the foot of the garden. Electricity is supplied and there is water from a community well or tap. There may be chickens; other livestock such as a goat or milk cow would belong to permanent residents. Some of the outlying villages contain a mix of small farmsteads and old houses that have been rehabilitated into dachas.

Nancy J Scarth (Canada)

the place became a popular summer holiday destination for Moscow's élite. From 1890 to 1910, Pushkino became known as Russia's summer arts capital with a renowned theatre. While the theatre has gone, the five-cupola St Nicholas Church built in the 1690s remains.

Km36: Pravda Правда
To the left of Pravda station, which translates as *truth*, is the village of Zavety Ilicha (Заветы Ильича). This name, which figuratively means the Commandments of Ilich Vladimir Lenin, was a popular name for not only dozens of Soviet towns, but also for collective farms, metro stations and ships.

Km57: Abramtsevo Абрамцево
About 3km from the station is the Abramtsevo Estate, one of the most important centres of Russian culture in the second half of the 19th century. Today, the Abramtsevo estate is a museum and well worth a day trip from Moscow (see p166).

Km59: Khotkovo Хотьково
This town (pop: 23,400) has a well preserved historic section on the high bank of the Pazha River which flows through the centre of the town. The most impressive building here is the large **Intercession of Khotkovo Monastery** which was founded in 1308. Most of the original buildings in the monastery were replaced during the 18th century. The classical **Intercession Cathedral**, built between 1811 and 1816, is decorated with four Corinthian columns and crowned with a massive rotunda and four cupolas.

The train crosses over the Pazha River just before it reaches Khotkovo station and you can see these buildings on the left.

Km73 (N): Sergiev Posad Сергиев Посад   [See p178]
Have your cameras ready for the stunning sight of the blue and gold domes of the cathedrals of Sergiev Posad (pop: 110,000), known as **Zagorsk** between 1930 and 1993. Look north back to the city just after you leave the station. For many years this was the seat of the Russian Orthodox Church (until it was moved back to Moscow in 1988) and one of the most important seminaries in the country is here. The beautiful buildings of the seminary are much visited by tourists.

Km112: Aleksandrov (●) Александров
This little-known town was, for nearly two decades in the 14th century, the real capital of Russia. From 1564 to 1581, Ivan the Terrible lived here and directly ruled the half of the country which he called *Oprichnina* while abandoning the other half to the authority of *boyars* (nobles) and monasteries. The oprichnina was policed by *oprichniki*, mostly low class thugs, mercenaries and foreign adventurers who murdered, pillaged and destroyed at their pleasure.

Ivan ruled from Aleksandrov's **Trinity Fortress Monastery** which was a complex of dungeons, churches, barracks and warehouses. Ivan the Terrible certainly deserved his soubriquet. In his dungeons here he devised and supervised some of the cruellest tortures imaginable. There were racks which broke bones, iron cages for burning victims, pits for burying people alive and frames for whipping prisoners with a *knout* (leather truncheon) which could kill in three strokes. Ivan was a vicious practical joker and would even release his ravenous bears on his own unsuspecting courtiers.

The city's most notable building is the monumental brick **Trinity Cathedral**, built in 1513 in the style of early Moscow architecture. It has two brass doors pillaged from two other churches by Ivan the Terrible during his sacking of Novgorod and Tver.

Despite its vibrant history, Aleksandrov is most famous today for the Rekord brand of TV produced here in enormous numbers. Rekord and Gorizont are Russia's two biggest TV manufacturers.

In the yard just east of the station (N) are six old **steam locomotives**.

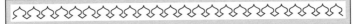

❏ The Golden Ring
You are now passing through Russia's most famous historical region; it was from this area that the mighty Russian state was born. The major Golden Ring cities along the Trans-Siberian are Sergiev Posad, Rostov-Yaroslavski and Yaroslavl.

Following the collapse of Kievan Rus, which was the first feudal state in Eastern Europe, its capital was shifted from Kiev to the Golden Ring town of Vladimir in 1169. At that time, Vladimir and the other Golden Ring towns were little more than villages but over the next 200 years they all rapidly grew into political, religious and commercial centres.

The typical Golden Ring town of the 11th to 18th century consisted of a *kremlin*, a *posad* and a *sloboda*. The kremlin, meaning fortress, usually occupied an elevated position and was originally ringed by earth embankments topped with wooden walls. Watch towers were positioned strategically along the walls. Over time, the earth and wooden walls were replaced by stone and brick. Inside the kremlin were the prince's residence, religious buildings and administrative complexes. Outside the kremlin was the undefended posad which was the merchants' and artisans' quarters. Often next to the posad was a sloboda, a tax-exempt settlement. Sloboda were often established to attract a new workforce.

After the decimation of Russia following the Tatar-Mongol invasion in 1236, Moscow's power had grown even faster since it was the Tatar-Mongols' centre for tax collectors and in 1318 its prince was granted the title of Grand Prince by the invaders. This symbolized the transfer of regional power from Vladimir to Moscow. Gradually Moscow annexed the Golden Ring principalities and used their economic and military power to expand its domination. By the end of the 1500s, Moscow had become a large powerful principality and was fighting to become the capital of Russia. While several of the Golden Ring cities continued to have commercial importance due to their locations on major trading routes, the golden era of these cities was over.

The train now enters **Yaroslavskaya Oblast** (administrative district), an area of 36,000 square kilometres in the upper Volga basin, famous for its cheeses and dairy farming. Oats, flax and vegetables are also grown in this region.

Km145: Berendeevo Берендеево There is a 21km branch line to the west from here to the Golden Ring town of Pereslavl-Zalesski.

Km200: Petrovsk Петровск About 15km east of Petrovsk, you will see **Lake Nero** on the right. Rostov-Yaroslavski sits on the western shore.

Km224: Rostov-Yaroslavski Ростов-Ярославский   [See p183] (pop: 37,000) This is one of the most pleasant Golden Ring cities to visit. It's an interesting place, relatively compact and attractively located beside Lake Nero.

About five minutes west of the station you cross over the Ishna River. Five hundred metres downstream (S), where the river flows into Lake Nero, is the **St Jacob Monastery** which guarded the city's southern approach centuries ago. The northern approach was protected by the **St Avraamy Monastery** which you can see about three minutes after leaving the station, on the right by the shores of Lake Nero.

Km240 (N): Amidst the fields and quite close to the track is a sadly neglected but **picturesque church** with five dilapidated domes and a tower.

Km284: Yaroslavl Ярославль (●)   [See p188] (pop: 637,000) Yaroslavl was founded in 1010 by the Christian King Yaroslavl the Wise. It grew quickly into an important trading centre on the Volga shipping route. Many of the ancient cathedrals still stand in spite of the heavy fighting that went on here during the Civil War.

About five minutes after entering Yaroslavl's outskirts, you pass the suburban station of **Kotorosl (Которосль)** and on the left you can see the **Church of St Peter and St Paul** with a 58m bell-tower beside it. The church was built in 1736 by a wealthy textile factory owner, in honour of Peter the Great who was a valuable customer. The church is constructed in the popular St Petersburg Baroque style and, in a final sycophantic gesture, it was designed to look like the Cathedral of St Peter and St Paul in St Petersburg. During the communist era it was used as a club.

A minute or so later you cross over the Kotorosl River giving you a good view of several landmarks. On the right of the train, on the southern river bank just before the road bridge is the 15-domed **Church of St John the Baptist**. On the left of the train also on the southern bank is the **Church of St Nicholas by the Water Mills**.

From the square in front of the station, you can see the **Church of the Vladimir Mother of God** built in 1678.

Km289: Volga River   About five minutes after leaving the station, the train changes direction from the north to the east and crosses over the mighty Volga River. The river is about 1km wide at this point. In times gone by Russians regarded this river with such high respect that they would stand and take off their hats to Mother Volga, as the train rattled onto the first spans of the long bridge. Rising in the Valdai hills, **Europe's longest river** meanders 3700km down to the Caspian Sea. It is to Russia what the Nile is to Egypt: a source of life and a thoroughfare. On the right side of the river you will see the main road bridge across the river and quays on both side of the river. You get a good view of the city of Yaroslavl and its cathedrals looking back south as you go over the bridge, which was built in 1910.

Km356: Danilov Данилов (●●●) (pop: 19,000)   A change of locomotive allows time for buying provisions from the traders on the platform. In the town is the Kazan Mother of God Cathedral which was consecrated by the Patriarch Tikhon in 1918. In the early years of the communist state, Lenin was forced for expediency to tolerate such practices but once power was consolidated, churches were rapidly closed.

Km358 (N): Junction with the line to Vologda and Arkhangelsk.

Km370-378: Some quite good views on both sides of the train in the breaks between the trees. The train soon enters Kostromskaya Oblast, a 60,000 sq km plain in the middle Volga basin. Most of the northern part of the oblast is covered with taiga (swampy forest). There is some cultivation (flax and oats) in the south. Main industries are linen-making and timber-processing.

Km394: Lyubim Любим   Lyubim's population is decreasing – down 10% since 1980 to about 6000. This makes the town typical of the Russia-wide migration trend from rural villages to large cities. The main reasons for this are the lack of jobs and limited education choices in the country. Following the easing of movement restrictions, many families moved away from country farms.

——————— Km 420-1266 TIME ZONE MT + 1 ———————

Km450: Bui Буй (●) (pop: 32,800)   There is nothing of interest in this industrial town, specializing in cheese, flax and mineral fertilizers.

Leaving the town, the train follows the southern banks of the Veksi and Holya rivers connected to the Galich Sea which you will see as you approach the town of Galich. The very beautiful lake is ringed with resorts for Moscow's rich and famous. Rotting silt (sapropel) is extracted from the lake and dried to be used as fuel or made into fertilizer.

Local time is now Moscow time + 1 hour. Note, however, that the dining-car sometimes continues on MT+0 until Km1267: check opening times.

Km501: Galich Галич If you drive a Lada and need a new door handle, get off the train here. Because of the centralized planning of the communist system, products were often made in huge numbers in only a few locations. Galich's speciality was car door handles.

The town is very ancient and was populated by the Merya tribe of Finno-Ugric peoples before the ethnic Russians arrived. The first mention of the town was in 1238 when the **Galich fortress** was destroyed by the Tatar-Mongol leader, Khan Baty. The fortress was rebuilt and in 1427 amazingly withstood a four-week siege by the Tatar-Mongols. The walls of the fortress can still be seen ringing the central part of the town. The town's centre is a 15-minute walk north from the station. After departing from the station, on the right (S) you pass **Paisiev Monastery**.

Km651: Manturovo Мантурово (pop: 22,400) After leaving this industrial and forestry town, the train crosses the Unzha River (Km654) where you may notice the remains of large pits on the banks. These are from the shale oil and phosphate mining operations of a few decades ago.

Km698: Sharya Шарья (●●) (pop: 26,900) There is usually an 8-10 minute stop at this station where a Lenin bust still graces the platform. Some steam locos are stored here (L and Er classes) but numbers are dwindling. This town is the biggest timber centre in the region. It has a few interesting old buildings and a Museum of Local Studies.

Km818: Svetcha Светча Roughly mid-way between Sharya and Svetcha, you enter Kirov-skaya Oblast. Most of the 120,000 square kilometres of this region are within the basin of the Vyatka River. Since the greater part of the oblast is made up of taiga, the main industry here is logging.

Km870: Kotelnich Котельнич (pop: 38,000) This station sits at the junction of the Trans-

MAP 2

Монаково
MONAKOVO
Антролово
ANTROLOVO
Николо-Угол
NIKOLO-UGOL
Николо-Полома
NIKOLO-POLOMA
Номжа
NOMZHA
Еленский
YELENSKIY
Нея
NEYA
Нельша
NELSHA
Брантовка
BRANTOVKA
Петрушино
PETRUSHINO
Костриха
KOSTRIKHA
Мантурово
MANTUROVO
Вочерово
VOCHEROVO
Шекшема
SHEKSHEMA
Варакинский
VARAKINSKIY
Шарья Vetluga R.
SHARYA
Зебляки
ZEBLYAKI
Якшанга
YAKSHANGA
Бурундучиха
BURUNDUCHIKHA
Супротивный
SUPROTIVNIY
Метил
METIL
Гостовская
GOSTOVSKAYA
Шабалино
SHABALINO
Свеча
SVECHA
Юма
YUMA
Капиданцы
KAPIDANTSI
Ацвеж
ATSVEZH
Даровица
DAROVITSA
Котельнич
KOTELNICH
Быстряги
BISTRYAGI
Оричи
ORICHI
Стрижи
STRIZHI
Лянгасово
LYANGASOVO
Чухломинский
CHUKHLOMINSKIY
КИРОВ (KIROV)
Поздино
POZRINO
Полой (POLOY)
Бумкомбинат
BUMKOMBINAT
Просница
PROSNITSA

Siberian and the Kirov–Nizhni Novgorod–Moscow lines. If you are changing from one line to the other, don't get off here. Instead go 87km to the east to the major city of Kirov where tickets are much easier to get.

Kotelnich is an ancient trading city on the right bank of the Vyatka River, a major trading route between Arkhangelsk and the Volga region.

Finding your way around the town is not easy as it lies in three ravines with only the town centre being laid out in an orderly fashion. Here the major thoroughfare is ul Moskovskaya and along part of it are a number of buildings built in Vyatka Provincial Style from 1850 to 1880. Sights include the John the Baptist (Predtichi) Monastery and the Presentation of the Virgin (Vvedenski) Nunnery. The town has a museum.

After leaving the station, the train crosses over the **Vyatka River** which is the 10th longest river in European Russia. It meanders for 1367km and the Trans-Siberian crosses over it several times. When the train first reaches the Vyatka River Basin a few kilometres to the west of Kotelnich, there is a noticeable change in the landscape as the forests give way to fields and more villages.

Km890: Maradykovski Марадыковский Probably sensible not to break your journey here. At the nearby airforce base are stored 7000 out of Russia's 40,000 tons of chemical weapons agents (mustard gas, lewisite, hydrocyanic acid and phosgene). The government has approved a plan for destroying its stocks of chemical weapons but this won't be completed until 2005 at the earliest. It's ironic that the name of the settlement around the station is Mirny (Мирный) which means peaceful.

Km957: Vyatka/Kirov Вятка/Киров (●●●)   [See p195]
(Pop: 492,000) Vyatka, formerly known as Kirov, was founded in 1181 on the banks of the Vyatka River and was originally named Klynov. A branch line runs north to the Kotlas area which was where Alexander Solzhenitsyn's *A Day in the Life of Ivan Denisovitch* took place. The book describes 24 hours in the life of a Siberian convict.

Km975: Pozdino Поздино The town around the station is called Novovyatsk (Нововятск) and boasts one of Russia's largest ski factories. During Soviet times, the factory produced 20 per cent of the nation's skis.

Km995: Bum-Kombinat Бум-комбинат This unfortunately-named town gets its name from its principal employer, the paper complex.

Km1052: Zuevka Зуевка (pop: 15,700) Founded in 1895 with the construction of the railway; during WWII hundreds of Leningraders settled here. Their descendants manufacture swings and see-saws.

Km1127: Yar Яр About 20km before this station, you leave Kirovskaya Oblast and cross the administrative frontier into the heavily industrialized

Udmurtia Republic. Yar is the first town here and has a number of Udmurt speakers. It sits on a steep river bank (*yar*). There has been a small metallurgical plant here for over 230 years but nothing else of note.

Between Yar and Balyezino there are many market gardens set in this rolling, open countryside. You pass vast fields of grey-green cabbages, and long rows of greenhouses covered in plastic sheeting line the track in some places. There are tiny villages of log cabins with brightly painted front doors.

Km1136: Balyshur Балышур Just before arriving at the station, you pass a steam train storage depot.

Km1165: Glazov Глазов (●) (pop: 110,000) Originally an Udmurt indigenous village, Glazov soon became infamous as a desolate and impoverished place of exile. All this was to change with the arrival of the railway and by 1900 there were 102 enterprises and within a few more years the town grew into the region's largest flax, oats and oakum trading centre. Oakum is a fibre used for caulking the seams of ships.

There are still a few wooden Udmurt log huts remaining. Known as *korkas*, they are positioned along an open paved courtyard. The courtyard had a massive gate, which, like the hut, was often decorated with carved geometrical and plant designs. Glazov has a history museum.

Km1194: Balyezino Балезино (●●) A change of locomotive gives you a chance to stock up from the traders on the platform.

Km1223: Cheptsa Чепца Two kilometres west of this station, the line crosses the Cheptsa River (Km1221) which the route has been following for the last 250kms. The train begins to wind its way up towards the

Urals. Between Cheptsa and the next station of Vereshchagino is the frontier between the Udmurt Republic and Permskaya Oblast. Permskaya's 160,000 sq km are, like those of Kirovskaya Oblast, lost to the swampy forests of the taiga. However, Permskaya has greater prizes than its millions of pine and birch trees, for the region includes the mineral-rich Ural Mountains. Main industries include mining, logging and paper-making. Agriculture is confined to market gardening.

Km 1267-2496 TIME ZONE MT + 2

Km1310 (S): Vereshchagino Верещагино (pop: 24,900) Vereshchagino was founded at end of 19th century as a railway depot and today its main industry is still railways. There is a preserved FD21 steam locomotive on a plinth about 1km to the west (Moscow side) of the station near the main rail depot. The town is named after Russia's greatest battlefield painter, VV Vereshchagin, who stopped here on his way to the Russo-Japanese war front in 1905. It was his final and fatal commission.

There are some quite good views south, a few kilometres after Vereshchagino.

Km1340: Mendeleevo Менделеево The town is named after the chemist, Dmitri Mendeleev (1834-1907), who developed the periodic table. He often visited this town during his inspections of the region's metallurgical plants. There is a Mendeleev museum in nearby Tobolsk.

Km1387: Chaikovskaya Чайковская
This station is named after the composer Peter Tchaikovsky (1840-1893) who was born about 180km south-east of here at a factory settlement around the Kamsko-Votkinsk industrial plant. Until recently it was believed that Tchaikovsky died of cholera but researchers have revealed that he was blackmailed into taking poison to prevent his liaison with the nephew of a St Petersburg noble being made public.

The nearby town (a construction settlement for the hydroelectric dam) is called Maiski.

From here to Perm, there are excellent opportunities to get photos along the train as it snakes along the winding railway.

Km1410: Overyata Оверята An 11km branch line leads to the dirty industrial town of Krasnokamsk (Краснокамск) to the south. It was founded in the 1930s and has a large cellulose mill. Surprisingly near the town is the popular Ust-Kachka health resort with medicinal mud baths.

Km1429: Perm freight yard Пермь-Сортировочная This is one of Russia's largest, handling up to 135 trains simultaneously.

Km1432: Kama River Речка Кама Just before the train reaches Perm, you cross over the Kama River. From the 900m bridge which was built in 1899 you can see Perm stretching into the distance on the left. The mighty Kama River flows over 2000kms from the Urals into the Volga and is one of Russia's great waterways. Near the bridge, the river banks are lined with cranes and warehouses. A short distance west of Perm station (to the north of the line) there's a turntable and beside it an ancient green **'O' Class locomotive** (OB 14). Engines of this type were hauling the Trans-Siberian at the turn of the century.

Km1436: Perm 2 Пермь 2 (●●●) [see p197]

This city of more than one million inhabitants was founded in 1723 when the copper smelting works were established here. Because of its important position on the Kama River, the Great Siberian Post Road and later the Trans-Siberian Railway, Perm quickly grew into a major trading and industrial centre.

Before the railway reached Perm most travellers would arrive by steamer from Nizhny Novgorod and Kazan. RL Jefferson (see p103) cycled here from London in 1896 on his Siberian bike ride and was entertained by Gospodin Kuznetsoff, the 60-year-old president of the Perm Cycling Club, and 50 enthusiasts. On 20 July 1907, the cyclists came out to escort an equally sensational visitor, the Italian Prince Borghese, who had just driven across Siberia from Peking in his Itala and was on his way to Paris, where he would win the Peking to Paris motor rally. One of the wheels of the car was damaged and, when the Prince's chauffeur had replaced some of the wooden spokes, he declared that the wheel needed to be soaked to make the wood expand before the repair could be completed. A local official advised them to send it to one of the bathing establishments along the Kama River. A bathing-machine (of the type used by Victorian swimmers at English sea-side resorts) was hired and the wheel spent the night taking the waters.

Unfortunately, the centre of Old Perm is out of sight, 5km away from Perm 2 station at which the Trans-Siberian train stops. This is a pity as the

MAP 3

approaches and area around Perm 2 are dominated by dilapidated industrial enterprises.

Shortly after leaving the station, the train crosses a small bridge over a busy street. This street was once the Siberian *Trakt* (Great Post Road) which passed through Perm from 1863.

After leaving Perm, the landscape changes abruptly and forests give way to meadows and fields.

Km1452: Ferma Ферма The attractive, green-domed church (S) might make a good photograph.

Kms1460-1777 The train winds its way up to the highest point in the Urals. One would expect the range of mountains that divides Europe from Asia to be rather more impressive than these hills but they rise up not much more than 500m/1640ft above sea level in this area. Colin Thubron describes them as 'a faint upheaval of pine-darkened slopes' (*In Siberia*).

RL Jefferson wrote in 1896: 'The Urals certainly are not so high or majestic as the Alps or the Balkans but their wild picturesqueness is something to be seen to be appreciated.' Their wild picturesqueness is somewhat marred and scarred today by open-cast mines at Km1507 (N) and Km1509 (N). There is a large timber-mill at Km1523 (N).

Km1534: Kungur Кунгур Just outside the town is a fascinating and virtually unknown tourist attraction – the **Kungur Ice Caves** (see p198). The stockade town of Kungur was founded in 1648, 17km from its present site. By the 18th century, the town had become one of the largest centres in the Urals as it was a transit point on the Siberian Trakt. It had three big markets a year, numerous factories and the first technical college in the Urals, which opened in 1877. Today the town is much less important but it is still well known in Russia for its guitar factory.

Soon after leaving Kungur, you see the steep banks of the Sylva River which mark the start of the Kungur Forest Steppe. This area is characterized by rolling hills which reach 180-230m, a landscape pitted with troughs and sinkholes, and copses of birch, linden, oak and pine interspersed with farm lands.

Km1537 (N) A picturesque church stands alone on the hill across the Sylva River. The line follows this river up the valley to Km1556 where it cuts across a wide plain. The trees close in again from about Km1584 but there are occasional clearings with villages and timber-mills at about Km1650 (N).

Km1672 Shalya Шаля (pop: 26,900) A forestry town of no special interest. Fifty kilometres west of here, you enter **Sverdlovskaya Oblast**. It covers 195,000 square kilometres, taking in parts of the Urals and extending east onto the Siberian plain. Like most of the other oblasts you have passed through, this one is composed almost entirely of taiga forests. From the rich deposits in the Urals are mined iron ore, copper, platinum, gold, tungsten, cobalt, asbestos and bauxite as well as many varieties of gemstones. The soil is poor so there is very little agriculture in the region.

Km1729: Kuzino Кузино
Surprisingly, the statue of Lenin on the platform near the station building has not been removed and was still standing in summer 2000.

East of the large marshalling yard here the line rises once more, passing a little town built around a freshly whitewashed church with a green dome. After about 10km, the train reaches one of the most attractive rivers in the Urals, the Chusavya River. The line follows the course of the river for some 30km.

Km1748: Krylosovo Крылосово
A large factory with rows of apartment blocks for its workers looks a little out of place amongst the forests up here in the Urals. From Km1764 east the area becomes quite built up.

Km1770: Pervouralsk Первоуральск (pop: 148,000)
The city's name translates as The First Ural as it was here in 1727 that the first factory in the Urals was opened. Following the success of its cast iron works dozens of other factories sprang up and today the city is home to numerous heavy engineering complexes including one of Russia's largest pipeline factories. With the current economic difficulties many are either facing closure or have already closed.

You can see Pervouralsk's main tourist attraction, the **Europe-Asia border obelisk** from the train so there's no reason to get off. If you do, about the only place to stay in the city is *Hotel Pervouralsk* at pro Ilicha 28 (bus No 10 from the station). The hotel has a good restaurant and the other recommended choice is *Restaurant Talaktuka* at ul Trubnikov 52. The city boasts a **Museum of Folklore**, ul Lenina 65.

Km1777 (S): Europe-Asia Border Obelisk
People begin collecting in the corridor long before you reach the white stone obelisk which marks the continental division at this point in the Urals. The obelisk is about 15m to the east of the small Vershina (Вершина) railway platform.

When R L Jefferson reached the point near here where the road crosses the Urals (also marked with an obelisk) he wrote enthusiastically of the view: 'Hills piled upon hills, shaggy mountains and gaunt fir trees, and beyond them dwindling away into the mist of the horizon the great steppe lands of Siberia.' George Kennan wrote in 1887: 'The scenery of the Urals where the railroad crosses the range resembles in general outline that of West Virginia where the Baltimore and Ohio railroad crosses the Alleghenies; but it differs somewhat from the latter in colouring, owing to the greater preponderance in the Urals of evergreen trees'. Unfortunately you won't get much of a view from the train today.

Km1816: Yekaterinburg Екатеринбург (●●●)   [see p199]

(pop: 1,300,000) As soon as you reach the suburbs of Yekaterinburg you see a large lake on the right (Kms1807-9) which feeds the Iset River running through the city. There's a **locomotive depot** west of the station. The train halts in the largest city in the Urals, for a change of engine. Yekaterinburg was formerly known as Sverdlovsk.

❏ The U2 Affair: USSR 1, USA 0

The U2 affair represented an unprecedented Cold War embarrassment for the West. On 1 May 1960, an American U2 spyplane was shot down from a height of 68,000 feet, some 45km south of Sverdlovsk (as Yekaterinburg was then known). Its pilot, Gary Powers, baled out without activating the plane's self-destruct mechanism for fear that he would blow himself up (criticisms were later raised in Congress that he had not killed himself, either by destroying the aircraft or by pricking himself with the poisoned needle so thoughtfully provided by the CIA). He was picked up shortly after reaching the ground.

Four days later the USA announced that a U2 'meteorological aircraft' had 'gone missing' just north of Turkey after its pilot had reported problems with his oxygen mask. In a detailed press announcement it was speculated that he had fallen unconscious while the plane, automatic pilot engaged, might possibly have flown itself over Soviet territory. Shortly after this announcement, Khrushchev told the Supreme Soviet that a U2 'spyplane' had been shot down over Sverdlovsk. US presidential spokesman Lincoln White commented that 'this might be the same plane', and did his best to cool the situation by explaining the oxygen supply theory again. He concluded: 'there was absolutely no deliberate attempt to violate Soviet airspace and never has been', and he grounded all other U2s to 'check their oxygen systems'.

On 7 May Khrushchev addressed the Supreme Soviet again: 'I must tell you a secret. When I made my first report I deliberately did not say that the pilot was alive and well ... and now just look how many silly things they (the Americans) have said'. Khrushchev exploited his position, revelling in the details of the American cover-up: he was in possession of the pilot ('alive and kicking'), the 'plane, the camera, and had even had the photographs developed. He also had Powers' survival pack, including 7500 roubles, other currencies and gold rings and gifts for women. 'Why was all this necessary?' he asked, 'Maybe the pilot was to have flown still higher to Mars and was going to lead the Martian ladies astray?' He laughed at the US report that the U2 had a maximum height of 55,000 feet: 'It was hit by the rocket at 20,000m (65,000 feet). And if they fly any higher we will also hit them'.

The U2 Affair brought the 1960 Paris Summit to a grinding halt. Following the arrival of the first U2s in England in August 1962, Moscow remarked that they ought to be 'kept far away from us'. In the USSR, Powers was sentenced to ten years but released in exchange for Rudolph Abel, a KGB spy, in 1962. Soviet press maintained that Powers had been sent home as an 'act of clemency'. No mention was made of the exchange. The wreckage of the plane is now on display in Yekaterinburg.   **Dominic Streatfeild-James** (UK)

After the train leaves the station, on the right along the Iset River a mass of chimney stacks pollute the horizon. This is Yekaterinburg's main industrial region.

For about 70km east of Yekaterinburg, the train winds down and out of the Urals to the West Siberian plain. You are now in Asia (not quite in Siberia yet) but the scenery and houses look no different from those on the European flank of the mountains.

Km1912: Bogdanovich Богданович There is nothing of interest in this town unless you want to pick up some fireproof bricks which are the town's biggest products. Clay quarries and other factories make this town and region very ugly.

About 16km from Bogdanovich are the **Kurinsk mineral springs**. The *1900 Guide to the Great Siberian Railway* states 'They are efficacious for rheumatism, paralysis, scrofula and anaemia. Furnished houses and an hotel with good rooms are situated near the baths. There is a garden and a promenade with band; theatricals and concerts take place in the casino'. Such frivolous jollities are hard to imagine in this rather gloomy region today. There's still a hotel, however.

Km1955: Kamyshlov Камышлов The town was founded in 1668 as a fortress and is one of oldest settlements in the Urals. The original buildings have all gone and today the architecture of the town is predominantly late 19th and early 20th century. There is a museum here dedicated to the locally-born poet SP Shchepachev and the writer PP Bazhov, who lived here on and off from 1914 to 1923.

About 6km to the west of the town, on the banks of the Pyshma River, is the Obukhov sulphur and chalybeate mineral water sanatorium which has been famous since 1871.

Km2033: Talitsa Талица (pop: 20,100) The town is famous for its Mayan (Маян) brand of bottled mineral water, believed to be good for stomach disorders. The town, which is 3km south

MAP 4

ЕКАТЕРИНБУРГ
YEKATERINBURG
Шарташ
SHARTASH
Путевка
PUTEVKA
Косулино
KOSOLINO
Гагарский
GAGARSKIY
Баженово
BAZHENOVO
Грязновская
GRYAZNOVSKAYA
Богданович
BOGDANOVICH
Пышминская
PISHMINSKAYA
Еланский
YELANSKIY
Камышлов
KAMISHLOV
Аксариха
AKSARIKHA
Ощепково
OSHCHEPKOVO
Просёлок
PROSELOK
Талица
TALITSA
Юшала
YUSHALA
Бахметское
BAKHMETSKOYE
Тугулым
TUGULYM
Кармак
KARMAK
ТЮМЕНЬ
TYUMEN
Войновка
VOYNOVKA
О-Андреевское
OZERO ANDREYEVSKOYE
Винзили
VINZILI
Богандинская
BOGANDINSKAYA
Ялуторовск
YALUTOROVSK
Tobol R
Заводоуковская
ZAVODOUKOVSKAYA
Новая Заимка
NOVAYA ZAIMKA
Вагай
VAGAY

SVERDLOVSKAYA OBLAST

TYUMENSKAYA OBLAST

of the station, also produces another drink which is less beneficial: watered down industrial alcohol which is sold as rough vodka.

Km2064: Yushala Юшала   The sailors from the battleship *Potemkin* were shot here and buried at nearby Kamyshlov station.

Km2102: Siberia (Сибирь) begins here (ends here, for those going west). The border between Sverdlovskaya and Tyumenskaya Oblasts is the frontier between Siberia and the Urals. Tyumenskaya Oblast comprises 430,000 square kilometres of flat land, tundra in the north, taiga in the south. Until oil was discovered in the region twenty years ago, the inhabitants were engaged in reindeer-herding in the north and farming in the south. Many people have been brought into the oblast recently to work in the petroleum and construction industries.

South of the railway line, the point where the Great Post Road crossed Siberia's frontier was marked by 'a square pillar ten or twelve feet in height, of stuccoed or plastered brick', wrote George Kennan (on his way to research *Siberia and the Exile System* in 1887). He added: 'No other spot between St Petersburg and the Pacific is more full of painful suggestions, and none has for the traveller a more melancholy interest than the little opening in the forest where stands this grief-consecrated pillar. Here hundreds of thousands of exiled human beings – men, women and children; princes, nobles and peasants – have bidden good-by (sic) forever to friends, country, and home ... The Russian peasant even when a criminal is deeply attached to his native land; and heart-rending scenes have been witnessed around the boundary pillar ... Some gave way to unrestrained grief; some comforted the weeping; some knelt and pressed their faces to the loved soil of their native country and collected a little earth to take with them into exile ... Until recently the Siberian boundary post was covered with brief inscriptions, good-byes and the names of exiles ... In one place, in a man's hand, had been written the words "Prashchai Marya" (Goodbye Mary!) Who the writer was, who Mary was, there is nothing now left to show ...' (see p93).

Km2144: Tyumen Тюмень (●●) (pop: 496,000)   **[see p208]**
Tyumen is the oldest town in Siberia, founded in 1586. It was built on the banks of the Tura River, the site of the former Tatar town of Chingi Tura, said to date back to the fourteenth century. The Russian town was named by Tsar Feodor Ivanovich after Tyumen Khan, who formerly ruled this region. It grew quickly as a trading centre with goods arriving and being shipped on from the large port on the Tura River.

At least one million of the people who passed through this town before 1900 were convicts and exiles. Many were lodged, under the most appalling conditions, in the Tyumen Forwarding Prison. When George Kennan visited the prison in 1887, he was horrified by the overcrowded cells, the dirt and the terrible smell. He wrote: 'The air in the corridors and cells.....was laden with fever germs from the unventilated hospital wards, fetid odors from diseased human bodies and the stench arising from unemptied excrement buckets.....' After a miserable two-week stay here, convicts were sent on prison barges to Tomsk. Conditions were not much better for the 500,000 emigrants who flooded through the town between 1883 and 1900, but they at least had their freedom. When the new railway reached Tyumen in 1888 prisoners from Russia were no longer herded over the Urals in marching parties but travelled in relative luxury in box-cars used also for the transport of cattle and horses.

Tyumen is becoming increasingly important because of oil and gas discoveries in the oblast. Other industries include ship building and timber processing.

Km2222: Yalutorovsk Ялуторовск (pop: 37,000) The town sits on the bank of the wide, 1591km-long Tobol River. In 1639 it was the most easterly fortress of the Tsar's expanding empire. It later became one of the places of exile for Decembrists, who opened the first Siberian school for girls here. It's now a museum and is next to the Decembrists' museum, the house of the most famous exile, Muravev-Apostol.

After crossing over the Tobol River, you will see dozens of small, mostly salt lakes on both sides of the railway.

Km2431: Ishim Ишим (●●) (pop: 65,800) The town sits on the left bank of the Ishim River which was a major trading route before the arrival of the Trans-Siberian at the turn of the century. The strategic location of the town resulted in it hosting one of the largest trading fairs in Western Siberia. The Nikolsk fair was held every December and it attracted more than 2000 traders some from as far away as China. The town was founded in 1670 as Korkina village but its name was changed to Ishim in 1782.

North of Ishim, up the Ishim and Irtysh Rivers, lies the city of **Tobolsk**, one of the oldest settlements in Siberia. Yermak (see p89) reached the area in 1581 and established a fort here. The Tsar hoped to develop the region by encouraging colonization but to the Russian peasant, Siberia was as far away as the moon and no voluntary mass exodus over the Urals occurred. The policy of forced exile was rather more successful. The first exiles that arrived in Tobolsk were former inhabitants of the town of Uglich, who had been witnesses to the murder of Tsarevich Dimitri. With them was banished the **Uglich church bell** which rang the signal for the insurrection that followed the assassination. The bell was reconsecrated in Tobolsk church but in the 1880s the Uglich Town Council decided it would like its bell back. Tobolsk Council refused and the case eventually went to court. The judge ruled that as the bell had been exiled for life and it was still calling the people to prayers, it had not yet completed its sentence and must therefore remain in Tobolsk.

❏ **German spy in Ishim**

George Kennan recounts an amusing incident that occurred in Ishim in 1829, when Baron von Humboldt was conducting a geological survey for the Tsar. The famous explorer (who gave his name to the Humboldt Current off the west coast of South America) had by then become more than a little annoyed by the petty Siberian officials who kept him from his studies. He must have been rather short with the police prefect in this little town for the man took great offence and despatched an urgent letter to his governor-general in which he wrote 'A few days ago there arrived here a German of shortish stature, insignificant appearance, fussy and bearing a letter of introduction from your Excellency to me. I accordingly received him politely; but I must say I find him suspicious and even dangerous. I disliked him from the first. He talks too much .... despises my hospitality .... and associates with Poles and other political criminals .... On one occasion he proceeded with them to a hill overlooking the town. They took a box with them and got out of it a long tube which we all took for a gun. After fastening it to three feet they pointed it down on the town .... This was evidently a great danger for the town which is built entirely of wood; so I sent a detachment of troops with loaded rifles to watch the German on the hill. If the treacherous machinations of this man justify my suspicions, we shall be ready to give our lives for the Tsar and Holy Russia.' Kennan adds: 'The civilized world is to be thanked that the brilliant career of the great von Humboldt was not cut short by a Cossack bullet .... while he was taking sights with a theodolite in that little Siberian town of Ishim.'

Km2497 This is the administrative frontier between Tyumenskaya and Omskaya oblasts. **Omskaya** is on a plain in the Irtysh River basin, occupying 140,000 square kilometres. The thick forests of the taiga cover the northern part of the oblast. In the south there is considerable agricultural development, the main crops being spring wheat, flax and sunflowers. As well as sheep and cattle farms, there are numerous dairy farms. This has been an important butter-producing region since the nineteenth century, when butter was exported to as far away as Turkey and Germany. It is said that butter-making was introduced to the region by the English wife of a Russian landowner. There are many swamps and lakes in the oblast which provide the habitat for a multitude of water birds, including duck, coot, grey goose, swan and crane.

─── **Km 2497-3478 TIME ZONE MT + 3** ───

Km2565: Nazyvaevskaya Называевская (●●●) (pop: 14,400)
Founded in 1910 with the arrival of the railway Nazyvaevskaya rapidly grew with an influx of new agricultural workers during the Khrushchev's Virgin Fields campaign. The plan was conceived following years of

chronic grain shortage after WWII and involved the cultivation of 25 million hectares of land in south-western Siberia and north Kazakhstan. To put the size of this massive undertaking into perspective, the total surface area of the United Kingdom is only 13 million hectares. By the 1960s over-intensive farming had reduced five million hectares to desert. The Trans-Siberian runs through the very north of the area which, unlike the more fragile south, is still fertile.

This area is famous as much for its insects as for its agriculture. In 1887, Kennan found that travelling through this marshy region was a singularly unpleasant experience. He wrote: 'We were so tormented by huge gray mosquitoes that we were obliged to put on thick gloves, cover our heads with calico hoods and horse hair netting and defend ourselves constantly with leafy branches.' You, however, should be quite safe in your compartment.

Km2706: Irtyshch River Речка Иртыш The Irtyshch rises in China and flows almost 3000km into the Ob River. It's joined here by the Om. The bridge is 650m long and built on granite pillars that came from the Urals and had to be brought 1000km by river to reach the construction site.

Km2712: Omsk Омск (●●●) (pop: 1,169,000) **[see p211]** Omsk is the second largest city in Siberia and great deal of effort has gone into making it the greenest. The 2500 hectares of parks and gardens cannot, however, disguise the fact that Omsk is essentially an industrial city.

Just before reaching the suburbs of Omsk, you see the airport on the left. The first suburban station you pass is Karbyshevo (Карбышево) and this is where the railway from Chelyabinsk joins the Trans-Siberian railway. The train then crosses the 500m wide Irtysh River which gives a view of Omsk to the left. The old centre of Omsk is on the right bank (eastern side). After the bridge, the train makes a left turn and on the right passes an old brick water tower for steam

engines, built during the early 20th century. This has been preserved as an architectural monument.

The stretch of line between Omsk and Novosibirsk has the greatest freight traffic density of any line in the world.

For the next 600km the train runs through the inhospitable **Baraba Steppe**. This vast expanse of greenish plains is dotted with shallow lakes and ponds, and coarse reeds and sedge grass conceal swamps, peat bogs and rare patches of firm ground. From the train it appears as if there is a continuous forest in the distance. However if you walk towards it, you will never get there as what you are seeing are clumps of birches and aspen trees that are spaced several kilometres or more apart. The lack of landmarks in this area has claimed hundreds of lives.

In spring, this place is hell as the air is grey with clouds of gnats and mosquitoes. The Baraba Steppe is also a vast breeding ground for ducks and geese and every year hunters bag about five million birds from this area. Below the steppe is an enormous natural reservoir of hot water, a geo-thermal energy supply that is currently being investigated.

❑ **The Kirghiz**
South of Omsk and the Baraba Steppe region lie the **Kirghiz Steppes**, the true home of the Kirghiz people. The area extends from the Urals in the west to the mineral-rich Altai Mountains in the south. The Kirghiz are direct descendants of the Turkic-Mongol hordes that joined Ghengis Khan's armies and invaded Europe in the thirteenth century AD. When SS Hill paid them a visit in 1854, they were nomadic herders who professed a mixture of Shamanism and Islam and survived on a diet of boiled mutton and *koumiss* (fermented mare's milk). They lived in *kibitkas* (felt tents or yurts), the doors of which were arranged to face in the direction of Mecca. Fortunately this alignment also kept out the southern winds that blew across the steppe. Of these people Hill wrote: 'The Kirgeeze have the high cheek bones.....of the Mongol Tatars, with an expression of countenance that seemed at least to us the very reverse of agreeable.' However he warmed to his 'new half-wild friends' when they shared their 'brave mess of *stchee*' (soup) with him.

George Kennan found them equally hospitable in 1887. Inside the tent he was offered a large container filled with about a litre and a half of koumiss. For fear of causing offence he swallowed the lot and to his horror, his host quickly refilled the container. Kennan wrote 'When I suggested that he reserve the second bowlful for my comrade, Mr Frost, he looked so pained and grieved that in order to restore his serenity I had to go to the *tarantas*, get my banjo and sing "There is a Tavern in the Town"'. This did not have quite the desired effect and they left shortly afterwards.

Km2760 (S): There is a locomotive storage depot here (mostly electric) and 3km east of it is the station of Kormilovka (Кормиловка).

Km2795: Kalachinskaya Калачинская (pop: 25,500) One of the more attractive towns in the Omsk Oblast, this town was founded in 1792 by Russian peasants who were distinct from other settlers because of their unusual dialect – *kalachon* means 'a sharp bend in a river'; *kalach* in modern Russian means 'a small padlock-shaped white bread loaf'. There's a useful bit of information.

Km2840 This is the administrative frontier between Omskaya and Novosibirskaya oblasts. The 178,000 square kilometres of **Novosibirskaya Oblast** extend across the Baraba Steppe region of swamps and lakes. Some of the land has been drained and is now extremely fertile. Crops include spring wheat, flax, rye, barley and sun-flowers with dairy farming in many parts of the Baraba region. You might see cowherds rounding up their stock on horseback.

Km2885: Tatarskaya Татарская (pop: 30,800) A rather uninteresting small town of apartment blocks and log cabins. The *1900 Guide to the Great Siberian Railway* was not enthusiastic about the place. 'The country is swampy and infested with fever. The water is bad, supplied by a pond formed by spring and bog water.' There was a church, a centre for emigrants, a school and 'the butter manufacturies of Mariupolsky, Padin, Soshovsky, Popel and Weiss, producing annually about 15,000 *puds* (250,000 kg) of cream butter'.

Km2883 (N) An attractive group of colourful log cabins. About fifty kilometres south of the line between Chany and Binsk lies Lake Chany, the centre of a fishing industry. Catches are smaller now but in the nineteenth century it was famous for its abundant stock of large pike (weighing up to 14kg/30lbs) and carp.

MAP 6

❑ **The West Siberian Railway (Kms 2716-3343)**
The original line started in Chelyabinsk, south of Yekaterinburg, and ran through
Kurgan and Petropavlovsk (both south of the modern route) to Omsk. Work
began in July 1892 under the direction of chief civil engineer, Mikhailovski. His
task was beset by problems that were also to be experienced along other sections
of the line: a shortage of labour and animals, a complete lack of suitable trees for
sleepers and inhospitable working conditions (eg swamps that swarmed with
insects). However, the first section from Chelyabinsk to Omsk was completed in
1894 and the Omsk to Novo-Nikolayevsk (now Novosibirsk) section opened in
October 1895. The total cost of the line was 46 million roubles, one million roubles fewer than the original estimate.

Km3040: Barabinsk Барабинск **(●●)** (pop: 36,400) Founded at the
end of the 19th century during the construction of the Trans-Siberian.
Twelve km to the north is the bigger and older town of Kuibyshev
(Kainsk-Barabinski).

Km3212: Chulymskaya Чулымская A large railway junction.

Km3322: Ob Обь Just before reaching this station, you can see
Tolmachevo Airport on the left which is one of the two airports which
serves Novosibirsk. The city of Novosibirsk is visible to the north-east.

Km3332: The Great Ob River Bridge After nearly a century of
operation, many of the steel bridges of the early Trans-Siberian are still
in use today. Known as hog-backed bridges because of the hump in the
middle of each span, they are supported by massive stone piers, each with
a thick buttress that slants upstream to deflect the huge ice chunks as they
float down the river in the spring thaw. The 870m-long Ob Bridge is a
classic hog-backed bridge made up of seven spans.

The writers of the *1900 Guide to the Great Siberian Railway* were
clearly impressed by the Ob Bridge, which at the time had only just been
completed. They devote almost a whole page to a detailed description of
the bridge, beginning: 'At the 1,328 *verst*, the line crosses the Ob by a
bridge 327.50 *sazhens* long, having seven spans, the I and VII openings
are 46.325 *sazhens*, the II, IV and VI, 53.65 *sazhens*, and III and V, 53.15
sazhens. The upper girders of the bridge are on the Herber's system.' If
you are unfamiliar with the Russian Imperial units of measurement, a
verst is 1.06km or 3500ft and a *sazhen* is 2.1m or 7ft.

Work started in 1893 on the bridge with construction of wooden false-
work which supported sections of the permanent steel structure until they

could be riveted together. Bridge-making proceeded all year round and was an extremely haz-
ardous occupation in winter. Gangs were perched
30 or more metres above the frozen river, bolting
and riveting without safety lines or protective
hoardings. More than a few dropped to their
deaths below.

The Ob River is one of the world's longest
rivers, flowing more than 4000km north across
Siberia from the Altai Mountains to the Gulf of
Ob below the Arctic Ocean.

As you are crossing over the Ob River, you
can see Novosibirsk city centre on the left and the
Oktyabrski port on the right. The passenger river
station is a further 800m upstream from the port.
On reaching the right bank, the train turns to the
north passing the city's long-distance bus station.
About 800m onwards on the right, you pass a
steam locomotive on a plinth.

Km3335: Novosibirsk Новосибирск (●●●)
[see p213] Novosibirsk (pop: 1,600,000) is the
capital of Western Siberia. Most trains stop long
enough for you to get a good look at Siberia's
largest station, an impressive blue-green, glass-
vaulted building that took from 1929 to 1941 to
complete.

Travelling east you pass through flat land of
fields and swamps with the dachas of Novo-
sibirskians in little groups amongst the trees.
Some are particularly photogenic (Km3409 (S)).
The line traverses an area of thin taiga to Oyash
(Km3424).

Km3463: Bolotnaya Болотная The town
was founded in 1805 as a stop on the Siberian
Trakt at a junction of a 250km road south to
Barnaul. The town's name means 'swampy',
which should please a certain British environmental activist.

───── **Km 3479-4473 TIME ZONE MT + 4** ─────

Km3479: The **administrative frontier** between
Novosibirskaya and Kemerovskaya Oblasts.

MAP 7

НОВОСИБИРСК
NOVOSIBIRSK
Мочище
MOCHISHCHE
Сокур
SOKUR
Мошково
MOSHKOVO
Ояш
OYASH
Чебула
CHEBULA
Болотная
BOLOTNAYA
Юрга
YURGA
Талыменка
TALMENKA
Яшкино
YASHKINO
Холкино Томск
KHOLKINO TOMSK
Тайга
TAIGA
Лихтач
LIKHTACH
Анжерская
ANZHERSKAYA
Яя
YAYA
Ижморская
IZHMORSKAYA
Берикульская
BERIKULSKAYA
Антибесский
ANTIBESSKIY

NOVOSIBIRSKAYA OBLAST
KEMEROVSKAYA OBLAST

Km3491: Yurga 1 Юрга 1 (pop: 94,300)   The town of Yurga 2 is 7km to the south of Yurga 1. A few kilometres east the train crosses the Tom River, which flows an unimpressive (by Siberian standards) 700km (or twice the length of the Thames) from the Kuznetsk basin into the Ob River.

Km3570: Taiga Тайга (●●) (pop: 25,900) This town once stood in the midst of the dense taiga forest. Nowadays the closest taiga is far to the east.

RL Jefferson was here in 1897 and wrote later: 'This little station was bang in the midst of the most impenetrable forest I had ever set eyes on....in the centre of a pit it seemed, for the great black trunks of pines went up all around and left only a circular space of blue sky visible.' Annette Meakin wrote a few years later that she, 'thought Taiga one of the prettiest stations in Siberia. It is only a few years old, built something after the style of a Swiss chalet.' Unfortunately it has since been replaced by a building that is rather more substantial but aesthetically less pleasing.

The station sits at the junction of a 79km branch line to the ancient city of **Tomsk**, and in retrospect the site of the junction was badly chosen. The basic problem is that there are no rivers or large reservoirs near Taiga so water had to be carted in to feed the steam engines. Tomsk was once the most important place in Siberia. It was founded in 1604 on the Tom River and developed into a large administrative, trading and gold-smelting centre on the Great Siberian Post Road. When it was originally bypassed by the railway, Tomsk began to lose out to the stations along the main line. It is still, however, a sizeable city of half a million people, the administrative capital of Tomskaya Oblast and a large centre of industrial engineering.

Tomsk was visited by almost every nineteenth century traveller who came to Siberia. The city was an important exile centre and had a large forwarding prison. Having almost succumbed to the stench from the overcrowded cells in 1887, Kennan wrote: 'If you visit the prison my advice to you is to breakfast heartily before starting, and to keep out of the hospital wards.' By the time Annette Meakin visited it fourteen years later, the railway had removed the need for forwarding prisons and she could write: 'It was not unlike a group of alms houses. We found very few prisoners.' Tomsk achieved international notoriety when at nearby Tomsk-7 on 6 April 1993 a radioactive waste reprocessing plant blew up contaminating an area of 120 square km.

Near the station is a **steam engine**, P-360192, built in 1956.

Km3602: Anzherskaya Анжерская (pop: 106,000) This ugly coal mining town is at the northern extremity of the giant Kuzbass coal field which contains a massive 600 billion tons of high quality low sulphur coal. The town, formerly called Anzhero-Sudzhensk (Анжеро-Судженск), was founded in 1897 during the construction of the Trans-

❏ **The Mid-Siberian Railway (Kms3343-5191)**
Work began on the Mid-Siberian Railway starting at the Ob River in the summer of 1893. Since Tomsk was to be bypassed, part of the route had to be hacked through the thick forests of the taiga regions around the station, which was aptly named Taiga. It would have been far easier to have followed the route of the Great Siberian Post Road through Tomsk but some of that city's administrators wanted nothing to do with the railway, since it would break their trade monopolies and bring down prices, damaging the economy as far as they were concerned. By the time they realized that the effect was quite the opposite it was too late to change the route of the line. Besides, the engineers had discovered that the bypass would save 90km. The tiny village of Novo-Nikolayevsk, (now Novosibirsk) situated where the railway crosses the Ob, grew quickly and soon eclipsed Tomsk as an industrial and cultural centre.

This was difficult territory to build a railway across. The swampy taiga is frozen until mid-July, so the building season was barely three months long. There was the usual labour shortage and 1500 convicts had to be brought in to help. In 1895 a branch line from Taiga reached Tomsk. Although only about 80km long, it had taken a year to build, owing to the virtually impenetrable taiga and the terrible swamps. In 1896 the line reached Krasnoyarsk and work began on the eastern section to Irkutsk. Numerous bridges were needed in this hilly country but by the beginning of 1898 the mid-Siberian was complete and the first trains rolled into Irkutsk. Total cost was about 110 million roubles.

Siberian which is also when coal mining started. From the end of the 19th to the beginning of the 20th century, 98 per cent of all coal from the Kuzbass came from here. Most of the original coal miners were Tsarist prisoners and their short and brutal mining life is documented in the Museum of Local Studies.

The railway branch line to the south from here leads to **Novokuznetsk** which is the heart of the Kuznetsk (or Kuzbass) Basin. In the early 1900s, a plan had been put forward to link these coal-fields with the Ural region where iron-ore was mined and coal was needed for the blast furnaces. This plan was not put into action until the 1930s when the so-called Ural-Kuzbass Kombinat was developed. Trains bring iron-ore to the Kuzbass furnaces and return to the iron foundries of the Urals with coal. You will have met (or will meet if you're going west) a good deal of this traffic on the line between Novosibirsk and the Urals.

Kms3613-3623: Several long views south across the fields. The line climbs slowly through birch forests and small fields to Mariinsk.

Km3715: Mariinsk Мариинск (●●●) (pop: 41,500) Founded as Kisskoe in 1698, this place was nothing more than a way station for postal riders who carried messages on the Moscow–Irkutsk postal road. In 1826, however, news of a massive gold find brought tens of thousands of fortune seekers. The gold rush lasted for decades and between 1828 and 1917 more than 50 tons of gold were extracted from the region. The town was renamed Mariinsk in 1857 after Maria Alexandrovna, the German wife of Tsar Alexander II.

Just west of the station there are large **engine repair yards** (S). Two kilometres east of the town you cross the Kiya River, a tributary of the Chulim. East of the river the line rises to cross the watershed at Km3760, where there are good views south. The line descends through the market town of Tiazhin (Km3779) to the river of the same name and then climbs over the next watershed descending to **Itat**, another agricultural town.

Km3820: This is the administrative frontier between Kemerovskaya Oblast and Krasnoyarski *Krai*. A krai is a large oblast, usually found in less developed areas of Siberia. This is also the border between West and East Siberia. **Krasnoyarski** is large, covering 2.5 million square kilometres (an area the size of Saudi Arabia) between the Arctic Ocean in the north and the Sayan Mountains in the south. Most of the krai is covered with taiga, though there is tundra in the region within the Arctic Circle and some agricultural land in the south. The economy is based on timber-processing but there are also important mineral reserves.

Km3849: Bogotol Боготол (●●) This railway town has a **museum** in its locomotive depot which is 1km to the west of the station. There is also a number of **steam locos** here. The town was founded in 1893 as a station on the Trans-Siberian although there is a much older village of the same name 8km away.

Near Bogotol are lignite (brown coal) deposits and open cut mines can be seen from the train scarring the landscape.

About 30km east the line begins to descend, crossing the **Chulim River** at Km3917. RL Jefferson arrived here in the winter of 1897 and described the river as 'rather a small stream when compared to the Obi, Tom or Irtish but still broad enough to make two of the Thames River at London Bridge'. At the time, the bridge had not been completed but engineers had the brilliant idea of freezing the rails to the thick ice, thus allowing the train to cross the river.

Km3917: Achinsk 1 Ачинск 1 (●) (214m/700f) Founded in 1642 when a stockaded outpost was built here, on the banks of the Chulim. It was burnt down by the Kirghiz 40 years later but soon rebuilt. In the 18th and 19th centuries Achinsk was an important trading centre, linked by the Chulim to Tyumen and Tomsk. Tea arrived by caravan from China and was forwarded in barges. To the north, in the valleys around the Chulim basin, lay the gold mines. The most valuable mines today, however, are those producing lignite. There's also a giant aluminium production complex which can be seen from the railway.

Kms3932-33 (S): Half-way point on the line from Moscow to Beijing (via Mongolia). There's a **white obelisk** to mark it on the south side of the line but it is difficult to see. The line continues through a hilly region of taiga, winding round sharp curves (Kms4006-12) and past picturesque groups of log cabins (Km4016).

There are occasional good views at Km4058 (N) and after the village of Minino (Km4072) at 4078 (N).

Km3960: Chernorechenskaya Чернореченская   The name of the town around the station is Novochernorechenskaya (Новочернореченский) meaning New Black River.

Km4098: Krasnoyarsk Красноярск (●●●)
[**see p222**] (pop: 929,000) This major industrial city was founded in 1628 beside the Yenisei River. (*Yenisei* is also the name of the Moscow–Krasnoyarsk Express which you may see standing in the station). A fort was built and named Krasny Yar. As an important trading centre on the Great Siberian Post Road and the Yenisei waterway, the town grew fast in the eighteenth century.

The railway reached Krasnoyarsk in 1896, some of the rails for this section of the line having been brought from England by ship via the Kara Sea (within the Arctic Circle) and the Yenisei. Murray would not recognize the town he described as 'pleasantly situated and sheltered by hills of moderate elevation', in the 1865 edition of his *Handbook for Russia, Poland and Finland*.

Local governor is ex-army hardliner, Alexander Lebed, who had stood against Yeltsin in the 1996 presidential elections but finally stood down and supported Yeltsin. Yeltsin no doubt had something to do with Lebed's successful election campaign in Krasnoyarsk.

MAP 8

Мариинск MARIINSK
Суслово SUSLOVO
Тяжин TYAZHIN
KEMEROVSKAYA OBLAST
Итат ITAT
Боготол BOGOTOL Ⓜ
Chulim R. Km 201
Критово KRITOVO
Ачинск ACHINSK
Чернореченская CHERNORECHENSKAYA
Козулька KOZULKA
Km 184
Зеледеево ZELEDEYEVO
Кача KACHA
KRASNOYARSKIY KRAY
Минино MININO
КРАСНОЯРСК KRASNOYARSK
Yenisei R.

Km4100-2: Yenisei River Речка Енисей Good views (N) and (S).
Leaving Krasnoyarsk, travelling east, the train crosses the great river that
bisects Siberia. The Yenisei (meaning 'wide water' in the language of the
local Evenki people) rises in Mongolia and flows into the Arctic Ocean,
5200km north of its source.

The river is crossed on a new bridge, opened in 1999. The old bridge,
which is almost a kilometre in length, dates from the 1890s and had to be
built on heavy granite piers to withstand the huge icebergs which steam-
roller their way down the river for a few weeks each year. The cement
was shipped from St Petersburg, the steel bearings from Warsaw. It took
94,000 workers three years to build. At the World Fair in Paris in 1900,
the bridge was awarded a gold medal. The other engineering feat to win
a gold medal that year was the Eiffel Tower.

The Yenisei is the traditional border between west and east Siberia.
For several kilometres after you've crossed the river the lumber mills and
factories blight the countryside. Opencast mining has slashed ugly gash-
es into the hills around Km4128 (N).

Km4117: Bazaika Базаиха There is a branch line to the north from
here to the closed city of Krasnoyarsk-26, a nuclear waste reprocessing
facility. The line goes through Sotsgorod station and terminates at the
Gorknokhimicheski Chemical complex. Neither this line nor the city
appeared on Soviet maps.

❏ **Evenki National Okrug**
About nine hundred kilometres due north of here lies the town of Tura, the capital of the **Evenki National Okrug**, 745,000 square kilometres of permanently
frozen land, specially reserved for the indigenous population. The **Evenkis**
belong to the Tungus group of people (the names are often used interchangeably)
and they were originally nomadic herders and hunters. After the Buryats and the
Yakuts, they form the next largest ethnic group in Siberia but they are scattered
into small groups, right across the northern regions. They used to live in wig-
wams or tents and survived off berries and reindeer-meat (a great delicacy being
the raw marrow sucked straight from the bone, preferably while it was still
warm). They discovered that Christianity fitted in well with their own
Shamanistic religion and worshipped St Nicholas as deputy to the Master Spirit
of the Underworld. After the Revolution they were organized into collective
farms and although most of the population is now settled, there are still some
reindeer-herders in the extreme north of the region.

Between Krasnoyarsk and Nizhneudinsk the line crosses hilly picturesque countryside, and the train climbs out of one valley and descends into the next. There are numerous bridges on this section. There are some good places for photographs along the train as it curves round bends at Km4165-7 and Km4176-4177; then the land becomes flatter.

Km4227: Uyar Уяр At the western end of the station is a strategic reserve of working **steam locos** and also a dump of about ten engines rusting away amongst the weeds. This town's full name is something of a tongue-twister. Try saying 'Uyarspasopreobrazhenskoye' after a few glasses of vodka. In 1897 the station's name was changed to Olgino in honour of grand duchess Olga Nikolaevna. In 1906 it was renamed Klyukvenaya after the railway engineer who built this section of the line but in 1973 its name was changed back to Uyar.

Km4262: Zaozernaya Заозёная (●) (pop: 15,600) A branch line runs north to the secret city of Krasnoyarsk 45 (also known as Zelenogorsk) where there's a space centre. East of the station there are huge opencast coal mines beside the track.

Km4343: Kansk-Yeniseiski Канск-Енисейский (●) (pop: 111,000) This big town, known just as Kansk, had an inglorious start. In 1628 the original Kansk wooden fortress was built about 43km away from the present site on the Kan River. The original site was badly chosen and in 1640, the fortress was moved. It was almost immediately burnt down by the Buryat indigenous people and although it was rebuilt, in 1677 it was again burnt down. Over the following two centuries the town became a major transit point for peasants settling in Siberia. The Russian author, Chekhov, wasn't very impressed with the town and said that Kansk belonged among the impoverished stagnant little towns famed only for an abundance of taverns. It's unlikely he'd change his view if he visited today.

MAP 9

КРАСНОЯРСК
KRASNOYARSK
Злобино
ZLOBINO
Зыково
ZIKOVO

Сорокино
SOROKINO
Камарчага
KAMARCHAGA
Балай
BALAY
Уяр
UYAR

Заозерная
ZAOZERNAYA
Камала
KAMALA
Солянка
SOLYANKA
Бошняково
BOSHNYAKOVO
Канск
KANSK
Иланская
ILANSKAYA

Ингашская
INGASHSKAYA

Тинская
TINSKAYA
Решоты
RESHOTI
Ключи
KLYUCHI
Юрты
YURTI
Бирюсинск
BIRYUSINSK
Тайшет
TAYSHET
BRATSK
Разгон
RAZGON
Алзамай
ALZAMAY
Камышет
KAMISHET
Ук
UK
Нижнеудинск
NIZHNEUDINSK

KRASNOYARSKIY KRAY

IRKUTSKAYA OBLAST

Km4375: Ilanskaya Иланская (●●●) (pop: 18,000) The site of the town was selected in 1734 by the Danish-born Russian naval explorer V Bering (of Bering Straits fame) during the Second Kamchatski Expedition to explore the coast of America. It may seem strange that Bering was surveying central Siberia but he was ordered to make himself useful as he crossed the country to the Russian Far East. There is a **museum** at the locomotive depot with a display of the history of the town.

Between here and Taishet, there are large deposits of brown coal. Our provodnitsa was well aware of this last bit of information and issued four of us with buckets to collect coal (for the carriage boiler) from the piles lying about the platform.

Km4453: Reshoti Решоты This is the junction for the line south to Abakan, an industrial centre in the foothills of the Sayan Mountains.

Km4473: Uralo-Klyuchi Урало-Ключи This small station's name translates as the Key to the Urals and it sits near the administrative frontier between Irkutsk and Krasnoyarsk oblasts.

———————— **Km 4474-5780 TIME ZONE MT + 5** ————————

Local time is now Moscow Time + 5 hours. The railway gradually swings round from the east to the south-east as you head towards Irkutsk. For the next 600km you will pass through one of Russia's biggest logging areas. Many of the rivers are used to float down the logs and you can often see log packs being towed down the river or the piles of loose logs washed up on the river banks. This section of the line is very impressive, the train constantly climbing and descending as it crosses numerous rivers and deep ravines.

Kms4501-02: The river here conveniently marks the **halfway point** for the Moscow to Beijing (via Manchuria) run.

Km4516: Taishet Тайшет (●) This town is at the junction of the Trans-Siberian and BAM (Baikal to Amur Mainline) railways. The 3400km BAM line (see p131) traverses Siberia from the Pacific Ocean to Lake Baikal and is the gateway to the rarely visited region known as the BAM Zone. The single track line is about 600 to 1000km north of the Trans-Siberian Railway, running parallel to it through pristine taiga, mountain tundra and wide river valley meadows.

Before the 1970s, the BAM Zone was virtually uninhabited taiga dotted with the villages of indigenous people. Today it has a population of about 300,000 involved in extracting natural resources from the region's enormous reserves. Only about 100 Westerners visit the region each year.

Taishet was founded when the Trans-Siberian arrived in 1897. There is nothing to see in the town even though it is famous in Soviet gulag literature. Taishet was a transit camp for Stalin-era prisoners heading east and west, and was a major camp of Ozerlag, the gulag complex which built the Taishet-Bratsk section of the BAM. The building of this section started in earnest following the end of WWII and at the height of construction there were over 300 camps dotted along the 350km from Taishet to Bratsk with a total population of 100,000 prisoners. In *The Gulag Archipelago*, Solzhenitsyn wrote that Taishet had a factory for creosoting railroad ties (railway sleepers) 'where, they say, creosote penetrates the skin and bones and its vapours fill the lungs – and that is death'. The factory which makes the ties still operates.

Km4555 (S): Razgon Разгон A small, poor-looking community of log cabins. About a kilometre east of here, the line rises and there are views across the taiga at Km4563 (S), Km4569 (N) and Km4570.

Km4631: Kamyshet Камышет It was here that George Kennan stopped in 1887 for repairs to his tarantass. While the wheel was being replaced, he watched the amazing spectacle of a Siberian blacksmith shoeing a horse. 'The poor beast had been hoisted by means of two broad belly-bands and suspended from a stout frame so that he could not touch the ground', he wrote. Three of the horse's legs had been secured to the frame and 'the daring blacksmith was fearlessly putting a shoe on the only hoof that the wretched and humiliated animal could move'.

Kms4640-4680: The train snakes its way through the foothills of the Eastern Sayan Mountains. The Sayan Mountain Range forms a natural frontier between Siberia and Mongolia.

At Kms4648-9, you have reached the **half-way point** on the line from Moscow to Vladivostok. There are some good views and a number of chances to take photographs of the whole length of the train as it winds

---

❏ The Tunguska Event

About 800km due north of here, on 30 June 1908, one of the largest (pre-atomic era) explosions in human history took place, in the Tunguska River region. Two thousand square kilometres of forest were instantly destroyed in what came to be known as the Tunguska Event. The sound of the explosion was heard up to 350kms away, the shock waves were registered on seismic equipment right around the world, and the light from the blast was seen throughout Europe.

Newspapers of the time proposed all kinds of theories to explain its cause, from the testing of new explosives to crash-landing Martian spaceships. Scientists now believe that it was caused by a fragment of Encke's Comet, which disintegrated as it entered the Earth's atmosphere, creating a vast fireball.

around the valleys. The best spots are around Km4657 (S), Km4660 (S), Kms4662-5 and Km4667.

Km4680: Nizhneudinsk Нижнеудинск (●●) (pop: 44,000)   The area is best known for sawmills, swamps and insects. Of the mosquitoes, Kennan complained, 'I found myself blotted from head to foot as if I were suffering from some eruptive disease.'

Near Nizhneudinsk is a famous Siberian beauty spot, the **Ukovsky Waterfall**, 18km upstream along the Ude River which flows through Nizhneudinsk. About 75km further upstream are the **Nizhneudinski Caves**, which contain ancient paintings.

Siberia's smallest indigenous group, the Tofalar (Tofy), live in the isolated village of Tofalariya, 200km from Nizhneudinsk. Less than 500 remain, living in and around this little settlement. There are no roads to this village and its only regular link with the rest of the world is the helicopter service from Nizhneudinsk.

Between Nizhneudinsk and Irkutsk the country becomes flatter and the taiga not so thick. The train passes through numerous timber-yards.

Km4789 (S): There is a large **graveyard** with a blue fence around it, standing close to the line. Some of the graves are topped with red stars, some with red crosses. Kennan wrote in 1887: 'The graveyards belonging to the Siberian settlements sometimes seemed to me much more remarkable and noteworthy than the settlements themselves.....Many graves (are) marked by three armed wooden crosses and covered with narrow A-shaped roofs.'

Km4794: Tulun Тулун (●) (pop: 53,800)   Tulun sits at the road junction of the M55 Moscow–Irkutsk Highway and the main road to the city of Bratsk, 225km to the north. Near the station is the town's centre which still consists of wooden houses. Tulun has a **Decembrists museum**.

The line follows the river, crossing it at Km4800 and passing a large sawmill at Km4804 (S) which might make a good photo with the town behind it. For once there are no wires to get in the way. At Km4809 (S) there is a large opencast mine. You pass through an area of large cultivated fields.

Km4875: Kuytun Куйтун   The town's name means 'cold' in the language of the Buryat people (see p345). There are cold springs in the area.

Km4940: Zima Зима (●●●) (460m/1500ft, pop: 39,400)   Zima means 'winter' and this was a place of exile at the beginning of the 19th century for members of the Sectarian sect. When the Tsarevich Nicholas visited Zima on 8 July 1891, the Buryats presented him with a model yurt cast in silver.

About 3km to the east of the town, the railway crosses the 790km long Oka River. The river runs brown as it cuts through seams of coal and copperas (ferrous sulphate). The mineral-rich water and earth have their benefits as the water was used to blacken tanned animal skins and, during epidemics of cholera, the copperas earth was used as disinfectant. However, it also causes goitre which many locals suffer from today. Down the Oka River near the village of Burluksk on the river banks are 1000 year old petroglylphs of cattle, horses and their riders.

As the line rises out of one valley, crosses the watershed and drops down to the next river you get several reasonable views: Km4958 (S), Km4972 (N), Km4977 (S) and Km4990 (S).

Km5000-40 You pass through the Ust-Ordinski Autonomous Okrug. There's another graveyard close to the track at Km5010 (S).

Km5027: Kutulik Кутулик This station is the biggest railway town in the **Ust-Orda Buryat Nationality District**. The Ust-Orda Buryats are related to the Buryats to the east of Lake Baikal and to the Mongolians but they have a different language and culture. The best time to be here is during the harvest festival of Surkharban when there are races, archery competitions and the Ust-Orda's peculiar brand of wrestling. Kutulik has a museum which contains information on the Ust-Orda Buryats.

Km5061: Cheremkhovo Черемхово (●) (pop: 73,500) The town revolves around the Cheremkhovo coal deposit, and various mining and industrial complexes are dotted along 10km of the railway. The first mine can be seen from the railway about 20km east of the station.

Thirty-one km to the south is **Belsk (Бельск)** where a blackened watchtower is all that remains of a wooden Cossack fortress built in 1691.

Km5087: Polovina Половина The station's name means 'half' and it once marked the halfway point on the Trans-Siberian between Moscow and Vladivostok. Today Moscow is 5090km away and Vladivostok is 4212km. The

MAP 10

Нижнеудинск
NIZHNEUDINSK
Хингуи
KHINGUY
Худоеланская
KHUDOYELANSKAYA
Шеверта
SHEBERTA
Утай
UTAY
Тулун
TULUN
Шуба
SHUBA
Тулюшка
TULYUSHKA
Куйтун
KUYTUN
Харик
KHARIK
Кимельтей
KIMELTEY
Зима
ZIMA
Тыреть
TIRET
Залари
ZALARI
Головинская
GOLOVINSKAYA
Кутулик
KUTULIK
Забитуй
ZABITUY
Черемхово
CHEREMKHOVO
Половина
POLOVINA
Белая
BELAYA
Усолье Сибирское
USOLE SIBIRSKOYE
Тельма
TELMA
Китой
KITOY
Ангарск
ANGARSK
Мегет
MEGET
Иркутск-Сорт
IRKUTSK-SORT
ИРКУТСК
IRKUTSK

IRKUTSKAYA OBLAST

UST-ORDINSKIY

V.A. OKRUG

❏ How the post was sent to Siberia

The building of the Trans-Siberian Railway revolutionized the carrying of mail across the vast Siberian steppes. By 1902 a letter could be carried from St Petersburg to Vladivostok in less than two weeks instead of several months as previously.

The first Siberian letter on record was that carried to Moscow in 1582 by some of Yermak's Cossacks, informed Tsar Ivan the Terrible that Siberia was now his. A regular postal system had been established in Siberia by 1600, Russian peasants being encouraged to emigrate to Siberia to work as Post House keepers and post-riders or *yamshchiki* (see p99). The post always had priority for the supply of horses and for right of way on the new post roads. Each Post House keeper had to keep some horses permanently in reserve in case the post should arrive, and on the road a blast of the courier's horn was enough to make other road users pull over and allow the post to pass. Indeed, the yamshchiki were not averse to using their whip on the drivers of carts which were slow to move out of the way.

In April 1829 the German writer, Adolph Erman, travelling down the still-frozen Lena River from Irkutsk to Yakutsk, wrote that he had 'the good luck of meeting the postman from Yakutsk and Kamchatka. At my desire he waited until the frozen ink which I carried with me had time to thaw, and a few lines to friends in Berlin were written and committed to his care. The courier, or paid overseer who attended the mail from Yakutsk to Irkutsk carried, as a mark of his rank and office, a sword and a loaded pistol, hanging by a chain from his neck. In winter he obtains from the peasants the requisite supply of sledges and horses; and when the ice-road is broken up he takes boats, sometimes, to ascend the Lena' (*Travels in Siberia*).

By the time Annette Meakin travelled along the Trans-Siberian Railway in 1900, she was able to send letters home speedily by train, but she had evidently heard about dishonest postal officials and she took pains to register all her letters. In *A Ribbon of Iron*, she wrote 'If you do not register in Siberia there is every chance that the stamps will be taken and the letter destroyed long before it reaches the border. You cannot register after 2pm, in which case it is advisable to use a black-edged envelope. Superstition will then prevent its being tampered with'. Black-edged envelopes were used during a period of mourning.

Much of the mail still travels by train, and passenger trains in Siberia often include a travelling post office coach in which mail is sorted. These have an aperture at platform level, through which letters and cards can be posted.

Philip Robinson (UK)

Philatelists may be interested to know that Philip Robinson is the author of *Russian Postmarks* and *Siberia – Postmarks and Postal History of the Russian Empire Period*. In 1999 he published a collection of railway postcards, *The Trans-Siberian Railway on Early Postcards*. Many of these postcards date from the 1890s and show scenes of railway construction and tunnel building.

Enquiries to the address on p2 concerning these books will be forwarded to Philip Robinson.

reason for this discrepancy is that the station was named at a time when the Trans-Siberian ran to Moscow via Chelyabinsk and not Yekaterinburg, and to Vladivostok through Manchuria not along the banks of the Amur.

Km5100: Malta Мальта
It was in a house in Malta, in February 1928, that farmer Platon Brilin was helping a comrade to build a cellar. While he was digging, his spade struck a white object which turned out to be a mammoth tusk carved into a female form. Excavations revealed dwellings with walls made from mammoth bones and roofs of antlers. He had discovered the remains of an ancient settlement, dating from the thirteenth millennium BC. A grave yielded the body of a child, still wearing a necklace and headband of bones. He may have been a young shaman (see p233) for the gods were thought to select their earthly representatives by branding them with some kind of deformity: the boy has two sets of teeth. Numerous figurines made of ivory have been found at Malta and also at the site in Buret, eight kilometres from here. Many of the excavated artefacts may be seen in the museums in Irkutsk. The oldest settlement in Russia that has so far been discovered is at Dering Yuryakh (1-2½ million years old) in northern Siberia near Yakutsk.

Km5124: Usole-Sibirskoe Усолье-Сибирское (●)
(pop: 106,900) This city, sitting on the left bank (western side) of the Angara River, is the salt capital of Siberia. Don't, however, expect to find Siberian salt mines here. Until 1956, all salt was produced by pumping salty water from shallow wells into pans; the water was then left to evaporate. These can still be seen on the left bank of the Angara River and on Varnichnoe Island. Nowadays the salt is produced at the **salt factory**, the biggest in Russia. It manufactures the Russian Extra brand of table salt, common throughout the country. The town's other big industrial plant is the 150-year-old **match factory**. Nearby, the **Usolye Health Resort** offers salt, sulphur and mud baths to cure afflictions of the limbs.

On the opposite side of the river is the nearly abandoned village of **Alexandrovskoe** which was renowned for the particularly brutal conditions of its Tsarist prison founded in 1873. In 1902 a failed revolt broke out here led by Felix Dzerzhinski. Many of the participants in the failed 1905 Revolution were imprisoned here.

Km5130 (N)
There is a large oil refinery here.

Km5133: Telma Тельма
Siberia's first textile mill opened here in 1731 and it still operates today, producing work clothing.

Km5160: Angarsk Ангарск (●)
(pop: 268,000) Although primarily an industrial city, Angarsk is well planned and still very attractive as the industrial and civic parts of it are separated by a wide green belt.

From the station, the industrial part is on the left (eastern side) and the civic area on the right. Angarsk's major industry is oil refining and oil is pumped here by pipeline from the West Siberian, Tatarstan and Baskir oil fields. This pipeline can occasionally be spotted running beside the railway.

The city has a river port and from here hydrofoils travel downstream to Bratsk. Ferries also run between Irkutsk and Angarsk, and coming here from Irkutsk makes a pleasant day trip.

Km5170: Meget Мегет Just north of Meget, there's a strategic reserve (N) of L and Ye 2-10-0s steam engines.

Km5178: Irkutsk Sortirovka Иркутск Сортировка This marshalling yard used to be a small station known as Innokentievskaya, in honour of St Innocent, Archbishop of Irkutsk, who was said to have been the first miracle-worker in Siberia. The **St Innocent Monastery of the Ascension** near here was founded in 1672.

The Tsar stopped here on his tour of Siberia in 1891 and the visit was thus described: 'After having listened to the singing, the Tsarevich (sic) knelt at the shrine of the Siberian Saint, kissed the relics and received the image of Innocent, presented to him by Agathangelius, Vicar of Irkutsk. At the same time a deputation from the Shaman Buryats expressed the desire of 250 men to adopt the orthodox religion and to receive the name of Nicholas in commemoration of the Tsarevich's visit to Siberia, which was thus to be preserved in the memory of their descendants. The Imperial traveller graciously acceded to this request.'

Km5182: Irkutsk Most Иркутск Мост Just east of this little station the railway crosses a bridge over the River Irkut, from which Irkutsk takes its name.

Km5185: Irkutsk Иркутск (●●●) [see p228]
(440m/1450ft, pop: 639,000)   Once known as the 'Paris of Siberia' Irkutsk is still a fascinating place and just 65km away is the beautiful Lake Baikal. From the railway you cannot see much of the centre of Irkutsk, located on the other side of the Angara River. In the distance, however, you can see the large Church of the Elevation of the Cross.

Km5214: Goncharovo Гончарово (pop: 49,300)   The town around the station is named Shelekhov (Шелехов) after the Russian merchant who led several trading expeditions to North America in the 1780s. He was made governor of the Russian settlement in America and become one of the richest merchants in Siberia, basing his empire in Irkutsk.

Passing through Goncharovo, you can see the town's main industry, the giant Irkutsk Aluminium Complex, founded in 1956. The train soon starts twisting and turning as it climbs the Primorski Mountains.

Winding through valleys of cedar and pine, and crossing numerous small streams, the train passes **Kultuk**, the junction for the old line from Port Baikal. At Km5228 (N) a giant etching of Lenin waves nonchalantly from the hill above. The line climbs steeply to Km5254 and then snakes downwards giving you your **first glimpses of Lake Baikal** from Kms5274-8.

After the tunnel (Km5290) there is a splendid view over the lake at Km5292 (N).

Km5297-8: There is a tunnel as the line curves sharply round the valley and descends to the water's edge. After the junction and goods yard at **Slyudyanka II** (Km5305) the train crawls along a part of the line that is prone to flooding from the lake and into the main station.

Km5312: Slyudyanka 1 Слюдянка 1 (●●) (pop: 20,100) The station is only about 500m from the lake which meant that when the train used to stop here for 15 minutes there was just enough time to run down to the water and dip your hand in for good luck (see p241). It now stops for only 10 minutes so only speedy sprinters should attempt this. Check with the carriage attendant that the train is stopping for the usual time and hurry down between the log cabins to the lake. You must be very quick; some people have been left behind doing this! ('The provodnitsas were horrified at your suggestion that it is possible to run down to Lake Baikal from Slyudyanka 1.' Howard Dymock, UK).

The station building was constructed in marble in 1904 to commemorate the building of the Circumbaikal Railway. There are usually interesting things to buy on the platform – sometimes even omul and boiled potatoes, or raspberries and bags of *orecha* (cedars seeds, the classic Siberian snack).

Although there are some photogenic log cabins near the station, Slyudyanka is a rather unattractive mining town; it does, however, have a basic hotel should you miss your train. It's a starting point for hikers and rafters who travel through the Khamar-

MAP 11

❑ The Circumbaikal Line

The original line from Irkutsk did not follow the route of the present railway but ran to Port Baikal. Until 1904 passengers crossed Lake Baikal on ferries which took them from Port Baikal to Mysovaya. In 1893 it had been decided that this short section of line along the mountainous southern shore of the lake would be impossibly expensive to build, and the plan was shelved in favour of the ferry link. From the English company of Armstrong and Mitchell a specially designed combined ice-breaker and train-ferry was ordered. The 4200-ton ship, christened the *Baikal*, had three pairs of rails laid across her decks for the carriages and could smash through ice up to four feet thick. A sister ship, the *Angara*, was soon brought into service. This ship has now been converted into a museum and is moored in Irkutsk (see p235).

The ferry system was not a great success, however. In mid-winter the ships were unable to break through the ice and in summer the wild storms for which the lake is notorious often delayed them. Since they could not accommodate more than 300 people between them, many passengers were subjected to a long wait beside the lake. The Trans-Siberian Committee realized that, however expensive it might prove, a line had to be built to bridge the 260km gap between the Mid-Siberian and the Transbaikal Railways. Further surveys were ordered in 1898 and in 1901 ten thousand labourers started work on the line.

This was the most difficult section to build on the entire railway. The terrain between Port Baikal and Kultuk (near Slyudyanka) was virtually one long cliff. Thirty-three tunnels and more than two hundred bridges and trestles were constructed, the task being made all the more difficult by the fact that in many places the labourers could reach the route only by boat. Work was carried on simultaneously on the Tankhoi to Mysovaya section.

The labour gangs hacked out embankments and excavated seven kilometres of tunnels but the line was not ready at the time it was most needed. On 8 February 1904, Japan attacked the Russian Navy while it lay at anchor in Port Arthur on the Pacific. Troops were rushed by rail from European Russia but when they arrived at Port Baikal, they found the *Baikal* and *Angara* ice-bound in the severe weather. The only way across the lake was a seventeen-hour march over the ice. It was then that the Minister of Ways of Communication, Prince Khilkov, put into action a plan which had been successful on several of Siberia's rivers: rails were laid across the ice. The first train to set off across the frozen lake did not get far along the forty-five kilometre track before the ice gave way with a crack like a cannon and the locomotive sank into the icy water. From then on the engines had to be stripped and their parts put on flatcars that were pulled over the ice by gangs of men and horses. Working as fast as possible, in all weathers, the Circumbaikal line was completed in September 1904 at a cost of about 70 million roubles. The first passengers found this section of the line particularly terrifying, not on account of the frequent derailments but because of the tunnels: there were none in European Russia at that time.

In the 1950s a short cut was opened between Irkutsk and Slyudyanka, which is the route followed by the train today. The line between Irkutsk and Port Baikal is now partly flooded and no longer used. The Port Baikal to Kultuk section, however, is still operational and makes an entertaining side-trip. See p244.

Daban Mountain Range to the south. Fur-trappers hunt sable and ermine in the forests around this area. From Slyudyanka, the 94km **Circumbaikal Railway** branch line runs along the shore of Lake Baikal to Port Baikal.

The train passes through a short tunnel and runs within sight of the water's edge for the next 180km. Some of the best views on the whole trip are along this section of the line.

Km5358: Baikalsk Байкальск (pop: 16,700) There is a basic hotel here, a base for walks and rafting in the Khamar-Daban Mountains.

About 3km past the town on the left is the **Baikalsk Cellulose and Paper Combine**, which makes an extremely strong cellulose used in air-craft tyres. Until recently it pumped its chlorine contaminated waste water directly into the lake which caused the number of crustacean species within a 50km radius of the factory to drop from 57 to 5. Not sur-prisingly, it was the brainchild of that environmental vandal Khrushchev who wanted to 'put Baikal to work'. It was Lake Baikal's biggest envi-

---

❏ **The Buryats**

The largest ethnic minority group in Siberia, these people are of Mongolian descent. When Russian colonists arrived in the lands around Lake Baikal, the Buryats were nomads who spent their time herding their flocks between the southern shores of the lake and what is now northern Mongolia, in search of pas-tureland. They lived in felt-covered yurts and practised a mixture of Buddhism and Shamanism.

The Buryats lived on fish from Lake Baikal, bear-meat and berries. However, their favourite food was said to be *urme*, the thick dried layer of scum skimmed from the top of boiled milk. They hunted the Baikal seal for its fur and in winter, when the lake was frozen, they would track these animals on the ice, wearing white clothing and pushing a white sledge as a hide. Back in their *yurts* the Buryats were not the cleanest of Siberian tribes, lacking even the most basic hygiene as the Soviet anthropologists Levin and Potapov point out in *The Peoples of Siberia*. Describing an after-dinner scene, they wrote: 'The vessels were not washed, as the spoons and cups were licked clean. An unwashed vessel was often passed from one member of the family to another as was the smoking pipe. Customs of this kind promoted the spread of various diseases.' Most of the diseases were probably brought by the Russian colonists.

Although at first hostile to the Russian colonists, the Buryats became involved in the fur trade with the Europeans and a certain amount of inter-mar-riage occurred. Some gave up their nomadic life and felt-covered *yurts* in favour of log cabins in Verkhneudinsk (now Ulan Ude) or Irkutsk. The Buryats, who number about 350,000, now have their own **Buryat Republic**, around the south-ern part of Lake Baikal. The capital, Ulan Ude, was opened to tourists in 1990 and is an interesting place to visit.

ronmental problem and because of the enormous cost of upgrading the plant and fitting filters, this destructive operation continued well into the 1990s. Despite the upgrading of the plant there are still occasional rumours of leaks of waste material into the lake.

Km5390: Vydrino Выдрино   The river just before the station marks the border of the **Buryat Republic**. This region, which is also known as Buryatia comprises an area of about 350,000 square kilometres (about the size of Italy). It was originally set aside for the Buryats (see p345), an indigenous ethnic group once nomadic but now adapted to an agricultural or urban life. Their republic is composed of mountainous taiga, and the economy is based on fur-farming, stock-raising, food and timber-processing and the mining of gold, aluminium, manganese, iron, coal, asbestos and mica. In fact, almost all the elements can be found here.

Km5421 (N):   The lonely-looking collection of ramshackle buildings by the water's edge might make a good photograph.

Km5426: Tankhoi Танхой (pop: 3000) Tankhoi sits in the middle of the 263,300-hectare **Baikalski Nature Reserve** which was created to preserve the Siberian taiga. Occasional ferries travel from here to Listvyanka and Port Baikal.

When Prince Borghese and his team were motoring through this area in 1907, taking part in the Peking to Paris Rally, they found that since the building of the railway, the Great Siberian Post Road had fallen into disrepair. Most of the post-stations were deserted and many of the bridges were rotten and dangerous. The Italians were given special permission by the governor-general to use the railway bridges. In fact they covered a considerable part of the journey here by driving along the railway line. However, their 40-horsepower Itala was not the only unorthodox vehicle to take to the rails. On his cycle-tour through south Siberia in 1896, RL Jefferson found it rather easier to pedal his Imperial Rover along the tracks than along the muddy roads.

Km5477: Mysovaya Мысовая (pop: 7200) This was the port where the *Baikal* and *Angara* (see p235) delivered their passengers (and their train).

When Annette Meakin and her mother disembarked from the *Baikal* in 1900, they were horrified to discover that the awaiting train was composed entirely of fourth class carriages. The brave ladies commandeered seats in the corner of one compartment but soon they were hemmed in by emigrating peasants. When two dirty moujiks climbed into the luggage rack above them, the ladies decided it would be better to wait at Mysovaya than spend four days in such claustrophobic conditions, and got out. However, the station-master allowed them to travel in an empty luggage-van, which gave them privacy but not comfort.

The village surrounding the town is known as Babushkin (Бабушкин) in honour of Lenin's friend and Irkutsk revolutionary. Ivan Babushkin was executed by Tsarist forces at the railway depot in 1906 and an obelisk marks the spot. While Mysovaya is still a major Baikal port, over 70 per cent of the village's population works for the railways.

Between Mysovaya and Petrovsky Zavod the line skirts around the lower reaches of the Khamar Daban Mountain Range. Around Km5536, the line enters the wide valley of the Selenga River, which it follows as far as Ulan Ude (Km5642).

Km5504: Boyarski Боярский The hills on the right of the station are all that remain of the volcanoes of the Khamar-Daban foothills. East of the station, the railway moves away from Lake Baikal.

Km5530: Posolskaya Посольская About 500m west of this station, the train crosses over a narrow, shallow river with the odd name of Bolshaya Rechka (Big Little Stream). Approximately 10km downstream from here the river flows into Lake Baikal at the site of the ancient village of Possolskoe. In previous centuries, Russian ambassadors travelling

❏ American soldiers die defending communists

During the Russian Civil War, American, Canadian and Japanese troops occupied parts of eastern Siberia and the Russian Far East helping the White Russian forces battling the communists. The undisciplined White Russians were often little more than bandits and murderers, and the allied forces were often put in the difficult position of supporting the White Army while trying to protect the Russian population from them. What happened at Posolskaya station in January 1920 was just one of many unpleasant incidents that resulted in the allied forces losing complete faith in the White Army.

The White Army General Nicholas Bogomolets arrested the station master at Ulan Ude and announced that he would execute him for Bolshevist activities. The American Colonel Morrow, based in Ulan Ude, threatened to call out 2500 soldiers under his command unless the innocent man was released. Bogomolets retreated with the railway official to Posolskaya in his armoured train, where he opened fire in the middle of the night on the boxcar barracks of a small American garrison comprising one officer and 38 enlisted men. These soldiers swarmed out of their quarters, dropped into a skirmish line and blazed away. Sergeant Carl Robbins disabled the train's locomotive with a hand grenade before being killed. At the cost of two dead and one wounded on their side, the Americans captured the train, the general, six other officers and 48 men.

Bogomolets was released for political reasons and emigrated to Hollywood before being deported to Latvia. Sergeant Robbins and Second Lieutenant Paul Kendall posthumously received the Distinguished Service Cross.

to Asian countries used to rest here and the rough village got a mention in the papers of Ambassador Fyodor Baikov when he visited it in 1656. In 1681, an abbot and a monk built a large walled monastery here but it has long since disappeared. Today Bolshaya Rechka hosts the Baikalski Priboi (Baikal Surf) Holiday Camp.

Km5562: Selenga Селенга The town was founded as a stockaded outpost in the 17th century on the Selenga River. Unfortunately the wood-pulping factories are rather more in evidence than the 16th century monastery which was the centre for missionaries attempting the conversion of the Buryats. The factories here and in Ulan Ude are notorious for pumping their industrial waste into the Selenga River which flows into Lake Baikal. Pollution from the Selenga and the once notorious but now upgraded cellulose and paper mill at Baikalsk has affected over 60 per cent of the lake and even if the pollution stopped tomorrow, it would take 400 years for the waste to be flushed out.

Km5596: Lesovozny Лесовозный The town around the station is called Ilnika (Ильинка). About 28km east of the station, the train crosses over Selenga River which provides an excellent photo opportunity. At Km5633-4 (N) there's an army camp with some abandoned tanks.

The train approaches Ulan Ude along the right bank (northern side) of the Selenga River and about 1km on the left before the station is a monument to five railway workers executed by the Tsarist forces in 1906 for revolutionary activities.

Km5642: Ulan Ude Улан-Уде (●●●)　　　　　　　[see p250]
(544m/1785ft, pop: 366,000) Ulan Ude is the capital of the Buryat Republic. Stretch your legs on the platform where there is a **steam loco** (Class Su) preserved outside the locomotive workshop (N) at the western end of the station. Turn to p370 for the **Trans-Mongolian route to Beijing**.

Two km east of the station, you cross over Uda River and after another 500m, you can see the Palace of Culture (N) and a WWII memorial.

Km5655: Zaudinski Заудинский The line to Mongolia branches off from the Trans-Siberian here.

Km5675 (N): Onokhoi Онохой There is a large number of **steam locos** at the west end of the station. From Onokhoi, the train follows the valley of the River Brian. From Zaigraevo (Km5696), the line begins to climb to Ilka, on the river of the same name. It continues to ascend the Zagon Dar range, reaching the highest point (882m/2892ft) at Kizha.

Km5734: Novoilinski Новоильинский About 20km past this station, the train crosses the **administrative frontier** between the Republic of Buryatia and Chitinskaya Oblast. The 432,000 square kilometres of the Chitinskaya Oblast comprise a series of mountain ranges interspersed with wide valleys. The dominant range is the Yablonovy (highest peak: Sokhondo, 2510m/8200ft) which is crossed by the Trans-Siberian near Amazar. The mountains are covered in a vast forest of conifers and the climate is dry. The economy is based on mining (gold, tungsten, tin, lead, zinc, molybdenum, lithium, lignite), timber-processing and fur-farming.

Km 5781-8183 TIME ZONE MT + 6

Km5784: Petrovski Zavod Петровский Завод (●●●) (pop 28,300)

Local time is now Moscow Time + 6 hours. The name of the station means 'Peter's Factory', after the ironworks founded in 1789 and still going strong. It was built to supply iron for the gold mines in the region. The factory was rebuilt in 1939 next to the railway and from the train you can see the flames from the open-hearth furnaces.

In 1830, the factory was operated by Decembrists brought from nearby Chita and housed in the factory prison. A **monument** and large memorial to them can be seen on the station's platform. There is also a **Decembrist museum** in the former house of Ekaterina Trubetskoi. Princess Trubetskoi (1800-54) was the first wife of a Decembrist to voluntarily follow her husband into exile. In doing so, she renounced her civil rights and noble privileges. Her name is immortalized in *Russian Women*, a poem by Nekrasov. Stretching along the railway in the narrow

---

❏ **The Transbaikal Railway (Kms5483-6532)**

In 1895 work was begun to connect Mysovaya (the port on Lake Baikal) with Sretensk, on the Shilka River near Kuenga, where passengers boarded steamers for the voyage to Khabarovsk. Materials were shipped to Vladivostok and thence by boat along the Ussuri, Amur and Shilka Rivers. There was a shortage of labour, for it proved impossible to get the local Buryats to work on the line. Gangs of reluctant convicts were brought in, although they became more interested in the operation after it was decided that they should receive 50 kopecks a day in return for their labour.

The terrain is mountainous and the line meanders up several valleys and over the Yablonovy range. Owing to the dry climate, work could continue throughout the winter, although water was in short supply during these months. Workers were also faced with the problem of permafrost which necessitated the building of bonfires to thaw the ground, or dynamite to break it up. A terrible set-back occurred in July 1887, when 350km of track and several bridges were swept away in a freak flood. The line was completed in early 1900 by which time it had cost over 60 million roubles.

river valley between the mountain ridges, Petrovskiy Zavod makes an interesting day-trip from Chita.

East of Petrovskiy Zavod, the line turns north-east into the wide, picturesque valley of the Khilok River, which it follows for almost 300kms to Sokhondo, crossing the Yablonovy range between Mogzon and Chita.

Km5883: Look out for the large graveyard of old steam locomotives.

Km5884: Bada Aeroport Бада Аэропорт The little town is clearly a product of the aerodrome and not vice versa: it's built around a large Soviet monument, a Mig fighter plane facing skyward. The runway (N) is interesting for the large numbers of old aircraft that congregate here. These might make an interesting photograph but discretion is advised.

Km5899 (S): A good place for a photo along the train as it travels on higher ground beside the river. Also at Km5908 (S), when the train winds slowly along the water's edge.

Km5932: Khilok Хилок (●) (805m/2640ft, pop: 13,700) East of this small industrial town you continue to climb gently up the valley beside the Khilok. There are pleasant views over the wide plain all along the river. North of the line are the Khogoy and Shentoy mountains, part of the Tsagan Khuntei range. Near the station a granite monument topped with a star commemorates 11 communists slain here during the Civil War.

The train now crosses the Yablonovy Mountains. The eastern escarpment is steeper than the western side and heavy freight trains travelling westwards invariably require extra engines.

Km6053: Mogzon Могзон (●●) (907m/2975ft) There's a steam dump in this dismal town and, for several km around this town, a number of heavily guarded prisons; there is one of these at Km6055 (N).

Km6093: Sokhondo Сохондо (944m/3,095ft) This station is named after the highest peak (2510m/8230ft) in the Yablonovy range. The line leaves the river valley and climbs over the Yablonovy. There is a long view at Km6097 (N). About 7km east of here you reach the **highest point on the line** (989m/3242ft). In the 1914 edition of his *Russia with Teheran, Port Arthur and Peking*, Karl Baedeker drew his readers' attention to the '93 yard tunnel inscribed at its western entrance "To the Great Ocean" and at its eastern entrance "To the Atlantic Ocean" in Russian', that was here. The line has now been re-routed up onto a huge grassy plain. It then descends steeply through Yablonovaya and there are several good views (Kms6107-9).

Km6116 (S): There was a graveyard of **steam locomotives** here but now most of the engines have been dismantled. West of the town of Ingoda, the train enters the narrow winding valley of the Ingoda River, which it follows for the next 250km east. The line passes through Chernovskaya, where lignite is mined.

Km6125: Yablonovaya (Яблоновая) At 1040m/3412ft this is the highest point on the line. About 20km south in the settlement of Drovyanaya (Дровяная) are 50 nuclear missile silos which house SS-17 or SS-19 inter-ballistic nuclear rockets.

Km6131 (S): The line crosses a picturesque meadow with a stream meandering across it. Good for a photograph when the flowers are out in May and June.

Km6197: (N) About 2km west of Chita is the 16 square kilometre Kenon Lake. Only 6m deep, the lake is warmed by the nearby power station and at its eastern end there's a popular beach beside the railway line.

  Further on the train crosses the small Chita River, and about 1km before the main station you pass through Chita 1 station where a railway factory is located.

Km6199: Chita Чита (●●●) [see p258] (655m/2150ft, pop: 376,000) Founded in 1655, the capital of the Chitinskaya Oblast stands beside the Chita and Ingoda rivers, surrounded by low hills. A stockaded fort was built here by the Cossacks at the end of the 17th century and the town became an important centre on the Chinese trade route.

  In 1827 a large group of exiled Decembrists arrived here and spent the first few months building the prison that was to be their home for the following three years. Many stayed on after they had served their sentence and the development of the town in the 19th century into an industrial and cultural centre was largely due to their efforts.

East of the city of Chita, the train continues to follow the left bank of the Ingoda River downhill for the next 250kms. The line passes through

MAP 12

Баляга BALYAGA
Тарбагатай TARBAGATAI
Ново-Павловка NOVO-PAVLOVKA
Толбага TOLBAGA
Хохотуй KHOKHOTAY
Бада BADA
Жипхеген ZHIPKHEGEN
Хилок KHILOK
Хушенга KHUSHENGA
Харагун KHARAGUN
Могзон MOGZON
Сохондо SOKHONDO
Яблоновая YABLONOVAYA
Лесной LESNOY
Ингода INGODA
Черновская CHERNOVSKAYA
Кадала KADALA
ЧИТА CHITA
CHITINSKAYA OBLAST
Khilok R.
Ingoda R.

Novaya, where the original community and the whole of the town were wiped out in the great flood of 1897. At Km6225 (S) there's a collection of log cabins (some of them quite photogenic), which looks rather vulnerable, being built on the edge of the river flood plain.

Km6265: Darasun Дарасун **(●)** Darasun is renowned for its carbonic mineral springs and the water from them has been exported to China and Korea for years. Near the station is a sanatorium where various cardiovascular and intestinal ailments are treated.

About 1km east of the station there's a good view as the train snakes along the river.

Km6270: Army supply base surrounded by a wooden stockade.

Km6293: Karymskaya Карымская **(●●●)** (605m/1985ft)   Small industrial town first settled by the Buryats.

Km6312: Tarskaya Тарская   Formerly known as Kaidalovo, this is the junction for the **railway to Beijing via Manchuria (see p381)**. A whitewashed church stands on the hill (S) above the village. Good views along the river at Km6316 (S) and across the wide plains for the next 100km, especially around Km6332 (S) and Km6369 (S). There are large fields around the river and bare hills to the north. The best views are all to the south, across to Mongolia.

Km6417: Onon Онон (515m/1690ft)   A few kilometres east of here the clear waters of the Ingoda River are joined by those of the muddy Onon, on whose banks the great Mongol leader, Genghis Khan, was born in 1162. The Onon and the Ingoda together form the Shilka River, a tributary of the mighty Amur. The railway follows the picturesque valley of the Shilka for the next 120kms.

Km6446: Shilka Шилка **(●)** (505m/1655ft, pop: 18,200)   This village on the Shilka River was founded in 1897 just to serve the railway. Two years later it became a popular tourist destination with the opening of the Shivanda Health Resort (*shivanda* means royal drink in the local indigenous language). Mineral water was and still is used to treat digestive and respiratory system disorders. A few years later the discovery of gold nearby brought more visitors. In 1954 fluoric spar, a mineral essential in chemistry and metallurgy, was discovered in the area.

There are several interesting-looking wooden buildings near the platform.

Crossing the Kiya River, the train continues over a great wide plain, grazing land for cattle that you may see being rounded up on horseback.

Km6496: Priiskavaya Приисковая **(●)**   The name means a mine, referring to the gold mining town of **Nerchinsk (Нерчинск)**, 10km down a branch line from here. It was here that the Treaty of Nerchinsk was signed in 1689, depriving the Russians of the valuable Amur region. The treaty gave the Manchurian emperor control over the Russian Far East for the next 170 years.

Nerchinsk was the centre of a rich silver, lead and gold mining district in Tsarist times. The mines were known to the Buryats long before the arrival of the Russians in the seventeenth century. In 1700, a Greek mining engineer founded the Nerchinski Zavod (Works) and the first convict gangs arrived in 1722. George Kennan visited the mine in 1887 and was shown around by one of the convict labourers. Not all the mines were the property of the Tsar and some owners became immensely wealthy. In one mansion he visited in Nerchinsk, Kennan could hardly believe that such opulence and luxury (tapestries, chandeliers, Oriental rugs, silk curtains and a vast ball-room) were to be found in one of the wildest parts of Siberia. From 1826 to 1917, the mines of Nerchinsk were a major Tsarist labour camp.

Today Nerchinsk has 17,000 inhabitants and some interesting sights. These include the early 19th century Resurrection Cathedral and the house of rich merchant, Butin, which was built in the popular Moorish style in the 1860s. Next door is the Hotel Dauriya (closed) where Chekhov stayed in 1890. There is a museum and basic hotel in Nerchinsk.

On the south side of Priiskavaya station is the small village of **Kalinino**. The famous Russian explorer Erofei Pavlovich Khabarov is buried under the walls of the old church. It is believed, however, that the corpse in the grave is actually his brother, Nikifor, the last resting place of Erofei remaining unknown.

Kms6511-2 (S): Standing just across the river is a large deserted church with another building beside it. In the middle of nowhere and with a thick forest of conifers rising behind them, these two lonely-looking buildings make an eminently photogenic scene.

MAP 13

ЧИТА CHITA
Песчанка PESCHANKA
Атамановка ATAMANOVKA
Новая NOVAYA
Маккавеево MAKKAVEYEVO
Дарасун DARASUN
Карымская KARYMSKAYA
Тарская TARSKAYA
Урульга URULGA
Зубарево ZUBAREVO
Размахнино RAZMAKHNINO
Солнцевая SOLNTSEVAYA
Онон ONON
Шилка-Пасс. SHILKA-PASS.
Холбон KHOLBON
Приисковая PRIISKOVAYA
Нерчинск NERCHINSK
Куэнга KUENGA
Укурей UKUREY
Чернышевск-Забайкал. CHERNISHEVSK
Сретенск SRETENSK
Бушулей BUSHULEY
Хоктонга KHOKTONGA
Зилово ZILOVO
Ульякан ULYAKAN
ЧИТИНСКАЯ ОBLAST

Km6532: Kuenga Куэнга (●) Junction for the line which runs 52km to the east to **Sretensk (Сретенск)**, which was the eastern end of the Transbaikal railway. Sretensk sits on the eastern bank of the Shilka River which flows into the mighty Amur River. The Amur marks the Chinese-Russian border for hundreds of kilometres, before passing through Khabarovsk on its way north to the Pacific. It was this river route that put Sretensk on Russian maps and it was a thriving river-port in the nineteenth and early twentieth centuries (considerably larger than Chita) before the Amur Railway was opened in 1916. Passengers transferred here to the ships of the Amur Steamship and Trade Company. Most of the forty steamers that plied between Sretensk and Khabarovsk were made either in Belgium or the Glasgow yards of Armstrong and Co. Waiting here with her mother in 1900, Annette Meakin caught sight of some Chinese men with their traditional pig-tails. She was not impressed and wrote, 'To me their appearance was quite girlish.'

Sretensk (pop: 10,300) is spread over both banks of the river with the centre on the eastern bank and the railway station on the high western bank. The two were joined only in 1986 when a bridge across the river was built. There is a museum and basic hotel in Sretensk. It's not as interesting to visit as Nerchinsk, however. In 1916 the Amur Railway was completed and Sretensk, bypassed, became a backwater.

The line leaves the Shilka River here, turns north, crosses the plain and climbs towards the eastern end of the Yablonovy Mountain Range.

Km6593:Chernyshevsk-Zabaikalski Чернышевск-Забайкальский (●●●) Nikolai Chernyshevsky (1828-1889) was a revolutionary who toiled for years at hard-labour camps in the region.

After this stop, the train ascends into the foothills of the Yablonovy range towards Zilovo.

Km6629: Bushulei Бушулей This is not the easiest area in which to build a railway as the Trans-Siberian engineers discovered. In winter it was bitterly cold and in the hot summers all surface water dried up. For most of the year, the ground had to be thawed out with gigantic bonfires before the track could be laid.

The complex around the station is a molybdenum ore enrichment plant. The mineral is added to steel to make it suitable for high-speed cutting tools. Scattered along the line are other molybdenum and gold mines.

Km6670: Zilovo Зилово (●) The town is called Aksenovo-Zilovskoe (Аксеново-Зиловское). To the south were the gold mines of the Kara region, also visited by Kennan, who found 2500 convicts working under the most appalling conditions. These mines were the property of the Tsar and from them and the other Imperial mines in Eastern Siberia, he could expect an average of 3600 pounds (1630kg) of pure gold each year.

Km6789: Ksenevskaya Ксеньевская The line continues across the forested southern slopes of the Eastern Yablonovy range for the next 200km with occasional good views over the trees.

Km6906: Mogocha Могоча (●●) (pop: 17,500) This ugly railway settlement, located in the Bolshoy Amazar River Valley, is probably one of the harshest place to live on the Trans-Siberian route because of the permafrost and the summer sun. In winter the top 10 centimetres of earth that thawed over the summer freeze over again in temperatures as low as -60°C (-87°F), killing all but the hardiest plants while the intense summer sun singes most young shoots. The town was founded in 1910 when this section of the Trans-Siberian was being built and later became the base for geological research expeditions seeking gold in the hills.

The town of **Olekminsk** on the Lena River lies about 700km due north of here (this being no more than a short hike to a Siberian, for as

---

❑ The Amur Railway (Kms6532-8531)

The building of the Amur Railway was proposed in the early 1890s but surveys showed that it would prove expensive, on account of the difficult terrain. More than one hundred bridges would be needed and many kilometres of embankments. Furthermore much of the region was locked in permafrost. In 1894, when the government signed the treaty with China allowing Russian rails to be laid across Manchuria, from Chita to Vladivostok, the Amur project was abandoned in favour of this considerably shorter route. This change of plan proved to be something of a false economy, for the East Chinese line, despite the considerable saving in distance, was ultimately to cost more than the whole of the rest of the Trans-Siberian Railway.

After Russia's embarrassing defeat by Japan in the 1904-5 War, the government realized the vulnerability of their East Chinese line. Japan was as keen as Russia to gain control of the rich lands of Manchuria and if they did decide to invade, the Russian naval base of Vladivostok would be deprived of a rail link with European Russia. A line within Russian lands was needed. The Amur project was reconsidered and, in 1907, approved.

Construction began in 1908 at Kuenga and for most of the 2000kms the line would follow a route about 100km north of the Amur River, out of range of Manchuria on the southern bank of the river. Winters are particularly harsh in this region and consequently track-laying could only take place over the four warmer months and even in mid-summer considerable amounts of dynamite were needed to blast through the permafrost. There were the usual problems with insects and disease but as the rest of the railway was operating it was comparatively easy to transport workers in from west of the Urals. By 1916 the long bridge over the Amur at Khabarovsk had been completed and the railway was opened. The Japanese were now Russia's allies and in 1918 (as allies to the White Russians) took over the running of the Amur Railway during the Civil War.

Intourist guides love to tell you, 'In Siberia a thousand kilometres is nothing to travel and a litre of vodka is nothing to drink', although they no longer add 'and a hundred roubles is nothing to spend' since it certainly isn't. As well as holding the world record for greatest temperature range – from minus 60°C (-87°F) to plus 45°C (113°F). Olekminsk was the place of exile in the eighteenth century for a bizarre Christian sect whose followers were known as the Skoptsy. They saw their salvation in abstinence and castrated themselves to be sure of a place in heaven. They lived in mixed communities, which they referred to as 'ships', each having a 'helmsman' and 'crew'. They avoided drink and tobacco and were excellent farmers. Since Olekminsk is experiencing something of a baby-boom at present it must be assumed that the more unconventional practices of the Skoptsy have been abandoned.

Km7010: Amazar Амазар **(●●)** There are the remains of a large strategic reserve of steam engines here. About 100km south the Shilka flows into the Amur River ('Heiling Chu' to the Chinese). The Amur rises in Mongolia and flows 2800km along the frontier with China into the Pacific at the Sea of Okhotsk. The river is exceptionally rich in fish and navigable for six months of the year. After initial explorations along the Amur by the Russians in the seventeenth century, following the Treaty of Nerchinsk with the Chinese in 1689, they were kept out of the region for the next 150 years. Colonization began in the mid-nineteenth century and the Cossacks established garrisons along the river. By 1860 there were 60 villages with a population of 11,000 in the Amur Basin. The Amur is still a vital communications link in the area.

Km7075: The **administrative frontier** between Chitinskaya and Amurskaya Oblasts also marks the border between Siberia and the Far Eastern Territories. **Amurskaya** covers 360,000 square kilometres in the middle part of the Amur basin and extends to the Stanovoy Range in the north. The southern region of the oblast is a fertile plain where wheat, soya-beans, flax and sun-flowers are grown. Most of the area in the north is under thick forest.

Km7119: Yerofei-Pavlovich Ерофей Павлович **(●●●)** Named in honour of the brutal explorer, Yerofei Pavlovich Khabarov (see p89). At the east end of the station (N) is a **preserved locomotive** (Em726-88) on a plinth.

The river through the town is called the Urka and it was down this that Khabarov travelled with his mercenaries in 1649 to reach the Amur River. The river route opened up a shortcut to the Russian Far East from Yakutsk.

This area is particularly inhospitable with frosts lasting from the middle of October to the beginning of April, with an average January temperature of -33°C. Patches of snow can be found on the shaded sides of mountains as late as July.

Km7211: Urusha Уруша (●) Running mostly downhill, for the next 100kms the line passes through an area of taiga interspersed with uncultivated plains, most of it locked in permafrost.

Km7266: Takhtamigda Тахтамыгда A small settlement with a view (N) across the river valley. The good views to the north continue for the next 150kms. About half a kilometre east of the village, also (N), stands a prison, surrounded with barbed wire and patrolled by guards in blue uniforms.

Km7273: Bamovskaya Бамовская This is a junction with the Little BAM, the line which runs north to join the Baikal–Amur Mainline (see p131). It is not advisable to get off a train here without knowing when your connecting train up the Little BAM will arrive as only a few head north each day. There is no hotel here.

East of the junction there are good views (S) between Km7295 and Km7300.

Km7306: Skovorodino Сковородино (●●●) (pop: 14,100) Named after a revolutionary leader killed here in 1920 during the Russian Civil War, Skovorodino is the first stop on the Trans-Siberian line for trains that travel down the Little BAM from Tynda to Khabarovsk. If you are getting off the Trans-Siberian to go up the Little BAM, Skovorodino is better than nearby Bamovskaya as there is a hotel. There's also the railway depot, forestry mills and the permafrost scientific research station.

You can see a lime-green P36-0091 **steam locomotive** by the platform of this station.

Km7323: Bolshoy Never Большой Невер On the left (N) side of the railway is the 800km long Amur Yakutsk Highway ('highway' being something of a misnomer) which ends in **Yakutsk** (see p248). Yakutsk is the capital of the Republic of Sakha, formerly known as Yakutia. This must be one of the least pleasant parts of the

MAP 14

Ульякан
ULYAKAN
Урюм
URYUM

Сбега
SBEGA

Ксеньевская
KSENEVSKAYA

Кислый Ключ
KISLYY KLUG

Артеушка
ARTEUSHKA

Раздольное
RAZDOLNOYE

Могоча
MOGOCHA
Таптугары
TAPTUGARY
Семиозерный
SEMIOZERNYY

Амазар
AMAZAR

Жанна
ZHANNA

Ерофей Павлович
YEROFEY PAVLOVICH

Уруша
URUSHA

Тахтамыгда
TAKHTAMIGDA

Бам
BAM   В.А.М.
Сковородино
SKOVORODINO

CHITINSKAYA OBLAST

AMURSKAYA OBLAST

❏ **The Yakuts**
These people, who number about 300,000, form the largest ethnic group in the
Far Eastern Territories. They were originally semi-nomadic herders who roamed
around the lands beside the Lena River. What seems to have struck nineteenth-
century travellers most about the Yakuts was their rather squalid lifestyle. They
never washed or changed their clothes, they shared their huts with their reindeer
and preferred their meat and fish once it had begun to rot. They drank a form of
koumiss (fermented mare's milk) which they froze, sometimes into huge boul-
ders. To give the Yakuts their due, they were considerably more advanced than
many other Siberian tribes. Although they were ignorant of the wheel (hardly
much use in such a cold climate), they used iron for weapons and tools. Most
Yakut clans possessed a blacksmith who was usually also a shaman, since metal-
working was considered a gift from the gods. The Yakuts were unique among
Siberian tribes in that they made pottery. Russian colonists treated the Yakuts
badly and demanded fur tributes for the Tsar. They have now almost completely
adopted the Russian culture and although some are still involved in reindeer-
herding, most Yakuts work in mining and the timber industry.

world to live in, for the region, which is about thirteen times the size of
Britain, is entirely covered with permafrost. Even in mid-summer, the soil
in Yakutsk is frozen solid to a depth of over 100 metres.

To the east the scenery becomes more interesting. There are good views
at Kms7318-25 (N) and around Km7335 (N). After the tunnel (Kms7343-
5) there's a long view (S) down the valley towards China. More views (S)
at Km7387 and Kms7426-28.

Km7501: Magdagachi Магдагачи (●●●)   The train continues to
descend gently, through Magdagachi, out of the taiga and onto a wide
plain. There may be a short stop at Tigda about 60kms after Magdagachi.

Km7602: Ushumun Ушумун   The border with China is no more than
forty kilometres south-west of here. The train turns south-east again and
soon crosses an obvious climatic boundary and a not so obvious one
marking the southern border of permafrost. From now on the larches
grow much taller, reaching 35m, and birches and oaks spring up. These
oaks are different from the European oaks as they do not lose their leaves
in winter but retain them even though they are stiff and brown.

   The train continues south-east across flat lands with small clumps of
trees.

Km7723: Shimanovskaya Шимановская (●) (pop: 26,500) Named
after a revolutionary hero, this town played an important part in the devel-

opment of both the Trans-Siberian and the BAM railways. There's a small museum in Shimanovskaya.

To the south the land becomes more fertile and parts of the wide plain are under cultivation.

Km7772: Ledinaya Лединая Hidden away in the trees just to the north of this station is the once secret Svobodni-18 Cosmodrome. Until the early 1990s, the base housed 60 SS-11 inter-ballistic rockets (which can each carry a single nuclear warhead 10,000km) but following the START missile reduction agreement, the base has become redundant. All but five of the missile silos has been destroyed. It will not be closed down, however, as the Russian space sector believes that the site has several advantages over the northern Russian Plesetsk Cosmodrome, one of which is that it is at a lower latitude (meaning smaller rockets for the same payload) than Plesetsk.

If you try to visit the site you will probably not get any further than the station. Good luck.

Km7815: Svobodny Свободный (●) (pop: 81,000) An attractive town sitting on the right bank of the Zeya River, Svobodny has a proud and tragic history associated with the railways. It was founded in 1912 and originally named Alekseyevsk, in honour of the Tsar's haemophiliac son, Alexis. It expanded rapidly into a major railway town with factories building carriages, and with a hospital, schools and an orphanage all sponsored by the railways. By the mid 1930s it was the headquarters of both the Amur section of the Trans-Siberian and the new BAM project. There's a **railway museum** here.

Beyond the town the line crosses the Zeya River the largest Russian tributary of the Amur River. In the rainy season the water level may rise as fast as 30cm an hour and 10m high floods have been recorded. The area beyond the river, called the Zeysko-Bureinskaya Plain, is the main granary for the Russian Far East. This is the most highly populated area of the Amur region with villages

MAP 15

СКОВОРОДИНО
SKOVORODINO
Б. Невер
B. NEVER

188

Талдан
TALDAN

Гонжа
GONZHA

Магдагачи
MAGDAGACHI
Сулус
SULUS

CHINA

Тыгда
TIGDA

Ушумун
USHUMUN

Сиваки
SIVAKI

AMURSKAYA OBLAST

372

Мухинская
MUKHINSKAYA

Берея
BEREYA

Шимановская
SHIMANOVSKAYA

Ледяная
LEDYANAYA
Бузули
BUZULI
Свободный
SVOBODNYY
М.Чесноковская
M.CHESNOKOVSKAYA
Серышево
SERISHEVO

every 10 to 20km, separated by fields of barley, soya beans or melons. The climate and landscape are very similar to parts of Ukraine and attracted many Ukrainians last century. Today over half the locals are of Ukrainian descent. You can easily spot the Ukrainian houses (*khatas*), which are white-washed. The solid log constructions with overlapping log ends are Russian.

Km7873: Belogorsk (●●●) Белогорск (pop: 75,000) Some of the older folk who make up the 70,000 inhabitants of this agricultural centre must find it difficult to remember the current name of their city as it has

❑ **The New York of Siberia**
Belogorsk is the junction for the line to **Blagoveshchensk**, a large industrial centre of 200,000 people. Sited on the left bank of the Amur River, it is the administrative capital of Amurskaya Oblast. Blagoveshchensk means 'Good News', for it was here in 1858 that Count Muravyev-Amurski announced the success of the treaty with China that granted Russia the Amur region. The city became a centre of colonization and grew fast in the second half of the nineteenth century. The locals called it the New York of Siberia because its streets were laid out on a grid pattern, American-style. It became the major port on the voyage between Sretensk and Khabarovsk in the days before the completion of the Amur Railway.

In July 1900, Blagoveshchensk was the scene of the cold-blooded massacre of the entire Chinese population of the town (several thousand people) by the Cossack forces. This was in retaliation for the murders of Europeans in China during the Boxer Rebellion. Annette Meakin wrote: 'The Cossacks, who were little better than savages, threw themselves on the helpless Chinese ... and drove them down to the water's edge. Those who could not get across on rafts were either brutally massacred on the banks or pushed into the water and drowned. The scene which followed was horrible beyond description, and the river was black with dead bodies for weeks afterwards. I have this from no less than five eye-witnesses.'

Good relations between the people of Blagoveshchensk and their Chinese neighbours across the river in the city of Hei-Hei have been cemented over the last few years with the development of a major trade route here. Siberian lumber and machinery is ferried across the Amur to be exchanged for Chinese consumer goods. Hei-Hei is connected by a railway to Harbin and Beijing. There is no bridge over the river but ferries travel six times a day between Hei-Hei and Blagoveshchensk. Currently, however, this border crossing is open only to Russian and Chinese nationals.

Blagoveshchensk has enough of interest to occupy a couple of days. The best accommodation is at *Hotel Zeya* (☎ 41622-21100), ul Kalinina 8. Travel agents can help organize the river crossing and rail tickets on the other side. They include Intourist (☎ 416 22-45772), ul Lenina 108/2, and Amurturist (☎ 416 22-27798, 90377, 23122, ▤ 27798, 23122), ul Kuznechnaya 1.

been changed so many times. It was founded in 1860 with the original name of Aleksandrovka. This stuck until 1935 when the local council decided it should be changed in favour of the rather more impressive Kuybyshevkavostochnaya. Just when everyone had got used to this exotic mouthful, it changed again, to boring Belogorsk.

There's a branch line from Belogorsk to **Blagoveshchensk** (see p360). In Belogorsk you can stay at the basic *Hotel Zarya* (☎ 24101-23750), ul Partizanskaya 23.

You can see a P36-0091 **steam locomotive** as you leave the station.

Km7992: Zavitaya Завитая (●) (pop: 22,300) This town is famous
for soya bean oil and soya flour. There is a 90km branch line to the south which terminates at Poyarkovo on the Chinese-Russian border. Only Chinese and Russian passport holders can cross here.

Km8037: Bureya Бурея (●) On the river of the same name, this town
was formerly the centre of a large gold mining region. It now produces tools for the coal mining industry.

The area was once inhabited by several different tribes most of whom were Shamanists. The **Manegres** were a nomadic people whose trademark was to keep their heads shaven, except for one long pig-tail. The **Birars** lived in hive-shaped huts beside the Bureya and grew vegetables and fruit. North of here lived **Tungus** (Evenki), who were hunters and the **Orochen** who herded reindeer.

To the east were the **Goldi**, described thus in the *1900 Guide to the Great Siberian Railway*: 'They are below average stature, and have a broad and flat face with a snub nose, thick lips, eyes shaped after the Mongolian fashion and prominent cheek-bones ... The women adorn themselves with earrings and pendants. Some of them, as a mark of particular elegance, introduce one or several small rings into the partition of the nose. The people of this tribe are characterized by great honesty, frankness and good will ... Their costume is very various and of all colours; they may at different times be seen wearing a Russian overcoat, a fish-skin suit or the Chinese dress.'

Km8088: Arkhara Архара (●●●) A long stop at the station here is
usual, with women selling snacks and fruit on the platform.

Km8118: Uril Урил On the right (S) side of the railway from here to
the next station of Kundur is the Khingan Nature Reserve. The sanctuary consists of swampy lowlands dotted with Amur velvet trees and Korean cedar pine woods with a thick undergrowth of hazel trees, wild grapes and wild pepper which is related to ginseng. The sanctuary is rich in Mongol and Siberian animals seldom encountered elsewhere, such as a raccoon-like dog.

Km 8150-8198: There are good photo opportunities on this stretch as the train winds around the valleys.

Km 8167: A second tunnel is under construction here.

Km8184: This is the administrative frontier between Amurskaya Oblast and Khabarovski Krai. **Khabarovski** is, like much of Russia east of the Urals, almost entirely composed of swampy taiga. In the far south, however, there is an area of deciduous trees. The krai is extremely rich in minerals but the economy is currently based on wood-processing, fishing and the petroleum industry.

—————————— **Km 8184-9289 TIME ZONE MT + 7** ——————————

Local time is now Moscow Time + 7 hours. East of this frontier you enter an autonomous oblast within Khabarovski Krai. Between Obluchye and Pryamuskaya, some of the stations have their names written up in Yiddish as well as in Russian, for this is part of the Yevreyskaya (Jewish) Autonomous Oblast, otherwise known as **Birobidzhan**, after its capital. This remote region was set aside for Jewish emigration in 1928 (the oblast being formed in 1934) but it never proved very popular. The Jewish population today stands at about 6000 – six per cent of the total number of inhabitants of this 36,000 sq km territory.

A glossy coffee-table book about Birobidzhan (written in Russian, Yiddish and English) used to be sold in the bookshops of Khabarovsk. After pages of smiling cement-factory workers, beaming miners and happy-looking milk-maids, the book ends with the following statement: 'The flourishing of the economy and culture of the Jewish Autonomous Region, the happiness of the people of labour of various nationalities inhabiting the Region, their equality, friendship and co-operation lay bare the hypocrisy (sic) of the propaganda campaign launched by the ringleaders of Israel and international Zionism, about the "disastrous situation" of Jews in the Soviet Union, about the "oppression and persecution" they are supposedly being subjected to. The working people of Jewish nationality wrathfully condemn the predatory policy of the ruling circles of Israel and give a resolute rebuff to the Zionist provocateurs.' What the book doesn't tell you is that in Stalin's anti-Jewish purges Birobidzhan's synagogue was closed and the speaking of Yiddish outlawed even here.

Km8198: Obluche Облучье (●) (pop: 11,700) The town is just inside the border of the Jewish Autonomous Oblast. The tunnel just after Obluche was the first in the world to be built through permafrost.

Km8234: Izvestkovaya Известковая The name means 'limestone' and there are large quarries in the area. This town sits at the junction of the Trans-Siberian and the 360km branch line to Novy Urgal on the BAM railway. Much of this branch line was built by Japanese POWs until they were repatriated in 1949 and Japanese graves litter the area. Izvestkovaya is a typical small town with a canteen, post office, dairy farm and market but little else. The old part of town, with its rustic wooden buildings and household garden plots, is hidden in the trees to the west.

Km8306: Bira Бира (●●) The obelisk on the platform commemorates the good works of local philanthropist Nikolai Trofemovich and his wife. The railway runs beside the Bira River for about 100km and passes through hills rich with the ingredients of cement.

Km8351: Birobidzhan Биробиджан (●) [see p262] (pop: 87,600) Originally known as Tikhonkaya, the capital of the 'Jewish' region was founded in 1928 on the Bira River. Once famous for its bright-red, self-propelled combine harvesters, made at the Dalselmash factory and exported to Cuba, Mexico, Iraq and China the town has been hard hit by the economic downturn. The few remaining Jewish people are leaving as fast as they can get their necessary papers organized.

Just east of Birobidzhan, on the left (N) you pass the huge **Iyuan-Koran Memorial** which commemorates a fierce Russian Civil War battle on this site in 1922. Near the memorial are mass graves of the fallen Red Guard.

Km8480: Volochaevka 1 Волочаевка 1 This small station is just a junction of the Trans-Siberian and the 344km railway to Komsomolsk-na-Amure. Volochaevka is famous as the scene of a major battle during the Russian Civil War, which took place in temperatures as low as -35°C. There is a panoramic painting of the battle in Khabarovsk's Museum of Local History. The town of Volochaevka is 9km from the station,

Km8512: Priamurskaya Приамурская This small town is just on the border of the Jewish Autonomous Region.

MAP 16

Серышево SERYSHEVO
Белогорск BELOGORSK
Возжаевка VOZHAYEVKA
Благовещенск BLAGOVESHCHENSK
Поздеевка POZDEYEVKA
Екатеринославка YEKATERINOSLAVKA
Завитая ZAVITAYA
Бурея BUREYA
Домикан DOMIKAN
Архара ARKHARA
Рачи RACHI
Кундур-Хабаровский KUNDUR-KHABAROVSKIY
Облучье OBLUCHE
Кимкан KIMKAN
Известковая IZVESTKOVAYA
Биракан BIRAKAN
Теплое Озеро TEPLOVE OZERO
Лондоко LONDOKO
Бира BIRA
Биробиджан BIROBIDZHAN

AMURSKAYA OBLAST
KHABAROVSKIY KRAY
Y.A. OBLAST

After crossing 3km of swamp and small streams you reach the 2.6km **bridge across the Amur River**, the longest on the Trans-Siberian and completed in 1998. It's a combined rail and road bridge, trains go underneath the road level. Before it opened, cars had to cross the Amur by ferry and trains used the bridge to the side, completed in 1916 and now being slowly dismantled. Khabarovsk stretches along the eastern bank of the river and the beaches here are packed with sunbathers at weekends in the summer. The main fishing port is 2¹/₂km upstream.

Km8521: Khabarovsk Хабаровск (●●●) (pop: 614,000) [see p263]

Khabarovsk was founded in 1858 as a military outpost against the Chinese. and today it is the most pleasant of the Russian Far East cities.

The train stops here for 20 minutes. Souvenirs and maps are sold in the Intourist Hall at the station. There's an impressive statue of Yerofei Pavlovich Khabarov, the city's founder, outside the station.

From Khabarovsk the line runs south to Vladivostok following the Ussuri River and the border with China. This region is a mixture of hilly country interspersed with wide flat valleys. Two hundred miles east of the line lies the Sikhote Alin mountain range, in which most of the rivers you will cross have their source. In the south, the firs and pines give way to a wide

❑ The Ussuri Railway (Kms8531-9441)

The first plans for the building of the Ussuri line, as this section between Khabarovsk and Vladivostok was called, were made in 1875 and the foundation stone for the whole of the Trans-Siberian Railway was laid in Vladivostok by the Tsarevich Nicholas in 1891. Priority was given to the Ussuri line as it was seen as vital to ensure that the strategic port of Vladivostok was not cut off by the Chinese. This was difficult territory for railway building. There was a severe shortage of labour. The local Goldi tribe, who at the time were happily existing in the Stone Age, were no help. They were unable to grasp the concept of paid labour and couldn't understand the point of the work, never having seen a train. Prisoners recruited from the jails of Sakhalin Island were not as co-operative as convicts used on other sections of the Trans-Siberian, preferring an evening of robbery and murder in Vladivostok to the railway camps. Like their fellow-workers on other sections of the line, the men here were plagued not only by vicious mosquitoes but also by the man-eating tigers which roamed the thick forests beside the line. Siberian anthrax decimated the already small population of pack animals, and rails and equipment had to be shipped from Europe, taking up to two months to reach Vladivostok.

In spite of these difficulties, the line was opened in 1897, 43 million roubles having been spent on its construction. It was double tracked in the 1930s and the branch line to Nakhodka was built after the Second World War.

range of deciduous trees. There are good views across the plains to China.

Km8597: The longest bridge on the Ussuri Railway. It crosses the Khor River, one of the widest tributaries of the Ussuri, whose turbulent waters made the construction of the bridge in 1897 extremely difficult.

Km8598: Pereyaslavka Переяславка The town around the station is called Verino (Верино) and was the site of a fierce civil war battle. In front of the station there is a war memorial. There's a museum in Verino.

Km8621: Khor Хор The train crosses the Khor River again. The river marks the southern boundary of the 46,000 hectare **Bolshe-Khekhzirzkiy Sanctuary**. The indigenous Udegeytsy people have a legend to explain why plants from both north and south Siberia are found here. Once two birds flying in opposite directions collided in thick fog and dropped their loads. They'd been sent by the Good Spirit of the South and Good Spirit of the North to throw seeds on the desert plains and mountains respectively. Since then, southern wild grapes wind around northern pine trees and the northern berry *klukva* grows side by side with the southern spiky palm *aralia,* with its metre-long leaves. You'll notice that the vegetation changes considerably with altitude. At the foot of the mountains broad leaf species dominate. On the slopes, cedar, Amur velvet ash (cork is produced from the black bark) and Manchurian nut trees take over while on the higher parts of the mountains, angular pine and fir trees dominate.

Km8642: Vyazemskaya Вяземская (●●) (pop: 18,200) This railway town was founded in 1895 and during the Russian Civil War there was fierce fighting around it. There are several memorials and a museum. To the west of the station is a plinthed **Ea series locomotive**. From about 20kms southwards the countryside changes dramatically with forests of maple, alder, willow, and elm.

MAP 17

БИРОБИДЖАН
BIROBIDZHAN

Y.A.OBLAST

135

ИН
IN

Волочаевка
VOLOCHAYEVKA

Приамурская
PRIAMURSKAYA
Красная Речка
KRASNAYA RECHKA
Николаевка
NIKOLAYEVKA

ХАБАРОВСК
KHABAROVSK

38

Дежневка
DEZHNEVKA

Amur R.

Корфовская
KORFOVSKAYA

Верино
BERINO

Хор
KHOR

Дормидонтовка
DORMIDONTOVKA

CHINA

Вяземская
VYAZEMSKAYA

KHABAROVSKIY KRAY

Розенгартовка
ROZENGARTOVKA

233

Ussuri R.

Бикин
BIKIN

Звеньевой
ZVENEVOI

Бурлит-Волочаевский
BURLIT-VOLOCHAYEVSKIY

PRIMORSKY KRAY

Лучегорск
LUCHEGORSK

Губерово
GUBEROVO

❑ **Decline of the Amur Tiger**

Once the scourge of the railway construction worker, the largest member of the cat family is now just another animal world statistic dwindling towards extinction. The tigers' habitat used to stretch as far west as Lake Baikal and to Beijing in the south but now only 250-350 cats remain in an area from Vladivostok north into the Sikhote Alin range.

Large scale forest clearance for timber sold to Japan and Korea forces tigers out of their territory. A male tiger can weigh up to 380kg (840lbs), almost twice the size of a lion, and requires about 400 sq km of hunting ground. A decline in their food source (deer and wild boar) has also reduced the population and forced remaining tigers to roam even larger areas for prey. In 1987, a train just outside Nakhodka was held up by a tiger that had strayed onto the tracks. An Amur tiger can be worth as much as US$10,000 in China, Korea and Taiwan for the medicinal value that parts of its body are believed to have, and for its skin. Poachers now slip across Russian borders that are no longer tightly patrolled.

The animals are found in and around several nature reserves in this area: Kedrovaya Pad (near Vladivostok), Lazo and Sikhote-Alin, but your chances of seeing a live Amur tiger here are close to zero. There are, in fact, about twice as many of the subspecies in zoos around the world as in the wild.

Km8756: Bikin Бикин (●●●) According to the *1900 Guide to the Great Siberian Railway*, the line crossed the river here and followed it south for 30kms. The book states that 'this is one of the most picturesque parts of the line offering an alpine scenery. The cuttings made in basalt rocks seem to be protected by columns of cyclopean construction. Wide expanses lying amidst the cliffs are covered with a most various vegetation, shading numerous Chinese huts. The river is enlivened by the small boats of the Golds and other natives, moving swiftly on the water's surface.' Unfortunately the line does not follow exactly the same route now, traversing rolling hills and marshy land strewn with telegraph poles keeling over at drunken angles.

The railway crosses the Bikin River. Two hundred km upstream is Krasny Yar, the largest village of the indigenous **Udeghe**. Known as the forest people for their lifestyle of fishing, hunting and gathering food from the taiga, the Udeghe are facing the end of their way of life because of the voracious logging industry.

Between Bikin and Zvenevoi is the **administrative border** between Khabarovski Krai and **Primorski Krai**. The Krai has a population of over half a million people.

Km8890: Dalnerechensk Дальнереченск (●) (pop: 34,600) Founded by Cossacks in 1895 this town quickly became a timber centre thanks to the large pine and red cedar trees there. There is a factory that is one of the few in Russia which still produces wooden barrels for salted fish and seal blubber. The town has a museum and a memorial to the guards killed in the 1969 border conflict with the Chinese over Damanski Island in the Ussuri River. There were several skirmishes and each country claimed the communist high ground as being the true Marxist revolutionary state. As both began preparing for nuclear war confrontation a political solution was reached when Kosygin, the Soviet premier, stopped off in Beijing on his way home from the funeral of Ho Chi Minh. Although progress has been made the border demarcation has not yet been finalized.

Km8900: Muravevo-Amurskaya/Lazo Муравьёво-Амурская/Лазо
This station is named after the explorer and governor of Eastern Siberian, Count Nikolai Muravevo-Amurskaya. It was formerly known as Lazo in honour of the communist revolutionary SG Lazo (1894-1920), who was captured in 1920 by the Japanese when they invaded the Russian Far East, and executed at the station allegedly by being thrown alive into a steam engine firebox. Two other revolutionaries, Lutski and Sibirtsev, met a similar fate and a monument to all three stands in front of the station.

Km8941: Ruzhino Ружино (●●●)
A long stop for the *Rossiya* here.

Km8991: Shmakovka Шмаковка
About 29km from the station is the mostly derelict Shmakovski Trinity-St Nicholas Monastery with a very mysterious history. Its land is now being fought over by two groups, both claiming to be its original owners. The Russian Orthodox Church maintains they built the monastery: the Russian military don't deny its religious past, but claim that they constructed the monastery as a front for an espionage academy. It does seem more than a little coincidental that ex-army officer Father-Superior Aleksei, who was commissioned to build the monastery, selected a site next to the remote Tihmenevo telegraph station. This was no ordinary relay station but one that was classified as a 'top secret military object' connected to Khabarovsk by an underground cable. And the monastery was certainly well equipped: there was even a printing press and photo lab. The military sanatorium here still operates today and the monastery is also home to 10 monks who are slowly rebuilding it.

Km9050: Spassk-Dalni Спасск-Дальний (●) (pop: 52,000)
Alexander Solzhenitsyn was imprisoned in this town, where he helped build the large cement works which still operates.

About 40km west is Lake Khanka which has a surface area of 4000 square km but its deepest point is only four metres. The lake is famous for the lotus flower *eurea* which has giant buds and leaves two metres wide.

Km9109: Sibirtsevo Сибирцево (●●●)
This area is the centre of an extremely fertile region where wheat, oats, soya beans and rice are grown.

Because of labour shortages, these are aerial sown and fertilized. The climate of the southern part of the Russian Far East makes most areas ideal for agriculture as the warm summer rains create a hothouse atmosphere.

A branch line runs from here through dairy-farming countryside to Lake Khanka. From Sibirchevo south, the line winds down to Ussurisk.

Km9177: Ussurisk Уссурийск (●●●) (pop: 161,000)

The fertile area around Ussurisk has been inhabited for over a thousand years, first as the legendary kingdom of Bokhai and then by the Manchus. In the mid-nineteenth century, European emigrants began to settle here. At that time the town was called Nikolskoe, in honour of the Tsar. The town stands at the junction of the Ussuri and the Chinese Eastern Railways. When the Tsarevich Nicholas visited it in 1891, there were three wooden churches, a half-built stone cathedral and a population of 8000 people, many of whom were Chinese. Ussurisk is a now an agricultural and engineering centre, home of the Okean brand of refrigerator.

From Ussurisk there are branch lines to Harbin in China via the East Chinese Railway and Pyongyang in North Korea. The scenery is very different from the Siberian taiga. The train winds through the hills in misty forests of deciduous trees (oak, elm, alder, and maple) and across European-looking meadows filled with Friesian cows and willow trees.

Km9221: Amurski Zaliv Амурский Залив

A branch line runs from here to the port of **Nakhodka**. Since most passenger ships now leave from Vladivostok there's little reason for visiting. For information on the line to Nakhodka, which is a further 175km, see below.

Km9246:

If you're heading east keep a look out on the right (S) for your first glimpse of the Pacific Ocean.

Km9255: Uglovaya Угловая (●)

The town here is known as Trudovoe (Трудовое) and it sits at the northern edge of the Uglovi Bay.

❑ The Vladivostok–Nakhodka Railway

Few travellers visit Nakhodka since the Japanese ferry which connects with Trans-Siberian trains now docks at Vladivostok, which is also the location of the only airport in the region. The 229km-journey from Vladivostok to Tikhookeanskaya (Тихоокеанская), the port 10km east of Nakhodka, runs through Uglovaya (Угловая) at Km47, the mining and industrial city of Artem-Primorski (Артем-Приморский) at Km56, Novonezhino (Новонежино) at Km104, Partizansk (Партизанск) Km183, past the vineyards of the Suchan River Valley to Nakhodka (Находка) Km219, and on to the terminus at Tikhookeanskaya (Тихоокеанская) Km229.

The pleasant beaches and the clean water make it a popular swimming spot for Vladivostok's day trippers.

East of the station the railway travels down a peninsula named in honour of the famous Russian explorer, Count Nikolai Muravevo-Amurskaya.

Km9262: Sadgorod Садгород Near Sadgorod (which means 'garden city') was the station called Khilkovo, named in honour of Prince MI Khilkov, Minister of Ways of Communication in the Tsarist government, who was one of the main supporters of the Trans-Siberian. Khilkovo station has long since disappeared. The accepted date for the start of the building of the Trans-Siberian Railway is 19 May 1891 although the Tsar's son, Nicholas, had already travelled 18km on it from the tip of the peninsula through Vladivostok to Sadgorod. Here he inaugurated it by tipping a barrow of ballast onto the embankment and then returned by train to Vladivostok to unveil a plaque announcing the construction of the railway.

Km9269: Sanatornaya Санаторная The hotels that rate as Vladivostok's best are located here but only local trains will make a stop.

Km9281: Vtoraya Rechka Вторая Речка Vladivostok's main long-distance bus station is here (buses for the airport).

Km9284: Pervaya Rechka Первая Речка According to the original 1880s plan for the Trans-Siberian, this was to have been the line's terminus and a small branch line would extend to Vladivos-tok. Despite the difficulties of building a multi-track railway along the steep shore, it was decided in the 1890s to extend the Trans-Siberian through to Vladivostok. Near Pervaya Rechka was a small settlement called Convicts' Hamlet, inhabited by exiled settlers who had completed their sentences.

Km9289: Vladivostok Владивосток (pop: 648,000) **[see p272]** The beginning or the end of your journey.

MAP 18

Trans-Mongolian Route

The branch line to Mongolia and China leaves the main Trans-Siberian route at Zaudinsky, 8km east of Ulan Ude. From here it takes five and a half hours to cover the 250km to the Russian-Mongolian border. Between Ulan Ude and the southern border, the train travels through the heart of Buryatia, the Buryat Republic.

Note that the line now swings due south from its east-west route. However, in order not to confuse readers we shall continue to use (N) and S) to show which side of the train points of interest are located, rather than changing to the more correct compass bearings. Thus (N) means left side of the train if you're coming from Moscow.

Km5642: Ulan Ude Улан-Удэ   [see p250]
The suburbs of Ulan Ude extend for several kilometres and there are good views back to the city at Km5659 (S) as the train climbs high above the east bank of the Selenga. The line follows the valley of the Selenga River all the way to the border with Mongolia. The scenery changes remarkably quickly to rolling green hills which are excellent pastures for the many cows in the area. Passing through the little station of **Sayatun** (Km5677) the line crosses to the west bank of the river at Km5689-90 and continues

---

❏ **The Trans-Mongolian Line**
This route to China is an ancient one, followed for centuries by the tea-caravans between Peking and Moscow. Travelling non-stop, foreigners and imperial messengers could manage the journey in forty days of acute discomfort. This was the route of the 1907 Peking to Paris Rally, the great motor race that was won by the Italian Prince Borghese and journalist Luigi Barzini in their 40-horsepower Itala. Until the middle of the present century, a rough track over the steppe-lands of northern Mongolia and the Gobi Desert in the south was the only route across this desolate country. In 1940, a branch-line was built between Ulan Ude and the border with Mongolia. After the Second World War, work started on the line from Naushki south, and in 1949 the track reached the Mongolian capital, Ulan Bator. The line between here and Beijing was begun in 1953 with a mixed work-force of Russians, Mongolians and Chinese. By the beginning of 1956 the work was completed and a regular rail service began between Ulan Ude and Beijing.

to climb through **Ubukun** (Km5732), stopping briefly at **Zagustay**.

Km5769: Zagustay Загустай The station sits in the ugly shadow of a factory belching out thick smoke. Six kilometres from this station is the large coal mining town of **Gusinozersk** (Гусиноозёрск). The town grew from nothing to today's population of 30,800 following the discovery of a huge coal basin in 1939. The name means 'Goose Lake Town'.

Km5771-99: Goose Lake Between the stations of Zagustay and Gusinoye Ozero the line passes along the western shore of Goose Lake. Until the Revolution, the most important *datsan* (lamasery) north of Urga (Ulan Bator) was at **Selenginsk**, 20km south-east of Gusinoye Ozero and overlooking the lake.

In 1887 George Kennan, who was researching his book on Siberian prisons, arrived in Selenginsk and visited the famous datsan. 'We were tired of prisons and the exile system and had enough misery,' he wrote. Nevertheless he found Selenginsk 'a wretched little Buriat town'. At the datsan, Kennan and his companions were entertained by the Khamba Lama, the chief lama, who claimed through the interpreter that they were the first foreigners ever to visit his lamasery. They were treated to a dinner and a special dance display. The Khamba Lama had never heard of America, Kennan's native land, and was confused when Kennan explained that 'it lies nearly under our feet; and if we could go directly through the earth, this would be the shortest way to reach it'. The lama was completely unaware that the earth was anything other than flat.

Today, the Selenginsk village datsan is operating again.

Km5780: Gusinoe Ozero Гусиное Озеро The line leaves the lake after this station and continues to climb from one valley to another, passing though **Selenduma** (Km5827) and still following the river.

❑ The old border town of Kyakhta

The border post for the railway is at the modern town of Naushki. However the old border for the tea-caravans was near the large town of **Kyakhta**, 20kms east of Naushki. In the 18th and 19th centuries this town together with **Maimachen**, the Chinese town beside it on the Mongolian side of the border, formed one of the most important trading centres in the world, based almost entirely on the tea trade. Great caravans of camels would transport the precious beverage from Peking across the Gobi Desert to Maimachen and Kyakhta. Kyakhta was a bustling town of wealthy traders and tea-barons but once the Trans-Siberian was built the tea was shipped via Vladivostok to European Russia. Maimachen is now named Altan Bulak.

On 24 June 1907 Prince Borghese and his team roared into town in their Itala and were entertained royally by local dignitaries. The morale of the tea-merchants had sunk with the recent decline in trade but was greatly boosted by the arrival of the car and they began making plans for their own motor-caravans. An earlier visitor to these border towns was George Kennan who attended a banquet in Maimachen, where he was served dog-meat dumplings, cocks' heads in vinegar and fried lichen from birch trees, washed down by several bottles of French champagne. He was sick for the next two weeks.

In January 1920 Kyakhta witnessed a particularly appalling atrocity when the sadistic White Army General Semenov despatched 800 people suspected communists using a different method of execution each day.

Today Kyakhta has a population of 18,000 and a large border-post garrison nearby. It's an interesting place to visit, however, with many crumbling old buildings and several vast churches hinting at prosperous times past. There's an impressive regional museum, and basic accommodation at the *Hotel Druzhba* (US$12 a room).

Km5852 (S): Dzhida Джида There appears to be a small air-base here with hangars dug into hummocks in the ground.

Km5895-0: Naushki Наушки (●●●++) At this **Russian border post** the train stops for at least two hours, usually for considerably longer, Customs officials collect passports, visas and currency declaration forms, returning them (often to the carriage attendant) after about half an hour. It would be unwise to get off the train before you've got your passport back since guards may not let you back on the train without it.

The station tends to be crowded with black marketeers and some may get on the train and start selling roubles to travellers heading west; don't buy too many as the rate is unlikely to be in your favour – and **watch your valuables** when these traders are around. There's a **bank** on the platform but the exchange rate here is not good (about 5% below the standard rate). Note that the bank is sign-posted in English but it's a long way down the platform (towards Mongolia). East-bound travellers should exchange any unspent roubles here as it's difficult to exchange them outside Russia. Note that the loos on the train remain locked until you leave the border. The station lavatories would not win any hygiene awards but are located in the building to the left of the station building. Have your insect repellent to hand as the air can be thick with mosquitoes in summer.

The **border** is marked by a menacing-looking electrified fence, about five kilometres beyond the Russian border post. Most trains are timetabled to cross this border at night, which is unfortunate since the landscape is attractive. To the south is the impressive Selenga River, prone to flooding in the late summer; hills reach up above the track to the north.

MONGOLIA

Distances given here follow the Mongolian kilometre markers. For cumulative distances from/to Moscow, see timetables: Appendix A).

Km21: Sukhbaatar Сухбаатар (●●●++)　At this **Mongolian border town** the immigration process used to be a fairly nerve-racking affair. Whole compartments would be rigorously searched, magazines confiscated and film ripped out of cameras. It's all rather tame now for foreigners, although the baggage of local travellers is thoroughly inspected. During immigration and customs procedures a diesel engine is attached. The Mongolian dining-car, however, is not put on until Ulan Bator.

Some travellers have managed to get Mongolian visas here (at a cost of US$50) but others have been refused: the situation is subject to change and also to the whims of the border official. Being turned back is not worth the hassle so don't rely on being able to get one here.

The station building is an excellent example of whimsical Mongolian railway architecture. It's an incredible mélange of architectural styles: mock Gothic, Moghul and Modern topped with crenellations and painted what looks like lime green in the artificial light. Strawberry pink is the other popular colour for station buildings in this country.

Situated at the confluence of the Selenga and Orhon Rivers, **Sukhbaatar** was founded in 1940 and named after the Mongolian revolutionary leader Damdiny Sukhe Bator. It grew quickly, superseding the border town on the caravan route, Maimachen (now named Altan Bulak). Sukhbaatar is now the third largest industrial centre in the country (although in a country as sparsely populated and industrially primitive as Mongolia this is not a particularly impressive fact). Matches, liquor and flour are produced here by some of the 20,000 inhabitants.

Km123: Darhan Дархан (Darkhan) (●●●)　It takes about eight hours to cover the 380km between Sukhbaatar and Ulan Bator. The train pass-

es through the town of **Darhan**, capital of Selenga *aimak* (district), which was founded in 1961 and is now the second most important industrial centre in Mongolia, after Ulan Bator. Darhan is a show town of planned urbanization and its population has increased from 1500 in 1961 to over 90,000. Main sources of employment are opencast mining, food production, construction and the production of leather and sheepskin coats. The town is an important communications junction with a branch-line running west from here to the big mining complex at **Erdenet**, and the port serves many villages along the Selenga and Orkhon Rivers.

About 120km west of Darhan, in the foothills of Mt Burenkhan is **Amarbayasgalant Monastery**. This vast eighteenth century temple complex, which once housed 10,000 monks and drew pilgrims from

❏ **Mongolia**

Mongolia is one of those countries, like Guyana or Chad, that rarely makes headline news, except when there's a dramatic change of leadership or policy. It's a sparsely populated place with only 2,650,000 people (34% below the age of 14) in an area the size of Western Europe or Alaska. Mongolia is changing fast but the capital, Ulan Bator, is changing at a much faster rate than the rest of the country. It's estimated that some 40% of the population lives below the poverty line.

Mongolia contains a surprising variety of terrain: the vast undulating plain in the east, the Gobi desert to the south, and in the west snow-capped mountains and extensive forests. Most of the eastern plain is at an altitude of 1500m and in this area the sun shines for around 250 days each year.

For many centuries the deserts and grasslands of Mongolia have been inhabited by nomadic herders living in felt tents (*yurts* or *ghers*). At certain times in the course of world history they have been bound together under a leader, the most famous being Genghis and Kublai Khan in the thirteenth century. Kublai Khan introduced Tibetan Buddhism to the country but it was not until the early seventeenth century that the majority of the population was converted and Buddhism gained a strong grip on the country.

By the end of the seventeenth century, control of Mongolia and its trade routes was in the hands of the Manchus. In 1911 the country became an independent monarchy, in effect a theocratic state since power lay with the 'Living Buddha', the chief representative of Buddhism in Mongolia, at Urga (now Ulan Bator). In 1921 the communist government that rules today took power and the struggle to modernize a country that was technologically in the Dark Ages began, with considerable help from the Soviet Union. Elections were held for the first time in 1990 and won by the People's Revolutionary Party (Communist Party), who pledged the introduction of a market-style economy. The presidential elections of May 1997 were won by People's Revolutionary Party leader, Natsagiin Bagabandi. The next elections are due in mid-2001.

The country is divided into 18 *aimaks* (districts) and the railway-line passes through three of these (Selenga, Tov and Dornogov).

many parts of Asia, was desecrated during the anti-religious movement in the 1930s but is now being restored with grants from the Mongolian government and UNESCO.

If you'd been doing this part of the journey in the not too distant past before the railway was built, you would now be swaying back and forth in the saddle of a camel, one of many in the caravan you would have joined in Kyakhta. In the 1865 edition of his *Handbook for Russia, Poland and Finland*, Murray gives the following advice: 'It is customary for caravans to travel sixteen hours a day and they come to a halt for cooking, eating and sleeping ... The Mongols are most trustworthy in their transactions, and the traveller may feel in perfect safety throughout the journey.' He also gives the following useful tips concerning local currency: 'The use of money is as yet almost unknown in this part of the country, brick-tea cut up into slices being the token of value most recognized; but small brass buttons are highly prized.'

Km 381: Crossing wide open grasslands with only the occasional yurt to break the monotony, the line begins to descend into the valley where Ulan Bator is situated. Looking south you catch the first glimpse (Km386) of the ugly factories on the outskirts of the city (Km396).

Km404: Ulan Bator Улаанбаатар (●●●+) [see p283]
(1350m/4430ft) The train spends half an hour at the Mongolian capital, a good chance to stretch your legs. There is a whole **collection of steam and diesel engines** standing outside the locomotive shed on the east side of the line (N). The display includes a 2-6-2 S-116, T31-011 and T32-508

❏ **Genghis Khan**
For many decades the name of this famous Mongolian conqueror has been taboo in his home country. The Russians saw Genghis Khan as a brutal invader to be erased from the history books but with their influence rapidly fading there has been a sudden rise in Mongolian nationalism. Genghis Khan, the founder of the thirteenth century Mongolian Empire, is a hero once more, lending his name to the most luxurious hotel in town and also to a brand of vodka.

Along with his rehabilitation have come a number of interesting characters each claiming to be his legitimate descendant. One of the best publicized was Ganjuurijin Dschero Khan, who claimed to have been smuggled out of the country to escape the Communists when he was four years old. Mongolians were intrigued to meet him, although they didn't quite know what to make of his appearance. He arrived in a military tunic, decked out with medals inscribed 'Bazooka', Carbine', 'Paratroopers' and 'Special Forces', which he claimed to have won in Korea and Vietnam. Support for him waned after it became apparent that he didn't speak Mongolian.

❦❦❦❦❦❦❦❦❦❦❦❦❦❦❦❦❦❦❦❦❦❦❦❦❦❦

❑ **The Gobi Desert**
This vast wilderness extends for 1000km north to south and 2400km west to east.
Most of the part crossed by the railway is not desert of the sandy Saharan type
but rolling grassy steppes. It is impressive for its emptiness: very few towns and
just the occasional collection of yurts, herds of stocky Mongolian horses and
small groups of camels or gazelles.

While it may not appear so, the Gobi is rich in wildlife although numbers of
some species are rapidly dwindling. This is mainly the result of poaching and the
destruction of habitat. There are large reserves of coal, copper, molybdenum,
gold, uranium and other valuable exports. It's estimated that up to 10 billion tons
of coal exist beneath the Gobi, and Japanese and Western companies are negoti-
ating with Mongolia to extract it using strip mining techniques, which could seriously affect the delicate environmental balance. An American conservation
group, Wildlife Conservation International, is helping the Mongolian Association
for Conservation of Nature and Environment (MACNE) to monitor species at
risk in the area. Among these are the 500 remaining wild Bactrian camels, the
Gobi bear, the *kulan* (Asian wild ass) and Przewalski's wild horse (the last
recorded sighting was in 1962).

❦❦❦❦❦❦❦❦❦❦❦❦❦❦❦❦❦❦❦❦❦❦❦❦❦❦

diesels, a 750mm gauge 0-8-0 469, and a 2-10-0 Ye-0266. They are
beside the public road but quite accessible even though there is a fence in
front of them. In the station building postcards (and weird Mongolian
stamps which leave little room for a message on a card) can be purchased
at the bar. Black marketeers may approach you on the platform to change
money. Don't change too much until you're sure of the rate. The dining-
car is attached here if you're en route to Beijing but is usually detached if
you're travelling in the other direction. For meals and souvenirs sold in the
dining-car both Mongolian currency and US$ are accepted although if you
want to use dollars the staff seem to make the prices up as they go along.

Km409: The city extends this far west. At around Km425 the line starts
to climb and for the next 50km, to Km470, snakes around, giving good
opportunities for photos along the train. Good views over the rolling hills
on both sides of the train.

Km507: Bagakangai Багакангай Airfield (S) with camouflaged
bunkers.

Km521: Manit Манит (●) The pink station with its tower and weath-
er-vane looks rather like a church.

Km560: Camels are occasionally to be seen roaming across the wide,
rolling plain.

Km649: Choyr Чоыр (●●●) Just behind this beautiful pink and white wedding-cake of a station is a statue of the first Mongolian cosmonaut, VVT Ertvuntz. He's had the all over silver paint treatment but still looks impressive. The Soviet airbase here has now closed.

Km733 (S): The pond here often attracts groups of camels and antelope.

Km751: Airag Аираг The train doesn't usually stop at this small station which is in the middle of nowhere and is surrounded by scrap metal.

Km875 (N): There's a collection of old **steam locos** on display just to the west of Sayn Shand station.

Km876: Sayn Shand Саын Шанд (●●●) (Sajnsand) This is the largest town between the capital and Dzamyn Ude on the southern border. Main industries include food-processing and coal-mining.

Km1113: Dzamyn Ude Дзамын Уде (Zamyn Uud) (●●●+) Mongolian border town with a station building that looks like a supermarket at Christmas with all its festive lights. There's a bank and a restaurant, both usually closed in the evening. Customs declaration forms and immigration forms are collected. Customs officers inspect the luggage of Chinese and Mongolian travellers but don't seem too interested in others. This process may take an hour and a half. If it's dark, you can try to spot the soldiers standing half concealed in the undergrowth by the tracks.

THE PEOPLE'S REPUBLIC OF CHINA

Kilometres below show distance to Beijing.

Km842: Erlyan (Erenhot/Ereen) (●●●++) Chinese station officials are obviously trying to outdo the show their Mongolian counterparts put on in the evening over the border, with a full-blown son-et-lumière. There's the *Vienna Waltz* blaring out of the speakers to welcome the train and the building's decked out in red neon and fairy lights.

Chinese customs officials come on board here. If you're travelling to Beijing you'll be required to fill in a health declaration form and baggage/currency declaration form. Passports are collected.

Bogie-changing The train spends about 20 minutes at the platform and is then shunted off to the bogie-changing shed. When you get off take something warm with you as it'll be about a couple of hours before you're allowed on board again. It may be possible to stay on the train until it gets to the shed, get off before they lock the doors (for safety reasons while raising the carriages), and watch some of the bogie-changing operations. The Chinese railway system operates on Standard Gauge (as do Europe and North America) and this is $3^{1}/_{2}$ inches narrower than five

❏ **Chinese trains**

Chinese trains ride on the left side of double tracks (unlike Russia which is right-hand drive). Km markers come in a variety of sizes (usually like little grave-stones down by the track) and there seems to be some disagreement between them and the official kilometre location (on timetables etc) for many places. I've followed the markers where possible but for the last 70km of the journey they are not reliable, altering by 25km at one point.

foot gauge used in the countries of the former Soviet Union and Mongolia. Giant hydraulic lifts raise the carriages and the bogies are rolled out and replaced. Photography is now permitted but take care not to get in the way or the authorities may restore the ban on photography which was in force for many years. You can walk back to the station building but you should be careful at night as the path is not well lit. There is usually a bunch of cycle-rickshaw men hanging round to take you, but bargain hard and make sure it's clear whether you are paying in yuan or dollars to avoid inevitable arguments at the other end.

Back in the station you can change money at the bank (passport not necessary but you do need to know your passport number), or visit the Friendship Store (Chinese vodka, Chinese champagne, beer, tea, Ritz crackers, and other snacks) and bar/restaurant (if open). The loos, how-ever, are usually in a terrible state. Upstairs is a foreigners' waiting room where fictitious literature (eg *Human Rights in China*) is provided free of charge. The platform is crowded with traders and food and drinks are also sold here.

The Age of the Steam Train has not yet passed in China and it is like-ly that the train will be shunted out of the bogie-changing shed and back to the platform by a puffing Class 2-10-2 locomotive built in Datong (see below). Passports are returned and you depart shortly thereafter, the whole operation taking anything from three to six hours.

Passing through towns with Mongolian names like Sonid Youqi and Qahar Youyi Houqi, you reach Jining in about five hours.

Km498: Jining (●)   The bulky white modernist station building is topped by a red flag. Beside it is an extensive goods yard full of working steam engines.

Travelling due south from Jining the train leaves the province of Inner Mongolia and enters Shanxi Province. This mountainous area was a great cultural and political centre over a thousand years ago. There are hills running parallel to the west and wide fields either side of the line. The train follows the course of a river which leads it into a valley and more rugged countryside after Fenezhen.

Km415: Fenezhen Between this drab town and Datong you pass through the line of the **Great Wall** for the first time. Occasional glimpses are all you will get until the spectacular crossing at Km82.

Km371: Datong (●●) This large city, found-ed as a military outpost by Han armies, has a pop-ulation of more than half a million and stands in the centre of the coal-rich Datong Basin. Its major tourist attraction is the group of Buddhist cave temples known as the **Yungang Grottoes** in the foothills of Wuzhou Mountain (16km west of the city). These caves, dating back to 460 AD, are richly decorated and renowned as one of China's three most impressive Buddhist complexes, the others being at Luoyang and Dunhuang.

If you're stopping off here, a visit to the **Datong Locomotive Works** is an interesting and educational experience. Until recently, this was one of the last places in the world where steam trains were made. In the 1980s they were turning them out at the rate of 240 locos per year. The manufacture of the Class QJ 8WT/12WT 2-10-2 engine (133 tonnes; max speed 80kph) ceased in 1986 and the Class JS 2-8-2 (104 tonnes; max speed 85kph) in 1989. Both classes are used for freight haulage and shunting work. The factory now produces parts for steam and diesel locomo-tives and has customers in many parts of the world. Tours are conducted twice a week and must be arranged through Chinese International Travel Service (CITS).

At Datong the line turns east and follows the Great Wall, running about 20km south of it as far as Zhangjiakou. One hundred kilometres west of Zhangjiakou you leave Shanxi and enter Hebei province. Between Km295 and Km272 (N) the Great Wall can be seen parallel to the line, on the hillside to the east. Best view is at Km284 (N).

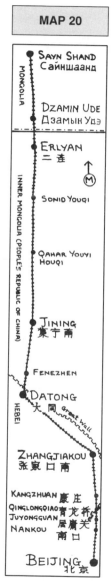

MAP 20

Km193: Zhangjiakou (●●) Founded 2000 years ago, this city used to be known by its Mongolian name, Kalgan (meaning gate or frontier). It stands at the point where the old caravan route between Peking and Russia crossed the Great Wall. Luigi Barzini described it as being like one of those 'cities one sees pictured upon Fu-kien tapestries: varied and picturesque, spreading over the bank of a wide snowy river'. He would not recognize it now; it has grown into an industrial city of over one million people. Yet he might recall the stink he'd noticed as he drove into town on 14 June 1907, for tanning and leather-work are still major industries here. About 15km south of the city a large factory pollutes the air with orange smoke.

From around Km175 the scenery becomes hilly and more interesting as the line rises over the mountains north of Beijing. There are small valleys of sunflowers, groves of poplars and even some apple orchards. At Km99 you cross San Gan River above which (N) can be seen a small isolated section of the Wall.

Km82: Kanzhuang (●) The train stops for a banking engine to be attached before the steep ascent up through the Great Wall.

Km73: Badaling The first of the stations for the **Great Wall**. To the east is a 2km tunnel beneath the Wall. Look up (N) to the east as you come out for a good view and be ready to get off for the short stop at Qinglongqiao ½km further on.

Km70: Qinglongqiao (●●) There are good views of the Great Wall high above this attractive station. After the stop the train reverses downhill through a spectacular series of tunnels alongside the road. Progress is very slow because of the tortuous bends and the need for heavy braking, which gives some people time to jump off the train and gather the wild marijuana plants which flourish near the tracks in this area. You pass the Tourist Reception Centre at Km68.

Km63: Juyongguan (●) Continuous application of the brake blocks makes them very hot necessitating a stop here.

Km53: Nankou (●●) The name means 'Southern Pass'. After a short stop to detach the rear engine the train speeds off across the fertile plain to Beijing. Something strange has happened to the km markers in this area, with 30km suddenly added around Km35.

Km0: Beijing Turn to p297 for more information.

MAP 21

Trans-Manchurian route

Km6199: Chita Чита (●●●) This is the last major Trans-Siberian station before the Trans-Manchurian trains branch off to China. Detailed information on Chita is on p259.

Km6293: Karymskaya Карымская (●) The branch line to Beijing via Manchuria leaves the main Trans-Siberian route at Tarskaya (formerly Kaidalovo), 12kms east of Karymskaya. Leaving Tarskaya, you cross the Ingoda River and head through open steppe-land. Twenty kilometres further south you enter the Buryat Republic (Buryatia).

Km6444: Olovyannaya Оловянная (●●) The 120-flat apartment block by the station was constructed by Chinese labourers using Chinese materials. It was one of many barter deals between the Zabaikalsk (Russia) and Harbin (China) railways. Since 1988, when the first barter contract was signed, most deals have involved Russia swapping fertilizers, old rails and railway wheel sets for Chinese food, clothes and shoes. As confidence has grown, Harbin Railways have provided specialist services such as doctors of traditional Chinese medicine for the nearby Karpovka railway workers, uniforms for Zabaikalsk workers, and the reconstruction specialists for Chita-2 and Petrovskiy Zavod stations.

Leaving this picturesque town you cross the Onon River, which flows north of the main Trans-Siberian line to join the Ingoda and form the Shilka. Genghis Khan (see p375) was born on the banks of the muddy Onon in 1162. Don't photograph anything from the train in this area as in the town's outskirts are silos housing SS-11 interballistic nuclear rockets and bunkers holding portable SS-20 nuclear rocket launchers. The SS-11 missiles can carry a single nuclear warhead up to 10,000km while the SS-20 can carry three 600 kiloton warheads a mere 5700km.

Between Olovyannaya and Borzya you cross the Adun Chelon mountain range, passing through Yasnaya (Km6464) and Birka (Km6477).

Km6486: Mirnaya Мирная At the western end of the station there are two small tanks whose guns appear to be aimed at the train.

Km6509: Khadabulak Хадабулак Small village below a large telecommunications tower on the hill. Long views across the plains to the hills in the north around this area.

Km6543: Borzya Борзя (●●) This town was founded in the 18th century and with the arrival of the railway became the transport hub of southeast Zabaikalsk region. A branch line from here to the west goes all the way to the city of Choibalsan in Mongolia. Black marketeers come aboard (if you're coming from Beijing) to tempt you with army uniforms, military watches and rabbit fur hats. **Watch your valuables**.

There are several opportunities for photographs along the train as it snakes around the curves between Km6554 and Km6570, and especially Km6564-5 (S).

Km6590: Kharanor Харанор There is a branch line from here to the east which runs to the military towns of Krasnokamensk and Priargunsk.

Km6609: Dauriya Даурия A small village surrounded by a marsh of red weeds.

Km6661: Zabaikalsk Забайкальск (●●●++) This town is within 1km of the border. Customs declarations and passports are checked on the train. If you are leaving Russia, you may still be required to produce your currency declaration form. Although they no longer seem to be enforcing this rule, any remaining roubles are subject to confiscation so don't admit to having them if you want some as souvenirs. The guards don't seem too bothered with the tourists but might check the Chinese traders.

The train is shunted into the **bogie changing sheds** at the south end of the station. You can either stay at the station, remain in the carriage or get out and watch the bogie changing. Taking photos in the bogie changing shed was once strictly prohibited but now it is possible.

The station has a **restaurant** which just about serves hot borsch and warm goulash if you are Russian, or with Russians, but will try to avoid serving anyone else. There is a **bank** upstairs with predictably poor rates. The black marketeers will catch you on your way in and it's probably the only time that it's worth using them. The **lavatories** are bearable if you hold your breath. In the building opposite the station and across the line there is a shop where vodka, champagne and palekh boxes are sold. There's a small department store next door. You will stay at the station for between two and six hours.

THE PEOPLE'S REPUBLIC OF CHINA

Note that the km markers along this route do not show the distance to Beijing until you reach Harbin. From the border to Harbin they show the distance to Harbin.

Km935 (Bei:2323): Manzhouli (●●●+)
(2135ft/651m) At this Chinese border town (formerly known as Manchuria Station) you're required to fill in a departure card and show officials your baggage and currency declaration form if you're leaving the country, or fill out this form as well as a health declaration form if you're just arriving. The train spends between one and three hours here so you can visit the **bank** and the **Friendship Store** (tins of good quality peanuts, Chinese vodka, beer and fake sports clothes). Postcards and stamps are also available. Puffing steam locomotives shunt carriages around the yard, a particularly impressive sight if you arrive in the early hours of a freezing winter morning. **Loos** stink, less so in winter.

Leaving the station you pass **Lake Dalai Nor** and roll across empty steppe-lands. You may see mounted herders from the train, as did Michael Myres Shoemaker in 1902 when he was passing through this area on his journey to Peking. Of the first Chinese person he saw, he wrote (in *The Great Siberian Railway from St Petersburg to Pekin*) 'these northern Celestials appear on the whole friendly, and are flying around in all directions swathed in furs, and mounted on shaggy horses.' European newspapers of the time had been filled with reports of the atrocities committed by the anti-foreigner Boxer sect in Manchuria, hence his surprise at the apparent friendliness of the local population.

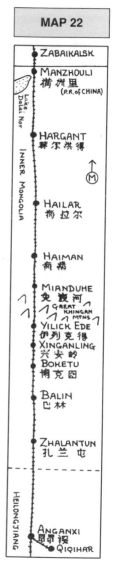

MAP 22

● ZABAIKALSK

● MANZHOULI
满洲里
(P.R.of CHINA)

Lake Dalai Nor

● HARGANT
蒙尔洪得

⊕ (M)

INNER MONGOLIA

● HAILAR
梅拉尔

● HAIMAN
梅燕

● MIANDUHE
兔渡河
GREAT KHINGAN MTNS
YILICK EDE
伊列克得
XINGANLING
兴安岭
BOKETU
博克图

● BALIN
巴林

● ZHALANTUN
扎兰屯

HEILONGJIANG

● ANGANXI
昂昂溪
● QIQIHAR

❏ THE EAST CHINESE RAILWAY 1897-1901

The route

The original plans for the Great Siberian Railway had not included the laying of tracks across territories that were outside the Russian Empire. However, when surveyors returned from the Shilka and Amur valleys in 1894 with the news that the Sretensk to Khabarovsk section of the line would prove extremely costly owing to the difficult terrain, the Siberian Railway Committee were obliged to consider an alternative. Their greedy eyes turned to the rich Chinese territory of Manchuria and they noted that a line straight across this province to Vladivostok would cut 513 *versts* (544km) off the journey to the port. Since the Chinese would obviously not be happy to have Russian railway lines extending into their territory, the Committee had to think up a scheme to win Peking over to the idea.

The Manchurian Deal

It did not take the wily Russian diplomats long to work out a deal the Chinese were forced to accept. After the 1894 Sino-Japanese war the victorious Japanese concocted a peace treaty that included the payment of a heavy indemnity by the Chinese. Knowing that China was unable to pay, the Russians offered them a generous loan in exchange for the right to build and operate a railway across Manchuria. They were granted an 80-year lease on a thin strip of land 1400km long and the project was to be disguised as a Chinese enterprise financed through the Russo-Chinese Bank. The rest of the world suspected Russia of flagrant imperialism and it proved them right in 1897 by annexing Port Arthur.

Work begins

Construction began in 1897 but it soon became obvious that the project was facing greater problems than any that had arisen during the building of other sections. There were difficult conditions (the Greater Khingan Mountains had to be crossed); there were not enough labourers; interpreters were needed to translate the orders of the Russian foremen to the Chinese coolies and the area through which the route passed was thick with *hunghutzes* (bandits). It was necessary to bring in a force of 5000 policemen to protect the workers. After the Boxer (anti-foreigner) riots began in the late 1890s it became necessary to protect the rails, too, for when they were not murdering missionaries the Boxers tore up the track and derailed trains.

Set-backs

After the annexation of Port Arthur, another Manchurian line was begun – from Harbin south through Mukden (now Shenyang) to Dalni (now Dalian) and Port Arthur (now Lushun). Work was disrupted in 1899 by the outbreak of bubonic plague although in spite of the Chinese refusing to co-operate with the quarantine procedures, only 1400 people died out of the total work-force of 200,000. In May 1900, the Boxers destroyed 200km of track and besieged Harbin. The Russians sent in a peace-keeping force of 200,000 men but by the time the rebellion had been put down, one third of the railway had been destroyed.

Despite these set-backs, the line was completed in 1901. It would have been far more economical to have built the Amur line from Sretensk to Khabarovsk, for in the end the East Chinese Railway had cost the government more than the total spent on the entire Trans-Siberian track on Russian soil.

Km749 (Bei:2137): Hailar (●●) (2030ft/619m) From here to Haiman the rolling steppes continue. If you'd been travelling in 1914, you would have the latest edition of the Baedeker's *Russia with Teheran, Port Arthur and Peking* with you and would therefore be looking out for 'the fortified station buildings (sometimes adorned with apes, dragons and other Chinese ornaments), the Chinese carts with their two high wheels and the camels at pasture'. Modern Hailar is an unexotic city of 180,000 people, the economic centre of the region. Local architecture is a blend of Russian and Mongolian: log cabins, some with yurt-style roofs. The average temperature in this area in January is a cool minus 27°C.

Km674 (Bei:2062): Haiman Also known as Yakoshih, this town stands near the foot of the Great Khingan mountain range which extends from the northern border with Russia south into Inner Mongolia. The line begins to rise into the foothills of the range.

Km634 (Bei:2022): Mianduhe (●) The train continues to climb the gently rising gradient.

Km574 (Bei:1962): Yilick Ede (●●) Note that the train does not stop here on the journey **from** Beijing.

Km564 (Bei:1952): Xinganling/Khingan (●) (3140ft/958m) This station stands at the highest point on the line. The long tunnel (3km) that was built here in 1901-2 was a considerable engineering achievement since most of the drilling was done during the winter, with shift workers labouring day and night.

Km539 (Bei:1927): Boketu (●●●) The line winds down through partly-wooded slopes to the town of Balin/Barim (Km7135/1866) and continues over the plains leaving Inner Mongolia and crossing into Heilongjiang Province.

Km270 (Bei:1658): Angangxi (●●●) Forty kilometres south is the ancient city of **Qiqihar** (Tsitsikar). By the time he reached this point Michael Myres Shoemaker had become bored with watching 'Celestials' from the windows of the train and was tired and hungry. He writes 'In Tsitsikar, at a wretched little mud hut, we find some hot soup and a chop, also some coffee, all of which, after our days in lunch baskets, taste very pleasant.' Over their lunch, they may well have discussed the nearby **Field of Death** for which the city was notorious. In this open area on the edge of Tsitsikar public executions were regularly performed. Most of the criminals decapitated before the crowds were *hunghutzes* (bandits). Since the Chinese believed that entry to Heaven was denied to mortals who were missing parts of their bodies, their heads had to be sewn back in place before a decent burial could take place. However, so as not to lower the moral tone of Paradise, the government ordered that the heads be sewn on the wrong way round, facing backwards.

Twenty kilometres east of Angangxi you pass through a large area of marshland, part of which has been designated a nature reserve. The marsh attracts a wide variety of water-fowl since it is on the migration route from the Arctic and Siberia down to southern Asia. The **Zhalong Nature Reserve**, 20km north of here, is best known for its cranes. Several of these (including the Siberian Crane) are now listed as endangered species.

Km159 (Bei:1547): Daqing (●) At the centre of one of the largest oil-fields in China, Daqing is a model industrial town producing plastics and gas as well as oil. Higher wages attract model workers from all over the country. Apart from the thousands of oil wells in this swampy district there's very little to see.

Km96 (Bei:1484): Song A small station in an island of cultivation amongst the swamps.

Km0 (Bei:1388): Harbin (●●●) (152m/500ft)   Crossing the wide Sungari (Songhua) River, a 1840km long tributary of the mighty Amur to the north, the line reaches Harbin, the industrial centre of Heilongjiang Province. It was a small fishing village until the mid 1890s when the Russians made it the headquarters of their railway building operations in Manchuria. After Michael Myres Shoemaker visited the town in 1902 he wrote: 'The state of society seems even worse at this military post of Harbin than in Irkutsk. There were seven throats cut last night, and now, as a member of the Russo-Chinese Bank expressed it, the town hopes for a quiet season.' The *Imperial Japanese Railways Guide to East Asia* (1913) recommended 'the excellent bread and butter, which are indeed the pride of Harbin' and warned travellers away from the numerous opium dens. After the Revolution, White Russian refugees poured into the town and the Russian influence on the place continued. There are few onion-domes and spires to be seen today in what is otherwise just another Chinese city: the Russian population is now small. The main tourist attraction is the **Ice Lantern Festival**, which takes place from January to early February. Winters here are particularly cold and during the festival the parks are filled with ice-sculptures: life-size elephants, dragons and horses as well as small buildings and bridges. Electric lights are frozen into these sculptures and when they are illuminated at night, the effect is spectacular.

At the station, good views along the track of the numerous steam locos can be obtained from the bridges between the platforms.

Km1260: The line crosses a wide tributary of the Songhua River. There are numerous small lakes in the area.

Km1146: Changchun (●●) (230m/760ft)

Between Harbin and Changchun you cross an immense cultivated plain, leaving Heilongjiang and entering Jilin Province. Changchun is the provincial capital. The station is quite interesting with white concrete sculptures of 'The Graces' and lots to buy from the snack sellers on the platform.

Back in 1913, the *Imperial Japanese Government Railways Guide to East Asia* was reminding its readers (all of whom would have had to change at this large junction) about 'the need of adjusting their watches – the Russian railwaytime being 23 minutes earlier than the Japanese'. From 1933 to 1945 Changchun was the centre of the Japanese puppet state of Manchukuo and it has now grown into an industrial metropolis of more than one million people. Local industries include the car factory (where Red Flag limousines are assembled: guided tours possible), the rail-carriage factory and the film studios. If you happen to get off here, the local delicacies include antler broth, hedgehog hydnum stewed with orchid, and the north-eastern speciality, *Qimian*, which is the nose of a moose. Changchun is, however, probably more popular with rail enthusiasts than with epicureans. RM Pacifics and QJ 2-10-2s are to be seen here and on the Changchun-Jilin line.

Km1030: Siping

Unattractive town but lots of working steam locos in the station. Ten kilometres further south the train crosses the provincial border into Liaoning Province.

Km841: Shenyang (●●●) (50m/160ft)

An industrial giant founded two thousand years ago during the Western Han dynasty (206 BC- 24 AD). At different times during the course of its long history the city has been controlled by the Manchus (who named it Mukden), the Russians, the Japanese and the Kuomintang until it was finally taken over by the Chinese Communists in 1948. Shenyang is now one of the largest indus-

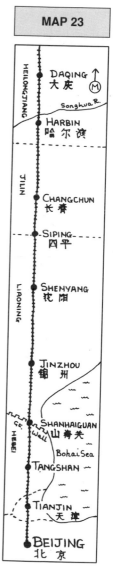

MAP 23

HEILONGJIANG

DAQING 大庆 ↑ Ⓜ

Songhua R.

HARBIN 哈尔滨

JILIN

CHANGCHUN 长春

SIPING 四平

LIAONING

SHENYANG 沈阳

JINZHOU 锦州

GT. WALL

HEBEI

SHANHAIGUAN 山海关

Bohai Sea

TANGSHAN

TIANJIN 天津

BEIJING 北京

trial centres in the People's Republic but there are several interesting places to visit between the factories, including a smaller version of the **Imperial Palace** in Beijing. There is also a **railway museum** situated beside Sujiatun shed. The station has a green dome and the square outside it is dominated by a tank on a high pedestal.

Km599: Jinzhou(●●) From here the line runs down almost to the coast which it follows south-west for the next 300km, crossing into Hebei Province. Beijing is just under eight hours from here.

Km415: Shanhaiguan (●●) As you approach the town from the north, you pass through the **Great Wall** – at its most eastern point. This end of the Wanlichangcheng (Ten Thousand Li Long Wall) has been partially done up for the tourists. Although the views here are not as spectacular as at Badaling (70km north of Beijing, see p300), the restoration at Shanhaiguan has been carried out more sympathetically – it is restoration rather than reconstruction. The large double-roofed tower houses an interesting museum.

Km262: Tangshan This was the epicentre of an earthquake which demolished this industrial town on 28 July 1976. The official death toll stands at 150,000 but it is probably as high as 750,000. Many of the factories have been rebuilt and the town is once again producing consumer goods. Locomotives are built here at the Tangshan Works: which until 1991 produced the SY class 2-8-2 steam engine.

Km133: Tianjin/Tientsin (●●) One of the largest ports in China, with a population of seven million. In the mid-nineteenth century the English and the French marched on the capital and 'negotiated' the Treaty of Peking which opened Tianjin to foreign trade. Concessions were granted to foreign powers as they were in Shanghai. England, France, Austria, Germany, Italy, Belgium, Russia, Japan and the United States each controlled different parts of the city, which accounts for the amazing variety of architectural styles to be found here. Chinese resentment at the foreign presence boiled over in 1870 when (during an incident that came to be known as the **Tientsin Massacre**) ten nuns, two priests and a French official were murdered. To save female babies from being killed by their parents (the Chinese have always considered it far more important to have sons than daughters) the nuns had been giving money for them. This had led the more gullible members of the Chinese population to believe that the nuns were either eating the children or grinding up their bones for patent medicines.

Km0: Beijing The beginning or the end? You are now 9001kms from Moscow. See p296 for information on the city.

This section contains basic information for those spending a few days in Tokyo, Hong Kong, Helsinki, Berlin, Budapest, Prague, Warsaw, Minsk, Tallinn, Riga or Vilnius at the end or beginning of the trip. Details of how to arrange tickets in these cities for the rail journey across Siberia are given in Part 1: Planning Your Trip.

JAPAN: TOKYO

General information

● **Visas** Visas are not necessary for passport holders from the UK, other Western European countries, North America and most British Commonwealth countries.

● **Money/costs** The unit of currency is the yen (¥). Japan has become one of the most expensive countries in the world for foreign visitors. You may need to allow for a minimum of £50/US$75 per day for the most basic accommodation and the cheapest meals.

● **Climate** Japan has four clearly-defined seasons: winter being cold and snowy, summer being hot and humid, and spring and autumn being warm.

● **Language** Since English is taught in the schools and the people are very keen to make contact with foreigners, you will almost always be able to find someone to help you. If you're stuck Japan Travel Phone provides assistance in English in Tokyo (☎ 03-3201 3331), Kyoto (☎ 075-371 5649) and has a toll-free number for everywhere in Japan outside these two cities (☎ 0088-22 4800; 09:00-17:00 daily).

● **Local transport** If you plan to spend some time touring the country, you should purchase a Japan Rail Pass – ¥28,300 (£190) for 7 days, ¥45,100 (£302) for 14 days, or ¥57,700 (£386) for 21 days. You must buy the pass before arriving in Japan. All stations have signs above the platforms in both Japanese and Roman letters.

Tourist information

Before you leave home, visit the branch of the Japan National Tourist Organization (JNTO) in your country. A wealth of useful maps and tourist brochures is provided free of charge. JNTO has a Web site at www.jnto.go.jp and some of their offices are at:

● **UK**: Heathcote House (☎ 020-7734 9638, ▭ info@jnto.co.uk, www.seejapan.co.uk), 20 Savile Row, London W1X 1AE

● **USA**: Suite 1250, 1 Rockefeller Plaza (☎ 212-757-5640), New York, NY 10020 (offices also in Chicago, San Francisco and Los Angeles)

● **Canada**: 165 University Ave (☎ 416-366-7140), Toronto, Ontario, M5H 3B8
● **Australia**: Chiefly Tower (☎ 02-9232 4522), Lvl 33, Sydney, NSW 2000

In Tokyo, the best place for information is Tokyo Tourist Information Centre (☎ 03-3201 3331) at B1F Tokyo International Forum, 3-5-1 Marunouchi, Chiyoda-ku, open 9:00-17:00 weekdays, 9:00-12:00 Saturday.

Arrival and departure

Flights are expensive in Japan so try to ensure you have made arrangements before arrival. For details of ferry services to China and Russia (as well as information about arranging **Trans-Siberian** tickets) see Part 1.

● **Narita Airport (Tokyo)** Transport to the city centre is expensive since the airport is 60km outside the capital. The cheapest way to get in if you don't have a rail pass is to take the Keisei Limited Express train from the airport to Keisei Ueno Station in Tokyo.

● **Niigata Port** Niigata Tourist Information Center (☎ 025-241 7914) is on your left as you take the main exit from the railway station. Niigata International Exchange Foundation (☎ 025-225 2777), Miyoshi Mansion 3F, 6-1211-5 Kami-Okawamae-dori, also has information and English-speaking staff; open daily except Wednesday 10:00-18:00. Note that the boat service between Niigata and Vladivostok does not operate in winter.

● **Niigata Airport** There are scheduled services to Khabarovsk, Vladivostok, Irkutsk and Shanghai. There is no flight between Niigata and Tokyo, but the fastest bullet train takes just over 1½ hours.

Where to stay

This can be expensive: a bed in a youth hostel will set you back US$20. Youth hostels are cheapest followed by *minshuku* (bed and breakfast) and then business hotels. *Ryokans* (Japanese-style hotels) are pricey but often include meals and are an interesting experience. The best way to find somewhere to sleep is to visit the TIC (see above) in Tokyo where there is a Welcome Inn Reservation Center. Reservations can be made here free of charge. Alternatively collect an accommodation list and a map and do it yourself by phoning the hotel/youth hostel (phone calls are reasonably cheap). Check prices and availability and then ask for directions. Some numbers to try for cheap accommodation in Tokyo are:

● *Tokyo International Youth Hostel (Iidabashi)* (☎ 03-3235 1107), 18F Central Plaza Building, 1-1 Kagura-kashi, Shinjuku-ku 162-0823
● *Asia Center of Japan (Akasaka)* (☎ 03-3233 0111, 🖷 03-3233 0633), 5-5 Saragakucho 2-chome, Chiyoda-ku
● *Taito Ryokan* (☎ 03-3843 2822, 🖳 jptaito@hotmail.com), Nishi-Asakusa 2-1-4, Taito-ku, 111-0035

HONG KONG

General information

On 1 July 1997, the British handed over administration of Hong Kong to China. The country is now a Special Administrative Region of China.

● **Visas** Entry regulations are changing gradually. The stay for British citizens is six months with no automatic right of employment and you may need to show proof of onward travel. Most other nationalities can stay for three months.

Visas for China are easy to get in Hong Kong. Either use a travel agent or do it yourself at the Visa Office (☎ 2585 1663) of the People's Republic of China, 5th floor, Lower Block, China Resources Building, 26 Harbour Rd, Wanchai. Remember that you will be without a passport while processing the visa, so if you need to cash travellers' cheques do this first.

● **Money** The currency is the Hong Kong dollar (HK$). The exchange rate is approximately US$1=HK$8 (£1=HK$11).

● **Climate** Mild with fairly hot and humid summers and cool winters.

● **Language** Cantonese and English.

Tourist information

The Hong Kong Tourist Association (HKTA) has branches in many countries, and in Hong Kong at the airport, Star Ferry terminal (Kowloon) and at Central, Hong Kong Island; these will provide you with useful maps and brochures. There is also a telephone information service with multilingual operators (☎ 2508 1234; open 08:00-18:00 daily) and a website (🖳 www.Discoverhongkong.com).

Arrival and departure

● **Chek Lap Kok Airport** The huge new airport is on the north side of Lantau Island. There is a very helpful information desk which you'll have to walk past as you arrive; accommodation can be booked at the HK Hotels Association desk. As in all airports, the rates the money-changers offer are bad so change only a little or use an ATM.

It's easy and hassle-free to get to Kowloon or Hong Kong Island from the airport; either catch the Airport Express Link (AEL) a high-speed rail link that takes 19 mins to Kowloon and 23 mins to Hong Kong Island, or take the airport bus.

● **By rail** To get to China you can take the 2¹/₂-hour, direct express train which runs between Kowloon (Hung Hom Station) and Canton (Guangzhou).

From China it is cheaper, however, to take local trains from Canton to Shenzen; there is also a bus service on this route. You walk across the border into Hong Kong and then take a local train from Lo Wu station to Hung Hom.

The new Beijing–Hong Kong and Shanghai–Hong Kong trains take 29 hours and run on alternate days of the week.

For **Trans-Siberian** tickets, see p35-6.

● **Ferry/hydrofoil to/from Canton (Guangzhou)** The eight-hour overnight ferry between Canton and Hong Kong arrives and departs from Tai Kok Tsui Wharf in Kowloon. There is also a 95-minute hydrofoil service between here and Canton. Book tickets from the China Ferry Terminal or through travel agents in Hong Kong.

● **Boat to/from Shanghai** There are about four departures a month for this delightful 60-hour trip. The service is popular and heavily booked in the summer, bookings must be made at least two weeks in advance.

Local transport
Most famous is the Star Ferry service which operates between Kowloon and Hong Kong Island. Ask the HKTA information offices for details of ferries to outlying islands. There is also a fast and efficient subway system and the old trams still operate on Hong Kong Island. Taxis are cheap but traffic is slow-moving.

Where to stay
For a cheap place to sleep, **Chungking Mansions**, Nathan Rd, is the best. In these blocks in Kowloon, near the harbour and a stone's throw from the famous Peninsula Hotel, there's a large number of small hotels with tiny rooms and low prices. Have a look at a few before you decide as the rooms vary in size, cleanliness and price. The *Travellers' Hostel* (☎ 2368 7710) on the top floor of Block A is a popular meeting place for backpackers and has cheap dormitory accommodation and a restaurant as well as a travel agency that can organize visas for China.

There's also a *YMCA* (☎ 2268 7000, 🗎 2739 9315, 🖳 room@ymc ahk.org.hk) next door to the Peninsula Hotel.

FINLAND: HELSINKI

General information
• **Visas** Visas are not necessary for passport holders from most countries including the UK, USA, Canada, Australia and New Zealand.
• **Money/costs** From January 2002 the unit of currency will be the euro, until then it is the Finnmark which is divided into 100 penniä. As in most Scandinavian countries, prices are higher than in many European countries.
• **Climate** Pleasantly warm in summer but winters are long and severe.
• **Language** There are two official languages – Finnish and Swedish (the Swedish name for Helsinki is Helsingfors). Most people also speak English.

Tourist information
There are Finnish tourist offices in many countries including:
• **Canada**: (☎ 416-964-9159), Box 246 Station Q, Toronto M4T 2M1
• **UK**: (☎ 0207-365 2512), 30-35 Pall Mall, London SW1Y 5LP (PO Box 33213, London SW1Y 5ZS)
• **USA**: (☎ 212-885-9737), 665 Third Avenue, New York, NY 10017

In Helsinki your first stop should be **Helsinki City Tourist Office** (☎ 9-169 3757), at Pohjoisesplanadi 19 on the Esplanadia (the park next to the water-side market square). It is open 08:30-18:00 weekdays, 10:00-15:00 weekends over summer and provides an accommodation list.

Arrival and departure
• **By sea** If you're arriving from Stockholm on a Viking Line Ship, or from Travemunde (Germany) on Finnjet, you will dock at Katajanokka on the east side of the bay.
    If you are arriving from Gdansk, from Tallinn, or from Stockholm on the Silja line, ships dock at Olympialaituri on the west of the bay. Both stops are a 15-20 minute walk from the city centre.
• **By air** Vantaa International Airport is situated 20km north of the city centre. There is a regular bus service (bus No 615 to the railway station). The journey takes about half an hour.
• **By rail** The railway station is six blocks west of the harbour and two blocks north.
    For booking the **Trans-Siberian** in Helsinki see p27-8.
• **By bus** Finnord Bus Agency and St Petersburg Express Bus Service operate daily bus services to St Petersburg. A ticket costs about US$45.

Where to stay
You can get information about accommodation and a list of youth hostels from the **Hotel Booking Centre (Hotellikeskus)** (☎ 9-2288 1400) at the railway station.

GERMANY: BERLIN

General information
● **Visas** Not necessary for most nationalities.
● **Money/costs** From January 2002 the euro, until then the Deutschmark (DM) is the unit of currency, divided into 100 pfennigs. Living and travelling costs can be high.
● **Language** It's useful to be able to speak a little German. Most Berliners study English at school and many speak it fluently.

Tourist information
Berlin Tourist Office (☎ 030-250025) in the Europa Center, Budapester Strasse 45 (the building with the Mercedes star on the top of it) is a ten-minute walk from Zoo Bahnhof (railway station) and is open 8:30-22.30 Monday to Saturday (10:00-18:30 on Sunday). There is also an information centre at Brandenburg Gate. The friendly staff will supply you with maps and brochures and book accommodation. In Zoo Bahnhof there is a EurAide desk which provides train information and has a room-finding service.

Arrival and departure
For cheap **flights** buy a copy of the weekly magazine *Zitty*, which has several pages of travel deals.

A system of **car-sharing** can be arranged through *mitfahrzentrale* agencies (🖳 www.mitfahrzentrale.de); you pay the agency a fee to find you a ride in a private car to other European cities.

Zoo Bahnhof (Zoo Railway Station; train info ☎ 01805-996633) is the station for international trains. There are left-luggage lockers and a bureau de change.

To make a booking on the **Trans-Siberian**, see pp27-8.

Where to stay
The cheapest places are the youth hostels which are luxurious by international YHA (HI) standards but comparatively expensive (DM30-50).
● *Berlin Jugendgastehaus* (☎ 030-261 1097), Kluck Strasse 3, W-Berlin 30 (Tiergarten)
● *Wannsee Jugendgastehaus* (☎ 030-803 2034), Badeweg 1, corner Kronprinzessinnenweg, W-Berlin 38 (Wannsee)
● *Ernst Reuter Youth Hostel* (☎ 030-404 1610), Hermsdorfer Damm 48, W-Berlin north (Hermsdorf)
● *Studenthotel Berlin* (☎ 030-784 6720), Meininger Strasse 10, W-Berlin 62, near Rathaus Schoneberg
● *Jugendgastehaus am Zoo* (☎ 312 9410), Hardenberg Strasse 9a. Under 27s only; accommodation from DM35. It is located very near Zoo Railway Station.

HUNGARY: BUDAPEST

General information

● **Visas** Visas are not necessary for passport holders from USA,. UK, Canada or most European countries. Australian and New Zealand passport holders can get a 48-hour transit visa or a 30-day tourist visa on arrival by air or road but not by rail.

● **Money** The Forint (Ft) is divided into 100 fillérs (f).

● **Language** Magyar is one of the world's more difficult languages to learn. Most people connected with tourism speak a little English though knowledge of German is more widespread.

Tourist information

Information can be obtained from **Tourinform** (☎ 1-317 9800, 💻 hun gary@tourinform.hu, www.hungarytourism.hu), Suto utca 2 (near Deak ter metro station). The office is open 08:00-20:00 daily.

Arrival and departure

There are train, plane and bus services to most destinations in Europe.

● **By rail** Most international services come into Keleti Station (East); Budapest Tourist has an information booth here. Nyugati Station (West) is used for trains to and from Prague and the East. Both have metro stations.

Tickets for the Trans-Siberian are no longer the amazing bargain they were when the communists were in power. For **Trans-Siberian** bookings see Part 1.

● **By air** The international airport is 20km south-east of the city centre. and there are shuttle buses every 30 minutes to the city.

● **By bus** There are three bus stations in Budapest. Erzsebet ter (metro Deak ter) serves destinations in central and Western Europe.

Where to stay

Budapest has a wide range of accommodation. At the top end there is the *Hilton* which blends well with the ancient walls of the castle tower it incorporates and stands on the hill above the city.

For budget travellers, the city's colleges offer their rooms during the summer holidays. All kinds of accommodation can be booked by contacting either of the offices listed below:

● **Welcome Hotel Service** (☎ 1-318 4848), 1052 Budapest, Apaczai Csere Janos u.1

● **Budapest Tourist** (☎ 1-317 3555), V Roosevelt ter 5

CZECH REPUBLIC: PRAGUE

General information

- **Visas** Visas are not necessary for passport holders from the UK, USA or Western European countries. Canadian, Australian, New Zealand, Japanese and Israeli citizens need a visa.
- **Money/costs** The unit of currency is the koruna (crown). German DM are accepted in some places. Prices for hotels and restaurants are low.
- **Language**   Many Czech people involved in tourism now speak English. German and Russian are other foreign languages spoken.

Tourist information

A good place for tourist information is **Prague Information Service** (☎ 544 444, ⌨ tourinfo@pis.cz, www.pis.cz). There are branches at 20 Na Prikope, Starometske namesti (Old Town Hall) and at the main railway station. They are open 8:30-19:00 weekdays and 9:00-17:00 weekends.

Arrival and departure

- **By rail** There are four railway stations: Hlavní Nádrazí (the main station, also called Wilsonovo Station), Holesovice to the north, Masarykovonadrazi near the centre, and Smíchovoske nadrazi to the south (mainly local trains).

    International rail tickets are sold at **Cedok** (☎ 02-2419 7616), 18 Na Príkope, where the queues are often very long. Bring your passport and hard currency. For **Trans-Siberian** bookings, see Part 1.
- **By air** The international airport is 10km from the city centre. There is a frequent bus service between the airport and the city centre.
- **By bus** The cheapest way to get to Britain on public transport is by bus, US$75 on Kingscourt Express, which takes 23 hours and there are daily departures except Sunday. You can get tickets in Prague at Havelska 8 (☎ 02-2423 4583), and in London at 15 Balham High Road (☎ 020-8673 7500).

Where to stay

There's a good range of accommodation but everything gets very crowded in the summer, so start looking for a place to stay early in the day.

   Pragotur (☎ 2-171 4130, ▤ 2-171 4127, ⌨ pis.pragotur@mbox. vol.cz), 186 50 Praha 8, Za Poricskou branou 7 has a booking service for accommodation. It's near Powder Gate and Metro Náméstí Republiky and is open 10:00-17:00.

   There are also several camp-sites around the city, some of which have chalets and dormitories. Full details are available from the tourist information agencies listed above.

POLAND: WARSAW

General information

- **Visas** are not necessary for passport holders from the USA, EU and most European countries who stay less than 90 days; Canadian, Australian and New Zealand citizens need a visa.
- **Money** The zloty is the unit of currency. Banking hours are 07:30 to 17:00 but cash can also be obtained from the many ATMs around the city. Travellers' cheques can be difficult to exchange. Credit cards are accepted in most hotels, restaurants and shops.
- **Language** Polish is the national language. Most people connected with tourism speak English, German or Russian.

Tourist information

Warsaw Tourist Information Centre (☎ 22-831 0464) on Plac Zamkowy 1/13 (Castle Square) and the branch in the main railway station can offer assistance.

Orbis is the national travel service, staff can provide information and make bookings for travel and accommodation. In addition to its offices in Poland, Orbis/Polorbis has branches in most countries in Western Europe and one in the USA.

- **UK**: Polish National Tourist Office (☎ 020-7580 8811), 1st Fl, 310-12 Regent St, London WIR 5AJ

  Polorbis Travel Ltd (☎ 020-7580 1704, 🖹 020-7436 6558), 82 Mortimer St, London W1N 7DE
- **USA**: Polish Travel Bureau Inc (☎ 212-867 5011, 🖹 212-682-4715), 342 Madison Ave, Suite 1512, New York NY 10173

Arrival and departure

International train and bus tickets can be bought from Orbis offices or at the train/bus station. ICIS student card-holders are eligible for a 25 per cent discount.

- **By rail** Warsaw is a major stopping point between Berlin and Russia. International trains depart from Warszawa Centralna Station.
- **By air** Many airlines fly to Warsaw and the national carrier, Lot Polish Airlines, has services to dozens of places.
- **By bus** Buses leave regularly for European cities and are cheaper than trains. In Warsaw, ask at the tourist information centre or at the main bus station (Centralny Dworzec PKS). From Britain, Eurolines National Express (☎ 020-7730 8235) at 52 Grosvenor Gardens, Victoria, London SWIW 0AC, can offer bus information and tickets.

Some Polish buses to Ukraine, Belarus, Lithuania and Russia use border crossings still closed to Western tourists: check before you buy your ticket.

Where to stay

Warsaw has a vast range of accommodation. Central and close to the station is the expensive *Forum Hotel* (☎ 22-210 270, 🖹 22-625 0476) on ulica Nowogrodzka 24/26; singles start from US$100. *Hotel Metropol* (☎ 22-6294 001, 🖹 22-625 3014) on ulica Marszalkowska 99a charges US$50 a room including breakfast. *Hotel Saski* (☎ 22-620 4611, 22-620 1115) on Plac Bankowy 1 has rooms from US$20.

For rooms in private homes contact **Syrena Travel Office** (☎ 22-628 7540) at ulica Krucza 16/22. Singles start from US$10 and doubles from US$20.

There are two good centrally-located *youth hostels* at ulica Smolna 30 (☎ 22-627 8952) and 5/7 Smyczkowa ulica (☎ 22-643 8621). They are, however, often full during the summer.

BELARUS: MINSK

General information

● **Visas** Visas are necessary for all passport holders except those transiting Belarus who need a Russian visa. To get a Belarusian visa, you need a visa invitation which can be issued only by travel agencies registered by the Belarusian Ministry of Foreign Affairs.

● **Money** The Belarusian rouble, better known as zaichiki (rabbit), has been the official currency since May 1992 though it is not certain whether it will be replaced again with the Russian rouble. In January 2000 a new currency (minus three zeros) was introduced; check you are given the correct notes.

The most widely-accepted foreign currencies are US$ and Deutschmarks. Make sure the notes are in perfect condition otherwise changing them may be difficult. In Minsk, you can cash travellers' cheques and receive cash advances on your credit card but it may be expensive and is not easy. Food and entertainment are cheap.

● **Language** In 1990 Belarusian became the country's official language. Belarusian is an Eastern Slavonic language related to Ukrainian and Russian. Russian is still spoken by the majority of people.

Tourist information

There are no tourist information offices in Belarus, only service bureaus and excursion offices within hotels.

● **Belintourist** (Belarus' version of Intourist) (☎ 017-226 9840, 🖹 017-223 1143) at praspekt Masherava 19, open 08:00-20:00.

● **Hotel Minsk** (☎ 017-220 0132) Praspekt Skaryny 11. This place has the best service bureau and they speak English.

Arrival and departure

● **By rail** Minsk has only one international train station which is south-east of the city. There are direct services to Vilnius, Warsaw, Moscow and St Petersburg. At the station is the metro station Ploshcha Nezalezhnastsi (formerly Lenin Square).

You can get **international train tickets** on the upper floor of the main railway station. A less stressful place to buy them is Belintourist (☎ 017-2269 840, 🖹 017-2231 143), Praspekt Masherava 19; the office is open daily 08:00-20:00. Another ticket office, at Praspekt Skaryny 18, between Vulitsa Linina and Kamsamolskaya, is also open daily.

● **By air** Minsk-2 airport, which is 40km east of the city, is used for most international flights. There is an hourly bus service to the city. Minsk-1 airport is nearer the city and is used for short-distance international flights.

The state-owned Belavia (Belarusian airlines; ☎ 017-229 2838) has an office at vulitsa Njamiha 14.

● **By bus** The central long-distance bus station is at Vulitsa Babrujskaja 12. There are two buses a day to Bialystok in Poland, and daily buses to Brest, Kaliningrad, Riga, Kaunas, Klaipeda and Vilnius. Vostochny Bus station services Homel, Vitsebsk, Pinsk, Polatsk and Warsaw. Bus No 8 travels between these two bus stations.

Where to stay

Hotel Minsk (☎ 017-220 0132), Praspekt Skaryny 11, has small but clean rooms starting from US$42 for a single. *Hotel Svislach* (☎ 017-220 9783) on Vulitsa Kirava 13 has rooms for as little as US$15 for a single. *Hotel Druzhba* (☎017-266 2481) at Vulitsa Tolbukhina 3 has very basic rooms for US$5 a night. One of the nicest hotels is *Hotel Kastrychnitskaja* (☎017-222 3289) at Vulitsa Enhelsa 13 where a single room with all amenities costs from US$70. *Hotel Jubileynaja* (☎ 017-226 9024), Praspekt Masherava 19, charges US$55 a single as does *Hotel Planeta* (☎ 017-226 7855), Praspekt Masherava 31.

ESTONIA: TALLINN

General information

● **Visas** are not necessary for passport holders from Australia, Canada, Japan, New Zealand, UK, USA and most European countries. If you do need a visa, you can obtain one on arrival but it's much cheaper if bought in advance.

● **Money** The unit of currency is the kroon (EEK). There are exchange offices at the airport and central railway station. If you are carrying hard currency exceeding DM1000, you need to declare it.

● **Language** The official language is Estonian. About 62 per cent of the population are native Estonian speakers but 30 per cent speak Russian.

Tourist information
The **Tourist Information Centre** (☎ 645 7777, 🖹 645 7778, 💻 turismi-info@tallinnly.ee, www.tallinn.ee) on Raekoja plats 10 (Town Hall Square) is open 09:00-17:00 weekdays and 10:00-16:00 weekends (closed on Sunday in winter). The centre has a wide range of information, maps and guides and the staff will book accommodation.

Arrival and departure
● **By air** Tallinn has air links with Riga, Vilnius, Helsinki, Stockholm, Copenhagen, Frankfurt, Amsterdam, St Petersburg and Moscow.

● **By ferry** There are daily ferries between Tallinn and Helsinki and Stockholm.

● **By bus** Buses between St Petersburg and Tallinn are cheap and operate daily. Routes to Latvia, Lithuania and Kaliningrad are also serviced.

● **By rail** Tallinn has direct services to Moscow, St Petersburg and Warsaw. Trains depart daily from Balti Jaam (Baltic Station). Tickets can be bought from window No 26 at the back of the main long-distance booking hall beside the platform (open 08:00 to 13:00 and 14:00 to 20:00 every day).

Where to stay
Tallinn has a variety of accommodation to suit all budgets. For details contact the tourist information centre (see above).

LATVIA: RIGA

General information
● **Visas** Visas are not necessary for passport holders from the UK and most Eastern European countries. Latvian visas are free to US citizens.

● **Money** The unit of currency is the lati. There are exchange offices at Riga airport and throughout the central city area. Most major banks will cash travellers' cheques and credit cards are increasingly accepted.

● **Language** Latvian is the national language.

Arrival and departure
● **By air** Riga has air links with many cities.including St Petersburg and Moscow. The airport is 8km south-west of the city centre. The information office on the first floor of the departure hall is open 9:00-21:00.

● **By rail** Riga Station is at Stacijas laukums. There are rail connections from Riga to St Petersburg and Moscow and to Berlin via Warsaw.

● **By bus** The bus terminal is a few hundred metres from the train station.

❏ **The Baltic States**

Estonia, Latvia and Lithuania lie within easy reach of Moscow and St Petersburg, and any of them makes an interesting staging post for entering or leaving Russia. The Baltics share a 'common visa space' where a visa for any of the three countries allows you to travel back and forth across the shared borders, though strict border-crossing procedures are maintained between Russia and the Baltic States. For in-depth information on the Baltic States useful guides are Bradt's *Baltic Capitals* and *Estonia, Latvia, Lithuania*; Lonely Planet's *Estonia, Latvia & Lithuania* and Insight's *Baltic States Guide*.

Tourist information

For travel assistance contact **Riga Information Centre** (☎ 704 4377, 🗐 704 4378, 🖳 tourinfo@riga800.lv, www.riga800.lv) at Ratslaukums 6, LV-1050.

Where to stay

There are hostels all over Riga and information on them can be obtained from the tourist office.

Viesnica Aurora (☎ 722 4479) on Marijas iela 5 is conveniently located opposite the station. Good choices are *Hotel Riga* (☎ 704 4222, 🗐 704 4223, 🖳 info@hotelriga.lv) on the outskirts of Old Riga at Aspazijas bulvaris 22, and the upmarket *Hotel de Rome* (☎ 708 7600, 🗐 708 7606 🖳 reservation@derome.lv) at Kalku iela 28. The only hostel in Riga that accepts the Hostelling International card is *Placis* (☎ 755 1824, at Laimdotas 2a.

For bed & breakfast from US$25 contact **Patricia** (☎ 728 4868, 🗐 728 6650, 🖳 tourism@parks.lv), Elizabetes 22-6, a short walk from the train station. The office can also reserve air, train and bus tickets.

LITHUANIA: VILNIUS

General information

● **Visa** Visas are necessary for passport holders from the UK, USA, Canada, Australia and New Zealand.
● **Money** The unit of currency is the litas. Money can be exchanged at the airport and the railway station. Banks and special currency exchange booths are also located all around town. Credit cards are accepted in places which cater for tourists.

Arrival and departure

● **By air** Vilnius has air links with Copenhagen, Warsaw, Frankfurt, Berlin, Hamburg, London, Zurich, Vienna, Budapest, St Petersburg and Moscow. The airport is 4km south of the centre in the suburb of Kirtimai. Bus No 1 runs from the railway station to the airport. For general flight information phone ☎ 2-630201.

● **By rail** Vilnius is connected by rail to Kaliningrad, St Petersburg, Moscow, Riga and Warsaw. There is also a service to Tallinn via Kaunas. The station is situated at Gelezinkelio 16, at the southern end of the Old Town.

● **By bus** Eurolines Baltic International (☎ 2-251377) operates services to most Western European cities. Services also link Vilnius with Estonia, Latvia, Minsk, Berlin and Warsaw. The long-distance bus station is at Sodu gatve 22, next to the railway station. Tickets can be bought in the main ticket hall of the bus station.

Tourist information

Vilnius Tourist Information Centre (☎/🖷 2-620762) at Pilies 42 and at Vilniaus 22 (☎ 2-629660) provides information, sells maps and books accommodation. The **Lithuanian Tourist Association** (☎/🖷 2-726191) is at Ukmerges 20, LT-2600.

Where to stay

For budget accommodation, contact the **Lithuanian Travellers' Union** (☎ 2-335930, 🖷 2-234255), Zemaites 6, LT-2600. This non-government organization also offers interesting travel options in Lithuania and can assist with all travel arrangements.

The centrally-located *Hotel Astorija* (☎ 2-220110, 🖷 2-221762) at Didzioji gatve 35/2 has doubles from US$150. *Ars Viva* (☎/🖷 2752495, 🖳 arsviva@post.omnitel.net), Liubarto 17, is a small guest-house with rooms from US$50.

The **Lithuanian Youth Hostels Association** (☎/🖷 2-262660, 🖳 lyh@jnakv.vno.soros.lt) can be contacted at PO Box 12, LT-2000, Vilnius (Filaretu g. 17, Vilnius).

APPENDIX A: TIMETABLES

Timetables for the most popular trains on the Trans-Siberian, Trans-Mongolian, and Trans-Manchurian routes are given below. Unless otherwise indicated departure times are shown; for arrival times simply subtract the number of minutes shown as the stopping time. Since the timetables are subject to change, you should consult the table posted on the wall of the carriage corridor to ensure times are correct. Published every two months, another useful source of information is the *Thomas Cook Overseas Timetable* (£9.50, available by post from PO Box 227, Peterborough PE3 6PU, UK). On the Internet – **http://gamayun.physics.sunysb.edu:8080/5** – you can get the latest Russian Ministry of Railways timetables by entering the train numbers as used here.

Notes: Times shown are departure times – subtract stop for arrival time
MT = Moscow Time; LT = Local Time
– = not stopping
1hr+ = 1 hour minimum stopping time but invariably much longer

Table 1 Trans-Siberian: Moscow–Vladivostok (Train Nos 1 & 2: *Rossiya*)

Departures are every other day in each direction.

Station		Km from Mscw	Stop (mins)	Eastbound No 2 MT	LT	Westbound No 1 MT	LT	Time Zone MT+
				Day 1	Day 1			
Moscow (Yaroslavski)	Москва (Ярославский)	0		15:26	15:26	17:00	17:00	0
Yaroslavl	Ярославль	284	5/5	19:22	19:22	12:50	12:50	0
Danilov	Данилов	356	20/15	20:56	20:56	11:36	11:36	0
Bui	Буй	450	2/2	22:16	22:16	10:02	10:02	0
				Day 2	Day 2			
Sharya	Шарья	698	10/10	01:56	01.56	06:37	06:37	0
Vyatka/Kirov	Вятка/Киров	957	15/16	05:43	05:43	02:57	02:57	0
						Day 7		
Balyezino	Балезино	1194	19/18	09:01	09:01	23:41	23:41	0
Perm 2	Прмь 2	1436	15/15	12:51	14:51	19:44	21:44	2
Pervouralsk	Првоуральсск	1770	–/–	–	–	–	–	2
Yekaterinburg	Екатринбургг	1816	30/30	19:04	21:04	13:44	15:44	2
Tyumen	Тюмньь	2144	15/15	23:35	01:35	09:02	11:02	2
				Day 3				
Ishim	Ишим	2431	12/12	03:08	05:08	05:15	07:15	2
Nazyvaevskaya	Называвскаяя	2565	15/18	05:14	08:14	03:26	06:26	3
Omsk	Омск	2712	25/25	07:13	10:13	01:28	04:28	3
						Day 6		
Barabinsk	Барабинск	3040	17/15	11:12	14:12	21:31	00:31	3
Novosibirsk	Новосибирск	3335	22/20	15:10	18:10	17:46	20:46	3
Taiga	Тайга	3570	25/25	19:08	23:08	14:05	18:05	4
Mariinsk	Мариинск	3715	20/20	21:26	01:26	11:41	15:41	4
Bogotol	Боготол	3849	8/10	23:28	03:28	09:14	13:14	4
				Day 4				
Achinsk 1	Ачинск 1	3917	2/4	00:28	04:28	08:01	12:01	4
Krasnoyarsk	Красноярск	4098	20/20	03:48	07:48	04:50	08:50	4

Table 1 Trans-Siberian: Moscow–Vladivostok (Train Nos 1 & 2: *Rossiya*) cont'd

Station		Km from Mscw	Stop (mins)	Eastbound No 2 MT	LT	Westbound No 1 MT	LT	Time Zone MT+
Zaozernaya	Заозёная	4262	2/2	06:24	10:24	01:36	05:36	4
Kansk-Yeniseiski	Канск-Енисейский	4343	2/5	07:38	11:38	00:25	04:25	4
						Day 5		
Ilanskaya	Иланская	4375	20/20	08:29	12:29	23:47	03:47	4
Reshoti	Решоты	4453	2/2	09:41	13:41	22:17	02:17	4
Taishet	Тайшт	4516	5/5	10:46	15:46	21:18	02:18	5
Nizhneudinsk	Нижнудинскк	4680	15/15	13:36	18:36	18:38	23:38	5
Tulun	Тулун	4794	2/2	15:09	20:09	16:52	21:52	5
Zima	Зима	4940	20/20	17:28	22:28	14:55	19:55	5
Cheremkhovo	Черемхово	5061	2/2	19:12	00:12	12:52	17:52	5
Usole-Sibirskoe	Усолье-Сибирское	5124	2/2	20:07	01:07	11:56	16:56	5
Angarsk	Ангарск	5160	2/2	20:33	01:33	11:31	16:31	5
Irkutsk Sortirovka	Иркутск Сортировка	5178	4/10	21:13	02:13	10:55	15:55	5
Irkutsk	Иркутск	5185	20/20	21:45	02:45	10:32	15:32	5
				Day 5				
Slyudyanka 1	Слюдянка 1	5312	10/10	00:07	05:07	08:07	13:07	5
Mysovaya	Мысовая	5477	2/2	02:38	07:38	05:26	10:26	5
Ulan Ude	Улан Уд	5642	20/30	05:18	10:18	03:09	08:09	5
Onokhoi	Онохой	5675	2/2	05:53	10:53	02:08	07:08	5
Petrovski Zavod	Птровский Завод	5784	20/20	07:47	13:47	00:32	06:32	6
						Day 4		
Khilok	Хилок	5932	2/3	10:15	16:15	21:50	03:50	6
Mogzon	Могзон	6053	15/15	12:20	18:20	20:03	02:03	6
Chita	Чита	6199	20/20	15:14	21:14	17:18	23:18	6
Darasun	Дарасун	6265	2/2	16:34	22:34	15:37	21:37	6
Karymskaya	Карымская	6293	20/20	17:29	23:29	15:00	21:00	6
Shilka	Шилка	6446	5/5	20:00	02:00	12:08	18:08	6
Priiskavaya	Приисковая	6496	2/2	20:49	02:49	11:13	17:13	6
Kuenga	Куэнга	6532	2/2	21:33	03:33	10:28	16:28	6
Chernyshevsk-Zabaikalski	Чрнышвск-Забайкальский	6593	18/18	22:55	04:55	09:21	15:21	6
				Day 6				
Zilovo	Зилово	6670	2/2	00:28	06:28	07:39	13:39	6
Ksenevskaya	Ксеньевская	6789	2/2	02:42	08:42	05:18	11:18	6
Mogocha	Могоча	6906	15/15	04:52	10:52	03:18	09:18	6
Amazar	Амазар	7010	15/15	06:39	12:39	01:23	07:23	6
						Day 3		
Yerofei-Pavlovich	Ерофй-Павлович	7119	20/20	08:57	14:57	23:19	05:19	6
Urusha	Уруша	7211	2/4	10:49	16:49	21:16	03:16	6
Skovorodino	Сковородино	7306	20/20	12:59	18:59	19:13	01:13	6
Magdagachi	Магдагачи	7501	18/18	16:26	22:26	15:46	21:46	6
Tygda	Тыгда		2/2	17:27	23:27	14:26	20:26	6
Shiimanovskaya	Шимановская	7723	2/2	19:43	01:43	12:09	18:09	6
Svobodny	Свободный	7815	5/5	20:59	02:59	10:24	16:24	6

Table 1 Trans-Siberian: Moscow–Vladivostok (Train Nos 1 & 2: *Rossiya*) cont'd

Station		Km from Mscw	Stop (mins)	Eastbound No 2		Westbound No 1		Time Zone
				MT	LT	MT	LT	MT+
Belogorsk	Блогорскк	7873	30/30	22:22	04:22	09:55	15:55	6
				Day 7				
Zavitaya	Завитая	7992	2/2	00:13	06:13	07:40	13:40	6
Bureya	Бурея	8037	2/2	00:53	06:53	06:56	12:56	6
Arkhara	Архара	8088	26/26	02:13	08:13	06:05	12:05	6
Obluche	Облучье	8198	3/2	04:16	11:16	03:40	10:40	7
Bira	Бира	8306	15/15	06:30	13:30	01:42	08:42	7
Birobidzhan	Биробиджан	8351	5/5	07:16	14:16	00:47	07:47	7
						Day 2		
Khabarovsk	Хабаровск	8521	36/26	10:15	17:15	22:21	05:21	7
Vyazemskaya	Вязмскаяя	8642	21/16	12:32	19:32	19:57	02:57	7
Bikin	Бикин	8756	22/20	14:30	21:30	18:05	01:05	7
Guberovo	Губерово		2/–	15:46	22:46	–	–	7
Dalnerechensk	Дальнереченск	8890	2/2	16:23	23:23	15:59	22:59	7
Ruzhino	Ружино	8941	18/15	17:33	00:33	15:07	22:07	7
Spassk-Dalni	Спасск-Дальний	9050	2/2	19:15	02:15	13:07	20:07	7
Muchnaya	Мучная		2/2	19:55	02:55	12:27	19:27	7
Sibirtsevo	Сибирцево	9109	20/20	20:36	03:36	12:04	19:04	7
Ussurisk	Уссурийск	9177	17/15	21:56	04:56	10:36	17:36	7
Ugolvaya	Угловая	9255	2/2	23:14	06:14	09:09	16:09	7
Vladivostok	Владивосток	9289		23:53	06:53	08:14	15:14	7
						Day 1	**Day 1**	

Notes: Times shown are departure times – subtract stop for arrival time
MT = Moscow Time; LT = Local Time
– = not stopping
1hr+ = 1 hour minimum stopping time but invariably much longer

Table 2 Irkutsk–Ulan Bator/Ulaanbaatar (Train Nos 263 & 264: *Angara*)

Departures are daily.

Station		Km from Mscw	Stop (mins)	Eastbound No 264		Westbound No 263		Time Zone
				MT	LT	MT	LT	MT+
				Day 1	**Day 1**			
Irkutsk	Иркутск	5185		15:10	20:10	03:28	08:28	5
Goncharovo	Гончарово	5214	2/2	15:38	20:38	03:01	08:01	5
Slyudyanka 1	Слюдянка 1	5312	10/10	18:13	23:13	00:32	05:32	5
						Day 3		
Baikalsk	Байкальск	5358	1/1	19:06	00:06	23:28	04:28	5
Vydrino	Выдрино	5390	5/5	19:36	00:36	23:03	04:03	5
Tankhoi	Танхой	5426	2/2	20:13	01:13	22:20	03:20	5
Mysovaya	Мысовая	5477	2/2	21:20	02:20	21:06	02:06	5
Boyarski	Боярский	5504	2/2	21:44	02:44	20:40	01:40	5
Posolskaya	Посольская	5530	2/2	22:09	03:09	20:18	01:18	5

Table 2 Irkutsk–Ulan Bator/Ulaanbaatar (Train Nos 263 & 264) cont'd

Station		Km from Mscw	Stop (mins)	Eastbound No 264 MT	LT	Westbound No 263 MT	LT	Time Zone MT+
Selenga	Селенга	5562	2/2	22:49	03:49	19:42	00:42	5
Lesovozny	Лесовозный	5596	2/2	23:20	04:20	19:12	00:12	5
				Day 2				
Ulan Ude	Улан Уд	5642	30/40	00:52	05:52	18:10	23:10	5
Zaudinski	Заудинский	5655	2/2	01:09	06:09	17:13	22:13	5
Zagustay	Загустай	5769	5/5	04:32	09:32	14:05	19:05	5
Gusinoe Ozero	Гусино Озроо	5780	2/2	05:13	10:13	13:16	18:16	5
Dzhida	Джид	5852	5/5	06:22	11:22	12:10	17:10	5
Naushki	Наушки	5895	1hr+	17:50	22:50	11:10	16:10	5
MONGOLIA						**RUSSIA**		
Sukhbaatar	Сухбаатар	5925	1hr+	21:10		08:45		
Darhan	Дархан	6023	20/2	23:30		03:50		
				Day 3		**Day 2**		
Ulan Bator	Улаанбаатар	6304		06:20		21:35		
						Day 1		

Table 3 Moscow–Irkutsk (Train Nos 9 & 10 *Baikal*)

Runs every other day, eastbound on odd dates and westbound on even dates.

Station		Km from Mscw	Stop (mins)	Eastbound No 10 MT	LT	Westbound No 9 MT	LT	Time Zone MT+
Moscow	Москва	0		**Day 1** 21:29	**Day 1** 21:29	15:17	15:17	0
(Yaroslavki)	(Ярославский)							
Aleksandrov	Алксандров	112	–/–	–	–	–	–	0
				Day 2	**Day 2**			
Yaroslavl	Ярославль	284	14/5	01:35	01:35	11:10	11:10	0
Danilov	Данилов	356	20/15	03:07	03:07	09:57	09:57	0
Bui	Буй	450	13/2	04:38	04:38	08:23	08:23	0
Sharya	Шарья	698	10/10	08:20	08:20	04:58	04:58	0
Kotelnich	Котельнич	870	–/–	–	–	–	–	0
Vyatka/Kirov	Вятка/Киров	957	17/15	12:09	12:09	01:18	01:18	0
						Day 4	**Day 4**	
Balyezino	Балезино	1194	20/20	15:28	15:28	22:03	22:03	0
Perm 2	Прмь 2	1436	16/18	19:19	21:19	18:05	20:05	2
				Day 3	**Day 3**			
Yekaterinburg	Екатринбургг	1816	15/15	01:16	03:16	12:04	14:04	2
Tyumen	Тюмньь	2144	15/15	05:45	07:45	07:35	09:35	2
Ishim	Ишим	2431	12/12	09:18	11:18	03:49	05:49	2
Nazyvaevskaya	Называевская	2565	23/24	11:24	14:24	02:00	05:00	3
						Day 3		
Omsk	Омск	2712	15/15	13:15	16:15	23:52	02:52	3
Tatarskaya	Татарская	2885	2/2	15:12	18:12	21:50	00:50	3
Barabinsk	Барабинск	3040	18/15	17:20	20:20	19:55	22:55	3
Novosibirsk	Новосибирск	3335	16/18	21:16	00:16	16:05	19:05	3

Table 3 Moscow–Irkutsk (Train Nos 9 & 10 *Baikal*) cont'd

Station		Km from Mscw	Stop (mins)	Eastbound No 10 MT	LT	Westbound No 9 MT	LT	Time Zone MT+
				Day 4				
Taiga	Тайга	3570	10/10	00:56	04:56	12:22	16:22	4
Mariinsk	Мариинск	3715	20/20	03:12	07:12	10:13	14:13	4
Bogotol	Боготол	3849	3/23	05:10	09:10	07:46	11:46	4
Achinsk 1	Ачинск 1	3917	2/2	06:10	10:10	06:21	10:21	4
Krasnoyarsk	Красноярск	4098	20/20	09:29	13:29	03:11	07:11	4
						Day 2		
Zaozernaya	Заозёная	4262	2/2	12:05	16:05	23:56	03:56	4
Kansk-Yeniseiski	Канск-Енисейский	4343	2/2	13:19	17:19	22:45	02:45	4
Ilanskaya	Иланская	4375	20/20	14:10	18:10	22:10	02:10	4
Taishet	Тайшт	4516	2/5	16:19	21:19	19:45	00:45	5
Nizhneudinsk	Нижнудинскк	4680	15/15	19:09	00:09	17:02	22:02	5
Tulun	Тулуп	4794	2/2	20:42	01:42	15:16	20:16	5
Kuytun	Куйтун	4875	2/2	21:54	02:54	14:08	19:08	5
Zima	Зима	4940	20/20	23:05	04:05	13:14	18:14	5
Zalari	Залари		2/2	23:56	04:56	12:01	17:01	5
				Day 5				
Cheremkhovo	Черемхово	5061	2/2	00:53	05:53	11:06	16:06	5
Usole-Sibirskoe	Усолье-Сибирское	5124	2/2	01:48	06:48	10:10	15:10	5
Angarsk	Ангарск	5160	2/2	02:14	07:14	09:45	14:45	5
Irkutsk Sortirovka	Иркутск Сортировка	5178	2/2	02:52	07:52	09:09	14:09	5
Irkutsk	Иркутск	5185		03:04	08:04	08:55	13:55	5
						Day 1	**Day 1**	

Notes: Times shown are departure times   subtract stop for arrival time
MT = Moscow Time; LT = Local Time
– = not stopping
1hr+ = 1 hour minimum stopping time but invariably much longer

Table 4 Trans-Mongolian: Moscow–Beijing (Train Nos 3 & 4)

One per week in each direction: currently ex-Moscow on Tues, ex-Beijing on Wed.

Station		Km from Mscw	Stop (mins)	Eastbound No 4 MT	LT	Westbound No 3 MT	LT	Time Zone MT+
				Day 1				
Moscow (Yaroslavski)	Москва (Ярославский)	0		23:42	23:42	14:10	14:10	0
				Day 2	**Day 2**			
Yaroslavl	Ярославль	284	–/–	–	–	–	–	0
Danilov	Данилов	356	15/15	04:55	04:55	08:53	08:53	0
Bui	Буй	450	2/–	06:15	06:15	–	–	0
Sharya	Шарья	698	10/10	09:55	09:55	03:59	03:59	0

Table 4 Trans-Mongolian: Moscow–Beijing (Train Nos 3 & 4) cont'd

Station		Km from Mscw	Stop (mins)	Eastbound No 4 MT	LT	Westbound No 3 MT	LT	Time Zone MT+
Vyatka/Kirov	Вятка/Киров	957	15/15	13:42	13:42	00:16	00:16	0
						Day 6	Day 6	
Balyezino	Балезино	1194	15/15	16:56	16:56	21:01	21:01	0
Perm 2	Прмь 2	1436	15/15	20:46	22:46	17:09	19:09	2
				Day 3	Day 3			
Yekaterinburg	Екатринбургг	1816	15/15	02:44	04:44	11:12	13:12	2
Tyumen	Тюмньь	2140	15/15	07:13	09:13	06:46	08:46	2
Ishim	Ишим	2431	12/12	10:46	12:46	02:59	04:59	2
Nazyvaevskaya	Называевская	2565	15/17	12:43	15:43	01:10	04:10	3
						Day 5		
Omsk	Омск	2712	15/15	14:29	17:29	23:13	02:13	3
Barabinsk	Барабинск	3040	15/15	18:20	21:20	19:26	22:26	3
Novosibirsk	Новосибирск	3335	15/15	22:10	01:10	15:41	18:41	3
				Day 4	Day 4			
Taiga	Тайга	3570	2/2	01:37	05:37	12:04	16:04	4
Mariinsk	Мариинск	3715	20/20	03:50	07:50	10:03	14:03	4
Bogotol	Боготол	3849	3/3	05:50	09:50	07:36	11:36	4
Achinsk 1	Ачинск 1	3917	2/2	06:50	10:50	06:31	10:31	4
Krasnoyarsk	Красноярск	4098	20/20	10:10	14:10	03:21	07:21	4
						Day 4		
Ilanskaya	Иланская	4375	20/20	14:44	18:44	22:30	02:30	4
Taishet	Тайштт	4516	2/2	16:54	21:54	20:04	01:04	5
Nizhneudinsk	Нижнудинскк	4680	15/15	19:44	00:44	17:27	22:27	5
Zima	Зима	4940	15/15	23:31	04:31	13:48	18:48	5
				Day 5	Day 5			
Angarsk	Ангарск	5160	2/2	02:34	07:34	10:37	15:37	5
Irkutsk	Иркутск	5185	25/15	03:46	08:46	09:49	14:49	5
Slyudyanka 1	Слюдянка 1	5312	10/10	06:08	11:08	07:29	12:29	5
Ulan Ude	Улан Уд	5642	20/29	11:16	16:16	02:35	07:35	5
						Day 3		
Gusinoe Ozero	Гусино Озроо	5780	2/2	14:03	19:03	23:22	04:22	5
Dzhida	Джида	5852	2/2	14:53	19:53	22:33	03:33	5
Naushki	Наушки	5895	1hr+	18:20	23:20	21:46	02:46	5
MONGOLIA						**RUSSIA**		
				Day 6				
Sukhbaatar	Сухбаатар	5925	1hr+	01:20		22:00		
Darhan	Дархан	6023	20/30	03:10		19:20		
Ulan Bator	Улаанбаатар	6304	35/40	08:50		13:50		
Choyr	Чойр	6551	15/20	11:31		08:20		
Sayn Shand	Сайн Шанд	7778	20/30	16:05		04:35		
Dzamyn Ude	Дзамын Уд	7013	1hr+	21:35		01:20		
CHINA				Day 7		Day 2		
Erlan		7023	1hr+	01:46		23:15		
Jining		7356	10/11	06:28		16:27		
Datong		7483	8/6	08:25		14:15		
Beijing		7865		15:33		07:40		
						Day 1		

Table 5 Trans-Manchurian: Moscow–Beijing (Train Nos 19 & 20: *Vostok*)

There is one departure per week in each direction currently leaving Moscow on Friday (Saturday from Mar 2001) and Beijing on Saturday but this may change.

Station		Km from Mscw	Stop (mins)	Eastbound No 20 MT	LT	Westbound No 19 MT	LT	Time Zone MT+
				Day 1	Day 1			
Moscow (Yaroslavlski)	Москва (Ярославский)	0		22:56	22:56	18:09	18:09	0
				Day 2	Day 2			
Yaroslavl	Ярославль	284	5/5	02:52	02:52	14:00	14:00	0
Danilov	Данилов	356	15/15	04:17	04:17	12:48	12:48	0
Bui	Буй	450	2/–	05:37	05:37	–	–	0
Sharya	Шарья	698	10/10	09:17	09:17	07:47	07:47	0
Vyatka/Kirov	Вятка/Киров	957	15/15	13:04	13:04	04:04	04:04	0
Balyezino	Балезино	1194	15/15	16:18	16:18	00:49	00:49	0
						Day 7	Day 7	
Perm 2	Прмь 2	1436	15/15	20:09	22:09	20:57	22:57	2
				Day 3	Day 3			
Yekaterinburg	Екатринбургг	1816	15/15	02:06	04:06	15:01	17:01	2
Tyumen	Тюмньь	2144	15/15	06:35	08:35	10:35	12:35	2
Ishim	Ишим	2431	12/12	10:08	12:08	06:48	08:48	2
Nazyvaevskaya	Называевская	2565	15/15	12:05	15:05	04:59	07:59	3
Omsk	Омск	2712	15/15	13:51	16:51	03:04	06:04	3
						Day 6		
Barabinsk	Барабинск	3040	15/15	17:42	20:42	23:17	02:17	3
Novosibirsk	Новосибирск	3335	25/25	21:42	00:42	19:32	22:32	3
				Day 4				
Taiga	Тайга	3565	2/2	01:09	05:09	15:45	19:45	4
Mariinsk	Мариинск	3715	20/20	03:22	07:22	13:44	17:44	4
Bogotol	Боготол	3849	3/3	05:20	09:20	11:17	15:17	4
Achinsk 1	Ачинск 1	3917	2/2	06:20	10:20	10:12	14:12	4
Krasnoyarsk	Красноярск	4098	20/20	09:39	13:39	07:02	11:02	4
Zaozernaya	Заозёная	4262	2/2	12:15	16:15	03:48	07:48	4
Kansk-Yeniseiski	Канск-Енисейский	4343	2/2	13:29	17:29	02:37	06:37	4
Ilanskaya	Иланская	4375	20/20	14:20	18:20	02:03	06:03	4
						Day 5		
Taishet	Тайштт	4516	2/2	16:29	21:29	23:38	04:38	5
Nizhneudinsk	Нижнеудинск	4680	15/15	19:20	00:20	21:01	02:01	5
Tulun	Тулун	4794	3/2	20:54	01:54	19:15	00:15	5
Zima	Зима	4940	20/15	23:15	04:15	17:18	22:18	5
				Day 5				
Angarsk	Ангарск	5160	2/2	02:24	07:24	14:07	19:07	5
Irkutsk	Иркутск	5185	25/25	03:36	08:36	13:22	18:22	5
Slyudyanka 1	Слюдянка 1	5312	10/10	05:58	10:58	10:51	15:51	5
Ulan Ude	Улан Уд	5642	20/15	11:06	16:06	05:57	10:57	5
Petrovski Zavod	Птровский Завод	5784	20/20	13:31	19:31	03:40	09:40	6
Khilok	Хилок	5932	3/3	16:00	22:00	00:58	06:58	6
						Day 4		

Table 5 Trans-Manchurian: Moscow–Beijing (Train Nos 19 & 20) cont'd

Station		Km from Mscw	Stop (mins)	Eastbound No 20 MT	LT	Westbound No 19 MT Wed	LT Wed	Time Zone MT+
Mogzon	Могзон	6053	15/15	18:05	00:05	23:11	05:11	6
Chita	Чита	6199	20/20	20:59	02:59	20:14	02:14	6
Karymskaya	Карымская	6293	20/20	23:10	05:10	18:00	00:00	6
Adrianovka	Адриановка		8/–	23:48	05:48	–	–	6
Sedlovoj	Седловой		–/2	–	–	16:49	22:49	6
				Day 6	**Day 6**			
Mogojtuj	Могойтуй		2/2	01:29	07:29	15:38	21:38	6
Olovannaya	Оловянная	6444	15/15	03:21	09:21	13:49	19:49	6
Borzya	Борзя	6543	15/15	06:15	12:15	10:58	16:58	6
Dauriya	Даурия	6609	2/2	07:57	13:57	08:59	14:59	6
Zabaikalsk	Забайкальск	6661	1hr+	14:06	20:06	07:39	13:39	6
CHINA								
Manzhouli		6678	1hr+	22:47		07:01		
				Day 7				
Hailar		6864	20/6	01:34		02:31		
						Day 3		
Boketu		7074	13/8	05:03		23:16		
Angangxi		7343	11/10	08:51		19:30		
Daqing		7454	6/6	10:23		18:00		
Harbin		7613	15/10	12:43		15:55		
Changchun		7855	8/9	15:47		12:53		
Shenyang		8160	15/15	20:03		09:20		
Jinzhou		8402	3/3	22:02		06:31		
				Day 8				
Shanhaiguan		8586	8/8	00:11		04:35		
Tangshan			3/3	02:21		02:22		
Tianjin		8868	8/8	03:59		00:48		
						Day 2		
Beijing		9001		05:30		23:10		
						Day 1		

Notes: Times shown are departure times – subtract stop for arrival time
MT = Moscow Time; LT = Local Time
– = not stopping
1hr+ = 1 hour minimum stopping time but invariably much longer

APPENDIX B: LIST OF SIBERIAN FAUNA

There are extensive displays of local animals in the natural history museums of Novosibirsk, Irkutsk and Khabarovsk but the labelling is in Russian and Latin. The following translation is given for non-Russian-speaking readers whose Latin is rusty or non-existent.

In the list below the letters given beside the animal's English name indicate its natural habitat. NS = Northern Siberia/Arctic Circle; SP = Siberian Plain; AS = Altai-Sayan Plateau/Mongolia; BI = Lake Baikal/Transbaikal region; FE = Far Eastern Territories. Where a Latin name is similar to the English (eg *Vipera* = Viper) these names have been omitted.

Accipiter gentilis	goshawk (AS/SP/NS/BI/FE)
Aegoceras montanus	mountain ram (AS)
Aegoceras sibiricus	Siberian goat (BI)
Aegolius funereus	boreal/Tengmalm's owl (BI/FE)
Aegypius monachus	black vulture (AS)
Aethia cristatella	crested auklet (NS/FE)
Alces alces	elk/moose (SP/BI/FE)
Allactaga jaculus	five-toed jerboa (SP/BI)
Alopex lagopus	arctic fox (NS)
Anas acuta	pintail (BI)
Anas clypeata	shoveler (SP/BI/FE)
Anas crecca	teal (BI/SP/FE)
Anas falcata	falcated teal (SP/BI/FE)
Anas formosa	Baikal teal (BI)
Anas platyrhynchos	mallard (AS/SP/BI/FE)
Anas poecilorhyncha	spotbill duck (AS/BI)
Anser anser	greylag goose (SP/BI)
Anser erythropus	white-fronted goose (AS/SP/BI/FE)
Antelope gutturosa/crispa	antelope (FE)
Arctomis bobac	marmot (AS/SP)
Ardea cinerea	grey heron (AS/SP/BI)
Aquila clanga	greater spotted eagle (SP)
Botaurus stellaris	bittern (SP/BI/FE)
Bubo bubo	eagle owl (BI/FE)
Buteo lagopus	rough legged buzzard (NS/SP/FE)
Butorides striatus	striated/green heron (FE)
Canis alpinus	mountain wolf (AS/FE)
Canis corsac	korsac/steppe fox (BI/FE)
Canis lagopus	arctic fox (NS)
Canis lupus	wolf (SP/BI/FE)
Canis procyonoides	Amur racoon (FE)
Capra sibirica	Siberian mountain goat/ibex (AS/BI)
Capreolus capreolus	roe deer (SP/BI/FE)
Castor fiber	beaver (SP/BI/FE)
Certhia familiaris	common treecreeper (AS/BI/FE)
Cervus alces	elk (AS/BI/FE)
Cervus capreolus	roe-buck (BI/FE)
Cervus elephas	maral deer (AS/BI/FE)
Cervus nippon	sika/Japanese deer (FE)

Cervus tarandus	reindeer (NS/FE)
Circus aeruginosus	marsh harrier (SP/BI)
Citellus undulatus	arctic ground squirrel/Siberian souslik (NS/BI/FE)
Cricetus cricetus	common hamster (AS/SP/BI/FE)
Cygnus cygnus	whooper swan (SP/BI)
Dicrostonyx torquatus	arctic lemming (NS)
Dryocopus martius	black woodpecker (SP/BI/FE)
Enhyra lutris	Kamchatka beaver (FE)
Equus hemionus	kulan/Asian wild ass (FE)
Eumentopias Stelleri	sea-lion (NS/FE)
Eutamias sibiricus	Siberian chipmunk (AS/SP/BI/FE)
Ealco columbarius	merlin (NS/SP/BI/FE)
Falco peregrinus	peregrine (NS/SP/BI/FE)
Falco tinnunculus	kestrel (SP)
Falco vesperinus	hawk (SP)
Felis irbis	irbis/panther (FE)
Felis lynx	lynx (SP/BI/FE)
Felis manul	wild cat (AS/SP/BI/FE)
Felis tigris altaica	Amur tiger (FE)
Foetorius altaicus	ermine (SP/BI)
Foetorius altaicus sibiricus	polecat (SP/BI)
Foetorius vulgaris	weasel (SP/BI)
Fulica atra	coot (SP/BI/FE)
Gallinago gallinago	common snipe (SP/BI/FE)
Gavia arctica	black-throated diver/loon (BI)
Gavia stellata	red-throated diver/loon (SP/BI)
Gazella subgutturosa	goitred gazelle (AS)
Grus cinerea	grey crane (SP)
Grus grus	common crane (SP/BI/FE)
Grus leucogeranus	Siberian white crane (NS/SP/FE)
Gulo gulo	wolverine/glutton (SP/BI/FE)
Gypaetus barbatus L.	lammergeyer (AS)
Haematopus ostralegus	oystercatcher (SP/BI/FE)
Lagomis alpinus	rat hare (FE)
Lagopus lagopus	willow grouse/ptarmigan (NS/SP/FE)
Larus argentatus	herring gull (BI/FE)
Larus canus	common gull (BI/FE)
Larus ridibundus	black-headed gull (BI/FE)
Lemmus obensis	Siberian lemming (NS/SP)
Lepus timidus	arctic hare (NS/BI/FE)
Lepus variabilis	polar hare (NS)
Lutra vulgaris	otter (BI/FE)
Marmota camtschatica	Kamchatka marmot (FE)
Marmota sibirica	Siberian marmot (AS/SP/BI)
Martes zibellina	sable (SP/BI/FE)
Melanitta deglandi	American black scoter (BI)
Melanocorypha mongolica	Mongolian lark (BI/FE)
Meles meles	Eurasian badger (AS/BI/FE)
Microtus hyperboreus	sub-arctic vole (NS/SP/FE)
Moschus moschiferus	musk deer (AS/BI/FE)
Mustela erminea	ermine (NS/AS/SP/BI/FE)
Mustela eversmanni	steppe polecat (AS/SP/BI/FE)

Mustela nivalis	common weasel (NS/SP/BI/FE)
Mustela sibirica	kolonok (FE)
Myodes torquatus/obensis	Ob lemming (NS)
Nucifraga caryocatactes	nutcracker (AS/SP/BI/FE)
Nyctea scandiaca	snowy owl (NS)
Ochotona alpina	Altai pika (AS)
Oenanthe isabellina	Isabelline wheatear (AS/SP/BI)
Omul baikalensis	omul (BI)
Otaria ursina	sea bear (NS/FE)
Otis tarda	bustard (SP/BI)
Ovis ammon	argalis (sheep) (AS)
Ovis Argali	arkhar (AS)
Ovis nivicola	Siberian bighorn/snow sheep (FE)
Panthera pardus orientalis	Amur leopard (FE)
Panthera tigris altaica	Siberian/Amur tiger (FE)
Panthera uncia	snow leopard (AS)
Perdix perdix	grey partridge (AS/SP/BI/FE)
Perisoreus infaustus	Siberian jay (BI/FE)
Phalacrocorax carbo	great cormorant (BI/FE)
Phoca barbata groenlandica	seal (NS/FE)
Phoca baicalensis	Baikal seal (BI)
Phocaena orca	dolphin (NS/FE)
Picoides tridactylus	three-toed woodpecker (SP/BI/FE)
Plectophenax nivalis	snow bunting (NS)
Podiceps auritus	Slavonian/horned grebe (AS/BI)
Podiceps cristatus	great crested grebe (AS/SP/BI)
Procapra gutturosa	Mongolian gazelle (FE)
Pteromys volans	Siberian flying squirrel (SP/BI/FE)
Rangifer tarandus	reindeer/caribou (NS/BI/FE)
Ranodon sibiricus	five-toed triton (AS/SP)
Rufibrenta ruficollis	red-breasted goose (NS)
Salpingotus crassicauda	pygmy jerboa (SP/AS)
Sciurus vulgaris	red squirrel (SP/BI/AS/FE)
Spermophilus eversmanni	Siberian marmot (BI)
Spermophilus undulatus	arctic ground squirrel (FE)
Sterna hirundo	common tern (BI/FE)
Strix nebulosa	great grey owl (SP/BI/FE)
Surnia ulula	hawk owl (SP/BI/FE)
Sus scrofa	wild boar (AS/BI/FE)
Tadorna ferruginea	ruddy shelduck (SP/BI/FE)
Tamias striatus	striped squirrel (BI)
Tetrao urogallus	capercaillie (SP/BI/FE)
Tetrao parvirostris	black-billed capercaillie (BI/FE)
Tetraogallus himalayanensis	Himalayan snowcock (AS)
Tetraogallus altaicus	Altai snowcock (AS)
Tetrastes bonasia	hazel grouse (SP/BI/FE)
Turdus sibiricus	Siberian thrush (SP/BI/FE)
Uria aalge	guillemot (NS/FE)
Ursus arctus	bear (SP/FE)
Ursus maritimus	polar bear (NS)
Ursus tibetanus	Tibet bear (FE)
Vulpes vulpes	red fox (AS/SP/BI/FE)

APPENDIX C: BIBLIOGRAPHY

Baedeker, Karl *Russia with Teheran, Port Arthur and Peking* (Leipzig 1914)

Barzini, Luigi *Peking to Paris. A Journey across Two Continents* (London 1907)

Byron, Robert *First Russia Then Tibet* (London 1933)

Collins, Perry McDonough *A Voyage down the Amoor* (New York 1860)

De Windt, Harry *Siberia as it is* (London 1892)

Des Cars J and Caracalla, JP *Le Transsiberien* (1986)

Dmitriev-Mamonov, AI and Zdziarski, AF *Guide to the Great Siberian Railway 1900* (St Petersburg 1900)

Fleming, HM and Price JH *Russian Steam Locomotives* (London 1960)

Gowing, LF *Five Thousand Miles in a Sledge* (London 1889)

Heywood AJ & Button IDC *Soviet Locomotive Types* (London/Malmo 1994)

Hill, SS *Travels in Siberia* (London 1854)

Hollingsworth, JB *The Atlas of Train Travel* (London 1980)

An Official Guide to Eastern Asia Vol 1: Manchuria & Chosen (Tokyo 1913)

Jefferson, RL *Awheel to Moscow and Back* (London 1895)

Jefferson, RL *Roughing it in Siberia* (London 1897)

Jefferson, RL *A New Ride to Khiva* (London 1899)

Johnson, Henry *The Life of Kate Marsden* (London 1895)

Kennan, George *Siberia and the Exile System* (London 1891)

Lansdell, Henry *Through Siberia* (London 1883)

Levin, MG and Potapov, LP *The Peoples of Siberia* (Chicago 1964)

Manley, Deborah *The Trans-Siberian Railway* (London 1988)

Marsden, Kate *On Sledge and Horseback to Outcast Siberian Lepers* (London 1895)

Meakin, Annette *A Ribbon of Iron* (London 1901)

Massie, RK *Nicholas and Alexandra* (London 1967)

Murray *Handbook for Russia, Poland and Finland* (London 1865)

Newby, Eric *The Big Red Train Ride* (London 1978)

Pifferi, Enzo *Le Transsiberien*

Poulsen, J and Kuranow, W *Die Transsibirische Eisenbahn* (Malmo 1986)

St George, George *Siberia: the New Frontier* (London 1969)

Shoemaker, MM *The Great Siberian Railway – St Petersburg to Peking* (London 1903)

Theroux, Paul *The Great Railway Bazaar* (London 1975)

Thubron, Colin *In Siberia* (Penguin 2000)

Tupper, Harmon *To the Great Ocean* (London 1965)

APPENDIX D: PHRASE LISTS

English-speaking travellers are unforgivably lazy when it comes to learning other people's languages. As with virtually every country in the world, it's possible to just about get by in Russia, Mongolia and China on a combination of English and sign language. English is spoken by tourist guides and some hotel staff but most of the local people you meet on the train will be eager to communicate with you and unable to speak English. Unless you enjoy charades it's well worth learning a few basic phrases in advance. Not only will this make communication easier but it'll also earn you the respect of local people. You might even consider evening classes before you go, or teaching yourself with books and cassettes from your local library.

The sections here highlight only a few useful words. It's well worth also taking along phrasebooks: Lonely Planet's pocket-sized phrasebooks in Russian, Mongolian and Chinese are recommended.

Russian

CYRILLIC ALPHABET AND PRONUNCIATION GUIDE

It is vital to spend the few hours it takes to master the Cyrillic alphabet before you go, otherwise you'll have trouble deciphering the names of streets, metro stations and, most important, the names of stations along the Trans-Siberian and Trans-Mongolian routes (Mongolian also uses Cyrillic script).

The Cyrillic alphabet is derived from the Greek. It was introduced in Russia in the tenth century, through a translation of the Bible made by the two Greek bishops, Cyril (who gave his name to the new alphabet) and Methodius.

Cyrillic letters	Roman letter	Pronunciation*		Cyrillic letters	Roman letter	Pronunciation*
А а	a	f<u>a</u>r		Р р	r	<u>R</u>ussia
Б б	b	<u>b</u>et		С с	s	<u>S</u>amarkand
В в	v	<u>v</u>odka		Т т	t	<u>t</u>rain
Г г	g	<u>g</u>et		У у	u/oo	m<u>o</u>ve
Д д	d	<u>d</u>og		Ф ф	f/ph	<u>f</u>rost
Е е	e	y<u>et</u>		Х х	kh	lo<u>ch</u>
Ё ё	e	<u>y</u>oghurt		Ц ц	ts	lo<u>ts</u>
Ж ж	zh	trea<u>s</u>ure		Ч ч	ch	<u>ch</u>illy
З з	z	<u>z</u>ebra		Ш ш	sh	<u>sh</u>ow
И и	i	s<u>ee</u>k		Щ щ	shch	fi<u>sh</u>
й й	i	bo<u>y</u>		ы ы	y	d<u>i</u>d
К к	k	<u>K</u>iev		ь ь	(no English – softens the preceding letter)	
Л л	l	<u>L</u>enin		Э э	e	l<u>e</u>t
М м	m	<u>M</u>oscow		Ю ю	yu	<u>u</u>nion
Н н	n	<u>n</u>ever		Я я	ya	<u>ya</u>k
О о	o	<u>o</u>ver				
П п	p	<u>P</u>eter				

* pronunciation shown by underlined letter/s

KEY PHRASES

The following phrases in Cyrillic script may be useful to point to if you're having problems communicating:

Please write it down for me Запишйте это для меня, пожалуйста

Help me, please Помогйте мне, пожалуйста

I need an interpreter Мне нужен переводчик с английского

CONVERSATIONAL RUSSIAN

Run the hyphenated syllables together as you speak and roll your 'R's:

General

Hello	*Zdrah-stvoo-iteh*
Good morning	*Dob-royeh-ootro*
Good afternoon/evening	*Dobree den/vecher*
Please	*Po-zhalsta*
Do you speak English?	*Gavar-iteh lee vy pa anglee-skee?*
No/Yes	*Nyet/da*
Thank you	*Spasee-ba*
Excuse me (sorry)	*Izveen-iteh*
good/bad	*haroshaw/plahoy*
cheap/expensive	*deshoveey/daragoy*
Wait a minute!	*Adnoo meenoo-too!*
Please call a doctor	*Vi'zaveete, po-zhalsta, vracha*
Goodbye	*Das-vedahneya*

Directions

map	*karta/schema*
Where is ...?	*G'dyeh*
hotel	*gastee-neetsoo*
airport	*aeroport/aerodrom*
bus station	*stantsia afto-boosa*
metro/taxi	*metro/taksee*
tram/trolley-bus	*tramvai/trolleybus*
restaurant/café	*restarahn/kafay*
museum/shop	*moo-zyey/maga-zyeen*
bakery/grocer's	*boolach-naya/gastra-nohm*
box office (theatre)	*teatrahl-naya kassa*
lavatory (ladies/gents)	*too-alet (zhen-ski/moozh-skoy)*
open/closed	*at-krita/za-krita*
left/right	*na-prahva/na-leva*

Numerals

1 *adeen*; 2 *dvah*; 3 *tree*; 4 *chetir*; 5 *p'aht*; 6 *shest*; 7 *s'em*; 8 *vosem*; 9 *d'evat*; 10 *d'e 'sat*; 11 *adeen-natsat*; 12 *dve-natsat*; 13 *tree-natsat*; 14 *chetir-natsat*; 15 *pyat-natsat*; 16 *shes-natsat*; 17 *sem-natsat*; 18 *va'sem-natsat*; 19 *d'evat-natsat*; 20 *dvatsat*; 30 *tree-tsat*; 40 *so'rok*; 50 *p'ad-desaht*; 60 *shez-desaht*; 70 *sem-desaht*; 80 *vosem-desaht*; 90 *d'even-osta*; 100 *sto*; 200 *dve-stee*; 300 *tree-sta*; 400 *chetir-esta*; 500 *p'at-sot*; 600 *shes-sot*; 700 *sem-sot*; 800 *vosem-sot*; 900 *devet-sot*; 1000 *tees-acha*.

How much/many?	Skolka?
rouble/roubles	rooble/rooblah/roobley *
Please write down the price	Nap' eesheet' eh, pazhalsta, tse-noo
ticket	beel-yet
1st/2nd/3rd Class	perviy/ftoroy/treteey class
express	express
What time is it?	Kato' riy chahs?
hours/minutes	chasof/meenoot
today	sevodna
yesterday/tomorrow	fcherah/zahftra
Monday/Tuesday	pani-dell-nik/ftor-nik
Wednesday/Thursday	sri-da/chit-virk
Friday	pyat-nit-sah
Saturday	sue-boat-ah
Sunday	vraski-sen-yah

*1st word is for 1 unit, 2nd word for 2-4 units, 3rd word for 5 or more.

Food and drink

menu	menoo
mineral water	meenerahl-noi vady
fruit juice	sokee
vodka/whisky	vodka/veeskee
beer	peeva
wine/cognac	veenah/kanya-koo
champagne	sham-pahn-skoya
Cheers!	Zah vasheh zdaro-vyeh!
caviare	eek-ry
salmon/sturgeon	lasa-seeny/aset-reeny
chicken/duck	tsy-plonka/oot-koo
steak/roast beef	beefshteks/rost-beef
pork	svee-nooyoo
veal	atbeef-noyoo telyah-choo
ham/sausage	vechinu/kalba-soo
bread/potatoes	khlee-ep/kar-toshka
butter/cheese	mah-sla/sir
eggs/omelette	yait-sa/amlet
salt/pepper	sol/perets
tea/coffee	chai/koh-fee
milk/sugar	mala-ko/sahk-har
bill	shchot

Questions and answers

What's your name?	Kak vahs Zavoot?
My name is....	Menyah zavoot....
I'm from	Yah preeyeh-khal eez....
Britain/USA	Anglee-ee/S-Sh-Ah
Canada/Australia	Kanadah/Avstralee
New Zealand/Japan	Novee Zeelandee/Yaponee
Sweden/Finland	Shvetsee/Finlandee
Norway/Denmark	Norveggee/Danee
Germany/Austria	Germanee/Avstree
France/Netherlands	Frantsee/Gollandee

Where are you going?	*Kudah vhee idyotyeh?*
I'm going to...	*Yah idoo...*
Are you married?	*Vee zhyehnaht/zamoozhyem?**
Have you any children?	*Yest ly oo vas dety?*
boy/girl	*mahl-cheek/de-vooshka*
How old are you?	*Skolka vahm l'et?*
What do you do?	*Shto vhee delayetyeh?*
student/teacher	*stoo-dent/oochee-tel (-neetsa) **
doctor/nurse	*vrach/myeh-sestra*
actor/artist	*aktor/khoo-dozh-neek*
engineer/lawyer	*een-zheneer/advokaht*
office worker	*sloo-zhash-chey*
Where do you live?	*G'dyeh vhee zhivyotyeh?*

*(feminine form)

RAILWAY DICTIONARY (Словарь железнодорожных терминов)

Ticket window
for tickets after 24 hours
for tickets within 24 hours

working from 08.00 to 20.00
open 24 hours
break from 13.00 to 14.00
technical break from 10.15 to 10.45

касса
предварительная касса
в день отправления касса
текущая продажа билетов
часы работы с 8 до 20
круглосуточная касса
перерыв 13 до 14
технический перерыв 10.15 до 10.45

Timetable
even days (ie 2, 4, 6, ... of May)
odd days (ie 1, 3, 5, ... of May)
weekends and public holidays
weekdays
departure
arrival
platform
station of destination

расписание
Чет. (четным числам)
Неч. (по нечетным числам)
вых (по выходным)
раб (по рабочим дням)
От. (отправление)
Пр. (прибытие)
Пл. (платформа)
станция назначения

Train
fast train
transit train
passenger train
suburban train
deluxe express train
train is late
train does not stop
train does not stop at the station

поезд
скорый поезд
транзитный поезд
пассажирский поезд
пригородный поезд
фирменный поезд
поезд опаздывает
поезд не останавливается
поезд не заходит на станцию

Station
station master
station attendant
information

вокзал, станция
начальник вокзала
дежурный по станции
справка

Carriage
2-berth compartment carriage

4-berth compartment carriage
open sleeping carriage
open sitting carriage
wagon which separates and joins
  another train part way through
  the journey

вагон
СВ (спальный вагон)
мягкий вагон
купейный вагон
плацкартный вагон
общий вагон
безпересадочный вагон
  or отцепной вагон

Ticket
one way
return
adult
child
berth number
upper berth
lower berth
pass such as a monthly pass
discount ticket for pensioners,
  students etc
price zones

билет
туда
обратно
полный
детский
место
верхнее место
нижнее место
проездной билет
льготный билет

зона

Time
Moscow time
local time

время
московское время
местное время

On the train
Train Captain (head conductor)

conductor
emergency stop handle
baggage rack
blankets
sheets
rolled-up mattress and pillow

на поезде
начальник поезда, начальник
  бригады проводников
проводник, проводница
стоп-кран
багажная полка
одеяло
белье
постельные принадлежности

Useful railway expressions
Here is my ticket
Please show me my place
Please wake me at ....
Please wake me an hour before
  we arrive at ....
Where is the restaurant car or
  buffet car?
Where is the toilet?
May I smoke here?
Please bring me a (another) blanket

What is the next station?
How many minutes will the
  train stop here?
I am late for the train

Полезные железнодорожные выражения
Вот мой билет
Покажите, пожалуйста, мое место
Разбудите меня в ...... часов
Разбудите меня, пожалуйста, за
  час до прибытия в ....
Где находится вагон-ресторан
  или буфет?
Где находится туалет?
Здесь можно курить?
Принесите, пожалуйста, (еще одно)
  одеяло
Какая следующая станция?
Сколько минут стоянка поезда?

Я опоздал на поезд

Mongolian

Westerners tend to have difficulty mastering the tricky pronunciation of the national language of Mongolia. Until very recently, Mongolian was written in the same script as Russian (see p415), with two additional characters θ (pronounced 'o') and **Y** ('u'). When Mongolian is transliterated into Roman script note that stress is indicated by doubling vowels. You will see Ulan Bator written as 'Ulaanbaatar' to show that the first 'a' in each word is stressed.

Hello	*Sayn bayna uu*
Thank you	*Bayar-lalaar*
Yes/No	*Teem/Ugu-i*
Sorry	*Ooch-laarai*
I don't understand	*Bi oilgokh-gu-i bayna*
What's your name?	*Tani ner khen beh?*
Where do you live?	*Th khaana ami-dardag beh?*
Goodbye	*Bayar-tai*
Where is ...?	*Khaana bayna veh....?*
hotel/airport	*zochid buudal/nisyeh ongotsni buudal*
railway station/bus station	*galt teregniy buudal/avtobusni zogsool*
temple/museum	*sum/moosei*
lavatory	*zhorlon*
left	*zuun*
right	*baruun*
soup	*shol*
egg	*ondog*
mutton	*honini makh*
rice	*budaar*
noodles	*goimon*
bread	*talh*
cheese	*byaslag*
potato	*toms*
tomato	*ulaan lool*
tea	*tsai*
coffee	*kofee*
beer	*peevo*
fermented mare's milk	*airag*
How much?	*Khed?*
cheap	*khyamd*
expensive	*kheterhiy unetiy yum*

1 *neg*; 2 *khoyor*; 3 *gurav*; 4 *doroy*; 5 *tav;* 6 *zurgaar*; 7 *doloo*; 8 *naym*; 9 *ee-us*; 10 *arav*; 11 *arvan neg*; 12 *arvan khoyor*; 13 *arvan gurav*; 14 *arvan dorov*; 15 *arvan tav*; 20 *khori*; 21 *khori neg*; 30 *guchin*; 31 *guchin neg*; 40 *doch*; 50 *tavi*; 60 *zhar*; 70 *dal*; 80 *naya*; 90 *er*; 100 *zuu*; 200 *khoyor zuu*; 1000 *neg myanga*.

Chinese

Particularly tricky. The problem with Chinese is one of pronunciation – so much depends on your tone and emphasis that if you do not get the sound exactly right you will not be understood at all.

The country's main dialect is Mandarin, spoken by about three-quarters of the population. Mandarin has four tones: high tone (–), rising (/) where the voice starts low and rises to the same level as the high tone, falling-rising (ˇ) where the voice starts with a middle tone, falls and then rises to just below a high tone; and falling (\) which starts at the high tone and falls to a low one.

READING PINYIN CHINESE

Pinyin is the system of transliterating Chinese into the Roman alphabet. Pronunciation is indicated by the underlined letters below:

Vowels

a as in far
e as in were
i as in tree or as in
   were after c,r,s,z,ch,sh,zh

o as in or
u as in pooh
ü as in cue

Consonants

c as in eats
q as in cheap

r as in trill
x as in sheep

h as in loch or the kh in an Arabic word, with the sound from the back of the throat
z as in plods
zh as in jaw

KEY PHRASES

The following phrases in Chinese characters may be useful to point to if you're having problems communicating:

Please write it down for me　　请 为 我 写 下 来

Help me please　　请 帮 帮 我

Please call a doctor　　请 叫 个 医 生 来

USEFUL WORDS AND PHRASES

General

Hello	Nǐ hǎo	你 好
Goodbye	Zài jiàn	再 见
Please	Qǐng	请
Do you speak English?	Nǐ huì shuō yīng yǔ ma?	你 会 说 英 语 吗?
Yes/No	Dùi/Bū dùi	对 / 不 对
(literally correct/incorrect)		

No/Sorry, but no	Méi yǒu	没 有
Thank you	Xiè xie	谢 谢
Excuse me (sorry)	Duì bù qǐ	对 不 起
Excuse me (may I have your attention?)	Qǐng wèn	请 问
Good/bad	Hǎo/bu hǎo	好 / 不 好
I understand/do not understand	Wǒ dǒng le/wǒ bù dǒng	我 懂 了/我 不 懂
UK/USA	Yīng guó/Měi guó	英 国/美 国
Canada/Australia	Jiā ná dà/Aó dà lia	加 拿 大/澳 大 利 亚
France/Netherlands/Germany	Fǎ guó/Hé lán/Dé guó	法 国/荷 兰/德 国
China	Zhōngguó	中 国
Foreigner	Wai guo ren/Guilo	外 国 人/鬼 佬
Translator	Fān yì	翻 译

Directions

Where is...?	Zǎi nǎr...?	在 哪 儿?
Toilet (ladies/gents)	cè sǔo (nu/nan)	厕 所
Telephone	diàn huà	电 话
Airport	jī chǎng	机 场
Bus station	chē zhàn	
Train	huǒchē	火 车
Railway station	huǒ chē zhàn	火 车 站
Taxi	chū zū qì chē	出 租 汽 车
Museum	bó wù guǎn	博 物 馆
Hotel/restaurant	fàn diàn	饭 店
Guesthouse	bīnguǎn	宾 馆
Post office	yóu jú	邮 局
PSB/CAAC office	Gōng ān jú/Zhōng háng gǒngsi	公 安 局/中 航 公 司
What time will we arrive at...?	Liè chē shénme shí jiān dào...?	列 车 什 么 时 候 到?
What station is this?	Zhè shì nà yí zhàn?	这 是 哪 一 站?
North	Běi	北
South	Nán	南
East	Dōng	东
West	Xī	西

Street names

Many of the street names throughout China are similar. In most of the cities you visit, for example, you will find a Renmin Lu (People's St) and Jiefang Lu (Liberation St). You will also discover that streets are named (usually) according to a system which divides them into sections: north, centre, south etc. Thus if the thoroughfare of the city is Renmin Lu, and it runs from east to west, it may well have three (or more) separate names: Renmin Rd West – Renmin Xilu, Renmin Rd Centre – Renmin Zhonglu, Renmin Rd East – Renmin Donglu. By way of an indication, the designation that is given to a particular avenue also indicates its size. Roughly the following equate to English terminology:

Street Lù 路   Road Jiē, Dàjiē 街，大街 Lane Qiǎng 巷

Numerals

1	yī	一
2	èr	二
3	sān	三
4	sì	四
5	wǔ	五
6	liù	六
7	qī	七
8	bā	八
9	jiǔ	九
10	shí	十
11	shí yī	十一
12	shí èr	十二
13	shí sān	十三
14	shí sì	十四
15	shí wǔ	十五
16	shí liù	十六
17	shí qī	十七
18	shí bā	十八
19	shí jiǔ	十九
20	èr shí	二十
21	èr shí yī	二十一
30	sān shí	三十
40	sì shí	四十
50	wǔ shí	五十
100	yì bǎi	一百
101	yì bǎi líng yī	一百零一
110	yì bǎi yī shí	一百一十
150	yì bǎi wǔ shí	一百五十
200	èr bǎi	二百
500	wǔ bǎi	五百
1000	yì qiān	一千
10,000	yí wàn	一万
100,000	shí wàn	十万
1 million	yì bǎi wàn	一百万

| How much? | Duō shǎo qián? | 多少钱 |
| That's too expensive | Tài guì le | 太贵了 |

Time

One o'clock,two o'clock...	Yī diǎn, èr diǎn...	一点，二点
Ten past one (1.10)	Yī diǎn shí fēn	一点十分
Quarter to two (1.45)	Yī diǎn sì shí wǔ fēn	一点四十五分
Two thirty (2.30)	Èr diǎn bàn	二点半
Monday/Tuesday/Wednesday	Xīng yī...yī/èr/sān	星期一/星期二/星期三
Thursday/Friday/Saturday	Xīng qī...sì/wǔ/liù/rì	星期四/星期五/星期六
Sunday	Xīng qī rì	星期日
Yesterday/tomorrow/today	zuó tiān/míng tiān/jīn tiān	昨天/明天/今天

Transport

ticket	piào	票
Hard seat/Soft seat	Yìng Zuò/Luǎn Zuò	硬座/软座
Hard sleeper/soft sleeper	Yìng Wò/Luǎn Wò	硬卧/软卧
Please may I upgrade this ticket...	Qǐng nǐ huan gao yī ji de piào	请你换高一级的票

Food and drink

menu	cài dān	菜单
Mineral water/tea/beer	kuàng quán shuǐ/chá/pí jiǔ	矿泉水/茶/啤酒
noodles/noodle soup	miàn/tāng miàn	面/汤面
bread/egg	miàn bāo/jī diàn	面包/鸡蛋
pork/beef/lamb	zhū ròu/niú ròu/yáng ròu	猪肉/牛肉/羊肉
chicken/duck/fish	jī/yā/yú	鸡/鸭/鱼
vegetables	shū cài	蔬菜
Do you have any vegetarian dishes?	Nǐ zhèr yǒu sù-cài ma?	你这儿有蔬菜吗?
steamed rice	mǐ fàn	米饭
fujian fried rice	fu jian chǎo fàn	福建炒饭
fried rice	jī chǎo fàn	鸡蛋炒饭
pork in Sichuan-style sauce	yú xiāng ròu sī	鱼香肉丝
sweet & sour pork	gu lao zhū ròu	咕老(猪)肉
pork and onion in soy sauce	hui guō ròu	回锅肉
pork in sweet thick sauce	táng cù lǐjī	糖醋里脊
beef chow mien	niú ròu chǎo miàn	牛肉炒面
spicy beef soup with veg	shui zhǔ niú ròu	水煮牛肉
chicken in Sichuan sauce	yu xian ba kuai jī	鱼香八块鸡
chicken chow mien	jī ròu chǎo miàn	鸡肉炒面
chicken with cashew nuts	yao guō jī ding	腰果鸡丁
fried tofu with meat and veg	jia chang dòufǔ	家常豆腐
green beanshoots	dòu miao	豆苗
vegetable chow mien	su chǎo miàn	素炒面
hot and sour soup	sūan là tāng	酸辣汤
Delicious	Hao chi	好吃
Cheers!	Gang bei!	干杯!

INDEX

Siberian BAM Guide – rail, rivers & road
Athol Yates and *Nicholas Zvegintzov*
416 pages, 20 colour photos, 50 B&W photos
ISBN 1 873756 18 6, *2nd edition*, £13.99, US$23.95
Comprehensive guide to the BAM Zone in NE Siberia. Includes
a detailed guide to the 3400-km Baikal Amur Mainline (BAM)
railway which traverses east Siberia from the Pacific Ocean to
Lake Baikal. Detailed information on how to take the train and
where to go in the BAM Zone. Plus Lena River routes.
  '...an encyclopaedic companion.' **The Independent**

❏ OTHER GUIDES FROM TRAILBLAZER PUBLICATIONS

Japan by Rail *Ramsey Zarifeh*
288 pages, 40 maps, 30 colour photos
ISBN 1 873756 23 2, *1st edition,* £11.99, US$18.95
With a Japan Railpass, travelling around this country can be surprisingly good value. This guide includes detailed route and planning information, where to stay, where to eat and the most interesting places to stop off along the way. Includes rail maps and town plans.

Vietnam by Rail *Tess Read*
320 pages, 45 maps, 30 colour photos
ISBN 1 873756 44 5, *1st edition,* £11.99, US$18.95
The 'Reunification Express' railway links the north and south and is the most popular way to travel the country. Includes a history of Vietnam's railways, a blow by blow account of the war, and a detailed route guide with 12 strip maps. Plus comprehensive guides to 24 towns and cities.

China by Rail *Douglas Streatfeild-James*
384 pages, 54 maps, 30 colour photos
ISBN 1 873756 15 1, *1st edition,* £11.95, US$17.95
The guide to China for rail travellers. Most visitors use the comprehensive rail system to get around. This guide takes in all the main attractions, with full details of where to stay and where to eat – for all budgets. Beijing, Hong Kong and 32 towns covered in detail.

Silk Route by Rail *Dominic Streatfeild-James*
320 pages, 37 maps, 30 colour photos
ISBN 1 873756 14 3, *2nd edition,* £10.95, US$17.95
First edition short-listed for the **Thomas Cook Guidebook Awards**. Covers the railway line which follows the old Silk Route. It's possible to travel by rail from Moscow via the Central Asian cities of Samarkand and Tashkent across western China to Beijing. Includes guides to 17 cities along the way.

Australia by Rail *Colin Taylor*
288 pages, 50 maps, 30 colour photos
ISBN 1 873756 40 2, *4th edition,* £11.99, US$19.95
Re-researched and expanded to include 50 strip maps covering all rail routes in Australia plus new information for rail travellers. Includes 14 town plans and six city guides: where to stay, where to eat and the most interesting places to stop off along the way.
Full of friendly advice, and spiced with humour – Network

Trans-Canada Rail Guide *Melissa Graham*
240 pages, 31 maps, 24 colour photos
ISBN 1 873756 39 9, *2nd edition,* £10.99, US$16.95
Expanded 2nd edition now includes Calgary city guide. Comprehensive guide to Canada's trans-continental railroad. Covers the entire route from coast to coast. What to see and where to stay in the cities along the line, with information for all budgets.
Invaluable – The Daily Telegraph